CEDAR MILL COMM LIBRARY

D0149655

CEDAR MILL LIBRARY

CRUCIBLE of COMMAND

CRUCIBLE *of* COMMAND

ULYSSES S. GRANT AND ROBERT E. LEE— THE WAR THEY FOUGHT, THE PEACE THEY FORGED

WILLIAM C. DAVIS

Da Capo Press
A Member of the Perseus Books Group

Copyright © 2014 by William C. Davis

All rights reserved. No part of this publication may be reproduced, stored in a retrieval system, or transmitted, in any form or by any means, electronic, mechanical, photocopying, recording, or otherwise, without the prior written permission of the publisher. Printed in the United States of America. For information, address Da Capo Press, 44 Farnsworth Street, Third Floor, Boston, MA 02210.

Editorial production by *Marra*thon Production Services. www.marrathon.net

Book design by Jane Raese
Set in 12-point Dante

Cataloging-in-Publication Data for this book is available
from the Library of Congress.
ISBN 978-0-306-82245-2 (hardcover)
ISBN 978-0-306-82246-9 (e-book)

Published by Da Capo Press
A Member of the Perseus Books Group
www.dacapopress.com

Da Capo Press books are available at special discounts for bulk purchases in the U.S. by corporations, institutions, and other organizations. For more information, please contact the Special Markets Department at the Perseus Books Group, 2300 Chestnut Street, Suite 200, Philadelphia, PA 19103, or call (800) 810-4145, ext. 5000, or e-mail special.markets@perseusbooks.com.

2 4 6 8 10 9 7 5 3 1

FOR BIRD, WHO GAVE ME THE IDEA

CONTENTS

List of Maps   *ix*

Preface   *xi*

Introduction: Icons   *xvii*

1   Sons and Fathers   *1*

2   School of the Soldier   *25*

3   Fighting on the Same Side   *51*

4   Times of Trial   *75*

5   A Crisis Made for Them   *104*

6   "What Has Become of Gen. Lee?"—
     "Who Is General Grant?"   *128*

7   Lee Frustrated and Grant Victorious   *160*

8   Shiloh and Sevens   *189*

9   Lee Victorious and Grant Frustrated   *221*

10   "What have we to live for if not victories?"   *252*

11   Two Rivers to Cross   *283*

12   July 1863   *314*

13   Hints of the Inevitable   *346*

14   "If defeated nothing will be left us to live for."   *373*

15   "A mere question of time."   *405*

16   Meeting Again   *429*

17   Grant and Lee in 1868   *455*

18   The Last Meeting   *481*

Notes   *495*

Bibliography   *593*

Acknowledgments   *609*

Index   *613*

MAPS

1. Grant and Lee's War, 1861–1865 — *xiv*
2. The Virginia Theater of the War — *xv*
3. Grant and Lee in Mexico, 1846–1848 — *55*
4. The Battle of Cheat Mountain, September 12, 1861 — *148*
5. The Battle of Belmont, November 7, 1861 — *155*
6. The Battle of Fort Donelson, February 15, 1862 — *187*
7. The Battle of Shiloh, April 6, 1862 — *204*
8. The Seven Days, June 25–July 1, 1862 — *217*
9. The Second Manassas Campaign, July 17–August 30, 1862 — *231*
10. The Battle of Antietam, September 17, 1862 — *245*
11. The Battles of Iuka and Corinth, September 19 and October 3, 1862 — *247*
12. The Battle of Fredericksburg, December 13, 1862 — *269*
13. The Battle of Chancellorsville, May 1–6, 1863 — *309*
14. The Battle of Gettysburg, July 1–3, 1863 — *327*
15. Grant's Approaches to Vicksburg — *332*
16. The Battles for Chattanooga, November 24–25, 1863 — *371*
17. The Battle of the Wilderness, May 5–6, 1864 — *399*
18. The Battles around Spotsylvania Court House, May 8–19, 1864 — *401*
19. Grant's Crossing of the James, June 13–16, 1864 — *410*
20. The Siege of Petersburg, June 1864–April 1865 — *421*
21. Grant's Pursuit of Lee to Appomattox, April 3–9, 1865 — *450*

PREFACE

A FEW WORDS about the approach to writing this book are in order. Those who actually consult the footnotes of the following bibliography will quickly note the heavy preponderance of primary sources used. Indeed, very sparing use has been made of secondary works, and most of those cited are for purposes of correcting errors found in them, or as recommended further readings. The secondary literature on Grant and Lee is vast and of dramatically varying quality. Of special note, Douglas Southall Freeman's monumental *R. E. Lee* is still imposing after three-quarters of a century, though Freeman's want of objectivity and occasional carelessness with sources somewhat dims its authority. Elizabeth Pryor's 2007 *Reading the Man: A Portrait of Robert E. Lee Through His Private Letters* is exhaustively researched and in the main an outstanding exploration of the inner Lee, often through writings not previously available, though she sometimes makes unwarranted leaps of interpretation from her sources. No counterpart to Freeman exists for Grant. Brooks D. Simpson's 2000 *Ulysses S. Grant: Triumph Over Adversity, 1822–1865* and his earlier *Let Us Have Peace: Ulysses S. Grant and the Politics of War and Reconstruction, 1861–1868* are together thorough, well researched, and generally balanced. Joan Waugh's recent *U. S. Grant: American Hero, American Myth* is an outstanding companion taking Grant from 1865 through posterity. Of course, William S. McFeely won a Pulitzer Prize for his *Grant, A Biography* in 1981, though it suffers from rather too much presentism.

These works, and the myriad others available, have been used sparingly or not at all, but not out of disdain. This is not a conventional biography. It is, rather, an exploration of the origins and development of Grant's and Lee's personalities and characters, their ethical and moral compasses, and their thinking processes and approaches to decision making—in short, the things that made them the kind of commanders they became. With that in mind, the safest course seemed to be to stay within the sources of their own time, written at the moment by those who knew the men and witnessed their acts, and as much as possible to use the directly contemporary writings of the men themselves. Hence, even Grant's incomparable *Personal Memoirs* plays little role here, for it was written twenty years after the fact, and inevitably influenced by fallible memory and the natural instinct for self-vindication. Lee left no memoirs, but even his few recorded postwar conversations about his campaigns see small use, for they, too, suffer from self-justification. Some may question this approach, for surely some later secondary writers and modern historians may have useful, even penetrating, insights into what made Grant and Lee great leaders. That is so, but the goal in *Crucible of Command* is for its conclusions to come as directly from the actions of the principals as possible, uninfluenced by the later interpretations of others. That may not make the insights here any better than others, but at least they have the virtue of coming directly from the men themselves and their immediate circles of friends and family.

Having said that this is not a conventional biography, it is worth emphasizing that there is much that is new here from sources ignored or newly discovered, especially on the all-important youth of both men. There are also numerous cases of attention given to correcting errors in some secondary works, especially Freeman and occasionally Pryor, on matters germane to the portraits here limned. This is done out of respect and solely to set the record straight, since in the future, as in the past, readers and students will rely most heavily on these classic and timeless works, making correction where needed all the more important.

Be bold, be bold, and everywhere be bold.

—Edmund Spenser, *The Faerie Queene*

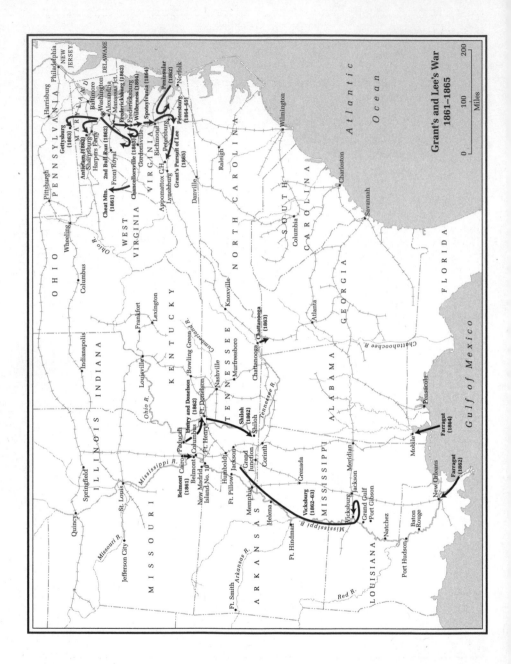

Grant's and Lee's War
1861–1865

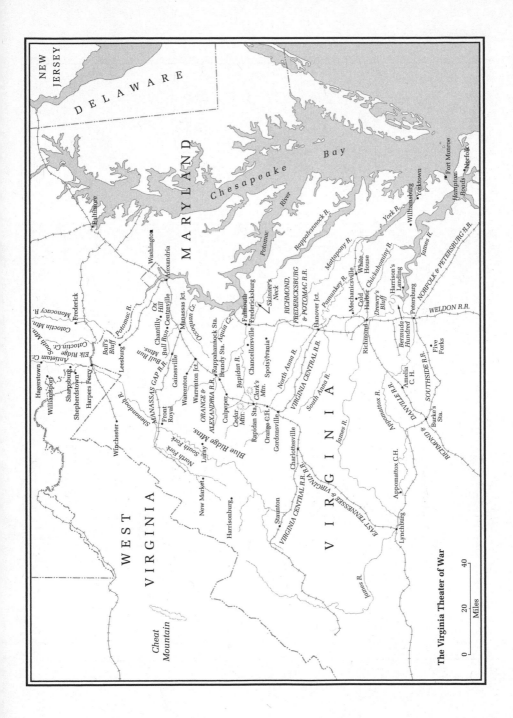

The Virginia Theater of War

INTRODUCTION: ICONS

IN THE SPRING of 1869 an enterprising merchant in Liverpool, England, tried luring customers into his showroom by mounting an exhibition of wax figures of distinguished Americans. A number beneath each bust referred visitors to a leaflet identifying the subjects. The likenesses were poor, but the leaflet even worse as it mismatched names with numbers. A head of recent Confederate president Jefferson Davis appeared on the sheet as Abraham Lincoln. More perplexing still, the guide reversed the descriptions for numbers 339 and 340, Generals Robert E. Lee and Ulysses S. Grant, misidentifying each as his archrival in the recent American Civil War. When visitors from the United States protested, the exhibitor refused to acknowledge error. He knew Grant from Lee, even if these silly Americans did not.[1]

❧

They first met as fellow soldiers in Mexico in 1847 in a moment both remembered and then forgotten by the time they met again in vastly different circumstances. No one then would have confused their identities or thought them remotely similar. Lee aptly stood for those fine old landed families now fallen on difficult times—the plantations gone or losing profitability, the wealth spent, their only influence now based on their names and the worth of their characters. The fortunes and small empires of the eighteenth century were dissolving in a new America. No wonder, then, that the longer Lee lived the more pessimistic became his view of a world in which he and his like were being displaced by a generation striving to replace the old order with a meritocracy of entrepreneurism, hard work, and imagination. Grant was one of those new Americans, and optimism was the fuel that drove him and his like.

Had there been no Civil War, Lee might have left a mark as a colonel of cavalry, or even a brigadier if he lived long enough. Grant likely would have made none at all, though both appeared, and would have continued to appear, in histories of the war with Mexico. The events of their generation created them and, call it coincidence or destiny, each proved to be the ideal man in the right place, and at the perfect moment. Then came *the* war, which accelerated everything both for them and their country at a pace seldom matched by plodding Time. That war made them both, and in it each revealed his singular attributes of personality and character. At the same time each demonstrated what few then or later chose to see: as thinkers and decision makers, as soldiers and as leaders, as men in *command*, they could be almost indistinguishable one from the other. They were hardly so identical as to give an excuse for numbers 339 and 340 being mistaken for each other, but take away the names and the faces and judge them by their acts, and their differences could be measured in motes.

The myths long ago replaced the men. Like favorite fairy tales that children beg to hear again and again, they give us portraits as we want them to be: familiar, comfortable, and unchallenging. Some are hardly flattering. Grant the butcher. Grant the drunkard. Grant the corrupt. Yet there is also Grant the magnanimous. Grant the peacemaker. Lee has fared better in mythology, even at the hands of his onetime enemies. Myths about him from his own time have now mostly disappeared—Lee the "woman-whipper"—replaced by the Lee who never called the enemy the "enemy." Lee the champion of reconciliation. For more than a century our eyes have teared at the oft-told tale of him, when president of Washington College after the war, threatening an instructor with dismissal if he spoke again disparagingly of General Grant—the great Confederate chieftain, still gallant in defeat, demanding respect for a noble and magnanimous victor. Yet almost certainly the story is just that: a myth.[2]

The mythology serves purposes darker than sentiment, nothing more so than the currently popular, and arrantly nonsensical, assertion that Lee freed his inherited slaves in 1862 before the war was over, while Grant kept his until the Thirteenth Amendment freed them in 1865. The subtext is transparent. If Southerner Lee freed his slaves while Northerner Grant kept his, then secession and the war that followed can hardly have had anything to do with slavery and must instead have been over the tariff or state rights, or some other handy pretext invented to cloak slavery's pivotal role.³ Losing a war is hard on the loser, but even more so when defeated while protecting an institution that Western culture has come to condemn unanimously. After decades of civil rights agitation in America have resulted in a vastly changed complexion to American society, an understandably defensive posture among many in the once-Confederate states welcomes anything showing Yankees like Grant to be venal hypocrites while Southerners like Lee were really committed to ending slavery. It is a powerful palliative to those displeased with the social realities of the present.

In this instance, of course, the reality is that Lee probably never owned any slaves after 1848, and those he freed in December 1862 never belonged to him in the first place. They were the property of his late father-in-law, who provided for their freedom in his will and made Lee his executor. In fact, Lee originally hoped to hold them longer than the will dictated, to enhance inheritances that went to his own children. As for Grant, he only ever owned one slave and that for just a year, and freed him in 1859 even when the failed Grant himself was virtually bankrupt and sorely needed the $1,000 or more the man might have brought him at auction. There were occasionally one or two slaves with his wife and family in the early war years when his wife joined him with the army in a slave state, but they belonged to her father who loaned them to her, and were all freed by state action nearly a year before ratification of the Thirteenth Amendment. In short, the slaves that Lee did free never belonged to him; the slaves that Grant supposedly failed to free were never his to free.

To earlier generations they were the greatest heroes of their time, deservedly the most popular and, if they wished it, influential men in their sections. The country needed both of them after the war, and into the century beyond. The South needed Lee—Lee the unbeatable, the very image of the cavalier warrior—as a focus for pride transcending defeat. Around him they could build a soul-sustaining ethos as they developed the mantra that the Confederacy was never really vanquished; it just wore itself out whipping the Yankees. The South also needed Grant, and a certain kind of Grant, too; a soulless, mechanistic disciple of numbers served slavishly by acolytes and myrmidons like Sherman and Sheridan, all willing to follow him in trading ten lives in blue for every one of gray, overwhelming by raw power and resources rather than skill as a commander. Defeat manfully fighting a leviathan contemptuous of the laws of civilized warfare was not defeat. Rather, it was a moral victory that took the sting from surrender at Appomattox. With Lee at their head, Confederates could face the years after 1865 with high-held heads. Even in the gloomiest hours of Reconstruction, Southern men were not acquiescent in their disfranchisement. Like Lee, they were simply being patient with the Yankees.

Ironically, the reunited Union needed a certain kind of Lee, too. There was no glory in besting a frothing rebel. Jefferson Davis would be vilified for years after the conflict as a tyrant and traitor responsible for the deaths of thousands of prisoners of war. He offered no texture, no nuance, to a North anxious in after years to have beaten the right sort of foe, and in the right way. Lee provided all of that, however. Defeating a knightly foe lent dignity to victory. From his supposedly anguished—and heavily romanticized—choice of loyalties in May 1861, through his series of near-miraculous victories, and on into his dignified and mostly restrained conduct after the war, he offered everything anyone could want in an enemy beaten. There could hardly be a greater irony than the fact that many Confederates would live into the next century to see the day when Lee's image appeared on United States postage, the nation honoring the man who came closer than any other to dividing it permanently. In romance the vanquished became a spiritual victor.

Of course, after 1865 the nation was perfectly happy with U. S. Grant. If the people understood rather little of the actual man, still he had provided most of their good news from 1862 through the surrenders. They liked the bulldog determination, the simple dress, the belligerent cigar, and the few yet unmistakable words. He seemed the culmination of the new American they wanted to be, emerging from the post-revolutionary generation with the "go ahead" optimism and energy to depend on their own sweat and merit rather than name and pedigree, determined to swallow the continent and make the world take notice. Moreover, an assassin had robbed them of the chance to exalt their Father Abraham, which left all of that unfulfilled adoration needful of another target, and Grant, in fact, was already arguably the most popular man in the Union, even more so than Lincoln, whose

Democratic foes even lauded Grant at least so long as they thought he might be one of them.

Until recently, time has been kinder to Lee than to Grant. Their meaning to a modern generation has shifted, driven largely by our own political and social divides. Some in the New South, even in Lexington, Virginia, where he is buried and enshrined, are faintly uncomfortable, embarrassed even, that the section's iconic hero rose to almost god-like stature in a contest ultimately rooted in slavery. They find it more difficult than their forebears to separate honoring a man for his intrinsic qualities of character, courage, and sacrifice, from distaste for the cause that propelled him into the American pantheon. Grant, on the other hand, after generations of being dismissed as a lucky general in spite of his failings, and a president so mired in corruption that his administration is best forgotten, has enjoyed a modest phoenix flight among historians, though the beating of its wings has disturbed little air in perceptions of the man among Americans in general.

Their legacies are inextricably intertwined. Only facing Grant brought out Lee's finest demonstrations of fortitude and resolution. Only defeating Lee made Grant second to Lincoln as the man of the century. They needed each other, and a nation divided in two and then reunited needed both of them in all their guises, often distorting the men themselves to suit a hunger for heroes and villains, not unlike the misshapen likenesses of those wax figures in Liverpool. After that first meeting in Mexico, they both had a long way to go to define the man each would be when they met each other again, and to determine whether they had the capacity to command.

CRUCIBLE *of* COMMAND

1

SONS AND FATHERS

A FATHER'S FAILURE shadowed the life of one; a father's success taunted the other. The first tried to make up for his father by making himself a model of respectability, application, and duty to rebuild his family's honor. The other struggled to live up to his father's expectations and boasts. The one was born to no wealth with a First Family lineage money could not buy. The other lived in the most affluent home in town, with a name and lineage that meant nothing. Yet even in youth they shared common threads, awaiting only the loom of history to weave them together.

Of Robert Edward Lee's youth we know little with certainty. He was born January 19, 1807, at Stratford Hall in Virginia's Westmoreland County.[1] His father was General Henry "Light Horse Harry" Lee, a hero of the Revolution. His mother was Ann Hill Carter, daughter of Charles Carter of ancient aristocracy in the Old Dominion. When the boy was ten Harry Lee recalled that "Robert was always good," but spent barely more than two years with his family after good Robert was born.[2] Arrested for debt in 1809, Lee spent more than a year in jail. Released in 1810 and nearly impoverished, he moved his family to a rented house at 611 Cameron Street in Alexandria, across the Potomac from Washington, where the family probably lived on Ann's income, and it was Ann who tugged on family ties a year later to persuade the leaseholder of her uncle William Henry Fitzhugh's "commodious dwelling house" at 607 Oronoco Street to sublet all or part of it to her family. It sat at the edge of town on a one-acre lot; it was an area some thought unhealthy, and Ann Lee was already unwell.[3]

When the second war with Great Britain came, the hero of the first one opposed it. In July 1812 Henry Lee went to Baltimore and bravely inserted himself between a pro-war mob and an anti-war newspaper. Authorities put Lee and others in the town jail for their own safety, but the mob would not be denied, and on the evening of July 28 it broke into the jail and seized Lee. They repeatedly stabbed him with pocket-knives. One assailant tried to amputate Lee's nose and left it a bloody mess. Others poured molten tallow into his eyes. The mob only failed to kill him from being too drunk.

He returned to Alexandria the ruin of a once-great man and stayed less than a year, broke, and broken in body and spirit. When Lee sat crumpled in the family pew at Christ Episcopal Church, his bandages made him a terrifying apparition to children.[4] He wished now only to get away, to seek peace and perhaps prosperity elsewhere. Counting on his relations and Ann's to care for his family, he left the country in the summer of 1813, never to return in life. His youngest son was just six, but Lee scarcely knew him.

Young Robert was born into debt. Less than three weeks after his birth his father advertised the auction of six thousand acres to settle just one debt of $16,666.[5] At least Ann Lee had independent income.[6] When Charles Carter died in 1806 he left his daughter more than £2,000 in cash, plus a share of a number of properties in Tidewater and north-ern Virginia, specifically providing that her inheritance go into a trust managed by his son and others to provide her income "free from the claim, demand, hindrance or molestation of her husband Genl Henry Lee or his creditors."[7] Then on June 8, 1807, her twenty-one-year-old sister Mildred died, leaving all but £60 of her estate to Ann, most of it in slaves. Mildred also stipulated that the monetary bequest go into a trust "free from the controul of her husband General Lee" until she passed it on to her children at her death.[8] Trustees converted both in-heritances to more than a hundred shares of stock in the Bank of Vir-ginia worth about $14,500. From 1807 onward the shares paid a yearly dividend of $1,440 until about 1812, and $1,210 a year thereafter, while Ann derived more revenue from hiring out Mildred's slaves.[9] With an-nual income of $1,800 or more, several times what most Virginians earned, she was not wealthy, but hardly destitute.[10]

Childhood is the forgotten chapter of biography. Robert Lee casts barely a shadow in his own story until early manhood. He was said to be an attractive child, teased by older sisters, and spoiled by rela-tions in Fauquier County where he was tutored with cousins.[11] If he returned a willful child it did not last long. At home he loved to play in the fenced yard among the viburnum "snowball" trees.[12] From the West Indies Henry Lee tried to exert some influence in shaping his older sons, and through them the youngest.[13] There was some degree of a breach between husband and wife that his years of absence hardly healed. More than once he asked Carter to tell him of his family in Alexandria. He could not remember his children's ages.[14]

Harry's letters to sons Henry and Charles Carter on life and character filtered to good Robert. He enjoined them to prefer "virtue to all other things," to shun falsehood and cherish truth, emulate the great men revealed in a study of mankind, and know right from wrong. He valued the sciences far less than the ethical development of their minds, quipping that "we are called to moralize daily, but we seldom turn to geometry." They should study life rather than nature and regard virtue as the greatest aspiration.[15] They should eschew profanity, especially with their social "inferiors," for it was low and degrading.[16] "Avoid all frivolous authors; such as novel writers," he said, something young Robert took much to heart. "I never could read a novel, because it was the narrative of imaginary action." He recommended particularly the *Meditations* of Marcus Aurelius, with its commentary on command of temper, modesty, piety, abhorrence of vice, and simplicity of diet.[17] Most of all, a man should win his reputation "without noise," be always master of himself, and never yield to passion. His sons must have "complete self-command," for that was "the pivot upon which the character, fame, and independence of us mortals hang."[18] They must stand for their rights and their beliefs, for often adversity brought forth "the greatest display of genius."[19] Years later Robert called these relics of the father he did not know "letters of love and wisdom."[20]

Young Robert Lee's tutorial instruction probably began around age eight, and for the next two or three years he got a sound introduction to Latin and Greek grammar and vocabulary, rhetoric, and perhaps some rudimentary elements of logic. At ten or eleven he was ready for secondary education, and it was not a good time for financial worries to erupt. Recession and a desperate shortage of cash followed the war with Britain. In May 1816 when Robert was nine, Ann told her son Carter that "there never was a period, when it was so difficult to procure money." She suffered a fright when it appeared that her Bank of Virginia shares dividend might be halved during a hard currency shortage.[21] Then that summer she and other Carter heirs were named in a series of suits to which her absent husband was also a party, which dragged on for a decade.[22] She had entered young Carter at Harvard College in 1815, carefully setting aside funds to see him to graduation when the expense of board and tuition approached $300 a year. She still had sons Sidney Smith and Robert to educate, house servants to maintain, and a nominal rent to pay for their house.

Ann was highly sensitive to debt, a concern exaggerated by the return of ill health.[23] "I, and my family, must greatly restrict ourselves," she wrote Carter that same summer. "We have no alternative." She hired out two more slaves and might do a third, and traded down her carriage horses to garner some cash. Unable to collect the money due her for slave hire, she feared she might have to tap Carter's college fund, though said that chiefly to admonish him to watch his expenses. Life with Henry Lee clearly made her something of a penny-pincher and alarmist. She even complained that every evening she and Robert and the others had to debate what they could afford to buy at market the next day for dinner, and rarely put two meat dishes on the table at the same time, Robert preferring veal when it was to be had. An unusual cold spell lasting into July forced her to burn more firewood than usual, and even that caused concern.[24] In May 1816, in the interest of economy, she moved the family just one block south from Oronoco to her brother-in-law Charles Lee's house at the corner of Washington and Princess streets. Before too long, however, the family moved back to Oronoco Street.[25]

She saw a possible solution in the slaves inherited from Mildred. As Ann said herself, slaves were "a species of property extremely inconvenient and disagreeable." She did not need them herself, but hiring them out was always precarious. The rates for hire fluctuated, and thanks to "the facility of their elopement" when out on hire, she had lost two as runaways in the past nine years. Meanwhile, she complained that the females had been "hitherto and will continue unproductive," meaning they bore no children. She feared that by the time her children inherited the blacks on her death, an estate of old men and childless women would probably be of no great value. She needed "a more certain, more punctual, and easily obtained, income for the maintenance of herself and the maintenance, education, and rearing of her said Children."

She asked the county court to allow her to sell the slaves and use the proceeds to buy dividend-producing stock to yield income now and for her children later. A local court denied the plea, but she soon had a petition before the legislature.[26] The petition reached the House of Delegates on December 17, and on January 7, 1817, a committee reported finding the petition reasonable. Finally on February 15, 1817, it passed.[27] While Ann may have kept a few of her sister's slaves out at hire, sale of the rest commenced as quickly as possible, and in the end raised enough capital for her to purchase several thousand dollars in shares in Alexandria's Potomac Bank. It is just as well that she did, for that summer she hired out two more remaining slaves and before the end of the year one of them ran away, putting Ann to the expense of offering a $40 reward.[28]

Fortunately the Bank of Virginia paid a dividend after all in 1816, though reduced by half that year, but with the addition of the Potomac Bank shares, plus income from slave hire and other lesser sources, Ann's family income in 1817 was about $3,000, and more than $4,000 in 1818.[29] For a change the timing was propitious, for in the fall of that year the family learned that Light Horse Harry had died on March 25, 1818, on the Georgia coast while en route to Virginia. There would be no revival of family fortunes from him. All he left his sons, through their mother, was several thousand valueless acres on the south slope of Buffalo Mountain in faraway Montgomery County in southwestern Virginia, as many more acres in Hardy County in western Virginia that he transferred to their names before his death to protect it from seizure, and surface rights to sixteen hundred acres at Harpers Ferry, Virginia, next to the U.S. Armory.[30]

The Lees had to move on, and Ann Lee had her own ideas about education. Her sons must learn to write well. "A man who cannot write a good letter on business, or on the subjects of familiar letters, will make an awkward figure in every situation, and will find himself greatly at a loss on many occasions," she warned. "Indeed I cannot imagine how he could pass through life with satisfaction or respectability." Writing well would be essential to eminence in any profession, so her boys "must write often now, in the days of your youth, and form a good style."[31] Over all, "attend to your studies," she told her sons. "A Man is of little importance in society without education. You will regret in after-life, if you neglect to lay in a store of knowledge now." Sensitive to her husband's disrepute, she wanted her sons to be respected. "Oh! Let me hear that all respect & love my Son," she told them, her most ardent wish for each being "that he should deserve the esteem of the whole world."[32] They must "repel every evil" and "indulge such habits only as are consistent with religion and morality." Robert inculcated her view of "the vanity of every pursuit, not under the control of the most inflexible virtue."[33]

She found an affordable school for Robert near at hand. George Washington helped to found the Alexandria Academy in 1786.[34] The town's most distinguished families composed its board of trustees, including Robert's uncle Edmund Jennings Lee.

In the winter of 1819 the trustees hired Irishman William B. Leary as principal, and during this period of transition Robert Lee probably enrolled for his first term.[35] Leary revised the curriculum, replaced history with English grammar, and held his first examinations on July 27, 1820, where two of Robert's cousins won distinctions.[36] In the fall of 1821 Robert E. Lee was quite definitely enrolled.[37] Again cousins won premiums after their exams, but not Robert.[38] Leary would win no prizes either. He could not manage the business of the academy and handle his classes, and the state of the institution began to deteriorate.[39] By May 30, 1822, it owed nearly $1,000, and its bank threatened to seize the property if not repaid. Finally on January 7, 1823, he announced that his school would move to St. Asaph Street for its spring term.[40] He moved yet again for the fall, but a bailiff jailed him on October 28 for debt.[41]

This near chaos was the backdrop for Lee's secondary education.[42] He applied himself to learning ancient history through the language of Caesar, Cicero, Sallust, Tacitus, Xenophon, and likely Herodotus and Thucydides. He studied rhetoric and writing in Longinus's *On the Sublime*, poetry in the odes of Horace and Virgil's works, and history and literature combined in Homer. Besides those titans, Lee read what he called "the small authors," as well as Andrew Dalzel's *Collectanea Graeca Minora* and *Collectanea Graeca Majora*, anthologies of classical Greek writings. If that were not enough, there was arithmetic, algebra, and the first six books of Euclidian geometry.[43] This diet did not form the man, but it informed him, fleshing a frame made by heredity, experience, and his free will. He would never be at disadvantage in learned company.

Ordinarily such a regimen took up to four years of study.[44] At the least, Lee spent three terms under Leary in 1821–1822, and probably more like three years, but not after Leary's arrest.[45] Since Leary taught both at the academy and elsewhere, Lee might have studied at any of his venues.[46] Withal Robert Lee managed still to be a boy. He ran in the hunt with his Fauquier cousins as the hounds chased foxes, loved riding, and acquired a thorough familiarity with horses.[47] He enjoyed an extended cadre of relations, especially uncle Edmund's boy Cassius F. Lee, as well as friends among the children of Alexandria's better families. Uncles Fitzhugh and Carter Williams treated him with paternal affection and, as he recalled four decades later, "made my days so happy."[48]

There was attention to the metaphysical, but neither parent stressed religious zeal. Henry Lee was an Enlightenment Deist, accepting a unique and benevolent god, but rejecting organized religion, revelation, miracles, and evangelism. He found God in reason and the natural world, but He did not interfere in its affairs, making prayer pointless. The Enlightenment shaped Ann Lee as well, but as a rationalist. Her God actively ordered human affairs and gave purpose to prayer, but still man was helpless in the face of God's will. Her religion arrayed virtue and morality in daily life to earn God's favor.[49] There being no formal ritual other than prayer, Ann joined family and friends in attending Alexandria's Christ Episcopal Church, where she saw Robert baptized, and where the Reverend William Meade often ran him through his Anglican catechism, though he never sought confirmation in his youth.[50] "Pray fervently for faith in Jesus Christ," Ann told her sons. "He is the only rock of your salvation, and the only security for your resurrection from the grave." She accepted a holy trinity and original sin, and that Christ was a god not a man.[51] Robert's faith lagged well behind hers. He might hope for Almighty favor, but expecting little, he expended little to secure it. Thus far his was a very conventional, rather arm's-length sort of Christianity.

He learned much more from his mother. When the navy gave Smith Lee a midshipman's appointment and he left home in 1820, thirteen-year-old Robert became the man of the family, and necessarily helped Ann run the house.[52] They suffered a substantial blow in 1819 when the

Bank of Virginia sustained a serious fall in the depressed economy. Its share value plummeted from $130 to $80, and in the next few years fell as low as $72. It paid no dividend at all for the first half of that year, and for the next two years paid barely half its previous yield. The financial crisis hurt the Potomac Bank less dramatically, but still its dividend fell more than one-third.[53] Fortunately both recovered in 1820, and over the next nine years Ann's annual income averaged almost $3,000.[54] Now an attorney, Carter moved his practice to Oronoco Street in 1823, probably to their house and sharing expenses, though she complained that if he made money, "little of it is seen at home."[55]

Even moderately constrained circumstances could be spirit break-ing for a daughter of the proud Carters. Willful from youth, high spir-ited and a bit of a snob, Ann Lee had also been active, witty, and popu-lar in a wide circle. The buffeting of the years reduced her now to what one cousin called a "great invalid," middle-aged, growing ever weaker and self-pitying, a mother who could trap a care-giving child.[56] Rob-ert looked a likely victim of the snare. With Carter at Harvard, older brother Smith off for the navy, one sister too frail to be of use and the other too young, caring for Ann Lee and tending household affairs fell to him. He went to market, oversaw maintenance of the house and grounds, helped the aged and inept slave coachman Nat look after the carriage horses, and held the keys of the house.[57] Almost daily he took Ann for carriage rides and conveyed her mail and messages about the town, recalling that "I was my mothers outdoor agent & confidential messenger."[58] She found him indispensable, and often said that he was both son and daughter to her.[59] People who knew them saw more of her than his father in young Lee.

All that responsibility came at a cost. Lee spent his teen years re-pressing feelings, a habit that proved hard to break in manhood.[60] He kept doubts, hurts, and disappointments to himself, resolved that he could show joy but not grief.[61] He could not open himself. "I am not very accessible," he confessed later, "and am as niggardly of my friend-ship as if it was worth having."[62] He had little time for that if he was to leave a better legacy than his father.[63] There would be many ac-quaintances, a few close friends, and one or two surrogate fathers, like "good old Uncle Fitzhugh" and George Washington Parke Custis of Arlington, whose paternal concern young Lee never forgot.[64]

It may have affected his studies, for his name was absent from the lists of top scholars.[65] Leary could be effusive praising students, as with Lee's contemporary William Maynadier, whom he extolled for "a desire to improve, to be preeminent in his studies, to yield to none the post of honour in the class."[66] His comments on pupil Lee were blandly economical. "I flatter myself that his information will be found adequate to the most sanguine expectations of his friends," the professor wrote. "I am certain that when examined he will neither disappoint me or his friends."[67] Leary praised Lee's "conduct and his literary information," and his "correct and gentlemanly deportment."[68] Yet he won no prizes even for that. Lee himself confessed that he found Leary's words "less flattering and rhetorical" than he might wish.[69]

There were things to experience beyond the confines of the school. Most exciting of all was October 16, 1824, and the visit of the Marquis de Lafayette, Revolutionary War hero and compatriot of Lee's father. Lafayette stopped in Alexandria to be greeted that afternoon with a gala, including a parade marked by the young Lee's first public appearance, representing his late father and family as one of several parade marshals.[70] More thrilling still, later that day the marquis called at the Oronoco Street home to visit the family of his old revolutionary compatriot.[71] There in the parlor Lee came face to face with someone who knew and admired his father from the heroic days before disgrace. At a dinner for Lafayette that evening, attended by Secretary of State John Quincy Adams, George Washington Parke Custis, and Brigadier General Alexander Macomb, the guests drank toasts to Lafayette, Washington, Patrick Henry, George Mason, Jefferson, and other great Virginians, but none to Light Horse Harry Lee.[72]

The aged hero's visit likely stirred something in Lee. Since boyhood he nurtured an ambition to be a soldier above all else.[73] His brother Smith was on his way to a solid naval career that should protect him from want. Robert had seen classmate William Maynadier secure an appointment to the United States Military Academy at West Point two years before, with the prospect of a free education. Perhaps he could do likewise. The Lees still had the right blood and political connections. Even his older half-brother Henry, so mired in financial and sexual scandal that he was dubbed "Black Horse Harry," maintained strong ties with the hero of the last war Senator Andrew Jackson of Tennessee, and Secretary of War John C. Calhoun, who held the power of appointment.

Only his mother dissented. She could have afforded to send him to college, for all her concern over her finances. In her frail condition, she did not want the son she so depended on to leave her. As for Robert, even if warned that army life might be very different from the rapid promotion and lively times his father experienced, it did not matter. Knowing that he was likely to be saddled with responsibility for his mother and sisters indefinitely, the loneliness of distant assignments did not daunt him. Besides, the Academy was what he really wanted, and no compromise because of money. "I thought & intended always to be one & alone in the World," he recalled a few years later.[74] A uniform would get him away from Alexandria and into a world of men.

He needed a quick decision, however, for if Secretary Calhoun could not give him the appointment, he had to find another career soon. Armed with endorsements from Leary, Fitzhugh, and others, Lee called on Calhoun in February 1824 in company with Custis's influential sister Nellie Lewis. The South Carolinian told the young man, as he did all applicants, to write him a letter stating his age and what he had studied to date. Lee left the meeting sensing that he needed to enlist prominent supporters. He and Mrs. Lewis called on Jackson, to whom Lee's name would not be unfamiliar.[75] Aunt Mary Fitzhugh could also have lent some aid, as she enjoyed high esteem among many in Washington's elite, including General Winfield Scott.[76] Two congressmen wrote letters of endorsement, and one circulated his letter to the whole Virginia delegation for signature. Lee's older brother Carter assured Calhoun that his brother's intellect "seems to be a good one," and, in what may have been an allusion to half-brother Henry Lee's peccadilloes, morally "irreproachable." "Black Horse Harry" wrote his own letter, based on the nation's debt to their illustrious father. Finally Jackson offered the trump card when, as the leading candidate for the presidency that fall, he sent an endorsement.[77]

On February 28 Lee himself wrote what he could expect to be one of the most important letters of his life. No wonder he misspelled a word, gave his birthday as January 29 instead of the nineteenth, and said he "completed" his eighteenth year that January when he meant to say "commenced." He gave a full listing of his studies, citing Leary's lukewarm endorsement, which he enclosed.[78] He need not have been nervous. On March 11 Calhoun gave him the appointment, but because the Academy's roster of cadets was full for the coming fall, Lee had to wait until July 1825. Calhoun let Jackson give the good news to Lee himself, and the young man immediately accepted.[79]

So Robert Lee would go to the Military Academy, but not for another sixteen months. He and his family agreed that an additional course of study would better prepare him, so first he spent time that fall with recent Yale graduate James Watson Robbins, who nurtured, if he did not awaken, in Lee a lifelong appreciation of flora, and may have taken Lee out gathering specimens in the Fauquier countryside that fall.[80] Meanwhile, Benjamin Hallowell and a partner announced their intent to open a boarding school in Alexandria to teach spelling, reading, writing, grammar, and geography, as well as arithmetic and several branches of math and their application to principles of natural science and chemistry. Of special interest was the announcement that they would admit a few pupils who lived in town as day students at greatly reduced rates.[81]

Better yet, Hallowell located in the house next door to the Lees.[82] Late in November his Alexandria Boarding School was ready to admit scholars.[83] A trickle of students commenced in January 1825 with Cassius Lee. Then in February Robert E. Lee paid $10 as a day student to spend the spring term studying mathematics.[84] In the ensuing months he found much to engage his interest and imagination.[85] Best of all was Hallowell himself. He was young, just past twenty-five, intellectually scrappy, but blessed with a keen mind and a passion for teaching.[86] He viewed English grammar as more than rules and emphasized what he called "the philosophy of our language." As a teacher he preferred books that exercised a pupil's judgment, not just his memory.[87] Hallowell also advocated opinions that mixed well with those of many of the Lees. The boys with whom Lee played and studied came from slave-owning families uncomfortable with slavery. In time they all espoused voluntary emancipation.[88]

As a Quaker, Hallowell condemned slavery as a curse to both races, and soon founded the Benevolent Society of Alexandria for "ameliorating and improving the condition of the People of Color." He was no abolitionist. Hallowell did not question the legality of slavery, but he did advocate ending it by gradual voluntary manumission, followed by colonization of the freed slaves back to Africa. Yet he also believed that blacks could not just be freed, for they were not the mental or moral equals of whites. They had to be taught how to think and act in their own best interests before they could be repatriated. Yet slavery must be ended, for he foresaw that it threatened "to sap the foundation of our free institutions" and would "involve us, or our posterity, in overwhelming calamity."[89]

He was a kindly professor, quaint with his Quaker "thee's" and "thou's," and formed a bond with Robert, who years later sometimes banteringly included those "thy's" and "thee's" in his own letters.[90] Hallowell saw how when the other boys left for a midday meal, Lee went home and made Ann Lee comfortable in her carriage against the cold, and took her for daily drives, bending every effort to keep her amused and entertained, while reversing their roles by giving her parental advice on staying cheerful despite her discomfort. When winter breezes gave her shivers, he made ersatz curtains for the coach's windows by cutting them from a newspaper with a large jackknife, much to her amusement.[91] In return she did what she could for him, even sending him to dancing lessons with his Lee cousins. She knew it would be a relief to him to get away even briefly, and he found it a respite from the pressures of home and school, where he found most classmates—"Hallowells boys" he called them—rather dull.[92]

But Hallowell was hardly dull. His tutelage inspired good performance from Lee. When Hallowell demanded rote memorization, Lee delivered as expected. Not surprisingly, his conduct and adherence to the school's rules were exemplary. If Hallowell noticed one thing in particular, it was that when Lee worked problems or drew diagrams on his slate, he did it with a finish and neatness suggesting it might be headed for the engraver rather than erasure. Even when demonstrating complex diagrams of analytical geometry, he drew every one with that same precision.[93] Lee worked unstintingly, brought discipline and pride to his work, and Hallowell himself declared that he held the young man "in great favor" on a basis of "warm personal friendship."[94] Lee never forgot the teacher. Years later he still appreciated Hallowell's instruction.[95]

When that term concluded, Lee had precious little time before he was to leave for New York. This departure marked an end to boyhood.

He had never traveled farther from home than summer trips to Fauquier County or Stratford. Now he was to go more than 250 miles to New York City and then steam up the Hudson to West Point. It was an adventure unlike any he had known before. If he succeeded, he would leave the Academy as a man with an education and a budding career. If his father and brother stained the Lee name, he might have an opportunity to cleanse it. He would not have been a normal young man if he did not feel excitement and anticipation, however torn he was at leaving his mother to be cared for by others. For Ann Lee it was to be no happy parting. "How can I live without Robert?" she complained. "He is both son and daughter to me."[96]

Whatever Lee chose to remember of his childhood, he said little of it in later years. There is no question that he understood duty. Of discipline and perseverance, as well as intellect, he had surely given good evidence thus far. Thanks to his mother he knew self-control and diligence, financial rectitude, and even the value of punctuality.[97]

Even if he did not win awards, still he won the good will and lifelong friendship of Leary and Hallowell. Testimony to his amiability suggests that a pleasing personality was formed, and his ability to make his mother laugh herself out of her black moods indicates an able sense of humor. Yet more shadows remain. Where did he believe he fit into the universe? Did he espouse the laissez-faire god of his father, or his mother's more active Almighty, or neither? Did men control men's affairs, or were events immutably ordained by God? How would he choose his friends and judge other men in that world beyond Alexandria? Would he love and marry? How steady was his moral compass? Were his ethics developing in ways that his father would approve? Did he have ingenuity? Was he cautious or brave? How would he make decisions? Could he be bold?

A host of shadows, and more questions than answers, but as Lee stepped out of the anonymity of childhood, more light gradually began slipping through. Soon the shadows would begin to shrink.

When Hannah Grant gave birth to her first son in a small cabin in the village of Point Pleasant, Ohio, on April 27, 1822, destiny promised nothing more for the boy than to become just one more faceless rural merchant. Ever a storyteller, Jesse Root Grant gave several explanations for his son's name. The earliest credited Hannah's stepmother with proposing Ulysses, she being a great reader of the classics, while Hannah's father simply liked the sound of the name Hiram. They named the boy Hiram Ulysses Grant, though Jesse called him Ulysses, and soon family and friends shortened that to 'Lys.[98]

Jesse Grant learned the tanning trade as a boy in Ohio and in Maysville, Kentucky, on the Ohio River, serving an apprenticeship in his midteens with Owen Brown, whose son John would one day help catapult Jesse's son to fame.[99] Later the young Grant started his own business, then moved to Point Pleasant where he married Hannah Simpson on June 24, 1821. Ten months later Ulysses appeared, and a year after that the Grant family moved to Georgetown, in Brown County, where Jesse's business prospered almost immediately. It was a middling village of fifty families where 'Lys did not want for playmates.[100] George P. Bailey lived virtually next door, Chilton A. White just two doors down, and the Ammens lived scarcely a hundred yards distant. Their son Daniel befriended young Grant, and surely shared stories of his older brother Jacob, then a cadet at West Point.

'Lys was a short, almost chubby boy by age eight, quiet and passive. He did not fight or swear like other boys, but that signaled no lack of daring.[101] Once old enough to wander beyond his mother's eye, Grant often joined his friend Ammen to fish in a modest creek near the village where 'Lys would crawl to the end of a slippery log over the stream to drop his hook. One day he fell in and nearly drowned before Ammen caught him.[102] Some boyish sports held no allure for 'Lys. Other boys could outrun and outwrestle him. He showed no interest in guns or hunting.[103] While friends terrorized squirrels with their rifles, Grant admitted that but for the occasional fish, he did not want to kill animals for either food or sport. When he joined friends for an extended hunt in the woods, he left them and came home without firing a shot, and never went hunting again. Years later, after sending hundreds of thousands of men into battle and possible death, he told Ammen that he had never in his life shot or killed any creature.[104]

He did not find his parents easy to deal with. Jesse was vain, boastful, overbearing, and more critical and harder to please than a parent should be. He thought himself a wit and composed satirical poems on

political affairs that he recited from memory, and sent caustic political letters to local newspapers. He had been friends with Thomas L.
Hamer, a fellow Jacksonian Democrat representing Brown County in
Congress, but the friendship soured when the anti-slave Grant wrote
letters condemning Hamer to the local press. Despite his prosperity,
Grant would never be a very popular man. Even his election as mayor
of Georgetown in 1837 probably had more to do with voters staying
on the good side of a difficult, if very successful, local businessman.
When Andrew Jackson left the presidency in 1837, Jesse Grant aligned
himself with Henry Clay's more progressive Whig Party, not least because of his views on slavery. He never identified himself as an abolitionist, but he regularly voiced his opposition to slavery before friends
and family.[105] In that household, 'Lys later recalled, "I was a Whig by
education and a great admirer of Mr. Clay."[106] Jesse Grant loved to
argue and make speeches, to hear his own voice.[107] Townsmen liked
to poke holes in his inflated ego, even at the expense of his eldest son,
making fun of the pretension of a name of mythic proportion like
Ulysses engrafted on an unprepossessing boy. Some played at cruel
anagrams and called him "Useless."[108]

Hannah Simpson Grant was cool and aloof, much under Jesse's sway,
and notably reticent, though she did not fear to speak her mind. Her
son mirrored her quiet and even-tempered nature.[109] What Ulysses and
the siblings to follow missed in her was affection. Surely she loved her
children, but she showed emotion sparingly. Young 'Lys told his friend
Ammen that he had never seen his mother's tears, either for sadness
or joy.[110] She was a devout Methodist, and Jesse joined the church in
1832, but neither parent forced their children to attend church or avow
faith other than to observe the Sabbath.[111] Hannah kept Ulysses well
dressed for school, but gave little evidence of her love beyond that.[112]
Perhaps that is why the boy became especially fond of her more affectionate mother, Sarah Simpson.[113] Grant heard his father's stories so
many times he never forgot them, but when he wrote his memoirs he
recalled not one detail of his mother's life.[114]

'Lys got a better than average education for his time and place. He
first attended Georgetown's small subscription academy, presided over
by a North Carolinian, John D. White. In winter the boys squirmed
on uncomfortable wooden benches before him, from just after dawn

until shortly before sunset. White was prone to fall asleep at his desk on warmer days. If the pupils woke him with their play, he took up a beech switch and swatted indiscriminately, assuming that a few blows were bound to hit the right boys. White could use a whole bundle of switches in a single day. "He only followed the universal custom of the period, and that under which he had received his own education," Grant recalled, never forgetting those switches and how "they performed that part of my education."[115] Recurring bouts with foot and leg cramps did not help 'Lys with concentration on lessons.[116]

The curriculum began with the alphabet, reading, and spelling, and later geography, grammar, and mathematics, though White undercut the math lessons by solving the difficult problems in his head without explaining the process.[117] Grant soon found that he could do them in his head, too. "His mind seemed exactly fitted for solving such problems on a moment's notice," recalled classmate James Sanderson. When others barely had the puzzler in their minds, Grant was already shouting the answer.[118]

Grammar was another matter, and he always believed he never really learned it.[119] He tried to avoid doing the brief 150-word essays his teacher assigned, yet produced a few of merit. Credit for that went to his reading. Though he claimed not to care for reading, he read well and grew to love books. Jesse Grant had perhaps three dozen titles at home, running from Washington Irving to tomes on Methodism. He encouraged his son to read them, even if 'Lys sometimes absent-mindedly scrawled his name on the fly leaves.[120] From the earliest surviving examples of his composition, it is clear that by reading and listening he absorbed sufficient style and grammar to express himself succinctly and precisely. Grant used words sparingly and chose the most direct approach both in writing and speaking. Schoolmates thought he was just dull, and teased him.[121] Actually he was revealing the beginnings of a style of his own.

Grant could scarcely speak in front of the class. After butchering a piece from George Washington's farewell address, he vowed never to speak in public again regardless of the consequences.[122] He did demonstrate one other skill, though, a fine eye for visual detail and a good grasp of proportion and perspective. Classmate Chilton White noted that "he could draw a horse and put a man on him."[123] In fact what his friends saw were the beginnings of a talent for pencil and brush, especially if a horse was in the frame—all early evidence of a quick visual study and power of observation.

Grant was "one of the quietest boys I ever knew," recalled Sanderson. Still, he was popular and usually up for a swim or a romp, but nothing excited him like riding.[124] 'Lys loved horses and from an early age revealed a notable rapport with the animals. He usually rode bareback or on a blanket at breakneck speed, sometimes down Georgetown's main street.[125] Occasionally a horse proved too much for him, as when Ammen's colt threw him over its neck into a stream, but that was an anomaly.[126] At horsemanship, as young Sanderson said, he was "the best anywhere in our locality."[127] A small circus on an Ohio tour in 1837 made a stop in Georgetown when Grant was about fifteen.[128] In one act a monkey rode a pony, and then the impresario invited boys to try riding the apparently docile animal. As soon as a boy mounted, the pony raced, twisting, turning, and bucking, until the hapless boy lay in the dust. When the handler asked for another volunteer, Grant stepped forward. The handler gave a sharp crack of his whip and the pony bolted off, then reared high on its back legs, kicked until all four were off the ground, and returned to a headlong gallop. Grant kept his seat through it all.[129]

Years later people told that story and others as metaphors for tenacity of another kind in Grant. Jesse recalled 'Lys driving a cow when he was twelve, only to have the animal bolt and run with him holding resolutely onto its tail. When the cow jumped a wide mud puddle, the boy fell in the mud. Jesse said it showed "the bull-dog pluck and tenacity with which Ulysses always held on when he got hold of a good thing," though Jesse often told tales that made his son look a fool as much as a hero.[130] Still, 'Lys revealed an early determination not to give up. A steep hill west of Georgetown often stalled teamsters, who found that the Grant boy could get their teams to the top for them. "I never got stalled myself," he supposedly told them, "and so my horses never got stalled either." From an early age he expected to accomplish what he set out to do.[131]

Ulysses gained a reputation for breaking horses and training pacers. Jesse retold many stories of his son's feats. In time he had young 'Lys harnessing a horse when barely old enough to walk himself, riding at age five standing on their bare backs, at eight doing it balanced on one leg, and at ten taking passengers forty miles by wagon to Cincinnati. Sometimes the posturing father's stories went beyond horses, to boast of his boy spending seven months at age twelve hauling huge logs to build the county jail. Like everyone else Ulysses knew his father's boasts were more about himself. Georgetown heartily wearied of what some called Jesse's "vain foolishness," and got even when a traveling phrenologist came to town. They watched in glee as Jesse submitted 'Lys to examination, and then believed the charlatan's discovery of a future president in the bumps on the boy's head. The joke never died, and Jesse never got it. Years later he still boasted of the prediction. His embarrassed son never mentioned it.[132]

If the father voiced approval, he usually ruined it quickly. When Jesse spoke of his son's work ethic, he added either that it sprang from his own, or went on to say that he could hardly ever get the boy to work in the tannery. Jesse said "he was a most beautiful child," then spoiled it by adding that "he did not grow up as handsome as our other boys."[133] Others saw how he treated his son, and years later Georgetown preferred to think that Ulysses got his brains from his mother.[134]

His father even told a humiliating story demonstrating his son's guilelessness, a lack of sophistication that often made him the butt of jokes. Schoolmaster White's son remembered thirty years after the fact how the boys teased 'Lys when in about 1831 Jesse sent him to buy a horse. He was to offer $50 and settle no higher than $60. At the outset Ulysses innocently told the seller how high he was authorized to go, and not surprisingly paid $60.[135] "It was a long time before I heard the last of it," Grant recalled years later. Late in life he still recalled his "great heart-burning" embarrassment when people told the story. "This story is nearly true," he confessed, but added context by explaining that he paid $25, not $60, got three years' use of the horse until it went blind, and then still managed to sell it for $20.[136] Offering no conclusion of his own, he let the facts say for him that it was not such a bad deal after all. The real lesson in the episode is that Grant adapted measures and wants to the conditions at hand, and assessed risk—in this case money paid—against a long-term return.

From about age eleven 'Lys managed a plow and horse, tended all the animals, and continued going to school, all a lesson in application and discipline, which he would never lack. However difficult his parents might be, they rarely scolded or punished him, and gave him wide latitude to do and go as he wanted when not at work or study. He could go fishing, ride to visit his mother's parents in the next county, and ice skate and drive the sleigh whenever the snow allowed. He enjoyed a golden childhood, free to stretch his mind and his muscle, and free from the constraints imposed on young Lee.[137]

'Lys's horizons expanded in 1836 when his grammar schooling ended, and he was at an age at which most boys left school for good and found employment. Two newspaper publishers, Samuel Medary of the *Ohio Sun* at nearby Batavia and David Morris of Batavia's *Chronicle of the Times*, each asked Jesse to let 'Lys come learn their trade. At odds politically with the Democrat Medary, Jesse occasionally wrote political pieces for Morris and might have favored his proposal had not Hannah protested that their boy was yet too young.[138] Meanwhile, Grant's friend Daniel Ammen left when Congressman Thomas L. Hamer gave him a midshipman's appointment in the United States Navy, evidence that there were worlds and careers beyond Georgetown and tanneries.[139]

Instead they enrolled 'Lys as a junior at the Maysville Academy across the Ohio in Kentucky.[140] It was twenty miles from Georgetown, but the boy had been farther from home than that, inspiring his reticent mother to offer the compliment that 'Lys was "always a good traveler."[141] Virginia-born William West Richeson ran the academy with partner Jacob W. Rand. Richeson was accomplished in English, Latin, and Greek, and passionate about math, which boded well for young Ulysses. When he started his studies he found a number of other boys of about his age, among them Thomas and William Nelson and Absalom Markland. Some became his lifelong friends. In the way of boys they gave each other nicknames. For reasons mysterious, young Grant became "Toad."[142]

Richeson read and lectured to them from the writings of Caesar, Sallust, and his favorite Juvenal, as well as the Roman poets Virgil and Horace. He took the students on long walks up Kentucky mountains, and Grant would have been especially impressed to find that the professor was a daring, almost reckless horseman.[143] Fellow students found "Toad" quiet, retiring, and studious, though the classics struggled to hold his attention. Sandy haired, freckled, still slightly chubby, the teenager seemed ever good-natured.[144] Surprisingly Grant joined the Philomathea Society, a literary and debating club, and sat on the executive committee. Despite his Georgetown resolution, he spoke in debates, defending propositions like "females wield greater influence in society than the males," "Socrates was right in not escaping when the prison doors were opened to him," or "intemperance is a greater evil than war." Despite Jesse's views, he won a resolution that "it would not be just and politic to liberate the slaves at this time."[145]

He stood well in all his classes by the time he finished his one term, but in 1837 Jesse called him home.[146] There was work to be done in the business, and 'Lys spent the next term back in Georgetown. He freely admitted he would much have preferred to be out with the horses, but he worked hard all the same.[147] Especially he enjoyed going away on business. "I had always a great desire to travel," he recalled of his youth. His father sent him on trips to Cincinnati and Maysville, even farther to Louisville and Lexington, Kentucky, to Chillicothe, 200 miles east to Wheeling, and 250 miles to Cleveland. By his midteen years 'Lys believed he was the best-traveled boy in Georgetown but for one other. At an age when young Robert E. Lee had scarcely been outside the immediate orbit of Alexandria, young Grant had traveled 1,500 miles or more, much of it on his own with responsibility for animals, wagons, and cargo.[148]

The experiences of those travels stayed with him. When Grant was just fifteen he went to Flat Rock, Kentucky, a seventy-mile trip, taking postmaster Hugh Payne to see his brother. Both Paynes, like Jesse, were Democrats turned ardent Henry Clay supporters.[149] Grant slept in Payne's store during his visit, and helped his clerk get ready to open for business in the mornings.[150] He also took a liking to one of William's saddle horses and proposed to trade it for one of the two pulling his carriage. By now Jesse Grant let his son do as he liked when it came to horses, and Payne agreed to the trade. He even paid Grant $10 in the bargain when the boy pointed out that the new horse was not yet broken to harness, while the one he offered was accustomed to pulling a carriage. The supposedly feckless 'Lys had made another good deal.

He believed he could break the horse by pairing him with the remaining animal on his carriage, the one steadying the other. It was almost a metaphor for the way a high-spirited man could be made productive by the lead of a steadier associate. The new horse did well until a barking dog spooked both animals, and they bolted and almost pulled the carriage over a steep bank. The forty-two-year-old Hugh Payne refused to ride farther and left, while the fifteen-year-old boy kept his head, tied a bandanna over the balky animal's eyes to calm it, and drove the rest of the way home on his own. Grant liked to recall the story in later life. He had made a good trade and met difficulty with calm and ingenuity.[151]

In the winter of 1838–1839 Jesse entered his son at the College of Ripley on the bank of the Ohio, which began auspiciously in 1830 headed by the noted abolitionist John Rankin.[152] Ripley had attracted some notoriety for once admitting a black to its theology classes.[153] It was barely holding on when sixteen-year-old Grant arrived. The school had little to teach him.[154] Besides, there were distractions. He had learned to dance and he enjoyed it, going to every party he could, becoming what one young lady recalled as "a great gallant among the rural girls."

Still, there were lessons to be had in the noted seedbed of abolitionist sentiment, and the very first stop for many runaway Kentucky slaves on the so-called Underground Railroad. Townspeople still talked of the winter just past when a slave woman who had run away from Kentucky with her infant child walked across the winter-frozen Ohio River to Ripley with her baby in her arms. The president sheltered her in his house until he could spirit her north to freedom. Years later Harriet Beecher Stowe used the anonymous woman as one of the prototypes for a composite character she called Eliza in her 1852 novel, *Uncle Tom's Cabin*.[155]

Ulysses Grant was apparently unimpressed by the story.[156] Neither was he impressed by the curriculum, which seemed to consist mainly of rote repetition of such basic axioms as "a noun is the name of a thing."[157] Grant was seventeen now, and though he later made light of his education, he knew what a noun was. He wrote easily and well, with a good vocabulary and facility of expression.[158] His spelling was well above average for his time and place, and his punctuation was better than young Lee's. Grant always showed some eccentricities in orthography, while Lee's spelling was more precise, befitting a man who would marry a cousin of Noah "Dictionary" Webster.

It took only one session for Jesse Grant to decide that the academy was not worth the $1.25 or so per week paid for his son's board.[159] A new prospect for a really practical higher education, with the potential for a life's career, and at virtually no expense, suddenly arose. There might be an unfilled appointment to the United States Military Academy. Jesse wrote to the War Department in Washington, but the reply was discouraging. Things had changed since Lee's day. Now Grant must persuade the sitting congressman for his district to nominate his boy, but that delegate was Thomas L. Hamer, whom Grant's fellow Whigs had recently denounced as a "double dealing political swaggerer."[160] Still, Grant boldly wrote Hamer immediately to ask that he nominate Ulysses for the cadetship.[161] Hamer wanted to heal the breach with Grant, and at the same time regain the support of one of his district's more prosperous and influential men.[162] Thus on March 22 young Grant secured the appointment.[163] Hamer had not been intimate with the Grants recently, and Georgetown had virtually forgotten the boy's full name, knowing him as only Ulysses, or just 'Lys. Amid all those sibilants Hamer thought he remembered hearing another, and sent his nomination in the name of Ulysses S. Grant.

If the young Ulysses to date felt any affinity for the Field of Mars he kept it well hidden. He had no interest in guns, and his amiability scarcely hinted that he might feel the spirit of aggression so vital in a successful military man, but Jesse Grant's children did what he told them. According to Jesse, when he asked 'Lys how he felt about going to West Point, his son replied "first rate."[164] As Ulysses remembered the story, his father told him he believed he would get an appointment, and 'Lys declared, "I won't go." Jesse said he rather believed he would, and Ulysses later confessed that *"I thought so too, if he did."*[165] It was neither the first nor the last little defeat at his father's hands.

'Lys returned to Georgetown briefly before leaving for West Point, and said little about it to his friends until a few days before his departure.[166] He always loved to travel, and a trip to New York would be his longest yet. The Military Academy placed a heavy emphasis on mathematics and engineering, and he could expect to find all of that interesting and challenging. Privately, however, he feared he might not pass his exams. 'Lys knew how his own father would take it if he failed to graduate.[167] Caught between the force of Jesse Grant's determination and fear of his father's wrath should he fail, Hiram Ulysses Grant prepared to leave for New York with probably less enthusiasm than any cadet-to-be of his time.

'Lys Grant enjoyed a happier childhood than Lee, though in a way they shared a common cause for such embarrassments as they felt—fathers. Lee never outgrew the impact of embarrassment over his father's bankruptcy and fall from a hero's perch; Grant suffered the frequent humiliation of a father constantly trying to make his son an extension of his own ego. Grant knew his father all too well, and his mother seemingly little at all. Thanks to having to be her doctor, nurse, coachman, and companion, Lee knew his mother perhaps too intimately, while his father remained little more than a name and a portrait. The boy Grant never knew want or the threat of insolvency. He lived rather an indulged, even privileged, childhood as the son of a rural magnate, and if Jesse was overbearing and Hannah cool and undemonstrative, still he did not have to contend with Lee's teasing sisters and the self-pity and possible hypochondria of Ann Hill Carter Lee. In the context of their times and places, the two young men received roughly comparable "academy" education. Certainly both were sufficiently prepared to pass their entrance examinations at West Point. Lee had distinguished connections in the East far greater than Jesse Grant's circle of Whig business and political cronies, but 'Lys's experience of urban and rural America outstripped Lee's limited Potomac horizons.

The differences between them were largely cosmetic, growing far more from accident of birth than individual character and ability. Each demonstrated industry, application, and self-reliance; Lee by being the man of the house from far too early an age, Grant by his assumption of extraordinary work duties for his age. The Ohioan was more curious about the world beyond home than Lee, but then the Virginian's responsibilities allowed him less opportunity to escape Alexandria. In tendencies mirroring their approaches to the world around them, Lee's temperament and nascent distrust of much of society turned him inward, allowing him scant scope for friendships, whereas Grant was open and outgoing, naive perhaps, with an ever-widening circle of acquaintances. Hard to anger, Grant got along with the easygoing and the difficult, an essential attribute for managing people, while Lee was already somewhat stiff and formal, muffled beneath protective layers, with a high temper that he sometimes struggled to control. Yet both types of personality could win loyalty, and both young men established lifetime friendships in these years. Lee revered his father, and all his life defended him, while trying not to be like him. Grant already sought to escape being Jesse's son. When he later told stories of his youth, he rarely included his father. If years later he had more to say of his father and his family than of Hannah and hers, it was recollection with an undercurrent of resentment against the grasping, bumptious, overbearing businessman of Georgetown. Each was more his mother's son.

Neither gave up on first encountering an obstacle. If he wanted something, he pursued it with determination, whether a coveted horse or better grounding in mathematics. Grant used ingenuity in problem solving, as well as trial and error, and had the capability of projecting solutions in his mind before putting them to the test. He made decisions by establishing in basic terms what he wanted to achieve and assessing his options as determined by resources and practicality. Lee as yet had less scope for demonstrating problem solving or decision making beyond the needs of coping with the care of his mother and sisters, yet he accomplished that effectively. Grant demonstrated daring and apparent fearlessness; if Lee did the same the memory was lost. Nothing suggests that their moral and ethical compasses were different. Neither professed interest in religion. Blood and experience instilled in Lee the nucleus of his later fatalism, while the happy-go-lucky Grant approached life with an almost innocent optimism.

Both boys had fun. Both loved to ride and felt affection for horses, though Grant's went deeper. Both enjoyed other boys' pursuits, but only Lee hunted game, while Grant avoided all blood sports. Neither showed a taste for telling jokes, yet each was developing a self-deprecating sense of humor; Grant's was further influenced by the vogue for rural humor then made popular by backwoods wits like David Crockett, while Lee's was sophisticated, involving wordplay and banter, often touched with an edge of sarcasm. Grant wanted to be a farmer. Lee wanted to be a soldier. Each was equipped to grow into a man of standing, just as two families in Virginia and Ohio expected. Just how considerable it might be, of course, would depend on what they did with the advantages given them, and the challenges and opportunities of events yet unforeseen.

SCHOOL OF
THE SOLDIER

IF LEE WAS a shadow through his childhood, at West Point he was a cipher. Almost nothing about him personally has survived beyond examination rankings, class standings, and records of special assignments. Yet there is a hint of his approach to learning. "I understand the *principle*," he said a few years later, "& when that is the case am never at a loss."[1] No wonder that first (or fourth class) year he finished fourth in math and fifth in French in a class of eighty-seven. Adding personal conduct, Lee emerged overall third in his class and sixth in the Academy.[2] The school operated on a demerit system for cadets who broke rules on uniform dress, church attendance, and behavior. Too many demerits and a cadet could be dismissed, but the demerits could be erased by an acceptable excuse or extra guard duty on Saturdays. Lee garnered not a single demerit during the year.[3]

It was an outstanding performance. His name appeared in the annual army register, then in June instructors promoted him to cadet staff sergeant.[4] Following a summer encampment full of infantry and artillery drill, he began his third classman year with more mathematics and geometry, French again, and drawing, while the infantry and artillery drill continued. He spent free time in the post library reading about Napoleon's campaigns, eschewing the novels his father condemned, though he imbibed enough of Shakespeare to quote from memory Falstaff's friends Nym and Bardolph from *Henry IV*.[5] He befriended a few fellow cadets like Joseph E. Johnston, another Virginian, though his closest friend surely was John "Jack" Mackay of Georgia. He won another honor with appointment as acting assistant professor of math—a tutor really.[6] As the year approached its end he had thoroughly enjoyed the Academy experience, and with pardonable pride wrote his mother of his leading achievements: rapid advancement in rank, his still demerit-free record, his assistant professorship, and the $10 a month it paid in addition to his cadet's monthly pay.[7] At the June 1827 examinations he advanced to second in his class behind Charles Mason, and seventh overall.[8]

The Academy allowed cadets one furlough after their third class year. Ann Lee had moved from Alexandria about the time Robert left for West Point, and now lived in a large house on Second Street in Georgetown built some years before by the developer Clement Smith.[9] Her health was now such that she could barely take part in managing the house. Her daughter Ann had married the year before and was gone, and only Mildred and Carter, whom Robert always called "the Captain," lived with her, and they spent most of their time reading and letting family business languish. No wonder she moaned that spring, "Alas! Alas! I wish I had my little boys, Smith and Robert, living with me again."[10] Robert's return must have been a tonic for her, as he passed much of his leave taking her to see family and friends at Eastern View in Fauquier County, where the graduate made quite an impression.[11] "He was dressed in the West Point uniform," a visiting fifteen-year-old girl recalled years later: "grey, with white bullet buttons, and I heard his beauty, and fine manners constantly commented on."[12]

Lee hoped to make a bigger impression on another young woman, his nineteen-year-old distant cousin Mary Anna Randolph Custis of Arlington House. Possibly some romantic bond began to tie them at Arlington on Christmas 1824, or even earlier.[13] Yet if his heart attached itself to her from his teen years, practical impediments kept it in check. His responsibility for his mother and sister Mildred added to his drive to find a profession, impelled him to rank duty over romance, and Lee accustomed his heart to the expectation that he might never marry.[14] Commenting on "that all-admiring & admired one Mr Lee" after he visited that August, Mary Custis told a friend that "he is so much occupied in the duties of his profession that he has but little time for the frivolous affairs of the heart," such things being "always *light* with him you know."[15]

Staff Sergeant Lee returned to the Academy and entered on chemistry and the physical sciences like mechanics, optics, electricity, astronomy, and geology. On the parade his class concentrated especially on artillery tactics. At examinations in January 1828, he finished second in natural philosophy, third in chemistry, and fourth in drawing, and improved on that in the spring term. Meanwhile, he expanded his reading to writings more recreational, among them a rather sensational self-laudatory autobiography by John Paul Jones, and Major General Charles de Warnery's *Thoughts and Anecdotes Military and Historical* on European wars of the previous century.[16] He finished the year as one of fifteen demerit-free cadets, ranked fifth in the entire school for conduct, while in his class he still stood second behind Mason, who seemed always one step ahead.[17]

Lee commenced his first classman year well when the commandant appointed him corps adjutant, the highest position a cadet could hold. The honor recognized Lee's surpassing soldierly deportment. Part of being a good officer was looking the part, and no one in the Academy excelled Lee in bearing.[18] Only in the first class year did cadets actually study the science of war: artillery tactics, grand strategy and field tactics, composition of armies and their movements, writing orders, and more, much of it with examples from military history. Lee read a translation of the military doctrine of Antoine-Henri, Baron Jomini, who argued that war was an art, not a science, and that while strategy might be reduced to some scientific principles, warfare itself could not. Rather he stressed that war's outcome, and even the result of its component battles, were influenced by popular passion, will, and motivation, the personalities of commanders, national martial heritage and pride, "and a thousand other things"—what he called "the poetry and metaphysics of war." Lee also read the *Federalist Papers* and other writings consonant with his father's views on the nature of government and the Whiggish sentiments of the Lees in general. It was an appropriate moment, for as Lee commenced his final year South Carolina pushed a doctrine of nullification whereby states could declare federal statutes null and void, with secession a possible alternative.[19]

In January Lee performed admirably and at the end of the final term emerged at the top in artillery and tactics, and close to the top in everything else. In a class now down to 46 cadets, he finished second, still behind Mason. Out of the 206 in the Academy, he tied with 5 others for top honors in conduct with not a demerit.[20] Lee's name appeared on the monthly list of those "distinguished for correct conduct" from the outset, and never went off.[21] For the fourth year in a row his name appeared in the army register. Better yet, given his choice of service, he selected the elite Corps of Engineers.

He had made himself a Lee to be proud of, and family in Virginia looked every day for his return from West Point, boasting to friends that "he graduates with much éclat." Letters from home dampened his spirits with the news that Ann Lee was sinking, now too ill to travel at all.[22] "I never calculate on living longer than from one season to another," she had told her sons two years before. "My disease is an unconquerable one."[23] By the time he reached Ravensworth, where her sister Anna Fitzhugh cared for her, she had just days to live. Lee became again nurse and companion, mixed her medicines, and stood at her bed night and day. If he left the room, she fixed her eyes on the door waiting for him to return. On July 10 her breathing stopped and her son found himself almost prostrated with grief.[24] Unable to control his feelings, he could not attend her funeral, and stayed in her room for hours pacing beside the bed.[25] Ever after, Lee attributed whatever in himself that was good to his mother.[26]

It was a scene far different from one almost exactly ten years later when another young man said farewell to his mother. Young Hiram Grant likely felt no pangs at leaving when he departed for West Point in the summer of 1839. He expressed some of his anticipation, and apprehension, in an acrostic poem for his friend Mary King:

> My country calls and I obey,
> And shortly I'll be on my way
> Removed from Home, far in the west,
> Yet you with home and friends are blest
>
> Kindly then remember me,
> (I'll also often think of thee)
> Nor forget the soldier story
> Gone to gain the field of glory.[27]

The soldier-to-be looked forward to two things when he boarded a paddle-wheeler for Pittsburgh on the first leg of his journey, and neither of them was the Military Academy. He wanted to see Philadelphia and New York, the largest cities in America.[28] Having done that he would have been content to turn around and go home. He transposed his name to Ulysses Hiram Grant when he reached West Point on May 31, 1839, hoping to avoid unnecessary teasing for his initials being H. U. G. The Academy somehow lost the Hiram and persisted in using Hamer's erroneous "S.," however, making him Ulysses S. Grant. The government in the end had its way, though it took him years to yield. He never used the "Simpson" represented by the new initial, and four years later comically observed, "I have an 'S' in my name and dont know what it stand for."[29]

When Grant stepped onto the Hudson River wharf at West Point, little had changed in the decade since Lee left. It was "the most beautiful place I have ever seen," Grant declared. "I do love the *place*." Inspiring sights reminded him of their revolutionary forefathers, as did the onetime headquarters of "that *base* and *heartless* traitor *to* his country and his God," Benedict Arnold. Even at seventeen Grant had a well-formed notion of treason's just deserts. After two months of summer encampment sleeping in a tent with only a single pair of blankets, he was still delighted. Once in barracks he spent free time on Sundays looking out his window on the scores of white sails dotting the Hudson, and despite predictions, was not the least homesick. He told friends that "I would not go home on any account whatever."[30]

That resolve did not waver even when he began to grasp the rigor of his studies. Fourth classmen like Grant spent their first year at French and mathematics, chiefly algebra. He found the classes long and hard, but halfway through the term he felt no great fear for the coming examinations in January. In fact the concentrated study made the time pass quickly, and the young cadet felt optimistic. "I mean to study hard and stay if it be possible," he told a cousin, for the army promised a good and secure career. "If a man graduates here he [is] safe fer life," Grant believed in September 1839. Should he not pass his exams, "very well," he mused. "The world is wide."

Regulations required cadets to attend chapel every Sunday or risk demerits, which Grant thought "not exactly republican." Those "black marks" as he called them were a sword over their heads.[31] Get more than two hundred and a man faced dismissal. The conduct system had changed little since Lee's time. Demerits received were only removed

by presenting a valid excuse to the superintendent, or by demonstrating error in awarding them. Grant's conduct his first month was perfect, but he got his first two in August, and twenty-six more by year
end.[32] He saw his share of what he called "big bugs" when they visited, men like President Martin Van Buren, General Winfield Scott,
and even one of his favorite writers, Washington Irving. Scott inspired
awe. "I thought him the finest specimen of manhood my eyes had ever
beheld," Grant later recalled.[33]

He would rather have seen a few women. After four months he had
not spoken to a single lady. "I wish some of the pretty girles of Bethel
were here just so I might look at them," he complained that fall, but
then dismissed his own complaint with "fudge! Confound the girles."
Besides, he hardly welcomed the idea of a pretty woman seeing him
as he saw himself at the moment. He felt laughable in his uniform,
his skin-tight pants threatening to split seams with a crack "as loud
as a pistol" anytime he bent over. His gray coat with its big buttons
fastened up to the chin made him feel "very singulir," and he feared
that on seeing him friends would wonder if he were fish or a mammal,
telling one "I hope you wont take me for a Babboon."

Withal he reported home that "I am happy, *alive* and *kicking*," and
hoped to last at least his first two years.[34] He passed his first term's
examinations well enough, below the median in French but above in
math. The next term challenged him more with algebra, plane geometry, trigonometry, and more, and he found his June 1840 examinations
difficult, especially after months of recurrent colds and sore throats.[35]
In a class of 60 he finished 49th in French and 16th in math. Despite
three demerit-free months, he finished the year with 51 and five-sixths
demerits, ranking him 27th in his class, and 147th of 233 in the school.[36]

With exams mercifully past, he went into summer encampment,
with some time to relax and enjoy a series of parties and balls, but
soon got an object lesson of another kind. At morning parade one
day a cadet officer reprimanded another for sloth at obeying an order.
That evening the offender dallied again and became insubordinate and
threatening when challenged. Arrested, he refused to remain in the
guard tent and sent the superintendent a dare to dismiss him, which
the superintendent obliged.[37] For all of those present, including Grant,
it was an object lesson in discipline and the hazard of unchecked

temper. Required to file a statement as a witness, Grant reluctantly obeyed. "Of all things I dont like to have to speak ill of a third person," he remarked a few years later, "and if I do have to speak so I would like as few as possible to know it."[38]

Grant advanced to the third class and commenced a new set of studies that summer, adding drawing and ethics to French and math, and applied himself a bit more successfully, though still he rarely read a lesson more than once. The post library drew him, but to shelves not visited by Lee. He loved novels like Alain René Le Sage's *Histoire de Gil Blas de Santillane*, but preferred his fiction in English. He read most of James Fenimore Cooper, Washington Irving, Walter Scott, Frederick Marryat, and Charles Lever, devoting more time to them than to his texts.[39] Other distractions drew him, and in January 1841 for the first time he committed an offense resulting in punishment when he got two extra tours of Saturday guard duty for being caught absent from his quarters visiting with Cadet Franklin Zantzinger of Virginia.[40] Still, in June 1841 he finished 44th of 53 in French, 23d in drawing, 46th in ethics, and an excellent 10th in math. At 24th overall, he stayed just above the midline in his third class, but was 144th of 219 in the Academy overall. Again he had three demerit-free months, but finished with 63 for the year, most for housekeeping and dress infractions.[41]

He went home on his eight-week furlough to find his family moved to nearby Bethel. He was fully grown now to about five feet seven inches tall, slimmed but still muscular, his hair a darkening sandy reddish-brown. He took little note of his appearance, but attracted the attention of others, especially among the boys of the town who listened to him tell stories of West Point in a rather diffident manner, with no evidence of brag or vanity. "He was shy with strangers, but among his friends he was always known as being a very good talker," recalled Melancthon Burke, who first met him that summer. Many noted the contrast between the modest young man and his overbearing father, who flaunted the fact that he was the richest man in town, had a piano in his house, wore gold spectacles, and had a son at the Military Academy.[42] When opportunity afforded Grant rode into the country to call on old friends like John W. Lowe of Batavia.[43] Surely he also called on some of the "girles" he had missed while away at West Point. Years afterward claimants to have been his sweetheart in these days were legion, but as yet nothing suggests that he had to date experienced young love.[44]

Soon enough the furlough ended and he was off once more to New York, arriving to find himself just barely chosen a cadet sergeant to help train a company at drill, the seventeenth of eighteen selected from his class.[45] Meanwhile, he met a largely new curriculum of sciences, including chemistry, optics, mechanics, astronomy, and electricity, as well as more drawing.[46] Now he numbered several other cadets as friends, both in his own and in other classes. A year ahead of him were William S. Rosecrans, John Pope, Daniel H. Hill, Gustavus W. Smith, Earl Van Dorn, and a Georgian named James Longstreet who became a close friend. Grant's own class included William B. Franklin, Rufus Ingalls, and his roommate and close friend Frederick T. Dent, while a year behind him was Kentuckian Simon Bolivar Buckner.[47]

Grant rose from the bottom third of his class to the middle in all of his subjects: 22nd of 41 in chemistry, 19th in drawing, and 15th in sciences, though his overall class rank was only marginally in the top half at 20th. He studied no more now than before, still preferring fiction to his texts. The daily two-hour drawing classes revealed a genuine talent at least as a copyist, painting bucolic countryside scenes—some with horses at which he excelled—European city and rural settings, and works by American painter George Catlin.[48] He showed a quick eye for detail and proportion, and a fine grasp of scale, all of which could serve a soldier well beyond the easel, but there were no demerit-free months this year, and twice more he would be punished. In February 1842 he did two extra Saturday guard tours for carelessness at drill, then in May was confined to his quarters for two weeks for "speaking in a disrespectful manner" to a superior.[49] No wonder his tally of demerits rose to 127, though 29 of those were later remitted.[50] In the corps as a whole he stayed in the upper edge of the bottom third at 157 of 213. Those demerits put an end to his cadet sergeant's stripes. "The promotion was too much for me," he later mused. He was to remain a cadet private to the end.[51] Still, that summer he was appointed a corps lieutenant to assist when the Department of Tactics taught third classmen a course known as the School of the Company. Then he moved on to his final year as a first classman, and at last the Academy began exposing him to military science under the instruction of Professor

Dennis Hart Mahan and Captain Charles F. Smith, as well as Lee's classmate First Lieutenant Miner Knowlton.

Like Lee before him, Grant studied engineering and the science of war, which included military and civil engineering, ethics, infantry tactics, artillery tactics, mineralogy, and geology. He had to master texts on field fortifications, permanent fortification, tactics of attack and defense, the nature and use of underground mines and other military "accessories," the organization and composition of armies, military strategy, civil engineering, architecture, and even stonecutting and machinery since permanent forts were built of rock or masonry. There were also ethics and rhetoric, so-called moral philosophy on the nature of right and wrong, and army manuals like Scott's *Rules and Regulations for the Exercise and Manoeuvres of the United States Infantry*.[52]

That was the most difficult year at the Academy, but still "U. H. Grant" acted as president of the Dialectic Society, the literary and debating club, and despite the heavy course of study he made time to read light fiction: Charles Lever's *Charles O'Malley, the Irish Dragoon* and *The Confessions of Harry Lorrequer*, comic works on military life in the Napoleonic wars, and Eugene Sue's *Adventures of Hercules Hardy*, a South American adventure.[53] By March 18, 1843, with just three months to graduation, pressure or impatience must have gotten to him and he took it out on his horse during cavalry exercise, which got him one week under arrest.[54] Despite that, he managed two demerit-free months, and closed the year with 78, of which 12 were remitted.[55] At the general examination on June 5, 1843, Grant faced a board headed by General Scott. Despite an illness that term that reduced him to 117 pounds, he still passed, finishing a lackluster 28th in ethics, the same in infantry tactics, and somewhat better at 25th for artillery tactics. However, in mineralogy and geology he ranked a respectable 17th, and 16th in engineering. His overall standing slipped to 21st of 39, but he made it into the middle third overall at 156th of 223.[56]

Suddenly what Grant later called "an interminable four years" were done, and somewhat to his own surprise, Ulysses S. Grant was a brevet second lieutenant in the United States Army.[57] His trip home on leave while awaiting assignment became something of a progress, stopping in Philadelphia to visit Daniel Ammen, then to Pittsburgh for the steamboat, stopping briefly at Maysville to visit Richeson at the Academy, and modestly declining an opportunity to step into a female classroom to allow the young ladies to view the uniformed graduate. At each visit he no doubt told all of his recent achievement.[58] Understandably he had hoped for a place in the mounted dragoons, but shortly after reaching Bethel he received notification of his commissioning in the 4th United States Infantry, with orders to join his regiment at the end of September at Jefferson Barracks at St. Louis. On July 28 Grant swore his oath of allegiance to the United States and three days later notified the adjutant general of his acceptance. For the first time he signed his name Ulysses S. Grant, another battle he decided to lose.[59]

e⁓

As similar as their West Point experiences were for both young graduates, circumstances set them on different personal and professional paths from the moment they took their commissions. Even while his mourning was fresh, Lieutenant Lee concluded that he was in love.[60] While in Georgetown he visited Arlington to see Mary Custis for the first time in two years. Their time together was brief, but they walked and rode over the grounds at Arlington, read together, and perhaps stole a few chastely private moments in its outbuildings.[61] By the time Lee left in August he was in the grip of an emotion quite new to him, as if his grief at his mother's death opened the door to other feelings.[62] His sister Mildred found him distracted and erratic, "uttering as he left the room, confused sentences about beauty and size," she wrote Mary, and "how little could be added to the former and how much to the latter." Teasingly she told the object of those feelings that "you know when one is much *agitated, their expressions are generally intricate and difficult to be understood.*"[63]

For the moment Lee could not press his suit, for on August 21 notice came of his appointment as brevet second lieutenant in the engineers, with orders to report in mid-November to Cockspur Island in the Savannah River to work on a new masonry seacoast defense called Fort Pulaski.[64] The ensuing months of hard toil on the hot, barren island passed slowly for want of anything but secondhand news of Mary. He still had not expressed the true depth of his feelings, and of course said nothing to her parents. No wonder loneliness surrounded him. After six months he told brother Carter that "I feel, and doubly feel, a hundred times more wretched than the day we parted," feelings enhanced when his uncle William Henry Fitzhugh died unexpectedly from what appeared to be an accidental poisoning. He urged Carter to tell Mary "she must write to me, & if she does not I'll tell her mother." Even if she only permitted him to write to her, then "she will have to answer me through common politeness."[65]

Lee returned to Virginia early in July 1830, though now he had no home there, and immediately went to Arlington. Within days Mary revealed her love for him, but Lee found her changed. An epiphany at their mutual uncle Fitzhugh's sudden death propelled her toward an evangelical fervor foreign to Lee, for whom religion was still an arm's-length affair. Seeing Fitzhugh die aged only thirty-two fixed her mind on the brevity of human existence, and in its way that may have accelerated her relations with Lee. "Strange things have happened here this Summer," he wrote brother Carter before he left Arlington late in September. "I am engaged to Miss Mary C." They had an understanding for a spring wedding, and already his family talked of marriage and him resigning his commission.[66] Father Custis gave his permission for them to correspond, but that was all. He liked Lee, but doubted his pampered daughter could make a happy army wife.

Even before taking ship for Georgia, Lee fell into a foul humor at separation, almost wishing he could refuse to go, though of course he would never consider disobeying an order. "I *will* go on," he told her, but he felt things keenly now that he had never felt before, and it amazed him that "I may give vent to them, and act according to their dictates, but this is fast recurring to me."[67] He worked hard at the business of love letters, and knew enough of French and the works of Cervantes and Goethe to include allusions demonstrating the breadth of his education and tastes, but he refrained from hypocritically implying familiarity with works that might pander to her evangelicalism.[68] Lee presented himself in his best light, but he would not pretend to be what he was not.

In response Mary revealed a divided agendum when she began pushing him toward a faith in keeping with her own.[69] She sent him books on religion, but when he looked at the pages all he saw was her.[70] Longing to read sweet endearments, he got more preaching than poetry. Lee told her she was too anxious and to be patient. "I am sure no one could have a greater inducement than I have," he admitted, "but Sweetheart don't expect miracles in my case." She must let time work to "make me feel what I desire, and so seek that I may find."[71] This young man who had no time for fiction and the world of imagination even fantasized about having a magic carpet to whisk him to her, only to have her scold him that the pain of parting would spoil the joy of reunion. All he wanted was to know what she was thinking and perhaps hear her laugh.[72]

As Christmas approached time became a burden. "It does go so slowly here," he told her. "The days appear to pass away, but the nights, the long nights, I sometimes think that day will never come again."[73] Feeling "a poor lone man as I am," he craved more flirting and less proselytizing.[74] "She writes me little sermons every time," Lee complained. Condemning men's earthly ambitions, the wickedness of soldiers and men, and his own shortcomings, "she boxes all around the compas, giving me no respite at all," he grumbled, excusing her only because "she is young yet & knows nothing of human nature." He credited her good intentions, but feared "she will make bad, worse."[75] He would not misrepresent himself nor give her false expectations. "Perhaps I may be better, but I see no prospect of it now," he told her. "I have always remained the same sinful Robert Lee."[76] She did not appreciate his sense of humor, and never would. It did not help that his banter often took a sarcastic turn, as when she scolded him when he told her he found her last lecture disappointing, then backpedaled in his next letter by assuring her that "I was not 'disappointed in my lecture this time' for I read it more plainly than it was written & felt it more deeply than was intended." Even flattery of "your great superiority to all in sweetness" did not deflect her. Yet within him there was a man wanting to have *his* way, too, frustrated with a fiancée who would not defer to him. "Recollect how *good* I am," he told her rather bluntly, "and do not *presume* to lecture."[77]

The fact that he persisted in spite of Mary's romantic diffidence and religious zeal is ample evidence that Lee genuinely loved her, but also of his determination to be a married man. If he felt more invested in their engagement than she, his youth may be held to account. She was his first and only love after years in an emotional desert. Still, sense of duty trumped his affections. When Mary hinted that her father's influence might get him assigned to Washington, he protested that "I could not ask another having a higher claim than myself to be set aside for my benefit."[78]

In time her tone changed, confidences became more personal, and the endearments more heartfelt. Lee even felt secure enough to begin writing about her weight—he wanted her to weigh more. He spoke of her becoming "fat & rosy," happy that "you are getting so fat," asking "are you *perfectly* fat," scolding her when she failed to put on pounds, and telling her that at their next meeting "I do expect to find you very fat."[79] In a letter to her mother he spoke of a friend whose fiancée weighed 140 pounds, saying, "Oh bountiful nature what a quantity of love the fellow will have."[80] Perhaps Lee really preferred plump women, or he equated a fuller figure with health, and Mary already showed signs of future chronic illness. Then there was childbirth, which seemed difficult for slender women, and Lee wanted a family.

Old Custis consented at last in March 1831, unfortunately at the same time that "Black Horse Harry" returned to the press accused of stealing millions while a diplomat.[81] Lieutenant Lee well knew of Mr. Custis's concerns about the reputations of his brother and late father. "Of these no one can be more sensible than myself, or less able to devise a remedy," Robert wrote Mary in April. "But should I be able to escape the sins into which they have fallen, I hope the blame, which is justly their due, will not be laid to me." This only made him the more anxious to set a date before Custis changed his mind.[82] Reassignment in May to Fort Monroe at Old Point Comfort, Virginia, less than two hundred miles from Arlington, only added to his anxiety.

By mid-May he told her "I declare I cannot wait *any longer*." He threatened to demand an immediate furlough, and if his superior refused, then "Uncle Sam may go to—France—For what I care." It was as close to profanity as Lee came, his only other occasional attempt being the anodyne "God knows for I don't." Though written in jest, it revealed his ill humor when he added that "I never expected You *would* be mine & you see how it has turned out."[83] Fearing she would take his insistence for bullying, he added that "I will not Consent that every body should yield to my wishes." His good humor returned, and by early June he could tease her that if she did not set a date, "I will be an old Man soon, Bald, toothless & every thing else."[84]

When finally she agreed on a date doubts haunted him. Two weeks before their nuptials he told her mother that "there is nothing I covet so much as the power of benefitting those I love, though I fear it will be many years, if ever, before my means will equal my desires."[85] A week later he wrote to ask Mary "if you are as anxious as I am." He feared she would be sorry she married him. "You have been so much at home & seen so little of mankind," he reflected, "that you will not be prepared to find them as they are, & the change from Arlington to a Garrison of wicked & Blasphemous soldiers will be greater & more *shocking* to you than you are aware of."[86] Nevertheless, on June 30 at Arlington, perhaps to Lee's amazement, it all happened without a hiccup other than an inconvenient rain. They spent a month on honeymoon at Arlington and Ravensworth, and then began Lee's real voyage of discovery as a married man. His brother Carter thought Robert's "fancy & recollections of the Arabian Nights," encouraged by Mary's red cheeks, would soon lead him to regard her as a new Queen Gulnare of the Sea.[87]

Surely there was joy, yet within months sides of Mary appeared that courtship, distance, and letters had concealed. He was punctuality to a fetish; she habitually late. He never left their quarters unless impeccably uniformed; her dress sense was, at best, casual, and often just inappropriate. He wanted neatness and order in his physical environment, as befit an engineer and a West Point graduate with no demerits; she was, by his own account, absent-minded, untidy, and lazy at housekeeping, forcing Lee to apologize preemptively to guests for the state of his home. A few years after their marriage she awoke one morning to find her hair badly tangled, so she cut it all off. Lee masked embarrassment by joking that he would find her one day completely bald.[88]

They were temperaments at odds. In response to the disorder of his youth, Lee wanted and needed control in all aspects of his life. He understood that, even if he could not always keep it in check, and sometimes it led to conflict. Barely thirty months after their wedding he apologized after an argument, saying, "I don't know that I shall ever overcome my propensity for order & method But I will try." Then he lapsed into the tones of defeat by adding, "yet for that as for anything else I am now unfit."[89] Scarcely more than a newlywed, Lee had learned resignation. "Do as you please Molly in all things," he told her.

Disagreeing over her dress, he gave up. "Since my taste is so difficult," he told her, "I will conform to yours." That was a man choosing his battles.[90]

Mary also showed her independence by going home to Arlington, and for long periods. Less than a month after her arrival at Fort Monroe homesickness set in. "I have a husband always ready to go with me when his duties will permit," she wrote her mother, and appreciatively confessed that "I must give him a little just commendation sometimes."[91] These were not separations in anger, but rather visits that seemed to last longer than Lee had expected. After six months at Fort Monroe, already pregnant, she returned to Arlington with her mother. She gave birth to George Washington Custis Lee on September 16, 1832, and after a brief visit to Lee, by November Mary and baby were back at Arlington. A year later they went again. Left to himself at Fort Monroe, he missed "My Sweet little Boy," as he called little Custis. "The house is a perfect desert without him & his mother & there is no comfort in it." He felt the absence of his bedfellow, confessing that "the want of so much that I have been accustomed to drives me from my bed sometimes before day."[92] It was scant compensation to help his boyhood friend Lieutenant Maynadier organize a dance at the post with cake, lemonade, wine, and harder spirits, if Mary was not to be there with him.[93] Even the arrival of the Sauk Indian war leader Black Hawk and the Winnebago prophet Wabokieshiek in April 1833, sent to prison at Fort Monroe after their failed uprising in the northwest, captured little of his attention, with his thoughts at Arlington.[94]

His tendency toward the didactic offended her independent nature. When Mary's parents tried to help them set up house, Lee admonished that they were just starting out and "ought to contract our wishes to their smallest compass and enlarge them as opportunity offers."[95] He scolded her for not showing good sense if she suggested anything conflicting with his duty. "I must not consent to do aught that would lower me in your eyes, my own & that of others," he told her. Rather, she must prepare to "cheer up & pack up; to lay aside unavailing regrets, & to meet with a smiling face & cheerful heart the vicissitudes of life."[96] In short, she needed to be more like him, but Mary was a wild card that did not easily fit the well-ordered pattern of his life as he saw it. Lee gradually softened his controlling impulses with

Mary. There was never a lessening of affection, but rather a growth of respect and tolerance on his part, mixed with resignation at what he knew he could not change but could live with, while for her part Mary did much the same. There were tender moments, too, and passionate ones, and almost every night he read aloud to her while she sewed clothes for their growing family.[97]

⁓

If Lee felt two years was too long a wait to claim his bride, Lieutenant Grant's road to matrimony seemed endless, though in other respects the two had much in common. 'Lys soon climbed back to 137 pounds, proudly filling out his new uniform until he saw the alcoholic stableman at the inn across from the Grant home parading in a pair of light-blue pants with a strip of white sewn down the trouser seams in mimicry of Grant's uniform. "The joke was a huge one in the mind of many of the people, and was much enjoyed by them," Grant ruefully remembered. "I did not appreciate it so highly."[98] What he did not see was that the mockery was aimed at his father, Jesse Grant being an unpopular man in town.[99] The son never entirely recovered from that hurt pride about his uniform. It left in him a "distaste" for military finery that never left him. With Grant, hurts felt were not soon forgotten, and sometimes never.

Showing his disinclination to stop at the first obstacle, Grant requested transfer to the dragoons just weeks after reaching Missouri, only to be turned down.[100] It is just as well, for Jefferson Barracks proved a happy posting, not least because his Academy roommate Frederick T. Dent's family lived only a few miles away. Weekly visits from Lieutenant Grant became daily after February 1844 when seventeen-year-old daughter Julia Dent came home from school in St. Louis. Neither a plain nor a handsome girl, she suffered strabismus, as one eye wandered out of focus, making her reluctant to be photographed. She lacked beauty, but her features were strong and illuminated by smiles and laughter.

If not immediately smitten, Grant soon was. For "two winged months," as Julia called them, they rode almost daily.[101] In April, before he left for home on a leave, Grant made a clumsy effort to propose that she somewhat flippantly dismissed. Then came orders for the 4th Infantry to leave for Louisiana, and Julia despaired of seeing him again. Grant was not to be deterred. On his way from Ohio to Louisiana he came by way of St. Louis to spend a week with the Dents, and asked her again more directly to marry him. Without saying yes, she accepted his West Point class ring as a token, saying she thought being engaged would be wonderful, but she was not sure about marriage. As Lee discovered more than a dozen years before, there was a game to be played, and it included long engagements, often long separations, and almost ritualized correspondence. Lee's game lasted just nine months; Grant's would be more than four years.[102]

A few weeks later he referred to his engagement as something "laughable, curious, important, surprising, etc."[103] No sooner did he reach Camp Salubrity near Natchitoches, than he worried that her parents might not consent. He was only twenty-two. Did they think him too young and inexperienced?[104] When her father objected to army life and argued that it would not suit his daughter, Grant tried to assure Julia that "soldiering is a very pleasant occupation," and would get better as he won promotion.[105] For the next several months his letters to her reflected his insecurity.[106] Economical with words, he often used the same wording whether writing to Julia or to a neighbor, and always there was that self-effacing modesty. He added his rank and regiment to a letter, "not because I wish people to know what it is," he said, but to make sure replies reached him.[107]

All he had on his mind was Julia. They had promised each to think of the other when watching a sunset, a time when he usually found himself on parade, fearful that he looked absent-minded to his superiors with his thoughts hundreds of miles away. When her letters failed to arrive when expected he told her "I took the Blues," and urged her to write more and more often.[108] He also begged her to find a name to go with the orphaned "S" in his name.[109] For her part, she called one of her bedposts for him, and every evening after watching the sunset she bid it good night.[110]

When he returned to Missouri on leave in the spring of 1845, he believed that he was close to a confirmed regular commission, his first step up the ladder.[111] The elder Dent was not impressed, but relented to allow them to continue their correspondence.[112] Grant's capability at expressing himself was every bit as good as Lee's, but when it came to telling her directly that he loved her, his pen hesitated. "What an out I make at expressing any thing like love or sentiment," he lamented to her.[113] Affection was an emotion so little displayed to him by his mother that he grew to manhood with no experience at expressing it. He begged her to write more often, and just as Lee had so often signed himself "R. E. Lee," so this suitor usually closed his missives "U S Grant."

In the fall of 1845 tensions between the United States and Mexico over the annexation of Texas resulted in the 4th Infantry being ordered to Corpus Christi on the Gulf of Mexico. The lieutenant saw little danger of war.[114] Rather he suspected Mexicans might lapse into revolution against near dictatorship, establish a more democratic government, and even welcome seeing the United States expand below the Rio Grande River to enfold them in the eagle's wings.[115] By October 1845 Grant still felt secure from imminent hazard. His greatest concern was his engagement. He and Julia had been betrothed well over a year. He did not like immobility. Inaction was defeat. He pressed Julia to give him a definite answer to marriage, offering to resign and enter civilian life if that would satisfy her parents. Her father asked what he might do if he left the army, and coincidentally his own ever-interfering father offered an alternative when he began urging him to resign that fall. Joseph McDowell Matthews, the founder and principal of the six-year-old Oakland Female Seminary in Hillsboro, Ohio, had approached Jesse Grant about employing his son Ulysses to teach mathematics to the ninety young ladies there enrolled at the state's first school offering a full college education to women.[116] Jesse continued pushing 'Lys in that direction through that fall and into the winter.[117] He certainly gave it much thought as a means of winning over Julia's father, but he liked the service. "I do not think I will ever [be] half so well contented out of the Army as in it," he told her. He urged Julia to agree to elope and marry even without her parents' permission. He even conquered his clumsiness over feelings and for the first time signed a letter "Your Devoted Lover Ulysses."[118] When Julia sent him her copy of Eugene Sue's *The Wandering Jew*, he found a passage she had marked and read it over and over again hoping she had meant him to see themselves in it: "for two drops of dew blending in the cup of a flower are as hearts that mingle in a pure and virgin love."[119]

Following more than a dozen years of marriage, Lee was past poetry. Eight months after the wedding his provisional or "brevet" rank
as second lieutenant shifted to full rank.[120] He stayed at Fort Monroe
until the fall of 1834 when ordered to Washington as an assistant to the
chief of engineers. Even with Arlington in view on the heights across
the Potomac, he took a room in a boarding house to be close to his
office while Mary and the baby stayed with the Custises. He worked
long days, and only visited Arlington after dark. When the War Department sent him to survey the contested Ohio-Michigan Territory
border, Mary was expecting again.[121] He came home in October 1836
to find her ill after giving birth to their second child, Mary Custis Lee.
Meanwhile, his only reward for the routine of office work was promotion to first lieutenant in September 1836. That was not enough. "I
am waiting, looking and hoping for some good opportunity to bid an
affectionate farewell to my dear Uncle Sam," he complained in February 1837. "I must get away from here."[122] In the capital he saw "so much
iniquity [in] more ways than one, that I feared for my morality."[123]

Relief came in April 1837 with assignment to St. Louis to combat
the Mississippi River's efforts to abandon the Missouri city. He left
just after Mary delivered their third child, William Henry Fitzhugh
Lee, and in the spring of 1838 brought his family with him.[124] They
stayed in what Lee liked to call "the Western Metropolis" for the next
year, where he quipped that "I have been studying mud and water
in the West."[125] Missouri was hardly the Old Dominion, and Lee did
not care much for the citizenry. "It is a rough country to bring them
to," he told Mackay, "but they smooth it to me most marvellously."[126]
However, within weeks of arriving he began to wish himself back in
Virginia.[127] The army had been good to him, but he bristled at "the
manner in which the Army is considered and treated by the country,"
telling Mackay that it "is enough to disgust every one with the service,
and has the effect of driving every good soldier from it." He saw how
politicians attacked the army for partisan motives, and grumbled that
"the miserable slander of dirty legislators is an insult to the Army and
shews in what light its feelings are estimated, and its rights sacrificed at
the shrine of popularity."[128]

Good news was promotion to captain and the discovery of another
pregnancy. Lee took Mary and the children back to Arlington in May

1839, then left before Anne Carter Lee was born in June. During these absences he sent Mary lectures on how to raise the children with discipline and "proper restraint." Lee himself tried to reason with his children, making it clear that he was unwavering in "my demands" for their behavior. Yet he feared that Mary did not support him. "You must assist me in my attempts," he urged. "You must not let them run wild in my absence." Mildness and forbearance, "tempered by firmness and judgment, will strengthen their affection for you," he told her, "while it will maintain your control over them." These were the words by which Lee had made sense of his own youth: restraint, discipline, and most of all self-control.[129] He missed his children. "I am sure to be introduced to a new one every Xmas," he told Mackay in November. "They are the dearest Annuals of the season, and I find something in every edition that I in vain look for elsewhere."[130]

Lee was happy to leave St. Louis when reassignment came in 1840.[131] Extended contact had not improved his opinion of the population, especially what he called "the lower class," who he thought "are a swaggering, noisy set, careless of getting work except occasionally." He dismissed most locals, even what he called "those of the higher order," as crass and grasping, while he thought their children filthy and ill-mannered, "demanding and dirty."[132] Even the local economic elite in Missouri were "new money." Men were obsessed with business and making money, and defaulting on debts, and he found the best of them far different from his class at home. They were not like his Virginians.[133] He described his departure as "my escape from the West."[134]

Still, the work on the Mississippi enhanced his reputation and reinforced his Whiggish outlook that the government had a role to play in promoting the expansion and economic benefit of the nation through internal improvements.[135] No one could escape politics, and Lee showed some interest as an officer must, since it affected his career. When the nullification crisis erupted he groused that Congress did "nothing" in the face of South Carolina's posturing and threats of secession.[136] "Nullification! Nullification!! Nullification!!!," he grumbled.[137] As a Whig he surely condemned it, just as he later abhorred secession. Lee was not especially politically aware as yet, but he paid attention to what might affect the army. On leave at Arlington in the winter of 1832–1833, he sat in the Capitol's Senate gallery to hear the debates on President Jackson's so-called Force Bill enabling him to use the military, and Lee, if necessary, to compel South Carolina to comply with the unpopular tariff of 1828. Lee heard now-senator John C. Calhoun's angry denunciation of Jackson for the measure, which he said threatened civil war.

Thirty-two years later, in April 1865, Lee recalled that Calhoun's eloquence "fell like a thunderbolt on an iceberg, glanced, hissed and was extinguished." Nevertheless, in 1833 the Force Bill could conceivably result in Lee facing fellow Southerners across drawn battle lines. He heard Daniel Webster stand in defense of Jackson, and remembered that he "never saw a more striking object than Webster in the Senate." A few years later, again in Washington, Lee heard Henry Clay speak in the Senate in denunciation of presumed British aggressions, and found him a natural orator. Of all that great triumvirate, however, in 1865 he regarded Calhoun as possessed of the greatest moral force, perhaps because the Carolinian had spoken of Southern rights against Northern aggression, a subject on which Lee's own position had shifted dramatically.[138]

Like so many officers, he tried to keep himself clear of politics and politicians. "I never mention politics," he told Jack Mackay in 1834, "thinking that you will see all the *Slang-whang* in the papers, & care & believe as much as I do."[139] In common with Whigs, he had little use for President Martin Van Buren and his weak administration's "bold front," yet watched without emotion as Southern Democrats gradually joined forces with those in the North to support a bill to take the government out of the banking system. By 1840 he believed the Whigs were "gathering head and are in fine spirits," yet congress seemed to do little but pass appropriations for their own salaries.[140]

He looked on from afar for several years as the Seminoles of Florida successfully stymied the army's efforts to contain them. The Seminole sore festered until 1842, replaced by vague threats of war with Britain over Canada, which Lee thought nothing but talk. "There will be no war with England this year," he predicted in February 1843. "Our worthy members of Congress have another opportunity to make belligerent speeches," he thought, but nothing more. He felt anxious about a bill to annex the Oregon territory, but most of all watched Congress and its budget reductions for military works with pessimism, despite the fact that fellow officers whom he styled "the boys in Wash[ington]" were optimistic. "No man can tell what Cong[ress] will do for the plain reason that they do not know themselves," he told Mackay.[141]

Even if Lee did not formally identify himself as a Whig, still he looked more favorably on their policies. They were the ideological heirs of his family's Federalists. They supported those internal improvements—the roads and canals and bridges—to be constructed and maintained by the engineers, meaning they were anxious to keep him employed. The Whigs buttered his side of the bread. In 1844 Lee even called personally on President John Tyler, a fellow Virginian and a Whig, to intercede on behalf of a young man seeking appointment to the Military Academy.[142] From early manhood Lee held a low opinion of politicians, and believed military men should stay out of politics. When a fellow officer ran for the office of city engineer in St. Louis, Lee chided him that "to become a political partizan would be derogatory to your office & profession," and that "your opinions & acts should be grounded by your judgment & not with a benefit of this or that party." He distrusted the common voters, especially the foreign born, as he viewed them as a clamorous mob cynically manipulated by scheming politicians, perhaps an echo of the mob that nearly killed his father. Any officer who entered politics, however well born, would have no choice but to "throw up your hat with the highest & hurrah with the loudest."[143] His brother Carter felt no such reluctance, and openly identified himself with the Whigs, making a Fourth of July speech in support of Clay's 1844 presidential candidacy. "I do not in general admire the introduction of party politics on such an occasion," Robert scolded, but he gladly passed a copy of a campaign song of Carter's on to the Henry Clay Club of Brooklyn while stationed at Fort Hamilton.[144] "We've been Whig and nothing else," went its refrain, "And now on fire for Clay!"

More and more the dynamo driving both speeches and songs was slavery, and Lee's attitude toward it mirrored his feelings about politics. If his family, friends, tutors, and other associations in Alexandria were almost unanimous in praying for an end to chattel servitude in America, still few if any favored governmental emancipation. In youth Lee had little personal interaction with slaves other than his mother's house servants and Nat the coachman, but Alexandria's many slave pens made numbers of them a common sight every day, while there were many more at Ravensworth and Eastern View. From his earliest expressions on the subject, Lee echoed his mother's view that slaves were "a species of property extremely inconvenient and disagreeable." He had no need of them as an officer in the field. His wife always had the use of her father's when she visited home, and when the newlyweds left for Fort Monroe in 1831, her parents sent Mary's "girl" Judy Meriday along. Judy and her brother Philip would be with them often over the years. When stationed in a free state like New York, Lee hired them out.[145]

Certainly the explosive potential of the slavery question came home to him early on. He barely got his new bride to Fort Monroe after their wedding before the famed Nat Turner slave rebellion erupted barely forty miles west of them, in Southampton County on August 22, 1831. Lee was not with the soldiers sent to quell the uprising, but when the detachment returned he heard stories of a scheme "widely extended," plotted in the slaves' religious gatherings that he thought "ought to have been devoted to better purposes." He made no comment on the broader issue of their bid for freedom, but there is no question that he believed the rebels deserved the harsh retribution they received at the noose. However, he spoke well of loyal servants who tried to defend their masters from the murderous assaults, and showed pity for one such whom he believed was mistakenly slain "from the inconsiderate & almost unwarrantable haste of the whites."[146]

Lee got his first actual experience trying to manage slaves on Cockspur Island, and it confirmed his ambivalence. Given charge of a gang of 150 hired blacks to excavate foundations for the future fort, he initially felt sympathy for what he called "my Black Walloons," almost regretting that he had to make the "poor creatures" work so hard.[147] But before long, he complained that "*no one* will do their duty without being made." Spending days knee deep in mud and water overseeing dilatory laborers, he grumbled that "I have to depend upon others, & if they would do as I tell them I should have no trouble, but this they will not do & I must let them have their own way."[148] When Mary suggested that he instruct the slaves in religion, he told her "I do teach those men something Good, for I learn them to do their work faithfully handsomely and scientifically."[149] He teased her for teaching "those little Plagues," the slave children at Arlington, and belittled her friends' efforts for another Custis emancipationist concern, the African Education Society.[150] If Lee did not endorse slavery now, he did not condemn it either. It was simply a fact of life in the slave states, like the weather.

And now he was a slave owner himself.[151] When Ann Hill Lee died in 1829 she bequeathed a few domestic slaves to her two daughters. The residue of her estate, to be liquidated as inheritance for her three sons, contained an unspecified number of others, all out at hire.[152] Her executor William Carter kept them rented while settling the estate, though it took some eighteen months before debts were cleared and Smith and Carter Lee agreed on a division among the three brothers in 1832, conveying to Robert sole title in four women, Catty or Cassy, Jane, Letitia, and a woman named Nancy Ruffin with her three children, as well as a man named Sam whom Lee in 1833 traded with his brother Carter for another slave named Gardner.[153] Lee called them "our Georgetonians" and "those people in Geotown," and had little use for any of them. Nancy was neither a good cook nor a washerwoman, and only Letitia was worth keeping at home. Coming into possession of them as he did soon after his marriage, he left their disposition to Mary immediately after she reached Arlington pregnant with their first son. She could keep, hire, or sell them, "but do not trouble yourself about them, as they are not worth it."[154]

They kept Catty, Jane, and Letitia no more than a couple of years, and by early 1835 Nancy and her three "plagues," as he called slave children, were "all of the race in my poss[ession]." He likely would have been happy to be rid of them as well, for he frankly admitted his belief that obdurance, stubbornness, and unreliability were typical of what he called their "sex, color & caste."[155] Oddly, Lee's comment about "all of the race in my poss" seemingly overlooked the slave he sometimes referred to as "my man Gardner," though he probably meant only those slaves actually with him and his family. His cousin Hill Carter in Charles City County had handled Gardner's hire for Ann Lee after 1822 at least, and Lee may not have seen him since, but the annual rent payments continued coming in to the executors, then to Carter Lee, and after 1834 or 1835 directly to Lee himself.[156] He had little interest in or patience with Nancy, but still kept her out at hire at Custis's White House plantation in New Kent County until 1847 or later.[157]

Lee was not entirely indifferent to the blacks themselves, regarding them much as he would children. Trying to help his aunt Fitzhugh find a new slave overseer, he emphasized that such a man should be "as attentive to their comfort and welfare, as to the discharge of their duties; and to be neither harsh nor severe in his discipline."[158] He personally went to some trouble for the welfare of old Nat, who came down with what was probably tuberculosis soon after Mildred inherited him. Robert had him sent to Georgia for his health, but a terrible twenty-five-day voyage only left him weaker with a terrible cough. Lee moved him into his quarters and began what he called an "experiment" with a treatment of his own concoction, as he had his mother.[159] When that failed, Lee moved him into Savannah with a physician, and thereafter called in on Nat when business brought him to town. As Nat sank, Lee blamed the doctor's medicines, and then on March 29, 1831, Nat died. "I was perfectly shocked to hear of his death," he told Mary. "So he too is gone," Lee mused, perhaps in sadness but also in sad reflection on the accumulating deaths of the faces of his youth: his father, his mother, Uncle Fitzhugh, and now Nat. Though reflective, he seemed unmoved, for immediately after penning those words, Lee abruptly moved on to talk of flower seeds, just as in a previous letter he shifted from Nat's health to the weather.[160] Of course he may have been suppressing his feelings again, too saddened to write more. In later years relatives recalled a heavily romanticized version of Nat's death that had Lee personally nursing him "with the tenderness of a son," and burying him with his own hands.[161]

Lee followed the gathering agitation over abolition, and by January 1840 believed with dismay that it was gaining ground.[162] As a soldier, however, his next assignment was of far greater interest. Besides its political ferment, Washington could be boring. "There is not much more doing in the gay world," he found in January 1840. "The Theatre is not much frequented, and parties are as yet few and far between.[163] He expected posting to New York or North Carolina, preferring the former, as "I should hate to see any friend of mine—in North Carolina."[164] Another child, Eleanor Agnes Lee, came that winter before Washington sent him to Fort Hamilton on New York harbor, where he arrived in April 1841. There, at least, his family could join him, and they lived there for much of the next five years, though Lee complained that "I never felt poorer in my life," and for the first time debts began to accumulate as his family grew.[165] Still, Mary went home to Arlington from time to time, leaving Lee lamenting that "I feel very forlorn without you & the house is very cold & cheerless."[166] In October 1843 the next child, R. E. Lee Jr., was born at the only secure home they had known to date. Meanwhile, Lee oversaw modernization and reinforcement of a finished fortress, major masonry projects that considerably broadened his experience and understanding. During the 1845–1846 winter Mary and the children returned once more to Arlington for yet another birth, their seventh and last, Mildred Childe Lee. Years earlier, feeling more secure in the idea of a family of his own without the taint of his father or half-brother, he began trying to devise a coat of arms to use as a seal on his correspondence.[167]

The year 1846 looked at its outset to be just like so many before—another child, more dull and unrewarding duty, more periods of family separation. Then politics stepped in to change everything. America was going to war. Tensions between the United States and Mexico had mounted ever since the annexation of Texas in 1845. President Polk deliberately posted American forces provocatively in contested land near the Rio Grande, and in April 1846 a Mexican command attacked and routed a small company of Americans on soil claimed by the United States. That meant war.

Lieutenant Grant was already there.

3

FIGHTING ON
THE SAME SIDE

WHEN GRANT'S REGIMENT moved toward the Rio Grande in February 1846 he estimated the chances of seeing a fight at even odds, but feared they would be defeated if the Mexicans attacked. When they reached Point Isabel on the Gulf Coast, their commander General Zachary Taylor set his soldiers to fortifying their base at Fort Polk, even as the Mexicans fortified themselves at Matamoras, a few miles distant on the other bank of the river. Grant believed they might attack at any moment, and thereafter dismissed any thought of resignation.[1]

On April 19 and 20, 1846, a contingent of 2,000 Mexican cavalry surprised a small party of United States soldiers in the contested area of Texas between the Nueces and Rio Grande Rivers, killing several and capturing others. Taylor responded by taking 2,000 soldiers out of Fort Polk on May 1; Grant's regiment marched in the column. Once at Point Isabel, Grant for the first time heard hostile fire: the distant sound of artillery as Mexican cannon at Matamoras bombarded Fort Polk behind them. "Dont fear for me My Dear Julia for this is only the active part of our business," he wrote his future wife on May 3. For the first time he expressed an attitude he would declare over and again in coming years, saying " the sooner it begins the sooner it will end."[2]

A few days later the lieutenant experienced action for the first time at Palo Alto on May 8 and at Resaca de la Palma the next day, the first battles of the war. The first was fought mainly by the artillery on both sides while the infantry like Grant's acted in support. Again he felt calm in the face of danger. "Although the balls were whizing thick and fast about me I did not feel a sensation of fear," he wrote three days later, "until nearly the close of the firing a ball struck close by me killing one man instantly." The foe withdrew during the night, and at dawn

Grant joined others in their first experience of the aftermath of battle. "It was a terrible sight to go over the ground the next day and see the amont of life that had been destroyed," he wrote Julia. "The ground was litterally strewed with the bodies of dead men and horses."

Later that day Taylor pursued the Mexicans, and found them in a dry creek bed and reinforced to twice his numbers. Now the infantry were in the thick of it as they advanced into combined Mexican artillery and infantry fire. After his first experience facing fire actually directed at him, Grant confessed to Julia that "there is no great sport in having bullets flying about one in evry direction but I find they have less horror when among them than when in anticipation." In the thickest of the fighting he found himself thinking of her.[3] The fear of battle could be far more terrifying than the actual event, the first of many valuable lessons he learned there and in the days ahead.

Writing a brief account of the twin engagements on the head of a captured drum, Grant took particular interest in other important matters. One was the human loss, of course, but he devoted much more time to assessing the logistical losses of the enemy: the number of cannon and small arms captured, the ammunition, sabers, and swords left on the field. More than that, he counted the wagons, mules, pack saddles and harness, camp equipment, and even bugles and drums. These were trophies, of course, but more than that he saw in them the materiel that kept an army in the field, and moved it to battle. He freely admitted the Mexicans had fought well, but he seemed more interested in how well prepared they had been for the campaign. That meant careful planning. In setting down his scant narrative of the fights and their aftermath, he also emphasized that initial impressions might be inaccurate, and resolved to keep his version brief until he could compare his facts with the accounts of others.[4] Accuracy seemed important to him.

Grant remained untroubled by fear for the rest of the war, telling his fiancée "do not feel alarmed about me my Dear Julia for there is not half the horrors in war that you imagine."[5] He told friends much the same. "I do not know that I felt any particular sensation," he wrote a few weeks later. "War seems much less horrible to persons engaged in it than to those who read of the battles."[6] Yet that hardly meant that he enjoyed it, despite its glorification in the popular literature he liked to read. Barely three months after his first actions he mused that "wherever there are battles a great many must suffer, and for the sake of the little glory gained I do not care to see it."[7] By September, he told Julia "I do wish this [war] would close," and a month later declared that "fighting is no longer a pleasure."[8] One year to the day after he first heard those Mexican batteries shelling Fort Polk, he told a friend back home that "I am hartily tired of the wars."[9]

Soon Grant began to see in newspapers from home how some officers, politicians given commissions in volunteer units, were lionized for their deeds in action, real or invented, and felt a growing cynicism toward such manufactured heroes. "I begin to see that luck is a fortune," he remarked in October 1846. "It is but necessary to get a start in the papers and there will soon be deeds enough of ones performances related."[10] Months later, after the fall of Mexico City, he grumbled about "the courage and science shown by individuals" in the press, adding that "even here one hears of individual exploits (which were never performed) sufficient to account for the taking of Mexico throwing out about four fifths of the army to do nothing." Worse was the way such journalistic heroics overshadowed the real bravery and sacrifice of the men and officers of the Regular Army.[11] When his name appeared for the first time in the Eastern press on a list of officers engaged at Palo Alto and Resaca de la Palma, he briefly acquired yet another orphaned initial when it appeared as "Lieut. W. S. Grant."[12]

It was the beginning of his lifelong suspicion of politicians and the press, especially after a newspaper caused him no little embarrassment. Jesse Grant read guests his son's latest letters from Mexico, then allowed a local newspaperman to publish one in which Grant described the shabby condition of a newly arrived company of volunteers from their own county.[13] When copies reached that company's men in Mexico, they raised a cry of indignation, including perhaps threats to Grant himself.[14] "Hereafter," he resolved, "I intend to be careful not to give them any news worth publishing."[15]

He approved of men distinguishing themselves in battle, of course, and perhaps dreamed of heroic deeds himself. Thanks to casualties among the company officers of the 4th Infantry, on July 22 he was assigned temporary command of Company C. That was a captain's post, and if he performed well, there was hope of promotion. After less than a month his colonel reassigned him to support duty as acting assistant quartermaster and commissary of the regiment, performing the vital tasks of keeping accurate account of uniforms and equipment, and making sure the soldiers were fed. Grant's own observations of the Mexicans' logistical attainments showed how well he understood that, but quartermaster and commissary was a rear-echelon posting. Supply officers might keep an army functioning, but there were few opportunities for action. Grant asked to return to his post in the field, but his brigade commander Lieutenant Colonel John Garland quickly replied that at the moment Grant was where he might best serve, saying that he chose him for that duty because of "his observed ability, skill and persistency." Major George Allen, commanding the 4th Infantry, agreed, and so did General Taylor.[16]

Quartermaster Grant could read a map. He saw that if Taylor took Monterey, some 225 miles due west near the upper tip of the Sierra Madre mountains, he would command all of Mexico northeast of the range, and be poised to move due south the 400 miles to Mexico City. Grant thought that might force the enemy to terms.[17] In so doing, he actually predicted Taylor's next move, and had ideas about conduct of operations. "We are very anxious to push forward for that is our only hope of a speedy peace," he told Julia. Having seen Mexicans overwhelm isolated detachments, he forecast that his outnumbered army could defeat anyone if concentrated.[18] Also they should move quickly. "If we have to fight," he said, "I would like to do it all at once and then make friends." An army wasting time wasted opportunity. He believed that delay was the Mexican strategy, retreating to draw the Americans deeper into their country until isolated and strung out maintaining supply lines over hundreds of miles of bad roads.[19]

When Taylor laid siege to Monterey on September 20, a frustrated Quartermaster Grant was three miles to the rear guarding his regiment's camp. "Curiosity got the better of my judgment," he later confessed, and the next day he rode to the front, disobeying—or at least ignoring—orders and abandoning his post and government property. He found the 4th Infantry on the verge of assaulting Mexican works. "Lacking the moral courage to return to camp," he admitted, he accompanied his regiment in the charge, being one of only a few mounted. At first the Mexicans drove them back with heavy loss, and

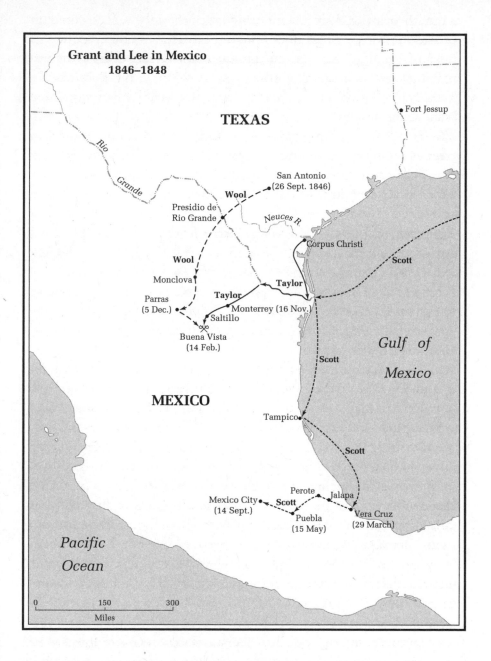

Grant and Lee in Mexico
1846–1848

Fort Jessup

TEXAS

Rio

Grande

San Antonio
(26 Sept. 1846)

Wool

Presidio de
Rio Grande

Neuces R.

Corpus Christi

Scott

Wool

Monclova

Taylor

Parras
(5 Dec.)

Taylor

Monterrey (16 Nov.)

Saltillo

Buena Vista
(14 Feb.)

Gulf of

Mexico

MEXICO

Scott

Tampico

Scott

Perote

Jalapa

Mexico City
(14 Sept.)

Scott

Puebla
(15 May)

Vera Cruz
(29 March)

Pacific

Ocean

0   150   300

Miles

as they reformed Grant saw the adjutant of the regiment, Lieutenant Charles Hoskins, one of Julia's one-time fleeting suitors, lagging in frail health and exhausted from running in the attack. Grant gave him his horse and then found another animal to rejoin the next assault. Hoskins was killed moments afterward, and Major Allen appointed Grant acting adjutant.

By September 23 the fighting was block-by-block through the city streets. Sniping from rooftops stopped Garland's brigade of the 3d and 4th Infantries just one square from the central plaza. When their ammunition dwindled, Garland asked for a volunteer to take a plea for reinforcements or more ammunition to Taylor, and Lieutenant Grant stepped forward. Wrapping an arm around his horse's neck and one leg around the cantle of the saddle, he left at a gallop, the horse's body shielding him from most enemy fire. He stopped momentarily at a house filled with wounded pinned down by the fire, promising to send them aid, then remounted and continued his gauntlet of fire. He reached safety uninjured, but before ammunition could be sent Garland's brigade withdrew.[20]

Grant showed bravery and initiative, not to mention youthful impetuosity in leaving his original post in the rear, but Garland ignored that. That evening Grant wrote to Julia, setting the mold for almost all his future correspondence when he made no mention of his daring ride other than to say that "I passed through some severe fireing but as yet have escaped unhurt."[21] The next day the city surrendered, the combatants agreeing on an eight-week armistice, and Grant feared they would advance no farther.[22] After two months of inactivity his frustration erupted. "Here we are, playing war a thousand miles from home," he said, "making show and parades, but not doing enough fighting to much amuse either the enemy or ourselves." Meanwhile, inured to being a quartermaster, he grumbled that the army had consumed enough rations in idleness to subsist them on a march to Mexico City. "If our mission is to occupy the enemy's country, it is a success, for we are inertly here; but if to conquer, it seems to some of us who have no control that we might as well be performing the job with greater energy."[23]

During those weeks he confronted the cost of war. A walk through his regiment's camp reminded him of those lost, sending him back to his tent with what he called "the Blues."[24] His close friend Lieutenant Charles Hazlitt fell in the first day's fighting not long after the two shook hands on the field.[25] Harder was the death from illness of his benefactor Congressman Thomas L. Hamer, who arrived as major of the 1st Ohio Volunteers, which included the company Grant's letter had offended. Theirs was a friendship that proved useful to Hamer, for he was entirely ignorant of the military, and West Point–educated Grant acted as his mentor despite the disparity in their ages.[26] In November Hamer came down with inflammation of the bowels and died on December 2.[27] Grant visited with him during his illness, and took the loss hard.[28]

Adding to Grant's disenchantment was Washington's management of the conflict. He did not vote in the 1844 election that put Polk in power, since he was on station far from Ohio.[29] Like many military men of all ages and ranks, Grant viewed politics through the limited lens of its impact on his profession and, of course, himself. Polk was not destined to be popular with professional soldiers. He gave too many high commissions to influential Southern or Democratic politicians with little or no military experience; men like his former law partner Gideon Pillow, or Franklin Pierce who was now a colonel in spite of never having worn a uniform in his life. Still, Grant actually became friendly with Pierce, however much he distrusted the policy that put him in the army.[30]

Then Polk generated perhaps Grant's first political comment. New regiments of volunteers were raised to augment the Regular Army in the conflict, and the first one ready came from Mississippi. To Grant's outrage, all of the officers in the regiment were themselves volunteers elected by their men, rather than professionals. "Mr. Polk has done the Officers of the Army injustice by filling up the new Regt. of Riflemen from citizens," he complained in June. "It is plain to be seen that we have but little to expect from him."[31] The "we" were the officers of the army, men like himself who might have expected to get promotions and assignments to lead those new volunteers. Instead, Second Lieutenant Grant would now find himself subordinate to any upstart politico who persuaded volunteers to elect him captain.

He still felt resentful a few weeks later when he told Julia that "after the way in which the President has taken to show his feelings for the Army, especially I think we have but little reason to want to see fighting."[32] Months later it still irked him. "If Mr. Polk does the Army another such insult as he did in officering the Rifle Regt. I think I will leave," he told Julia, then crossed out the words "I think" to make his determination unconditional.[33] It was a feeling born of disillusionment. By the end of 1846, Zachary Taylor loomed ever larger as a potential Whig candidate for the presidency in 1848. The senior professional officer, Major General Winfield Scott, was also a Whig, and feuding with Polk. The president wanted to put a man of his own party in charge of the war in hopes of boosting him to the White House instead of Taylor, but the highest-ranking Democrats in the army were unsuitable. "While the authorities at Washington are at sea as to who shall lead the army," Grant complained, "the enterprise ought and could be accomplished."[34] Then and thereafter he regarded the conflict as "a political war."[35]

Also pressing Grant to resign was his father, who repeatedly told his son that every officer ought to resign after Polk's civilian commissions. By April 1847 'Lys seemed to agree, telling Julia, "I believe he is right and if there is no prospect soon of the War closing I will go any how."[36] The separation was becoming intolerable. He had seen her just once since their engagement. She signed her letters with X's or the word "kiss" at the bottom, but kissing paper was scant satisfaction to a young man in love.[37] "I begin to believe like some author has said,that there are just two places in this world," he told her. "One is where a person's intended is, and the other is where she is not."[38]

Of the broader debate raging in the United States over the war, the accusation of the Whigs that it was a land grab to extend slavery, he said nothing. He grew up in an environment unfriendly to slavery, but was hardly unfamiliar with blacks, free and slave. When he first came to Texas with his regiment he had what he called a "black boy" attending as a hired servant, and even an adult male was still a "boy" to him and his circle, which only put him in the mainstream of American attitudes.[39] As with several matters of the mind and heart, like politics or religion, young Grant was at best indifferent to slavery at this stage of his life. However, as the war progressed he certainly revealed sympathy with one class of the poor and disfranchised, the common people of Mexico. On first contact they did not impress him much. "The people of Mexico are a very different race of people from ours," he told Julia. They looked and lived more like Indians than whites, which was not a compliment. He feared that *soldados* conscripted from that base might be uncontrollable, and expected cruel treatment if he were ever taken prisoner. As for enemy officers, he did not like the class system that produced most of them. "It is a great pity that [the] people [who] compose the Mexican soldiery should be made the tools for some proud and ambitious General to work out his advancement with," he lamented to Julia.[40] He believed that the great mass of the *soldados* had little understanding of why they fought.[41] "The better class are very proud and tyrinize over the lower and much more numerous class as much as a hard master docs over his negroes," he wrote, his earliest comment on the potential cruelty of slavery.[42]

What allowed that tyranny in Grant's mind was that the poor people of Mexico, though proud, were uneducated, subject to the will of an elite, "and they have no government to act for them."[43] To young Grant government was, or ought to be, an agency for the protection and benefit of all, not just those in power. "I pity poor Mexico," he wrote as the war approached its close. "With a soil and climate scarsely equaled in the world she has more poor and starving subjects who are willing and able to work than any country in the world." Yet poverty seemed universal and he saw beggars everywhere. The rich tyrannized the poor with "a hardness of heart that is incredible."[44] Just as disturbing was how he saw some of the undisciplined American volunteers in the army treating the Mexican people, especially Texans who combined racial intolerance with a spirit of vengeance dating back to their revolution of 1836. They "seem to think it perfectly right to impose upon the people of a conquered City to any extent, and even to murder them where the act can be covered by the dark," he lamented early in the war. Worse, some men enjoyed the violence. "I would not pretend to guess the number of murders that have been committed upon the persons of poor Mexicans."[45] Grant may not have regarded Mexicans, or blacks, as equals, but he clearly believed that the presumed superiority of his race conferred no license to deny human rights to another.

By February 1847 he was tired of the country, one of the reasons the subject of resigning kept recurring.[46] Grant wrote Julia in April

1847 that if "there is no prospect soon of the War closing" he would resign. As a quartermaster he was going nowhere. "I have been a very long time ballancing in my mind whether I would resign or not," he confessed. By this time he could have been in a comfortable and prosperous business with his father and married to Julia, or nearly as comfortable as a college professor.[47]

Happily, Grant's war took a different turn after Polk finally put Scott in command in January 1847. Scott ordered the bulk of Taylor's army to march to the mouth of the Rio Grande on the Gulf of Mexico, and then it moved by transports to Tampico where it met several thousand fresh soldiers coming with Scott, who would lead the combined force in a joint land and naval assault on the port city of Vera Cruz, the start of a campaign to take Mexico City itself. For the first time Grant and Lee began to revolve in the same orbit.

Lee stayed reticent about America going to war with Mexico. He believed it might have arisen from acts of either contestant, or "force of circumstances," observing only that if the United States did not understand the causes before going ahead, it should have. Before long he confessed a belief that Polk had "bullied" Mexico into war, and expressed himself ashamed of the fact, while in May 1846 he put himself squarely in the Whig camp when he said he doubted "the justice of our cause." Still, he went on to say that a soldier's duty was to implement government policy, not to try to influence it.[48] As a soldier he felt "it is rather late in the day now to discuss the origin of the war."[49] Still, it was a relief when war relieved him from more bureau duty in Washington. On August 19 orders sent him to report to Brigadier General John E. Wool at San Antonio, Texas.[50]

Before leaving Lee made out his will, leaving everything to Mary, including Nancy Ruffin and her children at White House. Little had changed in his attitude toward slaves. A year earlier Mary Lee had agreed to a proposition from Senator Albert S. White of Indiana to hire "her girl" Judy Meriday for a period of six years, "after which she will be considered as fully liberated."[51] But Lee was not giving her freedom. As an Arlington slave, she belonged to Mary Lee's father, and in arranging her hire and then freedom Lee simply carried out his father-in-law's wishes—and likely Mary's—for a favored servant, as he would do in future as Custis's agent. Lee himself no longer owned his only other slave. Gardner's hire had gone from $60 a year when Lee inherited him to just $30 in 1844, and though Lee wanted him hired in 1845, no one engaged him and he was still unemployed. Gardner was at least forty-nine now, possibly as old as seventy-two, and no longer an income-producing asset. Sometime during the past eighteen months Lee had either freed him, sold or given him to Hill Carter, or let him purchase his freedom with money Lee allowed him to earn over the years.[52] Now Lee stipulated that in the event of his death, Nancy Ruffin and her children were to be "liberated so soon as it can be done to their advantage & that of others."[53]

It was an equivocal sort of emancipation. He might have freed them that moment if he wished. By these terms they remained slaves as long as he lived and perhaps much longer. Should he die in Mexico, they could remain in bondage as long as Mary—or their children after her—wished, since they were the obvious "others" to whose advantage he referred. His intent was most likely to keep the slaves producing income for his widow and orphans, and leave it to Mary to decide when to emancipate them, probably when they became more trouble than they were worth. That was another reason for freeing or giving away Gardner now that he was not an earner, and might only be a headache for Mary to look after. The only implicit promise was that his heirs would not sell them. Beyond that he hinted at freedom, but gave nothing. Of course, he need not have mentioned liberation at all if he resolutely wanted the Ruffins to remain his family's property. Lee was still ambivalent toward voluntary emancipation. His mother had been content to have slaves if they produced income and caused no problems, and his attitude had been much the same, but he was evolving. The influences of his wife and her family, as well as others, had brought him to the place where he could contemplate manumission, even if only tentatively. It remained to be seen if he could travel farther down that road.

On September 21 Lee rode into the city of the Alamo to find Wool's forces gathering. He missed the Battle of Monterey, which commenced that very day three hundred miles to the south, but reconnoitered in advance of the column on its march to the Rio Grande, finding roads where there were any, making roads where there were none, and bridging streams. On October 12 Wool and Lee crossed the river into enemy territory only to learn of the eight-week armistice. Wool marched on to Monclova and halted to wait out the cease-fire, Lee the engineer meanwhile mapping the town for possible defenses, probably his first such exercise in the field.

The armistice lapsed on November 19, and Wool received word from Brigadier General William Worth that an attack on his command at Saltillo by a Mexican force seemed imminent. Wool immediately put his men on the march, and Lee again rode ahead to clear the road, but after a forced march to link with Worth they found that the feared Mexican attack proved to be only rumor. More false alarms followed, at one of which Lee and a Mexican guide rode some distance from the army looking for the enemy. Finally in the moonlight he spotted their white tents on a distant hillside, only to discover on closer inspection that it was really a flock of sheep. Still, he learned from the shepherds that *soldados* were some distance away and no immediate threat. Pleased at genuine intelligence of the foe's actual position, Wool added the duty of acting inspector general to Lee's brief as his ranking engineer officer.

Finally on January 16, 1847, General Winfield Scott, assuming overall command in Mexico, sent an order for Lee to join his staff as engineer for the campaign. Fortresses ringed Mexico City, and Scott needed an engineer to aid in their reduction. After a trip of more than 250 miles, Lee reached Scott at the mouth of the Rio Grande, where the general immediately placed him on his staff along with Lee's old friend Joseph E. Johnston. On February 21, after a rough voyage south along the Mexican coast, Lee saw the shores of the Island of Lobos near Tampico, Scott's staging area for the landing at Vera Cruz 200 miles farther south. "I shall have plenty to do there," Lee wrote his sons a few days later, "and am anxious for the time to come."[54] So was Lieutenant Grant, already there for some days. By March 3 they were at last ready to finish the voyage, Lee on a vessel named for a Northern state, the *Massachusetts,* and Grant on one named for a Southern state, the *North Carolina.* Two days later they both saw Vera Cruz.

Lee heard his first hostile shot when cannon mounted in the fort San Juan de Ulloa opened fire on his transport without harm. Five days hence, on March 9, Scott made the landing. The regulars went ashore first, Grant and the 4th Infantry among them, and incredibly there was no Mexican resistance whatever. The next day Scott and his staff went ashore, looked about, and concluded to lay siege to the fort rather than attempt a massed attack. A siege was engineering work, and Lee saw plenty of it in the slow but methodical preparation of lines of defensive works and gun emplacements. One day riding with Scott inspecting progress, they came upon a young officer walking alone in a field despite orders for officers to remain in quarters unless on assignment. The lieutenant said he had not received the order, but Lee peremptorily sent him back to his quarters, then rode away. Later that day Lee came to apologize for his abruptness, and he and Lieutenant George B. McClellan parted amicably.[55]

Lee positioned heavy cannon, constructed field works, and on March 24 actually directed the fire of naval guns from the *Mississippi* and a detachment of her sailors commanded by none other than his brother Lieutenant Smith Lee. In a twist of irony, the first bullet ever aimed at Captain Lee came from a fellow soldier's pistol during a reconnaissance when a trigger-happy American sentinel accidentally fired at him from a post so close that the flame from the muzzle singed Lee's uniform even as the bullet missed him.[56] Three days later the city surrendered, and when Scott filed his formal report of the operation, he included Lee among others for special mention. Thereafter Scott, who liked to quip that "boys are only fit to be shot," turned more and more to the Virginian, and the ensuing daily intimacy with Winfield Scott would be the making of Lee, provided he did not get shot.[57]

⸺ ℮⸺

There was no making of Lieutenant Grant at Vera Cruz, however. He felt little but frustration during the twenty-day siege. He saw and heard the army in action, but remained in the rear. "I had but little to do except to see to having the Pork and Beans rolled out," he complained to Julia.[58] Determined not to be left out of the action, Grant tried to resign the assignment as supply officer. "I *must* and *will* accompany my regiment in battle," he told Garland in a tone approaching insubordination, adding that he would willingly face a court martial should the government suffer any loss of public property while he was in action. Garland sternly told Grant that his current duty was "an *assigned* duty, and not an *office* that can be resigned." He needed Grant where he was. "However valuable his services might be, and certainly would be, in *line*," said Garland, "his services in his present assigned duties cannot be dispensed with."[59]

A supply officer was a bookkeeper, among other things, and Grant had a quick mind at mathematics. The maintenance and management of wagons and horse or mule teams was essential, and when it came to draft animals, especially horses, Grant likely had no superior in the army. His late friend Hamer reportedly spoke of how Grant once reduced "a train of refractory mules and their drivers to submissive order."[60] With those skills he could be an asset in a staff role, but that hardly made relegation to the rear during action any less galling. After the fall of Vera Cruz on March 29, and after Scott's army started the two-hundred-mile march toward Mexico City, Garland made Grant's appointment as quartermaster and commissary permanent.[61]

At least the march to Mexico City gave Grant a chance to see more of Mexico, and he determined to see as much as possible.[62] It also gave him a chance to refight the war in his mind. Barely had the conflict begun before he indulged in first speculation, and then as he grew more confident, second-guessing and even criticism, though none of it went beyond his letters to Julia. He had been frustrated even while en route to join Scott. "Just think in all this time there has been but three battles fought toward conquering a peace," he grumbled. "If we have to fight I would like to see it all done at once."[63]

After a few weeks the army set out to find the main Mexican army, or take Mexico City, or both.[64] Thanks to Lee's reconnaissance Scott was able to keep going. When the army approached Cerro Gordo, Lee's scouting took him so close to the foe that he found himself behind Mexican lines and had to hide beneath a fallen log by a spring while Mexican *soldados* came for a drink. In the end he escaped and reported a possible path for the army. The next day, April 17, Scott sent Lee to guide men of one division by his newfound route, while the rest of the army waited to advance until Lee's party routed the foe from their defenses. It worked almost to perfection, and the following day Lee ably positioned two batteries to pummel the foe, before Scott sent him to lead yet another party around Cerro Gordo to the enemy rear, to cut off an avenue of retreat. Lee succeeded in time for Scott's main assault to put the Mexican army and its commander General Antonio Lopez de Santa Anna to flight, resulting in the capture of nearly one-third of their numbers and the disorganized dispersal of most of the rest.

No man in Scott's army was more pivotal in the victory. In his first real battle as a soldier, Lee remained cool, acted judiciously, and showed more than the ordinary quotient of bravery. The dead and dying all about were the first casualties he had ever seen, and his impressions echoed Grant's. "You have no idea what a horrible sight a battlefield is," he wrote his oldest son a week later. At one point Lee helped collect Mexican dead and wounded and got them to one of their own surgeons, and then he heard the cries of a little girl and followed them to a hut where he found a *soldado* little more than a boy, his arm shattered by a musket ball. Lee got the boy to a doctor, to the sound of the girl crying *"mil gracias"* to him over and over again.

Again Scott singled him out for praise. Several months hence the war department gave Lee a brevet promotion to major for gallantry at Cerro Gordo.[65] For his part, Lee idolized Scott. "Our Genl. is our great reliance," he wrote soon afterward. "He is a great man on great occasions." Scott kept his eye constantly on his objective, never lost confidence in his strength and resources, took good care of his men, and did not send them into battle until after he had—often with Lee's aid—given them every possible advantage of position and intelligence. "His judgment is as sound as his heart is bold & daring," said Lee, who clearly had found his model of the great commander.[66]

Scott sent Lee ahead once more with the advance to take the town of Jalapa, and immediately afterward Lee moved on to La Hoya and Perote, where he surveyed more Mexican defenses. He was in Perote the first Sunday after the recent battle, and attended an Episcopal church service presented for the army's officers. "I endeavored to give thanks to our heavenly Father for all his mercies to me, for his preservation of me through all the dangers I have passed," he wrote Mary, "for I know I fall short of my obligations."[67] Lee may have been telling his wife what he knew she wanted to hear, but seeing the face of battle at last also may have started the process of impelling Lee to turn his face more heavenward on his own.

During that march Grant studied the landmarks of the battles they fought, like the Castle San Juan de Ulloa and the mountain pass at Cerro Gordo, which he thought impregnable.[68] Scott halted at Puebla on May 15 to refit and await reinforcements, while sending engineers like Lee out to reconnoiter.[69] The general also sent Quartermaster Grant out with a train of wagons and several hundred men as escort to collect foodstuffs from planters to sustain his army on the next march. It was Grant's first independent command in an enemy country, and a valuable experience in living off the land.[70]

Scott did not move again until August 7, and Lieutenant Grant put some of that time to use doing his own investigation of the campaign thus far and what lay ahead. Scott met and fought Santa Anna's army at a series of fortified positions of the Mexicans' choosing. Despite the American success, Grant wondered if there might be another route to approach Mexico City "without meeting such formidable obstructions, and at such great losses." At Cerro Gordo he saw how Lee's reconnaissance enabled Scott to bypass a fortified position and force the enemy to retreat without a severe battle, and that suited Grant's idea of strategy better than costly assaults. "If I should criticize, it would be contrary to military ethics, therefore I do not," Grant went on, but he left little doubt as to what policy he would have preferred.[71]

Grant got a map, interviewed scouts and friendly locals, and then noted the roads leading to Mexico City and what he could learn of the location and strength of its defenses. He concluded that instead of heading directly west and encountering the heaviest of the foe's defenses, the army could pass north of the city by an alternate route and then hit its northwestern suburbs where the foe anticipated no threat, without having to take any forts. Moreover, that route was over solid ground, whereas the direct approach crossed swamps, ditches, and other hazards before confronting heavily fortified positions outside the city. Grant sent his map and suggestions through the chain of command, but they probably never reached beyond Garland, if they got that far.[72] Grant never heard from headquarters. Rather than be offended, he assumed that "the opinion of a lieutenant, where it differs from that of his commanding General, *must* be founded on *ignorance* of the situation." Surely Scott knew better than he. Grant might daydream of being a commander, but he never lost sight of how to conduct himself as a subordinate.[73]

He also reflected on the contrasting management styles of the two army commanders he had served. He preferred Taylor. That general rarely if ever wore a uniform, and Grant himself already felt ambivalent about military costume. Taylor was plain and unaffected, which very much suited the lieutenant's temperament and personality. He did his own reconnaissance as often as not, cared little for a large retinue of staff officers, and wrote orders in brief, simple, unmistakable language so that there might be no confusion as to his intent. "He knew how to express what he wanted to say in the fewest well-chosen words," Grant later observed, "but would not sacrifice meaning to the construction of high-sounding sentences." Grant took that last to heart. Still, he saw much to emulate in Scott as well. Setting aside his ornate uniform and flashy staff—Lee included—Scott was also precise, though wordy in orders and pronouncements, as if conscious that he wrote for posterity. Grant admired both of them, yet concluded that while he was fortunate to serve *under* either, it was a pleasure to serve *with* Taylor.[74]

On August 10 Scott launched his army toward Mexico City. Two days later Lee began a series of reconnaissances that directed the army around heavily fortified Mexican positions, engaging a local guerilla leader named Dominguez and some of his followers to ride with him as scouts.[75] Their route took them south of the city via an indirect approach, to the village of Churubusco, and there on August 19 and 20 Lee repeatedly took a prominent role in placing artillery and directing its fire against enemy positions. He made two daring midnight traverses across a barren no-man's-land between separated columns to carry information, and went without sleep for a day and a half, the first evidence of his considerable physical stamina in the field. No officer in the army did more to pave the road to victory, and when the engagement was done, the way to Mexico City lay open and every high-ranking officer in the army paid tribute to his services. In due time, the war department produced another brevet to lieutenant colonel.

Mexico asked for an armistice and Scott granted it on the understanding that peace negotiations would resume, but after two weeks of inactivity he terminated the armistice at midnight September 6, and immediately called Lee to reconnoiter approaches to the city. Meanwhile, Grant still languished doling out "the Pork and Beans." He saw engagement after engagement from the rear, and finally got a chance for action again, though at first it seemed anticlimactic. On September 8 at Molina del Rey, he and other officers entered some mill buildings in their advance and he spotted *soldados* on top of one. Ordering a few soldiers to help him tip an abandoned cart upright against the outside wall, he climbed the cart's harness shafts to the roof of the building hoping to capture the riflemen, only to find that another infantryman beat him to it.

Lee only observed the fighting that day, then continued trying to find for Scott the best avenue of approach to take the city. A few days later the army marched toward the city in the distance, and Quartermaster Grant joined Worth's advance on the western approaches rather than remain in the rear. Suddenly a field piece backed by Mexican infantry halted them. Grant ran across the road to a stone wall extending some distance beyond their position and discovered a vantage from which snipers might suppress the enemy fire. Running to the rear he asked for a dozen volunteers to follow him, then led them forward under what Colonel Francis Lee called "the most galling fire," covered by musketry from the rest of the column.[76] Once behind the stone wall again, Grant led them forward to a position on the flank of the enemy cannon and infantry where "by a rush, and well directed fire" they disrupted the Mexican defenders and forced them to pull back. Grant had opened the road to advance once more.

Having been in the forefront thus far, he stayed there, up the street to the city gate at San Cosme Garita. He saw a church belfry that afforded a commanding view of the enemy rear if a cannon could be emplaced atop it, and on his own initiative commandeered a small howitzer and crew. The enemy still held the road leading directly to the church, so Grant and his men disassembled the howitzer and carried the gun over a field and through a series of ditches breast-high with water. Rather quaintly, instead of barging in when he reached the church, Grant knocked at the door. When the priest answered and declined to give him entry, Grant employed the little Spanish he knew to explain that he was coming in whether the *padre* liked it or not. That opened the door, and soon Grant's party had the howitzer atop the belfry, reassembled it, and began lobbing balls into the enemy rear, creating consternation.

General William Worth saw the gun's effect and sent Lieutenant John C. Pemberton to bring Grant to him. Worth complimented Grant and sent him back with another howitzer, hoping to double the effect, though Grant was unable to use it. Still, aided by Grant's gun and others similarly placed, Worth took the gate leading into the city before dark. That night Grant and others spent the hours cutting through walls connecting one house to another up to the gate to allow them to assault under cover the next day, but that night the Mexican army evacuated.[77]

Months of tedious garrison duty followed as peace negotiations dragged on. Grant's regiment moved to Tacubaya about four miles from Mexico City, with little for him to do but file forms and write reports. He let his reddish beard grow nearly halfway to his waist and enjoyed wonderful health, but found life oppressively dull. He rode into Mexico City almost every day to attend the theater, see an internationally famous juggler perform, and more. He indulged his traveler's curiosity by joining a two-week expedition up the great mountain Popocatepetl and explored a mammoth cave near Cuernavaca. Yet he could think only of Julia and three years of engagement during which he had seen her but once. "I have the *Blues* all the time," he wrote her in June. To pass the time he may have played cards occasionally, and of course there were taverns.[78]

His old friend John W. Lowe of Brown County, now a captain in the 2d Ohio Infantry, passed through in May 1848, and left afraid that Grant spent some of those idle hours drinking, though Lowe did not say whether he saw Grant imbibing or merely repeated hearsay. Moreover, Ohio volunteers resentful of Grant's earlier criticism might have retaliated by malicious gossip. Perhaps Grant did overindulge.[79] He was twenty-six years old, fifteen hundred miles from home, engaged to a woman he had not seen in years, bored and lonely, and surrounded by hundreds of others in the same situation—a virtual prescription for treatment by bottle. If he drank too much, no superior complained of inefficiency, and nowhere in a stationary army would such laxity show up more quickly than in a quartermaster's duties. Fred Dent saw Grant almost daily at Tacubaya. If he found Grant drinking too much, brotherly concern might have passed a warning to Julia, yet nothing suggests her awareness of such behavior. Soldiers away from home did drink frequently, and sometimes too much. Grant was a soldier away from home.

He certainly spent many of those idle hours reflecting on the recent successful campaign, and noted something about the soldiers his army fought. "The Mexicans fight well for a while, but they do not hold out," he observed. "They fight and simply quit." They had scant drill or discipline, inadequate rations, and little or no pay. Relieve those deficiencies, he believed, and "they would fight and persist in it." As it was, they fought as much as anything out of fear of their officers.[80]

Others looked back on his performance before Mexico City. General Worth singled out Grant for special mention in his report. Major Francis Lee, now commanding the 4th Infantry, complimented the lieutenant for distinguished gallantry. Grant's actions on September 13 took place early in the day and his spontaneous drive to the city gate was "the first and most advanced demonstration on the city," Lee believed. "I look on them as the most gallant acts of the day."[81] Garland added that Grant "acquitted himself most nobly upon several occasions."[82] In fact, he won brevet promotions to first lieutenant and captain, and at virtually the same time gained confirmed permanent rank as first lieutenant to fill a vacancy in his regiment.

Mexico and Mexicans impressed Lee far less than Grant, but Lee was not a traveler, and throughout his life no place or people compared to Virginia and Virginians. He did like the way Mexico City's women eschewed stockings and showed their "polished ankles," but even the *señoritas* posing on their balconies failed to interest him. "There is *ugliness* enough in this city to sink it," he thought.[83] He found the "miserable" populace "idle worthless & vicious," he wrote Mackay. Condemning the "power & iniquity of the church," Lee concluded that if the conquered nation was to progress, the influence of the Catholic church must be curbed, and free opinions of government and religion introduced instead.[84] This streak of anti-Catholicism grew in him in the years to come. Suspecting that the peace might break down, he promised "they will be taught a lesson." In fact, for the first time Lee revealed a hint of "manifest destiny" sentiment. "They will oblige us in spite of ourselves to overrun the country & drive them into the sea," he said. "I believe it would be our best plan to commence at once." European immigration could then bring an energetic and free-willed Protestant population to take the country from the Mexicans and develop it properly. "It is a beautiful country & in the hands of the proper people would be a magnificent one." Now that they were there, he believed they should occupy and hold all of it. If they simply defeated the Mexicans and then withdrew to the Rio Grande, they would be confronting them on the other side again soon enough. "By confining ourselves to the boundary we desire," he predicted, "we shall have a warlike peace, or a peacelike war for years.[85]

Lee had never spoken like an expansionist before. Even now he did not sound much like the typical Southern expansionist, usually a Democrat, bound on gaining new territory for the spread of slave-based plantation economy. Rather, he saw a promising country lying fallow under the stewardship of a lazy native population ruled by a corrupt Catholic aristocracy. If the United States was to be safe from further conflict, it needed a stable and prosperous democratic neighbor on its southern border. Only white Protestant Europeans, the stock that built his own country, could provide that.

To achieve it, however, the Americans would have to avoid fighting among themselves. Close as he was to army headquarters, he saw firsthand the unseemly jockeying for position and favor, the feuds between generals like Winfield Scott and Gideon Pillow over credit for successes. If he had not already been disdainful of such vainglory, this campaign made him so. "You will hear of many more things than have taken place," he told Mackay.

We are our own trumpeters, & it is so much more easy to make heroes on paper than in the field. For one of the latter you meet with 20 of the former, but not till the fight is done. The fine fellows are too precious of persons so dear to their countrymen to expose them to the view of the enemy, but when the battle is *won*, they accomplish with the tongue all that they would have done with the sword, had it not been dangerous to do so.[86]

The seemingly endless months of negotiations that followed left Lee "nauseated," especially when they resulted in a treaty that paid Mexico millions for territory already taken by conquest.[87] "We are the Victors in a regular war," he wrote brother Carter in March 1848. The Mexicans had been "whipped in a manner of which women might be ashamed," and the Americans had "the right by the laws of war of dictating the [terms] of peace and requiring indemnity for our losses and expenses."[88] More to the point, Lee could not forget the friends maimed or lost forever. He tried to be bravely flippant about it, writing a cousin that "there is a terrible deficiency of Arms & legs among them, but I have come to the conclusion that one of each is sufficient for a man, & its duplicate Superfluous," but he could not sustain the pose after burying three friends. He felt no exultation in victory. "Give me back our brave officers & men, & I will return all we have taken," he went on. "Their whole country cannot replace in my feelings what it has cost us."[89]

That disillusionment only grew when Scott brought charges against Pillow for insubordination and outrageous claims of credit for victories in which he scarcely participated. Lee tried to mediate between the two, but failed, and feared Scott would destroy his own reputation in the acrimonious feud. By March, Lee thought seriously of leaving the army to give more attention to his family when he returned home, but in May when Polk recalled Scott and Lee could have gone with him, he opted to remain longer to prevent Scott's enemies from accusing the general of taking good officers away from the army in Mexico.[90] Finally on May 21, 1848, he learned that one branch of the Mexican congress had voted final passage of a treaty of peace, and the other was expected to do likewise. "We all feel quite exhilarated at the prospect of getting home," he wrote his brother Smith.[91] The ratification of the Treaty of Guadalupe Hidalgo at the end of the month made that prospect a reality. Captain Lee had fought his war with sword, wits, and ingenuity, not his tongue, and everyone around him saw that, most of all Scott, who marked him. He would continue to watch Lee, even give his career a gentle boost when he could. He might have need of such a man in years to come.

When they left Mexico, Lee and Grant could reflect that each had experienced a good war. To the extent that Grant went home a hero, the names Palo Alto, Resaca de la Palma, and Monterey on his record made him already a distinguished veteran before Lee ever set foot in Mexico. For the first time Grant's name appeared in a few newspapers, and not just thanks to his father's promotion. Of course, the Mexican War made Lee professionally. He emerged to much more notoriety than Grant, thanks in no small part to the war catapulting him into the intimate orbit of Scott, who virtually became a father figure. The Virginian's contribution to the final victory was undoubtedly greater than Grant's, too. Lieutenant Raphael Semmes, commanding a sloop in the blockade of Vera Cruz, soon afterward declared that Lee was "endowed with a mind which has no superior in his corps," a peculiar instinctive grasp of topography that seemed intuitive, and "a judgment, tact, and discretion" that made him invaluable to Scott.[92] His name saw print virtually hundreds of times from Texas to Wisconsin, and Louisiana to New England, making him, if not quite a household name, easily the best known and most highly complimented engineer officer of the war. That, and the widespread acknowledgment that Lee stood higher than any other in Scott's esteem, propelled him to an almost exclusive stratum within the army. Engineers did not become field generals, and should he stay in his corps, he could expect little more than another promotion or two and an administrative position in Washington. Should circumstances and his reputation for energy, insight, and daring secure him a shift to a line regiment, however, advancement might be much more rapid. If another conflict came, that rise might be dramatic indeed.

Grant saw more action and wider service under both Taylor and Scott, but also more of the tedium of long weeks immobile during the armistices. Lee's war was compact, a single but climactic campaign. Taken together, their actions spoke well indeed for West Point, and for the initiative and bravery of the men of the United States Army. Sometime while they were in Mexico they met. Lee thought he recalled it but could never picture Grant's face, for diminutive, red-bearded "Toad" Grant was not then a man to remember. Grant never forgot their meeting, for the magnificent Lee was not a man to forget.

What remained to be seen was how well they readjusted to the tedium and inactivity that constituted the bulk of the real world of soldiering.[93]

4

TIMES OF TRIAL

In 1854 John Livingston, compiler of illustrated books on outstanding men of the time, approached first Grant and then Lee asking each to provide photographs and details of his war experiences for the new edition of his *American Portrait Gallery*. Clearly he regarded their exploits as on a par. Neither appeared in the final book. Grant may not have responded at all, while Lee declined, saying, "I fear the little incidents of my life would add nothing to the interest of your work nor would your readers be compensated for the trouble of their perusal."[1] For the first time their names were *almost* linked.

Captain Lee came home in the summer of 1848, with brevets to major, lieutenant colonel, and colonel, but disillusioned with the army after what he saw in Mexico. A soldier prepared for war all his career, but once it commenced "a Sett of worthless, ignorant, political aspirants or roués, are put over his head, who in spite of themselves, he has to tug on his Shoulders to victory."[2] It made him sick to witness. Henceforward leaving uniform for another pursuit came often to mind, but he could never make the break. Before long he was sent to Baltimore to oversee construction of Fort Carroll, where Mary and the children joined him and they spent the next three years.[3] Though Lee sometimes complained that "times are pretty dull," in fact he enjoyed those years. The construction challenged his ingenuity, but as he told son Custis, "all difficulties can be overcome by labour & perseverance."[4] Then in May 1852 orders reassigned him to the superintendence of the Military Academy. It was a comfortable post, and he could expect to be there for several years. He assumed command on September 1.

Immediate challenges confronted him. The best officers were often unwilling to serve there as faculty, his first experience at personnel management, and a problem that never went away.[5] He naturally gave close attention to removing temptations for cadets to misbehave, and kept parents fully advised when a son's demerits became a hazard, reminding them that demerits were military infractions, not moral misconduct. "I hope you will not allow yourself to be too much disturbed," Lee consoled one mother. "He is young, of fine capacity, & can succeed in whatever he applies himself to."[6] In serious disciplinary cases, he gave benefit of the doubt and allowed credit for good intention and sincere contrition, albeit along with appropriate punishment.[7] When cases went beyond forgiveness, he recommended court martial or dismissal.[8] "There must be a limit to everything," Lee declared.[9] When the punishment had to be imposed, he did not quail, explaining that "true kindness requires it should be applied with a firm hand."[10]

Lee believed a young man "must think, judge & act for himself, & not according to the say of pretended friends & fine fellows."[11] He set standards high and exemplified them in his own deportment, leading cadets to dub him the "Marble Model."[12] They admired him in spite of his expectations. "Our Superintendent Col. Lee is liked," one cadet wrote home in 1853. "He has the highest notions of military duty of any man I ever saw."[13] Every Saturday evening he held suppers for selected cadets, being himself quite particular on even the smallest matters of the table setting.[14] "He takes some interest in us," noted another young man. "He has an eagle eye and looks like a *man*."[15]

Besides dealing with discipline, Lee oversaw the maintenance of the physical plant at the Academy, striving to improve everything from the water supply to the library, and personally proofread Academy publications meticulously.[16] He accounted for every expenditure, himself calculating mileage allowances for the board of visitors when they came for examinations.[17] With an eye on boosting operating funds, he even recommended that a treasure hunter with a story of buried money on the grounds be allowed to dig if the post fund received half of anything found.[18] Lee pressed for expansion of the course from four years to five, and required everyone to attend chapel as he did himself. The current Presbyterian chaplain's sterner God may have accelerated his own shift toward a more providential faith.[19] When a cadet died, he told parents "you will find consolation in your loss, by reflecting upon his gain."[20]

After almost three years at the Academy he received promotion to lieutenant colonel and a shift to line service in the newly created 2d United States Cavalry, to serve under Colonel Albert Sidney Johnston.[21] He preferred to stay in the Engineers, "but so long as I continue an officer of the Army, I can neither decline promotion or service, & must leave to those in authority to say where my poor services can be best applied."[22] The prospect of active service suited him even though it would take him from family and friends. "A soldier's life is one of toil & self-denial," he confessed, but his only alternative was to resign when he could no longer stand the separation.[23]

He spent the next two years in Missouri and Texas building his new regiment and enjoying it.[24] Granted, he found little to say for the Plains Indians, an uninteresting race in need of humanization, made hideous by nature. He assumed everyone was an enemy until proven otherwise, and expected they would have to be killed, since violence was "the only corrective they understand." They meant only trouble and he thought them "not worth it."[25] As with Mexicans, Lee saw nothing in them to warrant his father's deistic notions of the natural dignity of all men. What sustained him on the frontier was that it was his duty. By now duty assumed the delineation of a faith for Lee, an obligation that was virtually God's will.[26] The tenuousness of life itself demanded every exertion to "fulfill our duties, & the work set before us, before we go home."[27] In fact, duty unselfishly performed was "the greatest happiness that any can enjoy in this world, for if done in its full sense, it holds out the prospect of happiness in the next."[28]

Duty unified all conflicts in his mind, especially religion. Shortly before marriage he thought Mary's notion of finding happiness only after death was unnatural.[29] He took his irreverent tone to war with him in 1846, joking to others that "I think a little lead, properly taken, is good for a man," yet at home Mary proudly read to others the Christian expressions in his letters as rather cynically he told her what he knew she wanted to hear.[30] Then the war itself changed him, and it came quickly. Returning home in June 1848, Lee told his brother Smith that "I have much cause for thankfulness & gratitude to that Good God, who has once more united us."[31] Just a year later he asserted that only obeying the Commandments and worshipping God as they prescribed could save him from "evil & calamity." Man was weak and selfish, drawn toward "folly, excess & sin" that made Lee "sometimes disgusted with myself & sometimes with all the world." He wanted to be better, yet even in prayer he felt inadequate. His only hope, he concluded, "is in my confidence, my trust in the mercy of God."[32] He might engage in a little hypocrisy for Mary's sake, but he had no reason to mislead his closest brother.

That trajectory over the next few years propelled him toward a providentialism that resigned him neither to resist nor resent the immutable will of God. All afflictions were the price of a better life to come. When his beloved mother-in-law died in 1853, grief accelerated his journey. He hardly saw how he could go on, looking on his remaining years with "apprehension & resignation."[33] He felt his life halted in its course, and he could not find the will to continue.[34] Of course he did continue, now with a wholly fatalistic view of man and God. In Texas his God promised protection even in the wilderness as he prayed and read the Bible, and accepted the Almighty's gifts of truth, justice, and duty to fight sin.[35] Even long absence from home was a divine gift to teach him and punish him for his sins. God scourged people to make them resist sin. "I acknowledge the justice of his afflictions," he told Mary in 1855, "& tremble to think how much mine may have contributed towards them."[36] Praying that he had the strength to seek comfort only in repentance, he began to speak of death as a release from life's sufferings, and that "the day of my death will be better for me than the day of my birth."[37]

Interestingly, Lee never wrote of Jesus by name, referring only occasionally to his "saviour," yet spoke often of the "Heavenly Father" and "Almighty God." His expressions sounded formulaic, and sometimes he sent the same sentiments verbatim to multiple people.[38] For a man prone to aphorisms, Lee easily adopted the argot of faith. Still, though he wrote often of "my prayers" or "our prayers" in a colloquial manner, he rarely mentioned himself actually kneeling in prayer, though surely he did. Perhaps that is because, ironically, his new belief in God's domination of man's fate rather neatly laced with the Deist view he heard in youth of a god who ignored prayer. In both man was powerless and must accept events as God's will. Lee even rationalized that unanswered prayer was a blessing, "a greater advantage than we imagine," because submitting to unrelieved suffering today brought promise of reward tomorrow.[39]

There was a streak of intolerance in his conservative Protestant-ism, one that may have been present before his conversion. He did not like Catholicism, thinking its ceremony ungodly, and its services "incomprehensible," a perversion of the teachings of Christ.[40] After attending a mass he left horrified at the icons and multiple offerto-ries and "the exhibition of ignorance & superstition in the worship of the true living God."[41] At a baby's christening he saw "the poor child pawed over, sprinkled, wiped & salted," while the mumbled Latin rit-ual meant nothing to those assembled.[42] He thought what he called "High Churchism" was elitist and un-American.[43] Even an Episcopal nativity service he found not to be as "simply and touchingly told as it is in the bible."[44]

By the summer of 1860 Lee believed his journey to faith was com-plete. "I cannot render due thanks for all the mercies bestowed upon me," he told Mary in June. "Such as I can I give, & heartily beseech God to accept my daily sacrifice of thanksgiving."[45] Though he may never have considered it, a universe in which man only proposed while God disposed was one where no matter what risk a man took, the out-come and the responsibility were preordained in His hands. In peace that release from responsibility was some comfort. For a believing commander in time of war it might be liberating.

Even in Texas Lee felt war's icy hand approaching. He shifted toward the Democratic Party in the 1850s thanks to perceived threats to South-ern slave-holding society. Being away from Arlington in 1852 and 1856 he did not vote in those elections, though in the latter he hoped that pro-Southern Democrat James Buchanan would win.[46] Knowing little of him, still Lee expected him to stand for the Union and the Constitu-tion, discourage the fanaticism that Lee saw both North and South, and subdue party partisanship gone out of control.[47] Buchanan did nothing, and what Lee saw instead was a Congress filled with extremists, the anti-slave Republicans and the ultra-Southern-rights crowd posturing over secession.[48] With Kansas in turmoil between pro- and anti-slave factions, he thought each courted explosion to serve its own ends.[49]

An unexpected event thrust him into the heart of the unrest. On October 25, 1857, George Washington Parke Custis died. As executor of Custis's will, Lee got leave to return to Arlington to settle the estate. What he found shocked him. Custis had so neglected his affairs that everything was in a precarious position. He bequeathed Arlington to his daughter Mary Lee for the rest of her life, and after her to Custis Lee, while other estates were to go to the other Lee sons, and the four daughters were to have $10,000 each. Further, Custis wanted his roughly two hundred slaves emancipated once his debts were paid and the bequests to his granddaughters fully funded. It would require the labor of those slaves to produce that money, so he stipulated that they might be retained up to five years after his death before being freed, or until October 25, 1862.[50]

Lee could only exclaim, "what am I [to] do?" when he saw the mess. He was a soldier, not a farmer.[51] Custis's creditors immediately presented demands, and he had to use his own money to meet the most urgent.[52] Before long he had at least $10,000 in debt tied to the properties, with more expected.[53] The house was run down and uninsured against fire.[54] The fields sat fallow and overgrown. Lee had no choice but to extend his leave, and when that expired, more extensions followed. Eighteen months passed, yet by May 1859 he expected it would take another year to get the properties in order and the debts retired, and that did not begin to fund the bequests.[55]

Then there were the slaves. There is no record of Robert E. Lee buying, selling, or freeing a slave of his own. Those few he owned he inherited from his mother and rented to others, and at least three of them were children whom he called "plagues" and "ebony mites."[56] He and Mary had the use of her father's slaves when at Arlington, but could not take any when stationed in New York. Lee hired one or two slaves when posted on his own in Texas, and in 1860 briefly considered buying a slave on a rent-purchase arrangement to replace the hired "boy" then acting as his servant, though confessing that "I would rather hire a *white* man than purchase if I could."[57] Even when they lived in Baltimore he was hesitant to take any from Arlington, fearing that "the abolitionists are very active here," and the opportunities for running away great.[58] Like her father, Mary was interested in the American Colonization Society, and in Baltimore her husband went to the society's offices in the fall of 1853 to make application for the family of thirty-year-old mulatto William Burke, whom Custis had freed several years before, to embark as colonists to Liberia.[59] Lee occasionally kept a body servant for himself when in Washington, Philip Meriday, one of the Arlington people, and rented him out when unable to take him to a free state.[60] Lee's views mirrored his mother's, that slaves were an untrustworthy nuisance, yet slavery was a necessary evil. By 1857 events began to add dimension to his feelings.

Three years earlier he read Joseph Glover Baldwin's *Party Leaders*, which spoke of the elevating effects of slavery on the lives of their masters, and accused abolitionists of retarding "the cause of humanity to these unfortunates" by fifty years.[61] Lee agreed and believed the book "richly deserved" wide readership.[62] When textile magnate Abbott Lawrence of Massachusetts died in August 1855, Lee said it was "a national loss, but his deeds live after him."[63] He failed to say what earned his admiration, but Lawrence, like Baldwin, stood strongly for the Union, personally opposed slavery's spread, but denied that Congress could regulate it, saying, "I have no sympathy with the abolition party."[64]

Then in December 1856, now-president Franklin Pierce accused the Republicans of planning to kill slavery by preventing its spread into the territories, and predicted that abolition would lead to civil war. Lee agreed, and something in Pierce's message impelled him to share his thoughts at length with Mary, though presumably she ought already to know how he felt about something so important. Believing that most Americans regarded slavery as "a moral & political evil," he argued that it was worse on whites than on the slaves. Slavery elevated them "morally, socially & physically." Their bondage was a "painful discipline" sent by God to prepare them for eventual freedom. In other words, slavery was their duty. Only God, not men, could free them, and it would come sooner "from the mild & melting influence of Christianity, than the storms & tempests of fiery controversy." If the abolitionists meant well for the slave, then they must not anger the master. Moreover, he accused Yankees of hypocrisy for honoring their Pilgrim fathers' immigration for "freedom of opinion," while they denied "the spiritual liberty of others." In short, somehow he conflated slavery with religious freedom.[65] Slavery elevated a race, preserved social order, and allowed white and black to occupy the continent peacefully until God decided the black's place in America.

Managing the Arlington slaves only confirmed Lee's beliefs. He had barely arrived before anonymous letters appeared in the local press saying old Custis promised immediate freedom to his slaves from his deathbed.[66] Much as he hated to see his name in the press, Lee responded that the will was available in the Alexandria County court for anyone to see, and that no one with Custis at the end saw him speak to the slaves about freedom.[67] He did not add that the will's wording was confused. Custis's statement "then I give freedom to my slaves" followed a stipulation that his plantations be cleared of debt and the Lee daughters' legacies be funded. The former seemed contingent on the latter, but in the next clause he stipulated keeping the slaves no more than five years after his death.[68] If the debts and legacies were incomplete by that time, were they still to be freed? Believing the will's intent was that the debts and legacies be settled first, Lee applied to the court for a decision, asking that the deadline be extended until all other obligations in the will had been met.[69] Even then Mary Lee thought it would be impossible to fund the legacies in even ten years. Meanwhile the slaves would be a burden, and when their freedom did come, it would benefit none but the Lees, "who will be relieved from a host of [the] idle & their useless dependents."[70]

Unidentified agitators told the slaves that they were free at Custis's death. Then Lee told them otherwise, and his troubles commenced. He wanted an overseer who while "considerate & kind to the negroes, will be firm & make them do their duty"; he had to act as overseer himself for months before he hired John McQuinn.[71] When Lee tried to get the slaves to work they accused him of being "a hard master," and he met resistance all through 1858 and on into 1859. One flatly refused to work.[72] The coachman ran away and had to be apprehended. Within weeks two women left claiming they had his permission, and they, too, had to be brought back at Lee's expense. Then others rebelled at working, and Lee may have had to use some force in subduing them. To keep the troublemakers from infecting the rest, he sent them to a Richmond broker to hire them out.[73] Slaves already working at hire ran away and Lee had to pay rewards for their apprehension, while one Arlington fugitive stole a jewelry box containing heirlooms of Martha Washington's.[74] The women irritated Mary, and Lee wanted them hired out if possible to relieve her.[75] Privately he feared for her safety if he returned to his regiment with the blacks still there.[76] Still, despite the trouble they put him to, he hoped to free the slaves as soon as possible. It was "justice to them," and meant freedom to him.[77]

That all made May of 1859 a bad time for twenty-nine-year-old Wesley Norris and his younger sister Mary to run for freedom.[78] With their cousin George Parks they struck north for the Mason-Dixon line and Pennsylvania and missed it by less than ten miles when authorities in Carroll County, Maryland, apprehended and jailed them in Westminster.[79] Lee sent a constable to retrieve and return them to Arlington in mid-June.[80] What happened next became a matter of public dispute that haunted him the rest of his life. On June 19 an anonymous letter in the New York *Tribune* said that "Col. Lee ordered them whipped," and that when the officer returning the slaves refused to lash Mary, Lee stripped her back bare and did it himself.[81] Two days later another letter added detail. Lee was known as a cruel master, cut the slaves' weekly ration of corn meal, stopped their fish allowance, and kept elderly women nearly a hundred years of age working dawn until dark sewing. He ordered the Norrises taken into a barn and stripped to their waists, whereupon the "slave-whipper" gave the men thirty-nine lashes but balked at whipping Mary, so Lee administered her lashes himself.[82]

"The N. Y. [*Tribune*] has attacked me for my treatment of your Grand Fathers slaves (he has left me an unpleasant legacy)," Lee wrote Custis a week later.[83] He would not reply, but the Alexandria *Gazette* tried to defend him, calling the story a "malicious fabrication."[84] Still, it took hold and reappeared again and again, with ever more lurid embellishments: Mary was only sixteen and Lee made her mother watch while he stripped and whipped her; the slaves dreaded Lee more than his overseer; the slaves had not run away but only went fishing; Mary was tied up by her hands so high she could only stand on tiptoe; Lee poured salt brine on her lacerated back after he whipped her.[85]

All his life Lee deplored conflict and confrontation, probably because to him it meant loss of control. Shortly before he returned to Arlington, he appeared as a witness at a court martial attended by Albert Sidney Johnston's wife. With some contempt she noted that he "humed and ha'd" when questioned, concluding that he equivocated because he feared "to become unpopular."[86] Had she known him better she would have realized that what she witnessed was his dread of public confrontation, of speaking ill of anyone to their face. Now the persistent defiance of the Arlington slaves made him a participant in a confrontation that forced him to a violent, though lawful, act. Surely Lee did have them whipped. After eighteen months of surliness, resistance, and insubordination, he was fed up. The plantation, the expense of hiring other workers, apprehending runaways, and paying for jails and rewards devoured his own cash. He had been on the verge of returning to his regiment, thinking he had things in hand.[87] The runaways dashed that hope, and now Lee feared for his family's safety. In that state of mind, he concluded that punishment and example were due. As Wesley Norris later said, Lee told them they needed "a lesson we never would forget."[88]

Lee may have resorted to whippings before, but it seems improbable.[89] Given the effect the Norrises' punishment had on their peers and the press, any others should have generated similar reaction. Lee stripping and whipping Mary Norris personally was just lurid invention for a hungry anti-slavery reading audience. Wesley Norris himself never claimed such a thing, and as for the brine, no mention of it appeared for years until a time when people in the North had other motives to demonize Lee.[90] Perhaps he ordered it; probably he did not. He had no patience with soldiers who shirked duty, while a quarter century earlier at Fort Pulaski he complained about slaves being lazy and uncooperative. The Arlington slaves were worse, for they violated trust, they lied, they stole his wife's jewelry, and they told malicious stories that embarrassed him in the national press. It was all consonant with the incessant agitation over slavery. Lee blamed the abolitionists, and had his conviction confirmed when events in the fall of 1859 embraced him in the greatest antebellum drama to date, and with a boyhood friend of Jesse Grant's.

When 'Lys Grant reached home in July 1848 he went first to St. Louis to see his fiancée and make their final wedding plans, then to Ohio where he was a local hero.[91] Two weeks later he married Julia on August 22, and the newlyweds spent the next three months on an extended leave before orders sent them first to Detroit, then almost immediately to Madison Barracks at Sackets Harbor, New York, on Lake Ontario, where he helped recruit a company of the 4th Infantry. Along the way his commission as first lieutenant arrived.[92] Early in March

1850 orders returned him to Detroit.[93] When he left, Julia went on a visit to her family, their first separation since marriage. Grant found Detroit dull, and discovered that already Julia was his anchor.[94] "You know dearest without *you* no place, or home, can be very pleasant to me," he wrote her, joking that since "I see no one I like half as well as my own dear Julia I have given up the notion." When her sister Emma teased him about marrying the old maid of the family, Grant told her with typical directness that "I got the very one I wanted, and the only one I wanted."[95]

The Grants spent two years in Detroit, probably their happiest posting. Like Mary Lee, Julia went home to give birth to their first child, Frederick Dent Grant, on May 30, 1850, and Grant later brought them back to Detroit where the next months passed pleasantly enough but for him taking a bad fall on winter ice.[96] He went to court to get the walkway cleared in winter and won his case, and in the process became acquainted with rising attorney Zachariah Chandler.[97]

The next spring Julia took their son to spend the season with her family. She loved her husband, and loved him even more as the years wore on, but dull Detroit was no match for St. Louis where she enjoyed the social life, her father's pampering, and living in ease. Grant indulged her, though it meant missing his son's first birthday. "I never dreamed that I should miss the little rascle so much," he told her.[98] Unfortunately, she was a poor correspondent. For six weeks he heard nothing from her, and in June he complained that "I have not had the scratch of a pen from you."[99] Meanwhile reassigned to Sackets Harbor, Grant indulged his favorite pastime, travel. He visited Niagara Falls, then got leave for an extended trip to New York City, West Point, Quebec, and Lake Champlain. He felt no hesitation at making "this little exkursion" on his own, and there was a difference between himself and Lee.[100] Despite the Virginian's worldly class, Lee had none of Grant's curiosity of the world. 'Lys was always anxious to see more.

When Julia came back they passed a delightful season until May 1852 when the army ordered the 4th Infantry to California.[101] Julia went to Bethel to await their next baby's arrival, while Grant prepared his regiment for the trip. He still found time to travel to Washington, which failed to impress him, as he wrote Julia that "the place seems small and scattering and the character of the buildings poor."[102] He most looked forward to his ocean voyage, hoping to see many South American ports, but on the day they sailed all he thought of was that "I never knew how much it was to part from you."[103]

Instead of sailing around Cape Horn, they landed on the Panama Isthmus and marched overland to the Pacific.[104] The War Department's failure to plan ahead left them largely to themselves. Seven companies went ahead, while Grant's followed with the baggage, arms, the band, a few officers' families, and a number of men sick with cholera. He took them by barge up the Chagres River to Cruces, only to find no transportation waiting for the baggage. Sending his company ahead, he spent days hiring mules to pack the sick. Daily he halted to bury the dead, then reached the Pacific on July 25 or 26 to find so many sick there that he was assigned the care of all. While tending them he also prepared the regiment for the voyage to California, miraculously avoiding the cholera himself. When the 4th Infantry left aboard the *Golden Gate* on August 5, at least eighty-four soldiers were dead.[105] Grant firmly believed that many of them need not have died if someone in Washington had better prepared for their journey, confiding that "there is a great accountability some where for the loss which we have sustained."[106] It was a tragic object lesson in the importance of being ready before launching any operation.

Landing at San Francisco on August 18, the regiment moved to Benicia Barracks.[107] "We are going to a fine country, and a new one," he told Julia.[108] Still, he keenly felt the separation, not yet knowing that he had another son, Ulysses Jr., born July 22.[109] "I am almost crazy sometimes to see Fred," he wrote a month later. "I cannot be separated from him and his Ma for a long time."[110] Her first letter only reached him on December 3 after three months. "You have no idea how happy it made me feel," he wrote in his joy, but the euphoria did not last.[111] To feel close to her, he kissed the leaves and flower petals that she had kissed and enclosed in her letter.[112]

Two things above all characterized Grant from youth: his industry and enterprise. He liked to work hard, his mind constantly focused on improving his situation. The setbacks he suffered never dulled his optimism. He simply looked for the next opportunity. He believed in using his sweat and imagination to make his own luck. It helped that he was by nature curious. At every new posting he explored the countryside, and here he embraced California and investigated ways to share in its promise.[113] "Alltogether I am, so far, a Calafornian in taste," he wrote Julia.[114] He saw no reason "why an active energeti[c] person should not make a fortune evry year." Still, he reined his optimism. His career was a certainty; California's promise "might prove a dream."[115]

Reassignment stunted that dream when orders sent him to Fort Vancouver on the Oregon coast.[116] Quickly the "prospects of the country" engaged his imagination, for its soil could grow produce that he could sell to immigrants at several times its value in the East.[117] Almost at once he made a deceptively quick profit with partner Elijah Camp when they bought a store on credit, then within weeks he sold Camp his share for a promissory note of $1,500.[118] After barely a month in the territory Grant was an enterprising entrepreneur. Traveling up the Columbia River to the spot where wagon trains portaged rapids, he bought livestock to sell to immigrants in the spring, and oxen to replace their teams, expecting thereby to double his money.[119] "It is necessary in this country that a person should help themselves," he concluded, but Oregon offered everything for the taking.[120] "So far as I have seen it it opens the richest chances for poor persons who are willing, and able."[121] He and other officers leased and cleared a hundred acres to sow potatoes and oats in the spring. Grant thrived on the work, gaining weight as he plowed the ground in a mild January.[122] He spent every dollar on seed potatoes.[123] He cut and sold timber to buy a wagon, horses, and tools, and planted twenty acres in potatoes and onions, then sowed more acres in grain. By March 1853 he expected that he could make enough to last his family for some years.[124] Still he expanded, buying cordwood to sell steamers on the Columbia, while he and Captain Henry Wallen of the 4th Infantry partnered to operate wagons hauling goods.[125] He also learned essential rules of management. "One is that I can do as much, and do it better, than I can hire it done," he wrote Julia. "The other is that by working myself those that are hired do a third more than if left alone."[126]

"Hard work and the climate agrees with me," he told her.[127] When she warned him to be careful of the local Indians, he dismissed her concerns. "Those about here are the most harmless people you ever saw," he told her. Echoing his attitude toward Mexicans, he added that "the whole race would be harmless and peaceable if they were not put upon by the whites."[128] The only natives were Klickitats, and occasionally Cowlitz and Dalles tribesmen, "and even this poor remnant of a once powerful tribe is fast wasting away before those blessings of civilization 'whisky and Small pox.'"[129]

He diversified beyond livestock, produce, and boiler wood. On a visit to San Francisco he called on a firm he dealt with as quartermaster and concluded an arrangement to alert them when he saw a rise in demand for an article in Oregon. They would then provide as much as he could take on credit to sell, splitting the proceeds.[130] "This dear Julia is the bright side," he told her in June. But then he confessed that "I have been quite unfortunate lately." Floods on the Columbia ruined some of his onion and grain crop before harvest, while to save his steamboat wood he paid to move it to dry ground, which almost eradicated his profit. Moreover, he had not outgrown his youthful naïveté, and trusted too easily. Elijah Camp left the territory owing him some $800.[131] Grant made substantial purchases on credit, and though at the end of 1852 he thought he had made $2,000, in fact much of that was in notes due to him. Soon a banking house sued him, and though he paid the debt, it was a sign of weakness as a businessman.[132]

Yet Grant was still the optimist. He salvaged some of the potato crop, bought a shipment of pork in San Francisco that netted almost $400, and expected more to yield $1,000 in June and the same in July, meanwhile making money wholesaling groceries and barrels of salt pork.[133] On his trips to San Francisco he visited Michael Phelan's Metropolitan Saloon and enjoyed watching Phelan, one of the finest billiard players of his era. While some thought Grant handy with a cue, he rarely played if others were watching.[134] He saw other potential in the game. Officers and gentlemen needed a club, a place to gather.[135] Grant, Wallen, and navy lieutenant Thomas H. Stevens leased part of the first floor of the newly opened Union Hotel at Kearny and Merchant Streets at $500 a month, and opened their own billiard saloon, charging fifty cents a game.[136]

Then the army put Grant out of business by reassigning him to Fort Humbolt on Humbolt Bay, California. He had no choice but to close all his enterprises, while the hired manager at the billiard hall closed it for him by embezzling its receipts. On Christmas Day 1853, in San Francisco about to leave for Humbolt, Grant authorized Wallen and

Stevens to sell his share of the tables and equipment.[137] He left Oregon owing at least $350 to creditors, soon referring to his business partnerships with Wallen as "our unfortunate San Francisco speculations."[138] Now he had small but mounting debts and on the very eve of departing borrowed $600 to satisfy creditors.[139]

Grant quickly found Humbolt Bay too confining to engage his entrepreneurial spirit. Instead, it all but shut it down.[140] The sudden interruption of his projects showed in his letters home.[141] "You do not know how forsaken I feel here!" he wrote two weeks after arriving. He just sat in his room and read or occasionally went riding. His last letter from Julia came just before he left San Francisco in January, but it was dated the previous October. His thoughts returned to the possibility of resignation.[142] "I think I have been from my family quite long enough," Grant wrote her in February. "The suspense I am in would make paradice form a bad picture." Though only thirty-two, he thought he looked half again older, and he soon went on the post sick roll.[143]

On the basis of what he knew, he seemed to miss Julia much more than she missed him. "You never complain of being lonesome," he wrote in March, "so I infer that you are quite contented." He dreamed of her often, but now in a dream he saw her at a party where she was too busy dancing with others even to talk to him. He seemed at risk of turning inward on himself. He became "so tired and out of patience with the lonliness of this place" that he scarcely ventured more than a hundred yards away for weeks at a time.[144] His imagination played on his fears. "I do not feel as if it was possible to endure this separation much longer," he wrote her, "but how do I know that you are thinking as much of me as I of you?" But then his old optimism returned and he assured her that "you write I am certain and some day I will get a big batch all at once."[145]

Occasionally he and others rode a few miles into the country, but that was all. Englishman Richard W. Brett ran the one good tavern in Eureka, with two billiard tables that perhaps drew Grant from time to time.[146] Occasionally he might have drowned boredom and loneliness with more liquor than was wise, but not habitually, and not to the detriment of performance of his official duties or his standing with his fellow officers.[147] He could ill afford to spend much on liquor.

"Living here is extravigantly high," he told Julia, "besides being very poor."[148] Unlike Robert E. Lee, who counseled his wife against excessive spending, Grant trusted Julia to use good judgment. "Do as you please with your money dearest Julia," he told her. "I know you are always prudent."[149]

By late March Grant was back in fine health and resolved to "find something to do."[150] Still, his even keel was fragile. He clung to the hope that a request for orders to Washington might be approved, so that he could settle the matter of a trunk containing $1,000 in quartermaster funds that was stolen in 1848 from a fellow officer's room, where Grant had placed it for safekeeping. No one blamed or suspected Grant, but it was nonetheless his responsibility until the government relieved him, making it one more debt on his mind. He would try unsuccessfully for years to get resolution. His frustration mounted when his request was needlessly delayed in San Francisco before going to Washington.[151]

Then on April 11 came notice of his promotion to captain. After ten years and eight months in uniform he had risen two grades, well ahead of the average eighteen years.[152] Even the exemplary Lee took almost nine years to make captain. Grant immediately accepted, but then, perhaps with the pen still in his hand, he wrote another brief communication to the adjutant general. Effective July 31, 1854, he was resigning from the army.[153] After nearly two years away from his family and a son he had never seen, he had had enough. As recently as March 6 he wrote Julia that "I sometimes get so anxious to see you, and our little boys, that I am almost tempted to resign." When he contemplated resignation, however, "*poverty, poverty*, begins to stare me in the face." All he needed to tip the scales was what he called "the certainty of a moderate competency."[154] In fact, the means were at hand, for Frederick Dent had recently given his daughter a hundred acres of his White Haven plantation.[155] A captain's pay would not support his family. Grant had always wanted to be a farmer, and this was his opportunity.[156] Moreover, Humboldt's climate set off malarial fevers, and he was on the sick list again.[157]

There was nothing precipitate in his resignation. Deliberately he weighed risks and advantages, and acted only when sure of his course. Grant had been heartily weary of what he called "that detestable Quar-

ter Master business" for some time.[158] Inspecting stoves and compar-
ing prices on maple versus hickory firewood hardly compared with a
gallop through the streets of Monterey under fire.[159] Still, he had handled the business well. He oversaw all materiel purchases, maintained
buildings, and even supervised the smithy, the tin shop, the saddler,
carpenters, and some two hundred pack animals, all with only one
clerk and no additional pay.[160] He outfitted two surveying expeditions
looking at possible routes for a transcontinental railroad, one of them
commanded by Captain George B. McClellan, an acquaintance from
West Point days.[161] He was responsible for more government money
than any officer in the regiment, as much as $38,000 at the end of
1853.[162] Grant handled all of this business on time, though occasionally
his accounts were late reaching Washington.[163] Sometimes the delays
were actually due to slow mails but, otherwise, when reminded he
produced the documents directly.[164]

Moreover, he showed effective leadership in the trip across Panama.[165] Soon afterward the Panama *Herald* published an article accusing the officers of the 4th Infantry of abandoning their men, specifically
naming only Grant.[166] The officers adopted resolutions condemning
the anonymous report and endorsing his conduct. Grant thought of
writing a defense for the home press, but changed his mind.[167] Taking
no notice of this first press libel established a policy that he followed
for the rest of his life.

Meanwhile, Jesse had been thinking of suggesting that his son resign
and come home, perhaps to run his store at Galena, Illinois. That fit
the thoughts on his own mind, but Grant told Julia that "I shall weigh
the matter well before I act."[168] That time had come. He made his
resignation effective July 31 to allow time to hand his responsibilities
to a successor and prepare final reports.[169] He also wrote one last note
to Julia, from whom he had not heard a word in seven months, telling
her simply that "I shall be on my way home."[170] The act stunned his father. Suddenly Jesse feared that his son "will be poorly qualifyed for the
pursuits of privat life," a sentiment at odds with his comment in 1848
that Ulysses "possessed a good deal of financial & business talent."[171]

Once back in St. Louis, Grant had his new son, the wife he adored,
and no immediate employment. He approached the challenge as usual,
with industry, perseverance, and optimism. While his family stayed at

White Haven, he cleared Julia's hundred acres. The following spring they moved to her brother Lewis Dent's farm, Wish-ton-wish. Alternately he cut timbers for a house and cordwood to sell in St. Louis. In the summer of 1856 he built a modest home he called Hardscrabble. Julia had little good to say of it, but Grant felt proud of his work. He wrested a farm from raw land with only a team of horses and his own and a hired man's labor. When not using it himself, he rented his team, making perhaps $50 a month, which helped. He expected that by 1858 he could be independent. "Evry day I like farming better and I do not doubt but that money is to be made at it," he told Jesse, believing that soon he would be hauling potatoes, sweet potatoes, corn, cabbage, beets, cucumbers, and more to St. Louis daily.

Until then, he hinted to Jesse that a loan of $500 would see him through.[172] Jesse Grant ignored the hint, regarding farming as beneath the family dignity. Then in February 1857 Grant abandoned subtlety. "I am going to make the last appeal to you," he wrote. "There is no one els to whom I could, with the same propriety, apply." He asked for $500 for two years. If he could not prosper with that, he was done. "I have worked hard and got but little and expect to go on in the same way," he said, but was determined to try "until I am perfectly independent."[173] Prosperity eluded him. On December 23 he went to pawnbroker J. S. Freligh and pawned his watch to give his family a Christmas.[174]

Grant later redeemed his watch, but that augured no improvement in his fortunes.[175] Julia's mother died in January 1857, and her father soon moved to the city. Grant then rented White Haven from him, paying in part by renting out Hardscrabble. Dent also rented two slaves to Grant, and sold or gave him a third, a thirty-five-year-old field hand named William Jones. The Grants moved in March 1858, and all that spring he hardly left the farm, working side-by-side with the Negroes. Meanwhile, Julia taught the children, and by now they had two more: Ellen born in 1855 and Jesse in 1858.[176]

The year did not improve. The whole family fell ill. They almost lost Fred to typhoid, Julia suffered chills, and Grant's recurring malaria lasted for months. He could scarcely work, and the farm fell behind.[177] His illness cost him 1858 without a cash crop; it was time for a change. He agreed to take a share of ownership in one of Jesse's businesses in the spring, but emphasized that he wanted a salary only temporarily, hoping to be in business for himself before long. "There is a pleasure in knowing that one's income depends somewhat upon his own exertions and business capacity."[178] That spirit took over in the spring of 1859 when he changed his mind and commenced partnership with Julia's cousin Harry Boggs in a general brokerage for real estate, securities, debt collection, and more.[179] Grant spent weekdays in a back room at the Boggs house, with only a camp bed and a chair, and weekends at White Haven.[180] Ever hopeful, he told Jesse that "I believe it will be something more than a support."[181]

In his new situation, Grant hardly had need of one field hand, let alone three. The two hired from Dent went back to the farm, but that left Jones, the only slave Grant ever owned.[182] His first real exposure to slaves in any number came in St. Louis, and even more in Louisiana. Julia's family owned many, and Dent gave her the use of servants both before and after her marriage. Grant's postings in free states meant those slaves could not accompany him even when Julia did. Only after his resignation did he live in a household attended by servants, who were still her father's property.[183] Then Grant somehow acquired title to Jones.[184] Since Dent gave his daughter the land for their farm, Jones was probably a gift, Dent hardly needing field hands when he moved to the city.

In the spring of 1859 Julia wanted to take the children to Covington to see the Grant family, but feared to take a servant since her boat would make stops in Ohio. After the recent Dred Scott decision affirmed that the federal government had no authority over slavery in the territories, anti-slave people were outraged, and it could be dangerous for a slaveholder to stop even briefly in a free state in company with a slave.[185] Just two weeks later her husband made a decision. Hard pressed to support his family let alone a slave, he went to the circuit court on March 29, 1859, and manumitted Jones.[186]

The slave could have brought him $1,000 or more, even as he confessed he "could hardly tell" if his commission business would succeed.[187] Grant had no strong feelings about slavery other than a general preference for the defunct Whigs, who opposed slavery's extension. His sympathy with Mexicans and Indians under white domination could suggest that he felt the same toward slaves, but it is not evident in his developing political consciousness. He closely followed the

1858 congressional campaign in St. Louis between Republican Francis Preston Blair Jr. and Democrat John R. Barret, who defended a bogus pro-slavery territorial constitution framed at Lecompton, Kansas. Grant viewed the Lecompton Constitution as invalid, putting him at odds with Barret, yet he accepted the Dred Scott ruling on Congress's authority.[188] Grant found Blair too extreme, but at the same time would have found Barret's weak stance on the Union unpleasant. Choosing the least of evils, he voted with a slim plurality electing Barret.[189]

That was an unlikely vote for a man who soon emancipated his only slave, yet it is equally unlikely that a man morally opposed to slavery would support the pro-slavery Lecompton. Still, there was a consistency to his ballot. He claimed that "I was a Whig by education," and the few glimpses of his political mindset certainly agree.[190] When Henry Clay died in 1852, Grant was moved to declare that "Mr. Clay's death produced a feeling of regret that could hardly be felt for any other man."[191] By his own admission, he thought little about politics in those years. Remote postings prevented soldiers from voting, which could only be done in a home county, so he missed the 1844 election when Clay lost to Polk. When Whig Zachary Taylor defeated Democrat Lewis Cass in November 1848, Grant was in Missouri and again unable to vote. Four years later when his friend Democrat Franklin Pierce defeated Winfield Scott, Grant was in Oregon.

Then came November 1856 and Grant, a civilian resident of Missouri, cast his first ballot at the age of thirty-four. The Whigs had split, pro-slavery elements aligning with the Democrats, while anti-slavery men framed the new Republican Party or joined the pro-temperance, anti-Catholic, anti-immigrant but also largely anti-slave American Party, better known as the "Know Nothings." Blair led the Republicans in Missouri but they were still amorphous, and a number of friends sharing what Grant called his "Whig proclivities" went over to the Know Nothings, who were themselves waning. Grant went to one of their meetings and allowed himself to be initiated as a member, but after learning more he never went again.[192]

Grant flirted with temperance pledges once or twice, and a few scattered incidents over the next decade might suggest resentment at coddling of immigrants in preference to native-born Americans. His year in St. Louis could account for that, since by 1856 foreign-born people, most of them anti-slave, comprised half the population.[193] The city also had a history of violent protest by nativists, especially as immigrants steadily took the city's public offices. Grant pawned his watch to the Jewish broker John S. Freligh. Soon he saw a county engineer's job that he wanted go to a Jewish immigrant from Prussia. Three anti-slave men on the hiring board chose the Prussian while the two Democrats went for Grant, reflecting party loyalty, but since immigrants held all but one St. Louis County office, Grant felt that foreigners enjoyed unfair advantage in public preferment.[194]

He feared that people misunderstood him. "I am strongly identified with the Democratic party!" he complained to his father in September 1859. "Such is not the case." He only voted for a Democrat once in 1856 when he cast for Buchanan what was in reality a vote against the new Republican candidate John C. Frémont, for Grant feared that a Republican victory might precipitate secession. Between a vote to contain slavery and a vote to avert disunion, he chose what seemed to him to be the greater good.

Ultimately, Jones's freedom represented personal motives. Frederick Dent was indulgent of his slaves.[195] No one in his family wanted to see servants sold into an uncertain future. Jones probably came with the proviso that he be ultimately returned or freed, but Dent could not use him in the city. That left manumission as the only alternative. There would still be slaves with the Grants, for Dent feared his daughter could not run a household without servants. He did the same for his daughter Emma, too, and it is evident that they were on loan, as Dent retained full control over them long after they left his home.[196] It is perhaps worth notice that while Boggs and Grant advertised themselves as agents for buying and selling almost everything, a conspicuous absence from their advertised portfolio was slaves.[197] If Grant did not actively oppose slavery, neither did he promote doing business in it himself. By the fall of 1859, when something exploded at Harpers Ferry, Virginia, slaves were the last thing on his mind.

Abolitionist John Brown and a score of followers forcibly occupied the United States arsenal at Harpers Ferry on October 17, 1859, bent on fomenting a slave uprising across the South. Since Lee was at hand,

General Scott ordered him to take a company of marines and local volunteers to apprehend the raiders. Lee reached Harpers Ferry to find them barricaded in a brick fire-engine house that he easily surrounded. He sent his aide First Lieutenant James E. B. "Jeb" Stuart to the door with a demand for surrender. When Stuart signaled his refusal, a brief assault killed several and captured the rest, including Brown himself, who was subsequently tried by a Virginia court and sentenced to hang. Lee also captured a cache of weapons that Brown hid in Maryland. "They had been prepared by a band of conspirators for the purpose of invading the state of Virginia and exciting rebellion in the South," he reported. That left not a jot of doubt in his mind that Brown and his men were traitors and deserved their fate.[198] On November 30 Lee returned to Harpers Ferry with a detachment to keep order at Brown's execution and prevent any disruption by the condemned man's friends, whom he described as "the *enemy*."[199] If he even recalled Lieutenant Grant from Mexico, he had no way of knowing that the man he watched drop from the scaffold had been a boyhood friend of Grant's father. The only threads connecting Lee and Grant were still gossamer thin.

The affair sent a shock through the slave states. Washington delayed Lee's return to his regiment so he could testify before a Senate committee investigating the incident.[200] Hence, he was still at Arlington when an invitation came from the military affairs committee of the state legislature to help them organize and arm state militia in reaction to the threat now posed. Lee suggested that others had more knowledge and experience than he, but the general assembly's call in a time of perceived peril should have told him that it regarded him as a man to look to in a crisis.[201]

Lee felt less sure of himself than the legislature. He was a man much changed from the young officer of thirty years before. "I see my own delinquencies now when too late to amend, & point them out to you," he told his children, warning that "you will find when you become old, it will then be too late."[202] Age and health preoccupied him. When first in Texas he stopped shaving and spoke of "my long grey beard" two months before he turned fifty.[203] Two years earlier he told Mary that his death might be "not far distant."[204] A year later he spoke as a man feeling old before his time, hoping his children would be able to take care of him and his wife when they could no longer care for themselves.[205] He complained of failing eyesight, could no longer read by lamplight, and needed large bold type for reading.[206] His memory seemed to weaken, and like his own father, he had to ask Mary to remind him of their children's birthdays.[207] He referred to himself now as "an old soldier," and suffered bouts of what he feared might be arthritis from "old age."[208] His legs ached, and then a pain in his right arm lasted through 1860, perhaps a sign of angina. "What a suffering set we are," he told Custis in the spring of 1859, and a year later lamented his "complaining mood" and general dissatisfaction.[209] By May of 1860 he was "tired & weary," a feeling that he thought "belonged to old people & that therefore I was entitled to."[210]

Worse, Lee felt isolated. In Texas he skipped meals with others to avoid "uninteresting men," wishing he was back by his campfire on the plains eating his meals alone.[211] He avoided sharing quarters and found that he "would infinitely prefer my tent to my-self."[212] In a group he felt more alone than out on the prairie, and that "my pleasure is derived from my own thoughts." He walked the banks of the San Antonio River with only the wildlife for company, the wilderness suiting his mood.[213] He rarely went anywhere, and rode across country rather than on the road where he might encounter other travelers. "I never call, or stop anywhere in my travels," he confessed. "Solitude seems more consonant to my feelings & temperament."[214] He sought little fellowship, for "I am a great advocate of people staying at home & minding their own affairs."[215] In such a country, "& such a population," he preferred to be left alone.[216]

He did not feel at ease even with his family. The months at Arlington went not well. "I was much in the way of every body," he wrote afterward, "& my tastes & pursuits did not coincide with the rest of the household."[217] Mary ignored her health, resulting in a relapse at the time of the Norris episode, and her frustrated husband complained that her behavior was "a great aggravation to me."[218] When finally orders took him back to his regiment in early February 1860, he was anxious to get away.[219] Once in Texas, he wrote her that "my presence is not necessary," and hoped that now "you have those around you whose Compy will give you more pleasure."[220] He told Annie that "now I hope every-body is happier." He was. Now he could "enjoy a life in the prairie & solitude again."[221] When he wrote Mildred that he led "so monotonous a life that I have nothing to tell you," he sounded pleased.[222]

His mood discolored almost everything. When a child died he called it a blessing that it was saved before worldly sin polluted it, while its death was a merciful reminder to the grieving parents to prepare themselves.[223] Seeing the hope in a newlywed couple, he gloomily told Mary he felt "sad to think how soon the clouds of disappointment darkens the prospect of lifes horizon," which she had to see as a reflection on their marriage.[224] When a fellow officer died just five months after his wedding, Lee told the new widow it was for the best, that "he has left the world before its brightness & pleasure had faded." She could remember him always "undisturbed by real or imaginary disappointments."[225]

During his quarter century of marriage, Lee's disappointments had been real enough. Mary complained; he assuaged. She stepped outside his rules of conduct; he scolded. She acted on impulse; he kept an iron grip on his totems of control and duty. They lived out a pattern of behavior sown in their courting days, and grew to full maturity with them. Lee chided her constantly over spending. He was no miser, but he kept careful account of his money, admonishing his children "never to *exceed* your means." She always overspent, kept no records, wrote checks on accounts with no funds, and bought "bargains" at twice their value.[226] He still could not get her to "array yourself as becomes a lady," while he bluntly told her that her efforts to manage housekeeping at Arlington were all but pointless after a lifetime of carelessness.[227]

Sometimes Lee tried to rekindle in Mary the joyful spirit of the girl he first courted. At Arlington he picked a rose in the mornings for her breakfast plate, but to little avail.[228] The week of Valentine's Day in 1855 the family had guests for dinner almost every night, and much as he disliked such parties, he convincingly pretended to enjoy them for Mary's benefit and their daughters'.[229] Her worsening physical infirmity, and his evolution from lover to hectoring protector, made her ever more complaining. Her self-pitying moods, even her physical condition, scolded a husband who seemed happier when away from her, and Lee fell into the role. Occasionally he responded to her complaints by holding a mirror to her, reminding her that "so clouded is our vision by narrow & selfish views" that people "often complain of what we ought not & blame others when the fault is in ourselves."[230] He pleaded for her to "take a happier view of things," and heard her complaints so often that he had no answers but platitudes: "We rarely know what is best for us, & as rarely see things as they really exist,"[231] "God helps those who help themselves," "Do not worry yourself about things you cannot help or change," "Be content to do what you can for the well being of what belongs properly to you," "Lay nothing therefore too much to heart," "Desire nothing too eagerly, nor think that all things can be perfectly accomplished."[232] He had become Polonius.

Even compliments could wound. Lee always preferred buxom women, and was pleased to hear Mary weighed 160 pounds, but then referred to her as "rotund" and reminded her that he only weighed 155 himself.[233] By the mid- and late 1850s his weekly letters became formulaic: advice on her health, finances, and the children, and what he saw around him of sickness and death.[234] In a neat reversal of their roles when courting, Lee lectured her on piety and resignation, telling her not to want too much in life, nor to take too much pleasure in happy moments, or grieve too much at misfortune. Passions must not guide them, but "what reason & religion dictates."[235] Surely passion was gone.

Perhaps only his sons and daughters cheered the lonely Virginian. "I have no enjoyment in life now but what I derive from my children," he told son Custis in May 1859.[236] He tried to shape them in the mold he applied to himself so successfully. Believing that children needed to learn "politeness, gentleness, courtesy & a regard for the rights of others," he advocated education from an early age, including the concept of kindergarten then in its infancy in Europe.[237] His sons would be men, and he had very definite ideas of manly deportment, while he wanted his daughters to live a "rational & religious life."[238] Toward those ends they needed his guidance, and he gave it, risking their resentment of "my old habit of giving advice."[239]

The eldest, Custis, was for the most part exemplary. General Scott got him an appointment to West Point, where he excelled from the outset. That is what Lee expected from his sons.[240] He hoped Custis would best his own record. "You must be No. 1," Lee told him. "It is a fine number. Easily found and remembered. Simple and unique. Jump to it, fellow."[241] Custis graduated first in his class in 1854 while his proud father was superintendent. Rooney Lee was his mother's child, indolent and impulsive, and Lee saw in him both her father and his own.[242] Lee intended to provide the best education he could, but refused to be "the means of indulging in extravagance folly or vice."[243] Lee entered Rooney at Harvard College in the fall of 1854, but after two years feared his son seemed "only to have time or thought for running about."[244] As a result, Lee sent one sententious letter after another until the boy stopped responding.[245] Rooney drank and smoked. His father had no objection to alcohol, and sometimes sent whisky as a gift to friends, though he also knew men who drank themselves to ruin.[246] He thought tobacco "dangerous to meddle with," and teased his son that kissing young women was a better use for his mouth.[247] As for other vices, Lee warned against "every immorality."[248] Thankfully, Rooney turned himself around and through General Scott's influence, gained a direct commission in a cavalry regiment in 1857. Meanwhile the youngest, Robert Jr., came in for fewer of his father's lectures.[249] "He has always been a good boy," Lee said, echoing his own father's words about him.[250] In 1860 Lee entered him at the University of Virginia despite reservations about its academic discipline and curriculum.[251]

"Our sons are fairly launched forth on the everchanging & tempestuous life they have selected," he told Mary, wistfully. "Probably they & I will never meet again."[252] Meanwhile, Lee left his daughters to their mother, though he wanted them to learn to dance and play the piano. Of course they should develop punctuality, which their mother never did.[253] They must be self-reliant, for as he had found, "no one will attend to your business as well as you will yourself."[254] He wanted them to be active outdoors, exercise, eat wholesome food, and, reflecting the era's obsession with bowels, "be regular in all your habits."[255] They could read amusing fiction; though the boys should eschew novels, which "paint beauty more charming than nature, & describe happiness that never exists."[256] That was Lee's father speaking. Above all he told them to "be careful of your conduct," and seek not what they should not.[257] Agnes and Annie delighted him in April 1857 when both become Christians, even when Agnes told him that "I see now I am far more vile and desperately sinful than I ever had the smallest idea of."[258]

He missed much of seeing them grow, and as he turned fifty Lee morbidly feared he might not see any of them again.[259] "When I think of your youth, impulsiveness, and many temptations, your distance from me, and the ease (and even innocence) with which you might commence an erroneous course, my heart quails within me," he told Custis in 1858.[260] Two years later in Texas his longing for them kept him wakeful at night, while during the day his focus drifted from his work to them. "I know it is useless to indulge these feelings," he confessed, "yet they arise unbidden, & will not stay repressed."[261]

Even the Texas wilderness had no comfort for Lee when he returned. 'I do not know where to fix myself now," he complained. Everything seemed so uncertain—the Union, his career, Arlington.[262] He even found fault with divine will. "How hard it is to get contentment, & to be quiet & gratified under all the dispensations of our merciful God!" he wrote Mary that April.[263] "Sad thoughts" oppressed him. He felt "rent by a thousand anxieties" as he contemplated the "divided heart I have too [long] had, & a divided life too long lived." Duty sent him away from home; his heart called him to Arlington. "I unfortunately belong to a profession, that debars all hope of domestic enjoyment, the duties of which cannot be performed, without a sacrifice of personal & private relations, & one or the other must be abandoned," he told a friend in 1857. "I cannot in honour abandon the former, while holding the office. I am therefore forced to relinquish the latter."[264] By 1860 he felt "small progress" in his life as a soldier or a man. "Thus I live & am unable to advance either." He had failed himself and his family.[265]

"A soldiers life I know to be a hard one," Lee admitted.[266] As he passed fifty he might expect one more promotion to colonel, perhaps, but probably that was all. Once he hoped for a staff position as inspector general that would allow him to live with his family, else he might have to resign, but that was before two years at Arlington soured him.[267] At the same time he took personally the criticism often hurled at the military. When politicians called on Secretary of War Jefferson Davis to disband Lee's regiment to save money, he scornfully declared that "they may suit themselves in everything relating to my services & whenever they tell me they are no longer required, they will not be obtruded upon them."[268] His patriotism was visceral and no folly of others could take that from him. He spent the Fourth of July in 1856 futilely trying to escape from a scorching Texas sun in the shade of a tent on the bank of the Brazos River. Miserable as he was, he reflected on the day and what it meant to him. "My feelings for my country were as ardent, my faith in her future as true, & my hopes for her advancement as unabated," he told Mary, "as if I felt under more propitious circumstances."[269]

Lee seemed not unlike his country itself. The optimism of youth was gone. His faith promised only trial and pain until death's release. Disappointed professionally, disillusioned personally, uncertain of the present and anxious for the future, he felt sad, occasionally depressed, racked by feelings of failure. He looked ahead with dread of infirmity, and anxiety for his children. "Our hardest lesson is self-knowledge," he told Custis at the close of 1860, "& it is perhaps one that is never accomplished."[270] His own lesson was far from complete. Lee now defined happiness as "independence, the success of our operations, prosperity of our plans, health, contentment, and the esteem of our friends."[271] He had no home of his own, little wealth, and no profession other than arms, and that might soon be the last post he wanted as America rushed to the precipice. By his own measure Lee was not a happy man, but that was God's will, a small comfort that the fault lay not in himself but in his stars.

If Lee felt a failure, Grant was one, and no constellation could take the blame. Grant should have known better than to think he could collect bills for others when he rarely collected debts due himself, and there was just enough work to support Boggs. Grant's application for the position of county engineer in August foundered on the anti-slave majority on the hiring board.[272] Jesse suggested he apply for a professorship at Washington University, but Grant dismissed that as impossible. "I do not want to fly from one thing to another, nor would I, but I am compelled to make a living from the start for which I am willing to give all my time and all my energy."[273] A month later he added, "I hope [for] something before a great while."[274]

Still, he resisted giving up. He traded Hardscrabble and his note for $3,000 for a house in St. Louis. Buoyed by that, he applied for a job as superintendent of the U.S. customs house and got a lesser job that paid $1,200 a year, but found it nothing but "a vacant desk."[275] A month later he left, still trying to find something to avert resort to his father. That winter he even sought a job as teamster to deliver army stores or drive a beef herd to New Mexico, and in February 1860 tried again unsuccessfully for the post of county engineer.[276] Now more than ever his words to Jesse the previous fall took on meaning: "What I shall do will depend entirely upon what I can get to do."[277]

Both Lee and Grant were inured to trial by now, yet the greatest trial of their generation lay just over the horizon.

5

A CRISIS MADE
FOR THEM

Fᴏʀ ᴜʟʏssᴇs ɢʀᴀɴᴛ there must come a time when optimism yielded to necessity. It came in the spring of 1860. Julia suggested that he go to Jesse one more time. "His father had always been not only willing but anxious to serve him," she recalled, though "in his own way, to be sure," by which she meant the father's overbearing and spirit-dampening control.[1] 'Lys Grant arrived at Covington with a crushing headache. "My head is nearly bursting with pain," he wrote Julia a few hours after arrival. Periodically he suffered such attacks, possibly migraine, and this one likely from stress as he waited to face his father. For four hours after reaching his parents' home he just sat in the dining room without leaving it, writing to Julia and talking with his seriously ill brother Simpson, as he tried to distract his mind from the pain.[2] In a few weeks he would be in Galena, a move that incidentally presented a new challenge to the Grants and the Dent slaves living with them. Julia wanted to take them with her, but she left them behind in Missouri. "Papa was not willing they should go with me to Galena," she explained years later, for "if I took them they would, of course, be free."[3]

When Grant arrived he found a small city of eight thousand sprawling over both sides of the Galena River where it flowed into the Mississippi. Galena's position as western terminus of the Illinois Central Railroad gave it trade with the entire northeast. Probably the city's most prominent citizen at the moment was Elihu B. Washburne, a founder of the Republican Party, friend of Lincoln's, and currently member of Congress representing northwest Illinois.[4] For $10 a month Grant rented a small two-story brick house on the west side of town some two hundred steps up a bluff from Main Street. Humble defined the place, and Julia felt embarrassed comparing it to the comforts of her father's White Haven. Their neighbors were respectable but hardly the elite: merchants, cabinet makers, a druggist, a mason, a blacksmith, and a few clerks. Now she, rather than servants, did the family's washing, cleaned the house, emptied the chamber pots, even sewed the children's clothes.[5] By the summer of 1860 she was able for a time to lodge a hired teenaged girl to help, but mostly Julia's hands ran the house.[6]

As for her husband, every day he went up and down those two hundred steps twice, once to work in the morning and return home in the evening, and the other to come home for his midday meal.[7] Those steps took him to the Grants' store in a four-story brick building at 145 Main Street running back to Commerce. Jesse Grant had opened the leather goods shop with E. A. Collins, and like most of his enterprises it prospered. When he and Collins dissolved the partnership, Jesse announced it in the local newspaper with one of his typical efforts at humorous doggerel:

TO THOSE WHO OWE US, WE WANT OUR PAY,
THEN BRING IT ON WITHOUT DELAY.

They dealt in leather hides, and a general line of harness, shoe parts, and other goods, but did not tan the hides themselves. In fact there was no tannery in Galena, and most of their hides came from Jesse's shop at Covington, or else they purchased them directly from regional farmers.[8] Simpson Grant had been running the store, but when he fell ill in 1859 with the cancer that killed him two years later, his younger brother Orville came to take over. People regarded Simpson as a man of ability, and thought Orville rather the opposite, hence it was good for the business when Ulysses arrived in May 1860.[9]

The new brother was not to be a partner in the firm, or not yet. Orville made him general clerk at $40 a month and there would be no raises, though Ulysses filled a genuine need with Simpson now gone.[10] Thanks to Orville's neglect Grant found the books a mess and spent his first three weeks straightening jumbled accounts, which appealed to his mathematical bent.[11] That done, Grant showed skill at oversight and management, beginning with the acquisition of stock. When farmers brought tanned hides to sell, he negotiated their purchase out on Main Street and himself often weighed and carried the heavy bundles into the store. Already prone to a careless, occasionally stooped gait, Grant stooped a little lower under those burdens. To protect his clothes he wore a short leather apron that often he forgot to remove when he went about town.[12]

Better yet from his point of view, he frequently took the firm's wagon into the country to buy hides at the source, which made them a little cheaper to acquire, and indulged his zest for travel. While the less-business minded Orville manned the sales counter in the store, 'Lys spent much of his time on trips up the Mississippi to their stores in La Crosse and Prairie du Chien, Wisconsin, and across the river in Cedar Rapids, Iowa. That was precisely the kind of travel that Grant always loved.[13]

When not in the country, however, Grant was one of two sales clerks in the store itself, a task that virtually all of Galena concluded he was entirely unsuited for, a majority that included Grant himself. "I was no clerk," he later confessed, "nor had I any capacity to be one." His idea of filing a paper was to stuff it in his coat pocket, and when Orville was away he preferred not to wait on shoppers at all.[14] If someone came in while the other clerk was out, Grant was likely to tell the person to wait a few minutes until he returned. If a customer refused to wait, Grant reluctantly went behind the counter to pull goods from the shelves, but then could not remember the prices, and guessed, often selling some below their value and others for more.[15] He was equally inept at wrapping purchases. When a customer asked how 'Lys was coming along, Orville derisively said that "he can do up a bundle after trying two or three times."[16]

Grant also foiled his brother's somewhat usurious practices. Paper money seriously depreciated in value in 1860, and the enterprising younger Grant used his cash box as a currency exchange, selling gold coin in return for paper at a premium. Among the things Captain Grant bought from farmers was pork, which the firm sent east to the New York market. When farmers brought him their hams and bacon sides, they asked if they could exchange their scrip for gold, since they had taxes to pay and the collector accepted only hard cash. The other clerk offered to sell them gold at Orville's inflated exchange rate, but hearing that, Grant interrupted and directed them to a local bank where the exchange would be fair, saving them money. "That was the style of the man," recalled one Galenan.[17]

Orville did not care for that style, especially as 'Lys was unable to live on $40 a month and Orville often had to advance more. He got even by taking opportunities to embarrass his brother. One day 'Lys asked him for $5 in front of a New York leather merchant and store clerk John Fishback. Orville gave him $3 and told him he had no business having more money than that. Grant quietly took what was given.[18] In front of a customer Orville sniped at his brother, "what are you good for?" Grant matter-of-factly confessed, "I don't know, but this business don't suit me."[19]

What did suit him was to sit in the office when there were no customers and talk. His friend John E. Smith, town jeweler, often stopped by on his way home at the end of the day, when the two lit their clay pipes and had a chat. Grant could converse on many subjects, his favorite being his experiences in Mexico.[20] If a veteran of that war happened to drop in, Grant might ignore his duties for hours, reminiscing.[21] His stories fascinated locals whose horizons never yet extended beyond their side of the Mississippi, and customers often asked Grant to regale them with tales of the land of the Monteczumas. Perched on the store counter, pipe in hand, he spent hours doing so, his enthusiasm for Mexico's beauty and resources still vivid even after a dozen years.[22]

Grant's time in Mexico was his only claim to celebrity in Galena. Otherwise, most of the population scarcely knew he existed. If ever there was a face in the crowd, it was his. Those who did notice saw a slender man of middle height in an old gray suit wearing a "plug," or slouch hat, and sometimes in a blue military jacket worn through at the elbows.[23] Thanks to the leather apron some people took him to be a porter.[24] He had a pipe in his mouth, occasionally a cigar, and held his head low, apparently lost in thought or determined upon some mission. Few people actually knew him, even among the merchants on Main Street.[25] Those who did called him "Captain," and all regarded him as a quiet, humble, unobtrusive man who mixed little in society and had few friends.[26] Mostly they saw him going from home to work and back, as one Galenan recalled, "a reticent, unpretending man."[27]

Grant did have friends, and he enjoyed a game of chess, being rated a fine player by opponents.[28] His favorite social pastime was a few hands of euchre with neighbors and business associates like the liveryman John C. Calderwood, the Illinois Central station agent Jack Booth, steamboat captain D. B. "Dick" Morehouse of the *Galena*, and the Swiss-born jeweler John E. Smith, soon to be elected county treasurer. He spent many an evening at the DeSoto House Hotel, where the players gathered in room 198 for conversation and cards, and Grant soon acquired a reputation as the best euchre player in the city. "He was very fond of the game," recalled one friend, while another noted that Grant "played every one of his cards for what it was worth." They played for drinks, though Grant often passed when he won, or took a cigar instead. Certainly he had no reputation as a drinker in Galena.[29] Despite his rough appearance, his manners were always impeccable. He listened well and attentively. He might tolerate and even laugh at an off-color story, but his own speech was clear, unblotted by profanity.[30]

He knew a few prominent men in town. H. H. Houghton, the editor of the Galena *Gazette*, was one of his closest friends, as was W. R. Rowley, clerk of the circuit court, and his neighbor the rising young attorney John A. Rawlins.[31] Rawlins represented the Grant store, and he had already heard a good deal about this new Grant brother from Hannah Grant's local half-sister, whose favorite topic was her nephew who went to Mexico and became a hero. Rawlins and Grant met just a few days after 'Lys arrived and they became fast friends, Rawlins joining the others in rapt attention when the Captain sat on the store counter and spoke of Mexico.[32] Grant also had a passing acquaintance with Washburne, who observed that he often seemed deep in thought on some abstract topic, impressing him as a man who was intelligent, reflective, and "large-minded."[33]

Otherwise, Grant seldom went out, and spent evenings at home with the newspaper, playing with the children, often reading aloud to Julia. Probably for the first time in his life, he frequently attended Galena's Methodist church where he enjoyed what he called, "feeling discourses from the pulpit" by the Reverend John H. Vincent.[34] He certainly favored freedom of faith, as his rejection of the Know Nothings showed, but whatever religious views he held he kept to himself and his family, and always would.[35] "Mostly he was a man of silence," said a friend, and another averred that he said "but little, and that to the point." One acquaintance thought him "utterly wanting in those characteristics which develop into greatness."[36] It was hard living on $40 a month, and generally Grant failed to make it work. Some described him as broken down, yet admired the fact that he did not give up.[37]

By late summer Grant believed that "I have become pretty well initiated into the Leather business and like it well." Moreover, the store thrived and he saw a fair hope of elevating himself "entirely above the frowns of the world, pecuniarily" in a few years.[38] He learned much and quickly, and by year's end hoped his father would make him a partner. "I am sanguine that a competency, at least, can be made at the business," he told a friend on the eve of 1861, and meanwhile he strove to keep expenses at a minimum to save enough to redeem his remaining obligations in the year ahead. That old abhorrence of debt never left him. "It is a matter that worries me incessantly that I should owe anything without the means of paying," he told one creditor, "but such is my position now and will be for some months to come."[39] Still, after several years of trial and failure, Grant's essential optimism and entrepreneurial spirit remained undimmed. His future looked brighter. Unfortunately, the same could not be said for the Union.

The Democratic Party split in convention into two wings in 1860: a Southern one supporting the Dred Scott decision and standing for the right of slave owners to take their property into the territories, with a reluctant John C. Breckinridge as its nominee; and a Northern wing championed by Stephen Douglas on a platform upholding the Union and asserting that a territory could determine the issue of slavery for itself when it framed its territorial constitution, and not just at the statehood stage. With a scattering of old Whigs and Know Nothings nominating John Bell as candidate of the head-in-the-sand Constitutional Union Party, the Republican nominee Abraham Lincoln was all but guaranteed victory as his opposition divided.

"I think the Democratic party want a little purifying," Grant told a friend in August, "and nothing will do it so effectually as a defeat." Galena was largely a pro-Douglas community, and Grant liked the "Little Giant's" stand for Union, but knew he could not win. He felt no sympathy for the Breckinridge wing, unlike his father-in-law Dent. The radicalism of some of the Republicans like Francis Preston Blair of Missouri put him off, and he told a Democrat friend that "I dont like to see a Republican beat the party." In the end, Grant could not vote because he had not been in Illinois long enough to establish residency, and he found being freed from having to make a choice something of a relief.[40] He took less interest in the national election than he did in the contest back in Missouri, where Barret ran for reelection against the former incumbent Blair. "I feel anxious to hear of Blair's defeat," Grant wrote the day after voters in his old district went to the polls, and early reports put Barret ahead, though Blair retook his seat.[41] Once again, as in 1856, Grant hoped that the defeat of the Republicans would at least preserve the Union for another four years, giving the sections time for passion to subside and to find some means of coexistence.

In such a politically charged year, Grant's friends felt curious about his leanings, yet had little idea of where he stood.[42] Rawlins found that "he was not an arguer on politics." Grant did say he had followed the Illinois senatorial contest in 1858 that produced the electrifying debates between Lincoln and Douglas, though he could not say for himself which of the two he thought got the better of the other. He admitted his generally Whig leanings, but also that he voted for Buchanan in 1856. Rawlins politicked in Galena and the county for Douglas, and he counted on Grant to vote as a Douglas Democrat, even though Grant confessed that he felt some admiration for Lincoln, if not the Republicans generally. In fact, Rawlins believed that Grant was somewhat disposed to be a Democrat and support Douglas, until he read some of the Little Giant's campaign speeches.[43] Yet Grant's father and his brother Orville were Republicans, and family pressure to follow suit must have been strong, for Grant was reported to have told a friend that he did not like to oppose his father's wishes.[44]

As just one instance of the seeming contradictions in Grant's political makeup, while he favored Douglas, but shared some of the old Whig ideas once prevalent with the Know Nothings, the man known in St. Louis for his Democratic associations spent rather a lot of time in the company of Republicans. Frequent torchlight parades by Douglas and Lincoln adherents cast shadows across Galena's evenings during the campaign. Grant's jeweler friend Smith secretly organized a para-

military band of Republicans on the pattern of the national group calling themselves "Wide-Awakes," and boldly paraded them in Galena
to protect the polls and make sure that Republican voters were not
intimidated. That mortified the dominant local Democrats, who organized their own Douglas Guard in response. Knowing Grant's military
training, Rawlins and a committee called on him and asked him to
train them as "sergeant," but he declined. An army officer, even one
not serving, should not hold such a position in a political organization,
he said, and besides, he was still new at his business and could not be
distracted.[45] In fact, he secretly met with the Wide Awakes a few times
and gave them instruction instead.[46]

When election day came, some townsmen believed Grant voted for
Douglas, while others thought he voted Republican with his family. Of
course, he did not vote at all.[47] That did not prevent him from spending the evening of election day at the store with several others watching for the election returns as they came into town on the telegraph.[48]
Through it all he felt a growing apprehension over what lay ahead.

Similar currents made Robert E. Lee even more unsettled at his choice
of trade. Now when others won promotion, he felt torn between pleasure at their good fortune and mild resentment. His reaction to Joseph
E. Johnston's recent promotion was complex, for Johnston's had been
a career of wire-pulling and politicking for rank.[49] "In proportion to
his services he has been advanced beyond anyone in the Army," Lee
grumbled in April 1860, "& has thrown more discredit than ever on
the system of favouritism."[50] Knowing that Secretary of War John B.
Floyd had virtually adopted Johnston's orphaned niece, Lee concluded
that Floyd gave Johnston the promotion "for his gratification," regarding it as an example that "much may be affected by influence."[51]

Then the position of quartermaster-general opened. General Scott
recommended Albert Sidney Johnston, Joseph E. Johnston, Lee, and
Charles F. Smith for consideration. Lee at least said he believed the first
Johnston to be the best man, denying that his opinion was influenced
by the fact that Johnston's elevation would put Lee in command of the
2d Cavalry and in line for promotion to full colonel. Not surprisingly,
Secretary Floyd gave the post to his favorite, the other Johnston. Such

army politics discouraged Lee, but by now he had no objection to a little discrete politicking on his own behalf. In October 1860, he told Custis to tell friends to "give me all the promotion they can."[52]

Lee might have hoped that his return to Texas in February 1860 would keep him away from the political turmoil, and Washington seemingly ignored his department. The Democratic breakup and the ensuing campaign were so far away in distance and time thanks to slow news that Lee might as well have been on another planet. He said little of the campaign other than a wish that if the Democrats would reunite behind Breckinridge, Douglas might withdraw and give them a chance to beat Lincoln. But then, as he said, "politicians I fear are too selfish to become martyrs."[53] His low opinion of the nation's state-craft only accelerated its downward march. Deploring what he called "policy, or tact, or expediency or any other end that was ever devised to conceal or mystify a deviation from a straight line," Lee blamed the radicals for the nation's disease. "Politicians are more or less so warped by party feeling, by selfishness, or prejudices, that their minds are not altogether truly balanced," he jotted to himself. "They are the most difficult to cure of all insane people, politics having so much excitement in them."[54]

As Lincoln's certain victory by a purely Northern vote approached, Lee feared the Southern reaction. "My little personal troubles sink into insignificance when I contemplate the condition of the country," he wrote Mildred in October, "& I feel as if I could easily lay down my life for its safety." He saw the lone-star flag of Texas flying everywhere in token of resistance, and angry Texans holding meetings to arouse themselves to action.[55] Following Lincoln's election Lee feared that "the Southern States seem to be in a convulsion." He could not foretell the outcome, he said, "but I hope all will end well."[56] Only half in jest he said his daughter Agnes, an emancipationist at heart, might be captured by the abolitionists during a visit to the North, "if she has been expressing any opinions inimical to their theories."[57]

Lee had no intention of remaining in the United States Army if there was a complete breakup. "If the Union is dissolved, which God in his mercy forbid, I shall return to you," he told Custis in October. He would go home to Virginia on leave of absence, or resign if he could not get leave.[58] A month after the election his new department commander, Major General David E. Twiggs, just arrived in San Antonio, told Lee he expected the Union to be dissolved in six weeks. Still, Lee did not yet abandon hope, or he would have left Texas immediately to go home. "I hope however the wisdom & patriotism of the country will devise some way of saving it," he wrote Custis, "& that kind Providence has not yet turned the current of his blessings from us." Buchanan's message to Congress on December 4 began with a contradictory declaration that secession was unconstitutional, but that the government had no authority to prevent it. He proposed appeasement, a constitutional amendment guaranteeing the right to own slaves and to take them into all of the territories, the repeal of personal liberty laws in the free states, and a reaffirmation of the Fugitive Slave Law. That meant the theoretical possibility of future new slave states. Lee believed the North and West would balk at such an amendment, but saw it as the last hope, vowing "I will cling to it to the last."

Admitting that he was educated to believe he owed his primary allegiance to Virginia, Lee saw fault and blamed extremists on both sides. He resented the North's efforts to deny the territories to slaveholders, and at the same time condemned the "selfish & dictatorial bearing" of the Deep South states, especially South Carolina when it threatened border states like Virginia with economic retaliation if they did not join in secession. If forced to choose a side, he would stand with Virginia, which it seemed had enemies in both camps, and that being the case he must do what he thought best for the Old Dominion. Meanwhile, his family should be prudent. "We must all take the risks of affairs, & lessen them to the extent of our means," he advised Custis. Expecting economic chaos in secession's wake, Lee kept most of his modest wealth liquid, to have something in case banks and shares collapsed. He cleared as much debt as possible to preserve his credit and secure property against seizure, realizing that the crisis could also interfere with selling part of the Custis estate and delay completing the emancipation of the Custis slaves. Fatalistic to the end, he could only conclude, "Gods will be done!"[59]

"I am not pleased with the course of the Cotton States," Lee wrote on December 14, a week before South Carolina's state convention was to meet to debate secession.[60] "I prize the Union very highly," he told Rooney, but now for the first time he added a condition. He would make any sacrifice to preserve it, "save that of honour."[61] Through more than thirty years of service to his country one fixed point in his universe was unwavering loyalty to the Union, but that was now conditional. "Save that of honour." He did not say what, related to honor, might make the exception, but that was coming.

There was no bright prospect to the new year. Lee saw everything "clouded by sad forebodings."[62] In mid-January he told a cousin that "if the Union is dissolved, I shall return to Virginia to share the fortune of my people." He believed that no state should go out unless the North rejected a fair proposal of the South's just demands. Equal rights to settle the territories was surely the greatest issue, but he believed the South should think before abandoning all the other benefits of the Union for the sake of that. "I am for maintaining all our rights, not for abandoning all for the sake of one—our national rights, liberty at home and security abroad, our lands, navy, forts, dock-yards, arsenals and institutions of every kind." If denied those rights, then "we can, with a clear conscience, separate," but he held no illusions of the consequence. "It will result in war, I know, fierce, bloody war," he predicted. "But so will secession, for it is revolution and war at last, and cannot be otherwise, and we might as well look at it in its true character." Again he would give all but his honor to see the nation preserved, "for I cannot anticipate so great a calamity to the nation as the dissolution of the Union.[63]

By January 1861 the Union was already dissolved, given that four states—South Carolina, Mississippi, Alabama, and Florida—had seceded, Georgia stood at the verge, and conventions in Louisiana and Texas would certainly follow. Something more than the secession of those states constituted dissolution to Lee, but he did not say what, nor did he say in what capacity he would return to Virginia, though the only inference is that he would no longer be a soldier. A week later, with Georgia seceded, he cleared the matter when he declared that "if a disruption takes place, I shall go back in sorrow to my people & share in the misery of my native state." He did not say why Virginia should be miserable because other states had seceded. The only meaning that fits is the contingency that Virginia herself might secede. That was "dissolution" to Lee. *His* Union was broken when Virginia seceded, and that severed his allegiance. He removed all doubt when he added that, except in Virginia's defense, "there will be one soldier less in the world than now." Should Virginia secede, he would be that "one soldier less."

The immensity of the crisis struck him all the more as he saw life-long friends in the army resigning to join what he derisively called "the Army of the Southern Republic!" It came home to him when Custis and Mary's cousin William Orton Williams told him they hoped for commissions in that new army, though as yet the seceding states had formed no confederation. Lee still believed no issue justified disunion, let alone civil war, but that resolve was weakening. "God alone can save us from our folly, selfishness & short sightedness," he told Williams's mother. "We have barely escaped anarchy to be plunged into civil war." He could not foresee the outcome, but knew that "a fearful calamity is upon us." They were about to destroy what the Founding Fathers had fought to create, and for that sin the country must suffer "a fiery ordeal." Lee wanted no government, no flag, no other song than "Hail Columbia." Yet honor was his line in the sand, and he could not betray his home and his ancestors.

He felt anxious to be home to protect his family and their property if an explosion came, but duty kept him in Texas, and as always, "we must all endeavor to do our whole duty," he said, "however far we know we fall short of it."[64] Then at the end of the month he told Rooney that "save in her [Virginia's] defense, I will draw my sword no more." Finally and unequivocally Lee affirmed that if Virginia seceded, and the Union should attempt by force to keep her, he would fight if he must against men now his comrades, and the flag he had served all his life. He would stay in the army for now, hoping for some providential accommodation to spare the Union, Virginia, and a career in a service he loved. "Secession is nothing but revolution," he told Rooney. In the early days of his father's republic it had been considered treason. "What can it be now?" he protested.[65]

The crisis occupied Lee's mind so much that he spoke of little else. "I feel the aggression" of the North, he said, but the territorial issue was one that could be settled by constitutional means; the nation should be able to survive this. Disunion was not a solution but "an accumulation of all the evils we complain of." Still, he set a price on his loyalty to that Union. He would not see men of one section denied a right extended to another solely because of the kind of property they owned. Yet he rejected secession as a remedy. The Constitution could not be "broken by every member of the Confederacy at will." He believed that the Founding Fathers intended a "perpetual union," not a mere compact, as Lincoln himself would say in his coming inaugural. The Union could only be dissolved lawfully by a convention of all the people, or else by revolution, and he thought "it is idle to talk of secession."[66] It might establish "anarchy," but not a government. Still, he told Custis, "a Union that can only be maintained by swords and bayonets, and in which strife and civil war are to take the place of brotherly love and kindness, has no charm for me."[67] He had just read Edward Everett's *The Life of George Washington*, and wondered how the "father of his country" would feel if he could see his child now. "We are between a state of anarchy & civil war," he told Mary. He often spoke of anarchy. To a man with his passion for order, nothing could be worse.

Ironically, Lee blamed democracy itself. A tyranny lurked within the will of a majority that lacked protections for the minority. "It has been evident for years that the country was doomed to run the full length of democracy," he said, "to what a fearful pass it has brought us." If the border slave states like Virginia, North Carolina, Tennessee, Maryland, Kentucky, Arkansas, and Missouri should secede, fourteen slave states would face sixteen free states. "One half of the country will be arrayed against the other," he said. Any attempt to maintain Federal authority must lead to war.[68]

Lee pinned small hope on Senator John Crittenden's proposed compromise calling for amendments to the Constitution reinstating the Missouri Compromise and instituting a number of protections for slavery, including a bar on any future amendments interfering with it. Though he thought them "fair & just," and hoped for popular support, he knew it was too late. Seceding states had already seized undefended Federal property within their borders, and to him that meant they were beyond compromise. "Their course is taken," he said, and should all the slave states array themselves in unison, no compromise could keep the peace now.

Lee wanted Virginia to stand the right ground. "I would wish that she might be able to maintain it & to save the Union," he told family in January, but at the same time advised them not to invest in state bonds, and to convert bank deposits into property or secure personal loans to protect it against financial collapse. They were all waiting on the turn of events, and for him in faraway Texas, where news came slowly, he feared the country could be at war for days before he found out. "God rescue us from the folly of our acts," he prayed.[69] Should Texas secede, he expected state authorities would order his regiment to leave, which was fine with him, affirming that "I have no desire to serve a foreign Govt." Meanwhile, his officers and men weighed allegiances. Lee found "all are anxious & uncertain," but as always, he felt powerless to do aught but "trust to the overruling providence of merciful God."[70]

Lee was a man in the middle, balancing his loves and loyalties, his patriotism, and his sense of where or whether he belonged in a Union no longer what he remembered from youth. "Our country requires now every one to put forth all his ability regardless of self," he told Custis at the beginning of February, yet Lee himself watched passively as events unfolded.[71] He had not lost his conviction that it was improper for soldiers to meddle in politics, and perhaps he felt that as a serving officer he should not speak out. In any case, there was little he could do except perhaps try to influence Virginia's course, and probably not even that. On February 23, 1861, with seven states out to form a new Confederacy in Montgomery, Alabama, he felt helpless, saying "I must try & be patient & await the end for I can do nothing to hasten or retard it."[72]

Two weeks earlier he had received orders to report to Scott in Washington. He reached Arlington on March 1 and met immediately with Scott, who no doubt informed him that Colonel Edwin V. Sumner of the 1st Cavalry in Kansas was being promoted brigadier general, and Lee was now to be full colonel to take command of Sumner's regiment. Kansas was still a tinderbox, and for some years the mission of the 1st Cavalry had been to keep the peace, a politically sensitive mission that warranted face-to-face consultation with Scott.[73] Lee's commission reached him on March 28, signed by the new president, Abraham Lincoln, but he waited two days before accepting.[74]

The state of the country constantly occupied his thoughts now. A Virginia convention had been debating secession for six weeks with no decision. Since his first loyalty was to his state, its actions must guide his. If secession was imminent, that could put him in an equivocal position should he accept a commission now and leave for Kansas, only to resign later. "Honour" meant good faith with the Union as well as the Old Dominion. Lee preferred to avoid inner conflicts just as much as personal confrontations, and mused almost wistfully that he might rather be a farmer, much as he had disliked managing Arlington. By March 30 the pro-Union forces in the state convention still appeared ascendant, and rumors in Washington suggested that Lincoln would back down from confrontation over Federal garrisons in Fort Sumter at Charleston and Fort Pickens at Pensacola. Events suggested that without a more direct challenge to the well-being of Virginia itself, the state was not going to jump, making it safe for Lee to accept his commission and hope for the best. It was a slim hope, for within two days of accepting he advised Custis not to resign his own commission "till I did."[75]

In fact, the Confederacy had offered him a brigadier's star in its new army two weeks earlier, and politicians from seceding states probably made similar overtures to him before they left Washington.[76] Lee quite properly did not respond. But then his two loyalties collided when Confederate batteries in Charleston Harbor opened fire on Fort Sumter on April 12 and the garrison capitulated two days later. He visited his Unionist aunt Anna Fitzhugh at Ravensworth just after the news reached Arlington. "I hope you are not going to leave your position in the army and go South," she told him. He replied that "I have no idea of such a thing."[77]

Lincoln issued a call on April 15 for 75,000 volunteers to put down the rebellion. Two days later the Virginia convention went into secret session one more time to debate secession. That same day Scott summoned Lee to meet on the morrow, and Lee received a note from Lincoln's advisor Francis Preston Blair, father of the St. Louis politician, asking him to call the next morning before seeing Scott. When Lee left Arlington for his meeting all he knew was that the convention was still in secret session late the previous afternoon. Rumor did circulate that it adopted a secession ordinance, but no one was yet sure.[78] He could expect that in this emergency his services would be needed, just as Scott called on him in the Harpers Ferry business. In fact, Blair offered him a soldier's dream. There were only four field-grade general officers in the army. Scott was seventy-five and John E. Wool was seventy-seven, both too old. William S. Harney, though only sixty, was a Tennessean not entirely trusted. Twiggs was the fourth, but he had already gone over to the rebels, replaced by sixty-four-year-old Sumner, now on his way to the Pacific Coast. Lincoln and Scott needed someone vigorous, experienced, reliable, and most of all loyal, to raise and energetically lead the new army. Scott thought only of Lee. A Virginian himself, Scott knew that a Southern officer could put duty to the nation above his native state. Blair conveyed to him Lincoln's offer of a major general's two stars and command of the new army. Only the aged Scott would outrank him, putting Lee in line to become commanding general within a few years at most.

Lee already knew his answer. He politely but firmly declined, assuring Blair that he deplored secession, but he opposed an invasion of the South to quell it, especially since any campaign must march across Virginia. Then he went to the War Department. While he waited in the anteroom, others there saw him pacing, unable to sit or stand still, clearly troubled and on his face what one thought an "expression of intense distress."[79] When he gave Scott his decision the old general was disappointed, but not entirely surprised. "He had fallen into that delusion [of] State rights," Scott said three years later, "and followed its lead, while his heart was with the old flag." Over the years he had seen in Lee no greatness in any one particular, but rather what he called "a combination of excellencies." He loved Lee and knew that Lee loved him.[80] But Scott, too, had come to a decision. An officer unwilling to accept any assignment given ought to resign, and he advised Lee he should do so immediately. It was a suggestion, not an order.

Lee went to the navy yard to see his brother Smith Lee, since the same dilemma confronted both. Hasty action now could needlessly end their careers if Virginia did not secede, and Lee was not yet settled on resignation. He asked his brother for his thoughts on "the correct course for me to pursue."[81] Since the only choices before him were resignation or taking the promotion and army command, Lee's struggle was to find a course that allowed him to accept. Smith Lee had been pondering the question all that week. "It was a severe struggle with him," his wife wrote soon afterward. He would be giving up a profession he loved in return for uncertainty, "taking sides, *North* or *South*, to fight against his own people or *for* them," she said, or "to fight *against your State*, where your kindred & children were, *or with them*."[82]

They parted still undecided, but not so Virginia. Lee went into Alexandria the next morning and learned that the convention had voted for secession in its secret session on April 17, but only now released the news. When he stopped in a pharmacy to pay a bill, he heard yet more fulminating on leaving the Union. Sadly, he told the apothecary that "I am one of those dull creatures that cannot see the good of secession."[83] A popular referendum on May 23 was to be held, and Lee saw a slim hope of averting resignation if the voters rejected the act.[84] Nevertheless, the convention had already asked Governor John Letcher to mobilize volunteers in defense, which meant that in a few weeks Virginia would have some kind of army just across the Potomac from Lincoln's.

Even while Lee was in Alexandria, Virginia volunteers took over the ruins of the United States Armory at Harpers Ferry, burned the day before by its evacuating garrison, while in Richmond state authorities seized Union vessels in the James River and the customs house and post office, acts that made avoiding a more serious clash before the referendum unlikely. "War seems to have commenced," Lee wrote brother Smith when he got back to Arlington, "and I am liable at any time to be ordered on duty which I could not conscientiously perform." Now his position was untenable. Even if he went to his regiment in Kansas, it would likely be ordered east in the emergency, and meanwhile he could receive orders at any moment that would pit him against Virginians then and there. To resign after receiving orders would be dishonorable. The only way to avoid that was to resign immediately. Early the next morning, on April 20, on coming downstairs from his bed chamber, he drafted his resignation and sent it to the War Department.[85] With it he enclosed a heartfelt letter to Scott, saying he would have resigned when they met "but for the struggle it has cost me to separate myself from a service to which I have devoted all the best years of my life." He hoped never to take arms again, "save in defense of my native state."[86] "I had to act at once," he told Smith. "I am now a private citizen and have no other ambition than to remain at home," he said. "I have no desire ever again to draw my sword."[87]

For some time afterward, Lee clearly felt he needed to explain his action to family and friends, and perhaps himself. "I suppose you will all think I have done very wrong," he told his family that morning after reading to them his note to Scott. He still hoped Virginia could avoid secession, but having refused a command, there was nothing else for him in the army that could save him from choosing sides, and he told them that "I thought I ought to wait no longer."[88] Hours later he told his sister Ann Marshall that "with all my devotion to the Union, and the feeling of loyalty and duty of an American citizen, I have not been able to make up my mind to raise my hand against my relatives, my children, my home." In an echo of his earlier aphoristic "save that of honour" exception, his explanations for resignation were virtually verbatim: "save in defense of my native state" and "draw my sword."[89] Asked to advise others on their course, he responded only that "I merely tell you what I have done that you may do better."[90] As before, he protested that if it had been left to him he would have "forborne and pleaded to the end for redress of grievances, real or supposed," though true to form, he declined to enter the public debate while in uniform. Even as a private citizen it would have been out of character for him to speak publicly, besides which he assumed—almost certainly correctly—that nothing he could say would sway Virginia's course, or the South's, or the Union's. They were all now "in a state of war which will yield to nothing."[91]

That same evening came a message from Letcher asking for a meeting. Lee could guess the import of that. The next morning he sat quietly at the end of his family's pew at Christ Church, but disappeared immediately after the service, so distracted that he left his daughter waiting outside in the carriage while he took a long walk along the canal with Cassius Lee, to share his uncertainty should the governor ask him to command Virginia forces. Cassius advised him to do nothing until and unless the referendum to secede was ratified. Lee preferred that course, but felt unsure that it would be possible to postpone yet another difficult decision.

Waiting back in her carriage, his daughter told a cousin that since her father's resignation, "it is like a death in the house."[92] The next day Lee rode again to Ravensworth to see his beloved aunt. When he found her still in bed asleep he decided not to have her disturbed. "Give my love to her," he told a servant, "and tell her that I am going to Richmond." When Anna Fitzhugh finally awoke and heard the news, she exclaimed, "I am so sorry that such a good man would take up such a bad cause."[93] On Monday April 22 he boarded the morning train for Richmond.

In the days and years ahead many who had known and loved R. E. Lee echoed her refrain, among them his old teacher Benjamin Hallowell. "It was a matter of great regret to me that he thought it right to take the course he did," he said, "but I never entertained the least doubt that he was influenced by what he believed to be his duty."[94] For the rest of his life Lee tried to convince people that he had done just that, but privately he feared they did not understand. "True patriotism sometimes requires of men to act exactly contrary, at one period, to that which it does at another, and the motive which impels them—the desire to do right—is precisely the same," he would say a few years hence. "The circumstances which govern their actions change; and their conduct must conform to the new order of things."[95] Circumstances had changed, and he had tried to do right. Still, he never forgot Dominguez, guerilla and sometime scout for Lee in Mexico, whose aid the army applauded even while he seemingly betrayed his countrymen. People often despised a traitor, while praising his treachery, which Lee thought "seems to be the universal sentiment of man."[96] How would the world regard him—as patriot or traitor? Anna Fitzhugh feared she knew, crying that "he has ruined himself forever."[97]

Sometime later Lee reduced his view of the case before him to an abstract. "Whenever propriety, talent & virtue are all on one side, & only ignorant numbers, with a mere sprinkling of propriety & talent to agitate them & make use of them, or misinformed or mistaken virtue to sanction them on the other side, an honest man can take time to deliberate which side he will choose."[98] In his mind now the South had that "propriety, talent & virtue," while the North had "ignorant numbers" and all the rest. He, the "honest man" in the middle, took his time and plotted his course carefully, deliberately, by a series of mileposts. First he positioned himself by the priority of his loyalty to Virginia. Then he established the limits within her course and Washington's that determined when he should or should not take action, which even left open the possibility of accepting army command. He made secession his last landmark, and then—and only then—did he commit the decisive act. As with every decision of his life to date, there was nothing precipitate or impulsive in his decision. Certainly he was concerned with appearances, with his perception of honor and his need for others to think him an honorable man, but in the end it was a rational decision based on his values and the circumstances before him. Ironically, considering the man he was to become before long, it was neither a bold nor daring act, for two-thirds of the other Virginia-born officers took the same step. He consulted with others, but made his decision himself. He took longer than some to make it, and did so in the absence of acceptable options rather than as a man taking a risk. It was the move of a conservative man joining a revolution.

Captain Grant watched that revolt unfold with dismay, as slave state radicals prepared to make good their threats once it was clear that Lincoln was elected. Now his evening reading to Julia was the speeches echoing in Congress and around the South. By December 10, 1860, he expected at least five of the slave states to secede and prepare to fight, if not more.[99] "It is hard to realize that a state or states should commit so suicidal an act," he wrote a friend, yet he predicted that "the present granny of an Executive," Buchanan, would do nothing. Rather, he feared the administration would somehow generate sympathy for the seceding states among those still in the Union. He kept his eyes on Missouri, where armed civil war threatened before a single state seceded. Rumors of an invasion by a legion of anti-slavery Kansans called "Jayhawkers" had prompted General Daniel M. Frost of the Missouri militia to lead several hundred pro-slavery volunteers to the western border to stop them. Frost was an old friend, one of those who endorsed Grant's application for county engineer, but he dismissed the campaign as "the farce no[w] going on in Southern Kansas," and feared having several hundred armed pro-slave—and presumably pro-secession—men at large. "Just a few men have produced all the present difficulties," he observed, "and I dont see why, by the same rule, a few hundred men could not carry Missouri out of the Union."[100] He had known many Southern men in the army, knew how they felt, and what they might do.[101]

As spring approached Grant became even more apprehensive over the ultimate result. Often visitors saw him pacing in the store, lost in thought, or walking the streets, the stoop-shouldered gait gone and his hat set squarely forward on his head. In his discussions with Raw-lins he mused on the North's ability to mobilize volunteers, and spoke more of his West Point education and Mexican War experience, and what they might fit him for in the crisis. He said he had a debt to his country.[102] Then came April.

Grant was in the store when he saw a newspaper account of the fir-ing on Sumter. On April 16, two days after Sumter's surrender, citizens held a public meeting at the courthouse. Mayor Robert Brand first rose to speak. The Breckinridge Democrat called for calming passions and compromise and proposed a peace resolution. Outraged citizens wanted more than that, and the following speeches stood strongly for the Union and an armed response. Then Rawlins took the stage. Standing beneath the Stars and Stripes, he spent nearly an hour declar-ing that the time for compromise was gone and they must "appeal to the God of Battles to vindicate our flag." One face in that crowd was Grant, who admired Rawlins's stand for the Union.[103]

The next day Lincoln issued his call for 75,000 volunteers to serve for ninety days in putting down the rebelloion, and the following day men met again at the courthouse to initiate raising a local company. The meeting wanted a military man to preside, and suddenly Galena re-membered Captain Grant. It needed prompting but he took the gavel, mumbled a few things about their reason for coming together, then called on speakers who held forth to arouse the crowd. Twenty-two men volunteered for a company they decided to call the Jo Daviess Guard. Someone logically nominated Grant as captain of the com-pany, but he declined, though promised he would help in raising and training the company in any way he could.[104]

When the meeting concluded, Grant walked out of the courthouse and down the steps with his father's friend C. R. Perkins. "I'll not do much more work in the store," he told Perkins. "I shall go into the army." Asked how he proposed to go in, Grant said he would "do any-thing—take the first chance that offers and work my way up." The nation had educated him and now it had a right to his services.[105] Yet he turned down the captaincy of the Jo Daviess Guard. The reason was simple. Illinois's quota was six regiments, and Grant told Rawlins and others that as an experienced soldier, even if only a captain, he hoped to get command of one. He thought a regiment was where he could best serve, and though he did not then say so, he had to know that whenever peace came, his prospects would be enhanced to some degree by being Colonel Grant.[106]

Over the next two days Grant, Rawlins, Smith, and others enlisted more men in Galena, and traveled to nearby Hanover and other towns, where Grant actually made a brief speech or two, his first since school. "In this season I saw new energies in Grant," said Rawlins, and Grant himself felt the change.[107] "Now is the time, particularly in the border Slave states, for men to prove their love of country," he said, telling his father that "evry one must be for or against his country, and show his colors." Democrats must work with Republicans, as did his friend Rawlins, and as Grant was doing insofar as he still felt himself a Democrat. Old party distinctions must yield to standing by the government and its laws. "Whatever may have been my political opinions before I have but one sentiment now," he said. There were only two allegiances, "Traitors & Patriots," and he predicted that the North would step forward in massive force. "I tell you there is no mistaking the feelings of the people," he told Jesse. He believed Lincoln could enlist ten times his 75,000 if need be, and rightly gauged Northern willingness to sacrifice not only men but money to support them.

Grant blamed the crisis on the South, while crediting Lincoln with restraint. "In all this I can but see the doom of Slavery," he forecast. Doubting that the North wanted to interfere with the institution where it existed, he predicted that Northerners would refuse to sanction slavery anywhere unless the seceding states came back. The rebellion would destroy the South's domination of the cotton trade by stimulating other nations to accelerate production to guarantee a steady supply, and that, in turn, would depreciate the value of slaves until they were not worth fighting for.[108] In rebelling to protect slavery, the South would destroy both it and itself.

By April 20 enlistments rose to eighty, and the Jo Daviess Guard tried once more to elect Grant their captain, yet again he declined. He believed that so many men would step forward to fill Illinois's quota that he would not be needed immediately. Meanwhile, he would do all he could to organize and equip the regiment, and agreed to take them to Springfield. His friend Smith had already been called there as an aide to the governor, and when he left Grant told him to tell the governor that "if I can be of any use to him in the organization of the regiments, I will be glad to do what I can."[109] Grant intended when he reached the capital to call on the governor in person to offer his services organizing volunteers. Meanwhile, Grant sought his father's approval of his conduct thus far, a habit he never entirely broke, and advised his parents to leave Kentucky if they feared any retaliation for Jesse's outspoken views on slavery. "I would never stultify my opinions for the sake of a little security," he said, and knew Jesse would not either.[110]

The old quartermaster in Grant came to the fore now as he consulted local tailors and seamstresses to make uniforms for the volunteers, spending much of his time overseeing their completion.[111] Remarkably, the men were all uniformed within a few days, and meanwhile from the morning after their enlistment Grant occasionally paraded them in a field, dividing them into squads and putting them through the elements of drill as they shouldered pine staves as mock muskets.[112] By the afternoon of April 25, just a week after its birth, the Jo Daviess Guard were ready to leave for Springfield to muster into state service and join other companies in forming one of the new regiments. The city gave the volunteers a grand parade filled by two bands, the local Masonic lodge, the city council, and more. Only after a ceremony presenting the company with a flag did Grant appear carrying a carpetbag with clothes for the two or three days he expected to be away. He marched on with the company, not at its head, but in the last rank, until they reached the Illinois Central depot.[113] As the volunteers boarded, Rawlins listened as Grant spoke of his hopes for getting a regiment and the right place for the faithful Rawlins in such a unit. When they parted Grant told him, "Rawlings [sic], if I see anything that will suit you I'll send you word."[114] He never really lived in Galena again.

⁓

Grant and Lee were not men of big ideas. They reflected little if at all on man and his place in the universe, the nature of democracy, or freedom, or liberty. They were two one-time Whigs turned quasi-Democrats, at least in spirit, with one of them now drifting in the crisis back toward the Republicans. Competing loyalties drove Lee, yet he always knew there was only one way for him to turn in the end. Even as he felt himself nearing the close of a career he regarded as largely unsuccessful, now he looked ahead to a service he dreaded but could not refuse, in a cause he deplored, and which he feared might only cap his professional failure with personal and regional ruin. He was not a happy man and had not been for some years. He saw nothing ahead but questions for himself and his people, all at risk of being answered disastrously. For his part, Grant knew the face of failure intimately, but was finally achieving at least a kind of basic security and domestic stability he had not known before. He may not have been prosperous, but he was happy. The crisis brought no tugs on his loyalties. From the moment of the firing on Fort Sumter he saw through all secondary matters, like family or party alliances, that there was only one question and only one answer, and his was the Union at any cost.

Each man embraced instinctive feelings about what it meant to be an American and what his country ought to be. Within a matter of hours in the bloom of springtime, each committed himself to war to try to give those feelings life.

6

"WHAT HAS BECOME OF GEN. LEE?"— "WHO IS GENERAL GRANT?"

GRANT DESCRIBED HIS trip to Springfield as "a perfect ovation."[1] At every stop crowds cheered the volunteers. During a three-hour delay at Decatur waiting for their connecting train, he took the company into a field near the station and drilled them to a crowd's delight.[2] When he delivered them to the rendezvous at Camp Yates, he expected to return to Galena but Governor Richard Yates asked him to inspect the state's arsenal.[3] Then on May 1 Yates assigned him to the state adjutant general's office to impose order on a mountain of paperwork. Though little interested in the job, Grant resolved that "I am in to do all I can and will do my best."[4] At least he understood the forms, but he grew restive at clerk's work in a dimly lit room with only a table and chair, seeing no one, for $2 a day. He told a Galena volunteer "I am tired of this" and resolved to return to Galena if need be. Prominent men in Galena even then advised Yates not to lose Grant and the governor listened, asked him to stay, and promised important work for him.[5] "I do not know that I shall receive any benefit from this but it does no harm," he told Julia.[6]

Meanwhile, he witnessed the mad log-rolling for colonelcies. "I was perfectly sickened at the political wire pulling for all these commissions," he told Jesse. Of the first six colonels Yates appointed, not one had any experience, and only one was a West Pointer. With governors handing out the commissions, other politicians stood front of the line for places. Had Grant taken the captaincy of the Galena company, he would now be a subordinate officer in a regiment commanded by some politico. "I shall be no ways backward in offering my services when and where they are required," he resolved, "but I feel that I have done more now than I could do serving as a Capt. under a green Colonel."[7] His time could yet come.

He saw determination all around him, believing "there is such a feeling aroused through the country now as has not been known since the Revolution."[8] Reflecting on the sort of conflict that might lie ahead, he concluded it would be a short war, something over ninety days, with little bloodshed. Just as in Mexico, he studied a map, and his instinct suggested that control of the rivers and coastal waters might be more decisive than grand battles, and thought Lincoln should strike first at the forts guarding cotton state ports like Charleston, Savannah, Mobile, and New Orleans. That would isolate the rebellion from foreign support and trap cotton in the South where it could not finance insurrection. He also looked at Cairo at the southern tip of Illinois, where the Ohio flowed into the Mississippi, making it vital to keeping both rivers open to Union traffic.[9] A Union victory would fatally cripple slavery, he concluded, and "the nigger will never disturb this country again." Concerned that slaves might take advantage of Confederate defeat to rise up in mindless insurrection, he foresaw Northerners working with Southerners to restore order. Apparently he expected slavery to die of its own weight.[10]

When Yates sent Grant to muster companies, he got close enough to St. Louis to see Dent, arriving late on May 9 to find the city in two armed camps.[11] Pro-Union citizens organized under Captain Nathaniel Lyon and Francis Preston Blair Jr. to protect the arsenal, while secessionists gathered at Camp Jackson commanded by Grant's old friend Daniel M. Frost with that arsenal in their sights. The next day he learned that the Unionists were marching on Camp Jackson. "I very much fear bloodshed," he scribbled to Julia, then went to the street himself.[12] He found Blair forming men for the march. The two had not met before, but after introducing himself Grant wished Blair success. When he later heard that Frost surrendered without a fight, Grant returned to the arsenal to welcome the victors, who were stoned and fired at by secessionists along their march. Among the onlookers now was the manager of a streetcar company, William T. Sherman, himself soon to don a uniform.[13]

Grant finally returned to Galena on May 23 and wrote to Washington to offer his services, suggesting that he could manage a regiment of infantry. Washington never answered.[14] Inactivity nagged him with a feeling that he was neglecting a duty to serve the Union, so he returned to Springfield, where he heard that some suggested he be handed a regiment he helped raise in Mattoon, now led by a colonel who could not cope. When he heard nothing more, however, he left for Covington and a quick visit to his parents.[15] En route he stopped in Cincinnati to call on McClellan, now a major general in charge of Ohio volunteers, to seek a place on his staff, but the new general kept him waiting until he gave up and left. On the return trip Grant stopped in Lafayette, Indiana, to stay with his West Point classmate Joseph Reynolds, now colonel of the 10th Indiana Infantry. That evening they dined with Congressman Daniel Mace, and someone mentioned a rumor of a slave insurrection in Louisiana.[16] An Ohio colonel declared that he would take his regiment out of battle, if necessary, to cooperate with Confederates in "reducing the slaves to obedience." Quiet until then, as usual, Grant spoke up to say, "I must tell you a man who can express such a sentiment as that is, is not far from being a traitor." Only Mace's intervention prevented an altercation.[17]

Unexpected news came that evening in a telegram forwarded from Covington. Yates had appointed Grant colonel of the Mattoon regiment. Presented with a command, he suddenly felt a bit overwhelmed. Could he handle 1,000 men? he wondered. His host's brother William Reynolds strongly urged him to accept, and ultimately Grant reasoned that he could do as well as many other new colonels he had seen.[18] Appreciatively, he wrote Julia that his friend Reynolds "has just the nicest family of brothers you ever saw."[19]

The first meeting with his regiment at Camp Yates was inauspicious. The men were not impressed with his appearance. "D—n such a Colonel," some said in his hearing, and one who made to shadow box at him behind his back accidentally hit Grant between the shoulders. He was not amused, and promised them not to judge a man by his clothes.[20] Still, he immediately went home and borrowed money to be fitted for a colonel's uniform, and when he returned he took command at once.[21] His predecessor had no concept of discipline, and the press declared that "a splendid regiment was being rapidly demoralized through the incapacity of their commander."[22] Grant combined discipline and leniency to turn them around, allowing no excuses for duties not performed, and promising swift punishment.[23] The first time men tested him by leaving guard posts, he arrested the offenders and announced that the prescribed penalty was death. He withheld it this time, but promised "it will not be excused again."[24] He soon found that the men respected his strictness, and insubordination quickly disappeared.[25] Grant and his officers themselves set example by abstaining from liquor and profanity. Word went out that Grant himself was a "total-abstinence" man and "bitterly opposed to profane swearing."[26]

He took his regiment, now designated the 21st Illinois, to Quincy on the bank of the Mississippi opposite Missouri. Instead of going by train, he marched them the hundred miles to give them seasoning, covering forty miles in the first three days. On the way Grant reinforced his example by personally driving away a liquor salesman who tried to do business near his camp.[27] When they reached Quincy on July 11, he found himself under the command of Brigadier General Stephen Hurlbut, one of the very political generals he hoped to avoid.[28] Three days later came orders for what might be Grant's first action. Mounted secessionists under Colonel Thomas Harris were threatening the North Missouri Railroad in the vicinity of Mexico, Missouri. Hurlbut told Grant to join two other regiments in driving them away. Resolved to do his best, he told Jesse that "I hope you will have only a good account of me," yet he felt a strange apprehension, the anxiety of the responsibility of command. "My heart is in the cause I have espoused," he wrote on the eve of leaving. "However I may have disliked party Republicanism there has never been a day that I would not have taken up arms for a Constitutional Administration."[29]

Then he learned that he and his five hundred would be alone facing Harris's reported twelve hundred, a number he thought exaggerated, but still he expected to be outnumbered. Nevertheless, he spoke confidently of dispersing the rebels, his optimism apparent again.[30] Approaching Harris's camp, however, he felt growing apprehension. Then as he crested a hill, immediate relief embraced him when he saw the camp abandoned. He had not considered that Harris might be just as fearful of him, as he had been of Harris. Grant learned by such experiences, and here he learned not to fear his foe. A day later he dismissed the episode as just "a little march south."[31]

Something more than a little march led two ill-trained armies to clash on July 21 in northern Virginia, near Manassas Junction. As much by accident as design the Confederates won a fine victory, sending a shock of humiliation and resolve even to distant Missouri, where Grant found that "since the defeat of our troops at Manassas things look more gloomy."[32] It might not be as short a war as he expected. "I have changed my mind so much that I dont know what to think," he told his sister Mary. The rebellion still could not endure for long. It might last through the spring of 1862, but he confessed "there is no telling when they may be subdued."[33] Visible evidence of that were the disloyal citizens in Missouri. His department commander, Major General John C. Frémont in St. Louis, gave no guidelines on dealing with them, so on his own authority Grant authorized seizure of wagon teams and provisions from the disloyal, but wanted it done "so as to make it as little offensive as possible," hoping not to further disaffect citizens much like Julia's father.[34] He forbore pressing charges when possible, understanding that leniency could keep opposition from moving from words to action.[35]

Grant soon assumed command of two more ill-disciplined regiments and began turning them around as he had the 21st Illinois. Then on August 3 he saw in the local newspaper a list of officers Lincoln had nominated for promotion to brigadier general, his name included. "This is certainly very complimentary to me," he told Jesse, pleased that he had not politicked for it.[36] In fact, the Illinois congressional delegation, chiefly Washburne and recent acquaintances John A. Logan and John A. McClernand, had pushed his promotion when he proved himself effective with Illinois troops.[37] Congress confirmed his commission on August 7, to date from May 17.

That meant Grant needed a staff to run his headquarters. Throughout the war such appointments went all too often to friends or family, and his early selections were comparable. Admiring the brilliance of William S. Hillyer, an attorney in the firm where Grant and Boggs rented space, he offered him a position as an aide. Thinking that he should have someone from the 21st Illinois, he selected Lieutenant Clark B. Lagow. He also wrote to Rawlins, reasoning that he needed someone from the city that had been the base for his rapid rise. He also liked and trusted Rawlins, and respected his organizational skills.

Rawlins would make a fine adjutant to run his headquarters. "I guess you had better come and take it," he wrote his friend.[38] Grant was not thinking much of managerial delegation and specialization as yet, and the fact that two of the three were lawyers probably meant he expected them to handle his paperwork, but by accident or design, Rawlins proved to be an inspired choice, one of the greatest adjutants of the war.

Now posted at Ironton in southeast Missouri, Grant concluded by August 12 that 5,000 rebels led by General William J. Hardee at Greenville, thirty-five miles south, and another 1,500 more than a dozen miles east, posed credible threats; their goal was to cut his railroad supply line north to St. Louis and force him to withdraw.[39] His response was telling. With no more experience at command in action than leading a few volunteers one afternoon in Mexico fifteen years earlier, Grant's instinct was to strike first, even while higher-ranking new commanders like McClellan and Frémont saw nothing but reasons not to move. On August 15 Brigadier General U. S. Grant wrote his wife that "tomorrow I move south."[40] He had been planning his first campaign for several days, intending to drive off the force to his east with one regiment and then have it move south to converge with him as he marched to meet Hardee. Then both columns were to converge from north and east to attack.[41] He expected to be outnumbered, but his perpetual optimism and a sense that delay favored the enemy propelled him. Here and hereafter, his instinct was to act quickly. No Union commander in this war would match his sense of urgency. He also made no plan for retreat. He expected to drive Hardee out of Missouri.

On the eve of moving out, politics stymied Grant. Brigadier General Benjamin Prentiss arrived to supersede him. A political appointee, Prentiss had done nothing thus far. Their commissions both dated from May 17, and Frémont was yet ignorant that Grant's prior army service gave him seniority. Grant went to St. Louis to protest being made junior to a man he actually outranked and Frémont redressed the matter, then put him in command of all of southeast Missouri and southern Illinois, with headquarters at Cape Girardeau on the Mississippi. Frémont ordered him to clear the district of the enemy by coordinating several commands, including Prentiss's. Grant took it in stride, telling his father that "all I fear is that too much may be expected of me." But Prentiss virtually mutinied, first failing to communicate, ignoring Grant's orders, then trying to negotiate who should command. Finally, in a pique, he sent his resignation to Frémont.[42] Grant simply arrested him and sent him to St. Louis.[43] In this, his first experience handling a difficult subordinate, he was patient, at first conciliatory, swallowing his feelings of humiliation at Prentiss's defiance, but he accepted confrontation when given no alternative. "A sacrifise of my own feelings is no sacrifise when the good of the service Calls for it," he told Prentiss, perhaps disingenuously, but he kept a journalist from publicizing the episode, hoping just to have the whole matter "buryd in oblivion."[44]

With his command and responsibility expanded, Grant moved headquarters to Cairo on September 2, where he shifted his gaze to Kentucky, which for the moment adopted an anomalous neutrality. He posted a company at Belmont, Missouri, to watch the bluff at Columbus, Kentucky, across the Mississippi. It was the highest ground north of Tennessee and artillery placed there could make a naval advance down the river impossible. The next day Grant learned that Confederate Major General Leonidas Polk had violated Kentucky's neutrality and occupied the place, commencing a buildup that would make it the most heavily fortified spot on the continent. Poised to respond, Grant recalled his company from Belmont and proposed to attack and take Columbus before Polk could consolidate his position. Then he would move down the Missouri riverbank to drive Confederates out of New Madrid to give Federals control of the river there.[45] Grant appeared to plan on taking one enemy position after another, using each in turn as a base to move on the next. Frémont withheld permission, but meanwhile Grant seized on the violation of Kentucky neutrality as pretext for what he intended to do next.

On September 5 Grant occupied the Kentucky side of the Ohio opposite Cairo to protect his base, then moved on Paducah thirty-five miles upriver. Paducah commanded the mouths of the Cumberland and Tennessee Rivers, the former flowing westerly from above Nashville, then north across most of west and middle Tennessee, and navigable all the way; the latter came out of the Appalachians above Knoxville and coursed south to Chattanooga, then across north Georgia and Alabama, turning northward across west Tennessee and Kentucky. It, too, was navigable along most of its length. Both were highways into the bowels of the Confederacy.

Grant knew Frémont would want Paducah, but he acted on his own initiative without orders, again demonstrating an instinct to move decisively. He put two regiments and a battery of artillery under the command of now–brigadier general McClernand aboard transports and two gunboats provided by Captain Andrew H. Foote, and only sent word of his action to St. Louis when it was too late for Frémont to recall him.[46] At eight-thirty next morning, in the war's first amphibious operation, Grant simply stepped ashore at Paducah. He ordered defenses established around the town, issued a proclamation assuring civilians of nothing to fear so long as they did not abet rebellion, and returned to Cairo by noon to find Frémont's authorization awaiting him.[47] In a bloodless stroke he had achieved one of the most significant strategic movements of the war.

The occupation made headlines across the North, rare good news for the Union that season. Newspapers put Grant's name in bold type and for a moment he was a man of minor note. He distrusted popularity and the press. "I do not let newspaper correspondents come about me," he told Julia, but that was going to be more and more difficult.[48] Three days after taking Paducah, Grant believed that the action "was of much greater importance than is probably generally known." He could have added that his own position was little short of incredible. In May he had been a civilian in a shabby coat and battered hat helping out on a $2 per diem, so insignificant that Washington did not bother to respond to him. Now he was a brigadier general, and thanks to geography and his own initiative, he commanded the most strategic point east of the Appalachians. By early October, Frémont reinforced Paducah until Grant had more than 20,000 men, the largest Federal force in Confederate proximity outside Virginia.[49] If not surprised, he should have been, but he focused now on what came next. "I would like to have the honor of commanding the Army that makes the advance down the river," he told Julia. His command, next to Virginia and Missouri, was the most important in the country. He knew there were envious unassigned senior generals, feared a higher-ranking officer might supersede him, and wanted to move quickly before that could happen.[50] A month after taking Paducah he was framing another campaign, proposing to Frémont to prepare for "a southern expedition."[51]

⤬

A delegation from the House of Delegates met Lee's train on the evening of April 22 and escorted him to the Spotswood Hotel where a crowd awaited. Lee spoke briefly, pledging to do his "duty and his whole duty to the land of his birth," and local press expected him to assume a high post.[52] That same day Confederate president Jefferson Davis wired to ask Letcher of Lee's intentions.[53] The governor offered Lee command of Virginia state forces and the rank of major general, and hardly needed to tell him that if Virginia joined the Confederacy, Davis would surely offer him an important post in the national army. The next day Lee appeared at the state house for unanimous confirmation of his appointment. In a few words he affirmed his gratitude, his doubt as to his capability, and his trust in the aid of the almighty, promising to "devote myself to the defence & service of my native State."[54] He assumed his command at once.

For the time being Virginia could only act defensively. Lee ordered commanders along the Potomac and Rappahannock Rivers to protect railroads and river crossings and rush the training of volunteers, but to leave the initiative to Lincoln. He urged Colonel Philip St. George Cocke to concentrate his volunteers along the Potomac at Leesburg and elsewhere to guard railroads leading to Alexandria. "Let it be known that you intend to make no attack," ordered Lee, "but, invasion of our soil, will be considered as an act of war." He feared no Yankee advance soon, but if "the enemy" did, Cocke must resist and then withdraw along the railroad to preserve his supply line. Just four days after resigning his commission, Lee's old army comrades were now "the enemy." On all sides he advised restraint. Virginia was not ready to fight.

Privately he still hoped for peace but his pessimism mounted. The day he resigned the editor of the Alexandria *Gazette* declared that Lee's name would make him a "tower of strength" in the crisis.[55] Seizing on that, his cousin Cassius Lee said publicly that if Lee took command of Virginia forces it might result in a settlement, reasoning that he could use his close friendship with General Scott to broker a peace.[56] That sparked Dr. James May of the Theological Seminary of Virginia to propose that Lee "may be raised up by God for such a time as this." Perhaps he could negotiate an armistice leading to a compromise convention? May knew Lee was a great soldier, and at Arlington during the last war he had heard Mary Lee read aloud the Christian expressions in her husband's letters. "God has put him in his present position to be an instrument of abating the storm," said May. Virginia gave birth to the nation through Washington. Could the Old Dominion bring peace now through Lee, if not reunion?[57]

Lee himself told May that "no earthly act would give me so much pleasure, as to restore peace to my country." Ironically, while calling Yankees "the enemy" he could still refer to "my country," meaning the Union. But only Providence governed events, he replied, not man, and certainly not Robert E. Lee. All they could do was "allow time to allay the passions and reason to resume her way." As he wrote he heard that Virginia might just have been admitted into the new Confederacy. If so, her course must now conform to a higher authority, and he could only "trust that a merciful Providence will not turn his face entirely from us and dash us from the height to which his smiles had raised us."[58] Those expressions of hope for compromise and peace conflicted with what he wrote Mary the next day, when he forthrightly said "war is inevitable & there is no telling when it will burst." She should leave Arlington and take as much as she could of the Washington silver and paintings for safekeeping. Until then she must "keep *quiet*" and attract no attention.[59] With his distrust of polyglot Northern society, Lee feared that "among such a mass of all characters" there would be plundering of Southern holdings, including Arlington. He spoke not of if, but "when the war commences," and forecast it lasting ten years. "May God preserve you all," he wrote, "& bring peace to our distracted country."[60]

Lee wavered in these early days, one moment saying war must come, and the next telling a young friend on May 5 that "a merciful God, whom I know will not unnecessarily afflict us, may yet allay the fury for war." He was still no friend of secession, nor did he as yet show any emotional stake in the confederation. That put him squarely in the camp of Vice President Alexander H. Stephens and other so-called reconstructionists who opposed secession until it became a fact, then went along in the hope that a united slave state front might impel the North to afford some compromise. Enemy or not, he maintained he felt no personal animosity toward the North. "Wherever the blame may be, the fact is that we are in the midst of a fratricidal war," he lamented. "I must side either with or against my section of country." He clearly foresaw that "the country will have to pass through a terrible ordeal, a necessary expatiation, perhaps, of our national sins."[61] While he had intended his April 20 resignation to be effective immediately, he learned now that Washington in fact dated it from April 25, two days after his commission from Letcher, leaving him in the equivocal position of having entered a seceded state's service while still an officer in the United States Army. If he received any pay for those five extra days, he returned it and advised others in similar circumstances to do the same.[62] If a peaceful reconstruction should miraculously come about, those days threatened to compromise his honor.

Visitors found Lee working in a small room on Bank Street near the capitol. After barely a week in office he lamented to Mary that "there is no rest for me to look to," and in time the load drove him to bed briefly.[63] He stayed in the Spotswood Hotel for weeks, with no time to find private lodging. Thanks to rumors of Yankee agents in the city, when he did look for something, friends advised him not to live close to the rail line north for fear he might be kidnapped and carried to Washington.[64] His face still wore its Texas tan, his hair gone slightly grayer along with his mustache, though as yet he had no beard. He dressed in a plain military uniform from his former army, but with all insignia removed. Callers found him grave but cordial. Occasionally he discussed the crisis, expressing the fear that the conflict almost upon them would last long, and at great cost. He knew the North and its people and resources, and they were not to be beaten easily. With no money and no credit, the Confederacy must raise an army and somehow assemble a fleet to protect its vital ports, while the Union had vast financial resources. Europe might not be so anxious to give them diplomatic recognition of their independence, or military and financial aid, because of antipathy to slavery, and the North would exploit that for all it was worth. The South might succeed, but the time required and the cost involved would demand the utmost in dedication.[65] He told friends who wrote with well wishes that "you have no cause of congratulation . . . I am sorry to say for the position I at present occupy." "If I had the ability, I have not the means to accomplish what is desired."[66]

In addition to building an army, Lee had to build his staff, exposing him for the first time to entreaties for favors from friends and family. "Persons on my staff should have a knowledge of their duties and experience of the wants of the service, to enable me to attend to other matters," he told an applicant.[67] As adjutant he appointed the officer who had served him in the same capacity at West Point, and soon added two aides and a military secretary, all that legislation allowed him at the moment, but he would add additional clerks and aides as opportunity and demand allowed. Lee understood the need for delegation, to preserve his time for matters most urgent. How well he would practice it would depend on the men he appointed, and his own ability to escape his belief that to do something well, he must do it himself.

He assumed that every avenue into the state could become the scene of active operations.[68] "Our opponents will do us all the harm they can," Lee wrote on May 2. "They feel their power & they seem to have the desire to oppress & distress us," and he concluded that they would do it.[69] He and Letcher looked for trouble in the western counties along the Potomac and Ohio, extending to Wheeling, havens of anti-secession sentiment, and at Norfolk near Hampton Roads.[70] To protect the latter, he concentrated heavy guns in shore batteries at Gloucester Point to contest any naval advance by the Federals.[71] More particularly they focused on Harpers Ferry on the Potomac, which controlled the Baltimore & Ohio Railroad and the Chesapeake & Ohio Canal connecting Washington with the Ohio Valley, vital arteries for moving troops and materiel. Small companies of volunteers already gathered there needed organization, so on April 27, in one of his first personnel decisions, Lee sent Colonel Thomas J. Jackson to take command.[72] A West Point graduate and veteran of the war with Mexico, Jackson had been an instructor at the Virginia Military Institute in Lexington, but he and Lee had only a passing acquaintance.[73]

Lee also felt concern for the sensitivity of Jackson's location. Just across the Potomac from Harpers Ferry, Maryland talked about secession, but any incident risked energizing Union sentiment, so Lee warned repeatedly against provocative acts. When Jackson crossed the river to occupy Maryland Heights, which commanded Harpers Ferry, Lee advised that "you may have been premature" and suggested that he withdraw. It was an early hint of a managerial style based on discretionary suggestions rather than emphatic orders to subordinates more familiar than he with local circumstances.[74] Still he admonished Jackson to "abstain from all provocation for attack as long as possible."[75] By May 21, however, Lee rationalized that Virginians had a right to hold Maryland Heights since pro-Southern Marylanders would not do it for them, and told Jackson to make his occupiers pretend to be Marylanders holding their own ground, a neat bit of political and diplomatic camouflage showing Lee's subtlety in areas other than military.[76]

By mid-May he felt that the eastern and western flanks of Virginia's border were secure enough that he could concentrate on its center, the line from Leesburg eastward to the Occoquan and in particular the vital rail junction at Manassas.[77] Early in May Lee ordered Cocke to post volunteers there where the Manassas Gap Railroad from the Shenandoah had its terminus with the Orange & Alexandria Railroad. If the Federals took the junction, they could use the Manassas Gap line to shift soldiers northwest to threaten Harpers Ferry and the Valley.[78] Meanwhile, he stationed volunteers in Alexandria where they could harass advancing Union troops and buy time for Cocke to prepare his defenses at Manassas.[79]

By this time Lee was a brigadier general in the new Confederate Army, the highest commission then mandated.[80] That put him in the peculiar position of directing both Virginia state troops and Confederate units sent into the state. Then Davis assigned another new brigadier, Joseph E. Johnston, to take command of Virginia volunteers at Harpers Ferry, superseding Jackson. Six days later Lee sent newly arrived Brigadier General Milledge L. Bonham with a brigade of South Carolina volunteers to the Manassas line, where Bonham replaced Colonel Cocke and began carrying out Lee's instructions to erect defenses there and at Alexandria.[81] On May 28 Lee finally escaped Richmond to inspect Bonham's preparations. Some of the haughty South Carolinians were not much impressed. Bonham's aide Samuel Melton thought Lee quite accomplished and "a splendid officer," noting that "the Virginians have great confidence in him," but feared that he was "slow—too slow," undoubtedly a reference to the time it took Lee to become a Confederate, which many Carolinians never forgot.[82]

Still, Lee acted fast enough to send units out east, west, and north, to give early notice of any movement toward Leesburg or Harpers Ferry. He also addressed something that may have been in his mind for some time. The Manassas Gap Railroad connected Manassas with Harpers Ferry. Lee foresaw Bonham using that link to reinforce Johnston in case of an enemy threat, which Lee seemed to think the most likely at the moment. Of course, Johnston could just as easily use it to reinforce Manassas, which the Federal occupation of Alexandria on May 24 suddenly made seem more likely.[83] As more units arrived, Lee sent most of them to Bonham, and on May 31 sent Brigadier General Pierre G. T. Beauregard to assume overall command.[84]

Letcher transferred all Virginia state forces to the Confederate States (CSA) on June 8, and Lee's command evaporated. In his brief tenure he enlisted 40,000 state volunteers, put water batteries on the James and York Rivers, and started defenses around Richmond. When he relinquished command he felt his efforts had been prudent, given what he had to work with.[85] Geography dictated his dispositions to protect avenues of invasion into the state, and any capable officer who could read a map ought to have done the same. Yet he revealed glimmers beyond the obvious, particularly his focus on the Manassas Gap Railroad. Lee addressed more than the possible strokes by the enemy. He looked for opportunities for counterstrokes.

He admitted to Mary that "I do not know what my position will be." He was a brigadier with no brigade, a bit confused about lines of allegiance. If Virginia still needed him, his duty was to serve, but he was also subject to the new nation's orders.[86] The Federal advance into Alexandria made armed conflict inevitable, and he took the Yankee occupation of Arlington as God's judgment against his family. "We have not been grateful enough for the happiness there within our reach," he told Mary. "Our heavenly father has found it necessary to deprive us of what He had given us." Acknowledging his own sins, he told her he would submit humbly to his punishment and advised her to do the same.[87] They could do nothing to influence events, and "in this time of great suffering to the state & country, our private distresses we must bear with resignation like Christians."[88] Lee seemed almost to find comfort in helplessness, a peculiar attribute for a general in war.[89] No wonder that on June 2 he took time to attend the first of many communions at St. Paul's Episcopal Church.[90]

Lee's future role in the war would be determined by President Davis, who arrived in Richmond on May 29, and two days later Lee met with him in the first of several days of locked-door sessions on resources and strategy.[91] They were the same age, knew each other from West Point, and exchanged some correspondence when Davis served as Pierce's secretary of war, but they had no sort of personal relationship. Lee probably regarded Davis with some suspicion for several reasons. Years later he lumped him with the extremists he blamed for the crisis, evidence that his perceptions were not always keen, for Davis came slowly to secession.[92] Also, Davis was not a Virginian. While Lee's paternal grandfather was a wealthy planter and a member of the House of Burgesses during the Revolution, Davis's had been an itinerant farmer wandering from Pennsylvania to Georgia. Lee likely regarded Davis as yet one more nouveau riche Southern demagogue. From now on they were often in daily contact, and became well acquainted, yet there would never be intimacy between them. Lee always remained muffled in expressing his opinion of a man who, for his part, came almost to worship the Virginian.

In their meetings Lee outlined the situation at Harpers Ferry, Manassas, and elsewhere.[93] He should have felt buoyed on June 10 when forces he had placed near Big Bethel Church drove back twenty-five hundred Federals advancing from Fort Monroe. He had alerted commanders at Yorktown and Norfolk to the threat, and now his vigilance and theirs gave the Confederacy a victory, albeit of minor consequence.[94] Lee was anxious to get into the field himself, but what he called "matters beyond my control" kept him in Richmond. That was the president. No one knew the full picture of Virginia's defenses as well as Lee, so Davis kept him in Richmond as an advisor with little to do while others led the battalions he helped create. Late in June Lee hoped to be sent into the field any day, yet no orders came, though he escaped for a quick visit to Manassas on June 29.[95] He arrived in time to see the men at dress parade, and for them to get their first glimpse of the man many would follow for nearly three years. Reactions were mixed. "Gen. Lee is a stout built, fleshy, rather haughty looking man," one volunteer wrote a few days later. "His fullness about the face and eyes would seem to indicate a fondness for drink, but it is said that he is perfectly temperate."[96]

In mid-July Lee asked to be sent to the western counties where an enemy approach raised serious concerns, but Davis refused.[97] What he did do was consult on refining the defense of Manassas, and when a Union army under Brigadier General Irvin McDowell marched out of Washington on July 16, Beauregard was ready for the clash that ensued on July 21 by the waters of Bull Run. Desperate to get to the scene, Lee stayed in Richmond, where Davis kept him to funnel reinforcements to the front. Lee wrote Mary that he felt "mortified" not to be on the field where he might have helped.[98] "I should have preferred to have been there than here," he told friends a few days later, "not that I could have done as well as was done, but I could have struck for my home and country."[99] At least he realized that his proposal to use the Manassas Gap Railroad to achieve a concentration of forces was the decisive feature, as Johnston arrived from the Shenandoah at the eleventh hour and precipitated the Federal rout. "That indeed was a glorious victory," he wrote Mary, assuring others that "the battle of the 21st was some evidence of our strength."[100]

With northern Virginia secure for the time being, Lee asked again to go to the western counties where a crisis brewed, largely of Davis's making. Finally the president assented but still did not send Lee as a field commander.[101] Rather, he was to be an inspector general to observe, coordinate, and facilitate, but not direct, the movements of the commanders in the department.[102] Davis had a habit of creating unwieldy assignments with wide discretion and few specific instructions, and Lee's would be his first. Still, it got him in the field at last. No one appreciated the extent of indifference or outright Unionism in the region. Lee's early efforts at recruiting in those counties failed, and attempts to stimulate loyalty by a display of force proved almost risible. The basic problem for Lee, as for Letcher and others in Richmond, was that he was not really a *Virginian*. Rather, he was an *eastern* Virginian. He had few friends or family west of the Appalachians. He had not even been in the region for more than twenty years, and he had no grasp of the culture or its people.[103] The subsistence farmers of the hollows, the hunters of the hills, and the merchants clinging to the great river were about as familiar to him as the Antipodes, yet he assumed that, being Virginians, they would think and feel as he did.

Most of them did not. On June 11 they met in a rump "convention" at Wheeling and declared a Union state government, with talk of declaring themselves an actual new state for the Union. Two weeks earlier General McClellan sent three columns to protect the Union hold on the Baltimore & Ohio, support the Unionists in the region, and threaten Harpers Ferry. Minor skirmishes followed, and then on July 11 Brigadier General William S. Rosecrans led 2,000 soldiers to defeat perhaps 1,300 Confederates at Rich Mountain. Another defeat two days later at Corrick's Ford killed the Confederate department commander Brigadier General Robert S. Garnett and lost the Rich Mountain–Cheat Mountain line, a significant barrier to enemy advance toward the east. Barely forty miles separated the Federals from passes into the Shenandoah.

Everyone in Richmond bungled affairs in the western counties. Lee and Davis sent too few reinforcements, too little supply and materiel, and too few competent leaders. Davis made brigadiers of two local politicians, former secretary of war John B. Floyd and Henry A. Wise, both past governors and ardent secessionists with powerful connections, but unfit for military command. Each had raised his own force—Wise's was called a "legion" since it had infantry, cavalry, and artillery. Davis had assigned Wise to the Kanawha Valley near the Kentucky border, and Floyd to southwestern Virginia. Neither cooperated with the other, each believing himself subject only to orders from the president. When Davis and Lee replaced Garnett with Brigadier General William W. Loring, they just added yet another inept martinet to the broth. Though he had no knowledge of the country, Lee tried to manage Loring's subsequent movements from Richmond. He wanted the three generals to converge their commands west of Staunton to protect the Virginia Central Railroad, and then make a counterblow against Rosecrans.[104] Instead, Wise and Floyd, each determined not to be superseded by a general of senior rank, made no effort to join Loring, or even communicate with him, creating an unhappy environment to await Lee when he left Richmond on July 28 to join them.[105]

Men who saw Lee that day found him erect in his carriage, and scrupulously neat in dress, with thinning hair gone almost completely gray, a heavy mustache, and dark though not black eyes. He spoke with a voice that was rather musical, his pronunciation resonant with the ancient Tidewater accents that turned "colonel" into "coronel," and "walnut" into "wonnut." Though he spoke about the war, he said nothing whatever of his plans or where he was going.[106] On arrival, Lee found part of Loring's command guarding the gap at Monterey leading to Staunton, and Loring himself at the next gap to the south at Huntersville. That eased his mind about those lines of approach, and he turned to concentrating Loring, Wise, and Floyd in a counterstroke to reclaim lost ground, virtually mirroring the instinct Grant soon revealed to seize initiative and hold it when grasped. Then he learned that thirty miles southwest of him Wise faced an enemy column aiming to strike the Virginia Central's terminus at Covington. Floyd's appearance with his brigade on August 6 just two miles from Wise's camps boded well for a concentration to force back the foe in their front. Instead, Floyd decided not to cooperate, but took his brigade sixty miles northwest to attack Federals near Charleston. Two weeks Wise's senior in rank, Floyd ordered him to provide reinforcements, and Wise all but refused, instead sending to Lee for an order recognizing his command as independent from Floyd.[107]

This was the pattern of the poisoned command system in western Virginia. Floyd ignored Lee and operated as if independent, while Wise implored Lee to set his command outside the chain of command. Uncertain of his authority with these political generals, Lee ignored Floyd's insubordination and mollified Wise with platitudes about the need for cooperation.[108] Eventually Floyd tried to take over Wise's command, and Wise ordered his officers to ignore Floyd.[109] Lee abhorred conflict, and felt uncomfortable in confrontations with subordinates just as he had dealing with the Arlington slaves. During his years in a profession riddled with egos, he had observed such clashes among others, but never as a participant. Back in Richmond he heard occasional muttering over thwarted ambitions, as when Colonel D. H. Hill complained that Lee assigned his regiment to a brigade commanded by another colonel actually junior to Hill in seniority, but there were no direct confrontations.[110] Lee's management style reflected his personality, leading by instruction and example, not fiat. Even his reprimands at the Military Academy came in terms of encouragement to do better. He was unequipped by nature to deal with men like Floyd and Wise, who did not share his allegiance to duty above self. Even as he attempted to make something of his feuding subordinates, he reflected that doing his duty was "all the pleasure, all the comfort, all the glory we can enjoy in this world."[111] He would have to find a more effective way of dealing with such men.

Weather and camp sickness made matters worse.[112] After several weeks he complained to Rooney that "I have been able to do but little here." As he told his son, "a battle must come off, and I am anxious to begin it." Finally the sun reappeared and the ground began to dry.[113] By that time Lee was camped almost thirty miles in advance of Loring's position, on a ridge overlooking the Tygart River valley twenty miles south of Rich Mountain. On the face of it, he and Loring got along, but one day as they stood behind two officers unaware of their presence, one asked the other if he saw any prospect of a move against the Yankees. "None in the world," responded the other, "unless somebody puts a coal of fire on the back of that old terrapin Lee." The "terrapin" smiled in good humor, but Loring broke into loud laughter that may have revealed more about himself.[114] He resented Lee's presence, and when Lee gently pressed him for several days to plan a campaign against the Yankees near Rich and Cheat Mountains, Loring stalled and protested.[115] For the moment Lee gave up being commander and reverted to inspector, riding ahead to scout Yankee positions, and for several days thereafter sent out reconnaissance patrols that he often accompanied. He also seemed to enjoy himself in the open air more than he had in months.[116]

Then on September 1 or 2 he learned that Davis had nominated him for promotion. To deal with the rapidly growing army, the Congress mandated four grades of general officer: brigadier, major, lieutenant, and full general. Lee was to be a full general, ranking in seniority third behind adjutant and inspector general Samuel Cooper and Albert Sidney Johnston, soon to be assigned to command in the Mississippi Valley.[117] Davis also wanted Lee back in Richmond as his advisor, but gave him freedom to decide when he should return and what steps to take to clear the region of the enemy first.[118] That suited his anxiety to bring on action already too long delayed. He had found a route to reach the Federals' rear and cut their supply line to Cheat Mountain, and learned of another path—difficult to be sure—that could get him on the mountain itself to strike the enemy's exposed right flank. If he forced them off the mountain and cut their route of retreat, Lee could have a crushing victory, albeit against a modest force. Wise and Floyd were too far away to be engaged, but still the total effective force for the operation was a little more than 7,500. Yankee numbers were probably more, though divided between 2,000 men on Cheat Mountain and a main force at Elkwater on the Tygart five miles west.[119]

Once more Lee planned a concentration of forces from two sides at once. He probably consulted with Loring in framing a plan of campaign that appeared over Loring's signature in an order on September 8. It would send part of one division on the night of September 11 to take a position fronting the Yankee line atop Cheat Mountain; there it would act as a distraction the next day while 2,000 men used the newly discovered path to hit the enemy flank on the summit at dawn on September 12. Meanwhile, another column was to cut off the enemy route of retreat, while two additional columns struck the Yankees at Elkwater to isolate them from the Federals on the mountain. Then all columns were to converge to drive the fleeing enemy back beyond Rich Mountain.[120] The plan suffered from too much complexity and too much contingency, especially for inexperienced volunteers in their first campaign, operating in largely unfamiliar and difficult territory. There were nine assignments, and if just one or two miscarried, the whole could founder, and the directive made scant allowance for the fact that the enemy might not react as expected. It left little discretion to subordinates, which did not sound like Lee. Most likely Loring drafted the details, Lee the commander disappearing in Lee the advisor.

Emphasizing how forgotten this theater was, at that very moment people elsewhere wondered if the Virginian had in fact disappeared. A Baltimore newspaper actually ran the headline WHAT HAS BECOME OF GEN. LEE? while a Charleston, South Carolina, paper alleged that he was no longer a Confederate general. Rumors said he had resigned over differences with Davis, or in a huff when Beauregard got the Manassas command instead of himself. Northern press said he regretted siding with the Confederacy and wanted to return to the U.S. Army and rally the loyal people of Virginia to fight for the Union. Some people accused him of abandoning Mary with no home or support, and others

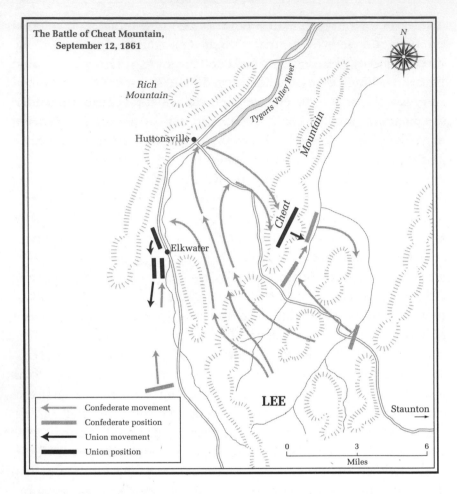

The Battle of Cheat Mountain,
September 12, 1861

Confederate movement
Confederate position
Union movement
Union position

alleged that in fact the two were separated, arising from the fact that she remained at Arlington and then Ravensworth until late May, and then moved on to Kinloch in Fauquier County, all within easy range of Yankee raids.[121] Lee dismissed such slanders, and discouraged Mary from giving one of his letters to the press to refute the charges. "I never write private letters for the public eye," he added. "Everybody is slandered, even the good," he told her. "How should I escape?"[122]

That same day he drafted a special order to his small force telling them that "the progress of this army must be forward."[123] Yet once launched, the campaign fell apart, and quickly. The several columns got in each other's way, they found the roads muddy and difficult to pass, a heavy night rain ruined most of their rations, and they had no tents to protect them. Lee moved with Loring and the main column aiming for Elkwater, and by nightfall on September 11 was in position. In spite of the obstacles almost every element was in its place, their signal to advance being the sound of the attack on the Cheat Mountain flank the next morning. It never came. Instead, the commander of that column called off his attack and withdrew, fearing his surprise was discovered. By ten o'clock that morning, Lee decided that surprise had been lost and ordered all units to retire, but now the Federals on the mountain and at Elkwater began to advance, threatening to take them in flank and surround them. It took much of the day for some of the columns to disengage and withdraw. Lee and Loring halted them to regroup, and for a time it seemed there might be some chance to renew their offensive, but in the end Lee did what he would do in the future after a battlefield setback. He spent the next three days keeping his men in position, daring the enemy to attack him and hoping for a chance to retrieve the lost opportunity. When the Federals did not move, he finally ordered Loring to withdraw.

Lee confessed his "regret & mortification" to Mary soon thereafter. "I had taken every precaution to ensure success & counted on it," he said. Lee blamed the night rain during their march that wore out the men and ruined their provisions. "The Ruler of the Universe . . . sent a storm to disconcert a well laid plan & destroy my hopes," he told her.[124] Putting the best face on it, two days later he issued congratulations to the army on what he now called a mere "forced reconnaissance," and claimed success for discovering all they needed to know of enemy defenses. Now they would be ready to achieve victory when opportunity afforded.[125] Few were fooled. "I think it is perfectly ridiculous, his having published a long account of a brilliant campaign which he intended to make if it had not failed," complained a staff officer at Manassas. "I think this shows vanity without greatness."[126] Lee could only say that "we must try again."[127]

Once Loring's command returned to its original camps, Lee left to see Floyd and Wise, expecting to find them united in the face of the enemy near the Gauley River. "I was very much struck with his fine soldierly and martial appearance," a visiting congressman wrote on Lee's arrival, and some were inspired to hope that Lee might bring about unity and cooperation.[128] Instead, Lee found that Wise had left

Floyd and moved to confront the foe on his own. Controlled in spite of his frustration, Lee told Wise that this was "the height of imprudence," and asked—but did not order—him to unite his command with Floyd's.[129] Wise complained that he felt unjustly rebuked, accusing Floyd of misleading Lee.[130] A few days later Davis finally ordered Wise to relinquish his command, and even then Wise asked Lee to advise him on whether to obey the order. At last Lee responded firmly to the point, bluntly saying, "Obey the President's order."[131] Soon afterward, under cover of night, the Yankees withdrew to the Gauley River and the danger in the western counties abated for the moment.[132]

For some time Lee held Loring near at hand to Floyd and Wise's old legion, now beyond question acting in overall command, and hoping to combine them for a stroke at Rosecrans. Then on October 20 he learned that Rosecrans might be advancing again, as were the Federals at Cheat Mountain. He sent Loring to meet that threat and encouraged Floyd to advance toward Rosecrans. Having done that, he decided to leave those turbulent officers to deal with the enemy as best they could. Lee could not wait to get away from western Virginia's generals. Behind him he left Staunton secure, and the coming winter weather would help protect the passes against the enemy. He was returning to Richmond.[133]

He took with him frustrating memories of western Virginia that must have shaken his confidence. A well-planned and executed campaign fell apart at the last moment on a critical element Lee overlooked: verification of the strength of the Federal right flank on Cheat Mountain. When the fight did start, Lee's only influence on the scattered skirmishing was to pull back and reform, and dare the enemy to attack him. Yet he was cool through it all. On a broader front, that spring and summer he demonstrated managerial skill in helping to raise volunteers, distributing armaments and materiel, assigning officers, and working effectively with first Letcher, and then Davis, with whom he laid the foundation of a fine working relationship. He was as much an architect of the victory at Manassas as any, and made Harpers Ferry, Norfolk, and the Manassas all safe. Even in western Virginia he left the three vital passes into the Shenandoah secure. If he failed to make Loring, Wise, and Floyd play well together, still he subordinated his own ego to the greater good by exercising patience in the effort, though the delay made some in the Confederacy wonder if he was resolute enough to be a good general.

Something else changed in Lee. Gone was remorse over disunion. Indeed, he had shed much of it by the time of the Manassas victory. "I have no regrets, far as I am concerned, for the past, and have no apprehensions for the future," he had written a friend on July 27. "I bear no malice, have no animosities to indulge, no selfish purpose to gratify. My only object is to repel the invaders of our peace and the spoilers of our homes." He left no room for doubt now that his resolve was fixed:

> I do not pretend to see the results of this conflict in which we have been forced, but leave its direction to a Merciful God, who I know will not afflict us unnecessarily. As far as my advice and my counsel goes, it will be continued on our side as long as there is one horse that can carry his rider and one arm to wield a sword. I prefer annihilation to submission. They may destroy, but I trust will never conquer us.[134]

Now the Federals were routinely "the enemy," especially after the death at Cheat Mountain of his adjutant Lieutenant Colonel John A. Washington. It was his first really close loss, and Lee took it very personally. "Our enemy's have stamped their attack upon our rights, with additional infamy," he fumed, "& by killing the lineal descendant and representative of him who under the guidance of Almighty God established them & by his virtues rendered our Republic immortal." Ironically, in the same sentence he spoke of Northerners as enemies, yet referred to the Union as "our Republic," though one hardly immortal at the moment. In his sorrow and anger he seemed to feel that the Yankees singled out Washington for death especially.[135] If his reference to "our Republic" was a slip, his emotional separation from the North was maturing rapidly, especially when he thought of Arlington under the invader's heel. Asked if the Yankees had vandalized his home, he acknowledged that he heard they had, and tears came to his eyes, his voice quavering as he confessed he never expected to see it again.[136]

He inspired few that season. "Lee has done nothing in the West," one officer complained. "I did not think him a man for the field.[137] Indeed, he had not yet commanded soldiers in a conventional combat, especially on the scale toward which this conflict rapidly escalated. As

a senior ranking field general of the Confederate Army, he was sure
to get the opportunity if the president ever cut him loose. Until then
many could wonder "What has Become of Gen. Lee?"

e⁓

Scarcely had Grant occupied Paducah before he told Frémont that
with a modest reinforcement he could take Columbus, then reiterated
the request five days later.[138] Paralyzed by timidity, Frémont stopped
communicating with Grant after September 28, then left St. Louis to
confront Confederates in southwest Missouri, leaving his adjutant to
act for him. Essentially, Grant was on his own.[139] Seeing firsthand the
evidence of sloth in high positions, he now told Julia that the war was
likely to last even longer than his last forecast.[140] For six weeks he went
without guidance or approval, compelled to scatter his forces as garrisons when he believed he should be concentrating against Columbus.
"What I want is to advance," he told Julia on October 20.[141] In their first
communications, Brigadier General William T. Sherman, commanding the Department of the Cumberland at Louisville, asked Grant on
October 16 to move against Columbus to divert Confederates at Bowling Green from his own front. Grant wanted to move immediately if
St. Louis allowed, but again no authorization came.[142]

He believed that his commands at Cairo and Cape Girardeau, totaling about 11,000, could move in combination with the 6,800 at Paducah
under Brigadier General Charles F. Smith and capture Columbus, isolating Confederates in southeast Missouri and forcing them back into
Arkansas.[143] It would also take the Mobile & Ohio Railroad, a vital
artery for the enemy army being assembled at Bowling Green, give
Grant a supply line for a move farther south, and put him in place to
strike at the rebels holding New Madrid and Island Number 10 in the
middle of the river. How far he could go beyond that was the stuff of
dreams, but his fixation on "going south" made it clear that a strategy
was germinating. At the same time he heard that President Lincoln
had taken notice of his operations to date, and Washburne was pressing for a second star for him. "I am not a place seeker but will try and
sustain myself wherever the authorities that be may place me," he told
Julia.[144] Hearing of others pressing for his advancement, he found it
gratifying but, perhaps with the ineffective Frémont in mind, he felt

no more such promotions ought to be made until brigadiers actually proved themselves deserving.[145]

At his headquarters in a Cairo bank, Grant perched at a cashier's window writing orders, making requisitions, and keeping orderlies busy running his messages. He started before dawn and often worked well into the night, leaving his hand painfully cramped, yet he thrived on the activity and felt healthier than ever. Occasionally he escaped for a brief ride, but that was all, and scarcely had time to mourn when his brother Simpson died on September 13. He was budgeting his time and delegating efficiently now, and by late September found that "I have reduced the duties of my office very much from what they were by being a little more exclusive than I was at first."[146] Still, Rawlins's arrival on September 8 to assume his duties as adjutant was most welcome, thereby relieving the general of much of the paperwork.[147] It also gave Grant time to attend to personal business. With a salary now of nearly $4,000, he was virtually out of debt and sending money home to Julia, with an injunction to save as much as possible to get them launched comfortably in peacetime.[148] He also learned to dismiss place seekers quickly, especially those his father often sent to him seeking appointments. Grant took the position that "I have none to give and want to be placed under no obligation to anyone." In his view, if he found a place for someone on the staff of one of his subordinates, he became responsible should that man fail in his duty and he might have to take away what he had given, offending both the appointee and whomever recommended him. "I want always to be in a condition to do my duty," he told his sister Mary, "without partiality, favor or affection."[149]

On November 2 Frémont notified Grant that 3,000 Confederates had moved into southeast Missouri and he wanted them forced back into Arkansas.[150] By now Grant had five brigades led by McClernand, Richard Oglesby, W. H. L. Wallace, John Cook, and Charles F. Smith. He sent two columns to converge on the rebels, and in his instructions revealed a difference between himself and his superior. The latter spoke of "driving" the foe; Grant told his subordinates "to destroy this force." Frémont was content to defer threats; Grant wanted them eliminated. As was now his habit, he left details to his subordinates' discretion.[151] "I do not want to cripple you by instructions," he said, "but simply give you the objects of the expedition and leave you to execute them."[152] And then Grant did something more. Ignored when he applied for permission to take Columbus, Grant assembled the permission he wanted on his own.[153] Two months earlier Frémont had told him to take Belmont, but soon cancelled that instruction.[154] Earlier Frémont had wanted Paducah, and Grant took it without orders, and with no reprimand afterward. Frémont had said nothing to imply he no longer wanted Belmont, so Grant decided to apply the Paducah precedent. By November 5, if not earlier, he resolved to "go south" immediately and make at least a demonstration, which could be a prelude to attacking Columbus next. Furthermore, persistent rumor said Lincoln was tired of Frémont and would relieve him any day now.[155] In fact, on November 2 he did. Grant did not know that as of November 5 but he knew his commander was an unpopular lame duck. It might be weeks before a successor took over. That left a command vacuum that gave Grant an opportunity.

Citing a November 1 order from Frémont to demonstrate toward Belmont without bringing on an engagement, Grant ordered McClernand to prepare for a reconnaissance in force, and told Smith that he intended "to menace Belmont," asking him to distract Polk at Columbus.[156] Grant was ready to go by midnight November 6 with 3,100 men, still evolving his plans, and sharing his full intent with no one. First he suggested that he might countervail Frémont's orders and recall the columns in southeast Missouri to join him at Belmont, which would swell his force to 9,000.[157] A risk like that suggested that he contemplated something more than a mere demonstration. A few hours later he actually did it, ordering both columns to "communicate with me at Belmont."[158] Though Grant later claimed this was only to make his demonstration more effective, he clearly intended to occupy Belmont or establish a foothold nearby.[159] Soon Smith cryptically asked "do you propose to carry out the idea & when," without saying what the "idea" might be. It is implicit that Grant proposed something contingent on a success at Belmont, most likely a move on New Madrid. Then across the Mississippi and north against Columbus itself, while Smith's approach from Paducah would squeeze Polk between them and cut off retreat.[160] Ultimately, Grant would have six distinct columns in motion across southeast Missouri and western Kentucky, the most complex

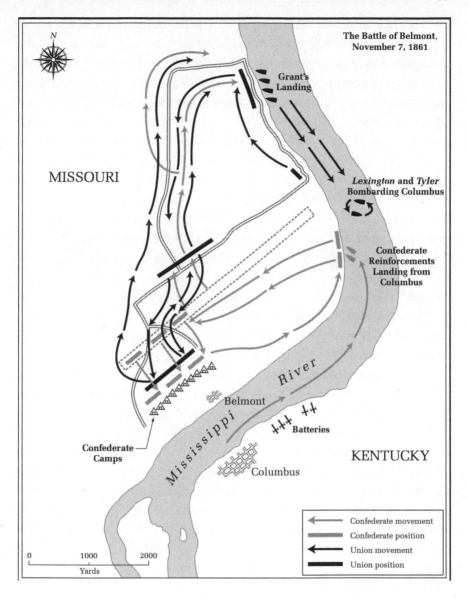

N

MISSOURI

The Battle of Belmont,
November 7, 1861

Grant's
Landing

Lexington and *Tyler*
Bombarding Columbus

Confederate
Reinforcements
Landing from
Columbus

Mississippi River

Belmont

Batteries

Confederate
Camps

KENTUCKY

Columbus

	Confederate movement
	Confederate position
	Union movement
	Union position

0   1000   2000
Yards

attempt at convergence of forces yet in this war, evidence that he had this plan awaiting an opportunity, and now it had come. Each column would support the other, positioning him to take quick advantage of any opportunity. There were risks, of course, the greatest to Grant himself if something went wrong.

His main column aboard six steamboats set off about six at night with the gunboats *Lexington* and *Tyler* in advance. Grant tied up for the night several miles south of Cairo, expecting to make Polk think Columbus was the objective.[161] Then he went to bed aboard the *Belle Memphis*. Either before leaving or during the night, Grant received information suggesting that Polk had reinforcements ready to cross the Mississippi, or were already over the river, to threaten Frémont or one of Grant's own columns. In either case, an attack on Belmont could distract those Confederates and draw them back, further reason to make more than a reconnaissance.[162] By eight the next morning they went ashore on the Missouri side just above a river bend that kept them out of sight from Columbus. A spatter of musketry from woods lining the bank meant that Belmont would soon know they were coming, so Grant put the infantry on its way immediately under McClernand and remained behind to get the artillery off-loaded. In just minutes, skirmishing began and then he heard the cannon of the *Lexington* and *Tyler* as they passed the bend to distract Columbus's batteries. Grant mounted his horse and posted a few companies down the riverbank as a reserve to protect the transports, then caught up with the infantry just as it went into the line of battle about two miles from Belmont's camps. Grant ordered an advance, then left McClernand to it and rode to survey his line. He and his staff stayed mounted behind the line as it advanced through the enemy camps, cheering the men and rallying the wavering until the rebels evacuated northward along the bank. Grant triumphantly ordered his men in pursuit.

Then it fell apart as men began leaving the firing line to plunder the rebel camps. To remove temptation, Grant ordered all the tents burned, only to hear sounds indicating that Polk had landed reinforcements upstream to launch a counterattack while cannon at Columbus opened fire on the Union position. As Grant and his officers struggled to get the men back in their ranks and into the cover of a heavy wood, he learned that at least two more steamboats had been spotted coming with yet more rebel reinforcements.

Grant never intended to stay at Belmont, but he had expected to stake a foothold nearby. Confederate reinforcements put an end to that. He had routed the enemy garrison, if temporarily, captured its artillery, burned its camps, and given Polk notice that Belmont was at hazard. His men had a taste of battle and he and his officers their first experience at command. With nothing more to gain, and much to lose if he remained too long, he ordered a retreat to the landing. Some men panicked and ran away, while others forgot their discipline and just wandered. Then the original Belmont garrison regrouped and erupted from the woods on their right as they retreated. The hazard of Grant's optimism became evident; having driven them off, he gave them no more thought. Taken by surprise, he saw his column at hazard of disintegrating. Then the obverse of that vulnerability emerged as he coolly rode ahead to collect the reserve he had posted earlier that day. Unfortunately, they panicked when they heard the counterattack, and were already at the transports. Virtually all who were ambulatory made it back to the landing, though they had to abandon the captured artillery. Supporting fire from *Lexington* and *Tyler* stalled the Confederates long enough for Grant to get his men on their boats and steaming north. Amid a last enemy lunge toward the landing, Grant himself rode his horse half sliding, half walking down a steep bank, and then coolly trotted across a plank, the last man aboard the last boat. He walked up to a cabin on the Texas deck and lay on a sofa to take a nap, probably exhausted by stress, but soon joined his officers in the main cabin. While they excitedly exchanged accounts of experience under fire, Grant sat silently by himself. Better than any, he knew what they had achieved, and how close they had come to disaster, his silence now perhaps reflecting uncertainty as to how his superior would react when they returned to Cairo.[163]

He found the town illuminated in celebration, and wired to St. Louis a brief statement of the attack and retreat.[164] The next day he put his total losses at about 250, adding that he believed his action prevented any Confederates from reinforcing those facing Frémont, and declared that "the victory was complete."[165] Destroying enemy camps counted only as an irritant, and of the six cannon captured he abandoned four in the retreat, along with about a thousand rifles dropped by his own soldiers when they ran for their transports. His actual loss came to 95 killed, 306 wounded, and 195 missing and presumably captured, double his first estimate, and 75 fewer than the enemy's. Between 2,500 rebels in the camps and an unknown number of those sent by Polk, the Confederates considerably outnumbered the Federals.[166]

Grant had much to reflect upon in his own conduct. He left the actual conduct of the forward movement to McClernand, as he should have. It was a risky management style that depended on good subordinates, and McClernand lost control in the camps and himself encouraged the looting. Grant also left the gunboats to act on their own, when they could have done good service distracting the fire from Columbus. Worse, he failed to take the enemy into account. Not worrying about what they might do made him vulnerable to what they did. Perhaps most puzzling of all was Grant's objective. Belmont had no value and the few hours he held it would hardly keep Polk from threatening Frémont or Grant's other columns if he wished. The attack made sense only as a step on the road to something else, but just what he expected, and how he expected to do it, he kept to himself.[167]

Still, his planning had been audacious, his execution swift. His campaign gave him multiple options based on anticipated contingencies. His misdirection by keeping so many columns in motion at once masked his real intent, yet all were poised to converge on his own should he wish. His second combined operation reinforced a cooperative spirit with the navy, while steam transport afforded swift movement. He learned that he could manage a complex operation and retain considerable control over its components. He disobeyed Frémont's orders not to bring on a battle, but unlike Lincoln's commanders in the East, and Frémont in the West, Grant showed the imagination to conceive a bold plan, and the courage to take risks.

Grant issued a congratulatory order on November 8 thanking his men for their performance.[168] He did not, of course, mention his own, and when he wrote Julia and his father that same day he said virtually nothing about himself. He did tell them that "taking into account the object of the expedition the victory was most complete," and that he "accomplished all that we went for, and even more." He said nothing about moving farther south than Belmont. The battle put an end to that for the moment. This time he added no injunction to his father not to share his letter with the press, expecting Jesse to do just that. Belmont had been a close-run affair. All he had to show for it were a couple of captured cannon, several score prisoners, and the hope that he had disrupted Polk's plans. Even though he learned of Frémont's removal when he returned to Cairo, Grant could expect criticism of his actions, and getting his own version of the story before the public early would do no harm.[169] Jesse did as expected, and soon the letter appeared in papers around the North. Belmont briefly captured nationwide attention, and the same day that Grant's letter to Jesse first appeared in print, the New York *Evening Post* ran a headline asking WHO IS GENERAL GRANT? Its answer was a scant paragraph noting only that he was from Galena, attended West Point, fought and won distinction in Mexico, and left the army in the 1850s.[170] That paragraph was soon republished around the North, fuelling curiosity. The nation would not have to wait very long to learn a good deal more.

7

LEE FRUSTRATED AND
GRANT VICTORIOUS

JEFFERSON DAVIS WAS still learning how to use Lee. By seniority he should have commanded in northern Virginia rather than Johnston, but his value marshaling state forces was too vital. By the time he was free of that, Johnston was the victorious general at Manassas and could hardly be superseded. The other Johnston, Albert Sidney, was now in place in the territorially vast department west of the Appalachians, so at the moment there simply was no open command commensurate with Lee's rank. Yet with the steady organization and expansion of the war department in Richmond, need for Lee's administrative services lessened. While President Davis was not always the most perceptive executive, he recognized that a desk wasted Lee's skills, especially as the president jealously held all the real reins of his war machine. Thus when Lee returned from western Virginia, the president had another job for him right away.

Lee's beard had grown in full and almost entirely gray, and on getting back to Richmond he decided to keep it that way.[1] He wanted Mary to see it, but she was visiting on the lower James River. Davis wanted him to leave right away for another trouble spot even more complex and poisoned than the last, so Lee had to leave without seeing his wife. The Yankees were poised for mischief along the Confederate Atlantic coast. They never gave up Fort Monroe, which positioned them to threaten Hampton Roads, afforded a potential base for operations against Richmond itself, and could support expeditions farther south. In fact, a substantial naval fleet left there on October 20, clearly intending a landing somewhere in the Carolinas. By the time Lee reached Richmond the fleet was already off Port Royal Sound, South Carolina, ready to attack the forts protecting that back door to Charleston and Savannah. Meanwhile, a command maelstrom at least as complicated as the Wise-Floyd-Loring situation prevailed in the area. Brigadier General A. R. Lawton commanded Georgia forces in Savannah, while Brigadier General James H. Trapier commanded South Carolina forces in Charleston. Neither had much use for the other, while governors Francis W. Pickens of South Carolina and Joseph E. Brown in Georgia guarded their own prerogatives. Everyone thought he was in charge, no one really was, and each worked against the other while guarding his own patch.

Of such divided counsels the enemy could make much, and on November 5 Davis asked Lee to go immediately to order before the Yankees gained an advantage. This time there would be no uncertainty about authority. Davis officially combined the two states and the eastern part of Florida into a single military department, placing Lee in command, while the new secretary of war Judah P. Benjamin informed generals and governors that "General Lee has full power to act" with "all the means of the Government within his reach."[2] There was no equivocation in that, but a few at least feared that his time as a desk soldier fitted him for nothing more now. "Though reputed to be an accomplished & great officer," Virginia secessionist Edmund Ruffin wrote on hearing of the new appointment, he feared Lee was "too much of a red-tapist to be an effective commander in the field."[3] Writing from Johnston's army at Manassas, an artilleryman mused that Lee "has lost ground in the army." He might be popular with the generals and officers but was regarded as "too cautious by the army and lacking in confidence in volunteers."[4]

Lee himself had no illusions about what lay in store, dismissing it as "another forlorn hope expedition," if anything, "worse than western Virginia."[5] Still, he left at once and by November 8 established headquarters in a deserted house on the Coosawhatchie River a few miles upstream from Port Royal Sound.[6] He arrived to find the Yankee fleet already pushing its way into the sound, the forts and batteries evacuated, and most of their guns and equipment abandoned. Worse, the Georgia units at the forts returned to Savannah without orders.[7] General Lawton wrote to welcome Lee and his assistance in the emergency, but was too busy to come see him and suggested that his new commander come to Savannah instead.[8] Trapier wanted permission to declare martial law in Charleston.[9] Governor Brown insisted on the return of Georgia troops to protect their own state, and Pickens demanded arms for South Carolina regiments not yet in existence.[10] Learning from his last experience. Lee asked for explicit definition of his authority. Benjamin replied that he could command soldiers, munitions, supplies, and "the entire resources of South Carolina and Georgia that are under control of the Confederate Government."[11]

Armed with that, Lee visited Savannah and Charleston to inspect their defenses, then went on to Fernandina, Florida. He knew how to judge the strength and readiness of masonry forts like those in and around Charleston Harbor, and he had overseen some of Fort Pulaski's construction thirty years before. The Yankees made no further advance, instead consolidating their gains at Port Royal to begin the buildup of a secure base. That gave Lee time to set in motion improvements, and he began making changes after just a week in the department. He first addressed immediate personnel and defensive necessities. Lee sent Trapier, a West Point–trained engineer, to Fernandina to see to its defenses, replacing him with Brigadier General Roswell S. Ripley, whom he ordered to continue the fortification of Charleston Harbor. It was Lee's first important personnel change of the war, on its face a good one, for Ripley had experience as an officer and performed well in Mexico. Only later would his penchant for liquor and insubordination become apparent. Lee also mustered and armed as many South Carolina volunteers as Pickens would release, and assumed temporary command of unassigned Confederate naval officers at Charleston to detail them to the harbor's water batteries.[12]

That done, Lee moved to the broad scale and made a pragmatic decision. He commanded more than three hundred miles of coastline with something fewer than 25,000 soldiers. Obviously, he could not attempt to defend all of it or he would spread himself so thin that he might not hold any of it. He decided to fortify only the most important points: Charleston and its vital harbor; Savannah and its approaches via the Savannah River and Fort Pulaski; Brunswick, Georgia, and St. Simons Sound; and Cumberland Sound at the mouth of the St. Mary's River, the border between Georgia and Florida. Lee put men to work shifting seacoast artillery from other locations to those points, a calculated risk based on his expectation that the enemy would want them as ideal spots for bases to supply the blockading squadron and launch campaigns into the interior. Given a month, he believed he could have their defenses ready to meet what the Yankees threw at him.[13]

Lee's new command now thrust him into the seedbed of the fire-brands and zealots he blamed for fomenting disunion. South Carolina was secession's womb. So radical were some of its offspring that when Virginia failed to secede in the first rush, men like Robert B. Rhett eyed it with distrust, suggesting even that it should not be allowed to join the Confederacy. They extended that suspicion to Lee personally, especially when the stories of his hesitance to resign his old commission became current, followed by the rumors that he had hoped for peaceful reunification.[14] When Lee first met Pickens, he did not know that the past summer the governor suspected both his commitment and his capability, claiming that the Yankee army defeated at Manassas would not have gotten even that far "if Lee had been the man his reputation makes him." Privately Pickens declared that "the truth is, Lee is not with us at heart, or he is a common man, with good looks, and too cautious for practical Revolution."[15]

A civilian population fearful of invasion tested Lee's diplomatic skills. Early in December those in the vicinity of his headquarters petitioned him to declare martial law along their coast. Lee politely demurred. The civil authorities functioned adequately and there was as yet no military emergency. Nowhere had the Confederate military declared a suspension of civil law as yet, and he believed it should be done only "as a last extremity."[16] Yet Lee did, for the first time, step outside his province and into the political realm. Asked for his views on South Carolina's defenses, he sent the state convention a letter declaring that the state must mobilize as many volunteers as possible, and not for a year's enlistment like so many of the current regiments, but for the actual duration of the war. This conflict was not going to be over in a season, and "we cannot stop short of its termination, be it long or short," he declared. In spring 1862 the enlistments of all the twelve-month volunteers raised in the early days of the war would expire. Their army could evaporate in the face of the enemy. "The Confederate States have now but one great object in view," he said. "The successful issue of their war of independence." Everything worth possessing depended on that, and "everything should yield to its accomplishment." Moreover, Lee pleaded that volunteers be enlisted only in individual regiments of infantry and cavalry and batteries of artillery as now prescribed by regulations, and not in "legions" or independent brigades like Wise's and Floyd's. He warned, from his own experience, that "special corps & separate commands are frequent causes of embarrassment."[17]

Sounding very much as if he expected to be quoted publicly, he warned that the enemy grew stronger all the time, and would act soon. "Where he will strike I do not know," he said, "but the blow when it does fall will be hard."[18] Lee revealed a clear appreciation for the benefit of influencing public opinion, even if it meant violating his aversion to seeing his words in the press, for more than once now he wrote with the popular ear clearly in mind. When the Federals brought a fleet of old merchant ships loaded with stone to the mouth of Charleston Harbor and sank them in the main channel on December 20, hoping to close the harbor on the anniversary of the state's secession, Lee responded immediately with venom greater than any of his words to date. "This achievement, so unworthy any nation, is the abortive expression of the malice & revenge of a people which they wish to perpetuate by rendering more memorable a day hateful in their calendar," he wrote. "It is also indicative of their despair of ever capturing a city they design to ruin, for they can never expect to possess what they labor so hard to reduce."[19]

When the Yankees raided the smaller bays and estuaries, destroying anything of military value, the masters fled and the slaves stole or destroyed what remained.[20] That made work on the defenses only the more vital. With legislators' approval, Lee employed slaves on the military works, and put picks and shovels in the hands of mustered white volunteers. He anticipated that when the enemy advanced he would send infantry to cut the Charleston & Savannah Railroad near its Savannah River crossing; this would prevent the two cities from reinforcing each other while the Yankees concentrated other columns and warships first on one city and then the other. Lee thought subtly and expected his foe to do the same, fearing that "this would be a difficult combination for us successfully to resist," but he prepared to meet it should it come.[21] He designed an interior defensive line so placed as to protect the approaches to the railroad, and at the same time safely out of range of Yankee gunboats coming up the river. That meant even more spadework, which did not make him popular with the new recruits.

After a month in command, Lee reorganized the South Carolina portion of his department into five separate districts for more stream-lined management that allowed the commander in each to react more immediately to threats on his own front.[22] At the same time his diplomacy with Pickens—aided by a helpful, perhaps planted, rumor that conflicts over state or national control of South Carolina regiments caused him embarrassment—elicited from the governor an acknowl-edgment that all South Carolina soldiers were "without any reserva-tion" under Lee's Confederate control; this was an important conces-sion from the leading state-rights state.[23]

By year's end Lee had made progress on every front without a shot fired, as the Federals continued to give him time, though hardly for leisure. Lee had hoped Mary might join him, or at least find lodging in Charleston or Savannah where they could see each other occasionally. She actually wanted to stay with him at Coosawhatchie, but he chided her for rejecting two very comfortable and genteel cities in favor of what he called "a decrepid & deserted village." If she saw the place, he believed she would desert it like its former inhabitants. As close as it was to Federal lines, she might not escape in an emergency, especially as she always moved so slowly. Lee felt good enough to banter with her again, joking that if the enemy approached, she would tell him to give her "just a minute," and be captured while still getting ready. "Well it shows the perverseness of human nature," he concluded.[24] She never came to South Carolina, and when Christmas arrived he could only write to her in recollection of more than thirty holidays past. "We must be content with the many blessings we receive," he wrote that day. "If we can only become sensible of our transgressions, so as to be fully penitent & forgiven, that this heavy punishment under which we labour may with justice be removed from us & the whole nation, what a gracious consummation of all that we have endured it will be!"[25]

He still spoke of "the whole nation," though by now he had aban-doned hope of a rapprochement. By Christmas he had been out of his old uniform just eight months, but his experience since, his frustration, and his shifting loyalty showed in his attitude toward the object of his former allegiance. His comments on the United States hosted not just anger now, but vestiges of distaste, even detestation, and a burgeoning sense that Yankees were of a lesser order. A few weeks after his condemnation of the North for sinking the stone fleet at Charleston, he told Custis that he believed "no civilized nation within my knowledge has ever carried on war as the United States government has against us."[26] His investment in his new nation rapidly tarnished the luster on his love for the old Union. He spoke now of "the great principle for which we are contending," without saying specifically what that principle might be.[27] He resigned his old commission because he could not fight against Virginia, friends, and family. When Virginia became Confederate, so did he, yet still he clung to hope for peaceful reconciliation founded on political compromise on an issue—slavery's protection in the territories—that meant little or nothing to him personally. Sacred Virginia had been invaded, and the Yankee presence fouled its northeastern soil and western counties.

Worst of all, part of that foothold was beloved Arlington, the home cherished by both him and his wife, however much of a headache it had been for him. Stories of his family's possessions being pillaged, the theft or destruction of precious George Washington artifacts, and grounds lacerated to build defenses and campsites raised his gorge. Even if the vindictive Yankees failed to destroy it, he doubted his family would ever recognize it again. Arlington would probably be uninhabitable when the war ended now that the main house, his family's home, was occupied by enemy soldiers. The Yankees dishonored their own Constitution's Third Amendment prohibiting quartering soldiers in private houses, and had "foully polluted" Mary's beloved home and his son Custis's birthright. Even his daughter Mildred's cat was still there at the enemy's mercy. Lee advised his family to abandon hope of ever returning, and to cherish their memories of Arlington before the Yankees came. "They cannot take away the remembrances of the spot, & the memories of those that to us rendered it sacred," he told them. The Federals and their war made the Lee family virtually homeless.[28] Personal loss is a powerful negative motivator of loyalty, and at this point it helped make Lee in heart as well as sword a Confederate, a conversion effected far more by circumstances than political conviction. Still, though he might deplore Yankee actions and attitudes, he did not hate them, for hatred meant loss of control.

It is as well that Mary did not come to Coosawhatchie, for Lee spent little time there. When not off on distant inspections, he filled his days observing local troop dispositions and enemy positions, often not returning to his house until late, and then official correspondence occupied him until midnight.[29] There was little time for leisure, though he enjoyed riding a new horse named Greenbrier, remarkably calm and good on long trips. For that reason Lee would rename him Traveller.[30] He cut his personal correspondence to a minimum, paid few social visits in Savannah and Charleston, and only occasionally managed to attend church. "One of the miseries of war is that there is no Sabbath & the current of work & strife has no cessation," he lamented to his daughter Annie. "How can we be pardoned for all our offenses!"[31] During an inspection of the Florida defenses in mid-January 1862, he did make a special and very personal visit to Dungeness, home of Revolutionary War general Nathaniel Greene. His father, Light Horse Harry Lee, lay buried there in the family cemetery. Yet when he wrote Mary of his visit, he remained oddly detached, spoke of no feelings or emotions on this first visit to his father's grave, and spent far more time describing the Greene house and garden than he did penning a single sentence, simply mentioning the marble slab and its bare inscription. When he wrote of the Dungeness visit to his son Custis he made no mention whatever of his father or his resting place.[32] Clearly torn between a yearning to admire his father and the inevitable embarrassment, perhaps even resentment, of what the old hero had done to his own family, Lee still did not know what to think of Light Horse Harry.

Such interludes were few. Lee's expectations for the war vacillated according to the news and his mood. When a Union warship stopped a British steamer carrying Confederate diplomats abroad and arrested them on November 8, the resulting international incident had many expecting war between the United States and Britain. This was a distraction that at the least would aid the Confederacy, and one that some hoped might lead to Britain granting diplomatic recognition and military assistance to the South. From the first Lee expected it to come to nothing, however. Granting that Lincoln and his cabinet "are not entirely mad," he forecast that when it came to a choice of war or releasing the Confederate diplomats, the Union would let them go. "No one will help us," he told Mary. In fact, he disdainfully complained that "the cry is too much for help." It mortified him to hear public and press pleading for foreign assistance. "We want no aid," he declared. He distrusted the entanglements and compromises that might be necessary to alliances. "We must make up our minds to fight our battles & win our independence alone," he wrote on Christmas. If they did, they could win if they were patient. "It is not a light achievement & cannot be accomplished at once."[33] Lincoln decided to release the prisoners and the crisis subsided just as Lee expected. By mid-January he expressed cautious hope that another year might bring the conflict to an end, then wavered again, and at the end of the month spoke of the war as something that might outlive him.[34]

From the time of his arrival, Lee felt first alarm and then dismay at the lassitude of the people along the coast and through South Carolina and Georgia generally. There was no war on their soil, despite the Yankees at Port Royal. The war was in Virginia where they had sent regiments, and now with no more battles in Virginia since Manassas, surely that war was all but over. Yet somehow it still dragged on, and the government expected them to make more sacrifices. Behind his confident public face, Lee hid his frustration when volunteers came forward slowly, and the population seemed more concerned with getting its livestock and cotton and slaves to safety in the interior. "The people do not seem to realize that there is a war," he complained to his daughter Annie.[35] The volunteers still signed up only for twelve months, and the governors continued letting them do so.[36] If South Carolinians enlisted slowly, Governor Brown seemed bent on keeping all Georgia volunteers under his personal control.[37] "I am dreadfully disappointed at the spirit here," Lee confessed at the end of the year. "They have all of a sudden realized the asperities of war, in what they must encounter, & do not seem to be prepared for it." Worse, the volunteers objected to laboring on defenses while the enemy made almost daily landings and minor raids to pillage and burn. "Still on the whole matters are encouraging," Lee felt by mid-January. If he only had a few veteran regiments he believed he could rally volunteers around them and hold his ground unless overwhelmed by raw numbers.[38]

Lee was in Charleston in late January when another fleet of old merchant vessels arrived to be scuttled in one of the main ship channels in another effort to close the harbor. He doubted it would be any more effective than the first such effort, but it added to his growing expectation that the Yankees would move first against Savannah, since an attack on Charleston using warships would need to use those blocked channels. Taking Savannah would give the enemy a foothold from which to launch a campaign approaching Charleston from the interior, perhaps to lay siege while the Union navy blockaded the port. The almost daily landings and petty raids along the Georgia coast confirmed his expectation as they seemed designed to cut off Fort Pulaski from communication with Savannah. "There are so many points of attack, & so little means to meet them on water," he lamented to Mary, "that there is but little rest."[39]

That only made his manpower needs more critical. When a commander in neighboring North Carolina appealed for help, Lee answered that he had too few men himself, some not yet armed, and faced constant threats along his own coast.[40] Compounding that, by early February something Lee had long feared and predicted began to materialize. The one-year enlistment of some of his South Carolina volunteers manning Fort Pulaski expired, and the men refused to reenlist and simply went home, while more units were due for expiration in the coming weeks. His command could evaporate in the face of the foe. "Neither the sentiment of the people, or the policy of the State seems to favor the organization of troops for Confederate service," he lamented to Benjamin. As for the volunteers still in the ranks, he had too few experienced officers to train them, especially gunners for the artillery that he believed would be the backbone of his defense. "Artillerists cannot be made on the eve of a battle," he complained.[41] On his next visit to Savannah he found defensive works that ought to have been finished still incomplete, and his officers seemed helpless to make the volunteers work harder or faster. "It is difficult to arouse ourselves from ease & comfort to labour & self denial," he told Mary, grumbling that "it is so very hard to get anything done, & while all wish well & mean well, it is so difficult to get them to act energetically & promptly." That meant more work for him. He had too much to do already—more, he feared, than he could accomplish well.[42]

There were tough decisions to make now that enemy activity pointed to Savannah as the point most at hazard. He must take some guns from his coastal defenses to strengthen the city. More than that, he had to abandon some points in order to concentrate his forces to meet the greatest threat. "I exceedingly dislike to yield an inch of territory to our enemies," he notified Benjamin, but on February 10 his orders went out to withdraw units and artillery from the least essential positions.[43] The first to be evacuated was St. Simon's Island protecting the water approaches to Brunswick, Georgia, which drew an immediate protest from Governor Brown.[44] A few days later Lee ordered the evacuation of Brunswick itself, but that was not all. The small town was a summer resort with a salubrious climate and ample buildings that could be turned into barracks and hospitals and other comforts for soldiers, while its harbor could host a small fleet of warships. Lee believed that if the Federals occupied the place, they would use it as a base for future operations against his other defenses. Months earlier he had warned Mary that military necessity in this conflict might result in acts that in peacetime would be deemed barbarous. "Many enormities will be committed I fear on both sides," he confessed.[45] Now he proposed one himself. Rather than leave Brunswick for the foe to convert to his own benefit, Lee proposed to destroy the town when the enemy approached, even though it was all private property. Doing so, he argued, would show the enemy their willingness to sacrifice, and their determination to be independent. He may also have known that much of it actually belonged to Northern capitalists, which would surely lessen his sorrow at such a move, but still his proposal would result in the largest destruction of civilian property in the war to date. No wonder he sought sanction both from the war department and Governor Brown before acting. No answer came from Richmond, but Brown emphatically supported Lee's proposal, which fortunately he never carried out.[46]

Expecting the enemy to strike in force when he moved, Lee asked Ripley and Trapier to abandon nonessential points, contract their lines where possible, and concentrate their commands far enough back from navigable rivers and estuaries that Federal naval cannon could not be brought to bear, thus taking them out of the equation so that "we can meet on more equal terms."[47] Governor Brown responded by refusing to send two Georgia regiments to the aid of Florida, and Governor John Milton of Florida protested the evacuation order and demanded that Lee send reinforcements to hold ground instead of abandoning it. The ugly face of the state-rights doctrine leered at Lee in a critical moment.[48] Then on February 8, events hundreds of miles to the west interfered with his plans. "News from Kentucky & Tennessee is not favourable," he wrote Mary.[49] He learned that two days earlier Fort Henry on the Tennessee River had fallen to the Yankees. Later, word of more loss out there only darkened the horizon. "Disasters seem to be thickening around us," he lamented on February 23. For the first time taking note of what Grant was doing, though not by name, he confided to his son Custis that Grant's victories demanded greater exertion and sacrifice on their part. Otherwise they might well be overrun for a time "& must make up our minds to great suffering."[50] Even before then, orders came from Richmond to contract his lines and abandon all islands along his coastline to protect the interior, while sending a regiment to Tennessee to reinforce General Albert Sidney Johnston as he assembled an army to try to hold Tennessee.[51] A few days later Benjamin ordered Lee virtually to abandon Florida and send more regiments to Johnston, and by March 1 Lee had them on their way.[52]

For the first time Lee felt at long distance the reverberations set in motion by Grant. This only reinforced his conviction that now they faced a long and hard contest. "The whole country has to go through much suffering," he wrote Mary. "It is necessary we should be humbled & taught to be less boastful, less selfish, & more devoted to right & justice to all the world." They must resolve themselves to accept defeats when they came, and use their wits and resources as best they could to overcome them, and in the end to "be resigned to what God ordains for us."[53]

Reduction of his own forces hardly made Lee's task on the coast any easier, but then he began to suspect that the enemy had no immediate plans to advance on Savannah, or else meant to deceive him regarding that city, while really moving on Charleston. He put Ripley on the alert, yet still held artillerists ready to come to Savannah immediately to man its guns should he be mistaken. Regardless of where the foe moved, Lee expected him first to try to cut the Charleston & Savannah Railroad to isolate the cities and garrisons from each other, and then to move inland to complete that isolation by cutting the Augusta & Savannah and the South Carolina Railroads at Augusta. Lee had just asked Governor Brown to support building a quarter-mile connection to link the two lines where they terminated at Augusta, and could not afford to lose either now. Consequently, he ordered the Savannah River to be obstructed inland below Augusta to prevent enemy boats from coming upstream to threaten the rail lines.[54] By the end of the month he believed he had done all he could with his small means and persistently slow workers, whom he still pushed to complete his interior defense line.[55]

At the dawn of March the Virginian seemed suspended between hope and despair, and in that dilemma he took refuge once again in resignation. What God had foreordained, man could not alter or halt.[56] "It is plain we have not suffered enough, laboured enough, repented enough, to deserve success," he told daughter Annie. "Our people have not been earnest enough, have thought too much of themselves & their ease, & instead of turning out to a man, have been content to nurse themselves & their dimes, & leave the protection of themselves & families to others." He could not help hearing the complaints that he did nothing but pointless digging, or the epithets of "Spades Lee" and "King of Spades" being murmured. His soldiers refused to see the necessity of their labor or that "it is better to sacrifice themselves than our cause."[57] Back in Virginia, some who had hoped he might accomplish something in South Carolina were now disillusioned. "Lee is very cautious—too much so, it is said by some," observed an artillery officer at Manassas. "This remains to be seen."[58] Lee complained privately that the people of his department "have been clamorous in criticising what others have done, & endeavored to prove that they ought to do nothing." They could not see what he saw: that now whenever the Yankees launched a campaign against Charleston or Savannah or the vital railroads, there would be a chance of repelling the invader, not by the storybook heroics of chivalrous "Southrons" in headlong battle, but thanks to miles of hard-built earthworks and bastions to protect those inexperienced and ill-equipped men.

Hardly had he written those words when a telegram came from Richmond. President Davis wanted to see him as soon as possible. Lee prepared to leave immediately on what he assumed would be a temporary visit, placing Major General John C. Pemberton in temporary command, and leaving three of his staff officers to continue pressing on with the work. He left on the evening of March 3 with much done, and much yet undone.[59] The night before he left he wrote his daughter Annie that "if our men will stand to their work we shall give them trouble & damage them yet." In the end surely God would give them the victory.[60]

◦‿◦

Confederate newspapers had asked WHAT HAS BECOME OF GEN. LEE? because of his reputation and unrealized expectations. When the New York *Evening Post* asked WHO IS GENERAL GRANT? after Belmont, it was because he had neither reputation nor expectations.[61] Suddenly the public wanted to know something of an obscure general associated only, if at all, with the occupation of Paducah. Even a correspondent in Cairo could barely begin to fill in the picture. "General Grant is a man of plain exterior," he wrote a few days after the engagement. "He is plain and retiring in his manners, and never wastes a word with any one, but pays strict attention." Reckoning Grant one of the best officers in the western theater of the war, the reporter predicted that he would "take an active part in the service of his country."[62]

"The battle of Belmont, as time passes, proves to have been a greater success than Gen. McClernand or myself at first thought," Grant wrote Washburne a fortnight after the fight, a pardonably proud assessment that few others then or later shared.[63] The day after the engagement Grant simply referred to it as "the skirmish of yesterday," when he sent a message to Polk seeking leave to collect his dead and wounded and exchange prisoners.[64] The Confederate was perhaps surprised, having heard that Grant was killed in the action, but the Federal's choice of words stunned him.[65] "Skirmish?" Polk supposedly exclaimed. "Hell and damnation! I'd like to know what he calls a battle!"[66] On November 13 Grant and Polk met aboard a steamboat anchored midstream between Cairo and Columbus and spoke at length on final terms of a prisoner exchange, neither government having yet worked out a cartel.[67] Polk did not think much of him. "He looked rather sad like a man who was not at ease and whose thoughts were not the most agreeable," the Confederate told his wife two days later. At length Grant smiled, but still Polk concluded that he was "rather second-rate, though I dare say a good enough man."[68]

Once back at Cairo Grant dove into administrative responsibilities of a kind that rarely troubled Lee thus far. His men needed clothing and stores badly, yet his quartermaster had no money to pay vendors, while outstanding government debt in his command hovered around $600,000 and few would extend any more credit.[69] He tried several expedients to give retailers confidence that they would be paid, then discovered that some of the problem was outright fraud in his headquarters.[70] Captain Reuben Hatch, his quartermaster, apparently bought goods at low bid prices, but submitted high bid invoices to the war department and pocketed the difference. Grant told Hatch he would be replaced, but Hatch did his best to impede an investigation when Grant asked that an inspector be sent.[71] Grant annulled Hatch's deals. "I am tearing all corrupt contracts," he said, yet the more he looked the more he uncovered.[72] "Extravagance seems to be the order of the day," he declared in January 1862. Thereafter, he personally examined and approved all contracts issued in his department. No matter was too small to catch his eye; he even replaced a corrupt bread contractor, in the process saving one-eighth of a cent per pound, which amounted to $50 a day.[73] He would not be lured into a conflict of interest, and when his father sent him unsolicited price quotations for leather harness, Grant tersely informed Jesse that "I cannot take an active part in securing contracts."[74] Meanwhile, he proposed that guilty contractors be forced to enlist in the army.[75]

All of this distracted Grant from his primary goal. Back on October 31 he and McClernand met with Congressman Washburne. Grant reiterated that Cairo was the key position for any expedition moving down the Mississippi, and argued that his district ought to be set apart from Frémont's. With headquarters at Cairo, that would make his command the logical one for any assignment to move south. He had been planning such a campaign for months, recently with help from McClernand, whom he probably enlisted more for his political influence. Grant well understood that Washington might hand such an important command to someone senior, but he was willing to take the risk. Washburne promised to work for him in Washington, and it can hardly be coincidental that one week later Grant attacked Belmont. A success in a small expedition launched from Cairo might just persuade the war department that Cairo was the base and Grant was the man for something more ambitious.

In fact Washburne made some progress in the capital, perhaps helped by public reaction to Belmont, and thought prospects good for authorization to launch Grant's campaign.[76] Then on November 9 the War Department announced a new arrangement of military districts that had been in the works for some time. It left Grant's district in its current department, and announced that Major General Henry W. Halleck would be Frémont's replacement.[77] That was an end to Grant's immediate hopes, though McClernand continued pushing the idea for the rest of the year, coveting the command for himself. The day after Halleck assumed command Grant asked for orders to meet with him in St. Louis, ostensibly to discuss the needs of his command, but more likely to press his case for the move down the Mississippi. Halleck said no.[78]

"My inclination is to whip the rebellion into submission," Grant wrote his father a week later, and Halleck's refusal to meet made him suspect that the old policy of delay would continue. He also feared for his own tenure. "I am somewhat troubled lest I lose my command here," he confessed. Regarding his district as strategically the most important in the entire department, he felt apprehensive that Halleck might give it to some senior.[79] He soon found his worries groundless, however. Apparently Halleck was satisfied with his subordinate. Certainly he could not fault Grant's industry. The brigadier worked from breakfast until well after dark seven days a week, and only wrote personal correspondence if he finished his official letters before midnight. His staff had grown and he had able men in adjutant Rawlins, aides Clark Lagow and Hillyer, and Colonel J. D. Webster, his chief of staff who doubled as chief engineer. He also had a quartermaster, a chief commissary, an ordnance officer overseeing artillery, a medical director and assistant, and a paymaster.[80] Including a volunteer aide it amounted to eleven men, most of them specialists, which relieved a considerable burden from Grant's shoulders, and from the first he had no difficulty in delegating authority and did not share Lee's nagging fear of things going undone if not under his personal supervision.

It was a huge command: all of southern Illinois, Kentucky west of the Cumberland River, and the Missouri counties south of Cape Girardeau; an area of twelve thousand or more square miles, all but its northern reaches bordering either the Confederacy or questionable portions of Missouri and Kentucky. "There is not a sufficiency of Union sentiment left in this portion of the state to save Sodom," he complained after a visit to Missouri.[81] He kept constantly busy dealing with illicit trade between the lines, Unionist refugees from the South, and Northern businessmen wanting to get to the Confederacy for profit. Secession was killing Union men now, one of them his boy-hood friend George B. Bailey, murdered or drowned after being shot in a surprise attack three days after Belmont.[82] For the sake of the sol-diers, Grant believed it imperative to cut off communication between the sections.[83] After mid-November he allowed passage south only to those bearing passes from Halleck himself.[84] However, he welcomed Unionist refugees from the Confederacy into his lines and temporarily provided for them until they moved north, and even dealt lightly with disloyal residents so long as they committed no hostile acts other than express their opinions. His goal was "to visit as lightly as possible, the rigors of a state of war upon noncombatants," and allowed press free-dom even when others objected to disunion sentiments appearing in some Missouri and Kentucky papers.[85]

Like all Union commanders, he had to deal with runaway slaves, but faced a special problem some others did not. While a secessionist's slave might be legitimate contraband, Kentucky and Missouri slaves were still protected as property by the Constitution. "I do not want the Army used as negro cat[c]hers," he declared on Christmas Day 1861, "but still less do I want to see it used as a cloak to cover their escape." So long as the Fugitive Slave Law remained in effect, regula-tions required the runaways' return to loyal men on application. Grant dealt with the distraction by ordering the expulsion of any fugitives found in his camps, staying out of the business of returning fugitives to loyal or disloyal men alike.[86] He still saw this as a white man's con-flict over loyalty, not slavery, and condemned press efforts to make it into a war for emancipation. "If it cannot be whipped in any other way than through a war against slavery, let it come to that legitimately," he argued. "If it is necessary that slavery should fall that the Republic may continue its existence, let slavery go." But he regarded those clamoring for a war for abolition as enemies to the country.[87]

Amid all this it helped to have Julia and the children join him for much of November and December, but they had scant free time together, and it helped that his father did not visit. Grant wearied of Jesse's self-serving requests and ill-informed complaints about virtually all Union generals, to whom his son quickly gave benefit of the doubt.[88] 'Lys chided his father that "there is a desire upon the part of people who stay securely at home to read in the morning papers, at their breakfast, startling reports of battles fought." They did not understand why troops had to be trained, logistics arranged, groundwork laid, and more. "You are very much disposed to criticise unfavorably from information received through the public press," Grant told him, and "I am very tired of the course pursued by a portion of the Union press."[89]

A few days before Christmas Grant unwittingly found himself in a minor controversy with Halleck; Grant acted on a hoax telegram that countermanded an order by Halleck, who sent him a heated reprimand and would not be mollified by explanations.[90] It was a small matter with wide repercussions commencing the very next day when Grant learned that William J. Kountz had arrived in Cairo to oversee river transportation and government claims in the department. He failed to present his orders to Grant first, and soon Grant heard of him making inquiries about matters that Grant thought none of his business. Having just been scolded by Halleck for being gullible, Grant was not in a mood to be taken in by anyone else. He ordered Kountz to explain himself. Kountz was known to be stubborn, interfering, and querulous, and not a man to be reprimanded. He was also a serial slanderer and libeler, and would be taken to court by at least one victim of his intemperate tongue.[91] Moreover, his appointment came from McClellan, a man whose associates often mimicked his self-importance. McClernand intervened and cleared any confusion, but Grant had made a noisy and vengeful enemy.[92]

He had little time to fret about Kountz, for within a few days it looked like there might be activity ahead. Grant never yielded his urgency about Columbus as he monitored the enemy buildup. He read the Confederate Memphis *Appeal* when he could, and learned much from its pages.[93] Then in December he sent a spy into Columbus to prepare a detailed map showing its defenses, and the man returned with not only the chart but also circumstantial reports that the Confederates had left the place garrisoned by militia.[94] In the first week of January further reports came in that the Columbus garrison was reduced even more.[95] By this time Grant's command of about 20,000 were virtually all armed and equipped to take the field.[96] Once again he asked for orders to come to St. Louis to meet with Halleck, but that same day an order came from his commander.[97] He wanted Grant to make a demonstration into western Kentucky, putting out the story that his real goal was Dover on the Cumberland River just below the Tennessee line, where rebel batteries commanded the river approach below an earthwork named Fort Donelson. He was also to hint that he might be headed up the Cumberland to Nashville, which would cut off the rebels at Donelson from communication with the enemy army then assembling at Bowling Green, Kentucky, under Albert Sidney Johnston. Probably aware of Grant's exceeding orders in his attack on Belmont, Halleck emphasized twice that he was to avoid a battle, though he could skirmish a little here and there to give his men experience.[98]

In fact, Halleck was responding nominally to pressure from Lincoln to advance, but he felt no hurry to take the field. He sent the order by mail rather than telegraph, and gave Grant no date for the movement. Strangely, he asked Brigadier General Don Carlos Buell, who had replaced Sherman at Louisville, to cooperate and pick a date that suited him best, but suggested that he "put it off as long as possible."[99] Grant did not share Halleck's timidity. Less than twenty-four hours after receiving his order, he had his expedition ready to go. After pondering such a move for so long, he had a campaign outline ready whenever opportunity arose, as always, allowing himself leeway to adapt on the road as contingencies arose.[100] Again he left detailed management to the judgment of his commanders.[101] Bad weather and Halleck's interference delayed the movement, and then Kountz reappeared. Grant and Foote wanted to make a quick reconnaissance down the Mississippi toward Columbus before the infantry started, but Kountz had so alienated local rivermen that Foote was short of volunteers to man his gunboats. Regarding himself as a law unto himself, Kountz refused to take orders from Grant until the general had him arrested.[102] He remained under arrest until early March when Halleck ordered his release, but he would retaliate well before then.[103] Grant had no problem dealing with confrontation, and at the same time finally ordered the arrest of quartermaster Hatch as well.[104] He also had no problem admitting error and righting a wrong. More than a year later, when a full investigation completely exonerated Hatch, Grant wrote directly to Lincoln recommending him for promotion from captain to colonel, adding that "I regard it as a positive act of duty to him to give this testimonial."[105]

Finally by January 17 his columns were deep in Kentucky, Grant himself personally doing much of the reconnaissance to find passable roads.[106] This time there would be no exceeding orders, and the next day, having made his "demonstration," he began pulling his men out.[107] He was back at Cairo late on January 20, unsure of the impact of what he facetiously called "the great expedition into Kentucky." He and Foote met and concluded that the moment was prime for them to repeat the movement, but this time amphibiously up the Tennessee to take Fort Henry, just a dozen miles from Fort Donelson on the Cumberland River. Foote could take gunboats and troop transports up the Tennessee and bombard the fort from his gunboats while Grant marched a column overland and the two of them then pinched the fort between them to force its surrender. Holding Fort Henry would open the Tennessee to Union warships all the way to the Muscle Shoals near Florence, Alabama, and position Grant to isolate the Columbus garrison from supply, force its evacuation, and endanger the supply line and security of Johnston's army at Bowling Green. The plan revealed his focus beyond the immediate battlefield to calculate the maximum capital to be made from taking a strategic position. "I have now a larger force than General Scott ever commanded," he wrote. Now was the time to act, and he warned his sister that "I expect to see but little quiet from this on."[108]

He left for St. Louis late January 23 to put his case to Halleck, who reacted slowly and probably reluctantly. Grant left a few days later with neither assent nor refusal, though in fact Halleck, McClellan, and Buell all had the river forts in their sights. There was little genius in the concept. A good map revealed the advantages of taking control of the twin rivers. A few weeks later Grant himself said it was pointless to argue about who first conceived this line of campaign. Their gunboats had been going up and down the rivers for months keeping an eye on progress on the forts, and practically illustrating how troops could be transported to attack. Grant felt certain that Halleck had thought of it, and that "I am shure I did."[109] The genius lay in the execution if it worked. Grant and Foote met again and decided to wear down Halleck. Both sent telegrams saying Fort Henry could be taken and asked for permission to act.[110] The next day Grant sent a follow-up letter pointing out that from Fort Henry he could move on Fort Donelson, or Columbus, or even Memphis, while setting his soldiers' boots on rebel territory would have a good effect on morale.[111] Grant and Foote might not move Halleck to quick decision, but McClellan did. He informed Halleck on January 29 of reports of a major reinforcement on the way to Bowling Green. Implicit was the suggestion to take Fort Henry and have Foote steam up the Tennessee River to prevent the reinforcements' use of the railroad bridges at Decatur and Stevenson, Alabama, to get to Bowling Green.[112] Halleck immediately ordered Grant and Foote to take Fort Henry and cut the railroad linking Fort Donelson with Memphis.[113]

Even before he received the order, Grant had his command ready, and intended to start on February 2, just three days after getting Halleck's nod. Foote's gunboats would escort his infantry on transports to a landing on the east bank of the Tennessee as close to Fort Henry as possible, then Grant would march overland to hit the fort from the land side while Foote moved in to bombard from the river. At the last moment Halleck sent him further instructions to take control of the road linking Fort Henry and Dover, thus cutting off reinforcements from that quarter. He made no mention of Fort Donelson.[114]

Amid the flurry of preparations, Grant did not need more trouble from Kountz. Bent on revenge, Kountz sent Halleck a series of invented charges accusing Grant of being repeatedly drunk on duty in December. Halleck may not have seen them before they were referred back to Grant, and he in turn gave them back to Kountz telling him to submit a copy to his office according to regulations. Grant sent the original on to St. Louis the same day that orders came for the expedition against Fort Henry.[115] That is all he did. His mind fixed on the looming campaign, he did not allow himself to be distracted, an example of Grant's capacity for compartmentalizing issues. Years before, while struggling to stay afloat economically, he still left financial woes behind in the evenings when he devoted himself to reading with Julia and playing with his children. He would hear more of Kountz, who was already elaborating his libels to implicate Grant in the contract frauds at Cairo.

McClernand's division of eleven regiments and several artillery batteries were aboard the gunboats and transports on their way up the Tennessee by dawn on February 3. Twenty-four hours later the flotilla landed three miles downstream from the fort and the troops went ashore, whereupon Grant went upstream with Foote and three gunboats to test the range of Fort Henry's batteries. Then he took the transports back to Paducah to board another eight regiments and more artillery under Brigadier General Charles F. Smith, making in all something over 15,000 men in the operation. On the way he had time to pen a hasty note to Julia. "I do not want to boast," he told her, "but I have a confidant feeling of success."[116]

The next day saw him back on the Tennessee with McClernand's division on the east bank and Smith's on the west. He ordered McClernand to move out late in the morning of February 6 to take control of the road to Dover as Halleck instructed, and be ready to move west against Fort Henry if so ordered. Smith would take two brigades and march south to a bluff opposite the fort and occupy an unfinished earthwork called Fort Heiman, emplacing artillery to defend it and to play on Fort Henry. Meanwhile, another brigade was to move quickly down the east bank to a position from which it could launch an assault on the fort itself.[117] Operating on barely three hours' sleep, Grant spent the balance of February 5 watching what movement he could see in Fort Henry. "Tomorrow will come the tug of war," he wrote Julia.[118]

The next morning all he could do was set things in motion and try to keep up with developments. At eleven o'clock Foote's gunboats moved up to occupy the fort's guns while the infantry began its march, but then unanticipated circumstances changed everything. During the night all but a few score Confederates evacuated the fort, which the high water made virtually untenable, to march to Fort Donelson. The remainder manned a few cannon for an hour, then before the infantry could arrive, the fort surrendered to Foote. Grant sent word back to Halleck, then closed it by adding, "I shall take and destroy Fort Donaldson on the 8th."[119] It was a statement, not a request for authorization, and setting his attack two days hence meant he might take the fort before Halleck even got his letter. He ordered remaining units at Cape Girardeau and elsewhere to rush to him, sent a steamer upriver to destroy the Memphis, Clarksville & Louisville Railroad bridge a dozen miles above the fort, and finished a busy day by sending Julia a brief note. "Fort Henry is taken," he told her. "This is news enough for to-night."[120]

Grant had devised to move his army by river as close to his objective as possible without exposing his men to enemy fire, then march inland to cut off routes of escape and approach from one or more land sides while the gunboats engaged the fort's attention. It was Belmont with variations, and now he planned to use it again to take Fort Donelson. The strengths of the plan were manifest. It assayed not to drive the Confederates in retreat, but to capture the entire garrison and fort and take both out of the war. One fact apparent in northern Virginia was that the victory at Manassas decided nothing. Six months later the contending sides were preparing to fight for the same ground again. By contrast, in taking Fort Henry Grant took control of more than 150 miles of the Tennessee River, and at high water light draft gunboats could steam upstream even farther. He cut off virtually all Confederates west of the river, including Columbus and Memphis, from direct access to Johnston's army at Bowling Green, imperiling their tenure in their positions. In return, Grant's only real exposure was his supply line, but so long as he controlled the river back to Paducah, with sufficient water for Foote's gunboats to operate, he could get supplies as needed. Still, there was a risk. Confederates at Columbus seventy miles to his west, the garrison at Fort Donelson just twelve miles to his east, and Johnston's growing army ninety miles northeast at Bowling Green heavily outnumbered Grant's 15,000 should they concentrate, but he could calculate on having time to react should they try.

However, Grant reckoned without the weather. Thanks to the inundated countryside, at dawn on February 8 he found himself "perfectly locked in by high water and bad roads."[121] Time was now his enemy as much as the Confederates. "I intend to keep the ball moving as lively as possible," he wrote his sister Mary, and had something of a premonition that he would succeed.[122] What he took for a presentiment was really the optimism that defined so much of his life. He planned well, he executed his plans well, he acted quickly and allowed himself and his subordinate commanders latitude to cope with the unexpected. In fact, the only serious hazard to Grant at the moment came from behind his own lines. Having been forced reluctantly to authorize an offensive, Halleck now rushed to assume credit for the success. His telegrams to McClellan conspicuously omitted Grant's name, saying rather that "I will take Fort Henry" and even that "I will threaten Nashville." When he told McClellan that the Fort Henry bombardment had commenced, he mentioned neither Grant nor Foote.[123] After the surrender Halleck triumphantly wired that "Fort Henry is ours." Not a word about Grant and Foote. The clear message was that Halleck himself had managed the whole affair, and was now handling the move to take the other fort.

Halleck had wanted to replace Grant with Ethan Allen Hitchcock since late January, though Hitchcock was not even in the army yet.[124] The very day of Fort Henry's fall, Halleck reiterated the request to McClellan, and made the proposal two days later directly to the secretary of war.[125] He had eight brigadiers whose commissions all bore the same May 17 date, including Grant, McClernand, and William T. Sherman, which did create potential for command conflict since none was senior to another. But then Halleck embroidered by adding that he found "each unwilling to serve under the other." That would soon apply to McClernand, but was a fabrication where Grant and Sherman and others were concerned. If another major general were sent to the department, that would give Halleck a senior officer who could assume command immediately anywhere by virtue of rank. Hitchcock was an inexplicable choice, a sixty-three-year-old officer who graduated from West Point before all but two of Halleck's brigadiers were born. Yet Halleck wanted him to take over the "Tennessee line" immediately.[126] He also wanted Grant's district expanded to include west Tennessee and designated the "Department of the Mississippi." If he could not have Hitchcock, then he wanted Sherman promoted to supersede Grant.[127]

It was an amazing request. At the very moment of one victory and poised for another to follow, Halleck wanted to replace the general who to date had more command experience than any of his other brigadiers. He gave no explanation, but two present themselves. One is that Halleck gave some credence to Kountz's charges and rightly feared that Grant could compromise his gains thus far. The other, and far more likely given Halleck's personality, is that he was jealous of Grant's modest successes and feared being overshadowed, something evident in his virtual omission of Grant's name from his correspondence immediately after Fort Henry's fall.

Unaware of the menace behind his lines, Grant felt secure in trying the Fort Henry template on Fort Donelson, with variations. On February 10 he ordered the gunboats to steam back down the Tennessee to Paducah, then up the Cumberland to take on the water batteries at Fort Donelson, while he marched his men across the strip of land separating the rivers and attacked the fort from the rear. "There should be no delay in this matter," he advised Foote as he anxiously awaited word of progress.[128] Meanwhile, he assembled his senior officers in conference that afternoon, Grant's first "council of war" in the field, and though what they discussed is unknown, almost certainly he outlined his plan for them. If he opened discussion to suggestions from others he had good reason. The night before, McClernand sent him a lengthy and overly detailed proposal for an advance on the fort, though it stopped at the point that units were to go into line facing the Confederates without proposing any tactics. Significantly, it involved only McClernand's division, it being implicit that he would conduct the fight without Smith.

Grant made no written response to McClernand.[129] Still, when he issued his own marching orders the next day, he incorporated McClernand's basic suggestions. He sent one brigade by the most direct road with orders to halt and form a line two miles from the fort. At the same time the other two brigades would take a southerly road leading to Dover to halt and throw out a line two miles from the village, connecting with the other brigade on their left. Grant then fleshed out the plan by ordering Smith's division to follow immediately behind on the Dover road, and if possible occupy Dover itself and cut off any chance of the Confederate garrison escaping by the river. That was all. Using the two roads simultaneously gave them the best chance of forces converging on the fort and Dover nearly at the same time. Grant did not expect surprise, assuming that the enemy expected him. What he did not know was enemy strength, and thus informed his generals that "it is impossible to give exact details of attack." Those he would decide on the field.[130] That evening he wrote to Julia and warned her that "quite an engagement may be expected," hinting that the campaign might continue beyond Donelson, which could only mean a move toward Nashville. He always thought one move ahead.[131]

The first of the gunboats left Cairo that evening, and Grant asked its commander to fire a few shells at Fort Donelson when he came within range to announce his arrival. Grant started the infantry at eight on the morning of February 12 on an easy march. Shortly before noon he heard the gunboat's guns to the east, and pressed on to within three or four miles of his objective when he met Confederate outposts on the Dover road. Grant left it to McClernand to handle them, and by three that afternoon the rebels pulled back into their lines. Meanwhile, Grant made headquarters in a cabin just off the road used by Smith about a mile west of the Confederates' outer works, as his first brigades took position; McClernand on the right from the river just upstream of Dover around to the west, while Smith's two brigades extended the line to the left facing Fort Donelson itself. Grant ordered them into line of battle, and when skirmishing began McClernand drove the rebels back into their main works, extending his own line to his right to cover the Forge Road, the only Confederate land route to Nashville. Grant inspected the line around dusk and found all well. He had Dover and the fort isolated from reinforcement or escape. Swollen creeks covered his flanks, and his only real concern was that McClernand was stretched so thin he could not entirely cover a gap between his left and Smith's right. He could chance that, since any Confederate thrust in that direction risked being caught from two sides as McClernand and Smith responded.

February 13 brought Grant's first real experience at battlefield management, and like most new commanders he did not have a sure feel right away. He probably spent most of the day at his headquarters keeping a steady stream of orders going out.[132] He told Smith to probe the enemy earthworks at eight in the morning, to get a sense of their numbers and artillery positions. The demonstration escalated out of control before Smith was forced to retire, but still Grant learned that the Confederate right flank was well defended. He so informed McClernand, who perhaps interpreted it as a suggestion for him to advance on his own front, though he did so without Grant's knowledge.

Fifteen minutes later the foe repulsed him, too, and Grant was not happy, though he may not have said anything to McClernand at the time. Increasingly, the Illinois politician showed a penchant for acting on his own in hopes of winning personal glory.[133]

That night Grant learned that 4,000 soldiers commanded by Lee's troublesome General John B. Floyd had arrived at Dover earlier that day. As senior, Floyd now commanded, seconded by Pillow and Grant's old friend Simon Bolivar Buckner, and Grant feared that his arrival boosted the Donelson garrison to more than 20,000. Moreover, the Confederates sat behind earthworks erected in depth over many months, and his probes revealed the strength of those works. Fortunately, word came from Foote that the gunboats would arrive in the morning. Buoyed by that, Grant concluded to commence a combined naval bombardment and infantry assault at ten o'clock on Valentine's Day morning, the infantry to pin the rebels down while Foote bombarded them into submission.[134] Before bed he just had time to write to Julia that he still expected to take the fort and garrison, but figured it would take him until February 16 to accomplish.[135]

That night the weather turned vicious, and amid snow and freezing rain the temperature plummeted to 12 degrees by Grant's estimate.[136] It had been so warm during the march from Fort Henry that the inexperienced volunteers dropped blankets and overcoats along the way, which Grant did not see from the head of the column. As a result his men passed a miserable night huddled around fires to avoid freezing. Yet come morning Grant felt confidant despite believing himself outnumbered.[137] When another division commanded by Brigadier General Lew Wallace arrived, Grant placed it in the gap in his center. More regiments arrived during the night on the gunboats, and at nine that morning Grant rode to Foote's landing with a guide to take them to the field.[138] With a fight imminent, he concentrated every man. Foote expressed uneasiness at sending his gunboats against the Confederate water batteries, but Grant persuaded him that he could knock out the enemy guns handily, and Foote reluctantly agreed to go ahead. Grant thereby defeated one of a commander's greatest foes: his subordinates' second thoughts on the eve of battle.

Foote appeared at the bend below the water batteries at two-thirty that afternoon, and Grant perched on the bluff beyond his left flank to

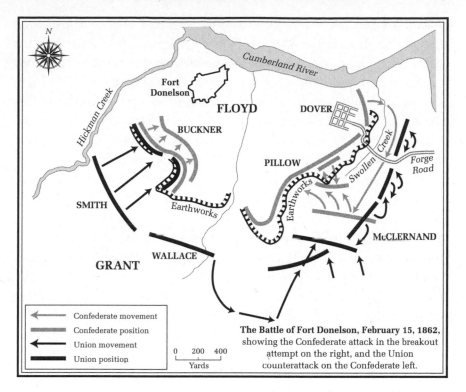

The Battle of Fort Donelson, February 15, 1862, showing the Confederate attack in the breakout attempt on the right, and the Union counterattack on the Confederate left.

watch the gunboats' approach, only to see deadly fire from the batteries put one after another out of action. Through it all Grant watched helplessly. It took scarcely a hundred men to man the water batteries, and even if he launched a diversionary assault on the Confederate defenses it would not pull them away from their guns' deadly work. There was nothing he could do. He had simply misjudged the power of those batteries.[139] Still, that night he could write that "I feel confidant of ultimate success."[140]

The next morning he went to Foote's anchorage and rowed out to the flagship to see how long it would take to get the fleet back in action, then on returning to shore he met an excited Hillyer bringing news that the Confederates had attacked McClernand and were driving him. Grant was far enough away not to hear the sound of the action opening. The Rebels were trying to break out. If they gained the Forge road they had a highway to Nashville and Bowling Green. Grant galloped back to his army, finding Smith's division in good order, and Wallace in position in the center. On the right flank he found

near chaos. As many as 10,000 Confederates had slammed into Mc-
Clernand at six that morning and kept up the pressure as the Federals
withdrew, many out of ammunition and some in panic. Grant found
them at one in the afternoon standing about in groups with little or
no formation, demoralized. Beyond them the Forge road was open,
but in a bizarre twist, the Confederates pulled back to their defenses
to pack their equipment and prepare for the march to Nashville. Grant
quickly realized three things: he could retake the Forge road easily and
keep the enemy trapped; to mass enough power to attack his right,
they must have weakened their line in front of Smith; he had to react
quickly if only for morale, telling Foote "I must order a charge to save
appearances." If Smith attacked now he might push into Fort Donelson, Grant told Foote, and if just a few gunboats appeared at the same
time, "it may secure us a Victory."[141]

Grant galloped to Smith and ordered an immediate advance that
captured the original rebel defensive line, while on the right Wallace
and McClernand reorganized and advanced. By dark they held the
Forge road again as McClernand reoccupied most of his original position. The Confederate army was back in its trap, its force spent in the
botched breakout. That night Floyd, Pillow, and Buckner concluded
that another breakout was doomed to failure, and their only options
were surrender or starvation in a siege. Floyd and Pillow ignomini-
ously abandoned the command to Buckner, and just before dawn the
next morning, Smith handed Grant a message from Buckner proposing an armistice for commissioners to discuss surrender terms. No
Confederate army had as yet surrendered. When Beauregard took
Fort Sumter he allowed the garrison to go home with banners flying and shouldered arms. Otherwise there was no template to guide
Grant, so he set the mold, and he probably had terms in mind already.
He sat down to write three simple sentences, asking Smith to read
them, and sent them to Buckner. There would be no armistice, no
commissioners. "No terms except an unconditional and immediate
surrender can be accepted," he said. "I propose to move immediately
upon your works."[142]

The accidental "S" in his name finally meant something. He was
about to become "Unconditional Surrender Grant."

8

SHILOH AND SEVENS

"I HAVE BEEN called here very unexpectedly to me & have today been placed in duty at this place under the directions of the Pres.," Lee wrote his brother Carter a week after arriving in Richmond. He came resolved to do anything for "the noble cause we are engaged in," but at least professed to crave a humble post in the field, fearing "I shall be able to do little in the position assigned me."[1] He went into conference with the president immediately on arriving, with barely time to visit Mary for the first time in a year, pleased to see her looking in better health than he expected.[2] It had been a season of disasters—Forts Henry and Donelson, the evacuation of Nashville soon afterward, the collapse of the whole west Tennessee line—and press and Congress demanded change. Davis would soon replace the unpopular Secretary of War Benjamin, and was himself engaged in a feud with P. G. T. Beauregard, while Joseph E. Johnston was proving impossible to control in northern Virginia.

To curb Davis's power, Congress created the office of general-in-chief, and many expected the president to hand Lee the portfolio. Instead, Davis assigned him to "conduct of military operations in the armies of the Confederacy," general-in-chief in essence but not in fact, for the position came with the clause "under the direction of the President," the reason Lee felt he could accomplish little.[3] Davis was his own general-in-chief and after appointing Lee he vetoed Congress's bill. He needed an appearance of change to quiet his foes. Lee was perfect. If he had no victories, neither had he defeats, and he was still widely respected. Response was mixed. The Richmond *Whig* said Lee's assignment "has revived confidence," but a week later retreated to saying he was the best qualified but "may not be a Carnot."[4] The Charleston *Mercury* praised faintly, "If he makes no advances, neither does the enemy. If he is not rapid and daring, he is energetic, and has forecast." Everyone realized Davis would still be in charge, and Lee was but an advisor.[5] The Richmond *Examiner* dripped sarcasm when it observed that "it is not known whether this important distinction has been conferred upon General Lee for his brilliant services in Western Virginia or his memorable defence of Alex[a]ndria."[6]

Lee understood his position and told Mary that "I do not see either advantage or pleasure in my duties," yet resigned himself to "do my best."[7] Once more he had to deal with governors unhappy that the president did not make generals of their favorites, or jealously hoarding new rifles in their state arsenals while soldiers in the field made do with old and worn-out arms.[8] Meanwhile, he familiarized himself with the war on all fronts. Joseph E. Johnston had pulled back from the Manassas line to the Rappahannock River. Forces that previously drubbed the Yankees at Big Bethel now dug in at Yorktown to protect Richmond from approach via the York-James Rivers peninsula. In western Virginia Confederates still guarded the approaches to Staunton and the Shenandoah Valley, while in the valley itself Major General Thomas J. Jackson, now dubbed "Stonewall," kept a watch. In the West Confederates held northern Arkansas, but the Yankees threatened Albert Sidney Johnston's army concentrating at Corinth, Mississippi, after leaving Nashville in the wake of Henry-Donelson. Charleston and Savannah were secure, but the enemy made continual inroads, and every Carolinian wanted to be a general, it seemed, and objected if Davis promoted anyone else first. Lee's advice to those so displeased was that if they thought themselves more qualified than others, then they must demonstrate their deserts "by increased diligence & zeal," an admonition that pleased no one.[9]

Lee quickly found himself in an awkward position with a general closer to home, Joseph E. Johnston. Davis's strategic policy was to hold every point. Lee knew that to be impossible, yet he had to reiterate that stance to Johnston, while on a tactical level he could give no orders without stepping on his prickly old friend's toes. Instead, he made recommendations couched in terms of "I request" and "I suggest."[10] At the same time, Lee had no idea if Johnston planned to fall back farther, as indeed he did, because that general consistently refused to communicate. When Lee hinted to Johnston to share his plans for defense, Johnston chose not to take the hint.[11]

Then the Virginia front exploded. General-in-Chief McClellan, setting aside his larger responsibilities, led the Army of the Potomac on a well-conceived shift from northern Virginia, via the Chesapeake, to Fort Monroe, which he would use as a base to campaign up the peninsula to Richmond less than 120 miles northwest. He achieved almost complete surprise. Lee wanted to go to the North Carolina coast after Federals took New Bern on March 14, but Davis did not give permission until March 23.[12] The next morning came the first sightings of a fleet of enemy transports disgorging soldiers at Fort Monroe. Lee believed that a major landing had taken place, and that either Norfolk or Richmond was the target, perhaps both. In the resulting consultation with Johnston over what could be done, Lee was reduced to being a mere conduit conveying messages back and forth between Davis and the general.[13] In the ensuing weeks he proved just as unsuccessful gaining cooperation from Johnston as the president, and meanwhile McClellan commenced a buildup to more than 100,000 soldiers. Johnston wanted a complete concentration on the peninsula, in spite of Davis's orders to protect the Rappahannock line as well, and eventually that is what he did without bothering to notify either Davis or Lee. Meanwhile, Lee coordinated the peninsula commands of Generals John B. Magruder and Benjamin Huger, on what appeared to be his own authority.[14]

Those were frustrating weeks. He learned that his son Robert was leaving university to enlist. "As I have done all in the matter that seems proper & right, I must now leave the rest in the hands of our merciful God," he told Mary. "I hope our son will do his duty and make a good soldier."[15] He feared for his wife, too, for an enemy advance might pass Rooney's White House plantation on the Pamunkey, where Mary was staying. He advised her to move, thinking the Yankees would persecute her for his sake. Respectable officers might protect her, but he doubted they could control their men, many of them foreign born and, in Lee's view, rabble.[16]

On April 4 Lee confessed that "all are anxious & expectant," and he still had no sure feeling of McClellan's intentions, or Johnston's. If the enemy used gunboats to move up the York and Pamunkey on one side, or the James on the other, or both, they could land heavy forces between Magruder and Richmond and cut him off. The next line of defense would then be the Chickahominy River, which flowed from Mechanicsville five miles north of Richmond, southeasterly nearly forty miles to empty into the James several miles above Williamsburg. That made the Chickahominy an obvious line of defense, and Lee was the first to see it, but when he advised Magruder, then holding Williamsburg, to prepare to occupy that line if necessary, Magruder read Lee's words as an order.[17] For the first time, his habit of writing avuncular suggestions rather than orders began to trouble him. Years later Lee said that "I am no great friend to adjectives," but now he used too many, at the expense of precision.[18] Meanwhile, Johnston used too few. Lee saw the president's mounting anxiety when the commander of his army refused to communicate, which only made Davis pester him more with requests. Soon the president began visiting the army after it shifted to the peninsula, which made Johnston more uncommunicative. There was a lesson there in how to manage a chief executive properly. Lee learned it while watching the dissolution of the relationship between the president and Johnston.

McClellan timidly took root at Yorktown until the end of April, giving Johnston time to get his army to the scene. He stood only three days before pulling back to Williamsburg to fight a delaying action before withdrawing once more, until by the end of May he had his army on the south bank of the Chickahominy, just as Lee had forecast. Through it all Lee had little to do but continue his futile efforts to facilitate communication.[19] Elsewhere he promoted operations that slowed McClellan's glacial advance even more. He coordinated three brigades in western Virginia, a brigade at Fredericksburg, a division not far away, and a division in the Shenandoah under Jackson to prevent remaining Federals in northern Virginia from reinforcing McClellan or moving on Richmond from the north. Johnston was their commander, too, but he had little time for them, and Lee stepped into the vacuum. Even before Lee got involved, Jackson attacked a force three times his strength at Kernstown on March 23, sending a shiver through the North. Seeing that, Lee brought those scattered forces together in a strategic concentration under Jackson. This led to a series of battles at McDowell, Front Royal, and Winchester by late May that panicked the Union and firmly pinned Union forces in place. While Jackson planned the campaign, Lee was the architect of the concentration, just as he had orchestrated Johnston's move to join Beauregard a year before.[20]

In Richmond itself Lee organized battalions for local defense, and struggled to keep ammunition and reinforcements rolling to Johnston's army.[21] Seeing the twelve-month enlistments of scores of regiments drawing near expiration, even in the face of the desperate need for more manpower created by McClellan's invasion, Lee concluded that a drastic remedy was needed. Under his direction a staff member composed proposed legislation making all able-bodied white males between the ages of eighteen and forty-five subject to national conscription, meanwhile extending by two years all current enlistments. The bill was a radical rejection of local rights and a dramatic expansion of national power, yet when Lee showed it to the president, Davis approved. He had it molded into a bill to go before Congress, where it was all but eviscerated.[22] Lee also dealt with events beyond the Old Dominion, especially Johnston's efforts to build an army at Corinth. Lee watched events there carefully, empathizing with Johnston in the challenge he faced in bringing together an army to stop Grant. Still, Lee felt hopeful in late March. Johnston's forces were almost united, while Grant and Buell were many miles apart. He urged Johnston to strike Grant before Buell could join him. He must keep the enemy divided.[23] By April 7 Lee knew that Johnston had struck the day before and all looked promising. Then came news of another disaster at the hands of a man he only indistinctly recalled from Mexico.

_____

Grant had told Julia he thought Fort Donelson would fall on February 16, and so it did. There is every reason to believe that he meant his threat to advance immediately on Fort Donelson. The bluff worked as Buckner, himself dazed by the failure of the breakout attempt, felt irresolute enough to fear that Grant might back his threat. For his part, Grant needed that bluff. He had improvised the Fort Donelson operation almost on the spot after taking Fort Henry, though he probably always had such a contingency in mind. He had the means at hand, command of the Cumberland approach, and momentum after Henry's fall, but he had to move quickly before Halleck's feet got chilly. His conduct of the operation was hardly flawless, though his strategic concept, mirroring the action at Fort Henry and even Belmont, had the merit of simplicity and concentration of force. A reconnaissance report a month earlier warned that gunboats steaming upriver against the water batteries would be at a disadvantage, but Grant pushed it anyhow in spite of Foote's last-minute hesitance. A second miscalculation came when the Confederates made their breakout attack. Once more he focused too little on what the foe might do, so unconcerned that he was with Foote when the breakout struck. Grant's genius lay in his reaction to the unexpected.

Grant may have had more than just a halt to the immediate fighting in mind when he dismissed making terms or conditions. Back in October 1861 Polk wrote to him seeking an exchange of prisoners. Grant at first declined, arguing that he had no authority to approve an exchange, and referred the matter to Frémont, adding that "I recognize no Southern Confederacy myself."[24] Apparently headquarters approved, for in the weeks following the battle of Belmont exchanges took place.[25] Prisoners gave their parole not to fight again until officially exchanged for an equal number from the other side. To date, the largest surrender came the previous September at Lexington, Missouri, when Confederates captured about 3,000 Yankees and released them the next day. Buckner had every reason to expect the same terms, but to Grant that meant 12,000 or more rebels would go to Johnston in Bowling Green, and in a few weeks he could be fighting them again. If he sent them north to prison war camps being hastily erected, then even if eventually exchanged, they would be out of the war and his way much longer.

As Grant sent his prisoners north and cared for his casualties, the battle in his rear continued. Kountz expanded his campaign of libels, accusing Grant of entertaining a prostitute in his hotel room, gambling with government money, and being publicly drunk on several occasions, including one when he had to climb stairs on all fours. "He can do me no harm," Grant told Julia the very day of the surrender. "He is known as a venimous man and is without friends or influence."[26] A few days after Donelson's fall Grant's chief engineer, Lieutenant Colonel James B. McPherson, advised him that "you will not be troubled any more by *Kountz*," who finally resigned March 13 and for the time being ceased to be a problem.[27]

Kountz might be neutralized, but not Halleck. The very day that Grant invested Fort Donelson, Halleck wired Buell to ask if he would come take Grant's command himself, offering to shift Grant to the Tennessee River line to remove the difficulty of him being senior to Buell.[28] Two days later Halleck paved the way for that by assigning Grant to the newly designated "Military District of West Tennessee," an amorphous command roughly covering the territory between the Cumberland and the Mississippi Rivers. This would be what Halleck called the "center column" in a reorganization of his department, and he intended to assume the direction of that column himself, relegating Grant to chief subordinate. Grant's promotion to major general on February 19, to date from three days earlier and Donelson's surrender, presented no obstacle to Halleck, since he would still command by seniority. It would be the best of two worlds. Halleck could capitalize on any success Grant achieved as his own, while should Grant fail, Halleck could leave the blame with him.[29] Grant knew nothing of this, of course. When he learned of the promotion he notified Julia at once, and asked "is father afraid yet that I will not be able to sustain myself?" It was as close to "I told you so, Jesse" as he ever came.[30]

Halleck then struck on a theme he pursued for the next fortnight. He complained on February 16 to McClellan that he had received "no communication" from Grant for the past three days, even though in the same letter he included details that came from the very communications he claimed not to have received.[31] When Grant telegraphed word of Donelson's fall, Halleck sent no response. In fact, he never sent a word of congratulation, though in St. Louis Halleck was jubilant, declaring that Grant had performed very well indeed. Instead, on February 17 Halleck sent a telegram to Lincoln all but ordering the president to place him in overall command of the region "in return for Forts Henry and Donelson."[32] He spoke of how a bolder enemy "could have crushed me at Fort Donelson," and complimented a subordinate for keeping Confederates from reinforcing Floyd, or else "I should have failed before Fort Donelson." Halleck claimed credit for sending reinforcements that only reached Grant too late for the fight, and though he praised Smith's counterattack, he made no mention that it was Grant who ordered it.[33]

Entirely unaware of this, Grant moved up the Cumberland to take Clarksville, and proposed to take Nashville itself in less than ten days if Halleck wished.[34] The next day Halleck notified Washington, "have taken Clarksville," without saying who took it.[35] In the next few weeks Johnston evacuated his army from Bowling Green and withdrew be- low the Cumberland, abandoning Nashville, the first Confederate state capital to fall to the Union. Halleck was a flurry of activity, boasting that he would "split secession in twain" in a month.[36] Then McClellan asked him for a statement of troop strength throughout the depart- ment, and Halleck found the club to beat Grant, or so he thought. He complained that Grant sent him none.

Grant optimistically overestimated the effect of his victories and thought there would be "one hard battle more to fight," but that it ought to be "easy sailing" after that.[37] Perhaps that is why he picked up a dropped Confederate pistol from the field at Donelson, his only sou- venir of the battle. There might not be many more opportunities.[38] He wanted to move again quickly but no orders came.[39] "I do not know what work General Halleck intends me to do next," he told Sherman on February 25, but feared delay. He had the enemy off balance and wanted to keep them running.[40] "These terrible battles are very good things to read about for persons who loose no friends but I am decid- edly in favor of having as little of it as possible," he wrote Julia. "The way to avoid it is to push forward as vigorously as possible."[41] He went to Nashville briefly to see Buell, now occupying the city, but hoped for orders any moment.[42] "I want to remain in the field and be actively em- ployed," he wrote his wife, and avowed he would serve in any capacity so long as he could fight the rebellion.[43] He still regarded Halleck as "one of the greatest men of the age," but confessed on March 1 that he craved an independent command where he would not be under the thumb of another.[44]

That very day he received orders to move to Corinth, Mississippi, to disrupt Confederate rail lines. Two days later Halleck told McClellan he had heard nothing from Grant for more than a week, that he went to Nashville without permission, and that satisfied with his victory at Donelson, he "sits down and enjoys it without any regard to the future."[45] McClellan authorized Halleck to arrest him at once and give his army to Smith.[46] The next day Halleck ordered Grant to relinquish command and return to Fort Henry, demanding to know "why do you not obey my orders to report strength." Grant was stunned.[47] He protested that he communicated almost daily with Halleck's adjutant, whom he logically assumed passed the information on.[48] Halleck fired back that he repeatedly sent requests for reports, though none survive. Grant in fact had heard nothing from Halleck until March 1.

Meanwhile, Halleck cryptically told McClellan of a rumor that after Fort Donelson Grant had fallen back on "his former bad habits."[49] The coincidence of this with Kountz's accusations is suggestive, especially since Halleck himself released Kountz from arrest within days of telling McClellan.[50] Yet virtually all references to Grant drinking during his old army days emerged only after 1862 and his rise to celebrity. Nothing suggests he had such a reputation in the old army, yet Halleck's reference to "former bad habits" assumed that McClellan would know what he meant without being explicitly told. If Grant had such repute, Halleck could have heard of it, since he served on the Pacific Coast at the same time, but McClellan did not. Moreover, the rumor said the "bad habits" occurred *after* the fall of Fort Donelson, while Kountz's allegations—and a few others clearly derived from him—all related to supposed events in 1861.

Grant had been at Fort Donelson without interruption since its fall, except for two days going to Nashville and back, so unless Halleck twisted Kountz's allegations, any rumor had to come from there, but no evidence survives and Halleck never repeated the charge.

Grant received the order to hand over to Smith while his father was visiting him to borrow money, something of a reversal. Thus Jesse witnessed the fulfillment of his prophesy that 'Lys would not be able to sustain himself in command. Jesse's smug claims of prescience added sting to Halleck's barb. "I feel myself worse used by my own family than by strangers," Grant told Julia in that day's letter. "I do not think father, of his own accord, would do me injustice yet I believe he is influanced, and always may be, to my prejudice." Grant confessed his foul humor. He was to be left behind with a small garrison while one of his subordinates moved south. "It may be all right," he told her in his gloom, "but I dont now see it."[51] Not for the first time, Grant's health reflected his spirits. He retained a bad head cold going back almost to the beginning of February, and by early March it had settled into his chest, probably a bronchitis to which he was prone most of his life. He also suffered severe and long-lasting headaches, and one appeared in early March. Only by willpower did he perform any duties.[52]

Two days later Grant asked to be relieved of duty and reassigned somewhere outside Halleck's department.[53] While waiting for action on his request, he sent telegrams or letters to Halleck once and often twice a day, making certain he would not be accused again of failing to communicate. Beyond his view, much had happened in the past three weeks. The twin victories electrified a Northern press and public hungry for good news. The first reports appeared in the papers on February 17, and a day later Grant's name was prominently in the headlines. Then the ball really began rolling with publication of his "unconditional surrender" response.[54] Soon a rumor appeared that Grant had cornered Johnston's retiring army at Murfreesboro, Tennessee, and once again he demanded unconditional surrender.[55] Headlines hailed Donelson as "the Great Victory of the War." Meanwhile, fleeting press suggestions accused McClellan, Halleck, and Buell of stealing credit for Grant's victories, hitting print on the same day that news leaked that Halleck might replace Grant for unspecified "bad conduct at Fort Donelson and elsewhere."[56]

None of that suited Halleck's purpose, and the men and officers of the Fort Donelson army made their displeasure known both in memorials to him and in quoted conversations with reporters.[57] Meanwhile, Confederates evacuated Columbus, Halleck's other subordinates won a victory at Pea Ridge, Arkansas, on March 8, which forced Confederates out of Missouri, and John Pope was even then moving against the next Mississippi bastions at New Madrid and Island Number 10. Thanks to Grant the Confederates gave up Kentucky, evacuated Nashville, and by March 10 were virtually out of the western half of Tennessee except for Memphis and a few fortified bluffs on the east bank of the Mississippi. Then Halleck suddenly lost interest in continuing his campaign against Grant. It was better, perhaps, to have Grant where he could keep an eye on him. Should he win more victories, some of the luster would still go to Halleck. If Grant lost, he could also shoulder the blame. On March 10 Halleck tersely informed Grant that reinforcements would be coming for the army on the Tennessee River, and that he should assume command again.[58] Notifying Smith of Halleck's change of mind, Grant confided that "I think it exceedingly doubtful whether I shall accept," and if he did it would not be before Smith had an opportunity to successfully complete the mission himself.[59] One way or the other, he did not expect to be at Fort Henry much longer.[60] However, by the end of the day when he wrote to Julia he had changed his mind and told her he would take the command. "Your husband will never disgrace you," he told her. "We all volunteered to be killed, if needs be," and all personal feelings ought to be shunted aside.[61] "We have such an inside track of the enemy that by following up our success we can go anywhere."[62]

Unfortunately, just two days after his decision to resume command, he received a delayed threat of dismissal from Halleck that reinforced Grant's conviction that his reputation and usefulness there were compromised. "There is such a disposition to find fault with me," he responded on March 13, "that I again ask to be relieved from further duty until I can be placed right in the estimation of those higher in authority."[63] Halleck replied that all was now well. "The power is in your hands; use it, & you will be sustained by all," he wired. Grant should take command of his army "& lead it on to new victories."[64] On March 14 Grant relented. For a change the timing was propitious. Two days before he landed the army at Savannah, on the east bank of the Tennessee about fifteen miles above the Mississippi border, Smith sustained an apparently minor leg injury that became infected and soon made it impossible for him to exercise command. Grant had to take over, and late on March 15 he was ready, set to leave the next day. "What you may look for is hard to say," he wrote Julia before he left. There might be a big fight, but "I have already been in so many that it begins to feel like home to me."[65]

Grant reached Savannah on March 17, and one of the first things to meet him was a report from a scout that enemy forces south of the river between Corinth and the Alabama line numbered 150,000, perhaps one-third of them at Corinth under Johnston's direct command. He dismissed the figures as exaggerated, but Halleck did not. Indeed, just the day before Halleck had enjoined Grant to "strictly obey" his orders not to bring on a general battle. Ordering Buell to bring a substantial reinforcement to converge with Grant's, Halleck directed that "we must strike no blow until we are strong enough to admit no doubt of the result."[66] Unlike Grant, Halleck wanted victory without risk, a policy that surrendered all the advantage of time to the enemy.

Grant planned to move the command down the west bank to Pittsburg Landing. From there Smith had intended to send an expedition to a point just east of the Confederate concentration at Corinth, some twenty miles south, then cut the town's rail lines and isolate Johnston from reinforcement and supply from every source except New Orleans and western Mississippi.[67] He found divisions under Sherman and Hurlbut already at Pittsburg Landing, with Lew Wallace's division at Crump's Landing six miles north, and McClernand's and Smith's divisions at Savannah. He sent all but McClernand forward to Pittsburg Landing. Within twenty-four hours he concluded that Johnston really numbered about 40,000, half at Corinth, an estimate that proved remarkably accurate.[68] On Grant's first full day at Savannah it was three in the morning before he had a moment to write to Julia telling her his next battle "will be a big lick so far as numbers engaged is concerned," and he felt entirely confident of success. He also found that the headache of the last few weeks was all but gone. Responsibility and activity were a tonic to his system.[69]

Over the next fortnight he addressed almost every facet of army organization just as he had when training the 21st Illinois. Grant the quartermaster reappeared, enforcing system and order on the disbursement of rations and equipment, and emphasizing that any property taken from the enemy belonged to the government and not to the men who took it. Interestingly, given his own behavior at Monterey, he directed that supply officers were "on no account" to leave their duties to go into the fight during battle.[70] He visited Sherman at Pittsburg Landing on March 19 to get the latest reports on Confederates at Corinth. At first he intended to lead Sherman's division in person to cut Corinth's communications, suggesting a subtle interpretation of Halleck's order not to engage the foe. "If a battle on anything like equal terms seems to be inevitable," he wrote, he would not retreat and risk demoralization, but move against another point so his men would feel they had fulfilled their objective. Implicit was that if he saw a chance to strike at favorable odds, he might take it, a subtle distinction that Halleck missed.[71]

Within twenty-four hours Grant got reports of more than 250 boxcars loaded with reinforcements arriving in Corinth. There was no

Jesse Root Grant, the father who both belittled his son and boasted of his future. *Library of Congress*

Standing at left is Brevet Second Lieutenant Ulysses S. Grant, in 1845 in Louisiana. Standing at right is Lieutenant Alexander Hays. *Library of Congress*

The cabin Grant built on his ill-starred "Hardscrabble" farm outside St. Louis.
Library of Congress

Brigadier General U. S. Grant
in October 1861 at Cairo,
Illinois. The gloves and sword
would be seldom seen in the
war, and the spadelike beard
was soon trimmed.
Library of Congress

Julia Dent Grant almost always posed with her left side to the camera, to hide the strabismus that caused her right eye to wander. Though it was operable, Grant preferred her just as she was. An early postwar image. *Library of Congress*

Grant's patron Congressman Elihu B. Washburne of Galena, in 1859. He was Grant's staunchest friend and supporter. *Library of Congress*

Brigadier General John A. Rawlins, standing at left, stood by Grant (center) throughout the war as guardian of his reputation and conscience, and was a brilliant staff officer. *Library of Congress*

Major General Henry W. Halleck went from jealous rival undermining Grant in 1862 to staunch supporter and friend by war's end. *Library of Congress*

Major General Grant at age forty sometime in 1862–1863. The calm eyes have seen Fort Donelson and Shiloh, and look to Chattanooga and beyond. *Library of Congress*

President Abraham Lincoln went from a slightly wary ally to an indomitable supporter of Grant, whom he made lieutenant general just one month after this February 9, 1864 portrait. *Library of Congress*

Elements of the Army of the Potomac crossing a pontoon bridge at Germanna Ford, May 4, 1864, for the inevitable meeting between Grant and Lee. *Library of Congress*

On May 21, 1864, two days after Spotsylvania, soldiers pulled pews out of Massaponax Church for Grant and his officers to confer. Grant sits cross-legged directly beneath the two trees, a bulldog look on his face, cigar in mouth. *Library of Congress*

ABOVE: The Massaponax conversation continues, messages coming in and going out. Grant is writing an order in a book while holding the ever-present cigar in his left hand. BELOW: Grant stands behind the pew at left, looking over General Meade's shoulder at a map while an aide reports.
Library of Congress

The iconic portrait of Grant, taken at City Point in August 1864. He is calm, businesslike, determined. *Library of Congress*

Grant, Julia, and their youngest son, Jesse, at his winter headquarters at City Point, Virginia, winter 1864–1865. *Library of Congress*

Major General William Tecumseh Sherman, Grant's closest friend in the high command, and his most trusted lieutenant. *Library of Congress*

Grant and some of his staff at City Point, winter 1864–1865. Rawlins stands immediately left of Grant. Colonel Ely Parker stands third from the right. *Library of Congress*

The home of Wilmer McLean at Appomattox Court House, April 1865, just days after Grant and Lee met in the front parlor to begin the end. *Library of Congress*

Lieutenant General Grant in May 1865, still wearing a black crepe band on his left arm in mourning for slain President Lincoln. *Library of Congress*

The dignitaries' viewing stand on Washington's Pennsylvania Avenue, for the Grand Review of the victorious Union armies, May 23–24, 1865. Grant is barely visible in the corner beneath the large star on the left. *Library of Congress*

General-in-Chief Grant visiting Fort Sanders, Wyoming, in late July 1868, during a trip to inspect progress on the transcontinental railroad. Grant stands beneath the pillar on the left; Sherman, in a dark suit, stands in profile in the center. *Library of Congress*

Grant's first inauguration as president of the United States, March 4, 1869. *Library of Congress*

President Ulysses S. Grant. *Library of Congress*

The dying Grant writing his memoirs on the porch at his Mt. McGregor house, June 27, 1885. *Library of Congress*

Grant at Mt. McGregor on July 19, 1885. Three days earlier he won his last battle when he finished his memoirs. Four days after this photo was made he was dead. *Library of Congress*

Grant's mausoleum shortly after its completion. There he would rest eternally with only his beloved Julia beside him. *Library of Congress*

chance of taking the town now without a battle, so he determined to wait for Halleck to send further instructions, telling Smith that he feared the Confederates were growing in strength as fast as Grant's own command, the price of Halleck's delay. "The sooner we attack," he said on March 23, "the easier will be the task."[72] That same evening he wrote Julia that "I want to whip these rebels once more in a big fight."[73]

Grant left the disposition of the troops at Pittsburg Landing to Sherman, who placed his own division in advance astride the Corinth road near Shiloh Church, and McClernand's division when it arrived several hundred yards to the rear on either side of the road. Hurlbut and Smith spread in a wide semicircle around the landing touching the river at both ends, and Wallace remained six miles downstream at Crump's Landing on another road to Corinth. Thus in a move against Corinth, Wallace and the main column could march simultaneously to converge a few miles above the Confederate position.[74] Grant expected that by March 27 Buell and up to 30,000 ought to be ninety miles distant, and thanks to soggy roads and destroyed bridges, at least a week from joining him. As the end of the month approached he confessed to Julia that he did not know when he might move the army. "A big fight may be looked for someplace before a great while," he told her. "You need not fear but what I will come out triumphantly."

Grant could have been ill at ease over his high command. Smith's health continued to deteriorate, and late in the month Grant had to replace him with W. H. L. Wallace, a brigadier for all of one day before he replaced Smith. Sherman's was the only one of the six divisions commanded by a West Pointer, and he at least had battlefield experience as a brigade commander at Manassas. Moreover, though the two were not yet close friends, they had known each other for some years before the war.[75] McClernand, the only one with combat experience in division command, was a politician and a growing irritant. Lew Wallace was a lawyer and small-time politician who scarcely concealed his disdain for Grant, while Hurlbut was a politician and a genuine inebriate. The commander of the new 6th Division was the same haughty Benjamin Prentiss Grant once arrested for insubordination.[76] Grant could see them pulling wires for self-advancement, particularly McClernand, but he refused to play the game. "I have no future ambition," he said.

He just wanted to end the war. If others wanted to scramble for credit, they were welcome to it.[77]

On March 31 Grant shifted his headquarters to Pittsburg Landing and learned that the head of Buell's column was still probably sixty miles distant, due to arrive by Sunday or Monday April 6–7.[78] They should have more than 70,000 when combined and Grant hoped Halleck would then let him move on Corinth.[79] So anxious was he that yet again he neglected to consider what the enemy might do first. After the fall of Fort Donelson Johnston achieved a brilliant concentration of troops from all across the Confederacy at Corinth, Mississippi, including regiments sent by Lee from the Atlantic coast. He intended to drive Grant all the way to the Ohio if possible. On April 1 Johnston ordered his corps on the alert to be ready to march within twenty-four hours.

Visiting Pittsburg Landing every day, Grant heard occasional firing in the direction of Corinth as his outposts encountered enemy cavalry patrols, then on April 1 Lew Wallace briefly skirmished with rebel infantry a few miles south of Crump's Landing. Infantry meant more than just patrols. Grant misread it as an attempt to cut communications between Savannah and Pittsburg Landing or else concentrate against Wallace, while diverting his attention by skirmishing with his main line at Pittsburg Landing.[80] Sherman dismissed virtually all such sightings as panicked exaggeration by inexperienced volunteers. Two days later when the first of Buell's divisions approached Savannah, Grant confidently wrote Buell that "all difficulties in our neighborhood will be remedied before your arrival."[81] There was no threat to his army. He reinforced Lew Wallace on April 4, and alerted W. H. L. Wallace to join him should he be attacked, though Grant told Sherman "I look for nothing of the kind." Still, he told Sherman to be vigilant for enemy movement in the direction of Crump's Landing.[82] The next day Grant inspected Sherman's lines, and felt no alarm over occasional skirmishing barely three miles in their front. Returning to Savannah he found a message from Buell that he expected to arrive the next day with one and perhaps two divisions, though he still had twenty-eight miles to march.[83]

Meanwhile, Grant reorganized the army to keep pace with its growth. He shifted cavalry and artillery units out of infantry brigades and reassigned them to divisional control, and put newly promoted brigadiers at the head of brigades.[84] Thus some of his nineteen brigade leaders had new and unfamiliar commands, and all of his division commanders had to manage cavalry and artillery as well as infantry. In reviewing the army he found it in good shape, despite a few units still in gray militia uniforms that might cause confusion in action.[85] They were all sensible actions to cope with the army's growth, but not changes to make on the eve of battle, more indication that Grant expected no offensive by Johnston. Buell was on his doorstep, and in a day or two his combined force should top 75,000. There was no confirmed intelligence of *major* enemy forces in his front, and thus no reason to fear that he was not master of the situation.

Grant was tired. "It would be a great relief not to have to think for a short time," he wrote Julia on April 3.[86] The next day his horse took a fall, badly spraining Grant's ankle and putting him on crutches for the next several days. But he did not let up. He hoped Halleck would let him move on Corinth soon. "When I do there will probably be the greatest battle fought of the War," he told Julia. Concerned for the inevitable casualties, he had no doubt of the result, feeling "as unconcerned about it as if nothing more than a review was to take place."[87]

Grant did alert subordinates on April 4 of what to do in case of an alarm, but neither he nor his division commanders had their men prepare even light defenses. Smith had said digging demoralized volunteers bent on taking the war to the enemy. Grant greatly respected his old mentor's views, and himself saw how digging earthworks impacted morale around Cairo. His time at Pittsburg Landing was better spent organizing and training this new army. That evening when Grant went to the scene of skirmishing a couple of miles to Sherman's front, he learned that infantry and artillery were with the enemy cavalry. That should have concerned both generals, but Sherman told him "I do not apprehend anything like an attack on our position." The next day Sherman sent more detail on the skirmish, adding that the enemy was "in some considerable force" barely four miles southwest of his camps. That ought to have commanded Grant's attention, for it was the first time that Sherman credited any information on enemy movements. Reports now suggested that the foe had grown to 60,000–80,000, but Grant cautioned that the information was not from reliable sources.

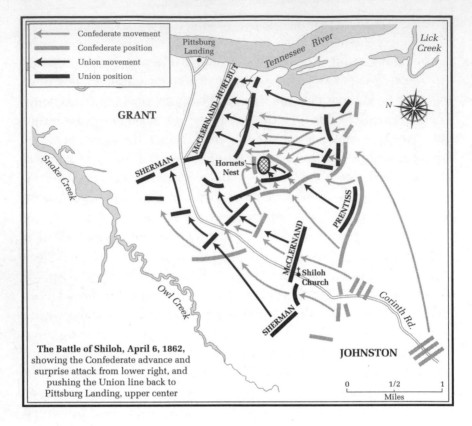

The Battle of Shiloh, April 6, 1862, showing the Confederate advance and surprise attack from lower right, and pushing the Union line back to Pittsburg Landing, upper center

His confidence only grew when Brigadier General William Nelson's division marched into Savannah and confirmed that Buell's other divisions would arrive on April 6 and 7. Grant wrote Halleck that "I have scarsely the faintest idea of an attack [general one], being made upon us but will be prepared should such a thing take place."[88] His strength now would at least equal Johnston's, and his men were better trained, armed, equipped, and motivated. For weeks deserters had given deliberately false reports of demoralization in Confederate ranks supposedly composed of men virtually forced into uniform, and Grant hardly expected such an army to perform well. Thus when he met Nelson, an old schoolmate from the Maysville Academy, Grant told him "there will be no fight at Pittsburg Landing; we will have to go to Corinth."[89]

He spent the night at Savannah. The next morning, April 6, Grant read his mail and then began breakfast shortly after seven o'clock when he heard something. Stepping onto a porch he recognized the sound of distant artillery. Cannon meant more than a skirmish. Immediately he walked with his staff to his headquarters boat *Tigress* and ordered her to get up steam, and meanwhile began rushing all available support to Pittsburg Landing. He ordered Nelson to march downstream opposite the landing, where transports would ferry him across, sent an order to Buell's other divisions to hurry to Savannah where transports would take them to the landing, and notified Buell that Sherman and probably McClernand were under attack. "I have been looking for this," he wrote, though he had not expected it for another day or two.[90] That hardly fit with what he told Nelson and Halleck just the day before. Yet again, as at Belmont and Fort Donelson, Grant had been surprised. He was human enough not to admit it. He never did.

As *Tigress* passed Crump's Landing, Grant yelled to Lew Wallace to be ready to march at his order, then in his cabin changed into full uniform, with sword, sidearm, and sash, rather than his usual simple blouse with insignia of rank. He judged that the more he looked like a general, the more confidence it would give his men. Around nine o'clock he reached the landing. As his horse was being brought off the boat he saw 2,000 or more wounded and demoralized men huddled below the bluff.[91] He mounted, tied his crutch to the saddle, and rode up to the plateau where officers informed him of the situation. The enemy had attacked in great strength and forced the Federals back some distance before Sherman got them in hand, and still he was being driven onto McClernand, while on the left Prentiss had been pressed back more than a mile.

The situation was not irretrievable if Grant kept his head. He organized a few regiments into line, set officers to reforming the panic-stricken, and placed artillery around the landing, expecting that if Johnston got that far, he would be himself so exhausted that this reserve might delay him until Nelson's division arrived that afternoon. Grant sent orders for Buell's other divisions to follow Nelson. He knew it would take them hours to arrive, by which time his command would be even more battered, but so would the enemy, whose numbers he now gauged at 100,000 or more. "The appearance of fresh troops on the field now would have a powerful effect both by inspiring our men and disheartening the enemy," he said. In his only acknowledgment of the seriousness of the situation, Grant added that they could "possibly save the day to us."[92] He also sent an officer to Lew Wallace to get his division moving at once down the river to come into line where Grant believed Sherman's right flank to be. Just getting those extra troops moving boosted confidence, and when he sent another order to Nelson to hurry he said nothing more about saving the day, but gave assurance that "all looks well."[93] After barely half an hour, Grant was in command of himself, and taking command of the defense.

He met with Sherman about ten o'clock, finding his line well in hand, then rode on to McClernand, whose division was hard pressed. Grant called up the regiments he left behind as reserve, while personally directing one of McClernand's units to advance, and continued riding on to see his other division commanders.[94] For the next hour or more he was constantly on the contracting lines. After eleven o'clock Grant grew anxious about Lew Wallace, who ought to have arrived by then, and sent a rider to find him, then rode to Prentiss's position. He found Prentiss and perhaps 1,200 men using the cover of a wood and a sunken road to repel Confederate assaults. If the enemy pushed through they might reach Pittsburg Landing, and if they forced Grant away from that base, his army would be cut off from Savannah and all but trapped with its back against the river. Grant ordered Prentiss to hold at all costs.[95]

He did, until about five-thirty, while Grant looked for Lew Wallace and Nelson. Nelson inexplicably dallied at Savannah and did not leave until one-thirty, while Lew Wallace took a wrong road and lost hours getting on the right one. Buell meanwhile showed no haste getting to a field where his command would be absorbed into Grant's.[96] Finally as Sherman, McClernand, Wallace, and Hurlbut began to give way about four o'clock, Grant saw Nelson's column approaching the opposite river bank. He had spent much of the afternoon forming a final line to hold the landing, so Nelson's arrival could not have been better timed. When Confederates finally surrounded Prentiss and he surrendered his position, soon dubbed the "Hornets' Nest," Grant had his battered divisions drawn up in a line extending three miles along the road to the landing, to protect his communications and keep the landing open for Buell's reinforcements and Lew Wallace's division when it arrived. When Nelson's first brigade crossed over Grant found it led by the older brother of his childhood friend Daniel Ammen, and personally placed it in the line.[97] Now fate reinforced the Federals, for Johnston fell mortally wounded sometime earlier, and the resulting lull in the action gave Grant invaluable time. When the Confederates' second in command Beauregard took over and launched another assault, the disorganized rebels were too few and too tired to be effective. Beauregard called off the fight for the night, thinking he had a victory. Even before that, Grant personally told each of his division commanders to be prepared to attack in the morning, though he gave few details. They had been stunned but so had the enemy. The army that remained resolute and struck first would win the field.[98]

He spent the night looking to his lines, reforming disrupted units, plugging Nelson's brigades into line as they crossed the river, and Lew Wallace's when they appeared shortly after seven o'clock. Soon the second of Buell's divisions began to arrive, and then the third. Grant pushed his line out to gain breathing space for the landing, and that evening officers found him confident, anxious to take advantage of his reinforcements and the enemy's condition. With his dispositions made, well after midnight he tried to get some sleep under a tree, but the heavy rain and the pain in his ankle kept him awake most of the night.[99]

The next day Grant had it all his own way as he expected. His army formed the right half of his line and Buell's the left. Halleck had made it plain to Buell that Grant, as senior, was to command, but Buell tried to act as if independent of Grant's orders. Sensitive as always to the awkwardness of such a situation, Grant did not assert his prerogative, but simply asked Buell to make an attack simultaneous with his own, just as in the days ahead his communications with Buell all came in terms of requests and suggestions.[100] Between eight and ten that morning both commands advanced and shortly after noon regained all the ground lost the day before. Late that afternoon Grant himself assembled fragments of regiments into a line and led them in a charge to dislodge one of the last enemy footholds.[101] By four o'clock the Confederates were in full retreat toward Corinth. Realizing that the foe could still sting, Grant determined not to continue the pursuit.

Soon satisfied that the enemy were concentrating back in Corinth and that his own position was secure, Grant hinted to Halleck on April 9 that this was the time to press on, unwilling to stop at one victory if a wounded foe could be struck again, perhaps decisively. He needed fresh troops, but believed the rebels could not make a strong resistance for two or three weeks.[102] Halleck's answer was to come to Pittsburg Landing two days later to assume command of both armies. This could be his time to lead an army and claim victory for himself.

Grant was always at his most frank with Julia. The day after the battle he told her he believed there had been no battle on the continent to match Pittsburg Landing—or "Shiloh" as some were calling it—and he was right. He believed the number killed and wounded on both sides could total 20,000, a fair estimate since the real number was close to 24,000.[103] His own were 13,000, virtually one-fourth of those engaged. Again his performance had been mixed. His calm demeanor gave courage to some of his dispirited soldiers on April 6. Knowing that, he consciously put himself at risk, especially in leading a charge on April 7. He let division commanders do their jobs and only managed in detail in isolated instances. His verbal orders to Lew Wallace, repeated through intermediary officers, became muddied, but his written orders were clear and concise, communicating what he meant as economically as possible.

Grant was not ready for the ferocity of the Confederate assault when it came. Twice now he had been taken off guard by enemy attacks. His measure hereafter would be settled if it happened again. Yet his response had been instant, positive, and decisive. He read the situation and went from reaction to stabilization, then consolidation of resources, reinforcement, and finally counterstroke, and accurately read the effects on the enemy of their own success. Thus far no other commander in the war had done that even once, let alone twice. The cost was heavy, but the gains dramatic. Johnston was dead, the cautious Beauregard commanded the Confederates, and the initiative was Halleck's to seize. "I am looking for a speedy move, one more fight," he told Julia, "and then easy sailing to the close of the war."[104]

Lee could well fear the same thing in the aftermath of Shiloh. "If Mississippi Valley is lost Atlantic States will be ruined," he telegraphed Pemberton on April 10 when the scale of the disaster began to be known in Richmond, and in his customary passive style asked Pemberton to send regiments to Beauregard "if possible."[105] President Davis gave Lee a free hand in dealing with his old department and he used it, relieving the troublesome Ripley of command and addressing the poor discipline reported in the Charleston garrisons. Frankly he told Governor Pickens to "let it be distinctly understood by every body, that Charleston and Savannah are to be defended to the last extremity." Should the Yankee gunboats enter their harbors, then "the cities are to be fought street by street and house by house as long as we have a foot of ground to stand upon."[106] Shiloh stamped urgency on all theaters of the conflict.

Lee had less patience with the living General Johnston, and adopted an almost peremptory tone on May 18 when he forwarded Davis's request for him to come confer on his immediate plans. The meeting produced nothing, and when three days later Lee conveyed Davis's renewed request for some statement of "the programme of operations which you propose," Lee suggested that Johnston do so in person. That would defeat any excuse of having no time to write, and allow Davis to respond immediately. To avoid a meeting, Johnston finally reported that he had 53,600 men in four divisions commanded by Major Generals G. W. Smith, James Longstreet, Magruder, and Daniel H. Hill, and cavalry under Brigadier General James E. B. Stuart.[107] As to his plans he remained mute, and Lee discovered yet again that he lacked a facility for managing difficult subordinates. To be fair, no one had ever managed Johnston. Nor would Lee have gotten further by opting for peremptory orders by raw authority, for Johnston never accepted that Lee was rightfully his senior. If anything, Lee's position as an intermediary only weakened him. The fact that the two Virginians had known each other since West Point counted for nothing, and Lee's distaste for Johnston's history of politicking for rank may have shown when they met, though he generally concealed all such feeling behind an iron mask. Lee had found a solution of sorts for difficult officers when he transferred Ripley, admittedly an indirect and incomplete remedy, for it merely shifted his ache to another head, but it was Lee's way of coping. Distance allowed him to remove conflicts he could not resolve.

He could hardly remove Johnston. He joined Davis on his almost daily rides to the Chickahominy line to see what Johnston refused to tell them. One day they found the right wing of the army pulled back from the river virtually into the environs of the city, and one corps of the enemy actually south of the river astride the Richmond & York River Railroad with a direct avenue to the capital. Davis may have threatened on the spot to replace Johnston, and asked Lee to join a cabinet meeting afterward to offer his advice. In words likely echoing his admonition to Pickens, Lee emphatically declared that they must not yield the capital. But then Lee did something Johnston would never do, a small gesture, perhaps unconscious or perhaps cunningly calculated, that helped to cement his working relationship with the president. He knew the pressure on Davis, and shared the frustration with Johnston. That bound them perhaps more than their daily meetings. Lee asked Davis what *he* thought they should do. He had read the man.

Davis agreed that Richmond must be held and that McClellan should be stopped before he crossed the Chickahominy where he could besiege Richmond. Lee's views matched the president's. He proposed that he make one more personal effort to glean what, if anything, Johnston proposed to do to defend the capital.[108] When the two generals met, Johnston told him he had set Thursday May 29 to attack McClellan's right flank, hoping to drive it back while more of his army crossed the river and hit the enemy center. Successful assaults should force the Yankees to pull back from Richmond, but beyond that Johnston offered no contingent plan to follow up on success. Then Thursday came and went with nothing more than skirmishing.[109] Johnston rescheduled his attack for May 31 and Lee came to the field early that afternoon when he heard firing break out in the direction of a crossroads known as Seven Pines. He met with Johnston briefly, and then Davis arrived and they both rode to the scene to find Confederates had driven the Yankees a mile toward the river, where the fighting was still brisk. Then late in the afternoon a messenger informed them that Johnston had been severely wounded, and the confused and ill-coordinated attack was sputtering.

The Confederacy's two major army commanders, both named Johnston, were out of action in just eight weeks. That left G. W. Smith the senior major general. Lee and Davis informed Smith that evening that he must assume command, but then the army's division commanders said they doubted they could hold a line north of the James, which meant giving up Richmond. Lee rarely played the wit, nor was he especially humorous even in easy times, but from young manhood he had the gift of what Davis's aide William Preston Johnston called "a quaint or slightly caustic remark." He could not restrain one now, replying sharply that pursuing their line of thought to its logical conclusion, the generals would just keep falling back "until they hit the Gulf of Mexico."[110] When he rode back to Richmond with Davis that night, neither felt easy over Smith's capacity.[111]

Lee arose early the next morning, if he slept at all, and before dawn read a note from Smith saying that he intended to renew the attack. "Your movements are judicious and determination to strike the enemy right," Lee answered at five that morning.[112] He was not up long before another note arrived, this one from Davis. Johnston's wounding forced the president to "interfere temporarily" with Lee's duties. He ordered him to assume field command in eastern Virginia and North Carolina, including the army on the Chickahominy.[113] Spending the morning forwarding more units to the front, where Smith had renewed the attack without success, Lee rode to the field and at about two o'clock reached Smith's headquarters. He found Davis already there, having just announced that Lee was assuming command.[114]

"I wish his mantle had fallen on an abler man," Lee wrote less than forty-eight hours later.[115] Lee always assumed that modest, almost diffident, posture, yet it is hard to square that with his frequent expressions of frustration over the peripheral nature of his commands in western Virginia and Georgia. In April 1861 he began building the nucleus of this army, and he as much as anyone could claim paternity. For almost three months he had struggled to see it fully equipped and manned, and strove to get it into action. Ever mindful of forces elsewhere in the Confederacy, he knew this one best. Friends and family peppered its ranks. Its generals had been his comrades in the old army, and younger officers still remembered him as the "marble model" of their Academy days. If Lee wanted only one command in the Confederacy, it was this. He never said so, but surely he believed he could do more with it than Johnston.

Lee brought with him a special order assuming command, exhorting the ranks to steel their resolve to win. He addressed it to the "Army of Northern Virginia," an unofficial appellation he had used occasionally.[116] The next day he gathered his generals and was disappointed to hear many say they should retreat before McClellan's advance. Once again Lee asked Davis what he suggested they do, but the president left the decision to him. The speed with which Lee then took charge and proposed a strategy suggests that, like Grant, he had devoted much thought to what he would do if given the chance.[117] On June 5 he outlined his plan. He proposed supporting Jackson's suggestion to "change the character of the war" by reinforcing and sending him across the Potomac into Maryland, even Pennsylvania, to create such panic that the Yankees would recall forces to protect Washington. Meanwhile, Lee read McClellan's treaclelike advance as evidence that he wanted to avoid battle and batter Richmond to submission by siege. Lee intended to counter that by having his own engineers create a defensive line to be held by a part of his army, while he kept the rest mobile to lure the Federals into the open where he could strike. Drive McClellan away from his Richmond & York Railroad supply line, and he could force him back to Fort Monroe. In the next four weeks that is precisely what he did.

First Lee had to overcome his reputation. When McClellan retreated from his front without Lee trying to stop him, some of his officers heard echoes of western Virginia and South Carolina, one Carolinian declaring that it "must forever stamp upon him the reward of an ignoble mediocrity."[118] When he set his soldiers to work digging on the current line and another to the rear should the army have to retreat, many remembered the great entrencher of Carolina, "Granny" Lee, the "King of Spades," "Old-stick-in-the-mud," as one diarist called him.[119] There was resistance and he protested to Davis that "our people are opposed to work." He warned against a spirit that ridiculed labor to preserve lives in earthworks, while extolling the inevitably higher cost of open field fighting. There would be enough of that, but better that it should come when he needed to take the risk. Moreover, thousands of his men were new recruits in regiments raised that spring, while the army as a whole had not yet fought a major engagement, and the performance of some division and brigade commanders at Seven Pines had been tentative, confused, and largely ineffective. Defenses, especially against McClellan's sloth, would buy Lee time to mark the good leaders, remove the bad, train the men, and then use them to best advantage. Fortunately, McClellan gave Lee ample time.

By late June he had four corps below the Chickahominy, and only one above the river and extending northwest to Mechanicsville.

As his army dug and drilled, Lee left the stage to Jackson. They scaled down his plan of operations and set him to further disrupting Federals in the Shenandoah. Jackson "is a good soldier," Lee told the new secretary of war George W. Randolph, "I expect him to do it," and so he did.[120] On June 8 and 9 Stonewall won stunning victories that cleared the Shenandoah of Federals, leaving him free to join Lee should he wish, and that is precisely what Lee wanted. Then Lee made a show of reinforcing Jackson, believing correctly that McClellan would conclude that Stonewall was to cross the Potomac rather than swoop down on his right flank above the Chickahominy.[121] Lee was perhaps ungrateful in fooling Little Mac, for on June 10 the Union general politely sent Mary Lee under escort through the lines. As her husband predicted, the Federal advance caught her, but contrary to his fears, the Yankees did not molest her, posting a guard for her protection.[122] Lee had sent a message to McClellan asking him to allow her to pass, and Little Mac agreed after cordially receiving Mary at his headquarters.[123]

Before he was ready for that, Lee reorganized his army. Instead of Johnston's two "wings" of two divisions each, plus a reserve, Lee produced six distinct divisions commanded by Major Generals A. P. Hill, Longstreet, Benjamin Huger, W. H. C. Whiting, Magruder, and Theophilus H. Holmes. In the offing he dissolved Smith's division, which left Smith without a command, Lee's way of removing him from his army.[124] Nearly 20 percent of the infantry units found themselves in new brigades or divisions. Reinforcements came from both Carolinas, and by late June there were regiments from every state in the Confederacy as well as Maryland and Kentucky. The Army of Northern Virginia had become a national army.

By June 10 Lee planned for Jackson to come from the Shenandoah and sweep down the north bank of the Chickahominy to cut McClellan's communications, while Lee kept him busy by attacking his main line. At the same time Stuart and the army's cavalry were to ride around the Federal army, further disrupting communications and spreading as much pandemonium as possible. Lee's army now totaled something over 92,000 men, the largest he would ever command, and he expected to use every bit of it. Davis approved the plan, and on

June 13 Lee set in motion Jackson's shift to the east. "The sooner you unite with this army the better," Lee told him.[125] Stuart performed his part brilliantly, boosting morale in the army at large. Believing Jackson to be on his way, Lee now framed his final plan of attack, and not just to drive McClellan back from Richmond, but all the way into Hampton Roads itself. In one of many similarities to Grant's thinking, Lee wanted more than immediate results. Every action must have contingent alternatives, and always he hoped that a crushing blow might dampen or even extinguish the North's willingness to continue the fight. He recognized the Union's vastly greater resources, but that would not matter if they defeated the Yankees' will to continue.

The magnitude of what Lee faced was greater than posterity has acknowledged. This would be his first battle of any kind under his hand, and his first action in nearly fifteen years. He would command the second-largest army ever fielded in the American hemisphere to date, only marginally smaller than the army it faced. Its organization was as new as its name, most of its soldiers and their officers not yet veterans. Lee's was a good and ancient name in Virginia, but thus far redolent only of failure in the western counties and tons of shifted earth on the southern coast. He had to prove himself to everyone. Still, he had advantages. This was home ground for many of his men, and not altogether unfamiliar to him, giving him the benefit of knowing the terrain. McClellan's supply line was many times longer than Lee's and vulnerable, as Stuart demonstrated. And at least a part of his army already had a tradition of victory, thanks to Big Bethel and Manassas and some action on the peninsula. Lee also had luck, for like Grant at Fort Donelson and the second day at Shiloh, he was fortunate in his opponent. He knew McClellan from Mexico, but their paths rarely crossed after the war. Lee watched "Little Mac" spend months throwing away time awaiting heavy artillery rather than use his strength in combat. He need expect no surprises. For Lee, McClellan was an open book, if dull reading.

On the afternoon of June 23 Lee convened Longstreet, the two Hills, and Jackson, who had ridden ahead of his command, and put the situation before them. It was time to strike McClellan before he laid siege to Richmond. These four Confederate division commanders were to concentrate against that lone Yankee corps north of the Chickahominy and drive it back down the peninsula, while Lee occupied the other

Yankee corps south of the river. That would concentrate 65,000 Confederates against perhaps 30,000 north of the river, which ought to be enough to shatter the Federals. The risk was that Lee with only 25,000 below the stream could hold McClellan with 60,000. Lee left them to work out details while he attended to other business, then returned to find them in agreement that, Jackson's command having the greatest distance to march, the time for the attack ought to be set for when he believed he could arrive, and he proposed dawn on June 26.[126] Lee agreed, though it was a managerial departure for him that involved some risk. Life had taught him that if something was to be done well he needed to do it himself, yet he left this crucial decision for his first battle to the judgment of these subordinates. All of them had more combat command experience than he, and the Cheat Mountain fiasco may have taught him that it was better for generals on the scene to set tactical details rather than a single more remote commander. Hereafter he would allow considerable latitude to senior commanders to conform their individual operations into his overall grand plan.

The campaign later called the Seven Days' Battles—though in reality they were one heavy skirmish and a brace of engagements, one of two days and the other of three—began June 25 with a minor action near Oak Grove when McClellan launched a tentative assault that Confederates handily repulsed. Lee spent the day from noon until after darkness on the lines, not eating his supper until ten o'clock, the first such day of many that he would have with his army, and even then he had much remaining to do. He gave up trying to get away to see Mary briefly, knowing he would only arrive in the middle of the night and have to wake her. Trusting that "a Merciful Providence may hear and answer" her prayers, he made do with a brief note expressing his hope that when this was all over they might "merit many happy days yet."[127]

The next day the real fighting began inauspiciously when Jackson was inexplicably eleven hours late getting his division in place. Lee spent hours on a height above Mechanicsville looking to see Jackson's legions approach, but when finally he heard firing and saw Yankees pulling back through the village, it was A. P. Hill's doing after he wearied of waiting on Jackson and launched the attack on his own. Lee immediately put Longstreet and D. H. Hill into their holding action, and though the Yankees repulsed the attack around Mechanicsville that first day, they still withdrew, followed by Jackson, Longstreet, and both Hills. Lee renewed the assault the next day around Gaines's Mill, but could not maintain effective control of his divisions because of mistakes over roads, bad maps, and Jackson being tardy yet again. By late afternoon Lee gained a better grasp of the situation and managed to initiate a combined—though far from simultaneous—assault by all of his divisions that hammered the Union V Corps, until at dusk it broke and retreated across the Chickahominy during the night. All the while McClellan remained frozen in his lines south of the river, obsessed with the fiction that Lee vastly outnumbered him. Lee had his first victory and the threat to Richmond was mitigated. Almost ecstatically he sent Davis a note that, "profoundly grateful to Almighty God," they had repulsed the Federals and he intended to give the enemy no time to regroup. He added that losses had been heavy, and he was right.[128] Outnumbering the Federals engaged more than two to one, his losses were about one-sixth greater than theirs, an arithmetic of battle he could not long afford. But he had the initiative.

By late afternoon on June 28 Lee felt certain that McClellan was abandoning his line of communications on the Richmond & York Railroad and withdrawing south to the James River, where Union gunboats could protect a new line of supply from Fort Monroe.[129] Since the four divisions from the previous days' fights were battered and disorganized, Lee ordered Magruder's fresh division to lead the pursuit on June 29, supported by Huger's equally fresh troops, and Jackson, but once again Lee discovered that generals marched faster in his imagination than on the ground. When Magruder finally encountered the Yankee rear guard that morning he stopped entirely for several hours awaiting reinforcements. Seeing his opportunity to demoralize a retreating foe fading, Lee sent Magruder an impatient note chiding him that "we must lose no more time."[130] Huger was just as tardy and never reached Magruder, while Jackson halted for the day in spite of his instructions, leaving Magruder on his own. Thanks to their failures, Lee saw his concentration squandered that afternoon when Magruder finally attacked two Union corps near Savage Station on the Richmond & York. Lee had planned to isolate those corps, a devastating blow if successful, but all three of his division commanders let him down, and the Yankees succeeded in continuing their retreat.

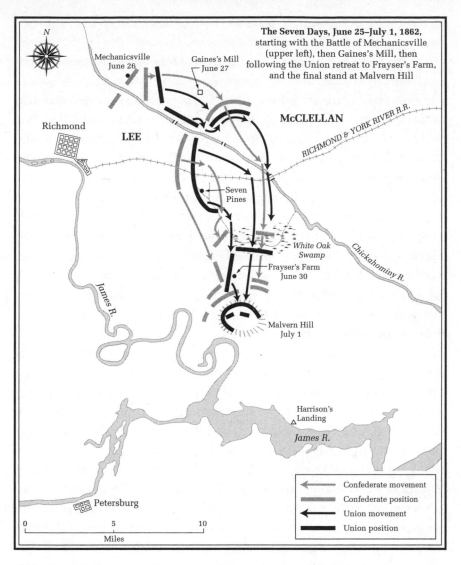

N

Mechanicsville
June 26

Gaines's Mill
June 27

The Seven Days, June 25–July 1, 1862,
starting with the Battle of Mechanicsville
(upper left), then Gaines's Mill, then
following the Union retreat to Frayser's Farm,
and the final stand at Malvern Hill

McCLELLAN

RICHMOND & YORK RIVER R.R.

Richmond

LEE

Seven
Pines

White Oak
Swamp

Chickahominy R.

Frayser's Farm
June 30

James R.

Malvern Hill
July 1

Harrison's
Landing

James R.

Petersburg

	Confederate movement
	Confederate position
	Union movement
	Union position

0   5   10

Miles

That day marked both Magruder and Huger as likely candidates for
transfer to oblivion with G. W. Smith. Jackson's performance had been
worse than any, though the importance of his Shenandoah campaign
would sustain him for now. Lee was starting to face some very tough
personnel issues at the worst possible moment.

He also rethought his own command style on the field that night.
He remained largely at his headquarters, which moved almost daily,
leaving it to his staff to communicate his instructions, though he failed

to use them to investigate Jackson's and Hill's galling delays. While that made him easy to find, it also meant he saw little of the overall field. Given his personality, that instinctive feeling of blame for what went wrong around him, he naturally assumed that some responsibility for the failure rested on himself. The way to counter that was to spend more time on the front. He also gave orders, and when they failed to be realized he just waited longer rather than actively seeking to discover the cause. That would have to change with better use of staff. On June 29 he changed his habit and established no fixed headquarters, meaning subordinates could not be sure where to find him to report or receive orders. That, too, would have to change. His staff performed well, but he did not use it well. Seven aides were not a lot, but they could be enough if properly employed.[131]

By noon on June 30 McClellan anchored his left on Malvern Hill, protected by a bend of the James River on its left, while his retreating corps, as they approached, extended his line northward four miles to White Oak Swamp, which protected its right. Once again Lee planned a convergence: Longstreet, the Hills, and Huger to hit the main enemy line, while Holmes's freshly arrived division would take Malvern Hill itself, and Jackson was to attack across the swamp to crush McClellan's right. Breaching Federal ranks anywhere should force the enemy to retreat to the bank of the James, and if Lee pinned them there before McClellan organized water evacuation, Lee might bag the entire army. He met during the night with Jackson about his role, called at Magruder's bivouac at dawn to do the same, and thereafter conferred in person with every division commander but Huger, trying to ensure no mistakes this time. Once the fight commenced he spent much of the day on the fighting line surveying enemy positions at no small risk. That afternoon while overlooking Hill's position, Lee's career as army commander very nearly came to an abrupt end when enemy artillery narrowly missed him as he spoke with President Davis, Longstreet, and others just behind A. P. Hill's lines.

But the machine was breaking down from losses, exhaustion, and confusion, and the test of stress on his commanders' abilities and stamina compromised Lee's best designs.

Huger was slow again. Magruder dithered and never reached the field. Where Jackson had performed better on June 29, on this day he was virtually useless, and again Lee failed to send someone to find out why. Only A. P. Hill and Longstreet actually attacked the Union line, at a spot locally known as Frayser's Farm, and though the fighting lasted for hours, they were too weak to break through. In a last gamble Lee attempted to coordinate Jackson hitting McClellan's right below the swamp while Holmes stuck the left at the hill. Then he went to the right of his line to try to hurry Holmes forward to Malvern Hill, which he reconnoitered first himself. The Yankees beat back Holmes easily, and once again Jackson failed to appear, as did Huger. With Magruder slowly on his way to Hill's support, Lee ably redirected him to the right to reinforce Holmes's attack, but in the event Magruder supported neither.[132] When darkness closed the fighting, Lee had gained nothing, and during the night McClellan succeeded in consolidating his corps on Malvern Hill in a formidable position.

Lee felt immeasurably frustrated, exclaiming to one general that McClellan "will get away because I cannot have my orders carried out."[133] Everyone but Longstreet and A. P. Hill let him down, and Longstreet lost valuable time in confusion about roads. Even if his hope of demolishing McClellan's army was unrealistic, still Lee's plans ought to have yielded more results. Like every army commander thus far in the war, Lee was learning that large columns of soldiers simply could not move fast, even on good roads in countryside they knew. Lee had tried everything, and still McClellan reached the James River and was within reach of Harrison's Landing, where he could easily reestablish supply and communications. Meanwhile, the Army of Northern Virginia was badly bloodied and bone weary, and Lee himself close to exhaustion. Any commander ought reasonably to question whether he and his men had one more push in them.

Lee decided to find out. He designed a heavy assault on Malvern Hill for the morning of July 1, and this time eschewed subtle tactics. Artillery was to drive back enemy cannon, and then he would send Huger, Jackson, and D. H. Hill up the hill in a massed frontal assault. He suspended the action when his artillery failed in their part, but then saw what he took to be signs that McClellan was evacuating. Lee thought the moment right to deliver a hammer blow and ordered the frontal assault again. Instead of moving up the slopes in unison, however, the Confederate divisions failed to coordinate their movements, and the Yankees succeeded in beating them back a division at a time with heavy casualties.

Lee decided that night that he had gained enough. "Our success has not been as great or complete as I could have desired," he told Mary a few days later. Ultimately, of course, it was out of his hands, for "God knows what is best for us."[134] In fact, the impact of Lee's achievement was seismic. Personally it saved his reputation from the doldrums and possible obscurity. The impact on Confederate morale could not be overstated. At the end of a long season of Confederate setbacks and outright disasters, Lee inflicted humiliating defeat on presumably the best the Union could send against him. He made spectacular and far reaching gains. A commander less than a month in office wielded an untested army against an opponent numerically his superior and in a steady offensive pushed it back nearly thirty miles, forcing it to make an unexpected change of base, and considerably demoralizing its already weak-willed commander. He relieved his capital from the imminent threat of siege, sent a fresh fright across the North to counter the optimism spawned by Grant's gains on the Mississippi and Tennessee Rivers, and electrified Virginia and the Confederacy. It came at heavy cost, perhaps 20,000 casualties, nearly one-fourth of his army, but Lee understood from the outset that this would be no short war. Time sided with the biggest battalions, and if the South was to overcome its disparity of odds with the North, it must be done by bold resolve, swift action, and sacrifice. Suddenly that seemed to be the very definition of Robert E. Lee. Goodbye to "Spades" and *stick-in-the-mud.*

9

LEE VICTORIOUS AND GRANT FRUSTRATED

The day after the battle closed, Grant congratulated his men in terms revealing that even he was not immune from hyperbole. The enemy had outnumbered them, he said, its army composed of "the flower of the southern army commanded by their ablest Generals and fought by them with all the desperation of despair." Still, there was no exaggeration when he told them that "no such contest ever took place on this continent."[1]

Grant sent Halleck almost daily reports of affairs, and apologized that it would be some days before he could submit troop strengths.[2] He would not again be accused of failing to keep his commander informed, and may have been especially sensitive as he could now expect an outcry over the battle. It came in less than a week when the press hinted that Grant was taken by surprise. As more details filtered north from Pittsburg Landing, a trickle became a rill.[3] Of course he had been surprised, and it availed little to point out that so had Sherman, who actually commanded on the front line. They knew a large enemy army was concentrated at Corinth. They knew significant portions of it had moved north. And they knew that skirmishes of the past few days involved not just the usual outposts and scouts, but some artillery and even infantry.

A year later experience would equip Grant to read those signs better. Every army commander in time would be surprised, as would Lee not too long from now. Shiloh was Grant's turn. He expected criticism, candidly admitting to Julia that "I say I dont care for what the papers say but I do." It annoyed him even more when he saw such reports causing her distress for his sake.[4] Grant was human enough to rationalize away the surprise of April 6. "We could not have been better prepared had the enemy sent word three days before when they would attack," he told a friend later that April. He could have initiated the battle a day or two before April 6, but waited for Buell. Even after the fight he still thought in terms of *his* intent to attack. That the foe attacked him, and caught him with no defensive works, did not signify. Without saying so, he implied that the foe drove his army back onto the landing by overwhelming strength of more than double his numbers; by May he escalated those odds to three to one.[5]

Grant had reports to back up his claim of 80,000 rebels in the battle, though soon he learned to discount such information. He never admitted the degree to which he was taken unawares, though, going only so far as to say the strength of the attack was greater than he expected.[6] His response to surprise, however, needed no rationalization. It was just as dynamic as at Fort Donelson. What mattered more was whether he had learned enough from the experience not to be surprised again. Would he restrain his optimism hereafter and spend more time thinking about what the enemy might do, assuming that he kept his command? The coming of Halleck on April 11 put that in some doubt.

Halleck's arrival was about Halleck's ambition, not Grant's surprise, and he seemed to take it thus. For the rest of the month he prepared for more action, expecting Halleck to let him move quickly for the battle to end the rebellion in the West. Instead, Halleck ordered Grant and Buell to prepare to be attacked again, which did not look like intent to advance. Grant saw a flurry of orders from Halleck covering everything from mounting guard to digging latrines, even the proper way to fold letters sent to headquarters.[7]

The outcry over the high casualties led Washington to ask Halleck if Grant or other generals were guilty of neglect or misconduct, but he withheld any comment.[8] The press was less generous. "The papers are giving me fits," Grant complained, and a fortnight after Halleck's arrival Grant told Julia that he was glad to be superseded. Perhaps now they would leave him alone. "If the papers only knew how little ambition I have outside of putting down this rebellion," he complained. He all but stopped reading the press, and felt better for it.[9] "The best contradiction in the world," he said, "is to pay no attention."[10]

Grant still did not suspect Halleck of envy or ill will.[11] When Halleck reorganized the army in late April he removed Buell's army from

Grant and left him to command only his own, now dubbed the "Army of the Tennessee," though as senior subordinate he was still nominally second in command of the combined forces. But Halleck then began issuing orders directly to Grant's subordinates without going through him, which soon led to speculation that Grant was essentially under arrest. He stood it for ten days, and then on May 11 asked Halleck to restore his full authority or relieve him of duty. Even then he suspected "a studied persistent opposition to me by persons outside the army," but not Halleck.[12] He considered resigning or going to Washington to argue his case. "I sometimes think it almost time to defend myself," he told Julia, and began speaking again of transfer to another theater of the war. "I have probably done more hard work than any other General officer," he told her. "I have had my full share of abuse too," and feared that his useful days with this field army were near an end.[13]

By now more than six months of intermittent criticism propelled him to step out of character to write to Washburne, who unbeknownst to Grant was already defending him on the floor of Congress.[14] Halleck finally met Grant personally on May 12 and somewhat mollified his subordinate. Meanwhile, Halleck commenced what proved to be a glacial advance toward Corinth. Week after week Grant forecast the next great battle soon, and week after week it came not. He even looked ahead to what he would do after victory in the war, perhaps commanding an occupying force in the South.[15] Then the army marched into Corinth at the end of May to find it empty, evacuated while Halleck dawdled.

Grant hoped for another campaign soon and an important role, preferably clearing west Tennessee of rebels, with his headquarters at Memphis where Julia could join him.[16] He wanted a brief furlough to see her, but even Halleck asked him to remain, and Sherman rejoiced. "You could not be quiet at home for a week, when armies were moving," he told Grant, and no rest would relieve him of the sense of injustice. Sherman was all for going to war with the press once they defeated the enemy, but Grant simply resumed his resolution to stay quiet and wait it out.[17]

Confederates surrendered Memphis on June 6. Four days later Halleck restored Grant to full command of his army, and by June 23 Grant did have headquarters in Memphis, and commenced fortifying it as a

major supply base for the next campaign. Halleck gave him no instructions for administering a civilian population, so Grant felt his way;
however, his chief objective was protecting the railroad leading south
into Mississippi for use as a supply line for his next advance. Sensing
his strength growing again, he became more assertive with Halleck in
pointing out contradictions in his superior's orders and expecting clarification.[18] He also suspended the Memphis *Avalanche* for publication of
critical articles on Union officers and men, despite his inclination not
to muzzle even the disloyal press.[19] By the summer of 1862, however,
he had taken as much as he could stand from editors, especially on the
festering issue of slaves.

When Julia and the children arrived in Memphis on July 1 after a
visit with his parents, Grant felt buoyed, but the presence of her old
slave nurse loaned by her father reminded him of a problem he confronted. Old Fred Dent's fortunes had declined and he feared his slaves
might be seized and auctioned to satisfy creditors. He sent his youngest daughter a bill of sale for the servants he loaned her to keep them
free from attachment. Grant suggested that his wife advise Dent to
do the same for the rest of his slaves. She could not keep hers much
longer in any event. They were not lawful in Galena, nor welcome in
Jesse Grant's home in Covington, and Grant preferred she not have
any slaves with her henceforward, since he doubted they would ever
live in a slave state again. Sharing the Dents' paternalism for their servants, he did not want them sold.[20] Julia would keep the nurse with her
awhile yet, but within a year she was free.[21]

Grant suspected by now that all slaves might not remain such much
longer. Runaways flocked to his army when he marched through the
country. He found half a dozen black men with the garrison at Fort
Donelson, and what he called the "Abolition press" accused him of
violating the law by allowing their Unionist owners from Kentucky to
reclaim their property.[22] In fact, those blacks were free men, and he released them at their own request to return to their homes. "So long as
I hold a commission in the Army I have no views of my own to carry
out," he told Washburne. The law was the law, and no officer ought
to put his personal views above it. Should Congress pass a statute he
could not obey, "I will resign."[23] Grant remained basically indifferent
toward slavery. "I have no hobby of my own with regard to the ne-

gro, either to effect his freedom or to continue his bondage," he told his father that August. "If Congress pass any law and the President approves, I am willing to execute it."[24] But he also saw that runaways hurt the Confederates. "Their *institution* are beginning to have ideas of their own," he told his sister. Consequently, rather than return runaways to owners, he gave them jobs in his army as cooks, nurses, and teamsters, "thus saving soldiers to carry the musket." There was the germ of an understanding of what more the slaves might do. "I dont know what is to become of these poor people in the end," he said, "but it [is] weakning the enemy to take them from them."[25]

Grant's handling of criticism matured alongside his management of discordant subordinates. It was one thing to arrest Captain Hatch in Cairo, and quite another to confront colonels and generals, but after a year of wearing his stars he did not hesitate. Having seen so many incompetents gain commissions, Grant spoke up even to Lincoln. Napoleon Bonaparte Buford, for instance, had joined Grant at Cairo as colonel of the 27th Illinois. He immediately revealed himself a crank by saying that the war would end with the Union adopting the British form of aristocracy, and that he would be a duke and his family nobility. At Belmont he disobeyed orders and almost lost his regiment, so Grant did not include him on the Henry-Donelson campaign. Still, Buford made brigadier, but when Grant read he might be promoted, he wrote directly to the president, averring that Buford was a "dead weight" who "would scarsely make a respectable Hospital nurse if put in petticoats."[26] Buford did not get the promotion.

There were worse than buffoons to deal with. Colonel Crafts J. Wright of the 22d Ohio had attended the Military Academy as Jefferson Davis's roommate, graduating almost last in his class with a compilation of demerits that placed him 204th of 207.[27] After leaving the army he had been both an attorney and a newspaper editor, often a volatile combination. He gave Grant trouble from the day he arrived at Cairo. He contested every fine point of military law and authority, then at Shiloh refused to obey orders from a superior whose seniority he questioned, and two days later similarly disobeyed orders to join the pursuit. Maintaining that "he has been the cause of more complaints from his immediate commanders than any six officers of this Command," Grant arrested him and convened an inquiry that resulted in Wright's dismissal.[28]

At the same time, Grant advanced those who showed promise, particularly Sherman, McPherson, Logan, and others. His judgment sometimes failed him as with Lew Wallace, whose tardiness at Shiloh Grant could not forget, but then Wallace was not a professional soldier, and except for Logan, Grant almost always favored West Pointers.[29] The more he saw of one subordinate, however, the more he needed to be on guard. McClernand's ambition came into the open after Fort Donelson, when his report exaggerated both his division's performance and his own, even claiming credit for ordering the February 15 counterattack.[30] This summer he challenged another general's authority to pass through an area nominally under his supervision, and Grant firmly dismissed any effort to claim territorial autonomy. "I command all the troops that are within, or that may come within, certain limits," he wrote back. His subordinates commanded troops, but not territory, and it would remain thus unless higher power overruled him. McClernand bristled, protesting he thought only of the good of the service, but still characterized Grant's response as "a boast of authority uncalled for," adding that "my actions . . . have lent luster to your authority."[31] Grant had not yet taken McClernand's full measure, nor did he know that the politician was still in touch with that useful slanderer Kountz.

Indeed, there was a risk with politician-subordinates. His most vicious critic after Shiloh was the Cincinnati *Gazette*. Until the later 1850s one of its owners and editors was that same Crafts J. Wright, and one of its correspondents with his army was Wright's friend Whitelaw Reid, who wrote a harsh attack on Grant for his conduct of the battle. Reid's article prompted Jesse Grant to send aggressive defenses to the *Gazette*'s main competitor, the Cincinnati *Commercial*. The resultant press controversy embarrassed the general, and he rebuked his father in terms charged by frustration pent up since childhood. Grant refused his father's suggestions that he write his own defense, and made it clear that he did not want the support of any Cincinnati press.[32] Nor did he want Jesse's. "I would write you many particulars but you are so imprudent that I dare not trust you with them," he scolded his father. "I have not an enemy in the world who has done me so much injury as you in your efforts in my defence." He wanted Jesse to stop, pleading "for my sake let me alone."[33]

Happily, Grant was soon rid of a difficult superior. Like Lee, he grasped the interconnected nature of events across the continent, and specifically asked to be telegraphed the latest military news from other points, especially McClellan's advance on Richmond.[34] His first word of Little Mac's defeat came on July 7 from jubilant secessionists in Memphis, and he doubted the news until Halleck confirmed it the next day.[35] Disheartening though it was, Lee's defeat of McClellan led Lincoln to relieve him as general-in-chief, and on July 11 Halleck got an order to come east immediately. Later that day Halleck ordered Grant to come to Corinth. Grant had been hoping for orders to move south against Vicksburg, Mississippi, two hundred miles downriver.[36] With the fall of New Orleans in late April, the batteries on Vicksburg's bluffs and letter emplacements at Port Hudson, Louisiana, were the only remaining obstacles to Union control of the river, keys to isolating the western third of the Confederacy and severing the flow of men and provisions eastward. It would also complete a water cordon surrounding the Deep South. Resentful at being called east, Halleck tersely told him "this place will be your Head Quarters." That meant Grant would not be going to Vicksburg. Bringing his family, he reached Corinth on July 15.[37] Even then Halleck told him nothing, and two days later Grant still did not know why he was in Corinth. He thought Halleck might be made general-in-chief, and believed it a fine selection, even though "he and I have had several little spats."[38]

Finally, Grant received a special order on July 16 placing him in command of the District of West Tennessee, including his own old Army of the Tennessee at Corinth and John Pope's smaller Army of the Mississippi then camped a few miles away. Lee's victories in the Seven Days served notice on the Union that it could be a long war after all, though Grant still did not think so. It frightened Washington into calling Pope east to command an army protecting the capital should Lee move north while McClellan took root on the James. It was a significant move, for it showed that Lincoln and Halleck were willing to shift successful commanders from one theater of the war to another. Pope's achievements to date had been solid, taking New Madrid and Island Number 10, and thus opening the upper Mississippi down nearly to Memphis. Though Grant's achievements were inarguably more significant and far-reaching, the idea of sending him east did not arise, no doubt because of lingering doubts thanks to Halleck's old accusations, and of course because with Halleck gone Grant had a greater command than that awaiting Pope. For the first time a glimmer of inevitability arose. A Confederate chieftain had emerged who could do the seemingly impossible, with whom disparity of numbers meant nothing. Ironically, Lee's victory boosted Grant's career by moving Halleck and Pope out of his department. If the war lasted long enough, if Pope should fail, or McClellan fail once more, then Washington might look again to the west. At the moment that could only mean Grant.

In Pope's place, Brigadier General William S. Rosecrans commanded. Grant in effect became department commander, reporting directly to Halleck. That meant greater freedom of action, of course, but with fewer resources since, before he left, Halleck sent Buell's army to eastern Tennessee. Grant's two armies combined numbered just over 63,000 spread over a wide line covering railroads, and thinning constantly by illness. Despite his numbers, he believed he dare not launch an offensive until reinforced.

A bright spot was Rosecrans. They knew each other at West Point, where "Rosey" finished high in his class a year ahead of Grant, though their paths never crossed again until May 1862 when Rosecrans arrived to relieve Pope. Rosecrans could be humorless and quick tempered, but Grant liked him. The two conferred frequently, often in person, and Grant especially credited his advice on defenses protecting Corinth. It appeared to be the beginning of a good friendship. Grant soon told Halleck that Rosecrans ought to be promoted to major general, "rank equal to his merit."[39] Still, McClellan had mantled himself in Rosecrans's success in western Virginia, which left Rosey resentful and suspicious of all superiors.

After a fortnight in command Grant believed that only about 20,000 Confederates, commanded by Major General Sterling Price, remained in his front at Tupelo forty-five miles south. He proposed to Halleck that he push Price back another fifty miles to Columbus, Mississippi.[40] Instead, Halleck chose to weaken his army by ordering divisions east to Buell's threatened army at Chattanooga.[41] As he began sending them, Grant grumbled to his sister that "I am now in a situation where it is impossible for me to do more than to protect my long lines of defence." Suddenly he thought Corinth too dangerous for his family to remain and packed them off to St. Louis on August 16.[42] The details of reinforcing Buell and preparing for action himself wore on him with Julia gone. "It is one constant strain now and has been for a year," he admitted, yet he saw no hope of getting away to rest and recuperate.[43] Two days after Julia left he wished he could be anywhere else "free from annoyance."[44]

By the end of August Grant had shifted three of Rosecrans's five divisions to Buell, even as reports suggested that Price was about to march on Corinth. Rosecrans had two remaining divisions protecting the Mobile & Ohio Railroad at Iuka, twenty miles east, and Grant soon pulled them to Corinth just in case. He was learning to discount exaggerated reports. "I never believe numbers to be equal to what they are reported," he had told Halleck.[45] By September 11 he expected Price to have 18,000–20,000 approaching Corinth in two days, not far from their actual 16,000.[46] As usual, he felt confident. "I am concentrated and strong," he told Julia, and he expected to repulse the foe. If the rebels did not attack, then he planned an advance of his own.[47] As he told Halleck, "stampeding is not my weakness."[48]

⁓

Sadly, that resolve was not universal in blue. If not exactly stampeded, McClellan all but cowered behind his defenses at Harrison's Landing, and Lee read the man well enough to believe he would take his time before moving again. His own army was too battered to risk another assault after the cost at Malvern Hill, so he pulled back to a strong defensive line to rest. They had confounded Little Mac "at least for a season," he believed, but still he begged friends to pray, trusting that "they will be heard and answered for our distressed country."[49] Thanking "our Heavenly Father for all the mercies He has extended to us," he was sorry not to have achieved more, but as he told Mary, "God knows what is best for us."[50]

In the ensuing days Lee exchanged prisoners with McClellan and arranged for the return of the wounded, but immediately had to turn his attention to reports that the Union army Pope assembled around Fredericksburg on the Rappahannock to protect Washington was showing signs of movement. By mid-July Lee could not as yet determine if Pope had designs on the Shenandoah Valley and the Virginia

Central Railroad at Staunton, or planned a move to strike Richmond from the north, perhaps in tandem with another push up the York-James Peninsula from McClellan. "It is difficult to learn the truth until too late to profit by it," he complained to the president on July 18.[51] He sent Stuart's cavalry north to glean more precise information, and earlier on July 13 sent Jackson with his division and General Richard S. Ewell's to block Pope if he could, while Lee remained with the army continuing its refitting and reorganization and watching McClellan. It was a risk. Jackson performed miserably during the Seven Days, yet Lee did not forget Stonewall's brilliant campaign in the Shenandoah in independent command. Moreover, Jackson and his men were better rested now. For the next three weeks he kept pace with Pope, and at first Lee felt he could not risk reinforcing him until he knew Pope's intentions, and whether or not Jackson saw an opportunity to strike a meaningful blow.[52]

Making things more difficult, by July 25 Lee would have risked sending A. P. Hill's huge division to reinforce Jackson, but Hill was under arrest at the moment, and Lee did not trust the capability of the next senior general in the command. Then on July 27 Lee got word from Stonewall of an opportunity worth the risk, and Lee sent Hill on his way, beefing Jackson's force to 30,000 or more. "I want Pope to be suppressed," Lee told him. He also hinted that Jackson relax his obsessive secrecy enough to let his subordinates know his actual plans so they could act more knowledgably. Hill was a temporary loan and he needed him back as soon as possible, for there was always the possibility that a sleeping McClellan might reawaken.[53]

Lee had adopted a very personal animus toward Pope by this time, for he had engaged in some acts and reprisals against citizens that outraged Confederates. Pope arrested Virginians who refused to take an oath of allegiance to the United States, allegedly forced others to take it, and allowed men wanting to escape Confederate service to swear oaths not to bear arms against the Union on pain of death. Lee sent a protest to McClellan alerting him that the Confederacy would regard none of those oaths as binding.[54] Pope also issued orders promising retaliation on the property of rebel sympathizers, which turned into something of a license for his men to pillage. Lee felt outraged, and took it so personally that when he learned that his nephew Louis Mar-

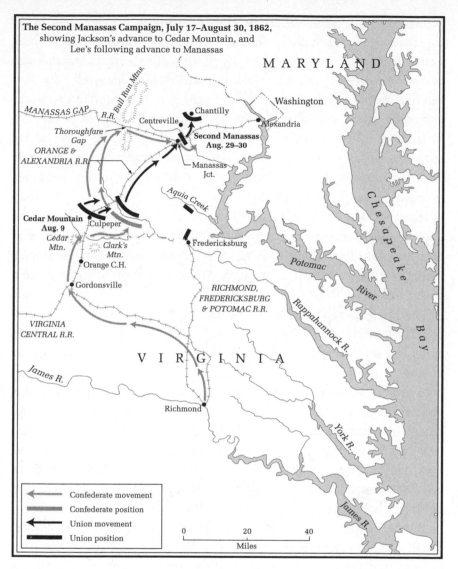

The Second Manassas Campaign, July 17–August 30, 1862, showing Jackson's advance to Cedar Mountain, and Lee's following advance to Manassas

shall had joined the Union army, he said, "I could forgive the latter for fighting against us, if he had not have joined such a miscreant as Pope."[55]

Jackson did not disappoint. He kept in constant communication with Lee, and though the latter did not always agree with Stonewall's assessment of a situation, he usually deferred to the man on the ground, saying "you ought to know."[56] Like Grant, Lee knew better than to try to impose his conceptions from afar. When he could send no more reinforcements, he left it to Jackson to decide if he should initiate combat. "Being on the spot you must determine what force to operate against," Lee told him on August 7. He suggested only that Jackson try to maneuver the enemy out of well-defended positions rather than try to take them by force, but again left the determination to Jackson. "I would rather you should have easy fighting and heavy victories," he told him. "Make up your mind what is best to be done under all the circumstances which surround us and let me hear the result at which you arrive."[57]

Again it was a hefty degree of independent discretion Lee gave Jackson, though in the event he had little choice. Stonewall was on the ground while Lee was more than a hundred miles to the southeast where he could hardly give direction. Any information he might act on was hours old before he got it, and by the time he could respond with orders the forces in the field might be miles from where he thought them to be. Happily, he had struck on just the right approach for managing Jackson, who was just as agile after Pope as he had been sluggish against McClellan. On August 9, at Cedar Mountain not far from Culpeper, he caught one of Pope's corps and gave it a severe battering. Lee rejoiced in "the victory which God has granted you."[58] More than that, he quickly read the signs of units leaving McClellan by transport. That told him two things: they were going to reinforce Pope, and a weakened McClellan was even less likely to move against Richmond. Now was the time to act, to take a greater risk. If Lee could concentrate enough strength against Pope, while still leaving Richmond protected, he might destroy one army and then turn back and take on McClellan.

On August 13 Lee ordered Longstreet's division off by rail to join Jackson, where as senior officer Longstreet would command. Within hours, however, Longstreet asked Lee to come assume command in person, and Lee spent August 14 making hurried preparations. He could not leave without telling President Davis, of course, and he notified him in a peculiar fashion. Instead of informing him face to face, Lee wrote a letter saying he would leave before dawn on August 15 "unless I hear from you to the contrary." Lee knew Davis well enough by now to know it was sometimes best not to give the president an opportunity to question. Yet at the same time Lee revealed what he had learned from Johnston's refusal to communicate. "I will keep you informed of everything of importance that transpires," he vowed. "When you do not hear from me, you may feel sure that I do not think it necessary to trouble you." Lee understood that Davis had a right to information from his commanders; indeed it was a necessity. He also sensed that an informed president was less likely to interfere. This would be the basic tenor of his relations with Davis for the rest of the war.[59]

Lee reached Gordonsville late the next morning and soon moved on to join the army at Orange Court House twenty miles south of Pope's army concentrated around Culpeper. His arrival caused something of a sensation among the soldiers, who were reconsidering "Granny Lee" now that he had led them to victory. An artilleryman who saw him in Gordonsville wrote his wife the same day that he thought Lee "silent, inscrutable, strong, like a God."[60]

The day before Lee told Longstreet that "it is all important that our movement in what ever direction it is determined should be as quick as possible," and on arrival he set out to do just that.[61] Though he believed himself to be outnumbered, in fact Lee and Pope were almost evenly matched at about 55,000 soldiers each, but Lee knew that large elements of McClellan's army were on their way via Washington and a landing on the lower Potomac at Aquia Creek. Lee had to make his move before they reached Pope in little more than a week, or else he would be too heavily outnumbered to risk engagement. He shifted the army east a few miles from Orange Court House to the south side of Clark's Mountain, which masked him from Pope's view on Cedar Mountain. He intended then to move north, keeping Clark's Mountain between himself and Pope, until he crossed the Rapidan River and pushed on to Culpeper. That would put him north of Pope, cut his line of supply and communications, and then Lee could turn south and strike the Federals. He set the movement for August 18, heeding his own injunction to be "as quick as possible."

The plan had the genius of simplicity. Lee based it on an accurate reading of enemy movements, a perceptive grasp of Pope's immediate situation, and his own excellent use of geography. It fit perfectly Lee's needs. Moreover, it lacked the complexity and coordination pitfalls that hampered him at Cheat Mountain and in the Seven Days.

Unfortunately, Lee timed the move before he could be ready himself, and did not reach the Rapidan until August 19, but his cavalry's failure to secure the crossing held him up another day, by which time it was all pointless. A Union cavalry raid on Stuart's headquarters at Verdiersville on the night of August 17 captured a copy of Lee's campaign plan; thus alerted, Pope pulled back north of the Rappahannock and all Lee could do was follow. For the next several days the armies faced each other over the river. Lee's splendid plan had come to nothing, and Pope's reinforcements were starting to arrive, boosting his strength to more than 70,000.

As with Grant, Lee's surpassing skill lay in his reaction to setbacks and the unexpected. Where most other commanders in this war might have handed the initiative to Pope, Lee instead thought in the boldest terms yet conceived. His problem had changed. Where it had been Pope alone, now it was Pope on north bank of the Rappahannock, and more than two fresh army corps at Fredericksburg, Aquia Creek, and Washington, bent on reinforcing him. Lee's solution was to hold Pope's army in place by a spirited demonstration; at the same time Jackson and 30,000 men, soon followed by Longstreet, moved up the right bank of the Rappahannock thirty miles, shielded from view on the east by the Bull Run Mountains, then turned east through Thoroughfare Gap another thirty miles to hit the Orange & Alexandria Railroad at or near Manassas, and cut Pope's line of communications. That would also cut off the reinforcements destined for Pope from Washington and, Lee hoped, force Pope to pull back to reestablish his supply line and give Lee an opening to attack at advantage somewhere in northern Virginia.

Lee's audacity was stunning, though not unduly reckless. Simple acceptance of the reality of his situation suggested that as the underdog he had no option but to take risks or else sit passively while the foe grew ever stronger. Jackson's success at Cedar Mountain repaired any erosion of Lee's confidence in his ability, and he thought no less of Longstreet. Pope was no McClellan, and Lee could expect him to move in response. It was a question of who moved faster. The danger for Lee was that if Pope beat Jackson to Manassas, he might be reinforced heavily in a day's time from Washington; then Lee's army would either attack at a disadvantage, or else have to retreat sixty miles by the same route they came on two sides of a triangle to Orange, while Pope could move in a straight line half that distance along the Orange & Alexandria to reach Orange first and cut Lee off from Richmond. The fact is that for the Confederates everywhere in this war there would be no gains without risks. Lee took risks in the Seven Days and despite almost daily disappointments, he accomplished much. That enhanced his confidence in himself and his army. And then in moments like this, even his fatalistic providentialism gave him strength in making a decision. If man achieved nothing God did not will, then in a way there was no risk. The Almighty guided his hand in making the effort, win or lose. If he suffered defeat, he was only a divine instrument. That gave him the freedom to gamble boldly.

It worked. Jackson covered all thirty miles the first day, and pushed his men hard enough on August 26 that by nightfall they reached Bristoe Station a few miles below Manassas and camped astride the railroad supplying Pope. That general did not suspect where the Confederates might be until the next morning, by which time Jackson occupied Manassas and was in the act of destroying Pope's mountain of supplies and materiel. Pope soon moved his army north and Jackson pulled back to a strong defensive position to hold on until Longstreet arrived, accompanied by Lee. By the morning of August 29 Lee and Longstreet had pushed through Thoroughfare Gap and were on their way to the field, arriving about ten o'clock, when Lee himself rode forward to the skirmish line to reconnoiter, as had been his habit of old. He returned with a red stripe on his cheek where a bullet narrowly missed killing him.[62]

Soon afterward he was reunited with Jackson and Longstreet, who went into line on Jackson's right, and essentially was not engaged the rest of the day as Pope concentrated on attacking Jackson's well-emplaced line. Seeing what appeared to be an exposed enemy left flank, Lee spent much of the morning trying to persuade Longstreet to hit it, but Longstreet repeatedly demurred, as he often would in this war, and Lee reluctantly yielded to his judgment, as he often would. Again in the afternoon Lee tried to launch a counterattack with Longstreet, but the presence of menacing Federal divisions on Longstreet's right front made it too risky. Having conducted a dynamic campaign to get here, Lee found himself fighting a defensive battle, something new to him. Late in the afternoon when the force threatening Long-street's right flank shifted toward the center of the battle line, Lee saw once more an opportunity for Longstreet to go forward, but again he objected that it was too late now, and the attack would be better made in the morning, and Lee agreed.

That night Lee made his plans for the daylight assault and sent a telegram to Davis reporting that he had cleared the Rappahannock of Yankees and so far repulsed Pope's assaults.[63] For the most part he allowed Jackson and Longstreet to conduct the battle that day, confin-ing his efforts to pressing for an attack on the Union left that circum-stances conspired against. He did not overrule Longstreet and it is well that he did not, for a repulse and strong counterattack would have jeopardized his army's position and hazarded all he had gained thus far, which was considerable. The movement to get his army here and reunited in the face of the foe was stunning. He had disrupted Pope's supply lines, destroyed millions of dollars' worth of supplies and mu-nitions at Manassas, and put Pope in the position of having to punch through Lee's line to reestablish his connection to Washington.

There was no morning assault, however. In the night Lee decided instead to attempt a wide sweeping movement by Longstreet around Pope's left flank to cut off his line of retreat and pin him against Bull Run. While getting the movement organized, Lee rode across Bull Run at dawn and dismounted on a patch of grass to let his horse graze. As Lee sat on a stump, an enemy cavalry movement got close enough to him that he ran to catch his mount and had just grasped the rein when the horse shied. Lee pitched forward, his feet tangled in his cloak, and he came down hard on both hands. The fall broke a bone in one and sprained the other, jarring his right arm to the shoulder. Though he caught his horse and rode much of the rest of the day, he was in severe pain. It would be months before he had the full use of his hands.[64]

Thus later that day he had to dictate a letter giving the president a more extended account of the campaign thus far. He had hoped to avoid a pitched battle with a stronger foe, and was trusting to maneu-ver to force Pope to leave central Virginia, which had worked. "We have no time to lose & must make every exertion if we expect to reap advantage," he closed.[65] Pope reopened his assaults on Jackson's line early in the afternoon, which preempted Lee's flank movement, but soon he found that Longstreet had no enemy in his front so Lee ordered him forward. Five divisions slammed into Pope's exposed left flank, then Jackson advanced in support and the stunned Union army fell back, ironically to the very hill where Stonewall earned his sobriquet thirteen months before. That evening Pope ordered a retreat to Centreville, and Lee's army was too battered from marching and fighting to pursue in the darkness. Still, he wired to the president that they had "a signal victory." He gave credit to his officers and men, but did not forget the one who perhaps gave him the courage to make the gamble in the first place. "Our gratitude to Almighty God for His mercies rises higher and higher each day," he wrote; "to Him and to the valour of our troops a nation's gratitude is due."[66]

On August 31 Lee tried another flank movement, sending Jackson across Bull Run in an effort to make a sweep to the north then east to get between Centreville and Washington, following with Longstreet the next day. On September 1, near a village called Chantilly, Jackson launched assaults against Pope's forces, but his men were so hungry and exhausted that their assaults had little punch. That was enough for the Federals, who pulled back, and the next day Pope began his retreat into the defenses of Washington. Lee suddenly had his second improbable victory. Having neutralized McClellan on the York-James Peninsula, now he virtually drove Pope out of Virginia. Again he benefited from facing a mediocre opponent, though Pope had more fight and determination than Little Mac to be sure, his real failure being his refusal to believe that he faced the bulk of Lee's army. Far more than in the Seven Days, Lee's surpassing contribution was his planning, for as a battlefield commander he exerted only minimal influence, unsuccessfully trying to launch Longstreet on what might have proved to be an ill-advised attack on the first day, then planning a flank march that never happened on the second. Yet he recognized the moment of opportunity that afternoon and sent Longstreet forward in the assault that decided the day. Above all else, however, Lee showed once again that he had in abundance a singular quality that he and Grant shared with few others: he was willing. It remained to be seen how he would act if his audacity and confidence put him in a position from which he could not escape.

Two weeks later that was the sort of position Grant hoped to catch Price in as it became evident that Iuka was his target.[67] By September 15 Grant knew he was there and expecting reinforcements to join in an attack on him. Calculating that they could not arrive before September 19, Grant decided to move first, drive him away from his reinforcement, and at the same time relieve Corinth of threat.[68] On September 17 he ordered Major General E. O. C. Ord, now commanding three divisions at Corinth, to march toward Iuka, while Rosecrans moved his divisions via a parallel road. Grant would travel with Ord, and the combined force of 15,000 should hit Iuka from two sides. When Rosecrans proposed an alternate route for his command, Grant agreed, assuming him to be better informed. Both columns were to be in place outside Iuka by nightfall September 18. Then Ord would strike after dawn from the northwest to distract Price while, at the sound of Ord's guns, Rosecrans struck from the southwest. They would pinch Price between them and destroy his army or force him eastward away from his reinforcements. Then Grant would turn on them as well. The plan offered multiple benefits, allowing Grant to respond to contingencies; its weakness was coordinating two forces separated by several miles.

Rosecrans got started late, slowed by rain and confusion regarding roads. By nightfall September 18 he was still twenty miles from Iuka, but told Grant he could still hit it hard by the next afternoon. That meant covering two miles an hour, easy for a man on foot, but difficult for a marching army over sodden roads in the summer heat. Grant altered the plan since Rosey would likely be late. Though behind schedule, Ord was only about six miles from Iuka. That night Grant ordered him to slow his march next day to give Rosecrans time to arrive, hoping they could still strike simultaneously and "do tomorrow all we can."[69] To encourage his men, he sent his commanders a telegram just received from Washington to be read to the soldiers. McClellan and Lee had fought a great battle in Maryland on September 17 and the Confederates were driven back, Longstreet and his whole corps captured, A. P. Hill killed, and Lee himself reported captured.[70] If Grant doubted the truth of all of it, it should nonetheless enspirit his men on the eve of their battle. A similar victory the following day might shatter the rebellion.

But Hill still lived, Longstreet was no prisoner, and Lee was at large and more dangerous than ever. Two days after Chantilly he wrote twice to Davis, once from the battlefield, and again later from Dranesville in sight of the Potomac. He wanted to cross the river. Defeat had demoralized McClellan and Pope, and though they were uniting around Washington, he believed it might be weeks before that army moved again. This was the moment to give pro-Confederate Marylanders the opportunity to rally to their banners. Lee probably had the idea germinating before he defeated Pope as a means to take pressure off Virginia by drawing enemy forces into Maryland, while subsisting his own there as well.

His army was not strong enough to conquer and hold territory. Still, he told Davis "we cannot afford to be idle." The tide of the moment flowed with them and they must run with it. He believed he could successfully raid into Maryland, especially if Beauregard's army, now commanded by General Braxton Bragg, advanced in tandem to prevent Buell from reinforcing McClellan.[71] General-in-Chief Lee was proposing a cross-department strategy, a gingerly inroad on prerogatives Davis jealously kept to himself, but now Lee knew how to manage the president. During the campaign just past he kept him well apprised of his movements. Moreover, when Lee first proposed the campaign against Pope, he emphasized his subordinate position by adding that "I shall feel obliged to you for any directions you may think proper to give."[72] Lee was never obsequious, but he knew Davis was more amenable when his authority was unchallenged.

Lee had launched his move north from Orange without waiting for the president's assent, and it worked. Now he tried it again. He could count on at least a three-day lead before any response from Davis might arrive, and that gave him freedom. A day after writing he had moved to Leesburg, putting the army close to one of the Potomac fords on a straight line to Frederick, Maryland. He weighed the benefits of crossing east of the Blue Ridge, which should pull most Yankees out of Virginia, or crossing west of the mountains above Harpers Ferry, hoping to pull Federals out of there and the Shenandoah. Either way he wanted to strike for Hagerstown twenty miles northwest of Frederick. Soon he revealed why.[73]

From Leesburg he wrote again, adding that he would move immediately unless Davis disapproved, an irrelevant contingency since his forward elements were already at White's Ford ready to cross. Then he mentioned one other thing: "I propose to enter Pennsylvania." That was why Hagerstown was his first objective. Cutting the Baltimore & Ohio Railroad along the way, he could cross the Mason-Dixon Line into the Cumberland Valley to fill his commissary and find good roads sixty miles northeast to Harrisburg on the Susquehanna, along the way breaking up the railroad that supplied Federals in the Shenandoah and Harpers Ferry. He could disrupt enemy communications all across the North, especially by wrecking the Pennsylvania Railroad's bridge at Rockville, severing the Union's most important east-west transportation link connecting New England and the mid-Atlantic states with Ohio and all parts west. If successful, it would be perhaps the most significant logistical blow the Confederates could attempt.

Lee also thought geopolitically. Marylanders might be more forthcoming with supplies if urged to cooperate by someone they respected, like pro-Confederate former governor Enoch L. Lowe, then living in Richmond. Lee asked the president to hurry Lowe to him. More than that, the advance of a Confederate army into Pennsylvania could shatter Northern morale weeks before the October–November election of Representatives in Congress, the selection of senators by several legislatures, and gubernatorial elections in New York and New Jersey. Lee well realized that the only way for the Confederacy to win was by persuading the Union to lose. That gave every battle political significance, which he realized could be a two-sided coin. Spreading panic in Pennsylvania might help defeat Republicans at the polls and cost Lincoln support for the war. Yet the raid could backfire if it so aroused Northerners that they became even more committed, as happened after the humiliation at the battle of First Manassas. Hence Lee wrote that he would not enter Pennsylvania if "you should deem it unadvisable upon political or other grounds."[74] By the time any "no" from the president arrived, Lee could be marching into the Keystone State.

Lee's letters may suggest that he was developing his strategy as he marched, but he may have been revealing his intentions gradually so as not to overwhelm the president. An invasion of Pennsylvania was not a new idea. Jackson had been talking of it for months, and back in June proposed moving as far as Harrisburg if reinforced. Lee then told Davis "it would change the character of the war," though nothing was done.[75] He gave it more thought over the next three months, and now barely three days' march from Pennsylvania, with a head start on the enemy, he would never likely be in a better position. When he wrote Davis again on September 5 there was no mention of halting if recalled. He wanted the president to hurry forward ammunition and supplies, directing that everything now go to him via the Shenandoah and Winchester. He also wanted bridges over the Rapidan and Rappahannock rebuilt in case he had to retire east of the Blue Ridge, so he would have rail communications with the capital. Like Grant, Lee did not start a campaign by planning his retreat, but prudence now could give his army strength in the event.[76]

By early September 6 Lee had two divisions across and expected to get the rest of the army over that day. He had cut the Chesapeake & Ohio Canal, and would soon break up the Baltimore & Ohio.[77] Unable to ride with his hands splinted and bandaged, he conducted the campaign from an ambulance. By September 7 virtually all of the army was on its way to Frederick, where he took position on the west bank of the Monocacy River. Most of the people welcomed their coming, and the army ate well again. Lee wanted to pay for the army's needs, and asked Davis to send hard currency at once, since some citizens were reluctant to accept Confederate paper. He did not really expect the people to rise up, whatever their expressions of sympathy.[78] Nevertheless, Lee distributed a broadside addressed "To the People of Maryland" that demonstrated his grasp of molding public opinion. Condemning "the wrongs and outrages" inflicted on Marylanders, he declared the sympathy of the Confederacy, to whom social, political, and commercial interests allied them. He came to help them regain the independence and sovereignty of their state. Exhorting them to join his army, he promised that "it is for you to decide your destiny, freely and without constraint." There would be no coercion. "This army will respect your choice."[79]

At the same time on September 8 he put his oar into political waters. The Confederates had held out for more than a year. He might soon be on Pennsylvania's Union firmament. This was the moment to propose recognition of Southern independence, he told Davis. In Mississippi Price was moving against Grant, and Bragg was moving into Kentucky. Across an eight-hundred-mile front the South was advancing. Offering peace now would demonstrate that all they wanted was freedom. Rejection would stamp responsibility for the war on the Republicans, and Northern voters might retaliate.[80] Four days later, probably with Lee's letter in hand, Davis drafted proposed proclamations for Lee and Bragg to issue declaring that Confederates invaded only to defend their homeland, that they wanted only an end to the war and recognition of independence, and hoped the people of the Union would persuade their leaders toward those ends.[81]

Lee proposed sending Jackson west through Sharpsburg to recross the Potomac at Shepherdstown, and then break the Baltimore & Ohio at Martinsburg, while two divisions captured the garrison at Harpers Ferry, which failed to evacuate as he hoped. Then the army was to reassemble at Boonsboro or Hagerstown to continue north.[82] Sometime that day he heard from Davis that he and Lowe were at Orange on September 7, and wanted to meet with him, most likely to discuss the draft proclamation and specifics on the campaign. Davis may have hoped to accompany the army, but that was the last thing Lee needed.[83] At once he wrote to dissuade Davis, saying it would be too dangerous for him to come, and Davis did not press.[84]

Within hours Lee's bandaged hands were contending with the breakdown of his plans. McClellan finally moved northward and reached Frederick on September 13. Then he found a lost copy of Lee's orders for the march and moved to get between Lee and Jackson at Harpers Ferry. Meanwhile, Lee reached Hagerstown, where on the morning of September 14 he learned that McClellan had found his order. He reacted immediately. Twenty miles and the Potomac divided the two wings of his army. McClellan was closer to Jackson and Harpers Ferry than was Lee. If the Yankees pushed hard they could cross Crampton's and Turner's Gaps on South Mountain, close the Potomac crossings, and isolate Jackson while turning overwhelming force against Longstreet. That news ended the raid. Now it was a campaign to reunite the army, meet and defeat McClellan, or withdraw to the Shenandoah.

Late that night the Federals took both gaps and began pushing through. Lee ordered a concentration at Sharpsburg to shield Jackson, planning to cross the Potomac to reunite with Stonewall and prepare to meet McClellan should he pursue.[85] Jackson did not capture the Harpers Ferry garrison until the morning of September 15.

Lee learned of it that afternoon, and the next day Jackson's divisions started coming into Sharpsburg, where Lee established his line just west of Antietam Creek, even as McClellan finally caught up to him and extended his own line on the other side. With fewer than 30,000 at hand, though more on the way, Lee faced close to 50,000 Yankees, and had no option but to stand on the defensive. He chose Sharpsburg hastily. Several bridges crossed the creek, and along his center and left the creek could be waded. As Jackson's divisions extended the army's left, he had to abandon crossings to the Yankees in order to anchor his left flank on the Potomac. Worse, higher ground on the Union side would allow McClellan's artillery full play over much of Lee's line. Worst of all, Lee's back was to the Potomac, with the only available crossing, Boteler's Ford, behind his right flank. If he lost that ford, the remainder of Jackson's corps, A. P. Hill and his division, would be cut off, and Lee could be squeezed between McClellan and the Potomac. He could have concentrated on the Virginia side, but if the raid was to impact Northern morale, he needed a combat above the river. The decision to stand on Maryland soil was a political one.

The fight came the next day, September 17. An unusually combative McClellan assaulted Lee's left in the morning, then the Yankees hit and broke his center. By noon his army's position was desperate, as only McClellan's caution prevented an assault that should have cut the line in two and isolated Jackson north of Sharpsburg. A few days later a battery commander who helped Lee prevent a rout told his wife that "I never saw Genl. Lee so anxious as he was at Sharpsburg."[86] That afternoon a fresh Union corps tried to push across the creek in front of Longstreet and by three o'clock was over the stream and pressing into the streets of Sharpsburg. Lee spent most of the day at his head-quarters shifting units to support Jackson on the left, then rode himself to the scene, an aide leading Traveller since Lee's bandaged hands could not manage a bridle. He was at or near the front in several places during the day, especially when his center was threatened. That afternoon as the Yankees began pushing his right flank back into town and away from the vital ford, Lee dismounted and recklessly exposed himself to enemy fire as he tried unsuccessfully to rally that flank short of a disaster, and was elated at that crucial moment to see A. P. Hill's column approaching from Harpers Ferry just after it crossed the ford.

By happy chance it rushed straight into the exposed flank of the advancing foe and brought them to a standstill. By late afternoon the exhausted armies stopped firing.[87]

Never again would Lee get himself into such a dangerous position. A competent general ought to have defeated him. A good one ought to have pushed him into the Potomac. Again Lee was a lucky commander, his luck in the man facing him. McClellan squandered everything, moving slowly after discovering Lee's plans, exerting little control over the battle, and at pivotal moments forfeiting the opportunity to strike decisively. Emphasizing that he little feared Little Mac, Lee stood his ground the next day daring McClellan to come get him. The Federal declined, and on the night of September 18 Lee crossed at Boteler's Ford unopposed and began a gradual withdrawal toward Winchester. It would be weeks before McClellan followed.

The Union undeservedly proclaimed victory. Tactically Lee repulsed almost every Federal assault. Given his situation, his mere survival makes the battle his victory. He held the same ground at the end of the day as at its outset, and it is evident that he defeated McClellan psychologically. Lee always knew he would withdraw into Virginia. It was a raid with specific goals, some of which he achieved. He drew the enemy army out of hard-pressed northern Virginia and replenished and subsisted his own in Maryland. He frightened Washington and Baltimore and perhaps strengthened Lincoln's opposition in the fall elections. He gave the pro-Confederate populace of Maryland an opportunity to rally and claim their independence. That they did not was due to them, not him. Granted, he did not draw the Harpers Ferry garrison out of its defenses. Instead he captured it there, with tons of munitions. The only failure in his stated goals was that he did not reach Pennsylvania.[88] Personally he made better use of his staff than before, using them to maintain communication among elements of his army during the campaign, though then and during the battle he still did not vest them with authority to give orders in his name.[89] Moreover, surely the whole campaign was too ambitious and fraught with danger, its gains arguably not worth the heavy cost. Lee lost more than 1,500 killed in action, and 8,700 wounded and missing, almost a third of the 33,000 engaged. Another such battle could reduce his army to a mere corps.

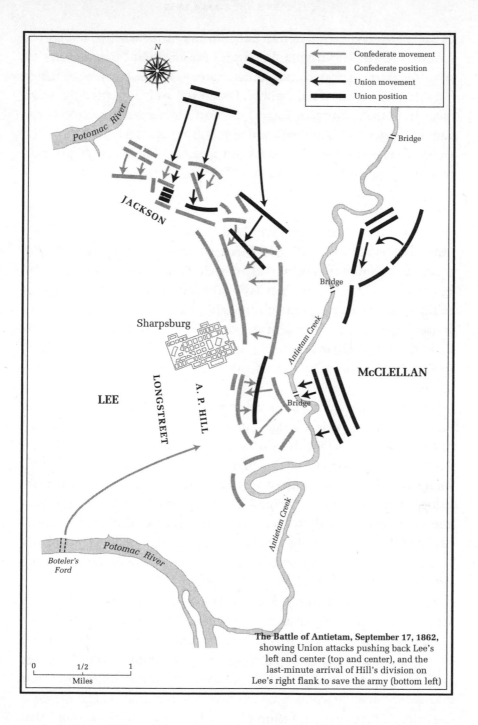

The Battle of Antietam, September 17, 1862,
showing Union attacks pushing back Lee's
left and center (top and center), and the
last-minute arrival of Hill's division on
Lee's right flank to save the army (bottom left)

But there was one intangible gain of incalculable worth. He gave the Army of Northern Virginia the luster of invincibility. In a season that soon saw Bragg defeated and Confederates in Mississippi repulsed, Lee fought McClellan to a standstill on Union soil and reoriented the war's focus from the suburbs of Richmond north to the Potomac. After the summer's victories, Antietam made this army and its commander the would-be nation's most important source of morale, national symbols of Confederate determination.[90]

Two days after Antietam Grant and Ord advanced only about two miles and halted to await news from Rosecrans, but as the day wore on began to doubt that he would arrive in time. Finally, Grant decided no attack could be made that day and instructed Ord to press closer to Iuka, but avoid engagement unless he heard from Rosecrans. Grant learned nothing more until a message from Rosecrans arrived that night telling him that as of noon he was still eight miles from Iuka.[91] In fact, by the time Grant read the dispatch, the battle of Iuka was already over.

After sending Grant that midday message, Rosecrans had kept advancing. He met Confederate outposts two miles below town, and after some skirmishing the Confederates came at him around four-thirty. That was not part of the plan. Rosey was supposed to wait until he heard firing from Ord, but he heard nothing. Then the skirmishing escalated and several hours of fighting ensued in which the Yankees held their ground, Rosecrans all the while listening for the sound of Ord's guns. Amazingly, Grant heard nothing, for an atmospheric anomaly called acoustic shadow caused by humid air and a strong north wind muffled all sound of the fighting.

Hence Grant was stunned just after eight-thirty the next morning when a message from Rosecrans announced the previous afternoon's fight and begged Ord to attack at once. Finally, Grant heard artillery in the distance and sent Ord forward at once. Then another message from Rosecrans asked "why did you not attack this morning?"[92] Of course, so far as Rosey knew, Ord was to have attacked the previous morning. There was confusion all around, and then they found that Price evacuated Iuka during the night using a road that Rosecrans ne-

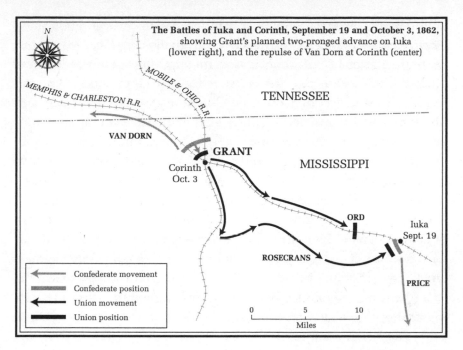

The Battles of Iuka and Corinth, September 19 and October 3, 1862, showing Grant's planned two-pronged advance on Iuka (lower right), and the repulse of Van Dorn at Corinth (center)

glected to hold as he advanced. The two generals met in Iuka about noon, with neither blame nor recrimination from either. Within hours Grant wired Halleck that "I cannot speak too highly of the energy & skill displayed by Genl Rosecrans."[93] It had been a messy operation, hampered by bad roads and weather, and communications compromised by messages being hours out of date by the time they arrived. Grant tried to do too much. Iuka was almost a mirror image of Lee's abortive efforts to coordinate his initial attack on McClellan in the Seven Days in July. Both generals were still learning the limitations of large movements, and the hazards of coordinating detachments without rapid communications.

There were gains from the fight, chiefly driving Price south and away from the 9,000 reinforcements approaching under Major General Earl Van Dorn. Grant wanted to move quickly fifty miles south to Tupelo, and then another hundred miles southwest to Greenwood on the Yazoo River to destroy Confederate gunboats sheltering there.[94] However, Van Dorn moved into west Tennessee, threatening Grant's communications between Corinth and Memphis, and he had to shelve the Yazoo operation and begin shifting forces to Corinth to meet this new threat. Van Dorn withdrew into Mississippi instead and joined Price twenty-five miles southwest of Corinth. By the end of the month more than 22,000 Confederates were moving north. Grant's line was anchored on the east by Rosecrans at Corinth with 23,000, Ord and Hurlbut with 12,000 forty miles northwest at Bolivar, Tennessee, and Sherman and 7,000 some fifty miles west of them at Memphis. Grant kept another 6,000 in reserve at Jackson, thirty miles north of Bolivar. By October 1 he concluded that Price and Van Dorn, the latter in command, intended to attack Corinth. "My position is precarious," he wired Halleck that evening, "but hope to get out of it all right."[95] The next day Grant rode to Jackson, where he could communicate quickly with all of his outposts. That evening Rosecrans proposed that he move out of his works and attack the approaching Confederates, and Grant gave him discretion to "move on them as you propose."[96]

In the morning on October 3 telegrams came into Jackson reporting cannon fire near Corinth, but then the line went dead for some time, and when a courier from Rosecrans rode in later, he had lost his dispatches on the way, so Grant knew nothing more than that Van Dorn had appeared before Rosecrans's advanced positions that morning and firing had been heard. Grant probably assumed that Rosey had attacked.[97] Thus Grant wired Hurlbut at Bolivar to send several brigades south to be in place to cut off Van Dorn's retreat, as usual expecting victory. He also put McPherson in charge of two brigades at Jackson and set him in motion to join Hurlbut, then changed his mind and directed them to Corinth instead.[98]

Grant spent the rest of the day trying to visualize events at Corinth, but the sketchy reports coming in gave him a poor picture. Confederate cavalry had reached and cut the Memphis & Charleston Railroad linking Corinth with Memphis, then retired. They also cut the Mobile & Ohio south from Jackson several miles above Corinth, so McPherson would have to march the last six to seven miles to reach Rosecrans. A man just in from near Corinth reported that "they are fighting."[99] At first Grant thought it might only be heavy skirmishing, and that the Confederates intended to launch their real attack on the morrow, but later in the day couriers from Corinth reported heavy fighting and the enemy attacking Rosecrans. That night Grant heard that in heavy fighting Price had pushed through Rosecrans's works and penetrated into Corinth itself before being driven back, with heavy loss on both sides.[100] He also learned that Hurlbut could not get on the road until at least three in the morning on October 4, meaning he could not possibly cover the forty-six miles to Corinth before October 5 at the earliest. Grant repeatedly hurried Hurlbut, regretting he had not sent him to Corinth a day earlier. "Rosecrans position is precarious," he urged. Believing the enemy numbered no more than 30,000, Grant said "he must be whipped."[101]

In fact, in heavy fighting on October 3 the Confederates pushed Rosecrans back into the defenses around Corinth and only nightfall kept them from pressing their advantage. Rosey himself conducted an erratic defense, planning well, then issuing contradictory orders and failing to maintain control. But he was not in bad shape. With the line working again, he sent Grant telegrams that his men had not fought well, but by midnight he believed he could hold the next day if attacked.[102] Grant still was not certain that this was not just a heavy demonstration to pin down Rosecrans, while the Confederates slipped away to move against Bolivar. Suddenly he realized that if the Confederates did that they would meet Hurlbut on the road and might overwhelm him. He wired Rosecrans that if Van Dorn fell back he must follow closely to prevent disaster for Hurlbut, admonishing "don't neglect this warning."[103]

He need not have worried. Van Dorn reopened his cannonade before dawn, but his renewed attack was tardy and ill coordinated. Rebel brigades hammered the Federal defenses, and in one or two places drove into town before being repulsed. There was heavy fighting until about one in the afternoon when the Confederate attack lost its energy, and a few hours later Van Dorn began a retreat eastward just as McPherson reached Corinth. Rosecrans wired Grant that they were badly beaten and promised to launch a pursuit in the morning.[104] "Push the enemy to the wall," Grant responded, hoping to pin Van Dorn against the Hatchie River a dozen miles west and bag his whole army, looking, as always, for the complete victory.[105] More urgent messages followed, warning Rosecrans that "if you do not bag the most of them it will be your fault."[106] Hurlbut and a detachment under Ord encountered the Confederates first on October 5, but could not prevent them from crossing the river to continue their retreat toward Holly Springs, Mississippi, fifty miles west of Corinth.[107]

The next day Grant again pressed Rosey to "capture and destroy the Rebel army to the utmost of your power," but by October 7 he concluded that the opportunity was gone.[108] Hurlbut and McPherson were almost out of rations and encumbered with wounded from the Hatchie fight, Grant had no more reinforcements in his department to send, and the enemy seemed to be moving faster than Rosecrans. Grant's forces were spread out across southwest Tennessee and northern Mississippi, getting farther from their bases of supply and the railroads they were protecting, leaving them increasingly exposed should the Confederates mount a counterstroke. Reluctantly, Grant ordered all of his forces to return to their bases. When Rosecrans objected, arguing that he could still take Van Dorn, Grant took his demurrer seriously enough to suspend the order pending Halleck's response to an appeal for reinforcements. Throughout October 8 he wavered on continuing the pursuit. Three times he ordered Rosecrans to fall back, believing that even if partially successful, Rosecrans would be drawn so far from his base that "disaster would follow in the end." Even then, however, he held open the option of taking command in person and pressing on as far as possible if Halleck wished.[109] A day later, hearing nothing from Halleck, Grant ordered Rosecrans's return to Corinth a last time.

Iuka fit the now-established mold for Grant the commander. Faced with a challenge, he seized the initiative and planned his offensive carefully, relying again on concentration of forces and convergence on the enemy from different points of the compass. He willingly altered his arrangement on the advice of the officer on the scene, and thought ahead to capitalize on success. Delays and miscommunication, and a freak atmospheric anomaly, disrupted his designs, but he improvised on the spot, though for the first time he did not command on the field after circumstances took the battle out of his hands and left it to Rosecrans before Grant arrived. "I had no more to do with troops under Gen. Ord than I had with those under Rosecrans," he said in assessing his role, "but gave the orders to both." And those orders were precise. Indeed, Grant was frustrated now with Hillyer, for often when he asked the aide to draft an order for him, the captain begged off by saying that no one could put things in so concise a form as Grant himself without possibility of misinterpretation.[110] He had planned to bag

Price's whole command, but circumstances foiled his hopes. Still, he blamed no one.[111]

Corinth was a departure. Grant left the initiative to the enemy. He had little choice until he knew Van Dorn's target, remembering now to think about what the enemy might do. Grant had over 45,000 in his department, but they covered a front 130 miles wide. Concentrating against Van Dorn risked exposing vital points if he misjudged the Confederate goal. Once he settled on Corinth, Grant still wondered if the real objective was Bolivar, perhaps because that is where *he* might have struck. A blow there could cut railroads, isolate Corinth, disrupt communications, put Memphis at hazard, and possibly force the evacuation of Corinth. When Van Dorn appeared there, Grant trusted Rosecrans to conduct his defense and spent his time forwarding reinforcements. If he erred, it was in those forces being too far away and counting on rail to get them to Corinth on short notice. With the battle over, his expectation of an immediate pursuit overlooked how disorganized even a victorious army could be. At Shiloh he had Buell's fresh divisions to commence pursuit at once; Rosecrans did not. Grant was still learning the practical capabilities of an army before, during, and after action. If he broke his own rule of relying on the judgment of the commander on the spot when he ordered the pursuit stopped, Grant respected his judgment enough to reconsider the decision.[112]

His appraisal of the result of the two battles was that the moral gains from the victories might outweigh the benefit of capturing Price's army, as he continued to fail to grasp the depth of Confederate resolve to resist. Optimistic as ever, he told his sister Mary in mid-October that "we now have such an advantage over the rebels that there should be but little more hard fighting."[113] He believed his role in ending the war was to "move south" again. Before the end of the month he framed the outline of a campaign to take Vicksburg.[114]

10

"WHAT HAVE WE
TO LIVE FOR
IF NOT VICTORIES?"

Lᴀᴛᴇ ɪɴ ᴛʜᴇ fall of 1862 a Springfield, Illinois, editor noted that while Grant's initials had been associated with Uncle Sam or United States, "they have lately been discovered, however, to mean 'Unconditional Surrender.'" He thought that "'Unconditional Surrender' Grant is a very good man to send after the rebels in Mississippi."[1] That was precisely what he wanted to do if only petty distractions did not beset him. For all the challenges of manning and maintaining his army, Robert E. Lee never had to cope with the political, economic, interpersonal, and command rivalry headaches that constantly distracted Grant.

The twenty-year friendship with Rosecrans was gone. On October 7 Rawlins issued on Grant's behalf a congratulatory order commending his army on the victory, but Rosey responded by protesting that the order seemed to hint that there might be jealousy between their commands.[2] Soon enough Grant learned that members of Rosecrans's staff actually did encourage feeling against him, and Rawlins heard that Rosecrans was trying to take all of the credit for Iuka and Corinth. Worse, unspecified "insinuations" were coming out of Rosecrans's headquarters suggesting that Grant was drinking at Iuka.[3] The culprit was William D. Bickham of the Cincinnati *Commercial*, which had often been critical of Grant. An aide to Rosecrans in western Virginia in 1861, Bickham stayed with Rosecrans's headquarters writing such glowing pieces that other correspondents branded him a "puffer" for Rosey.[4] His account of the fight at Corinth mentioned Grant only once, implying that victory would have been complete but for Grant halting the pursuit, and gave all credit to Rosey.[5] His attack on one division's performance led to threats that impelled him to flee the army temporarily.[6] Meanwhile, someone else seized on Bickham's reports to resurrect the charges of drunkenness in a forged letter to Washington.[7]

"For Heaven's sake do *something*," Rawlins's informant appealed, believing that Rosecrans angled for Grant's command, which was true.[8] Grant may not have thought so, but what he did hear coming from Rosey's staff did not dispose him well when that general accused him of giving preferential treatment to other portions of his army. Grant denied that vigorously, and then scolded Rosecrans for ignoring military protocol and communicating directly with Washington rather than going through him. "You regard your command [as] giving privileges held by others commanding geographical divisions," he wrote. "This is a mistake." Immediately backing down, Rosey protested that Grant "had no truer friend no more loyal subordinate," and blamed any misunderstandings on "mischief makers winesellers & mouse catching politicians."[9] Grant was not to be put off. Staff leaks and Bickham's articles encouraged jealousies between their armies detrimental to morale and cooperation, he charged, but Rosecrans blamed all such jealousies on Grant and his staff. "After this declaration I am free to say that if you do not meet me frankly with a declaration that you are satisfied," he wrote on October 21, "I shall consider my power to be useful in this Department ended."[10]

That was a conclusion Grant had already reached. The next day he wrote his final report on Iuka. On September 20 he sent a brief account to Washington stating that "I cannot speak too highly of the energy & skill displayed by Genl Rosecrans."[11] Now in this fuller report, drafted over several days by Rawlins but surely amended and approved by Grant, he might have been expected to be hard on Rosecrans. Grant was certainly human, and there were no effusions in this full report, no "cannot speak too highly," yet he was fair if restrained. He acknowledged Rosecrans's part in the campaign, without implying criticism, expressed "some disappointment" at his being late to reach the field, and offered explanations on Rosecrans's behalf for upsetting Grant's original plan.[12] If the report said rather less than Rosey deserved for his command's actions, it said more than he deserved after his recent behavior. That same day Rosecrans complained to Halleck and asked for a change of assignment, which Halleck granted the next day. In notifying Rosey of the change, Grant added that "I predict an

important command where in the course of events we may cooperate," and he was right.[13] Buell had been a disappointment, and Halleck now ordered Rosecrans to assume command of the Army of the
Cumberland.

Grant was relieved to be rid of him. "It is a great annoyance to gain
rank and command enough to attract public attention," he told Ord.
"I have found it so and would now really prefer some little command
where public attention would not be attracted towards me."[14] If he
must be in the public eye, he wanted himself and his command to be
fairly represented, and not as Bickham and Rosecrans's other supporters depicted them in the papers. "I have no objection to that [or] any
other Gen. being made a hero of by the press," he wrote Washburne,
"but I do not want to see it at the expense of a meritorious portion of
the Army."[15]

Still, Rosey was a minor irritant. Not so McClernand. He wanted to
be president, and being subordinate to a successful general was not a
fast track. McClernand criticized Grant in letters to Lincoln. In July he
tried to get reassigned to the Army of the Potomac, but denied that
he visited the president in person and pushed a plan to raise his own
army in Illinois to lead personally against Vicksburg, beyond Grant's
authority. In his anxiety for aggressive movement, Lincoln unwisely
approved, but gave Halleck some authority over the new regiments so
that Grant would have first crack at those he might need himself. Confused, Grant asked if he was to remain idle while McClernand raised
and led his expedition. With McClernand apparently an independent
authority inside Grant's department, was Sherman to be the same, or
would he still report to him?[16] Halleck tried to reassure Grant that he
commanded all forces in his department, but the "misterious rumors"
Grant was hearing left him unsettled.[17]

It did not help that Halleck gave no guidance. What he did do was
to reconstitute Grant's command into a new Department of the Tennessee, including Cairo, Forts Henry and Donelson, all of Kentucky
and Tennessee west of the Tennessee River, and as much of north
Mississippi as was in his hands.[18] Yet he told—or knew—nothing of
the plans of General Samuel Curtis commanding the Department of
the Missouri, or of Rosecrans in his new incumbency. Grant grasped,
even if they did not, that they needed coordination among them for

best results. Shortly after the fight at Corinth he had a rough total of 97,000 men of all arms spread through his department from Corinth to Memphis, and all the way back to Cairo.[19] Its force was blunted by not being concentrated, and he could not concentrate it without exposing a line of communications more than a hundred miles long. Doubting that he could resume offensive operations until reinforced, he proposed to shift his Corinth forces west to Grand Junction on the Mississippi Central Railroad, about fifty miles east of Memphis. With a small reinforcement. exclusive of McClernand, he would move down that railroad to Holly Springs, Mississippi, then on to Oxford, then Grenada. There he could isolate or destroy rebel gunboats sheltering on the upper Yazoo River, something he had in mind at least since September. Then he would keep moving south with Vicksburg in his sights. Grant suggested that the task would be easier if both sides of the Mississippi were under one unified command. He did not mention McClernand.[20]

With no demurrer from Halleck, Grant started units forward, rebuilding railroad and telegraph lines as they advanced, and hinting to McPherson that they might "go far south."[21] By November 4 he had about 31,000 men rendezvousing at Lagrange just west of Grand Junction. He intended for Sherman to move south from Memphis as a distraction, but postponed that when Halleck notified him that 20,000 reinforcements were coming. Again he asked for news of a rumored movement by Curtis toward the river, "so as to make the whole cooperate." Until he knew the whole picture in that theater, he could only make independent moves. Much as he liked that independence, he understood that he was part of a larger team. As for the reported 30,000 Confederates at Holly Springs, he believed he could "handle that number without gloves."[22] Indeed, "I have not the slightest apprehension of a reverse from present appearances," he told Halleck.[23] The Grant confidence and optimism remained undimmed.

Grant stayed at Lagrange almost to the end of November, long enough for Julia to come join him for a time.[24] His hope for a speedy move south was postponed by news that Curtis had sent a dozen regiments east to Memphis on their way to Grenada. He wanted Sherman to stay in Memphis to absorb them before the two columns started south, and meanwhile commenced a buildup of supplies, intending to keep at lease a million rations on hand. Otherwise, he intended that they would live off the land, taking whatever food and livestock they needed, but paying with vouchers that farmers could redeem at the end of the war.[25] Grant remained conscious of the need to deal fairly with civilians, for fear of alienating them. He threatened officers with serious consequences and enlisted men with death should they plunder private homes and property.[26] When regiments looted local stores Grant fined them to recompense the owners, punished the men involved, and dismissed their officers.[27] Meanwhile, he dealt with local cotton planters. Those deemed loyal he permitted to take their bales to Memphis for sale, while he simply seized for the government the cotton of disloyal or suspected growers.[28]

He also had to handle the fugitive slaves coming into his lines, now in wagonloads, presenting ever greater demands on his commissary. His solution to the growing problem was the innovative idea of commissioning a superintendent of contrabands to establish residence camps for the blacks, then find them jobs picking confiscated cotton in local fields under military oversight. Soon they were earning a little money, living securely and eating well, and making a contribution to the Union war effort. This was no social reform. Nothing suggests that Grant had yet developed any more discomfort with slavery than before the war, but by now he had encountered the real face of slavery far more extensively. As his attitudes toward Mexicans and Indians revealed, he felt sympathy for nonwhite peoples crushed by western progress. Moreover, Lincoln's announcement of a Preliminary Emancipation Proclamation the past September, and the promise of its going into effect on January 1, 1863, meant that tens—even hundreds—of thousands more slaves would be emancipating themselves by fleeing to Union lines.

He must be prepared to deal with them, if only to keep the human inflow from slowing the progress of his army. Grant knew from his own experience that blacks would work if motivated. If whites saw them willingly working as free men, in time black males might be accepted as soldiers should the Union need them. Once a man carried a rifle for his country, citizenship and even the ballot might follow. Organizing employment for these fugitives could have far-reaching effects. But that was Grant thinking out loud as he spoke with the man he made superintendent. This was purely a field expedient to deal with an immediate problem, but it was the sort of solution typical of Grant: direct, speedy, and aimed toward productive gain. "I was dealing with no incompetent," concluded the new superintendent after Grant explained his idea, "but a man capable of handling large issues."[29] Sensitive to the fact that slaves behind Union lines would remain slaves after promulgation of the Emancipation Proclamation, Grant directed that no slaves were to be lured away from their masters or forced into government service.[30] Loyal planters, or those not taking sides, must not be alienated.

As his army gradually grew Grant addressed matters of organization yet again, tried to make it more effective in action by securing arms of a uniform caliber throughout, and revised his staff to suit his needs. Appointing Rawlins both adjutant and chief of staff, he increased it to seventeen officers including specialized chiefs of cavalry, artillery, engineers, telegraph services, military railroads, ordnance, subsistence, quartermaster, medical, and topographical engineers or map making.[31] He also dealt with the inevitable empire builder, in this case the superintendent of telegraphs in the department, a man so imperious that he objected to any instructions from Grant and referred everything to his superior in the telegraph office in Washington. Worse, the man allowed paid commercial dispatches to occupy the army's line when Grant needed it for military communications. Grant was patient for some days, trying to work with the recalcitrant fellow, but again when nothing else seemed to break the impasse, he dealt with it directly by arresting him. When the superintendent of the military telegraph in Washington instructed his operators to take orders from no one but himself, Grant fired an angry response calling him "insolent" and thereafter ignored him, protesting that he had "neither the time nor the inclination" to waste effort better spent on more important matters.[32]

On November 20 Grant made a fast visit back to Cairo on just such a matter, to meet for the first time with Rear Admiral David D. Porter, the new commander of the Mississippi Squadron based there. Porter had contacted him sometime earlier to offer cooperation in his anticipated campaign into Mississippi, and at the same time may have told Grant a little more about McClernand's impending Vicksburg expedition, with which Porter was supposed to move in concert.[33] They met in the evening over dinner, and in the course of a few hours determined to ignore McClernand and act on their own.[34] The next day Grant stopped at Columbus, where Sherman met him, and they settled plans for the campaign. Sherman was to move on Holly Springs on November 26, Grant would advance from Lagrange three days later, and the forces coming from Curtis under Brigadier General Frederick Steele were expected to cross the river at Helena, Arkansas, and advance to Grenada. Grant asked Porter the next day to propose a plan whereby he might cooperate with them, and then Grant and Sherman both left for Grand Junction.[35] Grant felt confident of succeeding, but he expected a strong enemy in his front.[36]

The reason for the hurried activity was the enemy in his rear. Grant had decided that if he was to ignore McClernand, then he would launch his own thrust at Vicksburg first. On November 24 he notified Halleck that he had given orders for an advance. He gave the general-in-chief an opportunity to stay his hand, but Halleck wired back a terse approval, only warning him "don't go too far."[37] Grant might have pondered just what that meant, but in his experience Halleck was always advising him not to go too far. Either he was approved to move on Vicksburg or he was not, and Grant chose to assume that he was. Orders for the march went out on November 26, dividing his army into a right wing under Sherman moving from Memphis and a left under General Charles Hamilton with the forces at Lagrange.[38] McPherson's division formed a center between Sherman and Hamilton, all of them connected to him by telegraph. By Saturday morning, November 29, Grant rode into Holly Springs, recently evacuated by the enemy. Three days later he was in Abbeville, reestablishing rail and telegraph lines as he marched, and on December 4 he rode into Oxford.[39]

Now he was fifty miles into Mississippi, and very conscious of his exposure. "How far south would you like me to go?" he wired Halleck the day before he reached Oxford. It was out of character for Grant to ask such a question, but reflection began to chip at his optimism. Newspapers in the North estimated that McClernand's expedition, with which Porter must still cooperate by Lincoln's instruction, would be ready to launch downriver in less than a week.[40] When it did, its movement would leave Grant's right rear at Memphis exposed, opening the door to enemy cavalry to strike at his increasingly extended supply line on the Mississippi Central. He began to doubt that he could safely advance beyond Grenada and still maintain his line of communications. Rain had swelled streams and turned the roads into mires, slowing his advance. Perhaps it might be wiser for his command to hold the Confederates in his front somewhere below Grenada, while another force moved down the river on Vicksburg?[41] Grant did not say whose force, but Halleck certainly understood that he did not mean McClernand's. He advised that Grant not go farther south himself, but to get 25,000 troops back to Memphis for gunboats to take them south, promising that they would be reinforced by men from Curtis.[42]

Two days later Grant knew he had to stop, as the roads became all but impossible. Typically, if he could not move on land, he turned to the water. He suggested to Halleck that if he could command Steele's column, he would put Sherman in charge of it and his own wing and send them by transport to the mouth of the Yazoo River, a few miles upstream from Vicksburg. While Grant kept the main body of the Confederates commanded by Lieutenant General John C. Pemberton occupied in his front near Grenada, Sherman should have an easy time taking the river bastion.[43] By December 7 Grant was preparing to start sending divisions to Memphis, but a question remained. He asked Halleck who was to command the downriver expedition. "Do you want me to command," he asked, "or shall I send Sherman?"[44] Again, McClernand simply was not spoken of, as if he did not exist. Given the nature of the politician's independent command, they could do little else. Halleck wired back that Lincoln might insist on putting someone else in charge—he did not have to say it would be McClernand—but if he did not, then the choice was Grant's, though he favored Sherman. Halleck wanted Grant in north central Mississippi where he could protect Corinth in case Confederates from middle Tennessee should move west to threaten the vital rail junction and supply base.[45]

Before he had Halleck's response, Grant made the decision himself that Sherman should command an expedition of 40,000 to go to the mouth of the Yazoo, then upstream to land and cut Vicksburg's rail connection with Jackson. After that he would leave the manner of capturing the town to Sherman, while he cooperated from Oxford by keeping Pemberton occupied.[46] An erroneous report that Steele had actually crossed the Mississippi and captured Grenada reached Grant on December 8, and with it Halleck's authorization to assume command of Steele and any other forces of Curtis's then in his department. Thinking as he wrote to Sherman, he considered sending two divisions to Memphis, and thence downriver while he actually pressed forward his command at Oxford. If he did not, then he might push the entire combined force forward, establish a supply base at Grenada, and then move due south to take Jackson. His thinking was still evolving, but he rather preferred the waterborne option.[47] In fact, after that day he came to a decision and ordered Sherman to go to Memphis with one division and assume command of all troops there including any units of Steele's, and organize them into an army for Porter to transport to the vicinity of Vicksburg. Once there Sherman and Porter were to decide for themselves how best to take the city, and notify Grant so he could move in cooperation.[48] Before making up his mind, Grant issued an order assuming command of all of Curtis's forces then east of the Mississippi, and alerted Steele, who he discovered was actually at Helena on the west bank of the river, to send his men back to the Tennessee side to await Sherman.[49]

In the back of his mind always lurked McClernand. Grant did not hold back with Halleck in expressing his views on the politician-general. When he learned on December 9 that McClernand was just a few days from launching his expedition, Grant fired a telegram to Halleck saying that the expedition would "be much safer" in Sherman's hands, and then seemingly closed the matter by adding that in any case his expedition had already left.[50] In fact, Sherman was still at Memphis, but Washington did not know that. If Lincoln thought Sherman was already on his way he might check McClernand, whom Grant now regarded as "unmanageable and incompetent," dreading the thought that he might be attached to his command somehow.[51]

Consequently, that is what happened. On December 18 Halleck ordered Grant to organize his army into four corps, one commanded by McPherson, one by Hurlbut, one by Sherman, and McClernand's small army as a corps under himself.[52] Halleck further directed—at Lincoln's behest—that McClernand have command of the Vicksburg expedition, though under Grant's overall direction. Unfortunately Grant knew that McClernand would take little direction from him when he could go directly to the White House. His hope was that Sherman could embark and be at Vicksburg's doorsteps before Mc-Clernand arrived to take command. Dutifully, he wrote McClernand that same day notifying him of the orders. Wisely, he wrote a letter rather than a telegram. By this time Grant was well experienced at turning slow mail delivery versus near-instantaneous telegraphic delivery to his advantage. The later McClernand got notification of his orders, the more time that bought Sherman. By December 19 Grant hoped Sherman was ready to go, as in fact he almost was.[53] When he embarked the next day, McClernand was still in Springfield, Illinois, and would not reach Memphis until a week after the expedition departed. The Union needed good news now, for there was news of disaster on the Rappahannock.

In the weeks following Antietam Lee rebuilt his army in the northern Shenandoah, and McClellan did not interfere. Gradually his ranks grew above 80,000, and the Confederate Congress authorized the combining of divisions into army corps and the rank of lieutenant general for the new corps commanders, virtually replicating what Lee had been doing already. As a result, instead of commanding informal "wings" of his army, new Lieutenant General Longstreet would command the I Corps, and Lieutenant General Jackson the II Corps. Meanwhile, if he failed to get his army into Pennsylvania, he made his point with Stuart's cavalry, which he sent in mid-October on a ride around McClellan's army and all the way to Chambersburg, Pennsylvania. The raid accomplished no tangible damage to the enemy, but it threw McClellan off balance, boosted Southern spirits, and embarrassed Lincoln on the eve of the fall elections.

Tragic news quickly damped any elation at Stuart's feat. Thirty years earlier Lee had said a man should communicate his joy but conceal his grief. Now tragedy gave him a chance to practice his precept. Mary went to Jones's Springs in Warren County, North Carolina, that fall, taking their twenty-three-year-old daughter Annie with her. Neither was well, but Annie gradually sank until she died on October 20. It was not practical to take her body home—indeed, the Lees had no home to take her to—and so she was buried there.[54] The doleful news reached Lee a few days later. He knew his daughter had been ill but duty prevented him going to see her. "I cannot express the anguish I feel," he wrote Mary. He could offer no comfort but the belief that she had been called away "at the time and place when it is best for her to go."[55] For weeks thereafter in the stillness of the night his uncomforted grief crept over him until he felt all but overwhelmed. He had hoped a time might come with wars done when he could have a few years with her, "but year after year my hopes go out, and I must be resigned."[56]

No wonder that more and more Lee spoke nostalgically of "happier days" when he could enjoy his family's company. "Now that death has entered my home and nipped in the morning one of the flowers God had planted there," life's small luster was more dulled than ever, he told Carter. Despite all he and his army had achieved, "I feel as if nothing had been accomplished," he mused in his gloom, "but we must endure to the end." There was still so much to do if they were to be independent. "Nothing can surpass the valor and endurance of our troops," he told his brother Carter in late October, yet no sooner did he disperse one enemy army than another appeared in its place. "This snatches from us the fruits of victory and covers the battle fields with our gallant dead." Too many Antietams might bleed him to death. "We may be annihilated," he said, "but we cannot be conquered." And yet he asked, "what have we to live for if not victories."[57]

While Lee grieved, McClellan did not move again until October 26 when he commenced a glacial crossing of the Potomac just east of the Blue Ridge. Lee had anticipated the enemy would occupy Martinsburg and then move south into the Shenandoah, aptly guessing McClellan's original intent, but by the first week of November he believed the whole Union army was concentrating to the east.[58] His own army was divided, Jackson's corps of nearly 40,000 in the Shenandoah Valley around Winchester, while in response to McClellan's crossing Lee brought Longstreet's 45,000 east of the Blue Ridge to Culpeper Court House. For the moment he felt comfortable leaving Jackson on his own menacing the Federal flank from the valley. He did not have an accurate assessment of Federal strength, but he expected it to be well beyond his own—as it was—making the Yankees too strong for him to meet in battle. Consequently, Lee concluded to "baffle his designs by maneuvering."[59] If he could keep them uncertain along the Blue Ridge, perhaps dividing themselves to watch Jackson on the west and Longstreet on the east, then they might give him an opportunity to strike separate elements at advantage.[60]

By November 7 the Army of the Potomac had reached the vicinity of Warrenton, still north of the Rappahannock. Then Lincoln replaced McClellan with Major General Ambrose E. Burnside on November 7. Within a few days Lee knew that Burnside commanded.[61] By November 12 he expected the Yankees either to cross the Rappahannock to move against Longstreet, or else go to Fredericksburg, perhaps with a view of using Aquia Creek a few miles north as the staging area for another waterborne shift below Richmond.[62] For the next several days Lee watched and read what he could from enemy movements, considering the alternatives available to Burnside, and his own options, aware that his response might better be a little late than a little wrong. Three days later the Federals started moving southeast from Warrenton and Lee closely monitored their movements. Not until November 20 did he conclude that Burnside was going to Fredericksburg, and it was nearly too late, for by then the enemy army was already massing across the Rappahannock from the city.[63] Lee had been neither complaisant nor careless in waiting before moving, but he had been lucky. Had Washington not failed to get Burnside equipped with pontoons for building bridges, he might have been across the river and on the road to Richmond before Lee could stop him. Lee put Longstreet's corps in motion that same day, then rode ahead accompanied by his son Robert, and after midnight reached Fredericksburg.[64]

The town offered a fine place to an engineer's eye for defense. The Rappahannock ran too deep to ford here and Burnside would have to throw pontoon bridges over the stream to cross. Ordinarily those would make fine concentrated targets for a defender, but Stafford Heights on the north side of the river afforded enemy artillery a commanding field of fire over the town, meaning that any units Lee sent to contest a crossing could be shattered. However, just a few hundred yards west rose Marye's Heights with an equally commanding view of the town, and southeast of it Prospect Hill offered fine high ground to defend should the enemy try to cross downstream. Lee was too weak to strike at Burnside, even if he had means of crossing the river. With only half his army present Lee could only assume the defensive and make the enemy come to him as he had at Antietam. He could not keep Burnside from crossing the river, but he was confident he could keep him from getting on the road to Richmond.[65]

When Longstreet's column began arriving during the day Lee put it in line along Marye's Heights and high ground extending from either side. That same day Burnside's demand to city authorities that they surrender or he might start shelling the town erased any doubt Lee might have had of the Yankee's intent. Through most of the next day Lee employed army wagons to evacuate women and children from town and gave his promise not to occupy the city for military purposes, but to defend it should Burnside attempt to cross the river.[66] Meanwhile, he spent the days out in the cold and rain on his own heights with field glasses studying the Federal positions on Stafford. Then on the evening of November 22 Burnside moved his camps and supply trains to the rear, and by the following morning most of his artillery appeared to have left. Could Burnside be moving his army, intending to hold Lee here while changing base to strike west at Jackson in the Shenandoah or launch a North Carolina expedition? "They seem to be hesitating but are very numerous," he told Mary. "I do not now know what I can do."[67]

Fortunately, Lee read Northern newspapers when he could get them and knew that their public were fed up with delay, from which he concluded that Burnside did not dare delay action for fear of an outcry at home "equivalent to a defeat." He decided that Burnside had just pulled back to protect his camps from Confederate artillery, while establishing his communications line by rail and water back to Washington. When ready, the Yankees would cross the river and try to push through to take the road to Richmond. That being the case, Lee intended to delay Burnside to push any action deeper into the winter so that weather would make enemy movement more difficult. Of course that also applied to Lee's movements, but so long as he kept Burnside in his front he would have less distance to move than an enemy army trying to get around him. His readings on Napoleon at the Military Academy perhaps came to mind, with their account of how the Russians fell back before the emperor, drawing him deeper and deeper into a brutal winter. Still, Lee deferred to Davis, saying he would defend a line closer to the capital if the president wished. Unsaid was that Lee thought it would be foolish to give up any ground without a fight.[68]

He had 38,000 men on the heights under Longstreet, almost exactly one-third the enemy numbers across the river, and concluded now that it was time to call Jackson from the valley. Typically, Lee did not send an order. He merely laid out his view of the strategic situation at the moment, observed that he did not see what further good Jackson could do in the Shenandoah, and then suggested that if Stonewall agreed, "I wish you would move east." He did not even call Jackson to Fredericksburg, leaving it to him to decide where, though Lee favored Culpcpcr where he would be in speedy rail communication with Fredericksburg. While facing what could be a difficult defense in his front should Burnside move quickly, Lee still wanted to keep options open to the west, where Jackson's presence threatened Burnside's right flank.[69]

With the prospect of a battle imminent, Lee once more dealt with his most onerous task as army commander: handling an inadequate subordinate. Where Grant addressed such problems frontally, Lee recoiled from direct confrontation. For months now his division commanders had complained of Brigadier General Thomas Drayton. At Second Manassas he was so slow that his brigade missed the action. At Antietam his command all but dissolved. As one division commander after another complained of him, Lee had transferred his brigade repeatedly. He could not risk another poor performance in the next action, and reluctantly told Davis that Drayton "seems to lack the capacity to command." Yet rather than turn over the brigade to a better general, he resorted to the same roundabout means he used to get G. W. Smith out of his army. Citing Davis's preferred, though hardly universal, policy of composing brigades entirely of regiments from the same state, Lee notified the War Department that since Drayton's contained both South Carolina and Georgia units, he would dissolve it and reassign them to other brigades from their states. That, of course, left Drayton with no command. As he usually did with officers he did not want, Lee suggested that Drayton be sent to the Deep South or perhaps Louisiana or Texas.[70] It was certainly a way to solve Lee's problem. He seems not to have considered that he merely shifted his problem to someone else.

Unbeknownst to him, Lee had potential problems with subordinates much closer to his headquarters. There had been hints of friction between Jackson and Longstreet and their commands since the Seven Days. Then during the Antietam Campaign Jackson complained that the want of shoes and equipment hampered his movements, and after the battle he spoke privately of resigning in protest, especially when he believed Lee showed partiality to Longstreet in distributing guns and equipment. Apparently he said nothing of it to Lee, but as winter approached he remained upset with his commander.[71]

Meanwhile Longstreet, whose ambition far exceeded his ability, played a secret game of his own. He preferred Joseph E. Johnston's cautious and conservative style to Lee's aggressive, and therefore more costly, leadership. After Lee replaced the wounded Johnston, Longstreet maintained a correspondence with his former commander, making it clear that he wanted him to come back. "The men would now go wild at the sight of their old favorite," he told Johnston flatteringly—and erroneously—that October. "Although they have fought many battles and successfully under another leader, I feel that you have their hearts more decidedly than any other leader can ever have." Hearing that Johnston might be sent soon to the western theater to exercise overall command of the armies of Generals Bragg in Tennessee, Pemberton in Mississippi, and Kirby Smith in Kentucky, Longstreet objected and suggested that he come take command of the I Corps instead. "You are more than welcome to it," he wrote, "and I have no doubt but the command of the entire Army will fall to you before Spring." Not only did Longstreet express a surprising want of confidence in Lee, but also he went on to make naively transparent his own overweaningly self-interested motive by suggesting that he would go to the West in Johnston's place. It was seemingly a stunning display of naïveté, for Longstreet had no more authority to trade his corps command with another than Johnston did to assign anyone from Lee's army elsewhere, especially to a position of command. Longstreet was hinting that Johnston use his presumed political influence with a small but vocal bloc in Congress to return himself to the Army of Northern Virginia, and promote Longstreet to lieutenant general and send him to take one of those western commands, probably Kirby Smith's. Hinting that there was more he would impart, Longstreet wanted to meet with Johnston to discuss it all further, since they "cant always write what we would like to say."[72] Just days later Longstreet got his promotion to lieutenant general, a day before Jackson got his, but that only whetted his appetite for an independent command out from under Lee's oversight.

Unaware of these undercurrents, while not dealing with administrative problems, Lee personally examined the left bank of the Rappahannock for a dozen miles below Fredericksburg to spot the most likely places for Burnside to cross, and concluded that he might not try to cross at the town at all.[73] On November 27 he finally instructed Jackson to bring his corps to join Longstreet's, taking position downstream from town on and around Prospect Hill in extension of Longstreet's line.[74] There for nearly two weeks the army, now grown to 92,000 including Stuart, stared across the Rappahannock waiting for Burnside to move.[75] The weather turned colder and early snow fell. Lee had a few comforts against the cold. A local woman sent him a mattress and some catsup and preserves, but he found little pleasure in such things when he knew so many of his soldiers suffered barefoot and ill clad in the snow. When a woman sent him a cake, he set it outside under some trees for the young men attached to headquarters to share.[76] Then on December 9 the cold came even closer when he learned that Rooney's infant daughter had died, the second child lost to him that year. "You have now two sweet angels in heaven," he wrote Rooney's wife the next day. "What joy there is in the thought!"[77]

Those "sweet angels" would soon have a lot of company. Hours later, just before dawn on December 11, Longstreet sent word that the Federals were attempting to put down pontoons in front of town. Lee knew from the first that he could not hold the town, but with a major battle in the offing, he needed to buy time for Jackson's troops to march upstream to link with Longstreet, and assigned a Mississippi brigade to offer a stubborn resistance to the Federal crossing, first on the riverfront, then in Fredericksburg itself, before it withdrew to Marye's Heights. By late afternoon some bridges were complete and the Federals began crossing into the town. Lee had only moments to rush a few words to Mary, some mundane things about a bridle bit he needed, a brief description of the enemy movement, and then the hope that "we shall be able to damage them yet."[78] All that night he heard enemy infantry and artillery rumbling across the bridges, and then watched during the next day as they continued their crossing. There was little he could do but wait, leaving all initiative for the moment to Burnside. About noon he met Jackson and they rode forward to reconnoiter, satisfying themselves that Burnside appeared to be putting his whole army across. Later that day he wrote back to Richmond, "I shall try and do them all the damage in our power when they move forward."[79] He would be fighting on the defensive, which he did not like, but this was different than his stand at Antietam. There he had been on the move and McClellan just caught up to him, forcing a quick selection of ground. Here he had time to select and enhance his positions with the spade, even though he believed at the time that the south banks of the North Anna or South Anna Rivers offered more advantage.

About nine o'clock December 13 Burnside launched his attack, first on Jackson's position, where the fighting went back and forth throughout the morning as Jackson held his ground. Then about eleven o'clock four Federal divisions formed lines in the town and one after another marched up the slope of Marye's Heights to hurl themselves at Lee over and over for more than two hours without breaking through. Lee himself watched the fight with Longstreet from the top of Telegraph Hill just to the right rear of Marye's Heights, where he had a fair view of the terrible grandeur of Burnside's doomed assaults.[80] When Lee learned that the Federals in front of Jackson showed no sign of renewing their assault, he transferred several brigades over to bolster Longstreet, and that afternoon when fresh Union divisions repeated the effort to storm Marye's, the Confederates repulsed them with terrible losses. One last assault at dusk met the same fate, and the battle was done. Burnside suffered more than 12,500 killed, wounded, or captured, the majority of them on the bloody slopes of Marye's Heights. Lee's losses were 4,600, and most of those came when his men pursued the retreating Federals down the heights onto the plain below Prospect Hill where the Union artillery had full play on them.[81]

Lee hoped that Burnside would try again the next day, since he had fresh units and ammunition in readiness. When the Yankees made no move, he still hoped for a renewal on December 15, and again the 16th, but found that morning that the Federal army had pulled back across the river and removed its bridges. Lee confessed his disappointment. "They suffered heavily as far as the battle went," he wrote Mary that

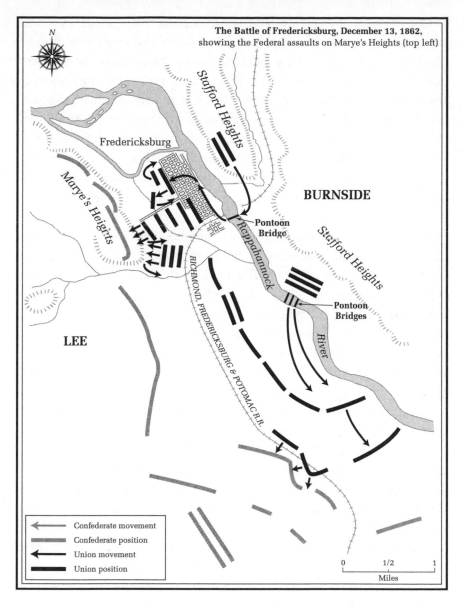

The Battle of Fredericksburg, December 13, 1862, showing the Federal assaults on Marye's Heights (top left)

day, "but it did not go far enough to satisfy me."[82] More than a week later he still nursed his discontent. "I was holding back all that day," he said on Christmas, expecting that the attack on December 13 was but prelude to a bigger effort. "Had I devined that was to have been his only effort, he would have had more of it." Still, since he might himself have suffered greater losses, he concluded that "I am content."[83]

But contentment did not mean complaisance. Just hours after find-ing the enemy gone from the south side of the river, Lee warned Richmond of "the contest which will have to be renewed, but at what point I cannot now state." Even after losing more than one-tenth of his army, Burnside still outnumbered the Army of Northern Virginia. There were several other places besides Fredericksburg where Burn-side could cross, and if the weather allowed, Lee expected him to do it. In the event, Lee preferred to withdraw to the line of the North or South Anna Rivers to draw Burnside that much farther from his base, extending a line of supply and communications that ought to be vul-nerable to Stuart's troopers.[84]

Now, at least, he could find moments to grieve for his lost grand-daughter, as well as the one who died before her, and his poor daugh-ter Annie. "I have grieved over the death of that little child of so many hopes," he wrote Mary when the Yankees had left the town. At least they were spared "the pains & sorrows of this world." Still, though this fresh victory might not be as complete as he hoped, "God has been so merciful to us in so many ways," he said, "that I cannot repine at whatever he does." Lee attributed Burnside's withdrawal to divine "interference."[85]

Then, writing even as his men removed the dead, the dying, and the wounded from the field, Lee turned in one of those abrupt tran-sitions so characteristic of the tight compartments of his mind, from the burden of one overwhelming responsibility momentarily lifted to another. Eighteen months of war and incessant responsibility had not displaced from his mind an old duty yet unfulfilled. Arlington might be overrun and other Custis plantations disrupted, but the emancipation of his father-in-law's slaves still weighed on him. One point remained unclear to him, and that was whether or not Custis's legacies to Lee's daughters were considered debts of the estate. If they were, then his reading of the will meant that the slaves must keep working until those legacies were funded even if it took more than five years from Custis's death. If the legacies were not debts of the estate, then the slaves must be freed whenever all other debts of the estate were paid or by the end of 1862, whichever came first. The Arlington slaves were beyond reach, of course, and any hire due for them could never be collected. "Nothing can be done with them," he told Custis in January 1862, but the slaves at White House and Romancoke could still produce revenue, and he advised Custis to keep them out at hire if possible.[86] Two weeks later he finally got a court ruling that the legacies were not part of the estate's debts, so the slaves must be emancipated at the end of five years. In June 1860, nearly three years after Custis's death, not a cent had yet been credited to the legacies as Lee retired debts.[87] That had meant the only way to fund his daughters' legacies was by sales of small properties, but he was far too occupied to be able to get them in shape for sale, and at the moment no one was buying land. At least one Custis property was occupied by the Yankees, so there was nothing to do with it, and as for its slaves, he confessed to Mary that he did not know what to do with them.[88] Many had already run away during the enemy occupation, panicked when Federals told them during the Seven Days that Lee was coming to cut their throats.[89]

Now on December 16, the day after the close of the battle, and midway through a letter describing the battle, Lee turned abruptly to the subject of the Arlington slaves. Custis died October 10, 1857, so the five years had already passed, but these recent months had been too filled with activity and movement to take action. Now he would have a respite. Almost miraculously all of Custis's debts were paid, and a start had been made on his daughters' legacies. He was the estate's only creditor now. "I wish to close the whole affair," he told Mary. "Whether I can do so during the war I cannot say now, nor do I know that I shall live to the end of it." He wanted now to advance that as much as possible. Many were already hired out in Richmond and the countryside, and might continue their employment in their own right once he gave them their emancipation papers. "I hope they will all do well and behave themselves," he said. As for the slaves at White House and Romancoke, he would give them their papers, too, and try to ensure they could support themselves there, but any who chose to leave would either have to find jobs elsewhere or leave the state, which did not permit unemployed free blacks. He knew the men could find jobs, but was concerned for the women and children not supported by husbands. "I desire to do what is right & best for the people," he added. Ideally he would like to ensure that they were employed at good wages and living conditions, but the war's demands on him made that impossible. The best he could do was give back to them any residue of their hire for the year after the debts and legacies were retired, and to increase that amount a little he would cancel the estate's debt to himself. As for the Arlington slaves, they were beyond his reach and already presumably free, but still he would get their papers to them if he could. It was time for "the liberation of the people."[90]

❧

That same day Grant wrestled with a racial issue of his own. If he nurtured a hostile attitude toward Jews prior to the war, he certainly kept it well concealed. When stationed at Sackets Harbor in the early months of 1848, he shopped at the Watertown dry goods firm of J. & H. Seligman's.[91] Either then or on his return to Sacket's Harbor in June 1851 Grant befriended Jesse Seligman in particular, a friendship he renewed later in San Francisco where Seligman started an import business, and Grant often visited while stationed on the Pacific coast.[92] It was an acquaintance and mutual respect that lasted the rest of Grant's life. A few years later, in December 1857, he pawned his watch to the Jewish broker J. S. Freligh in St. Louis, but later redeemed it, leaving no cause for a grudge against Freligh's people.[93] He was probably like many Americans of his time, at ease with the conflict between befriending Jews as individuals, while accepting stereotypical myths about them as a people.

In December 1861 he approved dismissal of a corrupt Jewish bread contractor at Cairo, though Grant may have been unaware of the man's ethnicity.[94] In July 1862, however, when speculators began paying planters in gold for cotton that they refused to sell to the government for Treasury notes, he saw that it would result in higher costs to Northern mills, while the hard cash itself would likely find its way to the Confederacy to be used against the Union. He issued an order forbidding such transactions, then the following day advised that all speculators coming into his department ought to have their baggage searched for suspiciously large amounts of specie. "Jews," he said, "should receive special attention."[95] Sherman, who was always outspoken in his prejudices, approved heartily, complaining of the "Jews and Speculators" and "swarms of Jews" trading gold for cotton in Memphis.[96] Worse, Union officers conspired with some of the speculators to share in the cotton fortune, compromising both law and morale.[97] Northern need for cotton led Washington to ask Grant to relent, which he did reluctantly.

Contractors and speculators badgered him constantly while he tried to keep his procurement departments free of fraud. He had heard so as to believe it that a syndicate of wealthy men had formed at the opening of the war to monopolize army contracts and make fortunes, boasting that they could "remove any General who did not please them." One of those profiteers, he believed, was Leonard Swett, with whom Grant grappled in 1861. In November he learned that Swett was close to Lincoln. Without actually saying so, Grant felt concerned that Swett would use his influence with the president to injure him.[98]

The rumor was false, but Grant believed it at the moment, even as he prepared for his move south toward Holly Springs, beset by applications from speculators for permits to follow him into cotton-rich northern Mississippi. The combination of the two concerns led him just two days later to issue orders to his commanders to refuse to honor all permits for travel below Jackson, Tennessee, for the immediate present. "The Israelites especially should be kept out," he urged, and followed the next day with an order to all conductors on the railroad above Lagrange that no Jews were to travel the road southward. They could travel north out of his command if they wished. Indeed, he encouraged that. "They are such an intolerable nuisance," he wrote, "that the Dept. must be purged [of] them."[99] Before he left Lagrange on November 28 Grant issued orders that no cotton buyers could move with the army, but they could follow in time and buy cotton in the rear. By December 5, however, he had had enough and told Sherman that "in consequence of the total disregard and evasion of orders by the Jews my policy is to exclude them as far as practicable from the Dept."[100]

He gave no such order then. Rather, when Washington ordered that shipping cotton out of the country be encouraged, Grant rescinded a subordinate's directive that "all Cotton-Speculators, Jews and other Vagrants" who were "trading upon the miseries of their country" without Grant's permission had twenty-four hours to leave.[101] At the same time, Grant allowed cotton trading to be resumed in their rear in Tennessee, but ordered that speculators trading in Holly Springs should be expelled.[102] If the orders seemed contradictory, they were not. Grant's intention was only to eject those who failed to buy at the established marketplace according to rules laid down by the Treasury Department.

The pieces were in place for Grant to make a decision that seemed operationally reasonable and in the government's interest, while being woefully impolitic. The problems with speculators had been coming to a head for some time. Back in August it was well known in Corinth that he intended to do something about the "sharks, feeding upon the soldiers," as one soldier characterized Jewish peddlers.[103] Now a letter forwarded from Washington arrived saying that as of December 1 "Jews are taking large amounts of gold into Kentucky and Tennessee."[104] One story in the press accused them of pretending to be peddlers while bringing forbidden contraband goods like medicines and paying local secessionists to store it for them until Union armies moved on, after which the goods were sold at inflated prices to the Confederate military.[105] Even across the lines the Confederate press excoriated Jews as "vermin" for speculating in tobacco.[106] The Cincinnati *Commercial* carried a satirical poem that lamented of Bolivar, Tennessee: "Thy cotton sold to Northern Jews."[107] That paper, never very friendly also intimated that "too much must not be expected of Gen. Grant."[108]

"I suffer the mortification of seeing myself attacked right and left by people at home professing patriotism and love of country who never heard the whistle of a bullet," he complained to his sister Mary on December 15 from Oxford. Especially he resented the assaults of "speculators whos patriotism is measured by dollars & cents," men for whom "country has no value with them compared to money."[109] Now he was about to enter the heart of Mississippi's cotton belt, and those speculators drooled more than ever. All Jews were not unpatriotic, of course. There were Jewish soldiers in his command, and at least a few officers who had heard the bullets' whistle. But he now regarded Jews who followed the army as speculators as a separate class, and definitely not patriots. If he needed proof it came that same December 15 when his post commander at Abbeville wired him that a man named Shultz had tried a new subterfuge. Finding a Confederate whose cotton had been seized, Shultz "bought" it from him for a fraction of its value and got a predated receipt to demonstrate his ownership prior to seizure. The officer in Abbeville called it whipping "the Devil around the stump," and refused to hand over the cotton, whereon Shultz brazenly lied that he had Grant's authorization.[110]

That same day he learned that his father was at Holly Springs with Julia and would reach him at Oxford in a day or two. On December 6 Jesse entered a partnership with the firm of Mack & Brothers of Cincinnati for what Simon Mack called "an adventure in the purchase of cotton." Jesse's role was to secure from his son a permit for the Macks' agents to come buy cotton and get his permission for rail or boat transportation of the bales to New York. In return the Macks would pay Jesse one-fourth of their profits. A week later Jesse left with Simon Mack and agent Solomon Goldsmith, reaching Holly Springs on or before December 15, where Goldsmith apparently began buying without waiting for Jesse to approach his son.[111] As yet Grant knew nothing of the purpose of Jesse's visit or of Goldsmith and Mack being along.[112]

He was feeling the weight of his responsibility more than usual. That same day he told his sister that "I am extended now like a Peninsula into an enemies country with a large Army depending for their daily bread upon keeping open a line of rail-road running one hundred & ninety miles." Thousands of lives rested on his judgment, and he did not have to add that the fate of the Union had a stake in his actions. For some time now he envied the man who could conduct his daily business and then "retire to a quiet home without a feeling of responsibility for the morrow."[113] Within hours he learned that Confederate cavalry had been seen near the Tennessee River, and on a path to threaten his communications via Jackson to Cairo.[114]

Then a telegram came from Jesse asking if he and "a friend" could come on to Oxford. Ordinarily Grant's aide at Holly Springs would have issued a pass. Jesse's approaching his son directly may have raised suspicion, soon confirmed when a telegram arrived informing Grant that Jesse's friend was "a Jew." Grant surely knew nothing yet of the December 6 partnership, but he knew his father's unerring instinct for conflicts of interest. He was also out of patience with his father for his rudeness to Julia, who simply could not please Jesse. "This is not pleasing to me," Grant told him a few weeks earlier. The bully in Jesse also picked on his grandson Fred, who was often sickly, and sensitive as a result.[115] Now Grant wired back that his father was welcome to come, but not his friend.[116]

Two days later something more arrived.[117] It may have been a telegram or a packet of letters referred from Washington. The import was yet another warning that Jews in particular were buying with gold and silver that would surely find its way to the Confederacy. An angered Grant took this as criticism of his management of the problem, and he could easily envision the outcry against him in the press if his own father got involved by using his son's influence. He responded to an assistant secretary of war, recapitulating his long concerns that "unprincipled traders" were routinely violating the Treasury Department's regulations, reminding Washington that he had tried to stop it by refusing "all permits to Jews" to come south, "but they come in with their Carpet sacks in spite of all that can be done to prevent it." They bought cotton themselves, or else acted as agents for someone who had a legitimate permit to buy cotton with Treasury notes, and then purchased the bales from them at discounted rates using gold. In short, there was nothing else he or any other department commander could do. He suggested that the solution was for the government to buy all cotton at an established rate and ship it North for sale. Then "all traders" could be expelled, for "they are a curse to the Army."[118]

Grant confronted the problem as he confronted all others, head-on and, he hoped, decisively. He drafted General Orders No. 11, the culmination of months of personal, military, and administrative frustration.[119] "The Jews, as a class" were to be expelled from his departmental command. He ordered post commanders to give them twenty-four hours' notice to leave on penalty of arrest. Moreover, no passes should be given "these people" to come to his headquarters to apply for trade permits, which should take care of Jesse's partners.[120] This was no sudden reaction to his father's appearance with Goldsmith or other frustrations. It was the logical extension of a policy he had been evolving for at least five months, though the irritants surrounding him may have prevented the mature reflection such a bombshell needed.

Since all speculators had been a besetting nuisance to him, it seems unlikely that he would act only against those who were Jews, for that addressed only a part of the problem, and in his letter to the assistant secretary of war that day he spoke interchangeably of Jews and "all traders." Yet he intentionally singled out Jews "as a class." His own degree of anti-Semitism, the fact that Jewish buyers seemed to stand out from the rest, the reinforcement of his feelings by Sherman and others, and warnings from Washington of the unpatriotic—if not treasonous—actions of traders providing gold, silver, or contraband goods that quickly found their way to Confederate hands, all seemed to call for a preemptive act to halt such practice.[121]

Grant later confessed that he issued the order "without any reflection, and without thinking of the Jews as a sect or race to themselves." They were just those most successful in "whipping the Devil around the stump" and had to be stopped.[122] He was not given to impulse, but it was his habit to confront a difficult subordinate or an administrative problem directly. Influences acting on him in mid-December clouded his judgment. Anti-Semitism did not impel him to issue an order, which was certainly needed, but it did influence his concept of the order's imposition. Far greater responsibility for Grant's misstep rests on exactly what he said, not enough reflection, and the desire to stop wasting time on this niggling and unpatriotic business so he could address the urgent matters before him. A host of trenchant reasons led him to the right decision—banishment of speculators—but promulgated with terribly wrong stipulations. He spent the rest of his life trying to cope with and overcome its repercussions.

Lee faced no such problem since his army did not occupy enemy soil, offering no opportunity for Confederate speculators to profit. He did, however, have a number of what he called "soldiers of the Jewish persuasion" in his army, mostly from Louisiana and South Carolina, and his notion that they were Jews by choice of faith rather than by birth suggests that his own personal feeling about Jews differed little from Grant's. He sought to maintain their good will and commitment to the cause, even when demands of the service forced him to deny a request just after Antietam from the rabbi in Richmond for a general furlough to "that class of soldiers" for the Rosh Hashanah and Yom Kippur holidays. Still, Lee encouraged individual Jews to apply to their regimental commanders to be furloughed as exigency allowed.[123]

If he did not share Grant's challenge with one ethnic interest, Lee's challenge with another continued. He collected all the names he could

from Mary and his sons and had an attorney draft a deed of manumission listing 201 slaves at Arlington, White House, and Romancoke,
among them familiar people like Wesley Norris and his sister Mary.
On December 29 Lee took it to the county court house in Fredericksburg and signed it before a justice of the peace.[124] Perhaps it was just
coincidental that three days later Lincoln's Emancipation Proclamation went into effect. By its terms if the Confederacy lost the war, the
resultant freedom of the Custis slaves would date from the proclamation. Punctilious as always, Lee wanted their freedom to date from
his manumission, the fulfillment of his responsibility to them under
Custis's will. Ironically, the proclamation applied only to areas still
resisting Federal authority, which no longer included Arlington and
Alexandria. Thus Lincoln did not free slaves at Arlington, but Lee did.

That was not an end of it, however. Lee needed to locate the slaves
and get their manumission papers to them before they could walk as
free men. He sent word to Arlington to inform the people there of
their freedom, and sent emancipation papers to an agent to distribute
at Richmond, White House, and elsewhere, meanwhile continuing the
search for more names.[125] He also enjoined his agents to help find the
people employment, emphasizing that any wages currently due them
were theirs to keep.[126] "I wish to emancipate the whole," he told Mary.
"They are entitled to their freedom and I wish to give it to them."[127] Still
sensitive to the accusations of violating Custis's will, Lee told his son, "I
wished to give a complete list & to liberate all, to Show that your Grd
Fathers wishes so far as I was Concerned had been fulfilled."[128]

The manumission put an end to Lee's use of the Custis slaves, a few
of whom had been with him in the field since his first command in
western Virginia in 1861.[129] Henceforth he would hire his servants, and
he continued to employ Perry Parks, who came to him from Arlington
in May 1861, despite his being "not entirely reliable." Lee complained
that Perry was slow, inefficient, and lazy in the mornings, yet "does
as well as he can." He did not expect to keep him indefinitely, hoping
that his next employer would take good care of him, but in fact Parks
remained with him at least another two years, for which Lee paid him
$8.20 a month. He also employed other Arlington slaves as cooks: first
Michael Meriday and later George Clarke.[130] Nothing suggests that
Lee still owned Nancy Ruffin and her children, but if he or Mary did

still have any slaves, he may have arranged their emancipation around this time as well.[131]

⁓

The storm of protest from both Jews and gentiles alike was predictable, but peculiarly delayed. Rumors of Grant's order did not reach the Northern press until New Year's Day, when a dispatch from Cairo said merely that he had issued an order for "all Jews in his department to leave."[132] The actual text did not appear until January 5, a day after Halleck directed Grant to revoke the order. Grant felt severely embarrassed, but kept it to himself, and thereafter avoided the subject. It was a valuable lesson hard learned, though he had his defenders.[133] Yet the storm all lay in the future, as Grant returned to planning Sherman's expedition. Then 3,500 Confederate cavalry led by Van Dorn swept out of nowhere onto Holly Springs on December 20, captured the garrison, and destroyed those million rations husbanded for the campaign. At the same time more rebel horse led by Brigadier General Nathan Bedford Forrest struck rail and telegraph lines elsewhere, nearly closing down the flow of information out of the department, and thus delaying word of General Orders No. 11 reaching the North.

Grant had his cavalry out looking for the rebels, who simply moved faster than his own troopers. As a precaution he temporarily postponed an advance on December 19 until he felt secure, but when word of the disaster reached him he immediately pulled in his divisions and began making plans to defend Corinth should it be threatened. As ever, Grant reacted aggressively. Falling back meant some of his divisions could be sent to Sherman, and Grant concluded to go with them himself in overall command. Being present in person, he would outrank McClernand when he arrived.[134] Thanks to the disruption at Holly Springs, however, he did not know if Sherman had embarked already. Grant's supply base was gone, the rebels almost captured Julia, who left Holly Springs the day before, his overland campaign was stymied, his communications disrupted, and he had no sure idea of where the Vicksburg expedition might be, or even if it would depart Memphis before McClernand came to make his life miserable. The only good news for Grant that yuletide were things his downed telegraph lines delayed. The North did not yet know about General Orders No. 11, and he did not yet know the full extent of Burnside's disaster on the Rappahannock the week before. Good news from Vicksburg would go a long way toward brightening Union spirits.

The aftermath of victory only dampened Lee's spirits. "I have no time to think of my private affairs," he told Mary. "I expect to die a pauper, & I see no way of preventing it. So that I can get enough for you & the girls I am content."[135] He felt a longing for an earlier period of his life. He missed Arlington, but now that was lost to them forever. Only one other place inspired that sort of affection in him: Stratford. Often his thoughts turned back to his father's house and his few memories of life there. Nostalgia made him daydream frequently of buying the place and spending his last years there if ever the war should end. There was not much left of the farm, he feared, but he expected they could produce enough corn bread and bacon to get by. A year earlier he had made inquiries to see if it might be for sale, and for how much.[136]

No wonder Christmas made him pensive. He thought of the happy holiday meals of past years, wistfully wishing they might all be re-united at Arlington.[137] The past year had seen innumerable evidences of divine favor. "I have seen his hand in all the events of the war," he said, and if only the Confederate people would put aside their "vain self boasting & adulation" and acknowledge their debt to Him, Lee felt he could have confidence in ultimate independence. "What a cruel thing is war," he lamented. It destroyed families and fostered hate rather than brotherhood. He prayed for Yankee hearts to turn to peace. He spoke of the recent battle, lamenting that if he had known Burnside would not renew his attacks on December 14, Lee would have given him "more of it" on the thirteenth. Amid Christmas lamentations over the loss of brotherly love, he was sorry he had not killed more.[138] With Mildred he was more playful, saying he was happy that "Genl. Burnside and his army will not eat their promised Xmas dinner in Richmond to day."[139] A few weeks later he told Custis that "if honour & independence is delt us I will be content," and hope seemed a bit brighter when Davis returned from a visit to Mississippi encouraged that they might hold that line against Grant, "and the integrity of the Confederacy may be thus preserved."[140]

If only the people and the government would put their country first. "The people must help themselves, or Providence will not help them," he had told Custis before the battle.[141] Governors still erected defenses against Richmond rather than bridges to cooperate.[142] For more than a year he urged that regiments be organized for the duration of the war and placed under Richmond's control, not the governors'. His strength at Fredericksburg had been his greatest since the Peninsula, yet he knew the Union could call forth vastly more. The easy victory changed nothing. Rather, it revealed to him that the South could not win preemptively. It could only persuade the North to lose, and to do that he must continue taking risks to even the odds. On the very day of the battle he wrote to Richmond that "the people must turn out to defend their homes, or they will be taken from them."[143] Soon he warned that the people did not feel the extent of their danger or the growing power of the North. The South had won signal victories, but he feared that made the people complacent. Against the might of the Union, more wins must cost "the most precious blood of the country," blood on the hands of those who failed to join their brothers in arms. Even after a great success his army had not the strength to press its advantage to its fullest, as at Antietam where "victory itself has been made to put on the appearance of defeat, because our diminished and exhausted troops have been unable to renew a successful struggle against fresh numbers of the enemy."

Lincoln's proclamation encouraged slaves to revolt, overthrow white rule, and bring anarchy and violence in vengeance for ancient grievances. Rape and perhaps even forced racial amalgamation would follow, a "brutal and savage policy" that left them "no alternative but success or degradation worse than death, if we would save the honor of our families from pollution, our social system from destruction."[144] A rumor had appeared in the Northern press of a letter Lee supposedly wrote Halleck condemning the proclamation as an incitement to servile rebellion, and promising bloody retaliation on Union prisoners. Some questioned the rumor when the War Department issued no transcript, though the letter's inflammatory nature had considerable propaganda value. By the end of the month the story died.[145] No one took credit for the hoax, if such it was, and Lee ignored it. "As to the attacks of the Northern papers I do not mind them," he told Mary.[146]

Still, he condemned Lincoln's act as a declaration of war on civilization itself that severed any remaining cords of attachment he felt to the old Union. Ironically, as the war pushed Grant toward embracing black freedom, it pushed Lee further away.

Lee became even more pessimistic when he learned that the Yankee Congress would authorize $900 million to finance the war and make as many as three million men subject to service. "Nothing can now arrest during the present administration the most desolating war that was ever practiced," he forecast. Only revolution within the Union could stop Lincoln, and that demanded "systematic success" on their part.[147] The enemy would strain every sinew to crush them by June, he believed, and they would have to exhaust every resource to resist.[148] In February he reiterated that prediction. "Our salvation will depend on the next four months," he wrote, yet their own Congress spent its time passing special acts to exempt men from service. In disgust he groused that "I shall feel very much obliged to them if they will pass a law relieving me from all duty and legislating some one in my place, better able to do it."[149]

Lee may have grown increasingly conservative and suspicious of central authority in the former United States by 1860, but as a Confederate faced with the necessities of survival, he was reverting to the federalism of his father. As he said in 1861, so he felt now still. Their only objective was independence. Everything they had depended on victory, and every interest must yield to that imperative.[150] They must disenthrall themselves and mobilize every asset they had, or soon they would have none to mobilize. Issues of state sovereignty paled in the face of annihilation. If he had to intrude beyond his bounds into the political and social world, he might do so. They had until the summer of 1863 to commit or evaporate.[151]

11

TWO RIVERS
TO CROSS

On the last day of 1862 Lee issued a congratulatory order to his army thanking them for their victory "under the blessings of Almighty God," though he also shared his opinion of its equivocal impact, telling them "the war is not yet ended." Still, divine mercy had blessed them all year, giving him hope that "the same Almighty hand" would bring more victories.[1] A few criticized Lee, saying he ought to have destroyed Burnside, one arguing that he should have hurled red-hot rocks into the stream to prevent the enemy crossing, turning the Rappahannock into a stew of parboiled Yankees.[2] His defenders replied that "we think Gen. Lee has pretty strong reasons both for what he does and fails to attempt."[3] One commentator averred that Lee, while "not possessing the first order of intellect, is endowed with rare judgment and equanimity, unerring sagacity, great self-control, and extraordinary powers of combination." Other generals might be as intelligent, and perhaps even better fighters, but when it came to planning and conducting a campaign, no one could surpass him in "the qualities of a commander."[4]

Confederates were trying to fit Lee into their popular culture. He was a hero, but that did not settle who they needed him to be. Anecdotes making him the avuncular bemused foil in episodes of camp humor gained no purchase in their imagination.[5] Neither did humor come at the expense of soldiers, as when the general supposedly tested a boy on obedience by ordering him to about face and forward march away from Lee's tent . . . and never said to halt.[6] Neither did the idea of Lee in political life catch fire. On the eve of Fredericksburg, Virginian colonel Edmund W. Hubard proposed that people consider Lee for the governorship in 1863, but no one took up the cry.[7]

Confederates found encouragement in his faith. They expected God to favor them as Christians.[8] The press commented often on Lee the "Christian man," the "Christian gentleman," the "Christian hero and patriot," and just days after Fredericksburg, the "meek and humble christian."[9] The *Southern Christian Advocate* proclaimed that "he is not ashamed to acknowledge the hand of God in his successes," and that Christians were gratified "to know that they have a man of prayer, and a servant of God, as leader to their armies." His trust in Providence was an omen of success.[10] Lee's letters to bereaved families often became public, wherein by extolling the sacrifice and Christian virtues of the slain, he exhorted others to emulate their example. At Fredericksburg Generals Thomas R. R. Cobb of Georgia and Maxcy Gregg of South Carolina both fell. The unpopular Cobb had been an ardent critic of Lee for months. "Genl. Lee has not the first feeling of a gentleman," Cobb complained back in July. "He is haughty and boorish and supercilious in his bearing and is particularly so to me." That may have been because the supremely conceited amateur took it on himself to tell Lee how to run the army. He further complained that Lee got even by giving him "all the dirty and hard work" while the best assignments went to family like Rooney and Lee's nephew Fitzhugh Lee.[11] In fact, Lee had recently approved transferring Cobb's command to Georgia in a move redolent of another problem solved.[12] Still, on December 18, 1862, Lee wrote of Cobb's "merits, his lofty intellect, his accomplishments, his professional fame, and above all, his true Christian character," saying the name of this "Christian statesman and soldier" should be "a holy remembrance."[13] Yet at that same sitting, Lee wrote regarding Gregg to Governor Pickens in South Carolina. Absent was any reference to Christian virtues, but surely Lee knew that Gregg professed no religion, making it untoward to impose it on him in death.[14] Lee would rarely act a hypocrite.

Editors conjured a tableaux of Lee anointed to lead them to freedom. When he visited the dying Bishop Meade, the press carried Meade's supposed last words. "I have known you, General, from a boy, and have always loved you," he said haltingly. Despite early reluctance to accept secession, Meade was now wholly committed to the "righteous cause," and Lee must do his utmost in its service. "You are a Christian soldier," he said. As Lee wept, Meade laid his hands on the general's bowed head, enjoining him to "trust in God, and God will bless you."[15]

Lee read the *Southern Churchman* every month. He contributed to support coleporteurs distributing Christian materials among the soldiers, averring that "the virtue and fidelity which should characterize a soldier can only be learned from the holy pages of the Bible."[16] A Methodist congregation gave him a life directorship in the Confederate States Bible Society, which he accepted gladly. God had given them victories and they owed "grateful acknowledgment of the presence and agency of a merciful Providence in our affairs," he wrote in thanks. He blessed them with victories, and His was the glory. As he quoted loosely from Chronicles, his own words sounded almost like scripture, declaring that "true patriotism, no less than piety, demands that the prayers of the faithful should never cease to ascend to Him who saveth not by many or by few, but giveth the victory to whom He will."[17] After Fredericksburg editors reminded readers that Lee was "a professing and consistent Christian," and that "with God above, and General Lee at their head, they feared nothing that man could do."[18] He might not sit at the Almighty's right hand yet, but Confederates expected him to have a seat at the table.

Lee wavered between hope of success and uncertainty. "Should it please Him eventually to establish our independence & spare our lives, all will be well," he told Mildred at Christmas.[19] A day later he wrote Agnes that "a kind Providence" would look out for them, for "so much virtue will not be unregarded."[20] He was more tentative with Mary. "I wish I could be sufficiently thankful for all He has done for us, & felt that we deserved a continuance of the protection & guidance He had heretofore vouchsafed to us," he wrote in March as a revival swept through his army's ranks. "I know that in Him is our only salvation. He alone can give us peace & freedom & I humbly submit to His holy will."[21] Theirs was a just god who would make all right in the end. "To Him we must trust," he told her, "& for that we must wait."[22] With campaigning weather's approach in late April, he became impatient of the waiting, confessing, "I hope God in His own time will give us more substantial cause for rejoicing & thankfulness."[23]

Visitors left him with impressions that enhanced the South's image of Lee the kindly yet slightly aloof father of his army. An army doctor who saw him early in April came away impressed that "he is so noble a specimen of men," tall, robust, handsome, "always polite and agreeable, and thinking less of himself than he ought to," a man who thought of nothing "but the success of our cause." The surgeon wished other Confederates would emulate the general's humility to "arrive at his excellencies and not in boisterous exclamations like those the eccentric Stonewall Jackson elicits wherever he goes."[24] He eschewed pomp and comfort in favor of tents for himself and staff, surrounded by scattered baggage wagons sometimes captured from the foe, and no guard stood outside Lee's tent, making him more approachable than lesser generals in his army and Grant's.[25] "He cares but little for appearances," said another visitor. Regulations called for him to wear a blouse with three stars within a wreath on a standing collar, the insignia for all general officers, and yet he wore a mere brigadier's blouse with the three unwreathed stars of a colonel on its inner lapels, which he turned down to conceal his proper insignia underneath.[26]

British journalist Francis Lawley found him erect and healthy in figure, calm and stately in manner. Lee's dark brown eyes directly met the gaze of visitors. He smiled little and laughed less, and spoke in a deep voice that was losing some of its musicality, with but little variety of tone or inflection. His thoughtful nature was evident, as was a sense that he deliberated long and hard before making decisions. Lee's "childlike guilelessness" struck Lawley, who asserted that "it is very rare that a man of his age, conversant with important events, and thrown to the surface of mighty convulsions, retains the impress of a simple, ingenuous nature." That only proved Lee's mastery of guile to put people at ease, especially newspapermen, with whom he knew to be careful.[27] Another British visitor, Major Garnet Wolseley, found that "when speaking of the Yankees, he neither evinced any bitterness or feeling, nor gave utterance to a single violent expression," a pose at odds with the angry, even vengeful, Lee of his letters to family and officials in Richmond. It suited his purpose to be a man motivated by patriotism and not rancor. To all he attributed his victories to "the blessing of the Almighty," and prayed for more.[28]

Three weeks after Fredericksburg, rumor said that "General Lee contemplates a movement northward."[29] It was a feeling echoed in Washington, where Senator John C. Ten Eyck of New Jersey warned on the Senate floor that Lee might lead his army on the capital and invite them all to go home.[30] Late in January a bizarre rumor briefly surfaced that Lee had gone to Washington as a penitent seeking Lincoln's mercy.[31] Thanks to nonsense like that, he told Mary that "I am overwhelmed with confusion when I hear of my name in the papers."[32]

Yet there was some flame beneath the smoke. Early in February Lee pressed his commanders to collect stragglers and cancelled all furloughs. Visitors found him "very cheerful," especially after yet another false rumor that France might grant recognition of Confederate independence, with military intervention to follow.[33] After his series of successes, including Antietam, he felt enormous confidence in his men, however ragtag and unmilitary they looked. Granting his embarrassment over their appearance in front of foreign dignitaries, he told Lawley proudly that "there is only one attitude in which I should never be ashamed of your seeing my men, and that is when they are fighting."[34] Everyone expected them to be fighting again soon. That month as the combatants faced each other across the Rappahannock, one Confederate yelled to the other side that "we are all going back into the Union before long." Mistaking his meaning, a Yankee voice replied, "Bully for you. When are you coming?" Amused that his foe had taken the bait, the rebel lad responded, "I don't exactly know, but they say that General Lee is aiming to invade Pennsylvania next Spring."[35] Lee had said something must be done by June, and it looked like he was preparing to realize his own prophecy.

Lee daily expected the Federals to move again, and began to doubt that he could hold his position if they made a concerted effort. Yet he feared that falling back would risk losing the morale built by the recent victory.[36] On the morning of January 9 he learned that elements of Burnside's army had crossed upstream before dawn before being forced back later that day.[37] He reasonably concluded that it was a probe to check fords the Yankees might use, but that was little from which to read Burnside's intentions. Still, the alarm punctuated concern for the necessity to increase Southern armies. He wrote the secretary of war an open letter calling on the people to rally and if need be conscript "from very shame, those who will not heed the dictates of honor."[38]

Lee was assembling a picture. The enemy was reinforced and had strengthened his supply line, meaning Burnside had no intention to withdraw, yet the Federals built no substantial winter quarters, signaling an intention not to remain in place through the winter. Lee learned that the enemy ordered people in the counties immediately across from him not to leave their homes, so they could report no Federal movements to the Confederates. The enemy newspapers Lee read were silent on army activity, meaning the Federals had clamped down on news leaks. "I have hoped from day to day to have been able to discover what is contemplated," Lee told Davis on January 13, yet he gleaned only that Burnside planned a move before spring.[39]

Lee had to consider that Burnside might shift his army below the James River. Occasionally Lee tried to "read" enemy commanders, and believed that strategically the Yankees favored advancing on Richmond via North Carolina. He had expected that prior to Fredericksburg and, though mistaken then, he reconsidered it as an option now. In North Carolina Confederates were too weak to do anything but act on the defensive, yet he believed that the Federals were in the same condition. "It is as impossible for him to have a large operating army at every assailable point in our territory as it is for us to keep one to defend it," he observed. "We must move our troops from point to point as required, & by close observation and accurate information the true point of attack can generally be ascertained."[40] If Burnside moved below the James, Lee would shift the bulk of his men to counter, sending the rest to clear the Shenandoah Valley to protect Richmond's back door. Lee thought enemy operations in North Carolina were distractions aimed at drawing some of his own forces away from Burnside's front, yet by mid-January he considered the threat sufficiently pressing that he briefly planned a trip to North Carolina.[41]

He resisted the idea of sending detachments from his army. Lee had worked hard at its organization, and the men were in the best condition ever, with morale high. "I think it very hazardous to divide this army," he told the secretary of war, though he did suggest reassigning Daniel H. Hill to his native state to help with recruiting. Hill had been ill, and Lee thought him depressed. A return home might cheer him, and allow him to combat the nascent Unionism and anti-war sentiment then spreading in parts of the state.[42] Lee did not say that Hill was becoming a problem. His headquarters had lost the order that gave McClellan Lee's operational plans prior to Antietam, and since then Hill spoke critically of Lee's management. Depression may have been a euphemism for an attitude Lee thought detrimental to morale. He found Hill's temperament so "queer" that Lee never knew from one day to another what to expect. Regarding Hill's constant fault finding, Lee further complained in private that Hill "croaked."[43] The situation in North Carolina gave him a pretext to remove another discordant element.

By January 19 he believed the Army of the Potomac was about to advance in his front and cancelled plans to send reinforcements south.[44] The next day he concluded that the enemy would cross the Rappahannock upstream. Burnside could move down the river and strike Lee's left flank, or he could send one detachment to hold Lee in place while marching the main army farther south and east to cut Lee's rail and road links with Richmond; then he could either move on the capital or turn north to hit Lee with his back to the river, or both. Lee prudently sent cavalry to the upper fords to slow any enemy advance and give him time to react.[45]

The winter turned angry when a cold wind blew in, and then a heavy rain that scarcely let up for three days. It stopped Burnside in his tracks in a miserable affair soon dubbed the "Mud March." On January 23 Lee still believed that even as Burnside was shifting men toward the upper fords he was also pulling back to his camps.[46] Learning that Burnside went to Washington to consult with Lincoln, Lee expected him to return with a new plan commencing as soon as early February.[47] In fact, Lincoln replaced Burnside with Major General Joseph Hooker.

Consequently, Lee would face his fourth Union commander in eight months. The same imperatives that forced him on the defensive in the last battle still commanded him. Numbers and the nature of their positions gave the initiative to the enemy, and he could only wait and watch, and react. "Genl Hooker is obliged to do something," he told daughter Agnes. "I do not know what it will be." The Federals demonstrated on the other side of the river, threatening a ford here or there, then pulled back, to do the same the next day. Lee called it "the Chinese game": an effort to spread alarm and confusion. It gave some entertainment to his men, who often jeered at the moving Yankees across the river, but fear that any one of these feints might be real kept Lee in a foul mood. Despite his reserve and self-control, he never mastered his temper as well as Grant. "I am so cross now that I am not worth seeing," he grumbled to his daughter, and so busy that "I cannot be relied on for anything."[48] That was frustration at being unable to seize the offensive.[49]

Learning that Hooker had sent a corps by water to Hampton Roads, Lee considered that the rest of the Army of the Potomac would seek another field of maneuver. Again he thought of North Carolina, his repeated concern there suggesting that it might be what he would have done himself.[50] Then he concluded that Hooker might hold him here to prevent his sending reinforcements to the Carolinas, where Wilmington and Charleston might be the real targets. He ordered Longstreet to take two divisions south, ready to reinforce North Carolina just in case, as well as to gather much-needed pork and other commissary and quartermaster stores.[51] "I owe Mr. F[ighting] J[oe] Hooker no thanks for keeping me here in this state of expectancy," Lee complained to Mary. "He ought to have made up his mind long ago." Unable to get scouts through Union lines, Lee had to wait on the enemy to act before he could react, a posture that ill suited him.[52] Hooker might stay in his camps through the rest of the winter.[53] Still, Lee believed Hooker's best option was to wait for better weather, then push his corps at Hampton Roads toward Richmond to draw Lee back to protect the capital, and then move his main army across the river and take the road to Richmond. Laconically, Lee told Custis, "Must defeat it."[54]

As March ended its first week Lee believed "the enemy may break out at any time," yet tried to remain optimistic.[55] "If we do our duty I trust we shall not be crushed," he wrote brother Carter Lee on March 24.[56] Yet he passed an unpleasant winter, dining outdoors with his staff, his fingers freezing to tin plate and cup as he ate his soup and hardtack, rarely escaping camp.[57] His hands had healed from the accident, but early in March he complained of getting older and sadder, and that considering where he might have done good to others in his life thus far, he found himself "filled with confusion & despair."[58] He was miserable in the cold and wet of the winter, "nor can I expect any pleasure, during this war," he lamented to Mary.[59] The weight of duty pressed ever more on that spirit. "Writing, talking & thinking" took up so much of his time that there was little left for rest, and anxiety ensured scant sleep when he found time for his cot.

"As for my health I suppose I shall never be better," he mused.[60] It troubled him that he had been too busy to escape to see his dying daughter, making all the more painful a false and mean-spirited rumor that Annie Lee died in North Carolina "alone deserted by all" and "an outcast from her home," because she remained loyal to the Union.[61] In that weakened physical and emotional state he fell easy prey to a cold, and by the last Sunday of the month felt too feeble to attend services and prayed alone in his tent.[62] At the end of the month he moved for a few days to a nearby house, where he suffered seizures of pain in his chest, back, and arms, from what he assumed was a violent cold, but which may have been something much more serious, either angina or a small heart attack. His doctors thumped his chest "like an old steam boiler before condemning it," he joked, and April was a fortnight old before he returned to his tent.[63]

During his own illness Lee worried about the health of his soldiers. The winter was bad, but worse was their dwindling ration. Hearing that soldiers in other armies were better provisioned, he protested to Richmond that "I think this army deserves as much consideration."[64] Part of Longstreet's goal in being sent south of the James was to gather provisions along the border with North Carolina.[65] Lee urged his brother Carter to "set all the farmers to work."[66] Meanwhile, Lee himself ate in Spartan fashion, and his headquarters table offered no bounty. "I am willing to starve myself, but cannot bear my men or horses to be pinched," he told Mary.[67]

The continuing manpower problem troubled him. No one ought to resign from the service now, he said, regardless of the reason. With Custis on the president's private staff, Lee even asked his son to use his influence somehow to get laggards to enlist, suggesting he approach Senator Louis T. Wigfall, an outspoken administration critic, to press the matter.[68] Lee crossed boundaries between the military and the political more frequently now, living up to earlier hints. On January 6, learning of Davis's return from a trip to the western theater, Lee even resorted to sycophancy. "I know that your visit has inspired the people with confidence, & encouraged them to renewed exertions & greater sacrifices in the defence of the country," he wrote Davis. At the same time, hearing first reports—that proved untrue—that General Bragg had achieved a signal success near Murfreesboro at the close of the year, Lee told the president that "I attribute mainly the great victory of Genl Bragg to the courage diffused by your cheering words & presence."[69] In fact, Davis's western trip did neither, but Lee needed to ask much from the president in the days ahead, and their relationship was new enough that he did not know that his actions had already won him more good will than any honeyed words.

"If Genl Hooker is going to do anything we shall hear from him soon," Lee believed on April 3.[70] Thinking the army would soon be engaged in active operations, he warned the rabbi in Richmond that he would allow the Jews in his army to celebrate the coming Passover as far as he could, but they might have a more immediate angel of death to confront.[71] Then Lee wondered if Hooker intended to stay in position through the summer to keep him occupied, while sending large-scale reinforcements to Kentucky or Tennessee to cooperate with Grant or Rosecrans. When Richmond asked him about supporting armies west of the Appalachians, Lee discouraged sending units from his own army. Instead, he suggested launching another invasion of Maryland.[72] Lee might be parochial in thinking first and foremost of his army and his department, but it had delivered the lion's share of Confederate success and there was good reason not to dissipate its strength to lesser commanders elsewhere.

By mid-April Lee began to press for an offensive himself. A speedy move to the Shenandoah and then into Maryland would clear the valley of Yankees, and force Hooker to withdraw north of the Potomac.[73] Rumors came that the Yankees were giving up on taking Vicksburg, Lee's first mention of Grant by name.[74] "I do not think our enemies are so confident of success as they used to be," he told Mary on April 19. "If we can baffle them in their various designs this year & our people are true to our cause & not so devoted to themselves & their own aggrandisement, I think our success will be certain." If they held out until the fall of 1864, he believed Northern voters would reject the Republicans and the peace party might be willing to make terms. "We have only to resist manfully," he predicted.[75]

As the month wore on Lee tried to glean some insight into Hooker's intentions, busy enough that he could not spare the few minutes to keep an appointment possibly arranged by Mary. He and Jackson were supposed to sit for Richmond photographer D. T. Cowell, who brought his camera to the army.[76] Cowell and his firm planned to reproduce the photo for distribution and sale to the public, something that would identify Lee with his cause in the public mind even more than his name in the papers. "My portrait I think can give pleasure to no one," he protested to Mary, "& should it resemble the original would not be worth having." He was already displeased with a woodcut of himself in the English press. Lee had sat for Confederate photographers before, and he would again, but at the moment his spirits were low. He felt "oppressed by what I have to undergo for the first time in my life," he confessed. Instead of the faces of sad old men, Mary should "get the portraits of the young, the happy, the gay."[77]

By April 27 Lee suspected Hooker might cross the Rappahannock, and if he did it would be by the fords above Fredericksburg. Almost daily Hooker sent detachments up and down his side of the river, trying to confuse Lee as to which was real and which a feint, and Lee took them as such.[78] But there was no mistaking the news that a large force of Yankees began crossing twenty miles upstream from Fredericksburg on April 28, nor that two Yankee corps crossed just below Fredericksburg almost in Lee's front. Reports of more crossings reached him, making it apparent that Hooker was on the move. Lee concluded that the corps in his front were to hold him in place while those upriver would hit his left flank and rear. At once he began a flurry of communications to the president, the adjutant general, and others, imploring them to send all available units, and to keep the bridges over the North and South Anna Rivers intact, implying that he might have to fall back to that line to protect Richmond and keep his supply line open.[79]

Again Lee was surprised, not from want of vigilance, but thanks to effective security in Hooker's army. Lee had no alternative but to shape his movements on Hooker's, and survival depended on how he reacted. While he pulled in his own right flank to face the Federal corps below Fredericksburg, he concentrated one division that evening several miles west at a small crossroads called Chancellorsville, in the heart of a tangled region of woods and brush known locally as The Wilderness. The enemy corps closing in on his left would have to pass through that first, and Lee hoped to delay them while he augmented and repositioned his army. With Longstreet away Lee had just over 50,000 men; he expected Hooker might have 160,000.

On April 30 the division at Chancellorsville could not hold its ground and withdrew. By late afternoon the Yankees had a clear road to Lee's left rear. Like Grant, Lee was again lucky in the man he faced. After conceiving a brilliant offensive, Hooker turned cautious and halted. Even before that benison, Lee decided to blunt the enemy advance with an attack. But which wing of the Army of the Potomac was the real spearhead—the crossing at Fredericksburg or the corps closing around Chancellorsville? The Union artillery on Stafford Heights commanding the ground in front of Fredericksburg persuaded him that he could accomplish nothing there, so he took the only alternative he had. He tried to push back the Yankees at Chancellorsville, and he guessed right. On May 1, leaving just a few brigades facing two Federal corps at Fredericksburg, Lee launched Jackson's 30,000 men and 15,000 in two divisions of Longstreet's still with the army, toward more than 70,000 under Hooker. Lee dared to court disaster to prevent one.

Grant's own disaster at Holly Springs forced him to pull back to the Tallahatchie River, but as usual, he reacted by considering "what move next to make" after he reopened his line of communications. Meanwhile, he learned something in the withdrawal. Denied the supplies destroyed in the raid, his men and his large wagon trains "fed entirely off of the country" during the retreat, and did so for some days thereafter.[80] That might be useful knowledge in the future.

As ever, he confronted problems directly, and even as he ordered his cavalry out to run down Van Dorn and Forrest, Grant began dealing with the commander at Holly Springs and others whose weaknesses emerged in the crisis. Doing what Lee would never do, he relieved officers of their commands immediately, including a colonel of cavalry for reluctance to obey orders, and taking Brigadier General Leonard Ross's brigade away for a similar offense. Yet on getting a reasonable explanation, Grant reinstated the colonel, and restored Ross's brigade, though only after a reprimand for acting in the heat of the moment.[81] By the end of December most of the damage to the railroad from Memphis to Corinth was repaired, but hearing that some citizens in

Memphis threatened to disrupt the line again, he vowed to depopulate northern Mississippi and evict every family in the city whose loyalty he doubted. For every guerilla raid on the rail line, he intended to eject ten prominent secessionist families from his lines.[82]

The disaster made Grant long for word from Sherman. On the last day of the year he heard that Sherman had taken Vicksburg, but he could get no details. On New Year's Day another report said Vicksburg had not fallen after all. A day later Grant decided to "make a dash" to cut Confederate communications in west Tennessee to allow him to send reinforcements to Sherman to finish the job. Finally, on January 3, a five-day-old letter from Sherman brought news of heavy fighting and some progress, yet reports elsewhere said that Sherman had taken the citadel. On January 4 Grant gave in to his optimism and prematurely wired Halleck that "Vicksburg has fallen," though he had no details. All he could get was rumor. Grant sarcastically spoke of an informant who claimed "he had heard somebody else say that some one he had forgotten who, had seen somebody else who had seen a Copy of the Chicago Times of the 27th which said that Lee was near Washington Halleck was removed the place offered to McClellan Cabinet dissolved and things generally in confusion."[83] For the first time Grant mentioned Lee by name, and in jest.

The absurdity of it punctuated Grant's hunger for real news from Sherman, a want of intelligence made more galling with the news that Rosecrans had repulsed the Confederate Army of Tennessee in year-end action at Murfreesboro south of Nashville.[84] It was an equivocal victory, but on the heels of Fredericksburg it boosted Union morale, which Grant had hoped to be doing on the Mississippi. Hearing nothing more direct from Sherman, Grant's confidence began to ebb, then on January 9, eleven days after the fact, he got definitive word that Sherman had been repulsed in two days of hard fighting just north of Vicksburg, and had withdrawn his command more than a hundred miles upriver to Napoleon, Arkansas. Grant decided to leave immediately for Memphis to "do everything possible for the capture of Vicksburg."[85]

He arrived the next day, and as one of his first acts sent an engineer to Rear Admiral David D. Porter's fleet. The engineer's instructions were to move down the west bank to survey the remains of an unfinished canal that cut across the west end of a tongue of land created by a tight bend in the river. At the eastern tip of the tongue sat Vicksburg.[86] Hours after learning Sherman had failed, Grant was planning a new approach to seize control of the Mississippi. His army lay split between northern Mississippi and Arkansas, fed by an attenuated supply line to Memphis. Porter was anxious to be of service but had nowhere really to go. Confederate cavalry threatened overland communications and cut off his one land route of approach to Vicksburg. Grant never intended to take it from the river side. His plan always was to move inland, take the state capital at Jackson, cut off Vicksburg's communications, isolate the garrison, and then move west to take it by storm or siege. Grant almost always preferred an indirect approach; in this case it was to take his army down the Arkansas and Louisiana side below Vicksburg, and then cross to strike for Jackson from below. That would also put him in supporting distance of Federals under Major General Nathaniel Banks, who was expected to come north from New Orleans to take the bastion Port Hudson, 140 miles south of Vicksburg. If either fortress fell, the victors could combine to take the other, and the river would belong to the Union. But first Grant must get his fleet of transports below Vicksburg to ferry the army across, and that meant facing those batteries.

What followed was a reprise of Lieutenant Grant of California and Oregon. Scarcely landed on the Pacific Coast, he looked for ways to profit from the opportunity, and by simultaneous alternatives. He would grow vegetables for hungry immigrants, raise draft animals to replace worn teams, operate a general goods store, explore lumbering and fur sales, operate a billiard saloon, and more. If one match struck no fire, another might, and even if none came to anything, the work kept him vigorous, mind stimulated and body fit, prepared to capitalize on any avenue that offered promise.[87] Coincidentally, while Grant looked at options for offense, Lee employed the same approach as he considered alternative responses to Federal movements. Their strategic vision was identical, conceiving options contingent on enemy actions and unforeseen opportunities. They differed in the atmospheres around their operations, and the risks of failure. No McClernand threatened Lee, no vocal politicians or press carped in his rear, no meddling Lincoln put the occasional stone in his path. Lee's army was larger than Grant's, fighting on home ground, and he knew his foe's goal was Richmond. Failure meant losing the capital, with spiritual, morale, industrial, and social costs perhaps too great to survive. Grant risked less: his army caught in enemy territory, the river left open to Confederate use, a serious blow to Northern morale, and a failure on his record that McClernand would surely use to his advantage. Lee faced national peril; Grant risked personal eclipse.

Then McClernand made his bid. Reaching Napoleon, he assumed command of Sherman's men and turned them to attack Fort Hindman near Arkansas Post, a few miles up the Arkansas River. Gunboats under its protection could steam down to the Mississippi and threaten McClernand's supply line to Memphis. He haughtily redesignated his command the "Army of the Mississippi" and, accompanied by Porter, took Fort Hindman on January 11. He intended next to move up the Arkansas to take Little Rock as a diversion to keep Confederates from concentrating on the defense of Vicksburg. Grant rightly viewed it as McClernand's diversion to attract attention to himself. He had "gone on a wild goose chase" to no useful end, Grant told Halleck.[88] To vent his anger, Grant resorted to a managerial tool sometimes used by Lincoln: writing a letter that he did not send. Stating his disapproval, he ordered McClernand to do nothing not directly connected to "the one great result, the capture of Vicksburg." Then Grant held the letter to give himself time to cool. Two days later he told McClernand of the letter, but only summarized its content in milder tones.[89] McClernand was murky ground. He still might be acting on authority from the secretary of war, or even the president. There was no profit in a confrontation until Grant was sure of his footing. He asked Halleck for clarification, and was told he could relieve McClernand and replace him with Sherman or take charge himself, as he chose. On January 18 Grant assumed command. McClernand wrote in heat to Grant and Lincoln, insisting that the president make his command independent, but Lincoln backed away, forcing McClernand to obey Grant's orders to return to the mouth of the Arkansas River.[90]

Grant met at once with Sherman, Porter, and McClernand, essentially ignoring the latter. Privately, Sherman, Porter, and others expressed their distrust of the man and his motives, erasing any doubts Grant may have had, and he so notified Halleck. He recommended again that both sides of the Mississippi be placed under a single general, and suggested that for maximum efficiency all departments in the region be united under one central command. As senior commander he had a claim on such a position, but preferred to retain direct charge of the Vicksburg campaign. Grant's modesty was usually genuine, but his past preference for action rather than administrative position argues persuasively that he was sincere.

Sherman and Porter agreed that Vicksburg could not be taken quickly. A series of fortified hills and bayous overflowing from heavy rains covered the upstream approaches, while the city itself was too well defended to be stormed directly from the river.[91] Grant already knew that, and had something different in mind. Before leaving Memphis he arranged for mining tools to be sent forward.[92] In the summer of 1862 Brigadier General Thomas Williams advanced on Vicksburg after taking Baton Rouge. He was forced to withdraw, but before leaving he spent a month digging an incomplete canal across that tongue of land. If Grant could complete and use it to bypass Vicksburg, he could get his army below.

He made his headquarters for the moment at Young's Point a few miles upriver, feeling good to be active again and away from the constant harassment of administrative details in Memphis. "Vicksburg will be a hard job," he told Julia on January 31. "I expect to get through it successfully however."[93] A first step was dealing with McClernand, who the day before accused Grant of subverting his authority by giving orders directly to his corps commanders without going through McClernand himself. Reiterating his authority from Secretary of War Edwin M. Stanton and Halleck, with Lincoln's endorsement, he asked that the question be referred to Washington. "Two Generals cannot command this army," he argued. Grant agreed, and the next day assumed immediate command of the Vicksburg expedition, effectively returning McClernand to command the XIII Corps, which he assigned to garrison the west bank of the Mississippi around Helena, Arkansas. McClernand demanded clarification, again citing his earlier orders from Halleck and Stanton. Grant responded dispassionately but succinctly that McClernand now commanded only his own corps. As for Lincoln's desires, the president was commander-in-chief and Grant vowed to obey any order of his, but he had seen nothing from Lincoln to prohibit his assuming command, and had Halleck's positive authorization to do so. McClernand agreed for the moment to abide by Grant's orders, but again asked that his protest be sent to Washington for official action. Seeking another way to regain independence, he asked to take his corps up the Arkansas to Little Rock and beyond, then move south to cooperate with Banks against Port Hudson, after which the combined forces could move against Vicksburg.[94]

Grant ignored McClernand's proposal and notified Washington that having seen the situation in person, he concluded that he did not feel McClernand could manage the expedition successfully. Lincoln and Stanton chose not to interfere, and there the matter rested, though McClernand had one more arrow in his quiver: his useful associate William Kountz. Late in February Kountz met with Stanton on McClernand's behalf, and on March 15 McClernand gave him an introduction to call on Lincoln. On the back of the document handed to the president Kountz had written that Grant had been "gloriously drunk and in bed sick" on March 14, and that "if you are averse to drunken Genls I can furnish the Name of officers of high standing to substantiate the above."[95] The accusation availed neither Kountz nor McClernand of any benefit. Kountz troubled Grant no more, and McClernand was demoted from threat to irritant.

When Grant's engineer saw the Williams canal, he found an unfinished ditch one and a half miles long that was too narrow and shallow. Worse, its entire length was within range of enemy batteries on the river bluffs at Vicksburg. When engineers commenced widening and deepening it, they counted on river water diverted into the upper end to deepen the channel. By the end of January water ran five feet deep in the canal but too slowly to scour it deeper, and the lower exit was still under enemy guns. On February 4 Grant decided the canal offered nothing for his strategic aims, but he continued the work since he needed to keep his army occupied to keep it fit, and because it forced the enemy to keep some of their guns occupied covering the exit, weakening the main batteries at the city.[96] The river broke through levees and dams, and by the latter part of March the Confederates had the range, and their fire forced him to close the work. Even then, had the ditch succeeded, his transports could only have used it after dark.

A template was set, however, and in fact Grant was refining it well before he abandoned the canal. He personally inquired about alternative water routes to get his army south of Vicksburg, and soon learned of Lake Providence, at one time a bend of the Mississippi forty miles north of the city, but now isolated by a shift of the river's course. Sluggish Bayou Maçon flowed southward from it into the Tensas River. That in turn fed into the Washita, which emptied into the Red River, whose waters coursed into the Mississippi more than 150 miles below Lake Providence. From that confluence Grant could choose myriad spots upriver to land his army on the east bank as close to Vicksburg as he dared. It needed only a short canal to connect Lake Providence with the Mississippi. Though the overall route would be close to 400 miles, he believed by January 30 that "some advantage may be gained by opening this," and sent a gunboat and a brigade of McClernand's to test the route's feasibility.[97]

Grant personally inspected the lake on February 5 and believed it to be the best means to bypass Vicksburg. He ordered McPherson to commence the canal, returned a week later to hurry the project in person, and by the end of the month had a river dredge on its way.[98] By March 7, however, he concluded that it would fail. The channel widened into cypress swamps choked with trees that had to be removed, and high water impeded the task. Still, he allowed the work to continue to keep McPherson's men busy, and by mid-March small steamers could enter the lake from the Mississippi and move down the bayou and rivers to the Red River.[99] Nevertheless, Grant concluded that the route was simply too long and vulnerable. Watchful for opportunities, he thought that he might later use it to send 20,000 men to cooperate with Banks.[100]

By this time all of his transport was committed to yet another simultaneous exploration. Back on January 22, noting the slow rise of the Mississippi's level, it occurred to him that the Yazoo Pass "might be turned to good account in aiding our enterprise."[101] Some 325 miles upriver from Vicksburg a levee cut Moon Lake off from the river, and a stream called the Yazoo Pass connected the lake with the Coldwater River, which flowed to the Tallahatchie River running southward more than fifty water miles to Greenwood. There it emptied into the Yazoo River, which was fully navigable to its confluence with the Mississippi just a few miles upstream from Vicksburg. It might allow him to get his army to Haynes' Bluff, high ground ten miles north of the city, which he could attack without fear of the batteries facing the river. All he need do was cut the levee. On January 29 he ordered it done, sending a party to explore the route's practicability, followed days later by Porter and some gunboats, along with 600 soldiers.[102]

It was typical of Grant to regard the newest alternative as the most promising thus far. "I expect great results," he told Porter on Saint Valentine's Day, providing the gunboats could make the trip.[103] Yet there were serious drawbacks, not least being that his troops stationed at Milliken's Bend would have to travel a total distance of nearly seven hundred miles to reach Haynes' Bluff. By February 23 a division was ready to board Porter's gunboats for the first phase of the operation, cutting trees to clear the channel, and a few days later he had a dredge on the way to clear the bottom. On March 5 Grant ordered McPherson to take his 25,000-man corps through the pass and head for Yazoo City, less than thirty miles from Haynes' Bluff, a force Grant believed sufficient to take the northern approach to Vicksburg, while Sherman would handle the rest.[104]

Meanwhile, Grant sent gunboats up the Yazoo River as close to Haynes' Bluff as possible, and near midnight on March 6 one fired a signal gun to let him know they were in position. They were to draw enemy fire in their direction while McPherson approached from the land side after navigating the waterways. Now all Grant had to do was wait for McPherson to reach his landing. While waiting, Grant confidently wrote Washburne on March 10 that "the Yazoo Pass expedition is going to prove a perfect success," and that "we are going through a campaign here such as has not been heard of on this continent before."[105] By March 17, however, he learned that Confederates had left Vicksburg and gone up the Yazoo to try to stop McPherson. He also could not get enough light draft steamers to convoy as many regiments as he had hoped, circumstances that determined him to countermand his orders and bring McPherson back to Milliken's Bend. A few days later he learned that Confederates had fortified the Yazoo above Greenwood and on March 11 the gunboats found they could not safely pass.[106]

Typically, Grant was already exploring one more option. On March 13 Porter took a gunboat up Steele's Bayou, which connected with Black Bayou a dozen miles upstream; Black Bayou connected with

Deer Creek, which in turn linked with the Rolling Fork. That stream flowed into the Sunflower River, which ran back south to enter the Yazoo a dozen miles above Haynes' Bluff. Grant might use that route to send forces up the Yazoo to cooperate with McPherson in getting past Greenwood, or go downstream to Haynes' Bluff. He personally inspected the route on March 15 and immediately realized its potential. At 130 miles, it was shorter than the Lake Providence or Yazoo Pass alternatives, by now all but abandoned. At once Grant ordered Sherman to reconnoiter the route thoroughly and clear the channel where necessary; he awaited only Sherman's word that the route was open before sending several brigades up the Mississippi to a spot where Steele's Bayou flowed barely a mile east of a river bend. There he would march them overland and board them on Porter's transports for the rest of their journey.[107] By March 17 Grant believed that here, finally, he had his route to high ground behind Vicksburg. Five days later, however, his hopes faded when he learned that Porter feared they might get no farther than Rolling Fork, which presented unanticipated problems for passage.[108] Six days later Grant confessed that "I cannot promise success to this expedition," and on March 27 admitted defeat when Porter said that Confederates had blocked the Sunflower almost within sight of the Yazoo, making clearing the route too dangerous to proceed.[109]

Grant found that the work had kept his men cheerful despite the wet weather, and he felt better himself than he had in months.[110] On Saint Valentine's day he told Julia "I am remarkably well." He ate heartily and slept soundly every night, though accidental loss of his false teeth made meals a bit of a challenge.[111] No doubt part of his good cheer came from the turnabout his salary made in his financial status, enabling him in February to invest $12,000 in United States bonds.[112] Even McClernand was quiet for a change. Still, Grant chafed at the passing time, though the only outward sign was the eighteen to twenty cigars he smoked every day.[113] Early in February, acknowledging that it would be some time yet before he could attack Vicksburg, he railed against rising river and heavy rain that threatened to flood not only his camps but also his works. Nonetheless, he told Hillyer that "I hope yet to fool the rebels and effect a landing where they do not expect one." Then "there will be a big fight or a foot race."[114] A week later, revealing much of his mental process with any problem, he told Julia that "we are not much nearer an attack on Vicksburg now apparently than when I first come down, but still as the attack will be made and time is passing we are necessarily coming nearer the great conflict."[115] He worked; so long as he worked he progressed; so long as he progressed he would reach his goal. "The reduction of Vicksburg is a heavy contract," he said late in February, "but I feel very confident of success."[116] It was all the same dynamic, whether digging potatoes in Oregon or canals in Louisiana.

Through the multiple setbacks, Grant never forgot something that happened weeks before on February 2. That morning before dawn, one of Porter's fleet of armored boats boldly ran down the river right under the guns of Vicksburg's batteries to ram a Confederate vessel and then moved on south past the remaining batteries to safety below. "This is of vast importance," Grant wired Halleck that afternoon, though for the moment he saw the main effect being severing Vicksburg's communications west of the Mississippi.[117] Seven weeks later on March 25 two more of Porter's rams ran the gauntlet in daylight. One fell almost to pieces when hit by a rebel artillery shot, but the other came through in good condition despite several hits.[118] This was no idle event. The fastest and most direct way to get below Vicksburg was to run past the city on gunboats and transports, yet Grant and Porter had assumed that the formidable batteries on the eastern bluffs were too deadly. Now two of three vessels had passed them relatively unharmed. Some truths became obvious. River current ran at four or five miles an hour, and a steamboat's engines could boost that to seven or eight miles an hour or more. Heavy cannon on the bluffs might get in only one shot as a target passed and could not reaim fast enough to try again with accuracy. If the vessels risked passing in the night, the chances of success mushroomed.

Late in February Grant ordered a reconnaissance in the direction of Warrenton, a likely landing ten miles below Vicksburg, where batteries covered the southern end of his first canal.[119] Almost a month later he decided to destroy them. He sent two gunboats and several small sailboats and transports past Vicksburg under cover of darkness; he then marched troops down the west bank to meet the small flotilla across the river from Warrenton, where the boats would ferry them over for the attack. After that the infantry would be ferried back to the west bank and return northward. It was a raid and nothing more.[120] Instead, the two rams ran past by themselves the morning of March 25 without notifying Grant, intending to do the ferrying themselves. He was irked, but not for long. "It may all be providential," he told Porter, "and I shall expect a change of apparent luck soon." For Grant that meant changing his luck himself.[121]

Within hours his concept shifted to something dramatically different. He sent a requisition north to forward to him "for purposes, that are of the highest importance," at least twenty-five flat boats, thirty or more yawls, a barge capable of carrying artillery and soldiers, and four or five Chicago tugboats for towing, all to be sufficient to carry up to 50,000 soldiers and artillery, with supplies, equipment, ordnance, and two regiments of cavalry.[122] By this time he had all but abandoned the Haynes' Bluff option. On March 22 Grant revealed an uncharacteristic concern. Having placed so much faith first in the Yazoo Pass gambit, and then in the stalled Steele's Bayou approach, he confided to Sherman that "I have made really but little calculation u[p]on reaching Vicksburg by any other [route] than Hains Bluff."[123] To his other confidant, Julia, he was even more open. "I am very well but much perplexed," he wrote her. "Heretofore I have had nothing to do but fight the enemy. This time I have to overcome obsticles to reach him."[124] On April 2 he made a final personal reconnaissance of Haynes' Bluff and concluded that any attack there would meet with "immense sacrifice of life, if not with defeat." That settled his mind, and he abandoned any idea of taking Vicksburg by its upriver flank. That same day he asked Porter to prepare to run gunboats and transports past the batteries as soon as possible.[125]

He knew what he was going to do. He would move 20,000 troops on shallow draft yawls down the west bank via a number of bayous he could open, establishing his camp at New Carthage, Louisiana, twenty miles downstream from Vicksburg. Then Porter would run gunboats and transports past Vicksburg by night to rendezvous at New Carthage and ferry his command over to take Warrenton, or else farther downstream at Grand Gulf just below the Big Black River. From there he would have a straight approach toward Jackson. By March 29 he had engineers at work making surveys for opening the bayous.[126] The next day his confidence was returned entirely. "There has been some delay in the attack," he wrote Julia, but "once landed on the other side of the river I expect but little trouble."[127]

Grant commenced one last canal connecting the Mississippi below Milliken's Bend with Walnut Bayou half a mile west. It would connect inland to Willow Bayou, which led to Roundaway Bayou and south to New Carthage. A week later the canal was half finished, but thereafter problems mounted. Debris clogged the bayous and the Mississippi began falling dramatically. By April 25 there was barely half a foot of water in the canal in places, and the bayous held little more. Another effort had failed, but by this time it did not matter, for on his orders McClernand's corps had cut a land route beside and across the bayous to New Carthage. That gave his army a road to take it below Vicksburg.

The day after coming to his decision, Grant told Julia that "I am doing all I can and expect to be successful."[128] He justified his decision to Halleck by explaining that "this is the only move I now see as practicable." For it to work he intended to hold his army compactly together and pay special attention to keeping his supply line open. Should he meet with a setback, it would not be "in any other way than a fair fight." Once across the river he expected to find good roads both directly to Vicksburg, and also to Jackson, giving him an option of targets. "The greatest confidance of success prevails," he told the general-in-chief.[129]

Grant had hoped for Porter to run the batteries the night of April 14, with transports sufficient for two batteries of artillery and 6,000 to 8,000 men. He sent orders to McClernand to board his men on the boats immediately on their arrival and cross the river to take Grand Gulf after Porter silenced its batteries. Rather than pursue the Confederates if they pulled back, McClernand was to consolidate his corps on the east bank, then be ready to move south to support Banks at Port Hudson, though Grant soon changed his mind and decided he could not spare men to cooperate with Banks just yet.[130] McPherson's first division would cross next.[131] Finally, on the night of April 16, Porter put a dozen boats in motion downriver in the night and though the Confederates discovered them and opened fire, hitting every one, all but one passed the batteries with only minor damage. Several nights later another eighteen barges and transports ran the gauntlet and eleven got through. It was enough. Almost everyone had opposed running the batteries, but Grant's boldness was vindicated.

"I am doing my best and am full of hope for complete success," he wrote Julia late April 21. "I never expect to have an army under my command whipped unless it is very badly whipped and cant help it."[132] The next day he arrived personally at New Carthage, and on April 24 he and Porter made a reconnaissance of Grand Gulf and its batteries from one of the gunboats, Grant concluding that if they moved within forty-eight hours they could take it easily.[133] The next day he sent one of his staff scouting up the Black River looking for a good route to high ground in the interior, once his army was across.[134] On April 27 he began loading McClernand's corps on their transports to be ready for a landing on the morrow. Porter would first bombard the batteries into submission, while transports full of infantrymen waited in the stream to go ashore. On landing they would form ranks, establish a beachhead on the best high ground available, and then reform to move forward into the interior.[135] There was no room for unnecessary animals, so most officers' horses, including Grant's, remained behind.

Leaving little to chance, he notified Sherman that a demonstration at Haynes' Bluff might be a useful distraction to cover his landing, though he left the decision to his trusted subordinate.[136] Meanwhile, another diversion had been under way for some days. On April 16, as Porter's fleet readied for its run, Colonel Benjamin Grierson led a body of cavalry on a raid south from LaGrange, Tennessee. It was a raid through the Mississippi interior that Grant designed to disrupt enemy communications, cut Vicksburg and Jackson's rail connections, and lure enemy cavalry away from Grant's route of advance once over the river. Grant had no idea of its progress as yet.

Bad weather delayed the bombardment and landing on April 28, and Grant fretted. Weather, roads, and water were, he complained, "all against me." Now he expected to get started on the morning of April 29. "I feel every confidance of sucsess," he wrote Julia, "but may be disappointed." He would be aboard a small tug in the river to watch the bombardment. If he took Grand Gulf, he told her, it would mean "virtual possession of Vicksburg and Port Hudson and the entire Mississippi river."[137]

Porter's guns opened at eight o'clock the following morning, and fired until one in the afternoon, but the Grand Gulf batteries could not be silenced completely. Grant made a quick field decision. He could not keep what was by now 10,000 men on boats in the river much longer. Sending them back to the Louisiana side, he put McClernand in motion marching down the west bank about nine miles, then asked Porter to escort all the transports downriver past the Grand Gulf batteries under cover of an evening bombardment. They made the run successfully and Grant sent word off to Halleck that "I feel that the battle is now more than half won."[138] On April 30 the infantry boarded the transports once more and crossed the river entirely unopposed to land at Bruinsburg. Grant himself crossed with Porter on his flagship *Benton*, and once on the east bank oversaw the transfer of more soldiers while McClernand formed his divisions and moved inland. His corps marched on after nightfall under a full moon, and finally at about two o'clock that morning on May 1 encountered Confederates hurried from Grand Gulf a few miles west of Port Gibson. After a spirited hour's engagement, the combatants skirmished through the night, and then at dawn McClernand moved forward. Having brought nothing with him but the uniform he wore, Grant borrowed an extra horse from one of his generals and reached the field by ten in the morning to find one flank doing well but the other held back, and called up enough reinforcements to drive the Confederates in retreat.[139]

Grant and McClernand rode over the field to the cheers of their soldiers, and Grant felt relieved enough to indulge McClernand's desire to make a brief speech to the cheering soldiers before suggesting that he ought to press the pursuit.[140] Five months of planning and struggle had all been to reach this moment. Grant was on the east bank with a secure foothold on high ground. Roads from Port Gibson led both to Vicksburg and Jackson. He had only about 20,000 men with him at the moment, with what he mistakenly thought might be three times that many of the enemy at Vicksburg, Jackson, and other locations ahead. But the rest of McPherson's corps and some of Sherman's were coming. On his ride from Bruinsburg he saw enough to conclude that he could subsist his men and animals on beef and forage from the countryside. The rest of what was needed he would draw from Milliken's Bend via the admittedly precarious route through New Carthage.

Even if he had to break free from his supply line for a time, "I have every confidance in succeeding in doing it," he soon wrote Halleck.

The first fight was scarcely over when a local came to Grant and told him that "Grierson has knocked the heart out of the State." The diversionary cavalry raid from LaGrange was a spectacular success. The horsemen had raced south through central Mississippi, cut the railroad east out of Jackson, then moved on to cut its rail link with Confederates in southern Mississippi and Louisiana, threatened Natchez, and were last heard of riding toward Union lines in Baton Rouge. Behind them the raiders left a desolation of broken rail track, burned bridges, destroyed locomotives and rolling stock, and tons of stores. Grant told Halleck that it was "the most successful thing of the kind since the breaking out of the rebellion."[141]

There was a long road ahead, but from that battlefield a buoyed Grant sent word back to Porter of success thus far, and that "our forces are on the move."[142]

As Grant's command moved from the battlefield, Hooker's renewed advance met Jackson in The Wilderness. After desultory fighting he pulled back around Chancellorsville and put his men to building defenses, surrendering all initiative to Lee. Hooker's fortified position was too strong to attack frontally, especially in The Wilderness, which seriously restricted all maneuver. The brigades left at Fredericksburg were hardly a match for the two Federal corps in their front, and in fact stood little chance of holding their ground if the Yankees attacked. Yet again Lee was lucky. A report came to him that Hooker's right flank was exposed and vulnerable. That evening he met with Jackson to discuss their options. For some time the two generals had what a nearby member of Jackson's staff called "earnest conversation." Once he had confirmation that Hooker was indeed vulnerable, Lee favored sending a heavy column secretly around the enemy right to strike it in flank and rear, even though that meant dividing his army. He had done that before and succeeded, but not against such heavy odds. Jackson liked the idea and said his corps could do it. Still, Lee felt natural hesitance at the enormous risk. He remained silent in thought for what seemed like a quarter of an hour. He was making one of the decisions

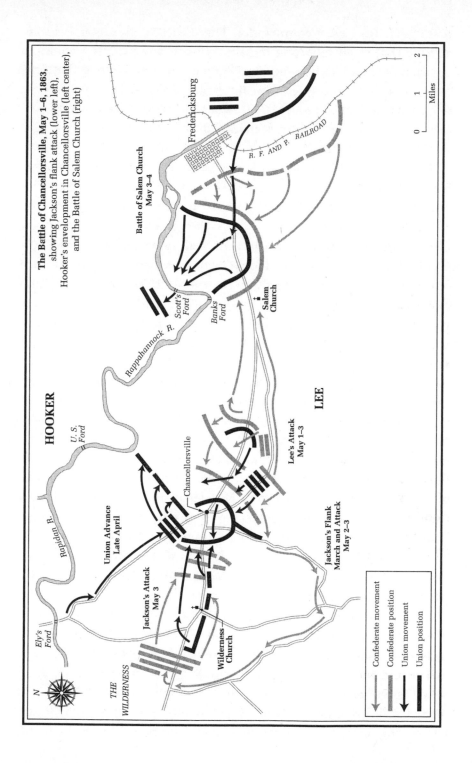

The Battle of Chancellorsville, May 1–6, 1863,
showing Jackson's flank attack (lower left),
Hooker's envelopment in Chancellorsville (left center),
and the Battle of Salem Church (right)

that made him a great commander. There was clearly an opportunity at hand that might not long remain. He believed his army could do anything. He had faith in Jackson. He had known all along that only great hazard held promise of great results, given the enemy's preponderant strength and resources. He would trust to audacity and Providence, though clearly the risk made him uneasy. "Well General," he said, "you may try it."[143]

The plan was a house of cards. One failure anywhere risked collapse. An even greater risk was Lee's decision to make the flank attack as powerful as possible by assigning almost three-fifths of the command at hand. He would himself hold perhaps 15,000 to keep the attention of the Federal center, and have Jackson lead 28,000 via back roads to a point just over a mile west of Hooker's flank, where they were to turn onto a turnpike leading directly to the exposed Yankees. They would have almost fifteen miles to march on poor roads. The route in places would take them within earshot of Federals. Jackson had failed him more than once on the James-York Peninsula. And yet, given what Lee knew at that moment, it represented a sensible, almost prudent, judgment. His alternatives appeared to be to stand his ground and wait for the Yankees to attack him, or seize the initiative. A direct assault on the lines in front of him was doomed. Since Hooker had stalled, a bold move could prolong that stall, and nothing was bolder than Jackson's march. If Lee hoped to knock Hooker off balance, the best way was the unexpected, and with enough power to force the enemy to rethink his position. It had worked against McClellan and Pope. It could work against Hooker. It was an objective approach to a serious problem that, in the circumstances, might have no other solution.

From the moment Jackson's march commenced the next morning, various Federals discovered it, yet no one took the threat seriously. After an exhausting march lasting most of the daylight hours, Jackson was in position and ordered the attack forward shortly before dusk. The impact crumpled the Union right back on itself as Jackson pressed onward for the next two hours, his own advance stalling thanks to exhaustion and the gathering darkness. In the confusion Jackson himself was wounded by his own men, then A. P. Hill went down, and by nightfall the attack sputtered out. A messenger that evening found Lee resting on a bed of straw, and brought news of Jackson's wound, reporting it as serious but not fatal. "Thank God, it is no worse; God be praised that he is still alive," Lee said. "Any victory is a dear one that deprives us of the services of Jackson, even for a short time." Rising to eat a bit of ham and hardtack, Lee immediately left on his own to make dispositions to renew the fight on the morrow.[144]

The next morning once again Lee was lucky, for all Hooker could think of was getting his army to a secure new defensive line. Confederate attacks from two sides hammered him through the morning before he pulled back, and then Lee maintained the pressure. He was actually preparing a fresh attack when a dispatch alerted him that the Federals opposite Fredericksburg had finally advanced, taken the town and Marye's Heights, and were pushing the defenders back. Though Lee had Hooker at bay, Federal divisions from Fredericksburg would have an open road to his rear and soon he could be caught in a vise.

Again, Lee's reaction to crisis marked his judgment. He could have withdrawn southward to Spotsylvania, consolidating with the brigades from Fredericksburg, and then taken a new defensive position some miles south behind the North Anna River. But that would give up territory to a foe whom he now considered spiritually beaten and demoralized. If he could damage Hooker this much while outnumbered more than double, then he could hold Hooker in place long enough to detach units to protect his rear. He subdivided one half of his already divided army to send four brigades hurrying eastward. By midafternoon they stopped around Salem Church, joining another brigade from town that had fought a sturdy defense there, ending the immediate threat.

Every day brought its difficult decision. During that night the main Union army dug in and bolstered its defensive line. That told Lee that Hooker did not intend to renew the offensive, making him no longer an immediate threat. Every hour that Hooker remained passive told Lee he had less to fear from that quarter. Again, he chose the most productive alternative. He would leave half his command under Stuart to hold Hooker, while he took the rest to deal with the Federals near Salem Church. It took most of the day to accomplish the movement, and anxiety made Lee short-tempered at delays to get the attack going. Finding the division commanders at Salem Church uncertain of who should do what, Lee assumed direct command and began putting units in place for an assault. By five-thirty in the afternoon all was ready. At the signal, Lee himself, his hat in his hand, stood with the 2d Georgia Battalion near the center of his line and led it forward for a few yards, a fair sign of his emotional intensity that evening.[145]

Ordinarily he was not reckless, prudently remaining behind the lines at a field headquarters, but this was a special circumstance. There was no corps commander present. He was impatient and aroused, and may have felt the men needed his presence in the front rank to boost spirits. Having spoken of the need for greater effort, even if it meant greater risks, he may have extended that to his own person. The assault soon broke down from confusion and the strength of the enemy works, yet as darkness fell Lee spoke of a night attack, a desperate act almost doomed to failure, and a sign that frustration, anxiety, and excitement momentarily clouded his judgment. Still, the Confederates had the Yankees backed into a bend of the Rappahannock where they held their ground until they escaped across a ford during the night.

Lee turned his column and hurried back on May 5 to rejoin the rest and try to push Hooker into the river. Stuart, temporarily replacing Jackson in command of the II Corps, wanted to risk a frontal attack that morning even before the army was concentrated. Lee advised him to be careful, but gave him permission to make the assault if he believed it could succeed. Of all his risks, this was the only one showing questionable judgment. After five days of action or marching, his men were exhausted, and nearly one-fourth of them were casualties. The Union line anchored at both ends on the Rappahannock. That meant frontal assaults against well-entrenched positions, which risked a repeat of the heavy casualties Lee suffered at Malvern Hill. Yet each risk taken had been rewarded thus far, and each emboldened Lee the more for the next. When faced with no alternative, he would resort to the frontal assault more than once.

In the next couple of hours, however, Lee's concerns grew, and he changed his mind. An assault now, in their condition, "might be beyond us," he warned Stuart. Expecting Hooker to retreat, Lee concluded that they could damage him severely as he fell back, with less chance of disaster to themselves.[146] Hooker did indeed retreat that night, but at dawn on May 6 Lee ultimately concluded that his army was too battered and exhausted to pursue. Before long both armies moved back to their old positions looking at each other across the river at Fredericksburg.

There was something near miraculous in the campaign. Certainly Lee saw a heavenly hand in it all, even the wounding and, on May 10, death of Jackson. "I do not know how to replace him," Lee lamented the next day, "but God's will be done."[147] If, as he believed, Providence disposed all and man had no agency in what happened on earth, then his victories were preordained, which could only mean that God favored the Army of Northern Virginia at least, if not the South itself, and the daring, even foolhardy, risks that Lee took time and again really were no risks at all, but the will of the Almighty carried out through his hands.

In that month of May Lee achieved and Grant commenced the most brilliant successes of their careers, and both through careful planning, quick reaction to setbacks and the unexpected, and unflagging audacity. Surely the season could not be far off when Lincoln or Davis would decide it was time to set one the task of stopping the other?

12

JULY 1863

THE WAR CONTINUED to harden Lee's heart against the North. When the Federals sent a message asking for the customary opportunity to come to the battlefield to remove their dead, he gave his permission, with an edge of bitterness after Jackson's death from pneumonia on May 10, remarking that he "did not want a single Yankee to remain on our soil *dead* or *alive.*"[1]

"I require efficient persons about me," Lee told Mary in February 1862.[2] No commander of an army could function without a headquarters staff, or without managing it effectively. The Confederate army recognized two distinct kinds of staff: personal and general. A commander appointed a small personal staff while the War Department assigned officers from its several bureaus to compose a general staff. The common expectation was that a commander used his personal staff in battle as couriers, but not the general staff, though Lee used both.

Two questions confronted him. Was his staff adequate for the job; and did he use them adequately? Lee saw some officers accruing virtual retinues of aides through nepotism, political ambition, and self-aggrandizement. Beauregard always had a bloated staff, and Magruder in fifteen months in Virginia went through nearly half a hundred, a virtual battalion.[3] Even Jeb Stuart put nine relatives on his staff, and A. P. Hill had five. By contrast, Lee appointed none, though in 1861 he asked Custis to recommend a useful relative, and repeatedly in the war opened the door for Custis himself.[4] In western Virginia he appointed his close friend Washington an aide, and in April 1862 named as an aide the son of his old army comrade Andrew Talcott.

Lee rather consistently limited himself to the number of aides prescribed by statute, always aware of himself as an example. While his soldiers slept on the ground he slept in a tent rather than a bed in a warm house. He ate almost the same fare as his men. He still wore a colonel's blouse, now well faded, and old blue flannel trousers that showed their wear.[5] When he wore through his trousers, he got replacements from the same bureau in Richmond that clothed his soldiers, and was indifferent about regulation officer's stripes on their outer seams. Where most generals wore gold braided kepis, he used a simple gray round-brimmed hat. He resisted posing for his photograph, but when he did he kept none himself.[6] A large staff did not fit this template, and the government only paid for a few aides. Any more must be paid from Lee's pocket.[7] Inspired by concern for economy, he said he needed no more than two or three, since "on the field all the members of the staff departments can perform the duties of aides."[8]

Lee began the war with staff handed him from state forces, and when he took over his army retained twenty-two-year-old Walter H. Taylor as his adjutant, an able headquarters factotum nearly the equal of Grant's Rawlins. Otherwise, in 1862 Lee selected staff who remained most of the war. Charles S. Venable had taught mathematics at three universities, and Lee used him as an inspector and sometime secretary. Of them all he was the most likely to dare approach when Lee was in a bad mood.[9] Charles Marshall had a master's degree from the University of Virginia, and acted most of the time as Lee's military secretary, composing orders and writing Lee's reports of campaigns compiled from the often conflicting reports of subordinates. Marshall had to confront the authors directly for resolution, saving Lee the embarrassment of questioning his officers.[10] Thomas M. R. Talcott served as aide and then engineer officer until he left in 1864, and Armistead L. Long was an aide until he became a brigadier in the fall of 1863. Thus from 1864 on Lee would have only Taylor, Marshall, and Venable on his personal staff.

Lee gave each man his assignment for the day, then left him to it. Thereafter as a task came to hand, he simply used the one most handy. From 1862 onward, however, he more strictly defined their duties. Taylor oversaw virtually all paperwork. Long and Marshall served as secretaries, while Venable and Talcott acted as aides, but in a pinch Lee still used any man for any task, and on the battlefield all became eyes, ears, and couriers. Outsiders complained he should have more seasoned men, but Lee preferred not to take such men away from field assignments. They rode with him on the march and camped closest to his tent. His speech could be quick and brusque in the tone of a man accustomed to giving orders, and some who saw him thought him "the stern soldier," and that included his staff.[11] If he lost his temper, they were most often the objects, Venable especially. By the summer of 1863 he thought of asking for assignment elsewhere. "I am too high-tempered to stand a high-tempered man and consequently I become stubborn, sullen, useless and disagreeable" he confessed, but then calmed as he usually did, remembering that "the old man has much to annoy and worry him and is very kind and considerate after all."[12] In equal candor, Taylor said that though he served Lee faithfully, he could never love him.

The odd man out was Robert H. Chilton, whom the War Department first appointed as Lee's inspector general, but who became chief of staff. He was an inattentive listener whose habitually confused orders contributed to the costly debacle at Malvern Hill, and at Chancellorsville on May 2 he garbled a command that would have left Fredericksburg virtually helpless had the Federals reacted. Aware of Chilton's shortcomings, Lee made no effort to replace him. Indeed, he seemed blind to Chilton's failings, recommending him for promotion to brigadier in October 1862, and again in 1863, telling him that "you have always been zealous and active in the discharge of your official duties." Perhaps it was another case of avoiding confrontation and not wishing to cause an old friend embarrassment.[13] If so, it was an ill-placed concern.

Lee accepted the officers Richmond appointed for his general staff and left them to their assigned duties. As he told Mary so often, he had to make do with what he was given. Most were competent, and some outstanding. Lee regarded supply officers as most important, and his commissary of subsistence and quartermaster stayed with him almost to the end of the war. His first inspector general monitored discipline and efficiency, qualities embarrassingly lacking in the army during and after the Antietam campaign, which led Lee to order brigade commanders to appoint their own inspectors and tribunals capable of swift punishment, but the War Department abolished them just after Chancellorsville. In Briscoe G. Baldwin, Lee had a fine ordnance officer through his entire tenure in command. He had a chief engineer but only intermittently, and while chief of artillery was not a staff position, he did have William N. Pendleton as such through the war, a well-meaning but ineffectual holdover from Johnston. Lee had no signals officer since, as recently as 1859, he thought battlefield signaling impractical.[14]

When it came to how Lee used his staff, his performance was mixed thus far. As superintendent at West Point and colonel of his cavalry regiment, he had only an adjutant, a supply officer, and an aide or surgeon. To him a staff was to implement plans, not make them. Rarely did he consult the general staff on strategy. Where by now Grant's general staff was evolving into an operations committee, Lee did virtually all planning himself.[15] As for his personal staff, he would hardly seek counsel from inexperienced youths no matter how intelligent. Lee knew the value of delegation, having argued for it with Richmond, yet often he failed to use the resources at hand. No wonder that his staff nicknamed him "the great tycoon."

That reluctance to make full use of his staff had its origins in his personality. From youth his instinct was to do things himself to see them done well. Delegation had not worked for him as a young officer, and doing tasks himself risked no confrontation with others for poor performance. No doubt his concept of duty influenced him, too. As with the emancipation of the Custis slaves, he regarded a duty undertaken as a personal obligation to oversee every detail. By 1863 he felt increasingly that Confederate fate rested on his army, making it imperative that everything he did be done properly. Even his sense of personal and professional failure may have impelled him to do more himself. Second Manassas, Fredericksburg, and Chancellorsville argued that he was doing something right, yet after each he felt a failure to accomplish more.

In the Seven Days he used staff erratically. Instructions were too complex for aides to convey verbally, and he began delivering them himself. He sent no staff to see why Jackson was tardy, or to act as guides. Giving orders to his commanders, he left no one behind to ensure they were carried out, in spite of the repeated miscarriage of his instructions.[16] By the fall of 1862 Lee verbally conveyed plans to Longstreet and Jackson, and then left it to them to execute, which worked well in the main but could be dangerous, as Chilton's garbling at Chancellorsville demonstrated. In the Maryland campaign Lee used his personal staff to communicate with separate columns, yet he did not empower them to give orders in his name to meet exigent circumstances. No one went with Jackson to Harpers Ferry to coordinate his movements, and at Antietam staff carried his verbal orders but lacked the authority to react on the spot in his name.[17] Considering its importance, the famed lost order should have been entrusted to one of his staff. At Fredericksburg he used Long, Venable, and Talcott to mass artillery against the Federal advance. He had men available to perform good staff work on the battlefield, if he would use them.[18] In fact, by midwar his staff, including all of the various support personnel not reporting directly to him, approached or exceeded 100 men.[19] Yet he still had no intelligence officer, choosing to be his own, reading enemy newspapers, sifting scouts' reports, and analyzing their meaning. Someone else should have been doing that.

After nine months in command of his army, Lee had ideas for staff reform that he believed would make his job easier, and himself more effective. He recognized the need for a systematic general staff system employing men specifically trained for their positions. "The more simple the organization of our Army the more suitable in my opinion will it be to our service," he told the chairman of the Senate Military Committee. He wanted the position of chief of staff formalized and occupied by a brigadier general senior to all other staff, empowered to coordinate their efforts, and able to give orders directly to all subordinates instead of Lee having to send such orders through the corps commanders. "Otherwise I shall have to give all directions," he explained, "which, in the field, in time of action, &c., may be the cause of delay and loss," not to mention compromising much of the benefit of having a general staff.[20] He admired the current French system of a permanent corps of career staff officers teaching others their duties and ensuring that orders were obeyed, and suggested it as a model for the Confederacy. "The greatest difficulty I find is in causing orders and regulations to be obeyed," he told the president. The French model might "shape the staff of our Army" to good ends.[21] Just days after Chancellorsville Lee directed that all orders from the heads of staff departments at his headquarters came with his authority.[22] In other instances, however, even as he called for reforms in staff functions, he failed to enforce them himself.

Though their numbers were lean—and no doubt Lee could have benefited from a larger military family—they were demonstrably sufficient in number and capability for the job of running the army, as evidenced by its performance to date. As for Lee's management of that staff, he steadily learned during his first year in command. Certainly he still did too much himself but that was a function of his personality, and not inadequate staff. Though he was doing better, his communication with his top subordinates was still haphazard, often too discretionary or imprecise even when not garbled by Chilton. A larger personal staff would have made life easier for Taylor, Venable, and the others, but with Lee as the governing hand, it seems unlikely that he would have done any less, or that his staff would have been any more effective.[23]

Now he was about to place greater demands on them, and himself, than ever before. Even in the flush of victory, the armchair generals complained. "We allowed the enemy to get off too easily," carped the Richmond *Enquirer*. "His whole force ought to have been captured," but the fault was not Lee's. On one point, the editor was emphatic. The pubic should insist that "General Lee shall never hereafter again expose his valuable life to the missiles of death." With Jackson gone, "our great hero and chieftain, owes it to us, if not to himself, to be where the shock of battle cannot reach." Other men could be replaced, "but if General Lee should fall who could take his place?"[24]

Confederates spent the weeks after Chancellorsville speculating on what Lee might do next, for they expected him to do something. "Genl Lee I believe has more brains than all the balance of our big men put together," one man wrote his wife.[25] That confidence spread steadily both in and out of the army. "What may be General Lee's plans are doubtless known only to himself," observed a North Carolina editor. "We are quite content that it should be so. *He* understands his business. *We* do not."[26] Certainly the Yankees expected Lee to do something. One Union observer accused him of "showing off" his army at Fredericksburg "as if with the design of deceiving our military."[27] In fact, following the battle Lee did not believe he could do anything but pull back to Richmond unless reinforced. Hooker's numbers were too great, and his own casualties had been severe, more than 10,000, with heavy losses of experienced officers aside from the irreplaceable

Stonewall. Lee saw so little possibility of an offensive that he rescinded the order calling Longstreet to him.[28] At the same time, he resisted Secretary of War James A. Seddon's request that he send men to reinforce Vicksburg. Mistakenly thinking that campaign would be over by the end of May or Grant would have to give up in the summer heat, Lee rightly argued on May 10 that weakening his own army risked greater danger to Virginia, presuming that Hooker would use his numerical advantage to cross the Rappahannock River again.[29]

Lee reassessed the military situation on May 11 when Longstreet visited for three days of strategic discussions. Both agreed they were winning battles but losing the war by attrition. Longstreet favored reinforcing the army in Tennessee to force Grant to withdraw from Vicksburg, but Lee thought otherwise. At the end of the day Lee wrote to President Davis that sources said Hooker was being reinforced substantially from other departments. That meant that "Virginia is to be the theater of action." Weakening his army now courted disaster. However, if he concentrated units from the Carolinas with his own he might move north first to lure Hooker to someplace where Lee could strike to advantage.[30] The noncombat losses in his ranks chagrined him more than ever. "Can not our good citizens get back to us our stragglers and deserters?" he asked brother Carter.[31]

Over the next two days Lee and Longstreet framed the campaign's objectives. They should cross the Potomac, marching as far as the Susquehanna River to draw Hooker's army out of Virginia. Heavily outnumbered, they would avoid battle until they selected ground favoring a successful defense, and then maneuver Hooker into attacking them as Burnside had at Fredericksburg. While Longstreet's corps defended that line, the rest of the army, emulating Jackson, would move around the Federals to strike them flank and rear. Lee's goal was not just to defeat the Army of the Potomac, but to erase it.[32]

He had few strategic blind spots, yet he persisted in the belief in the battle of annihilation, and the old Napoleonic notion of one great victory winning a war. The size, organization, and weaponry of Civil War armies, plus the heavy casualties even to victors in major engagements, made the former virtually impossible.[33] As Grant had shown, an army could be eradicated by siege and surrender, but not on the battlefield. As for the latter, the North's resilience after two years of defeat in the East ought to have taught Lee that a nation could absorb even disaster when it knew it still possessed overwhelming manpower, resources, and resolve. Lee realized that his victories crumpled civilian morale, and saw evidence of that in the Northern press, yet the seams of dissent and dissatisfaction there reported were narrower than he believed.

He left for Richmond immediately after his meetings, and on May 15 met with Davis and Seddon to outline his proposal. His army was hungry. He might implore his brother Carter that "labor is the thing to make soldiers," and implore the people to urge boys too young to enlist to soldier in the cornfields armed with hoes, but that could not feed his men now.[34] Invading Maryland and Pennsylvania would allow the men to forage and eat well again. Hooker's army was in flux, with scores of regiments' terms of service expiring, and thousands of their replacements new units with no experience. Hooker himself had been beaten badly, and might be at a psychological disadvantage. Moving north would force him to follow Lee, relieving the pressure on the Old Dominion and Richmond. From his analysis of the impact of the battlefield on political will and civilian morale, Lee firmly believed that the Republicans would be repudiated at the polls in the fall if he was successful.

Above all, he believed his men could do anything. A fortnight before Chancellorsville his spirits had been so high that he boasted openly about his army, telling a fellow general that he now commanded "the finest army" to date.[35] "There never were such men in the Army before, & there never can be better in any Army again," he wrote a congressman on May 21. "If properly led they will go any where & never falter at the work before them." With the right officers and organization, and with the spirit of Stonewall infusing the ranks, "indeed we shall be invincible and our country safe."[36] There would have to be another major battle. Indeed, he wanted one, but on his terms. The situation facing Lee dictated that he do something. This was the moment to strike, and perhaps this time realize the Pennsylvania dream. There was nothing ill-considered about it. It was the sensible thing to do. It is what Jackson or Grant would do.

Davis and Seddon agreed. Lee commenced a flurry of preparations, starting with the army's organization. Since taking command and organizing it into two corps he had come to believe that each was too unwieldy for a single commander to manage. However, he postponed doing something about it because he did not know suitable men for any new corps created by another reorganization. Jackson's death and a pending campaign prompted him to do it now. Longstreet would stay at the head of a reduced First Corps. Since Ewell was the senior major general in the army and senior officer in Jackson's corps, he would succeed to its command as the logical choice, though Lee's recommendation of him as "an honest, brave soldier, who has always done his duty well" hardly glowed. Then elements of both corps joined by a few brigades brought up from the South were to be combined into a new Third Corps for a recovered A. P. Hill to command. Lee told the president that he thought Hill the best major general in the army. If Lee did not think him ready for corps command before, why now? In the end, his elevation, like Ewell's, was chiefly a matter of seniority. He thought division commanders John Bell Hood and Richard H. Anderson were "improving," and would one day make good corps commanders.[37] To Hood himself Lee confided that capable commanders were scarce. "Where can they be obtained?" he asked.[38] One thing Lee did not do was reorganize his staff.[39]

"It is time I was in motion," he told the president just five days after their conference.[40] While asking that the capital's reserves be put in order for its defense, he continued concentrating his army.[41] Shifting regiments and brigades from the Shenandoah to the Carolinas, deciding which outposts he could leave undefended, Lee counted on the coming summer heat to discourage the enemy from active campaigning farther south. He was so busy at the task that he was short with Mary when she chided him for not writing. "You are relapsing into your old error," he scolded, "supposing that I have a superabundance of time & have only my own pleasures to attend to."[42] He also lost his patience with D. H. Hill, commanding southeast Virginia and northeast North Carolina. Lee gave him an order with discretion to select units to send north, but Hill refused it and asked for a specific instruction. "I cannot operate in this manner," Lee complained to Davis. Avoiding conflict once again, the general asked the president to send Hill an order.[43] A day later, Lee asked Davis to remove Hill's department from his command so he would not have to deal with him again. Having transferred

Hill once to get him out of the way, Lee would now transfer territory to achieve the same end.[44]

Days moved too swiftly with too little being accomplished, and Lee's discouragement showed. "I fear the time has passed when I could have taken the offensive with advantage," he told Davis on May 30. Expecting Hooker to make some form of two-pronged advance, he feared he could not handle both and might have no choice but to stay in his defenses, or else "there may be nothing left for me to do but fall back."[45] He still felt unwell, and the old sense of creeping mortality gripped him again when he told his daughter Agnes that if ever their family was together again, he feared that "it may be for a short time."[46] He turned a corner by the end of the month, and in a better mood told Mary that "I pray that our merciful Father in Heaven may protect & direct us." If the Almighty stood by him once more, "I fear no odds & no numbers."[47]

A few days later on June 3 the march began. He prayed that Providence "will watch over us, & notwithstanding our weakness & sins will yet give us a name & place among the nations of the earth."[48] Longstreet moved first, then Ewell, while Hill remained in the works at Fredericksburg to persuade the enemy that the whole army was there. Lee coordinated a host of elements ably, from having Richmond send reinforcements to meet the army on the march rather than via Fredericksburg, to establishing a line of couriers to keep Hill in constant communication.[49] He continued to argue that this was the right step. "There is always hazard in military movements," he told Seddon, "but we must decide between the positive loss of inactivity and the risk of action."[50]

Being on the move buoyed Lee's spirits. "What a beautiful world God in His loving kindness to His creatures has given us," he wrote on arriving in Culpeper. "May He soon change the hearts of men."[51] What he read in Northern papers reinforced his hope for the power of Lincoln's opposition, and he told Davis that they should "neglect no honorable means of dividing and weakening our enemies" to encourage the peace faction. He counseled subtlety, and made no distinction between those who wanted peace with no conditions and those who saw it as means to reunion. If the belief became widespread that peace would restore the Union, the war would lose its supporters "and that after all is what we are interested in bringing about." Lee felt so strongly in the matter that he wrote Davis of it twice on the same day.[52] The only damper on his spirits came on the evening of June 9, when he reached Brandy Station at the close of a major cavalry battle with the Federals to see his son Rooney carried from the field with a saber wound in his leg. Lee expected him to recover, happily. "He is young & healthy & I trust will soon be up again," he wrote Mary. "God takes care of us all & calls to him those he prefers."[53]

Lee was using his staff better now. Couriers kept the separate columns in communication with him and each other, so he knew where his corps were, or had been a few hours earlier. He sent Long to Richmond to make a verbal report on the army's progress, and to investigate reports of Federal movements on the James-York Peninsula.[54] After disdaining signal communication in 1862, he now used signal stations to transmit information, meanwhile asking Richmond to send his correspondence ahead to keep up with his advance. One erroneous press report of Brandy Station said the Yankees captured Lee's campaign plans at Stuart's headquarters, a pointed reminder of the danger of mislaid correspondence.[55] Lee had already destroyed personal letters he carried, explaining to Rooney's wife that "we can carry with us only our recollections."[56]

When Lee sent Richmond notice of Brandy Station on the evening of June 9, he headed it "Culpeper," and the War Department allowed its publication on June 12. Lee knew that as soon as the Yankees saw that they would know he was on the move.[57] Back in the Confederacy, people knew it too by now, but not where. Asking "Is General Lee Left-Handed?" a Charleston editor compared him to a boxer who led with his left. He led with his left on the peninsula and the same at Second Manassas, Harpers Ferry, and Chancellorsville.[58] Of course that left was lost with Jackson gone, but the speculation was that he was leading with it yet again, suggesting a move from the Shenandoah. None should worry, said an editor, "because we believe that, under God, he has arranged all that is necessary for success."[59] The Almighty was Lee's left now.

He traveled with Longstreet, a habit formed largely because in the army's history to date, Jackson was usually detached and operating in advance. By June 16 he moved north on the east side of the Blue Ridge, using Longstreet's corps to screen Ewell's, which had crossed into the

Shenandoah Valley to capture Winchester on June 15. Lee's rail link to Richmond for supplies ended there, so the army would be foraging hereafter. A day later Ewell crossed the Potomac, the first of 80,000 Confederates once more taking the war to the enemy.[60] In the first of several instances of confusion, Longstreet failed to keep part of his corps east of the Blue Ridge as a screen, and sent his whole column on the road for the Shenandoah. "I hope it is for the best," Lee told him, but chagrin was evident when he added that "at any rate it is too late to change."[61] Three days later he told Ewell that "if Harrisburg comes within your means, capture it."[62]

Couriers and staff officers rode back and forth between Ewell's column and Lee's headquarters constantly, bringing news not much more than twenty-four hours old. Meanwhile, Lee paid more attention to gathering intelligence of enemy movements. He read every Yankee newspaper found, generally seeing them no more than three days after publication.[63] Unfortunately, after June 23 there would be no intelligence from Stuart, who persuaded Lee that he could ride around Hooker's army as he had McClellan's, disrupting supply and communications, destroying wagons and equipment, and capturing valuable stores. Lee authorized the raid with the caveat that Stuart must protect Ewell's eastern flank, which he ignored.[64] Stuart left two brigades behind, too little to be of great use either as a screen or for gathering intelligence. Hereafter, the Army of Northern Virginia marched almost without eyes and ears, and after it was too late Lee rued his decision.

That same day he received positive news that Hooker was about to cross the Potomac.[65] He needed a diversion and had proposed to Davis the novel idea of creating a phantom or "effigy" army at Culpeper and placing Beauregard in command. "His presence would give magnitude to even a small demonstration, and tend greatly to perplex and confound the enemy," Lee reasoned, for the Yankees would assume no officer of Beauregard's rank would be wasted on a minor outpost. He placed so much importance on the move that he returned to it now on June 25, but nothing was done, in part because they had left it too late.[66] By this time Ewell reached Chambersburg, Pennsylvania, with Longstreet and Hill closing up behind him for a concentration, and Lee could no longer keep his courier line running back to Virginia. His last communication to the president expressed the desire that Hooker would follow him north of the Potomac so Lee could at least disrupt Federal plans for the summer before he returned to Virginia. It was not quite the decisive victory he spoke of on May 15. He closed with a hope that "things will end well for us at Vicksburg," where he had watched events with interest.[67]

Having given up his intelligence arm when Stuart left, Lee did not know until he reached Chambersburg on June 28 that Hooker's army was last known to be near Frederick, Maryland, just thirty-five miles south. By this time he could be much closer. Lee immediately recalled Ewell from the outskirts of Harrisburg and ordered all three corps to use roads converging twenty-five miles southeast of him at Gettysburg.[68] This was not what he had planned. Now he must race to concentrate. By nightfall on June 30 Lee camped at Greenwood, less than twenty miles west of Gettysburg, where he learned that Hooker had been replaced by Major General George G. Meade just three days earlier. Other than vague rumors, he still did not know where Meade was, nor did he expect to encounter him for at least another day or two. Once he had his army together, he could reconnoiter to find the dreamed of ideal defensive position from which to annihilate the foe. That evening he wrote Mary a few personal things of no moment. "It is doubtful whether this gets through," he told her. "Therefore I say nothing more."[69]

For the next three days he had no time to say more. Hill's advance encountered Federal cavalry at Gettysburg the next morning before Longstreet and Ewell arrived. Thereafter, despite Lee's instructions not to bring on a general engagement, magnetic forces sucked his army and Meade's into a meeting engagement that by July 2 involved virtually the whole of both armies, even Stuart, who arrived on July 2 exhausted from a daring ride of little profit. The battlefield was in the main a long low hill called Seminary Ridge on the west, facing parallel Cemetery Hill and then Cemetery Ridge close to a mile east. The town of Gettysburg capped the northern end of Cemetery Hill, while at the south end stood a somewhat commanding eminence called Little Round Top. Lee's army would take position on Seminary Ridge, and Meade's on Cemetery Ridge.

Confronted with a battle he did not want on ground not of his choosing, Lee exercised minimal control before he reached the field

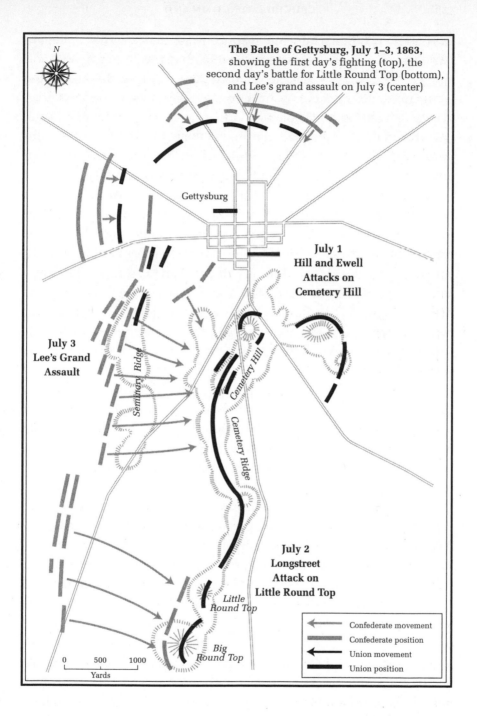

The Battle of Gettysburg, July 1–3, 1863, showing the first day's fighting (top), the second day's battle for Little Round Top (bottom), and Lee's grand assault on July 3 (center)

Gettysburg

July 1
Hill and Ewell
Attacks on
Cemetery Hill

July 3
Lee's Grand
Assault

Seminary Ridge

Cemetery Hill

Cemetery Ridge

July 2
Longstreet
Attack on
Little Round Top

Little
Round Top

Big
Round Top

0   500   1000
Yards

Confederate movement
Confederate position
Union movement
Union position

late on July 1. While struggling to concentrate the army, he could have sent staff to impose instructions on Hill and Ewell, but he did not, and left them to it. When he directed Ewell to take the key to the Union line on Cemetery Hill, he used the discretionary caveat "if practicable," an unproductive phrase with a mercurial general like Ewell. Once he established his headquarters on the field, Lee erratically communicated plans to his corps commanders. He met personally with both Ewell and Longstreet on July 1, but no staff officer went to hurry Longstreet to the field that night. The next morning when Longstreet got his orders to march to the right of the line to assault the Union left near Little Round Top, Lee had no maps to give him, but he did provide his engineer officer Colonel Samuel Johnston, who had reconnoitered Little Round Top just that morning. Yet Lee told Johnston only to accompany Longstreet, and that general failed to reveal their destination. "I had no idea where he was going," Johnston later recalled, a grave error by both Lee and Longstreet.[70] Lee gave his orders to his corps commanders but sent no staff with them to make certain his wishes were obeyed. As a result, Lee effectively lost control of Longstreet for the rest of the day and seemed strangely uninvolved. Lee still felt unwell, probably from the angina, now compounded by severe diarrhea, and his habit of dosing himself with quinine made it worse. A British observer found him sitting alone on a stump with almost no communications coming or going, and no aides standing ready for orders.[71]

Two months earlier at Chancellorsville Lee had explained his concept of battlefield management to a Prussian officer. He tried to make "plans as good as my human skill allows," he said. "I plan and work with all my might to bring the troops to the right place at the right time; with that I have done my duty. As soon as I order the troops forward into battle, I lay the fate of my army at the hands of God." Then, he said, "it is my Generals' turn to perform their duty."[72] That might have worked with Jackson, but Ewell and Hill were new to corps command, and Longstreet was balky at taking the offensive. Where typically Lee personally moved with Longstreet, in this instance he stayed on Seminary Ridge, closer to his new corps commanders, which was prudent. Unfortunately, he seems merely to have waited for Longstreet's attack to commence rather than sending an officer to regain control.[73]

On July 3, after failed attacks on the Union left and right, Lee reasoned that Meade might have strengthened his flanks at his center's expense, and concluded to mount a massive frontal assault. He had tried it at Gaines's Mill and saw it work, and again at Malvern Hill with terrible consequences, so his experience was mixed. Like many others in this war he did not yet realize that modern weaponry almost made the open charge obsolete. Yet his decision was not foolhardy. Meade might have weakened his center. A two-hour artillery barrage might disrupt the enemy line, but the war to date argued that it probably would not, especially since Confederate shells had an embarrassing habit of failing to explode. At best he could hope that solid shot might disable some Union field pieces. Nevertheless, if it had worked, Meade's army might have been driven from the field, in which case the assault would be hailed as genius. He had little alternative now. His army's ammunition dwindled. Maneuver and flank attacks had failed on July 1 and 2. Any chance for his battle of annihilation was surely gone, but still he could gain great morale advantage by any victory that drove Meade from the field. Win or lose, his raid into Pennsylvania was already over, with his supplies running low and his line of supply too attenuated to maintain securely much longer. His choices were either to retreat to the Potomac now, or take one more risk. In a campaign based on a succession of risks, the decision for Lee was an easy one. It was his most hazardous battlefield expedient yet, but then his men could do anything. Moreover, when he made any decision, success or failure lay not in his hands, but in His. If God meant for the assault to succeed, it would.

It did not. Lee and his staff sat their horses on Seminary Ridge and watched the mile-wide ranks of 12,000 men go forward, but from that moment he made no effort to coordinate or direct the assault.[74] In fact, Lee maintained only moderate control of his army during the entire battle. He did for the first time empower some staff officers to give orders in his name. They surveyed the field for him, and helped in some degree with the July 3 assault.[75] Still, in more than a dozen instances when his orders were not obeyed, he sent no one to investigate. It was an improvement on his performance at battlefield management, but he still had much to learn.[76]

After playing a key part in General Winfield Scott's victories in Mexico by his reconnaissance, Lee proved ineffective at it in this campaign.

He forfeited any long- or midrange tactical reconnaissance Stuart might have provided, and as a result had no grasp of the overall battlescape. He learned of Union movements too late to react, and never identified Meade's center of gravity in order to direct his own efforts to best effect. He let Hill bring on a major engagement despite instructions not to do so, and then gave orders too imprecise and discretionary to be effective. Five years later Lee offered two reasons for defeat: Stuart's absence left him blind; and he could not deliver the "one determined and united blow" that he believed would have assured victory. "As it was," he said, "victory trembled in the balance for three days."[77] What he did not say was that he was ultimately responsible. He let Stuart go, and his own laissez-faire management helped bungle the attacks on July 1 and 2. Two years after that Lee added another cause of defeat. "If Jackson had been there," he said in February 1870, they "would have succeeded."[78]

Every great general has his worst battle. Gettysburg was Lee's.

⌒

"The road to Vicksburg is open."[79] Grant felt cautiously jubilant on May 3 when he told Sherman of progress thus far, promising Halleck to pursue the foe "until Vicksburg is in our possession."[80] Grand Gulf had been taken, and Grant rode ahead of the army to start organizing it as a depot for supplies from Memphis. He saw for himself that the army's animals could subsist off the land, and he believed his soldiers could get all the beef and vegetables they needed, lacking only coffee, sugar, and hardtack. When he moved out of Bruinsburg he had but two days' rations per man, yet they stretched those to a full week by foraging, before Sherman collected tons of bacon and other goods to bring forward when he joined the army.[81] Every man would get three days' rations to last five days or more during the inland march. This same day he directed building a road to reduce the time supplies took to reach Grand Gulf, emphasizing that "every thing depends upon the promptness with which our supplies are forwarded."[82]

Popular mythology later asserted that Grant severed his own supply line and lived entirely off the land. What he was doing was hazardous enough, but little more so than Lee's army in Pennsylvania. He left Hillyer in charge at Grand Gulf and kept the wagons constantly moving between it and his advancing corps, telling Hillyer that speed was everything.[83] May 6 found him on the Black River sixteen miles below Vicksburg, waiting for the next wagon train, and again he issued three days' rations for the men to stretch to more.[84] He knew he could not keep his legions fully supplied, but he expected to get as much hardtack, coffee, and salt as possible, "and make the country furnish the balance."[85] No wonder Grant was irritated when he rode past McClernand's men and saw officers, enlisted men, and contrabands riding mules that should have been drawing supply wagons. When McClernand complained he did not have enough transportation to carry rations, Grant reminded him what those mules ought to be doing, chiding the general that "you should take steps to make the means at hand available."[86]

As he often did, Grant in his optimism believed he could move faster than he did, and expected he might take Vicksburg by the middle of the month.[87] Indeed, he became so confident that on May 9 he told Julia he expected the battle for Vicksburg to start in another three days, and for the first time mentioned the question of what assignment there might be for him after its fall.[88] To boost morale he issued a congratulatory order to the army on progress thus far. "Other battles are to be fought," he added, but they were only a few days from the "crowning victory over the rebellion."[89] By May 11 he had advanced almost thirty miles inland, attenuating his line of communications with Grand Gulf to the point that it was seriously vulnerable to enemy raid, so he simply closed it down. "You may not hear from me again for several days," he wrote to Halleck.[90] His men had about two days' rations and he warned corps commanders that they might have to last seven. "We must fight the enemy before our rations fail," he told McPherson, "and we are equally bound to make our rations last."[91] He still hoped to be in front of Vicksburg in a week. There he could extend his lines to the Yazoo River to open a new supply line.

A day later, however, Grant abruptly changed their objective.[92] McPherson took the town of Raymond in a sharp fight and exaggerated Confederate strength, so when they retreated to the northeast toward Jackson, Grant faced the prospect of a substantial enemy force on his right flank and rear if he continued in his course north. On the spot he made Jackson the next objective, but instead of McPherson,

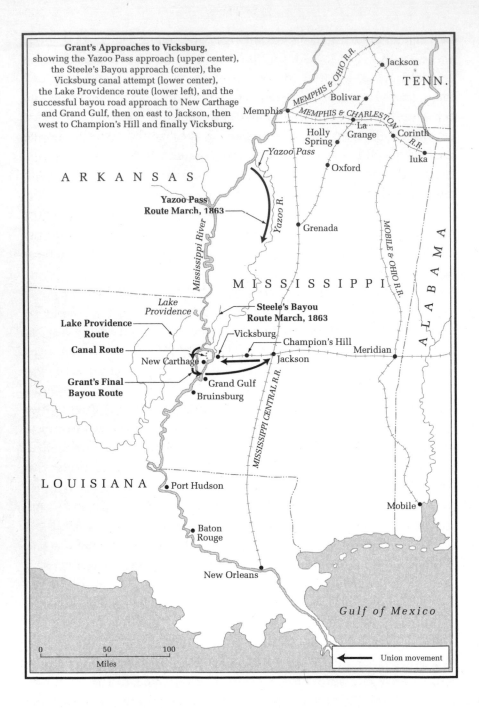

Grant's Approaches to Vicksburg, showing the Yazoo Pass approach (upper center), the Steele's Bayou approach (center), the Vicksburg canal attempt (lower center), the Lake Providence route (lower left), and the successful bayou road approach to New Carthage and Grand Gulf, then on east to Jackson, then west to Champion's Hill and finally Vicksburg.

TENN.

Jackson

MEMPHIS & OHIO R.R.

Bolivar

Memphis

MEMPHIS & CHARLESTON

La
Grange

Corinth
R.R.

Iuka

Holly
Spring

Yazoo Pass

Oxford

A R K A N S A S

Yazoo Pass
Route March, 1863

Yazoo R.

Grenada

MOBILE & OHIO R.R.

ALABAMA

Mississippi River

M I S S I S S I P P I

Lake
Providence

Steele's Bayou
Route March, 1863

Lake Providence
Route

Vicksburg

Champion's Hill

Meridian

Canal Route

New Carthage

Jackson

Grant's Final
Bayou Route

Grand Gulf
Bruinsburg

MISSISSIPPI CENTRAL R.R.

L O U I S I A N A

Port Hudson

Baton
Rouge

Mobile

New Orleans

Gulf of Mexico

0   50   100
Miles

Union movement

who was closer, he gave the assignment to Sherman, in whom he had more confidence.[93] Sherman moved quickly and on the afternoon of May 14 the capital fell, its defenders commanded by Joseph E. Johnston withdrawing to the north, but Grant suspected that they meant to move west to reinforce the Vicksburg garrison.[94]

When he decided to go for Jackson, Grant had sent McClernand's corps to Edwards' Station on the Vicksburg & Jackson Railroad, about twenty-eight miles west of Jackson and eighteen miles east of Vicksburg. He did it in part to get McClernand out of the way, expecting no action, but also as a feint to distract Pemberton.[95] Less than forty-eight hours after taking the capital, however, Grant learned that Pemberton had moved much of his army out of its defenses and was approaching the station.[96] After destroying anything of military use to the Confederates, Grant prepared to move west, buoyed by the prospect of catching Pemberton in the open field. His sense of urgency was evident when he sent a note to Sherman at five-thirty on the morning of May 16 to get every man in the field immediately, saying "the fight may be brought on at any moment."[97] Grant told McClernand to wait. He did not want him to bring on an engagement he could not handle. Before Sherman reached the field, other elements of McPherson's Corps came up with McClernand and found the Confederates in line across the road to Vicksburg, their center planted atop Champion Hill.

Grant arrived and ordered an attack. Hours of severe combat followed before overwhelming Union numbers put the Confederates to flight. In fact, Grant came close to destroying Pemberton on the spot. The Confederates lost almost 4,000 of 25,000 engaged, and made a scramble to get back to Vicksburg before the Federals cut off their retreat. "I am of the opinion that the battle of Vicksburg has been fought," Grant told Sherman. "We must be prepared however for whatever turns up." Pursuing as far as Edwards' Station that evening, he gave orders to advance again at dawn.[98] Speed, always speed.

The next day the Federal advance came upon Pemberton in line just east of the bridge over the Big Black River and put them to flight with another 1,800 casualties. In two days the Confederates had lost more than a fifth of their army, and Grant felt confident enough to tell Sherman to push into Vicksburg if he thought he could do so, and if not then to extend his lines facing its defenses, thinking he might still take it the following day.[99] On the morning of May 19, Grant gave orders for his entire line to move as close as they could to the defenses east of the city by two o'clock when, at a signal, they were to launch a general assault. At the same time, he asked Porter to commence a bombardment from his fleet on the river.[100] Only Sherman advanced at the signal, dooming the assault to failure, yet he did achieve one thing. With his lines reaching almost to the Mississippi north of town, he could now open a supply line via the Yazoo River. On May 11 Grant had hoped to be in front of Vicksburg within a week with his supply link renewed. It took him eight days, and but for hardtack and coffee his men never went hungry.[101]

Two days later Grant tried again. He ordered an all-out assault for ten o'clock on the morning of May 22, believing he could take the city and avoid a siege. Once again Porter would assist.[102] And once again it failed. Sherman and McPherson were stopped with heavy casualties by enemy artillery and rifle fire, but McClernand reported some success and suggested the moment was ripe if the general assault were renewed. Violating his own rule against believing the politician, Grant gave way to his optimism and ordered Sherman and McPherson to attack. The enemy repulsed them at heavy cost, as well as McClernand, who had overstated the strength of his position. At the end of the day Grant had a long list of casualties and a secure supply line, but he did not have Vicksburg. "I intend to lose no more men," he told Porter.[103] Seeing the strength of the enemy defenses, he wrote that evening to Halleck that "it can only be taken by a siege." Nevertheless, "it is entirely safe to us in time." He thought it would take another week.[104]

Grant had about 50,000 men for the job, and access to another 10,000 if he stripped west Tennessee, and within a few days ordered Hurlbut to abandon most garrisons north of Memphis to send men south.[105] "Concentration is essential," he avowed.[106] He needed cavalry to cover his rear from Johnston, reported to have 45,000 men, which he thought exaggerated, but he resolved to "do the best I can with all the means at hand."[107] He put engineers to work running siege works ever closer to the enemy parapets, and suggested to Sherman that they experiment with tunneling from their trenches to plant explosives beneath Confederate salients.[108] Meanwhile, he ordered artillery to shell the city occasionally to keep the Confederates anxious in case another assault should come. By June 3, with his works progressing well, Grant hopefully predicted that another five days ought to see his men in possession of the enemy parapets.[109]

He was so confident of success that he kept a box of wine in front of his headquarters tent for his officers to celebrate the fall of Vicksburg. That upset Rawlins, especially since he had heard that a few days earlier Grant drank a glass of wine with Sherman. Then on the evening of June 5 at headquarters, at an hour when Grant would ordinarily be asleep, Rawlins found him in conversation with others near an empty wine bottle. He feared that Grant had consumed too much, and thought he detected "the lack of your usual promptness of decision and clearness in expressing yourself in writing." At one that morning he wrote a long letter reminding Grant that in March 1863 he pledged not to drink for the rest of the war, and that "your only salvation depends upon your strict adherence." The general accepted the letter without offense or response, and Rawlins later wrote that he never had to remind Grant again.[110]

That is because he was not along on the evening of June 6 when Grant, James H. Wilson, and others rode to Haynes' Bluff to board a steamer to go up the Yazoo reconnoitering. Grant almost certainly had too much to drink that evening, Wilson noting in his diary "Genl G. intoxicated."[111] The next morning he awoke amazingly refreshed. No one was better aware that he should not start to drink than Grant himself, which perhaps explains why one of the first things he did on returning to his headquarters was to write to his wife, saying, "I want to see you very much dear Julia," urging her to come to Vicksburg as soon as she could.[112]

By the middle of the month, with the siege in its third week, Grant still had no doubt of success. Every few minutes his guns shelled the town, driving inhabitants to the cover of caves, while his siege works had advanced so close to the enemy defenses that a Confederate scarcely dared raise his head above the parapet. "They must give out soon even if their provisions do not," he told Julia, since every night deserters brought stories of soldiers on half rations and citizens starving. "Everything looks highly favorable now," he said, but his enthusiasm was tempered.[113] Had he been able to take Vicksburg with the May 22 assault, he believed he could have taken most of central

Mississippi by this time. Now with the summer heat and dust, he feared it would be difficult to find water for a marching army. Taking Vicksburg would open the Mississippi except for Port Hudson, but he had wanted more.[114] To the extent that he blamed McClernand, it was one more black mark against his would-be nemesis.

No one tried Grant's maturity as an executive more than McClernand, who had regarded Grant as an unsophisticated but useful tool and ally until he perceived in him a threat to his own ambition. For his part, Grant may have been suspicious of McClernand early on, but from at least the time of Fort Donelson he recognized that the politician had a personal agendum at variance with his own concept of their mission. Worse, the interference of Halleck, Stanton, and even Lincoln made McClernand a quasi power unto himself, or so it appeared, forcing Grant to find his way through shoals of conflicting authority as he tried to manage the man. McClernand's egotism made him a constant challenge, and though Grant would be accused often of political naïveté, his reading of the political situation with McClernand was clear. The support of others helped him put up with it, especially Sherman, whose opinion of McClernand was dramatically more outspoken than Grant's.

Grant had been spoon-feeding McClernand for some time now. When the corps commander left Milliken's Bend, he ignored his own sick, leaving them neither tents nor surgeons. On April 27 when the troops were supposed to be concentrated at New Carthage and ready to board their boats, McClernand caused delay by detailing one of the steamers to carry his new wife and her servants and baggage. Then he formed his corps in review for Governor Yates of Illinois to address, following that by firing an artillery salute in direct violation of Grant's orders not to waste ammunition that would be needed on the other side of the river. Grant forbore to reprimand him, but then on May 6 Secretary of War Stanton implied that Grant could relieve McClernand should he wish, and initially Grant determined to do so the day after Raymond, telling Halleck that he blamed his losses in that fight on the politician. "McClernands dispatches misled me as to the real state of facts and caused much of this loss," Grant declared. "He is entirely unfit for the position of Corps Commander both on the march and on the battle field." Sensing his own power now, Grant added that "looking after his Corps gives me more labor, and infinitely more un-easiness than all the remainder of my Dept."[115]

Then he changed his mind. Thinking that another few days would see him in Vicksburg, he determined to wait and then "induce" Mc-Clernand to ask for a leave of absence. Until then, Grant would con-tinue to supervise personally all movements of McClernand's corps.[116] He explained a few weeks later that "a disposition and earnest desire on my part to do the most I could with the means at my command . . . made me tolerate Gen. McClernand long after I thought the good of the service demanded his removal."[117] As an executive, Grant had a related concern. His other corps commanders were unanimous in their distrust and lack of respect for McClernand as a man and soldier. Yet should Grant be disabled or killed, the next senior officer was Mc-Clernand, who would succeed to command, at least briefly. The harm he could do did not bear contemplation.[118] Of course, Vicksburg did not fall, so Grant bided his time.

He did not wait long. On May 30 McClernand issued a congratula-tory order to the XIII Corps for its achievements to date. It slighted the rest of the army and was implicitly dismissive of Grant, referred to him only once by name, and more often as "the commander of the depart-ment." Scorning "indulgence in weak regrets and idle criminations" to explain the failure of the May 22 assault, McClernand implied that the fault was Grant's for refusing assistance.[119] A week later McClernand complained of a "systematic effort to destroy my usefulness and rep-utation" after hearing unspecified allegations of poor performance by him in the fight on May 22.[120] Then on June 9 he complained that a re-port in the Northern press attributed a decisive role at Champion Hill to one of McPherson's divisions rather than his own.[121] The rumors may have been indiscreet leaks from Grant's staff, or Sherman's or McPherson's, representing feeling in those quarters, but given Grant's history of confronting subordinates head-on, it seems unlikely.

Grant did not learn of the congratulatory address until Sherman sent a clipping from a Memphis newspaper on June 17, calling it "an effusion of vainglory and hypocrisy." By official decree, no such docu-ments were to be published without approval from Washington, with violation punishable by dismissal. Clearly, said Sherman, the real au-dience was not the XIII Corps but constituents in Illinois.[122] As soon as Rawlins showed Grant the clipping he sent it to McClernand with a terse demand to know if it was accurate.[123] The politician replied that it was correct and that he could support its claims.[124] His timing was poor, for that same day he submitted his report of operations from March 30 through the May 22 assault. Once again McClernand and his corps apparently did everything from opening the route to New Carthage to the victory at Champion Hill, while most of Grant's orders really were McClernand's ideas.[125] Grant found it "pretentious and egotistical," and riddled with inaccuracies.[126]

The combination of the two documents persuaded him to act, especially as Grant told a visitor that day that "most pernicious consequences" would result if McClernand should succeed him. On June 18 Grant issued a special order relieving him and ordering him to return to Illinois, explaining to Halleck that "I should have relieved him long since for general unfitness."[127] McClernand appealed to Stanton and Lincoln repeatedly over the following months, but they wearied of him, and he never again held a significant command east of the Mississippi. While Grant would encounter jealousy from other senior officers in the years ahead, the eclipse of McClernand ended any serious threat to his hold on this and future commands.

Three days after the landing, he wrote to Julia that "management I think has saved us an imense loss of life and gained all the results of a hard fight."[128] Like Lee and other West Point graduates before him, Grant received no training in the art of management, largely because scarcely one officer in a hundred ever rose to a command level calling for a staff. Working for Governor Yates on an informal basis, Grant had two volunteer officers helping out, but no real system. On taking command of his regiment he found no staff in place, and quickly engaged an adjutant and an aide who was also an engineer. Almost immediately on getting his commission as brigadier he replaced them with regular appointments—Rawlins as adjutant, and Lagow and Hillyer as aides—all of them, he thought, "able men."[129] That was the extent of his authority for appointments, though he could appoint unpaid volunteer aides. Grant resorted to a bit of nepotism when he tried to get a brother-in-law appointed brigade surgeon on his staff. Instead, the army medical department assigned Surgeon James Simmons, who had served in the 4th Infantry years before, so Grant was not at all displeased.[130]

He seems to have had some instinctive grasp of the benefit of a good staff, and of his own time management.[131] Intermittently during the first two years of the war he worked himself from dawn until well after dark, but after just a month in command at Cairo he saw his staff taking some of the workload from his shoulders, meaning he was learning to delegate.[132] After eight months Rawlins single-handedly took care of the majority of Grant's official correspondence, freeing him for more pressing matters.[133] Once he commanded a district Grant was entitled to general staff commensurate to his responsibilities, but those officers were not his to appoint. At the end of 1861 he had a quartermaster, a commissary of subsistence, a chief of ordnance, a chief engineer, a medical director and medical purveyor, and a paymaster. He might recommend someone he wanted to fill one of those posts, but the decision rested elsewhere, and he was often denied. However, with Colonel Joseph D. Webster already on his general staff as chief engineer, Grant was able to appoint him chief of staff.[134]

Beyond their usefulness at routine headquarters tasks, Grant used his staff vigorously in action when necessary. His performance and theirs was mixed in their first real action at Fort Donelson. In the crisis of the Confederate assault of February 15, while Grant was away visiting Foote, he left orders for all units to remain in place but left no overriding discretionary orders under his authority with his staff. Hence when the attack hit, none of the staff attempted to move reinforcements to McClernand's battered line. Webster performed admirably at Donelson, but otherwise the staff role was minimal.

Soon afterward Grant and Rawlins recognized the need to organize duties more formally, and either on his own or at Grant's instruction the adjutant issued a general order outlining responsibilities. Rawlins assigned himself the paperwork. Hillyer was to ensure that subordinates sent returns of strength to headquarters regularly, though Grant would use him as a jack-of-all-trades: mustering officer, inspector, prisoner escort, and more. Lagow was to handle passes into and out of the department, and monitor commissary and quartermaster stores, reflecting Grant's special emphasis—like Lee's—on high performance in his supply officers. Webster became Grant's special advisor and virtual intelligence officer.[135] At Shiloh Grant put him in charge of all of the artillery massed as a last line of defense. His chief engineer

McPherson surveyed the ground around the camps and made maps, and spent two days constantly in the saddle during the fighting. Grant kept his aides in motion carrying orders, looking for Lew Wallace, guiding regiments into position, and more.[136] Hillyer, Lagow, and Rawlins helped rally the fugitives early in the day on April 6; all sent messages on their own initiative to hurry Buell, while Hillyer actually got some of those reinforcements to the field by taking boats to Savannah for them, then wrote an order over Grant's name instructing other waiting units to march toward the battlefield. He had the confidence to assume authority on behalf of his commander, a discretion Grant must have given him. In that same battle volunteer aide George Pride kept the ammunition flowing constantly through the first day from an ordnance steamer on the river to the front ranks. Where Grant's staff had been largely idle at Fort Donelson, at Shiloh they were all over the field and exerting an influence on the battle's outcome on their own initiative as well as under Grant's supervision.[137]

It is evident that Grant had some embryonic idea of a staff keeping his army functioning even in his absence. "In the selection of my Staff," he told the adjutant general a few days before crossing the Mississippi, "it has been with a view to their competency and without reference to their present or previous party politics."[138] In the years ahead as his staff grew, he relied where possible on men whose capabilities were known to him. Grant and his staff evolved during the balance of 1862. While he devoted his time to operations planning, as well as administering his large department, he delegated principal field action to Rosecrans at Iuka and Corinth and did not immediately command on the field, but sent staff officers to urge him forward and to explain and reinforce his plans. Hindsight suggests he ought to have placed staff with Rosecrans throughout the campaign, but it is unlikely that Rosey would have accepted having surrogates telling him what to do. Meanwhile, Grant used staff in ways that expanded their authority, as when he made Webster commander of Memphis and then entrusted him with building defenses around the city, and in November put him in charge of all military railroads. At the same time he used Hillyer as provost marshal of Memphis, and kept Lagow on special assignments from escorting prisoners to investigating civilian traders.[139]

Near the end of 1862 Grant had seven officers on his personal staff: Rawlins, now chief of staff, six aides, and ten general staff officers handling specific functions from railroads to mapmaking.[140] He even used Hillyer and Lagow to verbally convey information between himself and Sherman, rather than risk letters or telegrams whose content might somehow reach McClernand.[141] Grant regarded Rawlins, McPherson, Wilson, and aide Theodore Bowers as especially indispensable, along with volunteer aide George Pride.[142] When they were away on detached duty he told Julia that "I have felt the necessity of staff officers, that is of a class that can do something."[143] In the Vicksburg operations he put Lagow in charge of the second fleet of transports that ran the batteries, left Bowers at Milliken's Bend in charge of that end of the line of communications, and of course had Hillyer forwarding supplies from Grand Gulf. During that march, Rawlins and Wilson even oversaw rebuilding burned bridges.

Grant made little complaint of the officers assigned to him, except in the supply departments. At the end of 1862 he told Halleck that his quartermaster and commissary were "all I want."[144] Then on the verge of his heading south, Washington assigned him five new assistant quartermasters, not one of whom had ever done a day's duty as a supply officer. He asked that they be replaced by four experienced men, and got what he wanted.[145]

A deep loyalty developed between Grant and his staff. It was two years before one of them resigned, when Hillyer, suffering from rheumatism, needed to attend to business back in St. Louis. Even then he stayed on an extra month to help arrange for men and supplies to get below Vicksburg for the landing. "I am lothe to lose him," Grant told the adjutant general in Washington.[146] Clark Lagow also left during the campaign to Vicksburg due to illness, never to return.[147] Grant watched the progress of others, and when he saw signs of greater promise he went out of his way to promote their careers even if it meant losing them from his staff. McPherson went from being his engineer officer to major general of volunteers and corps command under Grant's tutelage, and in time Wilson followed a similar path. Grant repeatedly recommended Rawlins for promotion for his capabilities, and Rawlins became so devoted that he virtually appointed himself Grant's conscience and protector, especially in the delicate matter of alcohol. When men like Hillyer and Lagow left,

Grant's replacements were not always of equal caliber, evidence that his judgment could be erratic and occasionally controlled by good, but unproductive motives. He made one underage boy an aide simply because he repeatedly ran away from home to be a soldier, and Grant thought he could at least protect him from harm by putting him on his staff. Another replacement during the Vicksburg campaign was Julia's cousin Peter Hudson, Grant's only truly nepotistic appointment.[148]

Beyond delegating to staff to free his time for more important tasks, Grant employed the same approach in dealing with field commanders. He placed greater trust in Sherman and McPherson than the rest, and most of all in Sherman. He told a cousin that McPherson "belongs to a class of men that we have to few of" and that "we cannot afford to lose them."[149] He was "one of my best men and is fully to be trusted," he told Washburne. "Sherman stands in the same category. In these two men I have a host. They are worth more than a full Brigade each."[150] His orders to them during the campaign were replete with stipulations like "I therefore leave it to you" and "I leave the management of affairs at your end of the line to you."[151] That had been his practice since October 1861 before Belmont when he told a subordinate, "I do not want to cripple you by instructions but simply give you the objects of the expedition and leave you to execute them."[152] Understanding that the officer on the scene saw and knew more than Grant could from a distance, and could react faster, he felt secure enough to delegate responsibility. That delegation did not always work, as with McClernand, which is why Grant gave him detailed orders leaving almost nothing to discretion, knowing that the politician was likely to exceed any authority no matter how limited.

One attribute he demonstrated must have come from simple common sense. Grant established an excellent rapport with officers of the navy's "brown water" fleet, especially the notoriously prickly Porter. Intraservice rivalry between army and navy was long established, but Grant gained full and enthusiastic cooperation from Foote, Porter, and others. In part it was because he made requests rather than demands, but even more it came from including naval officers in his designs from their inception, and taking their advice at full value.

In his dealings with officers and civilians alike, his demeanor mirrored his advice to Julia on settling an account with his sometimes difficult brother Orville. "Be patient and even tempered," he told her. "Do not expose yourself to any misconstruction from a hasty remark," but nevertheless "be firm."[153] Six years hence an observer looking back concluded of Grant that "he was what might be called a common sense General, displaying that mingled patience and promptitude, system, adaptation of means to ends, foresight and economy . . . which are accounted the main requisite for business prosperity." More to the point, it seemed to suit him comfortably, for "from the moment he fairly got at work in the field he went about everything with the easy and masterly vigor of a man who has found his place."[154]

There was an obverse to Grant's style, for he could be a true friend longer than he should have been. None of the officers he brought up with him to date would let him down, but before the war was out he would place great faith in a few men unequal to his confidence. If shown that he had misjudged an officer, Grant hurried to set things right, as he did with Quartermaster Hatch. Yet when he finally accepted that an officer or friend betrayed his trust, he could be unforgiving. Grant never again wrote or spoke of Rosecrans or especially McClernand without adding a critical caveat. When it came to officers he found incompetent or corrupt, Grant was wonderfully untroubled by getting rid of them directly. No manager should be anxious to dismiss subordinates, but neither should he be hesitant if circumstances dictate. Some months past he had arrested Brigadier General Willis Gorman in Helena when he was caught diverting a gunboat to carry cotton for his speculator son. Grant declared that there was "a disease that might be called *Cotton on the brain*" among people behind his lines. Finding that many speculators were lingering resigned or discharged officers, he ordered all of them out of his department "to remove as far as practicable all contagious tendencies of the disease."[155]

When it came to the firing of McClernand, Grant likely felt it deserved celebration, and in fact two days after relieving him, Grant ordered a general cannonade all along his line for the next day, but only because he thought it might reveal some weak spots.[156] He kept his men busy now to maintain morale. Then on June 25 soldiers captured a letter from one of Pemberton's generals, saying he thought the garrison could hold out another ten days at most. That supported Grant's belief that the city must surrender by the first week of July.[157] "During the present week I think the fate of Vicksburg will be decided," he wrote Julia on June 29. He set the date for its fall at July 4 or 5, though he still might have to fight Johnston soon thereafter.[158]

Finally, on July 3, a note from Pemberton came through the lines proposing an armistice for the two sides to arrange for commissioners to propose surrender terms. Grant would agree to an armistice, but there would be no commissioners and no negotiations. His terms were unconditional surrender or nothing. "Men who have shown so much endurance and courage as those now in Vicksburg, will always challenge the respect of an adversary," he said, implying that he would be lenient. He met Pemberton between their lines at three o'clock that afternoon.[159] Pemberton asked that his army march out in formation with their arms and flags before turning them over, and that officers keep their sidearms and personal property, all of them to be paroled. Grant agreed to send a response that evening. Then he met with his corps commanders to hear their views, one of the few times he ever held a council on a decision. But he went against their consensus and told Pemberton he would send a division into the city to make out lists of all men and officers and have them sign paroles. After that he would allow the Confederates to march out of their lines, the officers keeping their pistols and horses, and every man his clothing. They could also take any remaining rations, and whatever transportation they had to carry it all.[160] Grant made it clear that if he was not notified of acceptance by nine on the morning of July 4 he would resume the bombardment.[161] Pemberton had no choice but to agree.

To prepare for occupation of the city, Grant drafted special orders to govern the move. A brigade was to go in to prevent anyone entering or leaving, and Logan would take command, with a regiment stationed there to prevent looting. Guards were to be established to protect captured weapons and stores, and the black men were to be organized into working parties to police the earthworks. Still concerned that the tardy Johnston might advance against him, Grant ordered that his own artillery be moved into the Confederate works and trained outward.[162] Indeed, for more than a week intelligence had him concerned that Johnston might move against him, and Sherman had been ready to move out for a dozen days.[163] Grant told his aide Pride that he felt confidant that Vicksburg was so hemmed in that he could release most of his army to turn against Johnston if need be, though he added that "this is what I think but do not say it boastingly nor do I want it repeated or shown."[164] Now as he waited for word from Pemberton, Grant ordered Sherman and Ord to be prepared to turn eastward and march to meet Johnston the moment Vicksburg capitulated.[165]

The formalities and details took some time, but before the day was out Grant's officers counted 128 field pieces and more than 100 siege guns, while the rolls of paroled Confederates totaled at least 27,000 and were not yet complete. When Grant rode into the city he stopped first at the Warren County courthouse to see the national flag go up from its cupola, then down to the steamboat landing to greet Porter as he came ashore to thank him for his cooperation.[166] Half an hour after the surrender he sent a steamer south to Banks with the news, and another north to Cairo to telegraph Halleck that "the Enemy surrendered this morning." Reporting that Sherman would deal with Johnston, he said he would himself send troops to help take Port Hudson and free the Mississippi at last.[167] Vicksburg was a major milestone of the war, the greatest victory yet and a crippling blow to the rebellion, but the road led onward and Grant was ready to move.

13

HINTS OF THE INEVITABLE

Contrary to common opinion then and later, Gettysburg was hardly a decisive encounter in the East. Lee did not achieve his hoped-for battle of annihilation, but he did achieve one aim: the temporary disruption of summer campaigning plans by the Army of the Potomac. There would not be another major battle in the East for ten months. Moreover, Lee left the battlefield on his own terms just as he had at Antietam the day after that battle. He remained in his positions and dared Meade to attack him. It was more than stubbornness. Too weakened to renew the offensive, he could still inflict a heavy blow on Meade by doing what he originally intended, taking strong ground and letting the enemy attack him. Stuart was back at last, and if Meade tied up his infantry in attacking Lee's, then the largely unblooded Confederate cavalry could ride around a flank and strike the Union rear, gaining a Chancellorsville-like victory, even if it did not destroy the Union army. In one regard, however, the battle was decisive for the Army of Northern Virginia. The casualties among its experienced officers were so great that fully one third of his units at almost all levels would now be led by less seasoned men. The army would never again work as smoothly as before.

Outwardly, Lee refused to be discouraged. "Our success at Gettysburg was not as great as reported," he told Mary on July 12.[1] In fact, in his first message to President Davis written the day after the battle, Lee said nothing about defeat, but rather that his army had been "compelled to relinquish their advantage and retire."[2] He showed far greater concern when he retreated to the Potomac to find it so swollen by rains that he could not cross for a week. He would have to accept battle whether he wanted it or not should Meade pursue and attack.

Writing to Davis with a level of religious expression he had not used before in official correspondence, Lee told the president that "the result is in the hands of the Sovereign Ruler of the Universe, and known to Him only." He added that "I am not in the least discouraged."[3] Even more language of faith emerged when he wrote to Mary while waiting to cross the Potomac. "I trust that our merciful God, our only help & refuge, will not desert us in this our hour of need, but will deliver us by His almighty hand, that the whole world may recognize His power & all hearts be lifted up in adoration & praise of His unbounded loving kindness," he said. "We must however submit to His almighty will, whatever that may be."[4]

Lee's tone changed slightly when he crossed back into Virginia July 13–14. He had intended to remain in the North longer, he told Mary, but maintained that he had accomplished what he set out to do, relieving the Shenandoah Valley of Yankee presence and drawing Meade north of the Potomac. He said nothing now of climactic battles, however, only that he still hoped "to damage our adversaries when they meet us."[5] Greeting him in Virginia was the news of the fall of Vicksburg on July 4, and Port Hudson to Banks five days later. He told the president that they ought to fortify and provision someplace on the Mississippi so strongly that it could occupy Grant indefinitely, allowing Johnston's main army to operate against the Yankees' rear.[6] Given the limited options and resources available, and Johnston's demonstrated aversion to offensive action, it was an impractical and ill-informed notion, but then other things had occupied Lee's mind for some time.

A deepening gloom was settling over him. "I have no time," he lamented. He longed for God to forgive his "many & long standing sins" so that he could be with all of his family one more time "before I go hence & be no more seen." Reflecting on his life he saw how he had "thrown away my time & abused the opportunities afforded me." Feeling unable to help himself or others, he saw it as "the punishment due to my sins & follies."[7] Summing his assets at the age of fifty-six, he found that they came to "three horses, a watch, my apparel and camp equipage." The Custis estates were in enemy hands, the slaves gone, and outbuildings and fences ruined. "The land alone remains a waste," he told Custis.[8] In July a United States court ordered the official seizure of Arlington and its furniture, which of course had been occupied for two years, and by the end of August it would be done.[9] Very likely the Yankees would sell it, and in any event it already sat vandalized.[10]

The war was changing Lee. Gettysburg's near catastrophic casualties were the greatest yet. Coming as they did after more than a year of seeing the flower of Southern youth consumed in fire, the cumulative weight of it all must have been ever in his thoughts. He fumed at the plundered homes, including his own, and the destruction of private property. Nevertheless, Lee could, like Grant and most great captains—and many bad ones—compartmentalize his thinking and suppress the horror of losses in order to deal with the day ahead. Without that he and Grant could hardly have functioned. Of course, it took a toll. The relative objectivity of 1861 was gone now. He had ceased speaking of mutual responsibility for this holocaust. If he occasionally referred to the Yankees as "those people," they were always the enemy and by now he sincerely stereotyped and demonized them. No woman could keep a secret from them, for instance, because as he told Mary, "the yankees have a very coaxing & insidious manner, that our Southern women in their artlessness cannot resist."[11]

This year one calamity after another touched him and his family until it seemed the enemy targeted the Lees and their kin particularly. In May, reading what Northern newspapers he could get, Lee first would have seen that the infuriating business of the slave whippings was news once more, this time from Boston to the Mississippi and beyond. In April a soldier named Samuel Putnam visited Arlington and talked with Leonard Norris, father of Wesley and Mary. Old and infirm, and his memory faulty, Norris gave a garbled account that ended by saying "Gen. Lee was more dreaded by his slaves than were any of his overseers." He accused Lee of selling virtually all of his children away from him, whereas Lee sold not one, and then repeated the charge that Lee personally whipped Mary and poured brine on her lacerated back.[12]

The letter spread across the country's press. The Alexandria *Gazette* immediately condemned it as false, arguing that no story based on a slave's word could be trustworthy, and another unlikely defense came from a Northern pen, Mary Lee's half–first cousin William G. Webster, the son of Noah "Dictionary" Webster. He knew the Lees. In 1852 he gave a copy of the dictionary to the Military Academy, where Webster's son was even then a cadet known to Superintendent Lee.[13] The elder Webster often visited Arlington and he saw how Lee treated the Custis slaves, whom he described as an "indulged and good-for-nothing set." Lee sold none, he said, only sending the unruly elsewhere for hire for fear they might endanger Mary while he was away on duty. As for Lee whipping Mary Norris, Webster contemptuously retorted, "tell it to the marines." Whatever else Lee may have been, Webster still regarded him as a "dignified and thoughtful Christian" who could not be guilty of such a thing.[14] "Though his political sins are legion, his domestic virtues are unimpeachable."[15]

Putnam then escalated his accusation, responding that his sources told him that "Gen. Lee frequently whipped the slave *children* with his own hand."[16] Though written on April 16, Putnam's letter was not published for four weeks, suggesting that its appearance was in reaction to Chancellorsville. Anything that diminished Lee's growing stature as an invincible Mars was good for Northern morale. That may explain why the story ran for more than two weeks, including follow-up letters by Putnam, and still appeared as late as July 1 in a Pennsylvania paper at the same time that Lee was being drawn into battle at Gettysburg.[17] By that time one of Custis's offspring by a slave mistress told a story so garbled that when it appeared in the press it said she was actually the bastard daughter of Lee.[18] If he happened to see that item, it only added to his disgust with the slanderous Yankee nation.

By mid-June his cup of bile for the North overflowed, once more fuelled by a news item, this time the Richmond *Examiner* of June 13.[19] He saw a notice that William Orton Williams was dead, hanged by the Yankees as a spy. "Orton," it said mistakenly, "was cousin to General Robert E. Lee."[20] Lee had been fond of him, certainly, and he had been something of a fixture at Arlington before the war, especially attached to the Lees' daughter Agnes.[21] Lee recommended him as "faultless in his morals and character," and complimented his "inventive turn of mind," though for all his charm there was a headstrong recklessness about him, and Lee may not have favored a marriage.[22] Just three days after the firing on Fort Sumter, Scott made him a first lieutenant and attached him to his staff. It was he who warned Mary to leave when Federals were on the verge of occupying Arlington. That made him suspect and he was arrested and imprisoned until June 6, when he was released, resigned his commission, and went South.[23] Lee offered him a position as aide on his staff, but Williams took a place on General Polk's staff instead.[24] Handsome and flamboyant, he was a martinet rumored to have murdered a soldier who failed to salute him.[25] Instead of punishment, Williams finished the year commanding the Army of Tennessee headquarters cavalry escort.

Early in December 1862 Williams tried unsuccessfully to get transferred to Lee's staff, though not at his request, then legally changed his name to Lawrence W. Orton.[26] He also visited Agnes Lee, and it was clear at least to the children in the house that he was in love with her.[27] In April 1863 Lee expressed pleasure at hearing good accounts of him, for by then Orton was a colonel, destined for a small cavalry brigade command.[28] Then he claimed that he had married widow Francis Lamb, known to some as "the notorious Mrs. Lamb of Charleston," which dismayed Polk's nephew, who regarded Williams as a "d[amned] f[ool]," while others called him "half-crazy."[29] Meanwhile, men in his new command refused to serve under him, complaining that he was "out of balance, erratic, full of conceit, personal vanity, and had distorted views of his military importance and dignity."[30] Others thought his behavior due to "sheer lunacy," and what one called "the entire want of stability in his character."[31] On June 8 he suddenly appeared at Union-occupied Franklin, Tennessee, dressed as a Federal officer and calling himself Colonel Austin.[32] He was soon arrested as a spy and the next day, tried by a drumhead court-martial, he and a companion were hanged as spies. It took more than twenty minutes for him to die.[33]

Lee was stunned. "I see no necessity for his death except to gratify the evil passions of those whom he offended by leaving Genl. Scott," he wrote. He hoped the report might be a fiction "got up to gratify their revengeful feelings & to torture the feelings of his friends," yet the article contained so much detail, and was "in such accordance with the spirit of our enemies," that he feared it was true.[34] Two months later he told Mary that he thought the young men had simply gone on an adventure, and "evil passions" led to their execution "from a spirit of malignant vindictiveness, common in a cowardly people," a new language of invective when he spoke of the enemy.[35] He never fully escaped Williams's death. Three years later it yet haunted him with a memory still "as poignant now as on the day of its occurrence," as he wrote Williams's sister. "I cannot trust my pen or tongue to utter my feelings." He still felt the anger, too. "My blood boils at the thought of the atrocious outrage, against every manly & christian sentiment."[36]

Just three days after Gettysburg, Lee learned that Yankee raiders had visited the Williams home, Hickory Hill, near Ashland where Mary and his daughters stayed, and where Rooney had been taken to recuperate in company with his wife and children. They nearly captured Robert Jr. and put Rooney in a wagon and took him as hostage for captured Union officers. "We must bear this additional affliction with fortitude & resignation," Lee wrote Mary. "I must bear this as I have to bear other things."[37] Later he learned that the Yankees looted Hickory Hill then went to the nearby home of his maternal uncle, eighty-year-old Williams Carter, whom they beat to get information.[38] "We must expect to endure every injury that our enemies can inflict upon us & be resigned to it," he told Mary sadly. "Their conduct is not dictated by kindness or love."[39]

Had these things taken place a year or even two earlier, Lee's outrage surely would have been as great. Had they not come until a year later, or even not at all, there seems no reason to doubt that his gradually hardening attitude toward the North would have continued its ossification. Coming as they did now, and especially after months of ill health and the strains of Gettysburg, they suddenly and sharply accelerated his growing conviction that Yankees were a different and hateful people. Whatever his public demeanor toward the United States thereafter, Lee never forgot nor forgave. Mary Lee may have suggested that he retaliate for the capture of his son and the beating of his uncle, but he forbore. "I do not think we should follow their example," he told her. "The consequences of war is horrid enough at best," he said on July 12. "Why should we aggravate them?" To do so only risked even greater retaliation from the North. They could not help it, "& must endure it."[40] He also realized what Mary did not. Two Confederate officers had been executed as spies in east Tennessee, and Confederate authorities immediately selected two Union officer prisoners to be executed on August 14 in retaliation. That is why the Federals came for Rooney Lee, to exact potential retaliation on Lee's son and the son of another general then a prisoner. Rumors in Richmond soon said that Lee asked Davis to suspend the sentences of the doomed Yankees, even threatening that if the enemy hanged Rooney, he would resign his position and "leave the confederacy in disgust."[41] That was nonsense, of course, but still the danger to his son made the war intensely personal to Lee. "Our only course is to be patient & pray," Lee told Mary in August. "I grieve much at his position," he told her, but he could do nothing. "Any expression on my part would injure matters."[42]

In fact, Lee consistently opposed retaliation "except in very extreme cases." He thought it "better for us to suffer, and be right in our own eyes and in the eyes of the world."[43] That may have been a moral sentiment, or his practical realization that whatever Confederates did to retaliate, the enemy could respond in greater measure. To date he had only embraced one form of retaliation, and that had at least a shadow of lawful sanction. From the day they entered Maryland back in June, and especially after crossing into Pennsylvania, Ewell's soldiers and following units began seizing runaway slaves as well as some free blacks. They sent the runaways south to be sold or jailed until claimed by their presumed owners, while the freedmen went to military prisons in Richmond. The number taken is elusive, but could have been in the hundreds. This had been official policy since March, when the adjutant general's office issued a general order to that effect, and Lee reinforced it with an order to his generals. Since runaways were still Confederates' property, this did not violate his standing order against plundering.[44] Unspoken was the policy's retaliation for the Emancipation Proclamation and the arming of black soldiers to fight their former masters.

That fall, with still no sign of Rooney being released and exchanged, and his son's wife Charlotte's health declining, Lee felt even more helpless, though fears of execution were long past.[45] Then on Christmas Day Mary informed him that Charlotte was dying, and a day later she was gone. Lee blamed it in part on worry over her imprisoned husband, another credit to the Yankees' "spirit of vindictiveness" against his family. Their pleasure, he said, "seems to be to injure, harass, & annoy us." At least Charlotte was now with her dead children and his beloved Annie. "Thus dear Mary is link by link of the strong chain broken that binds us to earth, & smooths our passage to another world," he spoke in comfort. "Oh that we may at last unite in that haven of rest, where trouble & sorrow never enters, to join in the everlasting chorus of praise & glory to our Lord & Saviour!"[46]

In the face of that season of personal loss, it is no wonder Lee tried to find some gain in the recent campaign. He felt he had failed and became, if not defensive, then at least self-justifying. From talking of a battle of annihilation, he now implied that his goal had merely been to keep Meade's army north of the Potomac, and he failed only in that he did not keep it there longer. His army had done all it could. "I fear I required of it impossibilities," he told several people, yet "though it did not win a victory it conquered a success," a fine distinction he repeated to Davis when he said the army won "a general success, though it did not win a victory." It had the sound of a line oft used. Ordinarily Lee did not split hairs, nor did he fear responsibility for failure. He had badly bloodied Meade and once more shifted the war out of Virginia. His "general success" approach took away some of the sting for his officers and men, and afforded him a means to claim some benefit from the costly campaign, without facing the contradiction of calling a defeat a "success."[47]

He also prayed to have this cup taken from him. On August 8 Lee wrote to the president suggesting that he be removed from command. He sensed an undercurrent of discontent in the public and feared its spread to the army. Moreover, he knew better than anyone that he was not the same man he had been in June 1862. The effects of his illness that spring were still with him, his energy flagged easily, and he could scarcely perform a reconnaissance anymore. "I cannot even accomplish what I myself desire," he told Davis. "How can I fulfill the expectations of others?" He felt his powers of inductive reasoning failing as he took scouting reports and tried to forecast enemy movements and intentions. Davis should find a younger, healthier, more able man to take over.[48] Insecure managers often offer to resign, in secret hope of being reassured of their capability. Lee was surely sincere, however. The request fit his whole mood that summer. Also, fatalism took advantage of his weakened health to make him consider the possibility of ultimate defeat in the war. His prayer now was that "He will 'fight for us once again,'" suggesting that Lee faced the possibility that God was not with them at Gettysburg. A dramatic rise in desertions suggested that many of his men had the same epiphany. Feeling himself a failure as a father and husband, he may have hoped to avert one failure more should the Confederacy fall while he captained its premier army.

Of course Davis refused. If *Lee* was not a general, then he had none, a sentiment echoed in the Army of Northern Virginia. "My faith is in Providence, the troops, and Genl. Lee," an artillery commander wrote home that fall. With no confidence in corps commanders Hill and Ewell, he prayed that Lee would exert more personal control on the soldiers than previously, when he could depend on Jackson and Longstreet; "He should attend to the minutiae."[49] Disappointed—and perhaps reassured—Lee acquiesced, pleading that now his only goal in life was to care for his invalid wife, his three homeless daughters, and "the defense of our violated country's rights."[50] To that last end, he spent several days closeted with Davis at the end of August proposing plans to draw Meade from his positions above the Rappahannock so that Lee could try another offensive.[51] Instead, Davis gave in to Longstreet's politicking and sent his corps west to Bragg's army in Tennessee, hoping for a victory over Rosecrans to change the momentum of the war. He asked Lee to go in overall command, but Lee expressed a reluctance that came close to a refusal. He knew enough of the toxic, politicized command culture prevailing in the Army of Tennessee to doubt, wisely, that he could turn it around, and probably knew as well that powerful political influences—cosseted by an ambitious Longstreet—played a large role in Davis's plan. Besides, a bad cold and arthritic pain in his back so troubled him that he tried riding in a wagon instead of on horseback, to no avail. Early in September he told Mary that "if I cannot get relief I do not see what is to become of me."[52]

Longstreet's departure left the Army of Northern Virginia too reduced to make an offensive, so Lee pleaded to Davis that Bragg attack Rosecrans immediately so Longstreet could return.[53] His reduced strength was soon punctuated when Meade crossed the Rappahannock on September 13 to occupy Culpeper, and Lee had no choice but to withdraw below the Rapidan River. A day later he learned that the Federals knew of Longstreet's departure. "I begin to fear that we have lost the use of troops here where they are much needed," he chided Davis, "and that they have gone where they will do no good." Diplomatically he said he expected nothing from Bragg, that Longstreet would arrive too late to be of help, that Bragg might already have more men than he could handle—a rare instance of Lee implying criticism of a fellow army commander—and that if Longstreet was detained too long "it will result in evil."[54] It was as close to criticizing Davis's judgment to his face as Lee ever came. Once more he did not dare furlough "the 'Israelites' in his army to go to Richmond for their holy days, though he agreed to "allow them every indulgence consistent with safety and discipline."[55]

Davis was soon vindicated when news came that on September 18–20 Bragg had achieved the most crushing Confederate victory of the war at Chickamauga in north Georgia. Lee was delighted, to the point that he offered advice on strategy in Tennessee, suggesting that Longstreet move on the Federal garrison at Knoxville, which would reclaim east Tennessee, and then come east to rejoin him. Once more Lee almost lectured the president, arguing that "no time ought now to be lost or wasted" to get Longstreet back to him.[56] Despite the fact that it would be up to Bragg and Davis to decide when or if the I Corps returned, Lee understood enough of Longstreet's powerful political connections to appeal directly to him to "finish the work before you, my dear general, and return to me." Until the absent corps came back, he said, all he could do was try to delay Meade.[57]

In fact, Longstreet and Bragg had done that for him. Meade stopped his advance on learning of Chickamauga and sent two of his own corps to reinforce Rosecrans. That gave Lee an opportunity to take the initiative with something approaching acceptable odds. On October 9, still so sore from arthritis that he had to ride in a wagon, he crossed the Rapidan and, using Cedar Mountain to shield his movements, turned northeast to move around Meade's right flank, hoping to force Meade to retire toward Washington. Given a chance, Lee might then strike a blow to advantage, but Meade quickly withdrew, denying Lee any chance of cutting his line of communications and retreat. By October 14 Lee could only get at Meade's rear guard near Bristoe Station, when A. P. Hill's corps came up with the Federals and Hill launched an immediate and ill-prepared attack that saw his command severely battered to no gain. In keeping with his mood now, Lee did not try to conceal his frustration that Meade had escaped and Hill had lost nearly 2,000 men. The day after the fight, as Meade safely occupied earthworks at Centreville, Lee and Hill rode over the battleground where the hundreds of dead still lay. Hill tried to explain that two of his brigades performed badly but Lee cut him off. "Your line of battle was too short, sir & too weak," he said, in what amounted to a rare face-to-face reprimand. "Bury your poor dead; the less you say about that the better."[58] His staff heard him say of Bristoe that "We've grieved, we've mourned, we've wept, we never *blushed* before."[59]

Bristoe embarrassed more than Lee and Hill. "The army has lost prestige and confidence in its leaders," an artillery battalion commander complained, fearing that Lee "is too amiable a man to exercise the proper discipline with his officers."[60] Meanwhile, Lee increasingly felt his own incapacity. He could ride again, but he had not felt well since that spring, and was uncomfortably chilled in a cold and rainy October.[61] Even his uniforms shrank from exposure and added to his discomfort. Too weak to take on Centreville's defenses, and seeing thousands of his men with neither blankets, overcoats, nor even shoes, Lee could not expose them to further combat or the coming winter and pulled back below the Rappahannock.[62] He expected Meade to move south again, as indeed he did, but Lee could do little but wait for him, while the command morass in Tennessee worked against him. Longstreet wanted a campaign of his own, Bragg wanted to be rid of Longstreet, and many in that army wanted to be rid of Bragg. The result was that the I Corps would not be returning to Virginia after all, as Bragg sent Longstreet on a long and fruitless effort to take Knoxville, while at least one corps commander under Bragg appealed unsuccessfully to Lee to come take over.[63]

Meade made him more uncomfortable on November 7 when he began to cross the Rappahannock and captured most of two brigades in a surprise attack. Lee had no option but to withdraw again, back below the Rapidan where he believed the terrain worked more to his advantage. "I hope a kind Providence will prosper us & give us victory," he wrote Mary on November 11. "Our only trust is in [Him]."[64] Ten days later he was even more emphatic. "I am content to be poor, & to live on corn bread the rest of my life," he told her, "if a gracious God will give us our independence."[65] The next day he attended church in Orange with President Davis. Another worshipper that day thought him "burly & 'beefy' & fat," looking overall somehow "large & full & round." Lee held his head high and seemed "the very impersonation of dignity & manly power," thought the observer. "It makes one feel better to look at him."[66]

Yet Lee hardly felt content. Inwardly he agreed with the complaint that he did not control his corps commanders sufficiently, and just as his outburst at Hill had been out of character, now for the first time he directly relieved a senior officer. Ewell disappointed Lee at Gettysburg, and since then was indecisive and wont to vacillate between depression and elation. Lee had some cause to believe that the loss of a leg in 1862 had impaired the general's judgment and fighting spirit.[67] Now the stump of the missing limb troubled Ewell sufficiently that Lee proposed that he turn his corps over to Major General Jubal A. Early until recuperated. When Ewell argued that he would be fit again in a few days, Lee made it clear that his "suggestion" was an order. On November 15 Lee relieved him, saying in the hearing of others that "Gen. Ewell was doing no good for himself or the country."[68]

Then Meade moved again, crossing the Rapidan downstream from Lee and turning west in an effort to isolate him from Richmond. Lee reacted by laying out a line of works on the west bank of Mine Run Creek, and on November 29 was too occupied establishing positions to be patient when Ewell reappeared saying he felt well enough to resume his command. Lee refused, and scolded Ewell for even coming to the army in that busy hour.[69] For some days he concentrated his forces, hoping to launch a typical wide movement around Meade's left to cut his rail link to Washington, but when he was ready to go on December 2 he discovered that the Yankees were gone. "I am greatly disappointed at his getting off with so little damage," Lee wrote Mary two days later, "but we do not know what is best for us, & I believe a kind God has ordered all things for our good."[70] That late in the season the army would have to go into winter quarters and try to recruit itself for the spring. That same day, relieved of the stress of imminent combat, Lee restored Ewell to his corps, though he was probably already on the lookout for an opportunity to reassign him elsewhere.

His own and his army's performance had been unimpressive the past two months, and his future ability to meet the enemy effectively looked uncertain. Longstreet was still gone, but even when he returned, he had shown reluctance for Lee's style of warfare at Gettysburg and might again. Hill had revealed himself as erratic and too impetuous, and Ewell could not be counted on for resolution in a decisive moment. Given his own indifferent health and stamina, Lee could not even depend on himself to make up the difference if it came to that. Yet he knew that they would all have to be at peak performance come spring.

⟨⟩

Grant was a neat smoker. Despite his careless dress, no remnants of cigar ash soiled his uniform though he smoked almost constantly. Onlookers found that rather than appearing stimulated by tobacco, he puffed a Havana with "the listless, absorbed and satisfied air of an opium smoker." Smoking calmed him, which accounts for his using cigars at a faster rate during action than otherwise. He smoked during his meeting with Pemberton, and again when he rode into captured Vicksburg, leading one Confederate editor to declare that "a little stage effect is admirable in great captains."[71] Grant leaned slightly forward when he walked, and with a quick step if on business. When not immediately occupied, his sharp blue eyes still surveyed his surroundings constantly.[72] There was even less affectation in his dress than in Lee's, just a round brimmed hat and a simple private's blouse with his insignia of rank on the shoulders. One observer thought he made a "far less pretentious appearance than many a second lieutenant." If anything, some suspected that his dress was intentionally "a trifle, perhaps, *negligée*, as a man of his celebrity can very well afford that it should be." Dark brown hair, with now a few slivers of gray showing, crowned a brow that even admirers thought suggested "no unusual apparent capacity." He spoke in clipped sentences using words economically, and those to the point and without flourish, leading a New York correspondent to remark that "Gen. Grant has the substantial without the showy."[73]

Now he had Vicksburg, which was substantial indeed. Like Lee's defeat at Gettysburg, however, its significance was misrated then and later. In tandem with the fall of Port Hudson, it certainly opened the Mississippi's full length to Union traffic, and effectively closed any Confederate door to Texas, Arkansas, and west Louisiana. By this time, however, those distant regions had already stopped providing more than a trickle of men or materiel to the war effort east of the river, and Confederates essentially lost use of most of the Mississippi after the fall of New Orleans. Now the Union could move thousands of men quickly north or south as needed, and begin using the Mississippi's tributaries as highways farther into the Southern heartland, but to Grant the most significant achievement was taking 30,000 rebel soldiers, 50,000 rifles, and more than 170 cannon out of the war. By paroling them on the spot rather than convoying them to Northern prisons first, he left his river transports immediately available for his own use, either to go south to aid Banks at Port Hudson, or to return to Tennessee to go after Johnston.[74] He could also assume that thousands would leave the parole camps and go home. In either case, unable to serve again until exchanged, they would be an unproductive burden to the Confederate government and their own communities that had to feed them. In fact, two weeks after the surrender Grant saw that most of the parolees had already deserted the camps and gone home. Exchanged or not, he expected that many would never return to their regiments.[75]

He presumed he would not remain long in Vicksburg. "I do not expect to be still much however whilst the war lasts," he told Julia.[76] In fact, he had been impatient for months, chafing at the time his efforts took, and at the outspoken peace party at home that would retard his efforts. "My confidance in taking Vicksburg is not unshaken," he wrote Julia back in mid-February, but he worried that some of the people at home seemed miserly with their moral support. "They are behaving scandalously," he said of the anti-war Democrats called Copperheads in Illinois, Indiana, and Ohio, who encouraged soldiers to desert. "I want to see the Administration commence a war upon these people," he fumed, believing the disloyal press ought to be suppressed and the most vocal agitators confined until the end of the war.[77] Yet he drew a line at taking any such action himself without government sanction. When Hurlbut banned the anti-war Chicago *Times* from his department, Grant agreed that it was deserved, averring that several other Northern newspapers merited the same treatment, but since Washington did not suppress them everywhere, he doubted the propriety of doing it in his command alone and instructed Hurlbut to rescind his order.[78] He was ever mindful of the subordination of the military to the civil authority, and the Constitution.

Yet he could be provoked. Just as he decried what he regarded as the disloyal press, he ignored critics who thought he was too long at the task of taking Vicksburg. "I have no idea of being driven to do a desperate or foolish act by the howlings of the press," he told his father the previous April. "There is no one less disturbed by them than myself."[79] Still, he banished a New York *Herald* reporter from his army in April for attacking Sherman and that same month ordered the arrest of a correspondent from the Associated Press for writing a dispatch giving away the location of a battery designed to protect the lower end of one of the waterways bypassing Vicksburg. The next day, still in a mood, he ordered the suppression of all newspapers in Memphis for giving away his movements, and the arrest of one editor who published the plan to move via New Carthage and Grand Gulf. Grant suspected an engineer officer, an "incoragibly gassy man," of being the source, and was almost angry enough to arrest him first and look for supporting evidence afterward, but soon cooled.[80]

More important issues now held him at Vicksburg. Grant found hundreds of slaves freed by the fall of the city. At the beginning of the year when contrabands flocked to his lines, he had asked Halleck, "What will I do with surplus Negroes?" He employed as many as he could with the army, and sent several hundred others to Cincinnati to see them better cared for, as well as to relieve the pressure on his own resources.[81] A few weeks before Vicksburg's fall he wrote one of his few letters to date to Lincoln outlining his efforts to bring system and humanity to the treatment of the contrabands, asking the president to consider executive action to establish uniform policy for dealing with the freedmen.[82] Now he found a new host of them on his hands. "I want the negroes all to understand that they are free men," he directed. If any wanted to leave with their paroled masters, they could go, and might even do some good by telling others at home how the Yankees had come to free them. As for black males who remained, he was not at first ready to enlist them in the army, though black regiments were already in service elsewhere; but before the end of the month he began the enlistments, and soon found the new black regiments easier to discipline than many white units.

"This, with the emancipation of the negro, is the heaviest blow yet given the Confederacy," he told Lincoln in August. He sent cavalry into the country with recruiting officers to bring in black males who wanted to enlist. "I would do this whether arming the negro seemed to me a wise policy or not," he said, because it was an order, but in this instance he obeyed with enthusiasm. "By arming the negro we have added a powerful ally," he wrote the president. "They will make good soldiers and taking them from the enemy weaken him in the same proportion they strengthen us." He favored pushing the policy to raise enough to garrison all of the South that should fall into their hands, as well as to help in occupying more.[83] At first he envisioned using them for garrison duty to free white regiments for the field, but looking at the record of the few black units in combat thus far in his department, he attested that "all that have been tried have fought bravely."[84] Three of his corps commanders favored enlisting and arming blacks, and Grant had already told Halleck that he would carry out any policy directed by proper authority. Meanwhile, he put Confederate general Richard Taylor, commanding in west Louisiana, on notice that he expected captured black soldiers to receive the same treatment as white prisoners. Grant felt no more favor for a policy of retaliation than Lee, but should the Confederacy execute black soldiers taken prisoner, he warned Taylor that "I will accept the issue," and act accordingly.[85]

This harmonized with his evolving attitude toward the issue that had the nation at odds. "Slavery is already dead and cannot be resurrected," he told Washburne at the end of August. He doubted that it could be protected even if North and South made a peace with the right to own slaves guaranteed. "I was never an Abolitionist," he told the congressman, "[n]ot even what could be called anti slavery, but I try to judge farely & honestly and it become patent to my mind early in the rebellion that the North & South could never live at peace with each other except as one nation, and that without Slavery." Anxious as he was for peace, he made it plain that he would not accept any settlement that did not settle slavery first and forever.[86]

Looking beyond the new units that Mississippi's black men might provide, Grant thought about Union recruiting policy. Seeing that 300,000 new recruits were to be raised by conscription if necessary, two-thirds of them to form new regiments, Grant appealed personally to Lincoln to use the draftees to fill the gaps in veteran units instead, and made his case in dollars and cents. The veterans in the older regiments were seasoned soldiers even better than those of the professional Regular Army. "A recruit added to them would become an old soldier, from the very contact," Grant argued. Moreover, the existing regiments already had their officers and equipment, and adding a new recruit to them would cost only the man's pay and allowances. Creating new regiments, on the other hand, required new officers and the replication of all that equipment, as well as months of training that, from his personal observation, usually depleted a regiment by a third through sickness before it saw an enemy. "Taken in an economic view," he concluded, "one drafted man in an old regiment is worth three in a new one."[87]

Left unsaid was Grant's preference to wage his campaigns with veteran units rather than new ones, and he had another move in mind a fortnight after Pemberton's surrender. For some time now he had believed the next goal should be Mobile, Alabama, a target entirely consonant with his vision of this war from the beginning. Operating from Mobile, Union forces could move up the Alabama and Tombigbee Rivers to Meridian and Montgomery and beyond. Control of those streams, combined with the conquered Tennessee and Mississippi Rivers and the Gulf coast, reduced all of Mississippi, two-thirds of Alabama, all of western Tennessee and eastern Louisiana virtually to an island, accessible to the rest of the Confederacy only via a slim sixty-mile-wide doorway between the headwaters of the Alabama and the lower reaches of the Tennessee. Any Confederates remaining on that island must evacuate through that door or live off the land and risk being starved into submission. More than ten thousand square miles of Confederate soil and resources would fall to the Union, making Vicksburg pale in significance.

Throughout July and most of August he pressed the idea, even though it was outside his department, and offered to loan an army corps to General Banks in New Orleans for the task should he undertake it.[88] Banks, however, preferred to move up the Red River in western Louisiana and into Texas. His motives were mixed, one of them in large part being the lure of a great quantity of cotton there for the taking. Moreover, French forces had recently invaded and virtually taken over Mexico, and Lincoln felt the need of a strong Union presence in Texas to discourage France from carrying its adventuring north of the Rio Grande, or allying with the Confederacy. Early in

August Lincoln himself made that case to Grant, who immediately yielded the point, even though the territory that would fall under Union control if his Mobile plan succeeded, added to his conquest of the Mississippi, would render French intervention in Texas meaningless, for any aid from there would have to traverse nearly five hundred miles of Union-held territory just to reach Confederate lines in eastern Alabama.[89] As always, Grant observed the line of authority between commander-in-chief and a general in the field, and never questioned the president.

Moreover, he had cause to be grateful to Lincoln. Meade's failure to pursue Lee vigorously squandered a golden opportunity in the president's mind, and though Lincoln cooled, and declined Meade's offer to resign, the subject of replacing him in command of the Army of the Potomac stuck with Stanton, who suggested to Halleck and probably Lincoln that Grant be brought east to take over. At last the seemingly inevitable was in play, the Union striking first to bring its paladin to counter the Confederate champion. By July 18 a rumor got into the press that Grant would replace Meade.[90] Almost immediately, both Halleck and Charles Dana energetically stressed to Stanton that being ordered east would more sadden than satisfy the Union's most successful general, whereupon Stanton immediately shelved the idea. Grant, who may have known nothing about it as yet, felt immensely relieved when Dana told him. He understood the dynamics of command culture and the necessity of a harmonious senior officer corps to successful operations, having struggled to protect his own against McClernand's malicious influence. He was already seeing the effects of expelling that discordant element and replacing him with Ord at the head of the XIII Corps. "The change is better than 10 000 reinforcements," he told Dana. Now there was harmony throughout the top command of his army, though he realized that the XIII Corps had been governed so long by a spirit of ambition and insubordination that some of its generals might resent Ord. Grant was prepared to make changes in Ord's subordinate commanders until the malcontents were quiet or gone.[91] Grant recognized that Meade's army already had able officers with long experience in that body. "My going could do no possible good," he said. "To import a commander to place over them certainly could produce no good," perhaps just exchanging one problem for another. Though he would never refuse an order, he would have objected vehemently to being sent east. "I can do more with this army than it would be possible for me to do with any other," he believed. He knew the soldiers in his army would do what he asked. "I know the exact capacity of every General," he added, and where and how to place each for maximum benefit, which was to him "a matter of no small importance."[92] Lincoln could have insisted, and Grant would have gone, but he felt thankful that he did not have to deal with that now. Still, the seed was planted.

If he was not to go east, and with his Mobile plan dead, there remained a real question of what he should do next. Just the day after Vicksburg's surrender Grant asked Halleck for any instructions, and whether he was to cooperate with other department commanders in any grand scheme, or follow his own judgment.[93] After nearly two months of inactivity, Grant left Vicksburg on August 31 for what he expected to be a short trip to New Orleans to meet with Banks and discuss how he could help with the planned expedition into Texas.[94] He arrived two days later and was soon abed at the St. Charles Hotel when awakened by men singing in the street outside. Friends and admirers had come to serenade him, and though the only speech he made was an apology for not making one, he rose and dressed to shake hands with many.[95] The next evening Banks held a grand levee in Grant's honor at his headquarters, where most of loyal New Orleans turned out to see the hero of Vicksburg.[96] On the morrow he joined Banks in reviewing a corps, and was given a horse so strong and unruly that it took two men to hold him for Grant to mount. He handled the animal well through the review, but while they rode back to the city a carriage accidentally bumped the horse and sent it shying in panic. Incredibly, Grant stayed in the saddle, but the animal fell over on his right leg and side, severely bruising him from knee to chest, fortunately breaking no bones.

The next day found him bedridden in severe pain, unable to be carried to a boat to return to Vicksburg or even to write letters. Julia was not with him but several of his staff were, probably including Lagow, who had been there since July and had become overfond of liquor. On one of those trying days, possibly the day of the accident, confined to bed, frustrated at his inactivity, uncomfortable in the summer heat, Grant took the first drink, perhaps to ease his pain. Too many followed, and soon enough he was thoroughly drunk, though after that one event he passed the remainder of his convalescent time in New Orleans soberly.[97] He spent ten days in bed before able to be carried to the wharf to board a steamboat for Vicksburg, meanwhile trying to carry on necessary correspondence by dictation.[98] Back at Vicksburg on September 16, he sent for Julia, who soon came to nurse him, and perhaps watch that he did not get to a bottle again. Nine days after his return, and twenty days since the accident, he stood again with the aid of crutches, though still weak.[99]

It was just in time. Five days earlier Rosecrans suffered humiliating defeat at Chickamauga, he and his army rushing in a panic back to Chattanooga. Within a few days Grant sent off most of his army under Sherman toward Chattanooga, keeping just enough men to hold the Mississippi from Vicksburg to Banks's lines above Baton Rouge. Even then he thought wistfully of what he could accomplish if he had enough men to move against Mobile. As it was, he was staying behind to guard territory rather than following his desire to go out and conquer more.[100] Then on October 9 came instructions from Stanton that he should go to Cairo to await orders. When he arrived further orders sent him to Indianapolis.[101] Accompanied by Julia, Grant took a train from Cairo to Indianapolis and found none other than Secretary of War Stanton waiting for him. On October 18 they rode to Louisville, and en route Stanton revealed to Grant that he was holding a draft general order by Lincoln relieving Rosecrans of command of the Army of the Cumberland, and merging the Departments of the Cumberland, the Ohio, and the Tennessee into the newly created Military Division of the Mississippi. The command was Grant's if he would take it.[102]

He accepted immediately. Given the choice of retaining Rosecrans with the Army of the Cumberland or relieving him in favor of Major General George H. Thomas, Grant asserted the immediate necessity of replacing Rosecrans, whom he said would not obey orders. Stanton went ahead and issued the general order, and Grant sent off an order relieving Rosecrans and installing Thomas. Then in their discussion Stanton informed him of the Union objective in eastern Tennessee. The region hosted the Confederacy's only direct east-west rail line, held abundant natural resources for manufacturing, produced considerable staple crops, and was home to one of the largest concentrations of Southerners loyal to the Union. Burnside had been sent to take Knoxville at the upper end of the Tennessee Valley with a small army, and Rosecrans was to hold Chattanooga at the lower end, between them forcing the Confederate Army of Tennessee out of the state and protecting all those resources. Instead, Burnside took root at Knoxville and Bragg shattered Rosecrans at Chickamauga, and now had him almost surrounded and under siege at Chattanooga, with no more than two weeks' supply of rations.

Grant's first task would be to reopen a secure supply line for the Army of the Cumberland. He left for Chattanooga on October 21, but even before then gave orders for work to start on repairing a road connecting Chattanooga with Bridgeport, Alabama, on the Tennessee River, unaware that Confederates already commanded a vital river crossing on the road. He also placed Sherman in command of his old Department and Army of the Tennessee, and gave Sherman's corps to John Logan. Meanwhile, Washington ordered former army commander Hooker to come west with the XI and XII Corps from Meade's Army of the Potomac.

Grant reached Chattanooga well after dark on October 23, having to ride more than sixty miles through rain and mud from the railhead at Bridgeport, which inflamed the pain in his leg once more, especially after his horse stumbled on the slippery route and Grant fell to the ground. Directed to Thomas's headquarters on his arrival, he met a chilly reception. Never garrulous at the best of times, Thomas was taciturn and unwelcoming. Almost six years older than Grant, Thomas finished at West Point before 'Lys entered, and went into the artillery. Hence the two never met until the battle of Monterey in Mexico, if there. Certainly they met at or after the battle of Shiloh, where Thomas commanded a brigade in Buell's army, and they had occasional interchange in the weeks after Shiloh. There had been no contact between them at all for nearly eighteen months, and though nothing suggests any precise difficulty between them, their relations were and remained strictly professional. Grant may have been wary of Thomas because he was a native Virginian, though nothing suggests he was not wholly loyal to the Union. Thomas had also spent the past year in high command under Rosecrans, and Grant might reasonably fear that Rosey's conspiratorial and backbiting nature had rubbed off. As for Thomas, he may have considered himself the professional, and resented being placed under Grant. After all, he had spent twenty-one years in the army after leaving West Point, and was a full colonel in 1861 before the war commenced, whereas Grant never rose higher than captain before he resigned. The stiff-necked Thomas certainly heard the rumors about Grant's heavy drinking, and surely got an earful about Grant from Rosecrans and his staff, while after Shiloh Thomas could have been among those who held Grant responsible for the April 6 surprise.[103]

Quickly familiarizing himself with conditions at Chattanooga, Grant found Thomas's army hungry, tired, and dispirited. On his ride there he had seen all along the way the flotsam of Rosecrans's hasty retreat, and now he learned that the army was short on ammunition as well as rations, and had no secure route for resupply. Thomas had just started work on a plan to take Brown's Ferry on the Tennessee a mile west of Chattanooga, and Kelley's Ferry seven miles beyond, which crossed a loop in the river. If Federals from Chattanooga could drive away the enemy at Brown's, while Hooker's advancing column from Nashville could take Kelley's, a wagon road there offered a good link to Bridgeport, where steamboats could land supplies for the hungry army. Grant the old quartermaster knew that only victory built morale in an army faster than ample rations, warm uniforms in winter, and plenty of ammunition. He approved the plan at once. Brown's Ferry fell first on October 27, and Kelley's the next day, and soon supplies began to flow into Chattanooga. Rawlins had no doubt where credit belonged. Great schemes were fine, he wrote the night Brown's Ferry was taken, but it took "decisiveness and energy in action" to "make military genius."[104] Thomas and Major General William F. Smith were mainly responsible for the plan that opened this so-called cracker line, and even Rosecrans had a hand in it before he left. Yet nothing happened until the coming of Grant, who himself generously credited Thomas with the plan, and simply informed Halleck that "the question of supplies may now be regarded as settled."[105] For some days Grant concentrated on funneling supplies into Chattanooga, watching for Sherman's arrival, and trying to get an ossified Burnside to do something. Thomas's army was in no condition for an offensive, but would be soon.[106] By the first week of November he turned his attention to taking the initiative.

Chattanooga sat on the east side of a bend in the Tennessee River, commanded by the imposing height of Lookout Mountain less than two miles south, and by the long north-south range of Missionary Ridge an equal distance to the east. Grant's first goal was to reopen direct communications with Burnside in Knoxville, just over a hundred miles northeast. As soon as Sherman arrived with his two corps, Grant intended to take Lookout Mountain, which he believed would force the Confederates to fall back from Missionary Ridge and open the road to Knoxville.[107] Then he learned that Longstreet and his corps were on their way to strike Burnside, which meant that Bragg's army in his immediate front was substantially weakened. To capitalize on that unexpected development, he immediately gave Thomas orders on November 7 to attack and take the northern end of Missionary Ridge the next morning, and then move against Bragg's line of supply and communications back to Georgia. That, he reasoned, would force Longstreet to turn around. His written order to Thomas originally spoke of "if" he took Missionary Ridge, but in its place he inserted "when." Thomas needed to have the same certainty that Grant felt.[108]

Untypically, Grant had no sure idea yet of what the Army of the Cumberland could do, or the depth of its exhaustion. Supplies might be coming in, but they were not yet abundant, and the men were weary and weak from weeks on reduced rations. There were not enough horses to pull artillery and wagons, and many of those still living were emaciated, even dying, from lack of fodder, which the cracker line was not yet bringing in. Pressed heavily by Washington to save Burnside from being cut off or surrounded, he tried to rush Thomas too soon. That night Thomas came to Grant and told him forthrightly that he could not possibly have his army ready for several days, suggesting that they wait for Sherman's corps, which would be in better condition. Grant yielded and cancelled the attack, but began to have doubts about Thomas from that moment.[109] He could hardly forget that in his operations against Vicksburg his army marched and fought for more than a fortnight making three, or even two, days' rations stretch a week once he crossed the Mississippi. Thomas's army had been immobile for weeks on not much less, and Grant had to wonder why they could not do what his own veterans had done.

If he had not already, in that moment Grant apparently decided to depend foremost on Sherman for the heavy lifting thereafter. He hurried his old comrade toward him, intending for one of Hooker's corps to clear the west side of Lookout Mountain. Then Sherman would move into the valley between Lookout and Missionary Ridge, while Thomas advanced against the northern end of the ridge, which should force Bragg to retire. Grant would then move a force between Bragg and Longstreet, which ought to force the Confederates to withdraw from Knoxville. Grant told Sherman that, once Bragg fell back, "we will determine what is next to be done." On its face, that "we" seemed to exclude Thomas from the planning.[110]

Three days later, on November 14, Grant wrote Julia that "things will culminate here within ten days in great advantages with one or other parties." He felt confident and easy in his mind about his situation "and find no occasion to swear or fret." The only caveat he admitted was that he might be "failed by any officer in immediate command," possibly an oblique reference to nascent doubt about Thomas. His own people were working smoothly, though he had few aides with him. Two aides he left at Nashville operated with his authority to ensure that his orders for supplies were obeyed in the full, showing that he was grasping the fuller potential of a staff.[111] Grant calculated that he could not make the advance until November 19, the earliest date Sherman could reach him, and notified Halleck that he believed he could have Bragg in retreat two days later.[112] Much depended on Burnside's holding out now that he was besieged by Longstreet. Grant frankly told "Burn" not to abandon that position unless most of his army was destroyed. He declined even to discuss a possible line of retreat, reminding Burnside that his army was not the only one resisting Confederate advances at that moment.[113]

By November 18 Grant thought all was nearly ready. "There will be a big fight here," he wrote a friend, what he expected to be a "general skeedadle of the enemy," yet he did not expect overmuch. Another sound defeat ought to end the war, he thought, but added that "unfortunately I am not in a condition to give them that."[114] In fact, it took longer than expected for Sherman to get in position. On November 20 a bluffing Bragg advised Grant to get noncombatants out of the city, implying that he intended to shell or attack the Federals. Grant sent the note to Thomas noting that he thought it a "good joke" that Bragg would hold off an attack until nearly all Union forces were present, and in jest—or bluff—responded that "this I will not do; but I will attack you in your position to-morrow morning."[115] In fact he postponed the attack until November 23, and the frustration told on him. Only Sherman was really fully mobile. Two weeks after having to call off the first assault by Thomas, the Army of the Cumberland still could barely move its cannon, and would have to borrow horses from Sherman to move even one-sixth of its artillery. "I have never felt such restlessness before as I have had at the fixed and immovable condition of the Army of the Cumberland," Grant complained to Halleck.[116] The frustration clearly showed when he received a telegram from a general who protested willingness to lose his entire command if it would relieve the beleaguered Burnside, while actually moving not a muscle. "If you had shown half the willingness to sacrifice yourself and command at the start, [as] you do in your dispatch," chided Grant, "you might have rendered Burnside material aid."[117]

Bad weather and other contingencies postponed action until the afternoon of November 23, when Grant ordered Thomas forward to drive Confederates from two knolls between Chattanooga and Missionary Ridge, from which he expected to launch his next advance. By this time he had revised his thinking and directed Sherman to cross the Tennessee above Thomas's left to strike the right flank of Bragg's line on Missionary Ridge, while Hooker took Lookout Mountain on Bragg's left. Thomas was to move forward in support of Sherman when he attacked, and the Army of the Cumberland was either to take the enemy rifle pits at the base of the ridge and the ridge itself beyond, or shift left to concentrate with Sherman.[118] "A decisive battle will be fought," Grant wired Halleck after taking the knolls, and he expected it the next day.[119] Instead, fog and dwindling ammunition held up Hooker, though he advanced far enough to force Bragg to abandon Lookout Mountain that night, while Sherman got into position in front of the north end of Missionary Ridge, but could not attack before dark.

Grant's plan for November 25 was for Sherman to advance against the ridge at daylight, while Hooker pressed forward from Lookout against the southern end. It commenced well but soon slowed. Sher-

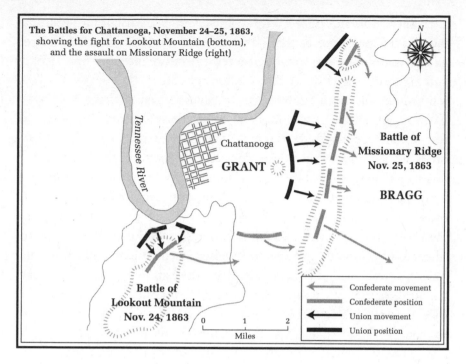

The Battles for Chattanooga, November 24–25, 1863, showing the fight for Lookout Mountain (bottom), and the assault on Missionary Ridge (right)

Battle of Missionary Ridge Nov. 25, 1863

BRAGG

GRANT

Chattanooga

Tennessee River

Battle of Lookout Mountain Nov. 24, 1863

N

0   1   2
Miles

Confederate movement
Confederate position
Union movement
Union position

man met tough resistance on the ridge, while Hooker lost time building a bridge to cross a creek before he hit the southern end of the
ridge and moved up it to start pressing northward. Grant and Thomas
watched the fighting from Orchard Knob, one of the two hills taken
two days before, and when Grant detected Confederates atop the
ridge shifting north to help stop Sherman, he ordered Thomas to send
forward three divisions to take the first line of rifle pits at the foot of
the ridge to try to keep Bragg from sending more.

Thomas's divisions moved forward and easily gained the line of
rifle pits, but they failed to stop there. Either Grant did not clearly
indicate to Thomas that he wanted them to halt and only move up
the ridge after Hooker appeared moving up on the crest—which is
unlikely given Grant's customary precision in written and oral instructions—or Thomas failed to hear him. Or more likely yet, his division
commanders recalled Grant's order to Thomas of the day before that
specifically said they were to "carry the rifle pits *and ridge* directly in
front of them." Seeing the Army of the Cumberland veterans swarm-
ing up the ridge, Grant was puzzled at first, commenting to those with

him that he had not ordered this. However, observing their vigor and the ground they were gaining, he decided not to call them back. Once he saw them carry the top, he ordered the entire line forward. Within half an hour Bragg's army dissolved in retreat.[120]

By nightfall Grant sent a wire to Halleck saying that "I believe I am not premature in announcing a complete victory."[121] Indeed he was not. The precipitate retreat of the Confederate army saw thousands left behind, others deserting, and Bragg himself faced with a disgrace that soon required his resignation. The Army of Tennessee would not reform until it came together in north Georgia. It was the most embarrassing defeat suffered by any Confederate army during the war, a consequence of Grant's planning, his soldiers' daring and resilience, and Confederate overconfidence in a formidable position they were too weak to hold effectively. With the battlefield still clouded by smoke, Grant began arranging that evening for Sherman and others to relieve Burnside and force Longstreet to withdraw, while he intended to pursue Bragg himself. Two days later he was at Ringgold, Georgia, nearly twenty miles south, but had marched ahead of his supplies and had little choice but to halt and return to Chattanooga.

"I have no expectation of spending a winter in idleness," he wrote Julia.[122] He could hardly make a winter campaign there in the cold, and suspected Washington wanted him to rest and wait for spring. "I do not feel satisfied though giving the rebels so much time for reorganizing," he told McPherson. He hoped to move yet again to press the enemy, and if allowed he intended to leave east Tennessee secure and then take Sherman's army and the white soldiers of McPherson's corps down the Mississippi to New Orleans, where in January 1864 he would resurrect his plan to take Mobile and fragment the Deep South.[123] If he succeeded in that, there would be little left of the Confederacy, and only one important enemy army—Lee's.

Inevitability.

14

"IF DEFEATED NOTHING WILL BE LEFT US TO LIVE FOR."

"**I** COULD HAVE marched to Atlanta or any other place in the Confederacy," U. S. Grant told a friend two weeks after the battle of Missionary Ridge. However, the extent of the collapse of Bragg's army took him somewhat by surprise, with no buildup of supplies for a long offensive.[1] The winter and roads in east Tennessee were bad at the best of times, and he preferred not to operate there, yet he wanted his army to stay busy. Hence he planned campaigns farther south, starting with taking Mobile in January, then moving up its rivers to seize all of Alabama and Mississippi, and part of Georgia. Grant still believed this gambit could end the rebellion by spring. Without saying so, he believed that Lee would see this as well, and thought the Confederates would abandon Virginia and North Carolina and move to defend this vital heartland.

Now he included the Army of the Potomac in his strategic thinking. Halleck told him that "nothing is to be hoped under its present commander," and he, Stanton, and Lincoln sought Grant's views for a replacement. He proposed William F. Smith or Sherman and favored Smith slightly, no doubt because he wanted to keep Sherman with him. Meade kept his job in the end, but Grant's influence was spreading eastward. Hereafter, nothing was likely to happen without his being consulted, and from now on he freely offered advice on what Meade should do.[2] Coincidentally, a week after Grant shared his plan of campaign, Washburne introduced in Congress a bill reviving the rank of lieutenant general, with Grant specifically in mind. Grant surely knew of it beforehand, and when he told Washburne on December 12 that "all is well with me" and that "every thing looks bright and favorable in this command," he could have added that things looked bright for U. S. Grant, as well.[3] Only George Washington had held that rank, and Winfield Scott by brevet. The fact that it took congressional action to revive it is a measure of just how the North had come to regard Grant, and what it expected of him.

Some expected even more. In several midwestern states, the Democratic Party divided between those supporting the war and those committed to peace at any cost. Soon after Grant wrote to Washburne, the chairman of the Ohio branch of the War Democrats asked if they could nominate him for the presidency. That stunned Grant. "The question astonishes me," he replied. "I do not know of anything I have ever done or said which would indicate that I could be a candidate for any office." He politely but firmly declined. They must crush the rebellion first, "and I will be content with whatever credit may then be given me, feeling assured that a just public will award all that is due." It was his first acknowledgment that he assumed some kind of reward would be coming at war's end.[4]

Yet nothing could subdue the presidential talk for the next few months. Days before the recent battle he was praised for being among the prominent Democrats supporting Lincoln and the war.[5] As early as December 11 the Democratic New York *Herald* mentioned him as a possible competitor when Lincoln sought reelection, then four days later declared that "Grant is the man for the occasion." In another week he was "the Universally Selected candidate."[6] Some Republicans eyed him as a successor after Lincoln's second term, and Washburne warned that "certain parties are attempting to make your name a foot ball for the Presidency."[7] Grant stubbornly resolved to stay out of it, which suited a wary Lincoln, watching to see if his general showed signs of becoming a rival. Satisfied by Grant's demurrers, the president felt easier about Washburne's proposed promotion. Rawlins advised Grant against the new rank if it meant an office in Washington in place of being with the armies. Press speculation continued, as well as entreaties to step forward, but Grant remarked that all such "very soon finds its way into the waste basket," since "I already have a pretty big job on my hands."[8]

While the political ferment bubbled, Grant grew increasingly frustrated over east Tennessee. He expected peace and reunion to come soon if they could act quickly against Longstreet, who retreated to Greenville for the winter.[9] Burnside needed prompting just to breathe, and even the addition of two divisions did not budge him. On December 9 Major General John G. Foster replaced him in command, but became too ill to launch a campaign. Grant foresaw what he called "the last great battle of the war" in east Tennessee, for if he pushed Longstreet into southwest Virginia and neutralized him there, Lee would be too weak to resist in the spring, and Grant could move against him with Meade.[10]

Nashville should be his base for a move against Longstreet and southwest Virginia, but when Grant arrived on December 19 what he found was discouraging. For several days he was a frequent sight walking briskly on the city sidewalks, or in an open buggy moving at a speed some thought recklessly fast as he made his inspections.[11] Thomas's staff departments were not functioning smoothly. Indeed, Thomas's imperious provost marshal even ignored Grant's orders. He allowed the inevitable speculators—"Jews and citizens generally," Grant called them—to travel in and out of the city as they chose, but refused to honor Grant's passes and actually arrested one of his staff's servants. Grant directed Thomas to replace the man, but not before he encountered the problem in person.[12] On the bitterly cold day after Christmas, wrapped in a huge overcoat, he went to the Nashville & Chattanooga rail depot to return to Chattanooga. As he started to board a car a guard stopped him, saying, "Here, sir, you can't go in there." Grant identified himself, but the guard insisted that he had orders to admit no one until after his pass was examined by the military conductor. Amused despite the inconvenience, Grant just smiled, replied "right, sir, right," and got in the conductor's line to wait his turn.[13]

Before leaving Grant set in motion a campaign to clear enemy cavalry from west Tennessee, and told Sherman to disrupt enemy communications in east and central Mississippi to keep the enemy from operating there that winter. He also wanted Thomas's army to advance into north Georgia. Only once that was all going would he undertake the Mobile operation.[14] Uppermost in his mind by the time he left Nashville was Longstreet, and it was evident to Grant that he would have to do it himself. Once back in Chattanooga, he made a hard ride on horseback over bad roads to Knoxville, but enjoyed it, telling Julia that "hard labor is the easiest duty I have to perform."[15] He arrived on New Year's Eve, only to find that Foster could not make even a brief campaign, despite all of Grant's efforts to get him supplied. The route from Chattanooga being so unreliable, the old quartermaster set out in person to find a more dependable avenue. It was not just hyperbole when Grant declared that a good quartermaster was "more important to the Government, than an Army Corps commander."[16] Over the next week, in subzero temperatures, he rode 120 miles from Knoxville through the Cumberland Gap into southern Kentucky and on to Lexington to see if wagon roads would serve to supply Foster; he also ordered units into position to move against Longstreet as soon as they were properly supplied. His ride convinced him that this route was no more reliable, and that for the time being Foster would have to live off the land while Grant explored other possibilities.

He kept pressing his main goal. Taking Atlanta would secure him much of west Georgia. Taking Montgomery would gain central Alabama. He could take the latter first by moving up the Alabama River from Mobile, and then be in position to move from there to Atlanta, using the Tennessee via Chattanooga for a supply line. At the same time Thomas could push directly south, drive the Army of Tennessee out of its winter quarters at Dalton, and force it back to Atlanta where he and Thomas would force it to withdraw eastward, giving up that major industrial and rail center. Meanwhile, Sherman's raid through central Mississippi could cooperate with Union forces in Montgomery to neutralize enemy movement in west Alabama and Mississippi. Grant would command one arm of that pincer, and Sherman the other.[17]

Grant's Henry-Donelson campaign had been sophisticated, and Vicksburg even more so, but nothing to date revealed the level of grand strategic insight that he displayed in this concept. Each of three forces could achieve much on its own, while each also could cooperate with another to double their gains, and all with secure lines of communications. He also envisioned that success here would impact Virginia as well. Unlikely though it might be that Lee would leave the state to rescue central Georgia and Alabama, Grant reasonably saw that as Lee's only alternative to finding Grant sweeping up from Atlanta through the Carolinas to threaten Richmond and his own rear while he faced Meade. Even if Lee did not take the bait, on January 19, 1864, Grant proposed a way for Meade to take care of Lee by himself.

Shunning his predecessors' avenues of approach, Meade should shift most of his army to Norfolk, use it as a base to concentrate in Suffolk, and then move southwest on Raleigh, North Carolina, 130 miles distant, destroying the rail lines concentrated around Weldon. Changing his base to New Bern or Wilmington, both closer and less vulnerable, Meade should move west from Raleigh to threaten the rail line at Greensboro. If the Yankees could cut that and hold Knoxville, they would isolate Virginia and Richmond from all communication with the rest of the Confederacy. Grant believed that rather than lose that rail line, Lee would send a large part of his army to protect it, virtually forcing the evacuation of Virginia and Longstreet from east Tennessee. With their state already rife with dissension, thousands of dispirited North Carolina troops would likely desert Lee's army. Thousands of slaves would run away to Union banners, Union armies could live off the country and still have good lines of supply, and Lee would be forced to give up well-prepared lines of defense to meet the Federals on unfamiliar ground, with no time to erect new works. The move would also isolate Wilmington, the South's last major Atlantic port for blockade traffic, and Meade would be in a climate where he could campaign without waiting for spring. Grant thought that 60,000 men could do it.

Some of the plan originated with General Smith and Lieutenant Colonel Cyrus Comstock just the day before, but Grant added the threat to the railroad west of Raleigh, giving it greater scope and greater potential gain.[18] As always, he sought an indirect approach to his objective, an opportunity for large territorial gains without major action, and concentration of force while making the enemy face him on his own terms. Events beyond his control would dictate that neither this plan nor his Mobile operation would ever launch as conceived. Of course either—or both—might not have worked, but it is unfortunate that two of the subtlest strategic concepts of the war were never tested. The other unknown was the Confederates' reaction. Grant consistently underestimated their determination. He might have remembered his own thoughts on the Mexican soldiers he faced in 1847. They had little drill or discipline, inadequate rations, and scant pay. Those deficiencies relieved, however, he believed "they would fight and persist."[19] Thus far the Confederates had outlasted the Mexicans at war by nearly a year. Convinced of the injustice of their cause, Grant could not see their motivation to protect home soil or defend the sacrifices made already, nor understand a growing Confederate nationalism. They were not going to yield easily.

His planning bore one practical result. Having commenced thinking in continental terms, he did not stop, yet it was Halleck's invitation that got him started. Thereafter, interest and ingenuity kept him at it intermittently, surely mindful of the possibility of another star. Characteristically, the most immediate attraction of more rank was the increased salary.[20] That would secure his finances more than ever, while with promotion yet undecided, Grant finally framed the "just reward" he hoped the country might offer. From the outset he knew that at war's end there would be a massive demobilization of the volunteers. Hundreds of generals would be civilians again, for all their battles won, and he could be back working for brother Orville in Galena. Commissions and promotions in the Regular Army were another matter, and Grant was now a major general in the regulars. Barring some legislation to the contrary, he should retain that rank and salary after the war and through retirement. That would be reward enough. "Through Providence I have attained to more than I ever hoped," he told a friend, "and with the position I now hold in the Regular Army, if allowed to retain it will be more than satisfied."[21] The war that had made him would sustain him thereafter.

He went to St. Louis late that month to see his son Fred, then dangerously ill with a fever. Finding the boy recovering, he accepted invitations to two dinners in his honor. At one he found himself in a crowd of hundreds including, uncomfortably, Rosecrans, now commanding in Missouri. Only their host sat between the two at the table, and while Grant kept quiet in his seat, Rosecrans did his best to upstage the guest of honor. Toasted as hero of the hour, Grant responded by saying, "it will be impossible for me to do more than to thank you," and sat down, after which Rosey spoke at some length on the heroism of the Union soldier, but pointedly failed to mention the guest of honor.[22] On leaving St. Louis, Grant wrote his father that he hoped not to "leave 'Dixie' again" until the end of the war. All the attention flattered, but it was embarrassing as well.[23] He daydreamed of going somewhere remote "where no body lives and where but few people are to be seen," and no one would know him.[24]

"Time sets very lightly with me," Grant wrote his friend Daniel Ammen in February. "I am neither grey nor bald nor do I feel any different from what I did at twenty-five."[25] His health was excellent, he had recovered fully from the accident in New Orleans, and he had the upper hand over alcohol. A week before the battles for Chattanooga he found some of his officers, chiefly Lagow, engaged in drunken revelries at headquarters and himself broke up one party at four in the morning. A few days later he allowed Lagow to resign rather than be dismissed. Grant himself may have had a drink or two in that period, but no more, and Rawlins gave him a refresher talk that cemented his resolve.[26] He had a fine staff of eighteen men well trained in their duties, and excellent relations with a cadre of top commanders starting with Sherman and McPherson, lower ranks like John Logan, and a new man he spotted at Chattanooga, Philip H. Sheridan. In Thomas he had a fine army commander, despite the absence of warmth between the two, and some concern about the man's reliability. Grant was mature enough to incorporate suggestions like Smith's and Comstock's into his own plans without feeling threatened. "He listens quietly to the opinions of others," wrote Major General David Hunter after three weeks at Grant's headquarters, "and then judges promptly for himself."[27] Awaiting guidance from Washington on his next mission, he worked to get his armies ready to move, at the same time advising Northern governors on how to have their new recruits ready for action as soon as they reached him. He still believed the war would end soon—it was always going to end soon—giving it until the end of 1864, but they must move quickly.[28] His hope for a winter campaign was gone, but by mid-February he expected operations to commence in early April.[29]

Events soon reshaped his expectations. Longstreet began a retreat back into southwest Virginia, with Major General John M. Schofield pursuing in place of Foster. Bragg's army, now commanded by Joseph E. Johnston, remained at Dalton. Then on February 26 Washburne's bill passed both houses of Congress, and Lincoln appointed Grant, who got the news at his Nashville headquarters on March 4, along with orders to report to Washington.[30] Grant initially mirrored Lee's concern about resentment and resistance if placed over an army he had not led. He also told Washburne early on that he wanted no position that kept him in Washington.[31] Expecting that he might have to oscillate between the two theaters of the war, he had no other inkling of his assignment.[32] Before leaving Nashville he offered thanks to Sherman and McPherson for making him a success. Sherman warned him to beware of the political swamp in Washington, imploring that he "continue as heretofore to be yourself, simple, honest, and unpretending."[33]

Reaching the capital on March 8, Grant went to the White House for his first meeting with the president, who that evening introduced him to a throng of guests by asking him to stand on a sofa for all to see, which Grant found embarrassing. The next day at a cabinet meeting Lincoln formally presented his commission, and later they discussed Grant's mandate. The president said all he wanted was for him to act, and to defeat Lee's army, promising all the assistance in his power. Grant pledged what he always did, that he would do his best with what he was given. He would determine his own operations now, and Lincoln did not immediately press him.[34] A friend in the city was less patient. "You mean to capture Richmond, I hope?" he asked the new lieutenant general. Grant's reply was simple, and typical: "I mean to beat Lee."[35]

Lee meant not to be beaten, but the collapse of the Army of Tennessee augured ill. Bragg resigned on November 30, but President Davis had only two full-rank generals available, and loathed both Johnston and Beauregard. Again he turned to Lee, the general he regarded most highly. The Virginian followed western events as he could through the newspapers, well aware that his sources were incomplete, often unreliable, and tainted by editorial prejudice. Still, what he called "impressions" told him the Yankees would aim deep into Georgia for supply depots and factories, meaning Atlanta. He knew there was risk in recommending Beauregard or Johnston for the command, but suggested the former cautiously as the better choice if he should be "considered suitable for the position." Beyond that he urged that the Deep South from Florida to Mississippi ought to be stripped to rebuild the Army of Tennessee, even if it risked points of secondary value. Lee further proposed that the slim forces defending southwest Virginia could reinforce Longstreet to attack Knoxville again. Finally, Lee proved Grant right to expect they might think alike. He perceived that if the enemy moved deeper into Georgia, then Savannah, Charleston, Wilmington, even Richmond would be threatened by Grant's advance as much as by Meade. It was the first time Lee ever mentioned Grant in relation to Virginia.[36]

Davis asked once more for Lee to take command of the Army of Tennessee, even temporarily, adding his own voice to the chorus expecting Lee and Grant to meet in the field.[37] As before, Lee begged off, saying it would be pointless unless he went in permanent command, and he doubted he could do much even then, believing that "I would not receive cordial cooperation." To that he added doubts in his strength or ability to be successful with that army, then wisely raised the matter of who could replace him in Virginia. His senior subordinate Longstreet was absent with his corps and Lee did not mention him, which could also indicate that Lee doubted his capacity for top command. Ewell was the next senior. Saying nothing of his expressed concern over that general's capacity, Lee argued that he was "too feeble" in health for the rigors of the position. Inevitably that brought them back to Beauregard and Johnston again. Genuinely fearing that Davis might peremptorily order him to go west, Lee reminded the president of what he would have to do in Virginia, and that forestalled any such order. From the outset Lee demonstrated keen subtlety in managing his president, and was getting better at it.[38]

Davis tried that skill two days later when he summoned Lee to Richmond for what proved to be more than a week of conferences.[39] Lee clearly feared that the peremptory order might be coming after all. "My heart and thought will always be with this army," he told Jeb Stuart before leaving, and his peculiar closing words, "I expect to be back," sounded like an expectation that it might only be a visit before going elsewhere.[40] If Davis pressed again for the command change, Lee continued his diplomatic resistance. When the depth of the president's animus to Beauregard became evident, Lee shifted to support Johnston. During their meetings reports arrived from Dalton that no imminent attack was expected. At the same time they learned that Longstreet had given up on taking Knoxville, that the enemy at Chattanooga appeared to be moving most of its army toward Nashville, and most disturbing, word arrived that Grant was moving east into Virginia.[41] With no means of sifting fact from rumor, Davis had to act on the information in hand and Lee's counsel as his chief advisor, and all of that worked to Lee's purpose. Now the Army of Tennessee's immediate front ought to be quiet long enough to give a new commander time to settle in. Longstreet's retreat and the Yankees' apparent pursuit presented a new threat to Richmond from a new direction, making Lee's presence essential with the only army that could hope to hold Meade and stop Grant.[42] By December 16 Davis yielded and appointed Johnston, and Lee let his staff know that he had dodged the assignment.[43]

Relieved of one concern, Lee returned to face another. His army was famished. Stuart's cavalry had received no issue of beef from the commissary since the summer of 1862, and in the interim virtually fended for themselves for meat. His infantry were down to a quarter pound of salt beef or pork a day, with just three days' supply of that, leaving him anxious that he might have to disperse the army to the interior for it to forage for itself. Reassembling it on call was not a task he could contemplate optimistically.[44] Lee had never been a supply officer like Grant, but he understood the critical importance of steady provisions. He also believed the problem was not availability, but distribution. Colonel Lucius B. Northrop, the commissary general in Richmond, had a well-justified reputation as hopelessly inadequate, an opinion Lee shared. Presented with Lee's complaints of empty bellies, Northrop actually suggested that Lee assume nominal control of Northrop's officers and impress what he needed from the civilian population, in essence doing his job for him. Lee refused, even more chagrined when he learned that while his men were on half rations or less, Johnston's in Georgia had plenty of everything.[45]

Late in January Lee issued a general order that amounted to an apology to his men for their short rations and an indirect protest that the responsibility was not his.[46] That same day he warned the secretary of war that declining morale and increased desertions were the inevitable result. Lee resorted to furloughing up to one-sixth of the army at a time so they could subsist at home and reduce the pressure, but that hazarded that some might not to return.[47] He dispersed his cavalry to get food for the animals, and the situation in some cases was so bad that in one division 400 men had no shoes, and more than 1,000 were without blankets for the winter.[48] Lee understood that wholesale impressments would produce disaffection in the short term, and the future probability that farmers would hide their livestock and produce from Northrop's agents. His insight into the ramifications of any kind of seizure was clear, but knowing that it was necessary, he pleaded that impressments be universally applied so that all suffered equally.[49] Happily, he found the quartermaster general both more cooperative and more competent, and set in train plans for the army to collect the hides necessary to make its own shoes, using ersatz ingenuity to make up for official shortfalls.

Lee lived simply, an acceptance of shortages as an immutable fact, and a means of setting an example. "I want nothing but a little bread & meat," he told Mary.[50] Grant rarely ever had to go hungry, not even when cut off from his supply line below Vicksburg, and except for Chattanooga, neither did his men. Lee's soldiers, however, frequently faced slim rations, while operating in countryside exhausted after supporting them and the occasional Yankee visitors for three years. Hence, the more food was on the soldiers' minds, the more Lee wisely ensured that his fare was not measurably better than theirs. Thinking it "criminal" to indulge daily in meat during times of shortage, he allowed it on his headquarters mess table only twice a week. Instead, his dinner was most often a head of cabbage boiled in saltwater and a pone of cornbread. One rainy day in April when several of his generals waited after a conference to return to their camps, Lee invited them to dine with him and ordered the usual cabbage, only with the addition of some "middling," or salt pork. What appeared was a heap of cabbage and, almost hiding on top, one slender slice of middling to feed several men. As the cornbread and cabbage went around the table, each guest in turn passed over the meat to leave it for someone else, until the cabbage was gone but the pork remained, which Lee would not eat in their presence. The next day he asked his servant Perry to bring him the pork, only to learn that his cook had borrowed it from someone else and "done paid it back," leaving Lee to eat cabbage.[51]

He did allow himself molasses with his cornbread if available. One of his officers somehow got five gallons of syrup from the commissary, but when Lee asked if that much was available for every other mess in the army, he was told no, and ordered the remainder of his to be returned, with orders that it go to the sick in hospital. Lee surely knew that in a rumor mill like an army, stories like that would spread, and Brigadier General John D. Imboden believed that hearing of Lee's self-denial "often reconciled a hungry, ragged Confederate to his hardships."[52] That is not to say that the general always handed over gift food. Cakes, fruit, pies, even wine occasionally appeared on his table, but always shared with his staff.

It was a cold and hungry Christmas that year. Typical of what his adjutant Taylor called Lee's "peculiar character," the Great Tycoon could have spent the holiday in Richmond with Mary, but instead returned to the army a few days before, which Taylor rather cynically thought was calculated "to show how very self-denying he is."[53] For the past six months Lee had largely controlled his impatience and not taken out frustrations on his staff, but this holiday he found that "the young men have no fondness for the society of the old Genl.," telling Mary that "he is too somber & heavy for them."[54]

The only good news that winter was Rooney's exchange and release in March. Lee still grieved over Charlotte's death, and consoled his son, saying "she is brighter & happier than ever, Safe from all evil & awaiting us in, her Heavenly abode." They should all pray that one day "God in his Mercy" would allow them "to join her in eternal praise to our Lord & Saviour." Grief was an indulgence ill afforded now. "Our Country demands all our thoughts, all our energies," he told his son. Powerful forces loomed. "If victorious we have everything to hope for in the future," he said. "If defeated nothing will be left us to live for." He expected the Yankees to move in the final week of April. "We have no time to wait," he warned Rooney. "We must strike fast & strong."[55]

The optimistic, like Adjutant Taylor, hoped spring would see them on the offensive and moving into Pennsylvania again, and this time "we'll *stay* there."[56] Lee had no illusions. He saw but two opportunities that at best might upset Union plans for the balance of the summer, his objective in invading Pennsylvania the year before. A reinforced Longstreet might march into Kentucky to threaten Grant's supply line to

Chattanooga, forcing the Federals back and allowing Johnston to take the offensive and regain Chattanooga, and perhaps even more of Tennessee. Alternatively, if Longstreet quietly rejoined Lee, they might drive Meade back on Washington. "We are not in a condition, & never have been, in my opinion, to invade the enemy's country with a prospect of permanent benefit," he told the president early in February, "but we can alarm & embarrass him to some extent." Perhaps it could be enough to forestall dangerous enemy enterprises.[57] He hardly need mention the fall elections in the North, ever mindful that Confederate independence lay in defeating the Union's will to continue.

Lee and Davis held more meetings in late February on strategy in the western theater, but the general soon returned to his headquarters at Orange Court House. Anxious to take the initiative before Meade and Grant were ready, Lee protested that without adequate supplies he could do nothing. With them, and with better horses for his cavalry, he told Davis, "I think I could disturb the quiet of the enemy & drive him to the Potomac."[58] Throughout the winter he recalled detachments, retrieved thousands of absentees, gleaned hospitals for men fit for duty, and exchanged convalescents for able-bodied men at nonessential posts. He juggled officers and shifted units to streamline his command and make his divisions more equal in size, and consolidated strength as much as possible, calling in several brigades from an expedition to North Carolina and urging Longstreet's return. He also begged the secretary of war to stop releasing his reports on battles to the press too quickly, for they contained information still useful to the Federals about his strength and organization.[59]

Meanwhile, he tried to divine enemy intentions. Lee distrusted what he read in Northern papers, expecting much of it to be planted to mislead, and initially his wariness betrayed him. The big news by late March was Grant's promotion, which he did not question, but he mistrusted the news that Grant would accompany Meade as bait to make him think Richmond would be the objective. Hence, Lee concluded that Johnston's army was the real target and that his own faced no imminent threat. Still, he advised vigilance and readiness everywhere, but no major troop movements east or west until the enemy gave away their intentions.[60] A few days later he accepted that Grant really would accompany Meade, which meant enemy concentration in Virginia.

Lee expressed no great concern that he would be meeting Grant on the field, though he knew enough of the Federal's past campaigns to warn Longstreet that deception "is part of Grant's tactics" and cautioned Longstreet that "it behooves us to be on the alert, or we will be deceived."[61] By the end of March he was convinced that Virginia was the real target, that Grant would move on Richmond, and that other Federals would advance into the Shenandoah Valley. Moreover, he believed Grant would invade on multiple lines. If Johnston did not launch an offensive to draw troops away from Virginia, Lee would have to concentrate everything available to meet the threat.[62] "We have got to whip them," Lee told his adjutant Taylor on April 3. "We must whip them and it has already made me feel better to think of it."[63]

First he wanted Longstreet in the Shenandoah, where he and Lee could concentrate to meet a threat on either side of the Blue Ridge, but by April 5 concluded to have him return to the army at once. He expected the Army of the Potomac to have 100,000 men or more, not counting those that threatened the Shenandoah, and feared that more might move up the York-James Peninsula from Fort Monroe.[64] By April 15 he felt certain he was right, and so he was. He knew of Banks's expedition up the Red River, and again correctly concluded that Grant's cherished Mobile operation was postponed. Fearing another incursion on the North Carolina coast, he advised that Beauregard's troops from South Carolina move north to meet it or hurry to the James River if necessary. Believing Richmond would be invested if Grant got that far, Lee advised that all nonessential civilians be evacuated, both to keep them out of the way and to stop their consuming food vital to a besieged garrison.[65] Continually he hammered at the War Department and even Davis for supplies. On April 12 he believed he had but two days' rations for his army. Food came in, but too little at intervals too long, while he knew that depots in Georgia bulged with rations, if only the useless Northrop would get them to him.

If Richmond could be securely defended, Lee proposed advancing against Grant and Meade in their positions along the Rappahannock River. "Should God give us a crowning victory there, all their plans would be dissipated," he told Davis, and the enemy would recall to Washington the small army preparing to advance up the peninsula. It was a desperate proposal, erected on a foundation of "what ifs," especially as Lee thought his own strength might be fewer than 60,000 versus twice their number. He could do no better, and not even that unless he brought his cavalry and artillery back to the army with enough fodder for a campaign.[66]

Longstreet was on his way by April 16, but would take days to arrive, while Lee expected an enemy advance almost daily, especially after scouts reported enemy engineers and bridge-building units moving below the Rappahannock. That could only mean a crossing of the Rapidan River. "Everything indicates a concentrated attack," he told Davis, as well as one and perhaps two raids into the Shenandoah.[67] Lee wisely kept his apprehensions to himself, for rumor around his headquarters held that he had said he would "try and wipe the enemy out" when next they met, one aide noting that "he is [not] given to boasting."[68]

That last week he asked President Davis to visit the army, hoping it would inspirit the soldiers on the eve of action, while Lee encouraged spiritual inspiration.[69] He always preferred that only the most necessary work be done on Sundays.[70] Beyond question he understood the value of a meaningful gesture, as well as the near-reverence his men felt for him. In the last phases of the abortive Mine Run operations, on a Sunday Lee and Hill with their staffs rode along the lines until they met a group of soldiers singing a hymn in a field service. Hundreds of men looked on from their earthworks, battle flags fluttered in the breeze, and artillery punctured the works awaiting action. Lee halted his retinue immediately and they all sat their mounts to hear the sermon. At the benediction Lee removed his hat to receive the blessing, then spurred his horse and they rode on. "It was a striking scene," Adjutant Taylor wrote a few days later, "and one well calculated to impress solemnly all who witnessed it." Seeing Lee beseech Divine assistance, Taylor felt "even more hopeful than before."[71] Hoping to multiply Taylor's feeling many thousandfold, in February Lee issued a general order that nonessential labor be scheduled for weekdays only, and that Sunday inspections avoid interrupting soldiers at worship.[72]

Small indulgences like this went a long way with his soldiers, who rewarded him with a host of nicknames in sign of affection: "Marse Robert," "Uncle Robert," and even the familial "Old Pap."[73] Fresh choruses of such greetings came when Longstreet's corps rejoined the army on April 22. "We had been absent seven months, but it seemed a year," wrote Longstreet's artillery chief E. P. Alexander. "Every one, officers & men, felt a keen personal delight in the re-union with our old comrades, & in the command of Gen. Lee." Lee honored them with a review on April 29, and they honored him, in turn, with an artillery salute. "The general reins up his horse, & bares his good gray head, & looks at us & we shout & cry & wave our battleflags," Alexander wrote in describing that reunion review, followed by "a wave of sentiment, such as can only come to large crowds in full sympathy." It seemed a holy moment, a renewed pledge of unwavering faith in their commander. In acts amounting to sacraments, the men clustered around him to touch his horse, the bridle and stirrups, even his boots, while tears welled in the general's eyes. An officer asked Lee's aide Venable if that expression of love did not make the general proud. "Not proud," Venable replied. "It awes him."[74]

On the eve of May Lee was himself more fatalistic than ever. "Our life in this world is of no value except to prepare us for a better," he told Mary as he awaited Grant's first move.[75] To the last there was no letup in his efforts. "I want for nothing but independence & peace to our distracted country," he wrote Mary on April 9, and spoke more emphatically with the president ten days later. "We have now but one thing to do; to establish our independence," he said. "We have no time for anything else."[76] Still, on April 30, with active operations surely just hours away, Lee returned a well-wisher's chicken sent to provide eggs, explaining that he would be in constant motion, and feared it might be injured during the campaign. Instead, he returned the bird hoping it could be put in a good run with others, "whereas with me he will have to be cooped up & have a dreadful time."[77] Given what he expected to come, Lee could have been speaking of himself and his army.

❧

Looking backward, Grant's rise in the war had something of the inexorable about it. By the end of 1863 there simply was no other Union commander with a record of success approaching his. At the same time, almost two years of disappointment in the field established that no Union commander in the East was likely to contain Lee. It was time to look elsewhere, as with Pope, for important as the West was strategically, the Confederacy could only be defeated *spiritually* in the East by beating Lee. By this point in the war, he *was* the Confederacy for Southern soldiers and civilians everywhere. Certainly Lincoln realized the gray chieftain's symbolic significance, and that taking Lee out of the war would knock the breath from the Confederacy everywhere.

Grant may not have grasped that quite yet, but in time he would. He spent March and April in a flurry of preparation. Now he had to formulate a spring plan for all Union forces. By mid-March it was still in embryo, but he knew he would direct that all forces act in concert to occupy Confederate armies and prevent one from reinforcing another. He advised his commanders to take more enemy territory if possible, but made it clear that defeating their field armies was "of vastly more importance." He also wanted his legions living off the country, easing pressure on the Federal commissary and increasing the burden on the foe's.[78]

He put Sherman in command of his old military division, and McPherson in command of Sherman's Army and Department of the Tennessee. Despite having an office in Washington, he made it clear that "I will not be there," but would be wherever he thought he was most needed.[79] He pored over maps showing the positions of Union forces across the country, studied the most recent returns of strength of the several armies, and revised his staff for the coming campaign. Rawlins remained as adjutant, with Bowers and the Seneca sachem Ely S. Parker, nicknamed "the Big Injun," as assistant adjutants, reflecting the increased paperwork of a general-in-chief. Among his aides he had the fertile-brained Comstock, Orville Babcock, Julia's brother Fred Dent, and Horace Porter, two military secretaries, and a smaller separate staff in Washington.

He also faced some liabilities of his new position. He would have to deal with some of the flotsam thrown up by a very politicized war. Lincoln had made influential political leaders into generals to bind their constituencies to the war effort. Some like Logan made first-rate commanders. Others like Frémont and McClernand were hopeless. To deal with them Grant gave them their orders, and then assigned senior officers of his choosing to "assist" them by handling their principal field operations, and sometimes one of his staff officers as well. He was already accustomed to dealing with Banks, and sent General

Hunter to make sure Banks obeyed his orders.[80] Grant bowed to Lincoln, allowing the expedition up the Red River and postponing Mobile, but expected small return.

Major General Franz Sigel, a hopeless incompetent who brought German-American votes and enlistments, commanded the Department of West Virginia. To get some use from him, Grant ordered him to enter the Shenandoah to take Staunton, destroy the railroad, and threaten Lee's left flank. When Sigel tried to communicate directly with Lincoln or a congressman rather than according to protocol, Grant immediately jerked him short. "It is time Gen. Sigel should learn to carry on his official correspondence through the proper channels," Grant told Halleck, making clear that it would not be tolerated in future.[81] He assigned Ord and other officers to "assist" by handling field operations while watching Sigel, and Babcock from his staff went to ensure no confusion about orders at Sigel's headquarters. Grant expected little. "If Sigel cant skin himself," he told Sherman, "he can hold a leg whilst some one else skins."[82]

Another liability was Major General Benjamin F. Butler, now commanding at Fort Monroe. While the Army of the Potomac made Lee's army its objective, Grant ordered Butler to send 30,000 men up the south side of the James toward Richmond, and assigned Major General William F. Smith and another general to take actual field command to keep Butler in the background. Should Grant push Lee into the defenses of Richmond, then the two Federal forces could unite or cooperate.[83] Grant sent Fred Dent to Butler's headquarters to ensure cooperation with Meade. It was a practical policy to make the best of a difficult situation.

No one needed to watch Sherman, and Grant left the campaign against Johnston entirely to him. Banks was to start as soon as possible and Butler and Sigel were to wait until Grant ordered them to move, by April 25 if ready. Again Sherman would decide for himself when to go. In the interest of security, Grant revealed his general plan of operations only to those who needed to know. Not forgetting the vital role played by Porter in his Mississippi operations, he also made early requests for cooperation from the navy for the move up the James.

Grant appeared at Meade's headquarters at Culpeper on March 24, pleased to see that the soldiers seemed happy with his coming.[84]

Meade was harder to read, and Grant was attuned to the difficulty of Meade's position. Grant's very presence could be taken as an implied criticism of Meade's past performance. He, too, had seen the press speculation that Grant would relieve him of his command. Fortunately Grant took pains to avert embarrassment, and issued orders through Meade himself, leaving as much as possible to his discretion. It was not an ideal situation, nor was Burnside's IX Corps reporting directly to Grant since it was not part of Meade's army, an organizational anomaly Grant ought to have redressed. Meade increasingly came to resent his position, but it was the right decision for Grant. Lee's was not just another Confederate army, and Lee was no ordinary general. Grant could trust Sherman against Johnston, and he knew that by this time defeating Lee virtually meant defeating the Confederacy. If Grant took the Army of Northern Virginia out of the war, it would end the rebellion itself. Grant was where he needed to be.

He also avoided going to Washington more than necessary, knowing that any appearance there generated rumor. For the first time he had to be conscious of personal security. A Confederate partisan raid on the Orange & Alexandria Railroad on April 14 narrowly missed bagging him on his way back from Washington. "I cannot move without it being known all over the country," he complained to Julia.[85]

On April 9 Grant outlined his matured plan to Meade. He would have preferred to move well south of Richmond, probably via the North Carolina coast, then advance inland near Lynchburg and approach Lee and Richmond from the southwest.[86] That meant abandoning his own supply line, but he had done that before. The plan resembled his earlier thought of launching a campaign out of east Tennessee into southwest Virginia and then onward. Such a move should force Lee to abandon northern Virginia to defend the capital, leaving it vulnerable to moves by Butler and any forces Grant assembled at Washington to move south. He concluded that such a move was too risky with an army he did not yet know, or for a nervous Washington that needed the security of a major army between it and the unpredictable Lee.

Grant understood that the North, having made him lieutenant general, expected him to confront Lee himself. "Lee's Army will be your objective point," he now told Meade. "Wherever Lee goes there you will go also."[87] Grant acknowledged that the campaign might end in laying siege to Richmond, and that they would aim to wind up south of the James to link with Butler.[88] By April 19 Grant hoped to give the signal to advance on April 30, but fresh rains forced postponement until May 1.[89] A few days later he set May 4 as the day, and there would be no more delays. "When I telegraph," he advised his commanders, "we will start rain or shine."[90] It was the worst possible moment to hear that Banks had failed already, his army defeated and sent in retreat on April 8. Grant had felt for nearly a year that Banks was a liability, and now suggested that his old friend Major General Joseph Reynolds replace him immediately, though political exigencies protected Banks for another month.[91]

Grant told Halleck that he would try to turn one or the other of Lee's flanks. Implicit was that he hoped to isolate Lee from Richmond and catch him in the open. But he also thought it possible that Lee would withdraw to Richmond's defenses without giving battle; in that case Grant would push forward and connect with Butler, both of them using the James River as a supply line. He knew the route he wanted to follow, but kept that even from Halleck, saying only that he wanted Butler and Meade to converge. He would launch with fifteen days' supplies, drawing enough from the land to stretch that to twenty-five, expecting to reach the James in that time. To be safe, he requested that a million rations be held on steamers ready to send where he might direct. He was prepared, it seemed, for everything, and anxious to begin.[92] "We are not yet off," he told Julia on April 30. "I am impatient to be off."[93]

On May 1 he thanked Lincoln for nearly three years of support. Should he fail, he told the president, "the least I can say is, the fault is not with you."[94] Next day he wrote his last letter to Julia. "I know the greatest anxiety is now felt in the North for the success of this move," he told her. He felt unperturbed by the enormous responsibility, then added that he only lost his presence of mind in the company of ladies, when "I know I must appear like a fool."[95]

The next evening Meade's legions began crossing the Rapidan River. Within a matter of hours Grant would know if Lee intended to fight.[96]

Lee's boyhood home Stratford Hall in Westmoreland County, which he always dreamed of recovering for his family. *Library of Congress*

One of Lee's several boyhood homes, his uncle William Fitzhugh's house at 607 Oronoco Street in Alexandria. Just visible at the left is the Benjamin Hallowell house where Lee attended classes in 1825. *Library of Congress*

The Custis home, Arlington House, where Lee wooed and married Mary Custis, shown in a wartime image. More than any other place, Arlington was "home" to Lee. *Library of Congress*

The earliest known photograph believed to be of Robert E. Lee, taken circa 1845–1846 in New York, with his son "Rooney" at his side. He was not quite forty years old. *Virginia Historical Society*

Lieutenant Lee's first assignment was initial construction of what became Fort Pulaski near Savannah, Georgia. *Library of Congress*

Mary Anna Randolph Custis Lee, circa 1845, with the Lees' youngest, Robert Jr. *Virginia Historical Society, Richmond, VA*

The man who more than any other helped influence and make Lee as a soldier, Major General Winfield Scott was virtually a surrogate father to him. *Library of Congress*

Lee's father-in-law, George Washington Parke Custis, who left him the unenviable task of saving the plantations and managing the slaves' ultimate emancipation. *Library of Congress*

Lieutenant Colonel Lee circa 1852 when he was superintendent at West Point. The uniform was added in 1861. *Library of Congress*

The slave pen at Alexandria where the captured runaway Arlington slaves were held until Lee had them whipped. *Library of Congress*

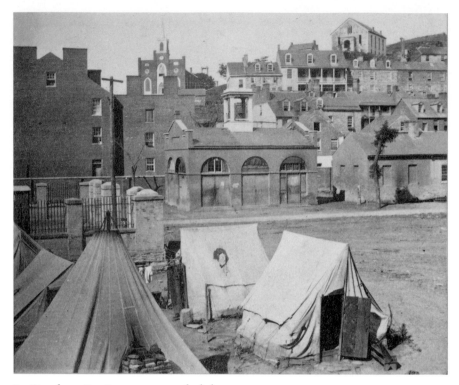

In October 1859 Lee commanded the company of marines who stormed this engine house at Harpers Ferry to capture John Brown and his raiders. *Library of Congress*

Before Lee could sit for a photographer after taking command of Virginia forces, someone doctored his West Point photo to add a uniform and a hat with "VA." *Library of Congress*

Lee built an excellent working relationship with President Jefferson Davis in spite of the Mississippian's prickly and sometimes obstinate nature. *Library of Congress*

Lieutenant General Thomas J. "Stonewall" Jackson became Lee's right hand until his mortal wounding at Chancellorsville, days after this image was made. *Library of Congress*

Lee's middle son, "Rooney," became an able cavalry general in his own right, and a source of much concern when he was wounded and a prisoner of war. *Library of Congress*

Vannerson's late-1864 portrait of Lee, probably his finest standing pose, with sash and presentation sword. Lee's famous perfect posture is manifest. *Library of Congress*

Lee thought his best wartime portraits were taken in early 1864 in Richmond by Julian Vannerson. *Library of Congress*

The table on which Lee signed the surrender terms proposed by Grant at Appomattox. *Library of Congress*

After Appomattox Lee returned to his family's home on Franklin Street in Richmond. He arrived April 15, two days before this image was made. From its window he watched Union soldiers marching past. *Library of Congress*

A few days later Mathew Brady brought his camera to Franklin Street to capture the old warrior, defiance still in his tired eyes, in his last photos as a Confederate general. *Library of Congress*

Lee was fifty-eight years old and not in good health, but still robust. Beside him is his son Custis at left, and adjutant Walter Taylor at right. *Library of Congress*

Lee did not like posing for the camera, even in good times, and always appeared stiff and formal. *Library of Congress*

The new president of Washington College, Lee in February 1866, and aging rapidly. *Library of Congress*

Lee's old friend and sometime rival,
General Joseph E. Johnston at left with Lee in April
1870, when Johnston was working on his memoirs,
and Lee had given up on his. *Library of Congress*

OPPOSITE ABOVE: The official dedication of Arlington National Cemetery
on May 30, 1868. Grant sits partially visible on the platform at center, later
to be somewhat apprehensive that he might be buried on Lee's old estate.
Just the day before, Grant accepted the Republican nomination for the
presidency, closing his acceptance with the words, "Let us have peace."
Library of Congress

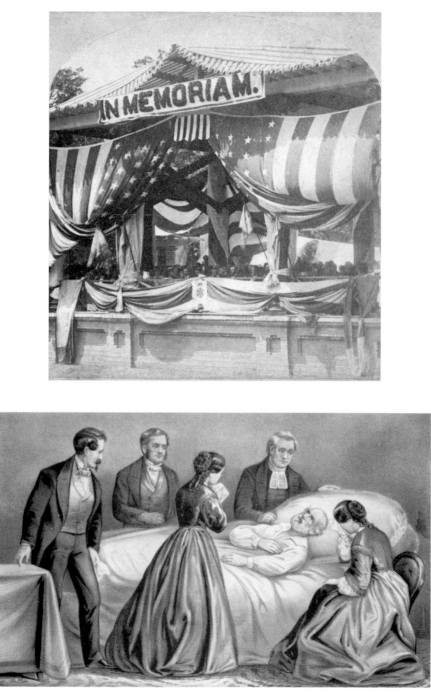

Currier and Ives created a print of Lee's death that suggested his apotheosis into sainthood. *Library of Congress*

The saint in his shrine. Recumbent of Lee by Edward Valentine in the chapel at Washington and Lee University in Lexington, Virginia. *Library of Congress*

On May 29, 1890, a crowd estimated at ten thousand gathered in Richmond for the unveiling of the Lee monument, an indelible link with the city, Confederacy, and Lost Cause memory. *U.S. Army Military History Institute, Carlisle, PA*

Rarely in history were two combatants more evenly matched. Both looked to preparation, careful planning, and especially supply to frame victories, yet remained ready on the instant to capitalize on unanticipated exigency. Both preferred the indirect approach and surprise to frontal combat. Both sought to follow up victory by pressing the foe for further gain, and more important, each reacted to unexpected setbacks with quick thinking and opportunism to regain initiative. Their views were hardly identical, and their personalities scarcely intersected, yet if ever they had fought side by side there would have been instant harmony. In most respects Grant enjoyed advantages in manpower and wherewithal; Lee had the benefit of acting on the defensive, an intimate knowledge of the men and officers of his army that he had molded for nearly two years, a tradition of victory, and his knowledge of the ground. Now both found themselves in a way pushed beyond their experience. Grant was not taking a bastion from an immobile foe, or using a river to push his advance, and he scarcely knew the Army of the Potomac as yet. Flowing northwest to southeast, Virginia's rivers offered Lee one line of defense after another, and Grant must force each crossing. For his part, a weaker Lee could only react to the enemy's first moves and then seize opportunities for counterstrokes; at Second Manassas and Chancellorsville he had shown just how devastating he could be. Grant's optimism and overconfidence might afford just such a chance. His days of being taken by surprise were done, but he reacted faster to the unexpected than anyone Lee had faced.

Grant was forty-two and Lee fifty-seven, Grant at the peak of health and energy, while Lee feared his weakening body and lagging faculties. Each was defending his notion of home. Grant by now was the most popular man in the Union, arguably more so even than Lincoln. Lee was easily the most important man in the Confederacy, his popularity and influence, had he chosen to use it, far outstripping Davis's. Unquestionably, they were at this moment the preeminent military figures in America, and arguably the world. All those past years of youth and education and experience brought them to this, along with chance and shifting fortune. Moreover, they embodied a mixture of the realities and aspirations of their respective causes, and America itself.

Grant was part of a generation that had been styled "Young America," the "go ahead" generation. Trade and industry and the spread of the free capital market that characterized the North were all in his blood, and framed his belief in the future of his country. Born in Ohio, matured in Missouri and then Illinois, he was at home anywhere Julia was, and he could just as well envision moving to California or even Mexico, his horizons limitless. For him the nation had been always a nation, not a confederation. For him civil war held few dangers of having to fight his own blood. If his name opened no doors as he grew to manhood, neither did it hold him with bonds. He was the self-made man, risen by his own talent and energy, and not a little good fortune. For all that his earlier enterprises had failed, through little agency of his own, he never lost his expectation of success. Now history put him in a position where those qualities could launch him. He had found the one thing he could do better than anyone else.

Alexis de Tocqueville, the French visitor who in his *Democracy in America* asked, "who is this new man, this American?" spoke of Grant and his kind, not Lee, for Lee was no new man. He typified both the reality and the cherished ideals of the Old South. His was a *name*, even if a little tarnished. He was tradition and sense of place. The idea of Lee living anywhere but Virginia was unthinkable; his horizons always were the Potomac, the Appalachians, the Chesapeake, and that North Carolina that he would not wish on a friend. No wonder that dear though the Union was to him, the Old Dominion was dearer. His network of extended family relations and alliances virtually guaranteed that he could never hope to avoid raising his sword against family if he accepted the command offered by Scott and Lincoln. He believed that slavery, even if an evil, was the best way for blacks to live amid white society.

Still, there was much in them that spoke for America as a whole. They both supported expansion. They both believed in a central government stronger than the old Jeffersonian ideal, though Lee had backed away some degree in his middle age. Each regarded representative democracy as a superior form for that government to take, differing only in their views of who should have the vote; Grant favored universal male suffrage, while Lee felt uneasy about even all classes of whites voting. When it came to this conflict, however, they were firmly united. This was a people's war. All the people had a stake in it. All the people had an obligation to put their hearts and wealth and blood into it. All would find their futures indelibly shaped by it.

Grant and Lee became commanders not by blood or accident of birth, or by favoritism and politics. A great general in history is often defined less by the battles he wins than by the defeats he can survive. Grant earned his chance at Lee by victories and demonstrated command capabilities that sustained him in spite of surprise at Shiloh and the embarrassment of Holly Springs. Lee deserved to be here about to meet him thanks to outstanding service in Mexico, his skill in building a new Confederate army from almost nothing, and a keener insight than any other general's into how the underdog had to approach this war. Serving under hesitant and inadequate superiors opened the door for Grant to rise, but even when viewed against the whole range of senior commanders in the first two years of the war, Grant still stood out by his energy and ability. As long as Lee kept beating the men Lincoln sent against him, Grant's turn at facing him was predestined. The accident of Joseph E. Johnston's wounding gave Lee command when it did, but Davis had already considered relieving him of his command; he would have sooner or later, when he could take no more of that general's insubordination and milquetoast leadership. Whenever that happened, Lee would be there, the only logical alternative.

And now everything depended upon them and what happened when they met again. Lee meant to contest every foot of ground. Grant meant to show Lee something new: a Federal army that did not turn back. The world was watching as America sat poised to leap forward to define the next century and more of Western culture. Grant and Lee were about to define what sort of nation America would become.

As the sun set just before seven o'clock on the evening of May 4, 1864, a thousand cook fires dotted the fields and woods south of the Rapidan. The armies did not need the fires for warmth; the temperature was still above 50 degrees when the men lay down for the fitful night ahead.[97] Rather, the blazes cooked rations and lent cheer to legions facing the unknown.

Two of those fires, away from the rest and ten miles apart, gave hot meals and perhaps cheer to two men in particular. They had met before, sixteen years ago in Mexico. They were a study in contrasts.

All that morning blue-clad soldiers waded the Rapidan at Germanna Ford. About midday something of an apparition rode across and up to a house just beyond, dismounted, and stepped onto the porch. He sat and wrote a telegram to go back to Washington: "The crossing of Rapidan effected."[98] With his mind on more important things than punctuation, he signed it "U S Grant Lt Genl." Then the general commanding all the armies of the United States watched rank upon rank of lean veterans march past him to their bivouacs, part of an army of 120,000.

At that moment General Ulysses S. Grant was a contradiction. Among the many things for which he was known by now, simplicity ranked high. He cared little for the pomp of war. On this day, however, he all but gleamed in finery. In place of the usual private's blouse he wore a blue frock coat with double rows of gleaming brass buttons grouped in threes, the only coat of its kind in the United States. His worn shoes or muddy boots were gone, replaced by polished black knee-length boots, his trousers neatly tucked into their tops. Despite disliking gloves, he wore new yellow ones matching the yellow sash around his waist, while a black felt hat with gold cord perched uneasily on his head. Like many officers, he thought a sword a clumsy nuisance, but a polished presentation saber hung at his side.

Grant in elegant dress was a rare sight even in Washington. In the army itself it ranked as a matter of wonder. Today he felt the occasion called for it, and because this army, still largely unknown to him, needed to think he looked like a general. He and they were about to contend with a legend made flesh. Perhaps Grant hoped his opponent would remember him this time. If so, the sense of occasion did not extend beyond his person. When he dismounted, everyone saw that he rode the same old saddle that for more than two years had carried him from victory to victory.

The rest of that day he stayed near the house, pleased at progress, but far from smug about what lay ahead. That evening he smoked cigars and talked until bedtime with his officers, some of whom felt uncertain that he was the right man for them. Instead of using the house, he slept in his tent; instead of a soft bed, he used a cot. Once he took off the finery Grant became again what he always was: a simple man of complex instincts. The man commanding half a million men across the continent washed in a tin basin precariously balanced on a tripod, with nothing more than a pine table and two folding camp chairs for furniture. Despite his almost meteoric rise, no one ever mistook Grant for a patrician.

That could never be said of the man at that other campfire more than a dozen road miles west of Germanna Ford at Verdiersville. Lee embodied the Confederacy to millions of its soldiers and civilians by 1864. He was not just *a* Virginian; he was *the* Virginian. Unlike Grant, he could never be a face in the crowd. From youth he never looked anything but a man intended by nature to lead, the envy of all who served with him, surely destined to become the finest soldier of the land. On him a formal uniform was a second skin, not because he loved finery but because it is what he was born to wear.

On this night any sense of occasion manifested itself not in his finest uniform, but in the preparations he had been making for more than two years as he faced one Union general after another. All that day he sent and received telegrams and hand-carried messages as he picked his ground for the contest to come, tried to divine Grant's intentions, and shifted legions approaching 70,000 strong, an army that revered him above all men. At nightfall he, too, sat by a fire in front of his tent, though the owners of a nearby house would gladly have given up their parlor and a bedroom for General Lee. His was a soldier's simplicity, as he sought to live in a manner that proclaimed to his soldiers, whose wisdom he did not always trust, that he was one of them, even if a general. Yet inside his tent visitors saw a marked contrast with Grant's. If Lee did not live in luxury, still he had a folding iron bed with at least something of a mattress, and more furniture than Grant. Lee's boots were always polished, his frock coat always an officer's, even if the elbows were worn. If outwardly he showed only the three stars of a Confederate colonel on his lapel, his general's insignia was still there beneath the lapel, immediately visible if he turned up his collar. Where Grant was a common man most comfortable as a common man, Lee was a patrician who knew the value of not flaunting his station.

Late into that evening messages from other legends came to Lee's campfire: words of encouragement from President Jefferson Davis and General "Jeb" Stuart's report that Grant's army was across the Rapidan, in the area near the scene of Lee's greatest victory at Chancellorsville, which all Virginians knew as The Wilderness. By fire's glow Lee read dispatches warning that other Union forces were advancing from east, northwest, and southwest into Virginia. He knew their goal was to cooperate with Grant to contain and then demolish his army, and he could not stop them all. Lesser Confederate commands must deal with them, for Grant was the main threat, and somehow Lee must stop him. If the mood was anticipation around that other headquarters fire that night, there was resignation at Verdiersville. Lee had been here before, not only in this situation but in this place, but never in as much peril. In the morning he would begin to learn just how much.

They had met once before. In a few hours they were about to give each other their undivided attention. Both would remember it this time.

Two days earlier Grant told Burnside that he intended to try first to get around Lee's right flank by crossing the Rapidan River between the Confederates and Fredericksburg; he hoped to force a retreat, which would give him a chance of an inside track to Richmond.[99] That meant Meade's army would pass through The Wilderness. Despite Hooker's experience, Grant seemed unconcerned about the terrain, probably because he half expected Lee not to fight. If he gained a one-day jump on Lee, he could be through The Wilderness and on better ground. Unfortunately, Grant was trying to funnel too many soldiers and supply wagons through too small an aperture. Late on May 4 two corps halted around Chancellorsville and Wilderness Tavern to wait for their supplies and much of their artillery. Worse, Grant and Meade failed to block the two roads leading into The Wilderness from the west.

Lee did not ignore those roads, though he was also negligent by having no units at the Rapidan fords to slow enemy crossings and buy time for him to get his army in motion. Hence, he rushed to catch up. "The long threatened effort to take Richmond has begun," he wrote Davis.[100] He put Ewell and Hill on those two roads, and started Longstreet in the same direction. On the morning of May 5 Grant told Meade to pitch into the enemy "if any opportunity presents," but Ewell opened the fight first when he collided with the Yankees west of Wilderness Tavern.[101]

What followed was so confused that neither commander had a full picture of the situation, or an appreciation of enemy strength, and nei-

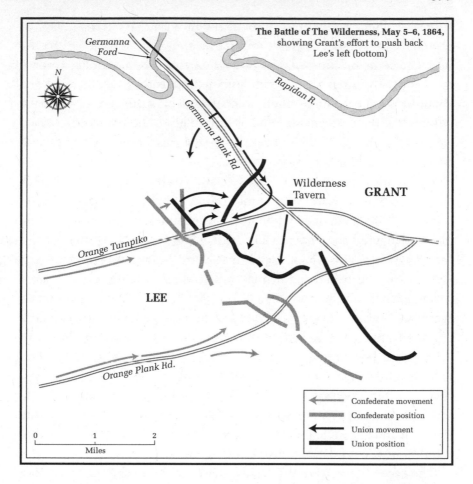

The Battle of The Wilderness, May 5–6, 1864, showing Grant's effort to push back Lee's left (bottom)

ther exerted real control. It became a series of isolated engagements in which the Confederates checked Union progress that day without gaining or losing much ground. Lee hurried Longstreet toward the scene all day, hoping to have him in line by morning to drive Meade's left away from the road to Germanna Ford, cutting the Federal line of communications and isolating him in The Wilderness. Yet again Lee reacted to the unexpected by seeking to turn it to his advantage. Failing that, he determined to strike Meade's left flank and push him across the Rapidan if possible.[102]

Grant struck first with a predawn attack on May 6 that almost crumpled Hill's corps on the Confederate right near Lee's headquarters. As Hill's line gave way, Lee rushed on foot and horseback to retreating groups trying to rally them, some thought with tears in his eyes. Just then he saw Longstreet arrive to send his brigades into the collapsing line. Lee came on the Texas brigade and broke his customary reserve to cheer them, then tried to ride just behind as they advanced, some thinking that he yelled for them to charge. Seeing the general about to risk his life, the veterans shouted at him to go to the rear, and grasped his horse's reins to lead him back, where he met Longstreet again and continued sending in reinforcements.[103]

By late morning both sides paused, and Grant sent word to Halleck that "there is no decisive result, but I think all things are progressing favorably."[104] That changed when Longstreet attacked Meade's left flank and endangered the Federals until their line held. Then friendly fire hit Longstreet, and Major General Richard H. Anderson took over. By evening the exhausted armies bivouacked virtually on the same ground where the fighting began the day before. "We can claim no victory," Grant reported to Halleck, but "neither have they gained a single advantage."[105] In fact, both commanders gained something. An ill-prepared Lee stalled Meade's advance, and delay worked to Confederate advantage. Despite underestimating the obstacle The Wilderness presented, Meade stood his ground and Grant did not fight and fall back like his predecessors. He consciously intended to show the Army of the Potomac that there was a different regime now: one that would give it confidence in itself and in him.[106]

The casualties in The Wilderness had been daunting, approaching 20,000 for Grant and 11,000 for Lee.[107] The armies rested the next day, while Grant reacted typically. Stopped in his advance, he abandoned attacking Lee frontally and decided to shift Meade eastward toward Spotsylvania Court House to get around the Confederate eastern flank and put the army between Lee and Richmond, and closer to the junction with Butler. As usual, he made no detailed plans for his route, leaving himself free to adapt from day to day.[108] When they saw that they were moving on south and not back toward the Rappahannock as so often before, Union veterans cheered Grant for the first time. Lee ably read the shift of pontoon bridges from Germanna Ford eastward to Ely's Ford as a sign that the Federals were heading toward Spotsylvania or Fredericksburg, and ordered Stuart to reconnoiter the roads he might use either to meet the Federal advance, or to get around

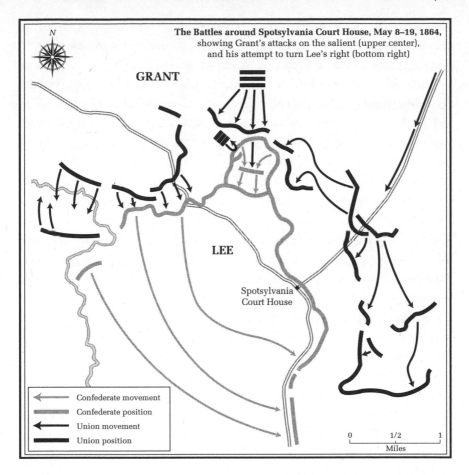

The Battles around Spotsylvania Court House, May 8–19, 1864, showing Grant's attacks on the salient (upper center), and his attempt to turn Lee's right (bottom right)

GRANT

LEE

Spotsylvania
Court House

Confederate movement
Confederate position
Union movement
Union position

0   1/2   1
Miles

Meade's flank.[109] By the evening of May 7 Lee had Anderson in motion to get to Spotsylvania first.[110]

The Yankees' leading elements were within three miles of Spotsylvania by eight that morning, but Anderson's got there first. Hours passed as both sides brought up more units. Meade launched a limited assault late in the afternoon to try to push Anderson out of the way, but nothing came of it. Adding to Lee's concerns now, Hill reported himself too ill to command. That meant two corps commanders lost in three days. Anderson had never exercised such command before, and Early only temporarily, while Ewell was already erratic at best. Indeed, a few weeks earlier Early had been under arrest after making a remark that Ewell found offensive, and Lee had to take the time to make peace between them so he could release Early to replace Hill temporarily.[111] Still, Confederate resistance that day persuaded Grant not to advance on May 9, though that did not mean he would be idle.[112] He promised Halleck, "I shall take no backward step."[113]

Instead, he reverted to the expedient that served him so well in the Vicksburg campaign, a cavalry raid around Lee's army to draw away Stuart, and then ride south destroying anything of use to the enemy. He did not have Colonel Benjamin Grierson with him, but still he had the man for the job. Philip H. Sheridan was a mere quartermaster on Halleck's staff in 1862 when Grant first met him near Corinth. They met again at Chattanooga where Sheridan, now commanding a division, stormed Missionary Ridge. Grant saw in him something he liked, and brought him east, not as an infantryman, but to command Meade's cavalry. It seemed an unwise move so far, for Sheridan mishandled his troopers from the first, but he had an attribute that Grant valued. He was ruthless, his determination rivaling Grant's.

Sheridan had 10,000 horsemen ready within hours and left on May 9. That night they reached the North Anna River, and the next day cut the Virginia Central Railroad, broke up ten miles of track, destroyed rolling stock and supplies, and moved on to the South Anna River. Stuart followed with less than half their number, and on May 11 came up with them at Yellow Tavern ten miles north of Richmond. In the engagement Stuart fell with a mortal wound, and Sheridan rode on to threaten Richmond before he passed around the east side of the capital, then turned north to cross the James at White House in sight of Rooney Lee's plantation. By the last week of May he was back above the North Anna. Grant had hoped Sheridan's raid would create a grand diversion in Lee's rear and destroy the Confederate cavalry. It failed to do either, but Stuart's death was a hard blow to Lee. "I grieve the loss of our gallant officers," he wrote Mary. "A more zealous, ardent, brave & devoted soldier than Stuart, the Confederacy cannot have."[114]

Meanwhile, Lee built formidable earthworks, and on May 8 Grant launched his first attack. This was the beginning of a series of battles that continued for ten days, the longest sustained engagement of the war to date. He tried to turn Lee's left, and briefly succeeded on May 10, but then learned of large numbers of Confederates shifting toward the danger. As he did at Fort Donelson, Grant reasoned that his flank attack had compelled Lee to weaken his line elsewhere. A concerted attack on Lee's center might split the enemy army and open the road to Spotsylvania and the James. When Grant's attack went forward, Lee's veterans and his excellent defenses repulsed it handily. Reporting that the fighting to date largely favored the Federals, for the first time Grant admitted that the campaign might not go as quickly as he had hoped, telling Stanton and Halleck that "I propose to fight it out on this line if it takes all summer."[115]

The Federals spent the next day preparing an attack on three sides of a salient in Lee's line, and on May 12 it drove back Lee's line in bitter combat, leading Grant to report that the foe "seem to have found the last ditch."[116] Once again in the heaviest of the fight Lee tried to lead an assault to stem the attack, and once more officers and men grasped his bridle and pushed his horse's flanks to turn him around, accompanied by cries of "Lee to the rear."[117] Tardy corps commanders frustrated Grant, and he briefly considered relieving one on the spot. He did not appreciate that this army had never seen fighting like this. By May 12 it had been in action six out of eight days, often against strong defenses, and not in the sort of open countryside Grant knew from Mississippi. Still, he felt pleased with Meade, and their relationship appeared to be working, in part because Grant scrupulously refrained from issuing orders to anyone in the Army of the Potomac except Meade himself. He advised Stanton that Meade and Sherman "are the fittest officers for large commands I have come in contact with."[118]

Lee was tiring, and reacted slowly when Grant shifted two corps from the right to the left of his line, hoping to turn Lee's right flank and push him away from Spotsylvania. Severe rain slowed the Federals long enough for Lee to shift his own lines in response. For the next three days both armies endured the rain with no major action, but Lee enjoyed positive gains when Major General John C. Breckinridge drove Sigel out of the Shenandoah Valley. That allowed Lee to summon Breckinridge and a few thousand infantry to him. Meanwhile, Beauregard had isolated Butler in a bend of the James from which he could not escape, meaning he would not be there to meet Grant if or when he arrived. Instead of holding legs, Sigel and Butler had been skinned. "He will do nothing but run," Halleck said of Sigel when he informed Grant of the defeat at New Market. "He never did anything else." All Halleck said for Butler was "dont rely on him."[119]

Lee addressed his army on May 14 hoping to boost its morale, citing all of the Yankee setbacks thus far. He even fudged in the interest of morale by calling Sheridan's return ride from the outskirts of Richmond a repulse. "The heroic valor of this Army, under the blessing of Almighty God has thus far checked the progress of the principal Army of the enemy," he congratulated them. "Your country looks to you in your gallant struggle with confidence and hope." Every man now must "resolve to put forth his utmost efforts to endure all and brave all, until by the assistance of a just and merciful God the enemy shall be driven back." They could win independence, he declared, and win "the admiration of mankind."[120]

If Grant was to best that determination, he must do it on his own, and now he had a fair idea of how difficult it would be. He agreed with Lee about the eyes of the globe. "The world has never seen so bloody or so protracted a battle as the one being fought and I hope never will again," he wrote Julia. "To loose this battle they loose their cause," he added. "As bad as it is they have fought for it with a gallantry worthy of a better."[121]

15

"A MERE QUESTION OF TIME."

"WE ARE STILL hanging about Spotsylvania C. H.," Grant wrote Julia on May 19. He had a plan to maneuver Lee out of his works, and as usual expressed confidence that his army could defeat Lee's "with one arm tied but as the two armies now stand we have both Arms bound."[1] Before he could set the plan in motion, however, Lee struck Meade's right flank such a blow that Grant delayed the advance. Once it launched, Lee withdrew to the south bank of the North Anna River, to defenses he had hoped to use before the battle at Fredericksburg. Just below the railroad crossing of the North Anna River the Virginia Central Railroad joined the Richmond & Fredericksburg at Hanover Junction, bringing the capital's rail connection with the Shenandoah Valley. "I should have preferred contesting the enemy's approach inch by inch," Lee reported to the president, but concern for Richmond impelled him to pull back.[2]

Grant and Meade soon followed, but not before Breckinridge arrived from the valley, and more Confederate reinforcements arrived from the James River where Butler was bottled up. It looked on paper like a classic concentration, smaller commands stopping or defeating the enemy's peripheral threats, then joining the main army to face Grant. "Whatever route he pursues," Lee informed Davis, "I am in a position to move against him." He suggested that if Beauregard, commanding the forces containing Butler, could possibly leave a minimum there for that task and bring the rest of his command, the two of them might unite and possibly crush Grant. "If it is possible to combine," he said, "I think it will succeed."[3] One benefit of pulling back was that Lee shortened his own supply line and lengthened Grant's. Writing to Mary, he added that "I begrudge every step he makes towards Richmond."[4]

Unfortunately, there was trouble in his army. Though Hill felt well enough to resume command of his corps, the mercurial Ewell approached collapse, while severe diarrhea virtually prostrated Lee, dulling his senses and forcing him to ride in a buggy. He remained indisposed until the end of the month, and his surgeon told him to drink wine to settle his stomach, which may have impaired his thinking a little more.[5] Somehow, Lee or Hill was careless and left an upstream ford ill protected. When the Federals arrived two corps were able to move up the right bank and push across, brushing aside Hill's tardy and inadequate defense. The next morning when Lee drove to see Hill, his foul mood was evident as he gave the corps commander a rare upbraiding in front of others.[6]

The Yankee crossing allowed them to cut the Virginia Central and then move down on Lee's left flank. That forced him to "refuse," or bend, his left back to face the threat, while confronting Burnside at the river. Another Federal corps had easily taken the Richmond & Fredericksburg bridge and were able to cross and force Lee to refuse his right flank as well. Then, however, little happened. Grant had moved quickly, as usual, only to find that he had moved too fast, and now his forces were spread in a wide arc and scattered on both sides of the river. If Lee were able to concentrate against one of his flanks, reinforcements from the other would have to cross to the north side, march more than a mile, then cross again to the south side to reach the other flank. Meanwhile, after Hill's recent performance, Lee apparently failed to trust Hill to strike effectively, or was himself too ill to think through a response to the opportunity Grant presented. Realizing his vulnerability, Grant corrected his mistake and on May 26 and 27 concentrated instead on tearing up the track of the two railroads.

By this time Grant's army was barely twenty miles from Richmond, and once again he attempted to sidestep Lee by shifting his columns south and east around Lee's right flank toward Old Cold Harbor, where Sheridan's cavalry awaited. Grant wanted to be there by June 1, but his legions slowed down, after almost a month of marching and fighting. The machine was grinding toward a stall, while casualties disrupted company and regimental headquarters. Grant always knew this was a risk, but still believed that the army's stamina would be fed by pride in its performance thus far. "Fighting, hard knocks only, could have accomplished the work," he would say soon afterward, yet even in his own headquarters the fatigue told.[7] For one thing, he was never more overconfident than now, though he had some cause. Captured Confederates looked like beaten men, their uniforms ragged, their shoes in tatters, and many of them malnourished. "Lees Army is really whipped," he told Halleck on May 26; "the actions of his Army shows it unmistakeably." Lee would not meet him in the open field, while Grant saw his own men marching and attacking with a new morale. "I may be mistaken," he said, "but I feel that our success over Lees Army is already insured."[8]

While Meade marched toward Cold Harbor, Grant directed that General Smith and the XVIII Corps be detached from Butler's stymied army and transported by boats to White House on the Pamunkey River, where they began arriving May 30. Lee raced to counter but Ewell had come down with diarrhea and handed his corps over to Early, a transfer that Lee sought diplomatically to make permanent. Fearful of losing his command, Ewell protested that he would soon return, but Lee told him he could not change corps commanders while the army was in almost daily action, something that in fact he had done at least four times in the past month. Ewell refused to take the hint and kept pressing, then took his case to the president, who sent him back to a painful conversation in which Lee obliquely, but unmistakably, made it clear that he had lost confidence in the general. It was the closest thing to a face-to-face dismissal of a senior officer Lee would perform in the war.[9]

By early June when the combatants reformed between the Chickahominy River and Totopotomoy Creek, neither army functioned well from the top down. Grant and Meade, already on ground unfamiliar, conducted haphazard reconnaissance. Not only was Lee's top command in flux after four changes of corps command in as many weeks, but division and brigade commanders fumbled assignments. When Lee sought to take the initiative on June 1, his designs collapsed, and the best he could do was entrench in a strong position with the two streams guarding his flanks. Grant had scarcely enough information at the end of the day's fighting to know its result. "The rebels are making a desperate fight," he wrote Julia that evening. "How long it will last is a problem," he told her. "I can hardly hope to get through this month."[10]

Grant planned a major assault for the afternoon of June 2, but postponed it until four-thirty on the morning of June 3 to give the men rest from the heat. Unfortunately, once again neither he nor Meade reconnoitered Lee's line with care, relying on anecdotal reports that led them to think that the portion of the Confederate line they would attack was not held in depth. As a result, when the assault jumped off on time on June 3, the Federals struck an enemy line heavily reinforced by Breckinridge, and well entrenched. Lee exerted almost no influence on the fight, being behind the lines ill at his tent. This was no battle of maneuver, but the simplest and most direct kind of attack and defense. In an hour of brutal assaults, the Yankees briefly broke through before being turned back, and then kept a tenuous grasp on positions in places barely fifty yards from the enemy works. Early that afternoon Grant did not yet appreciate the extent of his bloodying, dismissing it by wiring Halleck that "our loss was not severe."[11] Shortly after noon, when Meade's corps commanders declared that another assault would fail, Grant suspended the action.

Lee had Malvern Hill and Gettysburg and now Grant had Cold Harbor. He had not ordered a frontal assault since the early days at Vicksburg a year before. Doing so now represented a culmination of factors. The campaign was dragging, and summer heat and humidity allied themselves with Lee. Temperatures ran consistently in the eighties, and recently spiked into the nineties.[12] That sapped his soldiers' flagging energy. He wanted to be south of the James with a new base established on that river in time to uncork Butler and move against Petersburg and Richmond with a full campaign season ahead. At Cold Harbor for the first time Lee stood in a position that offered no opportunity for a flanking movement. Grant must either strike him head on or stop in his tracks. The only other alternative was to pull back, and he had sworn to himself and to Washington that he would not retreat. He had to make the effort, but in his own fatigue and his anxiety to keep moving, he had been careless. Grant later claimed that he regretted ordering that assault at Cold Harbor. The cost had been brutal, indeed, as over the next few days reports indicated more than 7,000 casualties. A higher price may have been the hesitation some senior officers felt from then on about making vigorous assaults against defended positions.

Still, Grant gained something. Five weeks of bludgeoning produced no victory and really no defeat since Grant always either held his ground or left it to advance farther. Yet he was now poised barely ten miles northeast of Richmond and just two days' march from the James. Generations later Winston Churchill, another warrior with intimate experience of winning and losing, quipped that "success is going from one failure to the next with no loss of enthusiasm." Stymied, Grant rested the army for a few days and then implemented a plan he had in mind all along. A position northeast of Richmond was impractical and difficult to supply. "My idea from the start has been to beat Lee's army, if possible, North of Richmond," he told Halleck, and then to transfer his army south of the James and move against Richmond from below, better supplied via steamers on the river and reinforced by Butler. Then he would steadily cut off the enemy capital and Lee's army from all sources of supply and communications.[13] Unless that movement brought on a fight, he reckoned the rest of the campaign would be a siege, which he would avoid if he could, but accept if he must.[14] Lee had sensed the same eventuality for some weeks. "We must destroy this army of Grant's before he gets to the James River," he told Early in May. "If he gets there it will become a siege, and then it will be a mere question of time."[15]

Grant "got there." Commencing after dark on June 12, Meade's army stealthily left its positions and marched by night east then south toward Wilcox's Landing on the James, the first elements arriving late in the afternoon June 13. The crossing began the next day by ferries, and meanwhile engineers built a 2,100-foot-long pontoon bridge in just eight hours. By June 16 Grant had four army corps on the south side of the James, with another transported down the York and up the James to land in support of Butler. And Lee had no idea what had happened. In fact, the day the Yankees began pulling out of their lines, Lee was feeling more confident than for some days, since he had Grant where he thought the enemy could not move. A Confederate surgeon who saw him that day found him cheerful and confident. "I have never seen Gen. Lee look more tranquil or cheerful than he does at present," he wrote. "Until I see anxiety and restlessness manifested in our great leader I shall be perfectly satisfied that all is going well."[16]

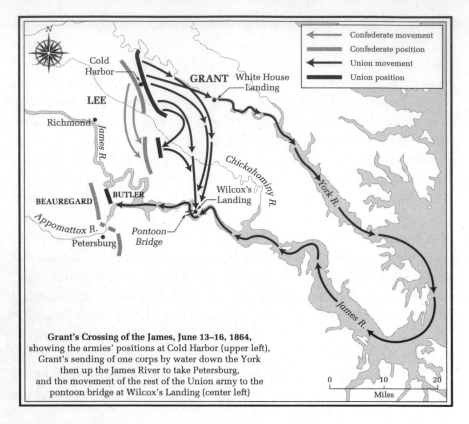

Grant's Crossing of the James, June 13–16, 1864,
showing the armies' positions at Cold Harbor (upper left),
Grant's sending of one corps by water down the York
then up the James River to take Petersburg,
and the movement of the rest of the Union army to the
pontoon bridge at Wilcox's Landing (center left)

Within hours that anxiety would be there to be seen. Lee discovered the Yankees' departure on the morning of June 13, when advance Union elements were already just miles from the James. By noon the next day Lee suspected Grant might be intending to cross the James, but thought it just as likely that he would go into the old fortifications at Harrison's Landing left by McClellan two years before and assume the defensive. Still, he also suspected that Grant might send some force directly up the James to try to take the transportation and industrial hub at Petersburg.[17] A few hours later he felt sure that Petersburg was the target, but even then hesitated and kept the main army in place throughout June 15, by which time the crossing was already well under way.[18]

In fact, by that time Petersburg had almost fallen. General Smith got there with his corps that afternoon and heavily outnumbered the scant 3,000 Confederates in his way, but he stalled, then launched an

attack that broke through and promised Petersburg as his for the taking until he stopped to await reinforcements. They came too late and
Smith postponed the attack until the following day. Then Grant and
Meade arrived with two full corps and attacked that evening, but the
defenders were reinforced, and though outnumbered more than three
to one, held their ground. More attacks on June 17 were turned back,
and when Grant ordered a maximum effort the morning of June 18
with close to 100,000 men on hand, Lee was coming into the defenses
before him. That afternoon Grant launched one more attack, but his
men were tired and uneasy about going against earthworks, and headquarters was too rushed to properly reconnoiter and coordinate their
efforts. Grant was satisfied that all that could be done had been. A
magnificent opportunity was lost by a matter of hours, but he still had
the upper hand; his supply line via the James was secure and he could
start spreading his left gradually south and westward to begin severing
the rail links connecting Petersburg and Richmond with the rest of the
Confederacy. "Now we will rest the men," he told Meade, "and use the
shade for their protection u[ntil] a new vein can be [s]truck."[19] In the
wake of this latest disappointment, he lost none of his enthusiasm. He
was still "Sam" Grant the Pacific Coast potato entrepreneur, looking
to make his next opportunity.

❦

One of the best weapons a much-relieved Lee had at his command by
this time was Jefferson Davis. After three years of working together they
had forged a model civil-military partnership. Lee likely had little to do
with Davis at West Point, where the future president was a year ahead
of him, for the Mississippian was no model cadet. Court-martialed and
dismissed once, then reinstated, and nearly dismissed again for partic-
ipating in a drunken revelry called the "Egg Nog Riot," Davis was not
the sort of cadet with whom the rigidly disciplined Virginian would associate. In the war with Mexico they might have met each other briefly
in early 1847 before Lee transferred from Taylor's to Scott's army, but
neither thought it worthy of later mention. In 1850 Davis was a senator from Mississippi. Approached by Cuban revolutionaries wanting
him to lead them in revolt against Spain, Davis begged off, but referred
them to Lee, then in Baltimore. He also declined, but evidently Davis

held him in some regard already. Of course, when serving as Pierce's secretary of war, Davis created the 2d United States Cavalry and made Lee its second in command. For his part Lee left little to suggest any opinion at all of Davis at this time other than a postwar declaration that he had thought the Mississippian "one of the extremist politicians," which put Davis in company that Lee largely disliked.[20]

During the first year of the war, the two men became better acquainted through almost constant association, though nothing suggests that they spent time together socially. Lee established the bedrock of their relationship early on when he made no issue of losing his seniority as major general of state forces by becoming a brigadier in the Confederacy. Self-effacement always marked Lee's character, but in working with this president in particular it became an asset, which Lee surely saw as he watched Davis's relations with Johnston and Beauregard progressively topple on the generals' egos and ambition. Beyond question, the president could be prickly, and had an outsized ego of his own, but he was also very intelligent, in some degree insightful, and possessed a grasp of military science and policy second to few. More to the point, he was also the commander-in-chief of a civil democracy, making it his generals' duty to get along with him rather than the other way around. No one understood or accepted that better than Lee. He had spent his entire professional life subordinate to someone, and not always to a superior he liked, especially in his early years. Yet his concept of duty fully encompassed subordination. Hence, from 1861 on he might disagree with the president, and freely voice that dissent in the give and take of open discussion, but he never challenged or dealt with him other than with respect and deference.

It helped that the two found common ground in their strategic thinking. He and Davis agreed in 1862 that Richmond must be defended at all costs. They also agreed that an opportunistic approach to defending the Confederacy was the best practical course: holding as much as possible while seizing any chance for an offensive to damage the enemy and sow consternation in the North. Both implicitly understood that the only likely path to Confederate independence lay in defeating not Northern armies, but the Northern population's will to continue. Moreover, to that end both accepted that all other considerations, state and local, must be subordinated to the one paramount goal. In what professed to be a conflict to preserve state sovereignty, Davis and Lee were willing to accept virtually total central control.

Other facets of Lee's personality strengthened that unity, for he was perfectly suited to work in accord with a man like Davis. He already distrusted newspapers, largely because of the business of the slave whippings at Arlington, and disliked seeing his name in print. Hence, he made no effort to court a favorable press. Davis appreciated that, though he had to deal with other generals who happily got involved with his opposition in the fourth estate. At the same time, Lee's mistrust of politicians kept him aloof from the political morass, even as he watched generals like Joseph E. Johnston, Longstreet, and others become unwitting tools for Davis's opponents. Lee also refrained from disputes with Davis's friends, starting with the barely capable Judah P. Benjamin, with whom Lee worked uncomplainingly during his western Virginia and South Carolina stints.

This was all part of the professional code he had followed all his life. In dealing with the president he took this two steps further based on his reading of the man. He set the tone at the cabinet meetings in May 1862 when Davis asked him to present views on Richmond's defense, and Lee concluded by asking the president for his ideas. Weeks later in June, when he assumed command of the Army of Northern Virginia, Lee again asked Davis what he thought should be their strategy, and thereafter did so again and again. As commander-in-chief, of course, Davis had the constitutional right and authority to dictate military policy, which he preferred not to do unless a general gave him no alternative. Still, being asked his views flattered him. Moreover, in communicating his own ideas, Lee routinely closed with qualifiers like "do you think anything can be done" and "I shall feel obliged to you for any directions you may think proper to give."[21] They reinforced Lee's awareness of his subordinate position, while flattering the president.

Seeing Davis's frustration with a man like Joseph E. Johnston, who all but refused to share his plans for a campaign, Lee divulged his own thinking fully, sometimes as it developed over a period of time as with what became the Gettysburg raid. "You should know everything," Lee assured the president, even if he felt he had to apologize for communicating too much.[22] Once Lee had the army in motion, he also wisely communicated with Davis as often as possible, keeping him informed of developments. During the march to Antietam Lee wrote almost once a day, sometimes just to say he had nothing to communicate. "When you do not hear from me," he told the president, "you may feel sure that I do not think it necessary to trouble you."[23] Lee understood that Davis had a right to be kept fully apprised, and that the better informed he was, the less likely he was to interfere. Despite a reputation for meddling with his commanders, Davis rarely did so if a general was actually in motion, and kept him abreast. During the march into Maryland in 1862 Davis wanted to join the army on the campaign, but by gentle persuasion and constant communication Lee kept him in Richmond and out of the way.

In return, Lee brought Davis victories, one after another, and more than all other Confederate commanders combined. More eloquent, however, were his defeats. When Johnston or Beauregard failed, it was everyone's fault but theirs. When Lee failed to destroy McClellan he told Davis that "I blame nobody but myself." After Gettysburg he offered to resign. "To ask me to substitute you by some one in my judgment more fit to command," the president responded, "is to demand an impossibility." Even then Lee asked him to keep his resignation, and invoke it anytime he thought necessary.[24] Already Davis addressed Lee as "My dear friend."

The chief executive's growing respect for Lee impelled him repeatedly to ask him to take over the troubled Army of Tennessee, and then weighed heavily in his decision to reinstate Johnston instead. The president was unwilling to order Lee to unwelcome duty, and placed enough confidence in his judgment to appoint instead a man Davis detested. Now, as Lee and Grant battled each other, Davis left the campaign in Lee's hands with confidence, devoting his own efforts to providing every support and succor. To Davis, by 1864 Lee stood alone, and when he spoke of him, it was clear all others were, in comparison to him, beginners.[25] No general and chief executive ever worked better together, and the credit belonged primarily to Lee, who never forgot the position of the military in a democracy, and who "read" the man in charge with unerring perception. If at times Lee's demeanor seemed flattering, verging even on the sycophantic, it was never for self-advancement, but done knowing that Lee's weapons were stronger with the president behind them, rather than in front.

Lee's need for the president's support grew increasingly desperate after the armies reached Petersburg and what became known as the Overland campaign ended in the growing stalemate of a siege. Three years of war, long separation from families, and months of inadequate rations and clothing, not to mention little or no pay, worked their evil on morale, and almost immediately his army began a slow disintegration. Or rather, the steady problem of desertion accelerated as discouragement and desperation set in.

Nearly a decade earlier Lee first dealt with deserters at Jefferson Barracks. "They are no loss," he said, condemning them as "dastardly & cowardly." Then he actually preferred that they flee during recruitment and training rather than in the field, after the time and expense of making them soldiers.[26] He did not get his wish then or now. Tens of thousands of Confederates, or about one in seven, would go absent without leave or desert during the war; especially in 1863 and afterward, as hopes for success ebbed, the desertion rate sometimes topped 25 percent. Lee made every effort to apprehend them, even detaching whole brigades from his army to pursue and bring them back, but once returned for justice, discipline and admonitory punishments were the only tools he had to discourage absenteeism.[27]

The maximum penalty for desertion was death, and a prevailing opinion was echoed by the officer of one Virginia deserter in 1863 who declared that "the only use that can be made of him is to shoot him as an example to others."[28] During the war Lee reviewed, approved, and passed on to Davis at least 245 such capital sentences, and almost certainly more.[29] In a minimum of 65 of those cases Lee sent them to the president with mitigating factors, and Davis remitted at least 29 sentences, while Lee himself set aside another 43 for various reasons. Of the 173 cases that Lee approved without such recommendations, at least 53 men were shot, while the 120 remaining condemned men escaped the firing squad for reasons ranging from death by disease to bureaucratic inefficiency.[30] In all, more than two-thirds of the sentences Lee approved were not carried out.

Part of the cause was that Lee viewed suspension of death sentences as a practical tool. Prior to Gettysburg he issued, with Davis's approval, a blanket amnesty for virtually all outstanding offenders. Thereafter in a single special order early in April 1864 he saved 27 men condemned to execution for mitigating circumstances ranging from youth, previous good character and performance to repentance and irregularities in their trials.[31] Yet he was also on the verge of the opening of spring campaigning, and needed every rifle on the line. Months later, in a higher position, and facing the coming of yet another, and surely final, campaign, he issued a blanket amnesty for all deserters who reported to their units within twenty days, making it clear that there would be no more amnesties in future.[32] Lee was not a cruel man, however much he detested deserters, yet it is hardly surprising that a man who could sanction whipping slaves for trying to run away to freedom could also impose a firing squad on those who ran away from their duty to comrades and country. Just over 20 percent of death sentences imposed in his army were carried out, virtually double the percentage for the Union army as a whole, but then the rate of desertion in Lee's army was almost ten times greater than in the Union army, where of 23,419 men convicted of desertion and 1,243 sentenced to death, only 140 went to execution.[33] Since the beginning of the year, Lee enjoined his subordinates if at all possible not to execute the condemned on the Sabbath.[34]

Grant had just as much impatience with misbehavior as Lee. When officers straggled behind the army, he ordered them sent forward to be publicly stripped of their buttons and insignia and then handcuffed to await trials.[35] Unlike Lee, however, Grant enjoyed periods of the war in which he did not have to deal with men sentenced to death for serious offenses. Prior to September 1862 he convened courts, but reviewing sentences and forwarding them to Washington was Halleck's responsibility.[36] Once he took over the Middle Military Division in October 1863, capital sentences were reviewed by the several army commanders under him and he rarely got involved, a procedure that continued now that he commanded all Union armies. Hence, unlike Lee, Grant's headquarters really only gave careful oversight for about a year in 1862–1863, though he always had the option of weighing in if a particular case came to hand that he thought required action.

At least a dozen capital cases for desertion came before Grant for review, the first just weeks after Halleck left him in command in Mississippi in October 1862. Grant approved the finding and sent it on to Lincoln, who commuted the sentence.[37] Like Lee, when possible Grant mitigated a sentence in light of previous good conduct in action, the condemned's youth, or family hardship.[38] He was also sensitive to technicalities in capital findings, but otherwise just like Lee he approved courts' sentences and sent them on to the president, who almost always commuted.[39] After February 1863 the law requiring capital sentences to be submitted to Lincoln no longer applied, though commanding officers were still free to suspend a sentence or to forward a case to the president, which Grant did in almost every instance.[40] Sometimes he attached his own recommendation for clemency, or a commutation to imprisonment for the remainder of the war.[41] However, when a soldier deserted in action he never recommended clemency, nor in any cases involving deserting to the enemy and taking arms against the Union.[42] Neither did he interfere in such cases when Meade approved the sentence.[43]

During the Vicksburg campaign trials for desertion were held within each division. Grant found that sometimes death sentences were carried out without coming before him for approval, while in other cases that he had approved he was not always informed whether the sentences had been executed according to regulations.[44] A stickler for military law, Grant preferred that the guilty go unpunished rather than be denied rigid adherence to code. Yet he seems to have understood that volunteers could not always be treated according to law. They were not soldiers, but civilians who had loaned themselves to the nation for the emergency, and humanity suggested some lenity. When more than 100 deserters came to Washington with the wounded from the first Spotsylvania fighting, Stanton wanted to send them back to Grant to be tried by drumhead court-martial and executed as an example.[45] Knowing what a disincentive harsh justice could be to future enlistments, Grant did nothing in the matter. If a Northern civilian ran to the Confederacy to escape the draft and then enlisted with the rebels, Grant was still likely to recommend pardon, especially if the man was a teenager.[46]

One death sentence for mutiny actually came under Grant's review after eight sergeants and corporals of the 11th Illinois refused further service under a despised lieutenant. All pled guilty and were sentenced to be shot, and he made no recommendation for mitigation when he forwarded the findings to Lincoln, who pardoned all eight. However, he did endorse a later petition for clemency, and all the sentences were commuted.[47] Before the fall of Vicksburg a private broke his rifle on the ground, shouting something about "damned abolitionists," then gave a cheer for Jefferson Davis and insulted his lieutenant when called to account. A court sentenced him to be shot, but Grant suspended the sentence on learning that the man had been drunk.[48] However, when another mutinous inebriate added striking his officer to his crimes, Grant merely passed the death sentence on to Lincoln to settle.[49] The murder of civilians or other soldiers never gained his recommendation for commutation.[50] If the victim was a Confederate it made no difference. At Memphis early in 1863 a lieutenant of the 2d United States Cavalry took a bribe from a Confederate prisoner to help him escape, then led the man through the lines and shot and killed him. Grant approved a death sentence without question.[51]

The practical result was that remarkably few capital sentences were carried out in Grant's immediate commands prior to his arrival in Virginia, and just thirty-one in Meade's Army of the Potomac after Grant became general-in-chief.[52] In fact, he occasionally acted as intermediary between Meade and Lincoln in brokering a reprieve.[53] Occasionally a Confederate soldier came before a court martial, and if the charge was murder, Grant made no objection to capital sentences regardless of the allegiance of the victim. When a Georgia lieutenant stabbed and killed a citizen, Grant approved hanging the culprit.[54] From his earliest command, Grant strove to show and encourage restraint toward Confederate citizens, and he carried that policy over into military justice. In the summer of 1863 when ten Missourians were caught for plundering and setting fires aboard a steamer, a military commission sentenced them to be hanged. Grant learned that the members of the commission had not been properly sworn in and so informed the president, recommending that the sentences be nullified.[55] When the crime was attempted murder or the murder of another citizen within his jurisdiction, Grant sought no mitigation in forwarding death sentences to Lincoln.[56] Neither did he show interest in clemency for guerrillas and partisans not regularly enlisted in Confederate service, though again Lincoln often commuted the sentences that Grant approved.[57] At the same time, however, Grant objected to executing Confederate soldiers in retaliation for murders committed by guerillas.[58] He even showed some reluctance to execute convicted spies, and before the war's end encouraged an arrangement whereby there should be no executions of such by either side until opposing authorities were notified and had time to offer explanations to justify a reprieve. In at least one case he and Lee exchanged correspondence in the successful effort to save a man's life.[59]

In all, Grant reviewed at least thirty-seven capital sentences, less than one-sixth the number addressed by Lee, and all but five from 1862 to 1863 when Grant commanded the Army of the Tennessee. He spared the lives of almost half of the condemned on technicalities or recommendations for mercy. The remaining nineteen—just over half—he approved and forwarded to Lincoln, surely knowing that the president routinely pardoned or commuted more than three-fourths of all death sentences. Lincoln did so in a dozen of Grant's cases, meaning only seven death sentences were confirmed, and possibly not all of those were carried out.[60] Thus, while Lee sought leniency in just under one-fourth of the cases coming to him, Grant sought it in just over half, and while again almost 22 percent of the cases Lee approved ultimately resulted in execution, in Grant's case it was 19 percent.

Grant was not more humane than Lee, though he seemed more reluctant to impose summary justice. Desertion never threatened national survival for the Union as it did for the Confederates. Moreover, deserters from the Army of the Potomac, now deep in enemy territory, had no friendly refuge to go to, and risked capture and a prisoner of war camp that could be more dangerous than the battlefield. Meanwhile, in Lee's already outnumbered army, any absence for any reason was felt all the more. The deep pockets of dissent and even disloyalty among units from parts of North Carolina and southwest Virginia posed a trenchant hazard of spreading demoralization and defeatism throughout the rest of the army, and no one in the Confederate military could think of a better palliative than the example of execution. Lee approved more capital sentences because more came to him, but both commanders had similar attitudes toward summary justice, well recognizing the fine line between salutary example and pointless death.

The failure of Grant's Petersburg attacks left his right flank based on the Appomattox River and his left slowly lengthening southward, matched by Lee's gradually extending right flank. Lee took advantage of the relative stalemate to take yet another daring gamble—his last of the kind—to ease the pressure in his front by forcing Grant to shift focus elsewhere. He detached Early's corps and Breckinridge to the Shenandoah Valley where they easily expelled a Federal raid and then launched a campaign down the valley to cross the Potomac into Maryland. They actually came in sight of Washington before its defenses forced them to withdraw, but the lightning raid forced Grant to detach a corps from his own front to protect his capital. It was exactly the sort of move that both generals conceived repeatedly, and usually with similar results. But Lee's boldness in doing it now was punctuated by the fact that it left him barely 25,000 men in the defenses at Petersburg facing more than 65,000 under Grant and Meade.

Thus on July 30, Grant tried an expedient he had used against Vicksburg, exploding a mine that blew a 120-foot-wide hole in Lee's works. Unfortunately, he compromised its effectiveness at the last minute by ordering Meade to send white troops into the anticipated breach, rather than the United States Colored Troops units originally assigned and trained for the operation. It was a pragmatic, political decision, for should the attack fail, it would play into the hands of Lincoln's opponents who claimed that blacks could not be soldiers. The incompetence and cowardice of Union subordinates entrusted with leading the planned follow-up assault saved the Confederates. After that, for the rest of 1864 the two sides settled down to relative inactivity punctuated by bloody bursts of action. Grant sent Sheridan's cavalry to the Shenandoah to deal with Early, which he did definitively. Through August Grant steadily extended his lines southeasterly, cutting the Weldon & Petersburg Railroad that linked Lee and Richmond to eastern North Carolina, and then that fall he went after the Southside Railroad west of the city, connecting it with Lynchburg, but A. P. Hill stopped him. After that cold weather halted virtually all operations.

Both armies were exhausted, and so were their commanders, especially Lee, whose health remained erratic throughout. Surely that had

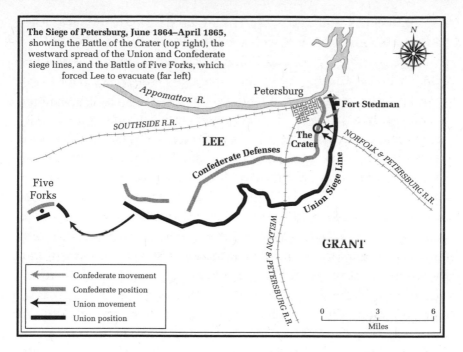

The Siege of Petersburg, June 1864–April 1865, showing the Battle of the Crater (top right), the westward spread of the Union and Confederate siege lines, and the Battle of Five Forks, which forced Lee to evacuate (far left)

an impact on his conduct of the campaign, but more significant was the fact that this was a wholly new kind of warfare for him: standing on the defensive, leaving the initiative to the foe, reacting rather than acting. He adapted quickly, carefully considering Grant's most likely options, and positing plans accordingly, though more than once he hesitated to commit himself fully to a course of action. As a result, he gave Grant a little extra time, which made the risks to himself all the greater, yet moving faster risked disaster should he react to the wrong enemy move. If Lee could not stop Grant anywhere until he found the ideal defensive line at Cold Harbor, still he made the Federals pay for every gain. In a way, the whole series of engagements from The Wilderness on were simultaneously victories and defeats for both generals, for neither got what he wanted. The frustration told on Lee, especially as his weakened and tiring army no longer reacted as once it had. With increasing frequency subordinates who failed to obey orders or stand their ground resolutely saw the angry glare in Lee's eyes that one observer thought looked as if he "might penetrate a two-inch plank."[61]

For his part, Grant planned brilliantly, but the old overconfidence, or perhaps just the effects of constant activity, made him unwontedly careless at times, and to his cost. His advance from the Rapidan River had been bloody to be sure, with about 60,000 total casualties, and critics in the Northern press and Congress castigated both him and Lincoln for the hard arithmetic of the campaign. Yet against an adversary as subtle and daring as Lee, there was no other way than what Grant had called "hard knocks." He tried maneuvering at every opportunity, only to find that his opponent often divined his purpose barely in time to thwart him, or his own subordinates failed to meet his expectations. At Cold Harbor his only alternatives were to strike head-on, stay put and lose time, or retreat. Still, those losses paled in face of the 100,000 or more suffered for nothing over the previous three years as Lee repulsed one after another of Grant's predecessors and held his ground. Now at a little more than half that terrible cost, and in a fraction of the time, Grant had virtually taken Lee and the Army of Northern Virginia out of the war as an open field threat. Not surprisingly, Confederate editors dubbed him "Grant, the Butcher" and "Butcher of the Wilderness."[62] However, the Democratic press in the North took up the sobriquet "Butcher Grant" as a weapon to use against Lincoln, and did more to spread it than even the enemy papers.[63] Yet the outcry over losses sustained followed strictly party lines, and the majority of the influence-making journals stood behind him, as did the voters when they reelected Lincoln that fall.

Grant's response to the critics was that "the Rebellion must be overcome, if overcome at all, by force; its resources destroyed; its fighting material obliterated, before peace could be obtained." In his own view, there had been but two failures: the abortive assault on Petersburg immediately after crossing the James and the botched attack following the mine explosion.[64] His own hasty planning and, for a change, imprecise orders contributed to the first; his last-minute changes had a hand in the second, though the bulk of the fault rested squarely with Burnside, who soon resigned. Grant understood the cruel arithmetic involved. Both sides were enduring terrible casualties, but Lee had nowhere to go for more men. "We loose to," he told a friend, "but can replace our losses."[65]

Despite the long months of developing siege, neither general had much opportunity for relaxation. Lee made time to go to church for the first time in weeks the day after Grant's last June assault, and occasionally thereafter. But most of the time when he was not at headquarters attending to business he was out riding along his lines, making corrections in positions, giving instructions for enhancing earthworks, or else in Richmond lobbying Davis, the War Department, and even congressmen for more men and supplies. By the fall he felt stiff and uncomfortable on horseback, and some days the rides took him more than thirty miles, but it had to be done.[66] Mary chided him that he exposed himself too much, and should forego his field tent for the greater comfort of a house. "It is from no desire of exposure or hazard that I live in a tent," he told her, "but from necessity." He felt his failing strength, and knew he could get a room or even a house, but that would separate him from his staff and delay business. He tried to shield himself from what he called "exciting causes," but asked her "what care can a man give to himself in a time of war?"[67] At least he did try to get a new tent in July. The one he used had been issued three years earlier, and he told the quartermaster general that it "has been my principal habitation ever since wherever I have been." The last two months in particular had ravaged its roof and walls, and now it scarcely afforded dry shelter. "I doubt whether it will hold together longer than the current summer months," he testified, and hoped a new one could be made for him that would close completely in front, with side walls all round, and "sufficiently capacious" for himself and others to meet inside.[68] In less than a week Richmond sent him a new one, but Lee complained now that it was too large for easy movement. More to the point, ever conscious of setting an example, he did not like the luxury of a capacious tent after he had confined his own staff officers to much smaller ones.[69]

There were a few pleasant moments even in the old tent. It was clean and cozy and Lee had a split-bottomed chair that he sometimes took outside where he donned his spectacles and sat to pore over newspapers from North and South. On quiet days he could hear a few chickens kept for eggs as they pecked around his nearby ambulance, one cock being a special favorite that had been with him for some time, despite his returning that other gift rooster in 1862.[70] Occasionally he got iced buttermilk, and on June 30 he could take a few minutes to write to Mary on their anniversary.[71] "Do you recollect what a happy day thirty three years ago this was?" he asked her. "How many hopes & pleasures it gave birth to?" In spite of all, God had been merciful and kind to them, leading Lee to muse on "how thankless & sinful I have been." He prayed that there might be a little peace and rest in store for them before they went to the better world.[72] Mary's health continued to trouble him, especially after she took a bad fall in July. When she left Richmond for a safer and less humid residence at the country home of a cousin, he felt some relief, though it made their visits infrequent. Christmas found him by himself at headquarters, but that hardly mattered. "I am unable to have any enjoyment of that kind now," he wrote her. He was happy just to be able to attend church that day.[73] It was a chance to acknowledge what "Him who alone controls the destiny of nations" had done for them, just as Lee did in publishing the president's proclamation of November 16 as a day for worship, suspending all but vital military duties to allow the men to worship.[74]

Such respites were few, however. "Grant seems so pleased with his present position that I fear he will never move again," Lee wrote Mary on July 10, but of course he knew he would.[75] There had been too many close calls thanks to the disparity of strength between them. "Where are we to get sufficient troops to oppose Grant?" he asked his son Custis a fortnight later. Lee offhandedly dismissed Grant's style of command by saying "his talent & strategy consists in accumulating overwhelming numbers," neatly ignoring the fact that regardless of manpower, Grant had more than once outthought him.[76] Yet that might not matter if only Lee could achieve something like parity in strength. "Unless some measures can be devised to replace our losses, the consequences may be disastrous," he warned Seddon in August. "No man should be excused from service." They must conscript more, and put arms in the hands of noncombatant soldiers. With only a few thousand new men he could hold his defenses, and use his veterans to deliver a real blow. "Without some increase of our strength, I cannot see how we are to escape the natural military consequences of the enemy's numerical superiority."[77]

Lee was receptive to any expedient. Barely a week after stopping Grant's assaults on Petersburg, he conceived the novel idea of sending the Maryland troops in his army north to the Potomac. There they would be ferried across to make an amphibious landing at Point Lookout, Maryland, to attack the Union prisoner of war camp maintained there and free more than 12,000 Confederate soldiers to return to his ranks. He believed that the prison garrison was almost all black soldiers, and assumed that the officers of such troops "would be poor & feeble" and offer little resistance.[78] Once free and armed with their captors' weapons, the prisoners and their liberators could then march around Washington and cross the Potomac somewhere upstream. Lee was hardly given to impractical schemes, yet this was easily the most fanciful idea he conceived during the war. It revealed his desperation, and his willingness to disenthrall himself of the conventional if it would solve his problem.

Later that summer he proposed to Davis that all men currently in the military but serving in rear-echelon positions should be sent to the front, their places to be filled with hired slaves and free blacks. "I think measures should be taken at once to substitute negroes for whites in every place in the army," he said, meaning use as teamsters, cooks, hospital orderlies, and the like. He did not suggest actually arming them as soldiers, or not yet, but that might be the logical extension of his argument. As further evidence of his desperation and improvisation, he also asked the president to call out the overage reserves and county home guard in Virginia and North Carolina, again to man defenses and garrisons so that his veterans could be available and ready to strike when opportunity afforded.[79]

Throughout that winter he made trip after trip to Richmond trying to motivate the War Department, and especially the quartermaster and commissary bureaus, to do something about his dwindling army and its miserly supplies. When he returned to his headquarters he groaned repeatedly that no one listened, and that members of Congress actually interrupted his conferences with the president and secretary of war to petition for furloughs for constituents, when he felt they should have been taking care of the army.[80] On the rare occasions when he could have dinner with Mary and his daughters in the house they rented in November on Franklin Street, he paced the parlor ranting that while his men starved, Congress thought it had nothing better to do than eat peanuts and chew tobacco.[81] When a senator from

Texas petitioned him to send one of the best brigades in the army home to the Lone Star State just as operations were on the eve of commencing, Lee responded that "such is our great want of men, that the absence of even four hundred would be severely felt, especially four hundred of our best troops." What he needed was for some of the many thousand soldiers lying largely idle west of the Mississippi to be brought east to him. Grant had brought many of the units that fought with him in the West, and Lee declared that "I think we must do the same with ours."[82]

Encouragements were few, though many came from his men when they passed resolutions that winter reaffirming their commitment to fight on. When that same Texas brigade sent him such resolves, he responded that "if our people will continue to sustain our soldiers as they have hitherto done, and face loss of property and deprivation of comfort with the unflinching fortitude that distinguishes their sons and brothers in the field, our success is neither doubtful nor remote." They must expect setbacks ahead, but the Yankees would only win if the people lost confidence and relaxed their commitment. "I trust that the noble sentiments of the army will pervade the country," he told the Texans, "and am confidant that under the blessing of God, all will be well."[83] "If our people will sustain the noble soldiers of the Confederacy, and evince the same resolution and fortitude under their trials which have characterized the army," he wrote a Virginia brigade, "I feel no apprehension about the issue of this contest." So long as those sentiments animated his soldiers, "our overthrow is beyond the power of the enemy."[84] For a change, he wrote intending for such letters to appear in the press.

Having dismissed the fighting capability of black soldiers in his Point Lookout plan, Lee nonetheless slowly came to endorse the ultimate expedient of enlisting blacks in the army. "We must choose between employing negroes ourselves, and having them employed against us," he warned Davis in September, though he was not yet speaking of using them as combatants.[85] The Confederate debate on using slaves as soldiers began almost immediately after the war started, but gained no traction until early 1864, and even then few gave it support. By that winter, however, the situation was so desperate that it emerged in legislation in Congress, and Lee was asked for his views. Little had changed in his feelings toward slavery and blacks. If "controlled by humane laws and influenced by Christianity and an enlightened public sentiment," slavery was the best relationship that could exist between white and black when they inhabited the same country, he replied. "I would deprecate any sudden disturbance of that relation." Ideally, he preferred to depend on white men to make their armies strong enough to counter the Federals, but he now believed that the white population simply was not enough. He had seen that slaves freed by enemy advances only swelled Yankee numbers as the males enlisted to help destroy slavery "in a manner most pernicious to the welfare of our people." Their own slaves would be used to hold them in place while the enemy completed his conquest.

"Whatever may be the effect of our employing negro troops, it cannot be as mischievous as this," he argued. "If it end in subverting slavery it will be accomplished by ourselves, and we can devise the means of alleviating the evil consequences to both races." Whites would still be in full control. If they lost, then Northern abolitionists would be in charge, slavery abolished, and society overturned, threatening white supremacy. It came down to a simple question. "We must decide whether slavery shall be extinguished by our enemies and the slaves be used against us, or use them ourselves at the risk of the effects which must be produced upon our social institutions." He argued that they should be employed without delay. They had the physical strength and endurance, and "long habits of obedience and subordination, coupled with the moral influence which in our country the white man possesses over the black, furnish an excellent foundation for that discipline which is the best guaranty of military efficiency." All that was wanting was a reason for them to fight, and Lee argued that it should be immediate freedom for the soldiers, freedom for their families at war's end, and "the privilege of residing in the South."

The Confederacy ought to implement "a well-digested plan of gradual and general emancipation." It would make the blacks who served more loyal, knowing that their families were to be free. It would also reduce the temptation of those at home to run away, not knowing if they would ever be able to return to their homeland, another reason for Lee's subtle suggestion of guaranteeing continued residence in the South. Accepting that the end of slavery was inevitable if the war lasted much longer, and certain if the Yankees won, Lee argued that they might as well adopt their own emancipation immediately. This would deny the enemy one of its most powerful weapons in world opinion, and make it incontestable that the Confederates' struggle was one for independence and not perpetuation of slavery.[86] Even before the law's passage in March 1865, Lee encouraged Davis to put it in effect immediately. They might not raise a large force at once, but if he could forestall Grant a few months, black regiments under white officers might become numerous given time.[87]

Time, of course, is what he no longer had.

16

MEETING AGAIN

"THEY WILL DYE HARD but dye they must," Grant wrote his father that summer of 1864. It appeared from deserters that the Confederates were putting old men and boys into the army now. "Their next resort for reinforcemen[t]s must be the womb," he quipped, "for they have already gone to the cradle."[1]

He enjoyed wonderful health that summer, the only one in his headquarters not sick a day since the campaign began.[2] That was well, because the physical and mental demands on him were considerable. Some days he spent a dozen hours writing in addition to the correspondence his military secretary and other staff handled.[3] The lion's share went to Halleck, Stanton, Meade, and Burnside, but addressees ranged the full extent of Union blue, even to the Pacific Coast. Julia always relieved his weariness, and he very much wanted her with him, but the summer heat and the uncertainty of his movements kept her mostly at Burlington, New Jersey, and he could not get away. "You know that of all persons I am the last one who can leave," he told her in September. Meanwhile, she cast about for some more permanent roost for the family. The citizens of Chicago wanted to raise money to give the Grants a house, and Philadelphia actually did, though it would not be ready before the end of the year. Grant preferred Chicago but since duty would require him in the East even after war's end, Philadelphia was the better choice. He hoped that when this campaign was over he could spend most of the winter there enjoying the home-cooked meals that he missed terribly. He might also spend the cold months visiting the other armies, leaving Meade in charge around Petersburg.

Philadelphia would also keep him in easy reach of army headquarters. "I have a horror of living in Washington and never intend to do it," he told her, but he could stand visits.[4] Looking to the future, he began planning investments designed, he hoped, to yield them an income of $6,000 a year, enough for his family live on comfortably even if something should happen to him.[5] He also invested in land that held the promise of oil, the old entrepreneur in him still alive and well. But when the other buyers asked to capitalize on his fame in attempting to resell the land with some hint of a certainty of its riches, he recoiled, replying that "I have a perfect abhorence of having any interest in anything which might prove speculative at the expense of a confiding public."[6]

Meanwhile, he dealt with that growing celebrity. "It is a terrible bore to me that I cannot travel like a private citizen," he complained after being almost mobbed in Philadelphia that fall.[7] Like Lee, he disliked being in the press, but unlike him, he began to find himself on a footing that Lee rarely faced. "Gen. Grant has met the fate that usually befalls celebrities," a Rhode Island editor wrote early in June. "He is in the hands of the anecdote mongers, and the newspapers teem with stories of his sayings and doings." It rather embarrassed him, especially since some of the anecdotes echoed Jesse's stories that made him out a bumpkin. "Anecdotes are like poems: they are either good or good-for-nothing," wrote that editor, and Grant largely agreed.[8] Hasty biographies appeared with titles like *Tanner-Boy, A Life of General Grant*, and *The Hero Boy*. Even the more serious like F. W. H. Stansfield's *The Life of Gen'l U. S. Grant* ran title pages attributing to him such prescient boyhood aphorisms as "Can't is not in the dictionary." If asked he refused to furnish information to prospective biographers. "It would be egotistical," he protested, "and I hope egotism is not to be numbered among my faults."[9] Worse, anecdotes appeared connecting him to the embarrassing biographies. A peddler selling one such book was supposedly accosted on a train by one of Grant's staff, who told him he could sell a copy to a nondescript-looking fellow sitting quietly off by himself. The peddler handed a copy to the prospect, who looked at it, then asked, "Who is it this is all about?" The incredulous salesman shot back, "You must be a darned greeny not to know General Grant," whereupon the man bought a copy. Needless to say, the buyer was Grant himself.[10]

Only in one regard did he cooperate with those wanting to publish any of his own writings. When Lincoln was renominated that summer, supporters asked if the general would allow some of his letters to be used to answer the charges Democrats leveled at the president. Grant heartily agreed, though warned that trying to answer every accusation would be like "setting a maiden to work to prove her chastity."[11] He fully supported Stanton's path-breaking plan to allow soldiers to vote in the field for the first time that fall, though he made it clear that he did not want stump-speaking politicians from either party flooding the armies, believing that his men knew the issues well enough to make their own choices.[12] When Lincoln won handily in November, Grant declared that "it will be worth more than a victory in the field," not least because it should quiet the constant dissenters in the North whom he believed abetted the rebellion.[13] "I try to look at everything calmly," he told Julia during the campaign, "therefore believe all we want to produce a speedy peace is a unity of sentiment in the North."[14]

From the time of their first meeting Grant and Lincoln got on well, though their personal relations never matched those between Davis and Lee. However, while Lee kept his inner feelings about his president carefully muffled, Grant openly displayed his warm loyalty and admiration. For his part, Lincoln differed more with his general on strategic issues than Davis, but never to the point of imposing his own ideas. It helped that Lincoln had watched Grant's campaigns and come to admire him before they first met. It helped, too, that both hailed from Illinois. Lincoln's was the greater intellect, Grant's the better adjusted personality, but not a glimmer of difference separated their convictions that preservation of the Union was the great issue. Moreover, their views on fighting the war were identical. "Hold on with a bulldog grip, and chew & choke, as much as possible," Lincoln told Grant in August.[15] Years later Davis would say of Lee that "he was my friend, and in that word is included all that I could say of any man."[16] Lincoln paid no such encomium to Grant, but repeatedly in their correspondence acknowledged his willing deference to his general's prowess. When they differed, Lincoln was big enough to admit when he was wrong. Lee later said virtually nothing in testimonial about Davis, while Grant's admiration for his president grew for the rest of his life.

Grant also learned from Lincoln, for the president's leadership and example more than anything else moved the general from his near-indifference to slavery in 1861 to the point where he viewed emancipation as a great weapon of war itself, and employment of black men as soldiers as a valuable missile in their arsenal. From his first use of black regiments at Milliken's Bend in the spring of 1863, Grant made it clear that he would carry out his government's instructions regardless of his own opinions, which he kept to himself. Initially, like most other Union commanders, he envisioned using black units mostly for labor and garrison duty to free white veterans for the field, and later to guard plantations and hold the west bank of the Mississippi when Sherman set out for Meridian in March 1864. Thus when new rifles became available, he gave them to his veterans and passed their used weapons to the black units.[17] Nevertheless, such new regiments being Washington's wishes, he insisted on the work being prosecuted vigorously. Fearing that one general would not conscientiously raise and train blacks, he recommended another in his place who will "take an active interest in this work," telling Sherman that "a Soldier does not consult his own views of policy when orders from his superiors intervene."[18] By early 1865 he had learned enough about considerations best suited for discipline and morale in the new outfits to order black regiments raised in South Carolina to be stationed near their homes and families.[19]

Grant sought white officers best fitted for the special demands of leading these path-breaking soldiers, and after the blacks' first actions he believed they had performed well and informed Halleck that "all that have been tried have fought bravely." Immediately after taking Vicksburg he wanted to raise and equip as many regiments of United States Colored Troops as possible. In August 1864 in the Weldon Railroad operations he told Halleck that "the Colored troops behaved handsomely," and that same month gave them a perhaps unintentional compliment when he averred that one of his trained black soldiers was now worth two of the white militiamen raised in the emergency caused by Early's raid on Washington.[20]

Grant's policy on the treatment of black soldiers by fellow whites required that only one standard should apply regardless of color. In the weeks before the fall of Vicksburg he preferred that white and black units be kept apart as much as possible, especially in their camps, to minimize bullying or worse from white soldiers.[21] The government having freed and armed the blacks, he saw no justice in "permitting one treatment for them, and another for the white soldiers."[22] When an officer was charged with whipping a white soldier who had abused the new recruits, Grant dismissed the charges.[23] He applied that same policy in dealing with the special concern over treatment of captured blacks, for if outraged Confederates did not shoot them immediately, they ran the risk of being returned to slavery as presumed runaways like the freemen taken by Lee's army in Pennsylvania. Hearing that black prisoners might have been hanged after the battle of Milliken's Bend, he informed local Confederate authorities that if this was their policy, he would reply in kind by hanging white prisoners until the abuse stopped.[24]

Early in October 1864 Lee proposed a massive prisoner exchange in the interests of relieving the captives of their hardships—and to return thousands to his army—but when Grant raised the issue of the Union's black soldiers, Lee could only say that those not believed to be runaways would be exchanged, while the rest were still lawful property and must go back to their masters. Denying that the Union recognized any difference in status within its black soldiery, or between black and white, Grant refused the exchange.[25] Later that month when Confederates forced captured black soldiers to work on the Petersburg defenses under fire, Grant put an equal number of captured Confederates to work on Butler's front. "I shall always regret the necessity of retaliating for wrongs done our soldiers," he wrote Lee. But when Lee attempted to argue in a lengthy legalistic defense that there was precedent for so employing those "who owe service or labor to citizens," carefully avoiding using the word "slaves," Grant dismissed it and informed him that "I have nothing to do with the discussion of the slavery question."[26] Only when the equitable treatment of all captured black soldiers was settled did Grant resume exchanges.

He was also quite aware of the manpower potential theoretically available to the Confederacy should it mandate enlisting slaves and free black males in its military. He told Thomas in December that he felt some apprehension on that score, and wrote an old friend that the enemy was so hard up for recruits that it could scarcely replace a thousand men "unless they resort to the darkey," adding that "him they are affraid of and will not use him unless as a last desperate resort."[27] By

February 1865 he instructed Major General E. R. S. Canby to enlist all the blacks he could in Louisiana before the Confederates forced them into their own ranks.[28]

Regardless of his personal feelings about blacks, which seem to have been the prevailing attitudes of his time and place, Grant never questioned their worth to the Union, both as soldiers in the cause and as labor denied the enemy. "Arming the negroes," he had told Banks in July 1863, "will act as a two edged sword cutting both ways."[29] Yet with the close of the war approaching, his policy of treating them as entitled to equal treatment while in uniform, and the growing laurels they earned in field and combat under his eye, were subtly changing his perceptions of where the black man might stand as a citizen in peacetime.

A great deal of his time not spent supervising the campaign in his front went to Grant's duties as general-in-chief, a position he filled actively. He studied organization and recommended reconfiguring some geographic departments for greater command efficiency, as well as to eliminate generals in whom he had no confidence. He created a new military division that included the Shenandoah Valley and put Sheridan in charge because, as he told Sherman, the man would "push the enemy to the very death."[30] He withheld ordering active operations in other areas when he doubted the aggressiveness of the officer in charge. He faced yet again the problem of Rosecrans, who he told Julia with some exaggeration "never obeyed an order in his life that I have yet heard of."[31] In October his one-time friend repulsed a haphazard invasion of Missouri by an army of ragged cavalry under Sterling Price. Meanwhile, Confederate general John Bell Hood had succeeded Johnston in command of the Army of Tennessee, and was then invading central Tennessee. On October 29 Grant ordered Rosecrans to send substantial reinforcements to bolster Thomas in stopping Hood. Knowing Rosey well, Grant specified that "immediate and prompt compliance with this order, is required." Grant even sent Rawlins to Rosecrans's headquarters to make sure of action, and with direct authority to issue the necessary orders if Rosey did not.[32] For a change Rosecrans cooperated and soon had the men in motion, but apparently not fast enough for Grant, who repeatedly recommended relieving him from command, and early in January 1865 actually suggested to the War Department that Rosecrans be dismissed from the service for violation of military articles.[33] No doubt Grant felt he had just cause. No doubt his own antipathy toward the man urged him to use it.

Then there was the problem of General Thomas and the Army of the Cumberland. After the fall of Atlanta in September, Hood's late fall invasion got to the outskirts of Nashville. Whatever the cause of Grant's reservations about Thomas, they had not gone away. Grant liked quick and decisive action. Thomas was deliberate, not slow so much as overly methodical, yet that approach did not suit the general-in-chief. Forced to slow his advance on Petersburg to send reinforcements to protect Washington and root out Early—"that Maryland raid upset my plans" he confessed to Washburne—he was not anxious to have to send more even farther away if Thomas let Hood get the upper hand.[34] "I have said all I could do to force him to attack without giving the possitive order," Grant grumbled to Sherman on December 6. "To-day however I could stand it no longer and gave the order."[35] That order was unmistakable. "Attack Hood at once," it said, and Grant planned to replace Thomas quickly if he did not obey.[36] In fact, Thomas did not move for over a week. Grant tried persuasion. "Now is the time," he said, for before him was a chance to destroy one of the enemy's three main armies. Grant withdrew the relief order and tried to explain to him that "it has seemed to me that you have been slow." Then again Grant tried the peremptory. "Delay no longer," he wired on December 11.[37] Then he sent General Logan with orders to relieve Thomas, and left for Nashville himself on December 15.

En route he learned that Thomas had finally attacked. With the result of the fight yet unknown, Grant wired ahead for Thomas to push Hood hard as far and as fast as possible, not to wait for his supply trains to get organized to follow, but to live off the land.[38] For Grant that was the measure of a field general. He had withheld an assignment from one general that summer because he did not believe the man could manage an army isolated from its lines of communication.[39] "What is wanted is a Commander who will not be afraid to cut loose from his base of supplies," he told Canby, "and who will make the best use of the resources of the Country."[40] That was not Thomas. "It has been hard work to get Thomas to attack Hood," Grant wrote Sherman three days later.[41] Then when Grant tried to get the Army of the

Cumberland to campaign actively in Alabama in concert with Sherman's march east from Atlanta, Thomas slowed down again. Resigned to the fact that the general was "slow beyond excuse," Grant worked around him by reassigning significant parts of his army to other commands and ordering Thomas's cavalry to cooperate in a move to take Mobile. For three weeks Thomas did nothing, and then Grant finally ordered him to prepare for an overland campaign into southwest Virginia and on to Lynchburg. He knew Thomas would never actually launch such a campaign, but at least he might have the preparations in hand so that at the proper moment Grant could replace him with someone more determined, probably Sheridan.[42] Perhaps he should have relieved Thomas, but that general's army loved him and Grant knew how important that was to morale. Thomas was popular in the North thanks to the battles of Chickamauga and Chattanooga. With the war's end not yet in immediate sight, wisdom said to endure a plodding hero.

Amid such challenges, men like Meade offered great relief, and none more than Sherman. He left Sherman to himself in planning and executing his spring campaign, and the taking of Atlanta was exactly what Grant had hoped for, though he grieved at the death of McPherson, the only army commander the Union lost in action. "To know him was but to love him," Grant told the bereaved family.[43] Meanwhile, he almost boasted that "I am glad to say that I appreciated Sherman from the first feeling him to be what he has proven to the World he is."[44] After Atlanta he complimented Sherman that "You have accomplished the most gigantic undertak[ing] given to any General in this War," then began talking of another campaign barely a week later. "We want to keep the enemy continually pressed to the end of the war," he wrote, suggesting an overland march across Georgia to Savannah as one option. Within a few weeks Sherman had the campaign planned and Grant gave his approval and left him to it.[45] So deeply did he believe in the value of Sherman's service that he began a movement for the citizens of Cincinnati to buy a house for him after the war. When Sherman took Savannah on Christmas Day, Grant had his final assignment ready for him: to march north across the Carolinas and, if possible, move into south-central Virginia to cooperate against Lee if he and his army were still intact.

Meanwhile, Grant paid attention to the other armies large and small, and suggested several command changes or reorganizations, some on concerns over competent generals, and others for reasons of efficiency. He asked that the Departments of the Northwest, Missouri, and Kansas be consolidated into one, and had no problem recommending the out-of-favor General Pope to relieve Rosecrans, because he would bring to bear "subordination, and intelligence of administration."[46] He also gave special attention to General Canby, who had replaced Banks in Louisiana, to whom Grant's old pet project of taking Mobile now fell. Beyond high-level concerns, he left conduct of operations very much to the individual commanders, adhering to his old assumption that no one knew the situation better than the man on the scene. Throughout, Grant continued to use his staff as eyes and ears, and even to exert his own authority. He sent Rawlins to try to budge first Rosecrans and then Thomas, and Horace Porter to confer with Sherman in planning the new campaign.[47] Looking completely across the continent, he feared that Confederate sympathizers in southern California might cross into French-occupied Mexico to organize and equip themselves to return as invaders. Should they do that, Grant authorized his commander on the Pacific to drive them back and follow them across the border. In fact, in his only contemplated incursion into international affairs, Grant suggested that any Mexican territory harboring the invaders ought to be occupied until its authorities provided an indemnity that this would not happen again. Beyond that, Grant expressed his opinion—though not an order—that "direct assistance on our part" ought to be given to expel French forces and their leader the emperor Maximilian to return Mexico's government to its people.[48]

Once Sherman began his scorching advance through South Carolina, Grant's optimism impelled him to tell Congressman Washburne that "a few days more of success with Sherman will put us where we can crow loud."[49] Even before that, Grant felt like crowing over the war machine that he, Lincoln, and the Northern people had built. "We now have an Army of Soldiers such as the world never saw before," he told a friend in January 1865. That said, he turned immediately to the inevitable peace, adding that "when we get this little job settled I hope there never will be occation for seeing so much of it again."[50]

Grant's most delicate challenge was dealing with Meade and the Army of the Potomac. He knew Meade in Mexico, and that officer thought well of him. "I think his great characteristic is indomitable energy and great tenacity of purpose," Meade wrote in December 1863 on learning of Grant's promotion, but he added that Grant had yet to face a general of Lee's capability.[51] When Grant came east he showed solicitude for the irascible Meade's feelings in a difficult situation, and thanks mainly to him, favorable relations between them commenced almost instantly. "You may rest assured he is no ordinary man," Meade told his wife in March. "Grant is emphatically an executive man, whose only place is in the field."[52] For his part, Grant sympathized over the way the press and Washington had treated Meade following the battle of Gettysburg. Further to bolster his confidence, Grant at first gave virtually no orders for the army and stayed out of its administration, yielding to Meade on almost every suggestion for planning the coming campaign. "I cannot but be rejoiced at his arrival," Meade concluded on the eve of action, "because I believe success to be the more probable."[53]

Grant also wisely stayed out of the army's internal politics, which had always been its besetting sin. Several subordinates tried to deal directly with him rather than through Meade, but he routinely referred them to him, putting all on notice that "the rising sun," as Meade called him, would not be politicked.[54] "Grant is not a striking man," thought Meade, who found him reticent, unworldly, and somewhat ill at ease in the presence of strangers. Nevertheless, "at the same time, he has natural qualities of a high order, and is a man whom, the more you see and know him, the better you like him." Grant reminded him of their Mexican-American War general Zachary Taylor, "and sometimes I fancy he models himself on old Zac."[55]

When the fighting began, Grant initially left maneuvers to Meade but gradually got more actively involved. Meade could have resented that, but instead understood that it was all but inevitable.[56] Before May was out, however, his persistent anxiety over recognition began to color his opinion of Grant. "I don't think he is a very magnanimous man," Meade told his wife late that month, though still he credited Grant with being "above any littleness." After the battle of Cold Harbor he believed Grant had "had his eyes opened," and soon expressed disappointment in him.[57] Still, Grant's strengths impressed him. "He is of a very sanguine temperament, and sees everything favorable in a strong light, and makes light of all obstacles," Meade found by that fall. "Grant is not a mighty genius, but he is a good soldier, of great force of character, honest and upright, of pure purposes." Above all, Meade saw that "his prominent quality is unflinching tenacity of purpose." Unintimidated by obstacles, Grant largely ignored them. He was almost too confident, and Meade also feared that his commander's guilelessness made him susceptible to the unscrupulous. Lacking the craving for approval himself, Grant failed often to see it in others, and unintentionally disappointed them, as he did Meade. Nevertheless, "take him all in all," said Meade, "he is, in my judgment, the best man the war has yet produced."[58]

As much as Grant thrived on the heavy load, he fell ill and bedridden just before Christmas, largely from overwork, sicker than at any time since the outbreak of war. "It would not do for me to get sick at this time when there is so much to do," he wrote Julia on December 22, "and when we have it in our hands to do so much towards the suppression of the rebellion."[59] Two days later, largely by his own power of will, he was better and back at work. "I believe determination can do a great deal to sustain one," he told her, adding with no trace of conceit that "I have that quality certainly to its fullest degree."[60] Through it all, his optimism never flagged. "I will work this thing all out right yet," he told Julia in October.[61] Richmond would fall as Atlanta had done. By the dawn of 1865 he believed Lee would never abandon Richmond, even if every other point in the Confederacy should fall.[62] Thus when he took the enemy capital, he would take Lee with it, and that would end the rebellion. By mid-February he felt confident as ever that "every thing looks to me to be favorable for a speedy termination of the war."[63]

Fearing the same thing, Lee's anger and animosity toward his foe only hardened during the siege. "How many happy homes have they destroyed, & turned the occupants adrift in the world with nothing," he lamented. "From how many hearts have they expelled all hopes of happiness forever." The Yankees planted "darkness & despair where flourished love & happiness before," and were nothing more than "cowardly persecutors."[64] He readily believed a rumor that Federals had torn down all the churches around Culpeper Court House, reusing the materials "often for the vilest purposes," and felt outrage that the pews of one church were hauled away to use in a theater.[65] Late in October when he heard a sermon on forgiveness of enemies, he granted that it was right and he ought to make an effort to do so, but told Mary that "it is a hard lesson to learn now," especially when he heard stories of Confederate citizens being placed on Union trains in northern Virginia as shields to prevent partisans from attacking.[66]

That anger, the frustration of siege, his inability to awaken Richmond to urgency, his bone weariness, and the near-constant sense of his own time running out all fed Lee's bent toward melancholy and fatalism. Daily he felt his lagging physical strength and energy. Though he might not admit that Grant had outguessed him more than once, he believed his mental acuity was dulled, and had to wonder if Grant could have matched wits with the Lee of 1862. Several times in the past campaign he almost courted death when he tried to lead men into battle. Meanwhile, the reaper's scythe had taken his daughter, daughter-in-law, and grandchildren. Then in August he learned of the death of his beloved old uncle Williams Carter, who had been so ill-used by the Yankees. Nostalgically, Lee spoke of him as "the last connecting link to the persons whom I enjoyed in my boyhood & who made my days so happy."[67] All of his bonds to happiness were being severed.

It would be too much to say that Lee had a death wish by this time, yet death would not have been unwelcome. His providentialism was so advanced that for years he had never spoken of the loss of a relative or friend without calling it a release from burdensome life to joyous afterlife. Convinced that he would be in Paradise with all of his loved ones past and present, he sometimes turned his thoughts from the inevitability of his passing to its manner. A soldier all his adult life, he considered how a warrior ought to die and one day mused about it on paper, remembering fragments from his boyhood classics:

The warmest instincts of every man's soul declare the glory of the soldier's death. It is more appropriate to the Christian than to the Greek to sing:

"Glorious his fate and envied his lot,
Who for his country fights, and for it dies."
There is a true glory, and a true honor. The glory of duty done—
the honor of the integrity of principle.[68]

To die as a soldier would be a good death. He might not seek it, but he would accept it should it come. Until then there was for him only the glory of duty.

By the early weeks of 1865 Lee's patience was about exhausted, both with politicians and even with the president. One day entering the executive mansion, he met Senator Benjamin Hill of Georgia coming out. With everyone mindful of the serious danger to Richmond, Hill asked Lee what he thought of moving the capital to someplace safer and easier to defend. As was his wont, Lee politely declined to comment on a matter outside his field of responsibility, but Hill pressed him that it was Lee's business, since if the Confederacy lasted long enough for Davis's six-year term as president to expire in 1868, surely Lee would be chosen as successor. "Never!" Lee recoiled, and as Hill remembered his words, added that "I think the military and civil talents are distinct, if not different, and full duty in either sphere is about as much as one man can qualify himself to perform." He would never do the people "the injustice to accept high civil office."[69] In fact, no popular groundswell to make Lee president emerged in the Confederacy as it did for Grant after Vicksburg, but with any theoretical election still more than three years distant, Confederates did not project Lee beyond his current role, and what little discussion there was about a next president centered on Breckinridge.

That suited Lee, for if anything, he was sick of presidents and presidencies. On February 25 Davis wanted to consult with Lee about rumors of the general's views on destroying Southern crops to deny them to the enemy, and suggested that *"if you can spare the time I wish you to come here."*[70] Relations between them seemed slightly strained by now, and Lee usually returned irritable from Richmond. After one such fruitless visit, he complained loudly of the difficulty of maintaining his lengthening line of defenses with an army the government seemed uncommitted to increasing. Venable asked the general why he did not simply abandon the capital for the open field. Lee turned his "two-inch plank" glare on him and shot back that if he did so he would be "a traitor to his government."[71] In such a mood he got the president's note to come talk of rumors, and replied that it would be difficult to get away at that moment, suggesting that the president send him written details and he would respond. That set Davis off. Angrily he replied, "Rest assured I will never ask your views in answer to rumours—your counsels are no longer wanted in this matter." Feeling the president's anger, Lee resignedly returned to Richmond, in part to mollify Davis, but also on sudden and potentially important business. He told no one what transpired at the meeting, but he returned a few days later visibly depressed.[72] The president calmed in time, but until then the tone of his letters was a bit chilly.

At some indefinite moment Lee concluded that the war was lost. Of course, from the outset he acknowledged the possibility of defeat. Every recommendation he made for strengthening Confederate arms carried with it an implicit suggestion of the unhappy alternative. Over time that evolved in Lee's mind from possibility to probability, an evolution that may have begun as early as June, when Grant began to lay siege and Lee found himself all but trapped in his defenses. Yet even after Atlanta's fall in September, Lee did not see the cause as irretrievable. "The fall of Atlanta is a blow to us," he told Mary at the time, but "not very grievous & which I hope we will soon recover from."[73] Then in November Lincoln's reelection dashed the Confederacy's last hopes of the North's peace faction taking over, and Lee's fear hardened toward certainty. Of course, Lincoln could still choose to make terms on the basis of Confederate independence, but why should he?

If what he saw by that time did not convince Lee that the cause was lost, the rumblings reaching him from political back rooms should have. Davis's opposition was essentially impotent, rarely able to be more than nettlesome, if loud. By January 1865 they were calling for Davis's impeachment. The speaker of the state house in South Carolina went further, proposing that Congress leave the president in office, but remove the commander-in-chief function from his powers and install Lee as "the military head of the Government."[74] In fact, rumors about making Lee a dictator surfaced at least as early as January 1864, and sporadically thereafter.[75] Later that year another South Carolinian, Robert Barnwell Rhett, actually proposed to Vice President Stephens that Congress remove Davis from office immediately without resorting to the impeachment process. Stephens ought then to step aside from succeeding to the presidency, allowing Congress to install Lee virtually as military dictator.[76] By November 1864 Charles Minnegerode, the rector of St. Paul's Episcopal Church where both Davis and Lee attended when possible, heard whispers in Richmond loud enough that he feared that "the idea of a military dictator in the person of General Lee seems to be predominating here."[77] In his newspaper the Charleston *Mercury,* Rhett hammered on into 1865 for Davis's replacement by a "high toned gentleman in the land, like General Lee."[78]

Stephens apparently ignored Rhett, and in any event Lee would never countenance such a plot. Still, though he carefully avoided correspondence with dissident politicians, some of their scheming was surely known to him, especially since by the end of 1864 two Richmond papers openly called for his installation as supreme leader. Lee said nothing in the matter, but it all spoke eloquently to him of the spreading rot within the Confederacy's civil authority.

In a half step toward crippling the president's power, the Senate on January 16 passed a bill creating the office of "general in chief of the armies," there being never any question who they expected the president to appoint. On the last day of the month Davis submitted Lee's nomination, which the Senate confirmed the next day.[79] Northern pundits thought Lee got the position as a reward for his "alliance" with Davis in supporting the war in spite of the desperate state of things.[80] That was nonsense, for Lee had been in effect general-in-chief since 1862, though he acted only in an advisory capacity on affairs beyond his immediate departmental command. Now Congress put him and Davis on notice that it expected him to manage all of the Confederacy's military operations actively, something that Lee himself protested as impractical.[81] Still, he assumed the command on February 9, complaining only slightly that he had no instructions and no idea what Davis wanted him to do.[82] Henceforth, orders to other department and army commanders did come from Lee for the most part, but the working relationship between the two men did not change, Lee remaining as deferential as ever. He continued watching events elsewhere, but other than putting Johnston again in command of the

Army of Tennessee in February, and advising Beauregard on the defense of Mobile in March, his exercise of his office bore only a slight resemblance to Grant's as he made little effort to exert influence beyond Virginia, which had always been his Confederacy.[83]

In 1861 Lee's fealty to the Old Dominion clearly overrode allegiance to the Union. Though it was never tested, the question remained of whether that same fealty might take precedence over his loyalty to the new nation. In North Carolina and Georgia there had been discontented rumblings of seeking a separate peace in the face of defeat, perhaps to exact better terms. No such movement emerged in Virginia, but still, though Lee might not be a dictator, he did now have the power to act unilaterally for all Confederate land forces, which made him the only warrior who could make a peace. Lincoln had been under pressure repeatedly to make overtures to Davis to end the war, and several inconclusive feelers followed. Most recently Francis Preston Blair Sr. came as unofficial agent to meet with Davis in Richmond on January 12, but to no avail. Lincoln's insistence on reunion and Davis's on independence were mutually exclusive. No sooner did Blair leave than on January 17 another even less official person arrived: James W. Singleton, a Virginia native now a prominent Illinois Democrat and friend of Lincoln.[84] He had been active in the peace movement, despite which in early January Lincoln gave him a pass to go to Richmond ostensibly to try to purchase Southern produce to ship north, but unofficially to approach Confederate leaders about reunion.

Singleton met, or claimed to have met with, Stephens, Virginia senator R. M. T. Hunter, Assistant Secretary of War John A. Campbell, Robert Ould, chief of the Bureau of Prisoner Exchange, and others, all of whom admitted that the war was lost. They also told him that Longstreet and Ewell, and even Lee, felt the same. The day after Singleton's arrival the Senate passed the resolution making Lee general-in-chief, which suggested to Singleton that Lee now had the power to make peace himself if he would order all Confederate land forces to lay down their arms. Coincidentally, General Breckinridge arrived in Richmond at the same time as Singleton, to be offered the position of secretary of war. Singleton knew Breckinridge and called on him, revealing his secret agendum, and Breckinridge arranged for him to meet with Lee.

On January 19, Lee's birthday as it happened, they met at army headquarters. When Singleton declared that further fighting only postponed the inevitable, Lee responded that he was "in the hands of Providence," and that though a soldier, he was a man of peace who wanted to stop the bloodletting, "and would go as far as any man in the Confederacy in his efforts to do so." The last thing he wanted to do was leave an unfinished war as a legacy to his children. It was his duty to fight on if he must—his only admission that he fought now out of duty, not expectation of success—but he would be glad to be spared that by a permanent peace. Lee left Singleton believing that a sixty-day armistice could produce a negotiated "reconstruction" on liberal terms, and that the South would give up slavery immediately in return for "fair compensation" and constitutional amendments protecting other rights of person and property. To that end he said he would be willing to meet with Grant to discuss a platform for peace.[85]

Singleton called Lee "the man with whom to treat," and others realized that as well.[86] Breckinridge assumed his portfolio as war secretary on February 7, and soon met frequently with Lee on matters relating to supplies and defense. Then in late February Longstreet came to Lee with a surprising proposal. During a meeting under flag of truce to discuss prisoner issues with General Ord, one of them changed the subject to how the commanding generals might end the war. Ord suggested that if Lee wanted to discuss the matter with Grant, he was sure Grant would agree to meet. It was this, as well as making his peace with the offended president, that brought Lee to Richmond on February 26 to see Davis, as well as Breckinridge. Three weeks earlier Lee had stated for public consumption that he did not see how the Confederacy could "by any compromise or negotiation" with the enemy abate any of the rights they claimed "without a surrender of the liberties we derived from our ancestors."[87] Privately, he now endorsed such a meeting, hoping there might be a possibility of peace without defeat if he and Grant could negotiate the points at issue and submit their recommendations to a military convention.[88]

For some time Breckinridge had believed the war was lost and reunion inevitable. Lee felt the same by now, and also Longstreet. Davis was not nearly ready to yield, but seized any hope for negotiation as a means of buying time. Lee wrote to Grant on March 2 suggesting a meeting, though he expected Grant to refuse any discussion not predicated on reunion. As Lee told Davis, he doubted that the Confederate people would accept reunion "yet awhile," a clear implication that he believed it must come eventually.[89] As expected, Grant replied that he could only meet with Lee on matters of a military nature. Still, he wrote in terms almost cordial, carefully explaining matters without the sarcasm and posturing that often infused communications between opposing army commanders. Mindful that such an approach could have been a ploy to postpone the commencement of active operations, still Grant believed that "peace must Come some day," and no peace feeler should be rejected out of hand.[90] The day that Lee received Grant's response, he met with Breckinridge and the quartermaster general and commissary of subsistence at the War Department to discuss the prospect for sustaining his army in the field that spring, and it was gloomy. Then they turned their conversation to peace. Davis was the obstacle, but Breckinridge believed that a strong and determined push from the Senate could force the president to address the issue, and Lee knew Hunter, the head of the Virginia delegation, well enough to approach him. They met and Lee suggested that Hunter introduce in the Senate a resolution calling on Davis to open negotiations with Lincoln looking toward an honorable surrender. Lee's own role, he told the senator, would be publicly to recommend opening negotiations, which he believed the armies and the people would regard as "almost equivalent to surrender." A later visit from Breckinridge emphasized the power of the general's personal prestige. This was no palace coup, but rather a design by constitutional means to nudge Davis to action. Unfortunately, Hunter refused.[91]

Set back but not beaten, the secretary and the general took a suggestion from Campbell, who agreed with them that any peace would inevitably come on terms of reunion and emancipation. On March 6 or 7 Lee and Breckinridge discussed it, and then on March 8, in his official capacity as war secretary, Breckinridge asked Lee to give him a written and candid statement of the military situation, to be handed to Davis and Congress. If Lee went on record publicly declaring that they were beaten, then surely the president would yield. The following day Lee delivered a report saying that their case was "full of peril." Confederate forces were ill equipped, ill fed, and outnumbered everywhere, and he entertained little hope of standing up to the foe in the coming spring. "It is not worse than the superior numbers and resources of the enemy justified us in expecting from the beginning," he added. The Confederacy had already held out "longer than we had reason to anticipate."

But then he temporized. The fall of Richmond and Petersburg would be a blow, but not necessarily fatal if the army in the field could be sustained. In fact, he did not say that their case was hopeless, and he did not mention opening surrender negotiations. Instead, he said everything depended on how much more sacrifice the elected representatives believed the people could sustain, the closest thing to a hint that Congress might conceivably act in the matter.[92] Lee fatally compromised the purpose of his report. Either he recoiled in the end from working with the politicians, some of them the same men whose failures brought on the war, or his loyalty to Davis and his duty trumped his conviction of inevitable defeat, which remained unchanged. Observers in the War Department and close to Davis detected an uncharacteristic caution in the report, and Campbell concluded that Lee "declined to do more than perform his military duty and would not assume to counsel much less to act upon the question of peace."[93] Davis sequestered the report, and only released a carefully edited précis that further weakened the document.

Still, Breckinridge probably showed the unexpurgated report a few days later when he met with several members of Congress to speak frankly of what he called "the final collapse." He suggested that even in their dire condition they still had a little power to negotiate for better terms than they might expect if defeated piece by piece.[94] He failed to move them to action before they adjourned on March 18, and that same day rode to Lee's headquarters to meet in private conference through March 21.[95] Their greatest bargaining chip remained at hand and under Lee's command, the Army of Northern Virginia. Breckinridge had been preparing in advance for the evacuation of the capital for weeks, and that exigency had been on Lee's mind for some time. When General Hood proposed a concentration of remaining armies in Tennessee, Lee responded doubtfully two days after his meetings with Breckinridge ended. "I believe it can be done though it would be attended with hazard & difficulty," he told Davis, for Yankees in east

Tennessee would be burning bridges to slow his westward progress, while Grant would surely pursue in the rear.

Still, he thought that "by energy & boldness the army might force its way to the borders of Tennessee." If Johnston's army from North Carolina and General Richard Taylor's in the Deep South could unite with him in central Tennessee, they would still number fewer than 100,000, especially after the inevitable straggling and desertion along the way. They would be too weak to occupy the country effectively, he said; "our continuance would depend upon victory." They would have to impress any supplies, having no means of moving their own where needed, and foraging would force them to spread out, thus lessening the advantage of concentration. He doubted they could reach the Ohio in any condition to invade the North and force Federals out of the Confederacy to meet them, and in any event their own transportation was such that they could hardly take more than enough ammunition for three battles.

In the end, he saw nothing to be gained that could not be realized with fewer complications by making the concentration in Virginia or North Carolina instead.[96] If Lee held off Grant long enough to remove supplies and materiel from the city, and then get his army away intact, he could try to link with Johnston's army now being pushed back in North Carolina by Sherman. Together they might turn on Sherman and perhaps defeat him before Grant caught up, and then turn to meet Grant. It was a plan that would have been delusional coming from any other Confederate at this stage of the war. Even coming from Lee it offered no realistic hope for more than a possible temporary advantage before the relentless Grant caught up to him. Nevertheless, Lee operating again in the open field posed a much more powerful argument in any surrender negotiations than he did bottled up in earthworks around Richmond.

On March 25 Lee launched a surprisingly powerful strike against the northern end of the Federal siege lines, reasoning that a breakthrough there would force Grant to contract elsewhere, which would open the way for Lee and much of the army to rush south to Johnston. Though the attack initially broke through, it soon lost momentum, not least because Grant's well-organized intelligence system had been informing him for some time that Lee was calling in outposts and guards from elsewhere, which Grant correctly read as a desperate buildup for an attack. "We are watching closely," he told Dana, and the watching paid off.[97] That left Lee with nothing to do but hope to get his entire army out in the field before the Yankees severed the last link out of Petersburg, the Southside Railroad to Danville.

A miserable rain soaked both armies at the end of the month, but Grant told Julia that bad as the weather was for his men, "it is Consoling to know that it rains on the enemy as well."[98] On April 1, however, Federal cavalry under Sheridan collapsed Lee's right flank at Five Forks. "I am feeling well and full of confidence," Grant wrote his wife after the news.[99] All the next day he pressed the whole Confederate line, and Lee knew he could stay in place no longer. He sent a telegram to Breckinridge saying he must evacuate during the night, and advised that the government prepare to leave Richmond. Soon a telegram arrived from the president with news that the government was not ready for a sudden move, archives had yet to be packed, and no one had arranged transportation. In fact, only the War Department was ready to go, thanks to Breckinridge. When Lee read the president's message he tore it to pieces, muttering to no one in particular that "I am sure I gave him sufficient notice."[100]

From the time his defensive lines first enveloped Petersburg, Lee felt painfully aware of the hardships of "its good people," and looking back on the city as he rode out in the night to march westward, he felt sorrowful for their lot as he abandoned them.[101] His hope was to outrun the Federals, reach supply depots at Lynchburg, and then turn south into North Carolina to link with Johnston more than a hundred miles away. Even more distant was any likelihood that he could make it happen. As his depleted legions made their way west, Lee's temper grew short from the frustration and anguish. Riding past a battery on the road, he saw a soldier exhibiting what he called "poor march discipline" and ordered him arrested, perhaps the only time in the war Lee ordered an arrest face to face.[102] Meanwhile, the Federals occupied first the abandoned Confederate works, and then Richmond on April 3. Grant admitted that there might yet be "some more hard work," but the prize was within grasp.[103] He communicated with Lincoln daily, and sometimes several times a day, the news in every telegram better than in the one before. On April 5 Lee reached Amelia Court House expecting to find a trainload of supplies, only to discover that Grant's

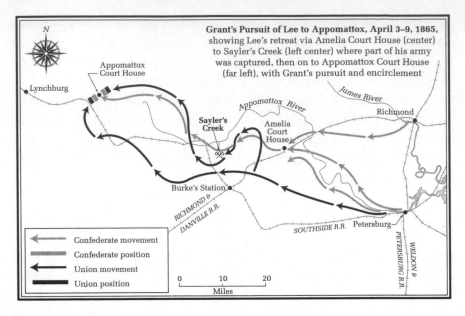

Grant's Pursuit of Lee to Appomattox, April 3–9, 1865, showing Lee's retreat via Amelia Court House (center) to Sayler's Creek (left center) where part of his army was captured, then on to Appomattox Court House (far left), with Grant's pursuit and encirclement

spies had diverted it. Forced to keep moving hungry, Lee pressed on the next day, and that morning Breckinridge caught up to him and they conferred briefly. That night they met again in Farmville, only after a third of the army had been lost at Sayler's Creek when it became isolated from the rest by the Appomattox River as the Yankees closed in. Lee had not much more than 25,000 soldiers remaining.

Lee met with Breckinridge again on the morning of April 7. Neither later divulged what they discussed. Surely much centered on avoiding battle if at all possible, and getting the remnant of the army away to link with Johnston. However, they also probably spoke of possible terms if Lee could not escape. Campbell had remained in Richmond hoping to meet with Lincoln to make their arguments for restoration. If brought to bay by Grant, Lee could try to make that same case with him if the reward were not just the Army of Northern Virginia, but all remaining Confederate forces. Coincidentally, just hours later Grant sent a note through the lines to Lee suggesting that further resistance meant only more useless bloodletting and asking Lee to surrender. Lee's reply reached him the next day, denying that the situation was yet that critical, but asking what terms Grant might propose before he considered the call for capitulation. *"Peace* being my great desire," Grant responded, he had but one condition: that on surrendering, the

Confederates go home and not take arms again unless properly exchanged, which he of course knew would never happen.

Lee wrote back asserting that "I did not intend to propose the surrender of the Army of Northern Virginia." Then he went on to add that since "the restoration of peace should be the sole object of all," he would like to meet with Grant to discuss how his proposed terms "may affect the C. S. forces under my command, & tend to the restoration of peace." Lee's meaning depended on how his note was read. Did he mean he would not discuss surrendering the army immediately facing Grant? Or had he not meant to limit his inquiry to just his army? He was willing to talk about something affecting "the C. S. forces under my command." Since he was general-in-chief, that meant the entire Confederate army, in effect the Confederacy itself.[104] Lee was attempting to do now what Breckinridge and Campbell had hoped he would do weeks before.

Lee said nothing about restoration of the Union or the end of slavery. Both were foregone conclusions, but there were other considerations of importance to Southerners, as there were many kinds of peace. Would Confederate officers and men be proscribed in any fashion, or would they have their full rights in a new Union? Would their leaders like Davis face indictment and trial for treason, or be left unmolested? Would they be secure in their real property, or face further confiscation as punitive retribution or to recompense the North for its war debt? Would their own war debts abroad be assumed by Washington? Most of all, could their sitting governors and legislatures be allowed to continue in office, and would they be allowed to send representatives to Congress with full rights? Would the relation of the states to the federal government be the same as before, or were they to be thereafter entirely subordinate to the central authority? Were they to have the Union of 1860, or something newer and less palatable?

By speaking of "the C. S. forces under my command," Lee hinted that in return for something approaching reunion on the basis of the prewar status quo, he would consider a universal surrender, though he probably hoped that talks with Grant might lead to an armistice followed by a voluntary dissolution of Confederate forces. This would mean not a defeat but a "withdrawal" with honor from the war. Further resistance in the interest of Confederate independence might be a fantasy, but with perhaps up to 150,000 men under arms between Virginia and Texas, the Confederates still had power to make the Yankees pay dearly in blood and treasure for victory. Like Breckinridge and Campbell, Lee regarded that as something to trade in return for some political and social concessions, and an end to conflict short of the humiliation of surrender. Most significantly, Lee hinted at all this with no consultation with Davis, who was trying to reestablish his government in Danville. Davis had been willing to negotiate before, and Lee could assume that he would again, though independence was always Davis's sine qua non. For Lee, in this extremis, it was not. He knew he proposed the death of the Confederacy in return for concessions. All of that he implied in those few brief words about restoration and the forces under his command.[105]

Grant quashed that immediately by responding on the morning of April 9 that "I have no authority to treat on the subject of peace," and therefore he saw no purpose served in meeting. While an isolated Lee could exercise considerable latitude in any negotiation, Grant could not. In a meeting with Lincoln just a dozen days before, the president made clear that he was to capture Lee's army or force its surrender on the terms Grant had already proposed, but nothing more. He was not to discuss questions of a political or social nature. All of that would be up to Lincoln and Congress afterward. If there had ever been a time when the Campbell-Breckinridge-Lee plan for peace had a hope, the time was past. Lee realized that when he received Grant's reply. By now his army was almost surrounded, starving, and his only route of escape to the west cut off by Sheridan's cavalry. His options were gone, and as soon as he received Grant's refusal at about eight-thirty that morning, he accepted the inevitable and responded by asking for a meeting to discuss the surrender of the Army of Northern Virginia.

Grant and Lee met in the parlor of a private home in the village of Appomattox Court House. Grant had hoped to avoid any formal surrender ceremony. "These are our people," he explained later. "They are not foreigners, but they belong to us and we to them, and all we want is for them to stop fighting, and for us all to live at peace and as a Union."[106] There had been no pomp at Fort Donelson or Vicksburg, and he wanted none now, sensing that it accorded with Lincoln's wishes. It would only humiliate the vanquished and do nothing to smooth their transition to citizenship. Still, there was no keeping several of his staff away, and a few of his generals, while for his part Lee arrived with only Taylor and Marshall.

The interview that followed is enshrined in American memory. It was the second time they had met since Mexico City. Lee claimed to remember Grant well, though that was more likely just courtesy. Certainly Grant remembered Lee. Neither was at his best. Grant had a migraine headache and later confessed to feelings of sadness and depression, as more than three years of anticipation of this moment released a flood of empathy.[107] This was not just the end of the Army of Northern Virginia, and presumably the war. It was also the end of the greatest, and only, sustained success of his life. Surely that was not on his mind just now, but his own future from this moment on was almost as uncertain as Lee's. Meanwhile, behind his dignified self-control, Lee felt almost overwhelmed. People who saw him then and the next day thought him depressed and his mind wandering.

Grant tried small talk to mask his ill ease until Lee brought them to the point. He wanted it over with. Grant reiterated Lincoln's terms. Lee agreed and asked to have them in writing. Handed the document, Lee read and approved, speaking only once to note the "happy effect" a provision for officers to retain their horses and side arms would have. Explaining that his cavalrymen and artillerymen owned their own horses, Lee observed that they were not covered in Grant's draft, a clarification amounting to a hint that Grant took. Thereupon Lee wrote a letter of acceptance, and was on the verge of leaving when he asked if Grant could provide rations and forage for his men and animals. Grant's immediate response was to ask how much he wanted and then told Lee to send his quartermasters and commissaries to get as much as they needed. After naming officers to work out the details of paroling the Confederates, Lee and Grant exchanged farewells and left, Lee first. As Lee mounted Traveller to return to his lines, Grant came out onto the porch and down a few steps to raise his hat, the officers behind him following his salute. Lee raised his own hat in response and rode away.[108] With him went an atmosphere of tension and discomfort that had pervaded throughout the interview.

Lee returned to his headquarters to break the news to his soldiers. Grant cut short an impromptu artillery salute in celebration. "We did not want to exult over their downfall," he wrote later. He knew enough of defeat and humiliation to know its sting. That done, he made plans to immediately go to Washington to halt the "useless outlay of money" on purchasing further supplies for his army. He never quite stopped being a quartermaster.[109]

17

GRANT AND LEE
IN 1868

Grant wanted to see Lee one more time, and without a room full of onlookers. The next morning he wired his friend and patron Washburne the news of the surrender, and then rode toward Lee's headquarters under a white flag.[1] Lee rode to meet him, but neither dismounted. They had met in war the day before. This was their first meeting in peace, and Grant wanted to expand it beyond Appomattox. The suddenness of the collapse somewhat surprised Grant, having thought the war in Virginia might last through the summer; nonetheless, he had assumed that when the Confederacy did start to topple, it would go quickly. On reflection he even thought it perhaps better that he had not taken Petersburg in June 1864. If he had, then Lee likely would have evacuated and withdrawn into the state's interior, possibly even resorting to the option of dispersing his army into guerrilla bands that might have prolonged the war for years.[2]

At the meeting Lee tried to negotiate subtly, observing that the South was a huge country, and though remaining Confederate forces could scarcely prevent an ultimate victory, the Yankees might have to move their armies across that landscape several times to complete their conquest. He hoped no more blood need be shed, but he could not tell what might happen. Presumably, he said nothing about an armistice and negotiations, but somewhere in there was a vague hint that generous terms, and perhaps some guarantees of civil and property rights afterward, might yield a full and immediate cease-fire. Grant had a wider peace on his mind, for he replied that he thought further fighting could be averted if Lee, as the one Confederate with more military and civil influence than any other, would "advise" all remaining Confederates to surrender. Loyal to the last to his subordination to his chief executive, Lee said he could not do that without first consulting Davis, which by implication suggested he was willing to do so if Davis agreed. Davis was unpredictable, and in any event they could not be sure if he was still in Danville—which he was not—raising the possibility that Lee wanted to buy time. Grant was not selling, however. As usual, he wanted something now, yet he also knew and understood enough of Lee to know he would not compromise when it came to his duty, and so did not press the matter.[3] They would not meet again for four years.

A few minutes later some Union officers including Meade visited Lee in his lines, and one staff officer noted not only the general's grave manner, but also that he seemed extremely depressed, "which gave him the air of a man who kept up his pride to the last, but who was entirely overwhelmed." Moreover, in speaking with Meade and others, Lee's mind seemed to wander, though he did aver that peace could be made at once if the Union adopted a conciliatory policy.[4] Perhaps his distraction resulted from trying to organize his thoughts for the tasks remaining to him. He needed to notify President Davis of his actions and it was his duty to file a final report. Harder still, he must find a way to say farewell to his loyal old veterans.

Lee gave Marshall the task of composing the farewell, while Taylor gathered such reports as he could from which to write a report of the last several days, the gist of which was that, outnumbered in his reckoning by five to one, his men unfed and exhausted, he felt he might have fought his way out of the encirclement to buy one more day, but a surrender would have been inevitable.[5] While that was in preparation, Lee edited Marshall's draft of what would be General Order No. 9 and had copies made to be read through the remnant of his army. They had fought heroically for four years, it began, and were now forced to "yield," but only to overwhelming enemy strength. He did so to save more blood. Grant's terms were honorable, and they could go home conscious of "duty faithfully performed." He said nothing about their fallen cause, which would only emphasize their situation and needlessly irritate the Federals, and closed saying, "I bid you an affectionate farewell."[6] That night he shared a last quiet supper with his staff, none of whom felt much like talking.

Lee chose not to be present at the formal ceremony two days later when his tattered legions marched past the victors to lay down their

rifles and banners. Early on the morning of April 12 he left in company with Taylor and Major Giles B. Cooke. His stopped to see his
brother Carter on the way, finally rode across the James bridge into
Richmond on the afternoon of April 15, and went immediately to the
house he rented on Franklin Street, though not without a few cheers
from civilians, and even a few Union soldiers, on the sidewalks.[7] Only
then, probably, did he learn that the night before President Lincoln had
been shot and was now dead. For the next several days he sequestered
himself at home with Mary, and was scarcely seen on the streets for
several weeks.[8] He slept as much as he could, and talked with Mary
and all of his children who gathered. He told them the story of Appomattox, how he had barely 8,700 men, and how they were all resolved
to cut their way out and fight on if Grant had demanded his usual
unconditional surrender. However, Lee said Grant's terms "were so
honorable" that he accepted, to save further loss of life.[9] That, at least,
is how he preferred to remember it at the moment. After a few days
he also concluded that he had one more duty to perform. As a paroled
prisoner of war, he no longer had authority over remaining soldiers
in the field, but he feared for their safety. On April 20, knowing nothing more than that Davis and his government had fled Danville after
his surrender, and were then in or near Charlotte, North Carolina, he
wrote a letter to the president. It was the sort of letter Campbell and
Breckinridge had hoped for in February, and the first step to realizing
what Grant sought in their April 10 meeting. Lee painted a frank picture of the demoralization of his army during the past winter, of how
their fighting spirit had left them, followed by the onset of epidemic
straggling and desertion. Almost 19,000 men had simply disappeared
in the final weeks. No Confederate army could now be reconstituted
in Virginia, let alone sustained, and he regarded affairs west of the
Mississippi as hopeless. Making no mention at all of Johnston and his
army facing Sherman, or of other scattered smaller forces in Alabama,
Lee regarded the only alternative remaining to them as a partisan war,
Confederate forces disbanding and taking to the hill and mountain
country and sniping at Union forces in small bands. He rejected that
out of hand as prolonging needless suffering, and as ultimately futile.
"I see no prospect," he concluded, "of achieving a separate independence." He recommended that Davis take steps to suspend hostilities,

meaning to secure an armistice leading to "the restoration of peace."[10] Even with his own army off the board, he felt that remaining Confederates might possibly gain something from negotiation if the Yankees would talk.

Lee may never have sent the letter, for even if he knew that Davis was in Charlotte, there was no way to get it to him, and soon enough the fleeing government was on the road again. Moreover, soon there was no point. Six days later Johnston surrendered to Sherman on terms similar to those given Lee. On May 4 the army in Alabama gave up, leaving only the Army of the Trans-Mississippi at large, and it was disintegrating and destined for surrender in three more weeks. Meanwhile, Federal cavalry captured Davis and his entourage on May 10 in Georgia.

More immediate matters faced Lee. He had no home of his own, no property but his clothing. Food was scarce and he had no money when it could be bought, and friends and well-wishers helped as they could by bringing produce to the house. The Lees even accepted some of the rations being doled out by Federal occupying troops to civilians, "just like the poorest negro in the place," thought one of Meade's staff.[11] Early in May Grant's army marched back through Richmond on its way to Washington to muster out. Meade called on Lee and the two old friends shared memories and discussed the future, Lee hesitant to commit himself until he knew what President Andrew Johnson's policy would be. Once satisfied that it would not be punitive toward the South, he said he would take the oath of allegiance, apply for the restoration of full rights of citizenship, and counsel others to do the same. For himself, he concluded to avoid all public controversy over the war and its causes, or current and future national affairs. He would stay out of the public eye and work to rebuild himself and Virginia.

The best way to accomplish that was to settle somewhere other than Richmond. Lee wanted to get his family to the country, perhaps near Rooney's place on the Pamunkey River, where they might be able to support themselves and find peace out of the way of constant reminders of their situation.[12] Punctuating that was the steady rumble of thousands of feet on the city streets as Grant's veterans, and then Sherman's, passed through headed to Washington. Occasionally a regiment marched down Franklin Street and a sharp-eyed Yankee looked up to see Lee in the window, partly veiled by the curtain, watching as they tramped past.[13]

Several of his old officers and soldiers called at his door, many seeking advice on whether to leave the country and go to Mexico or Brazil where colonies of former Confederates were to be launched. Brigadier General John Echols and Colonel Josiah Stoddard Johnston called and had a frank interview in which Lee said the South was in deplorable condition, its people without the protection of law, in financial ruin, and the children going without education. He discouraged all talk of emigration. Those who had been leaders in the Confederacy had an obligation to remain and share the fate of their people and help in the rebuilding, even at risk of their personal safety. "As to my own fate, I know not what is in store for me," he told his callers. "I believe the politicians at Washington are bent on the most extreme measures, and if they have their way will stop at no humiliation they can heap on me." He relied on Grant. "I have faith in his honor and his integrity as a soldier, and do not believe that he will permit the terms of my surrender or the parole given me to be violated."[14]

He also met with a few Yankees, among them the chaplain of the 80th Ohio Infantry, George W. Pepper, and in talking with them he weighed every sentence carefully before speaking. Pepper found that "his heart was grand and large" as he spoke, criticizing the politicians who brought on the war, including even Davis. Lee restated his opposition to secession and war, and how he resigned his commission to try to stay out of it. Lincoln's murder horrified him, but he had nothing but generous words for Grant. It was but "simple justice to General Grant" to acknowledge that his treatment of Lee's army was "without a parallel." Asked whom he thought to be the best of the Union generals, Lee diplomatically responded that "I have no hesitation in saying General Grant." He became more guarded when Pepper pressed him on the reasons for Confederate defeat. Lee said he was not a good extemporaneous speaker, "nor am I a very good extemporaneous answerer of questions." Superior manpower and resources beat them in part, he volunteered, but so did the vanity of the Southern people after early victories: "The cheering proved to be our folly."[15]

The constant callers made it difficult for him to stay out of the public eye. Early in May leaders of two Northern relief commissions, in

Richmond trying to feed the hungry, came to his door. Dressed in his old uniform, Lee met them in his dining room, saying nothing as they introduced themselves and extended their hands. Declaring theirs an unofficial visit, they merely called to pay their respects. Then one of the leaders said that he hoped Lee sympathized with their mission. The general spoke affirmatively, adding that such associations had done great good, and he hoped their efforts would succeed. They shook his hand again and left.[16]

Within days Lee's old enemy the New York *Tribune* condemned the "humanitarians" for meeting with Lee, and then reiterated the old Norris whipping story, now enhanced to have Lee working the slaves to pay his own debts, not his father-in-law's, and rubbing down the bloody brine-soaked backs of his victims with rough corn husks.[17] Less than a month later Senator Henry Wilson of Massachusetts spoke at Boston's Emancipation League and referred to Lee as "the woman whipper of Arlington."[18] It was Lee's first experience of the danger of speaking with even the most innocent callers.

When he did go out in public, he carried with him that same consciousness of the role he had chosen to play. For a start, when he was last in Richmond most of its black population were slaves. A few weeks later on his return they were all freedmen and the social balance had shifted dramatically. To be sure, whites still held all of the social, political, and economic power, but the door had been opened for blacks to make modest challenges to the old order. On Sunday June 4 Lee went to St. Paul's Episcopal Church for a communion service. While he was there, perhaps at the communion itself, an incident apparently took place involving a black communicant. Nothing more is known, but forty years later a witness still remembered that something occurred that would not have happened three months before.[19]

That may have been a part of the reason Lee wanted to leave Richmond, but mainly it was for peace and quiet, for Mary's health, and as he put it, to make a "quiet house in the woods where I can procure shelter & my daily bread if permitted by the victors."[20] When Elizabeth Randolph Cocke offered him a modest four-room cottage at Derwent near Powhatan, he gladly accepted and moved the family in the last week of June.[21] Soon he told his son Robert that "we are all well & established in a comfortable but small house, in a grove of oaks."

It was a poor region, but good for Mary, and he had some thought of trying farming at last.[22]

Before leaving Lee prepared an application for pardon and submitted it to friends in Richmond for their opinion.[23] In the process, he made clear that he acted willingly and only on his own behalf. His son Custis recalled him saying at the time that "it was but right for him to set an example of making formal submission to the Civil Authorities; and that he thought, by so doing, he might possibly be in a better position to be of use to the Confederates, who were not protected by Military paroles, especially Mr. Davis."[24] When word reached the press, speculation as to his motives ran rampant, but a few months later he explained his reason to Beauregard. "True patriotism sometimes re quires of men to act exactly contrary, at one period, to that which it does at another, and the motive which impels them—the desire to do right—is precisely the same," he wrote. "The circumstances which govern their actions change; and their conduct must conform to the new order of things."[25]

Lee was conforming to that "new order." However, just when his application was ready to submit, Federal Judge John Underwood in Norfolk unexpectedly handed down an indictment against him for treason on June 7. Lee doubted that there would be any trial, thinking himself protected from prosecution by the Appomattox surrender terms, but still engaged legal counsel. He sent his application to Grant, and asked if Grant believed he was liable to indictment. If so, he would not submit his application. If Grant did not so feel, then he asked him to forward it to the president. Telling Lee that he believed his own "good faith" was pledged to him, Grant endorsed the application on June 16 and took the matter personally to Johnson, finally threatening to resign unless the indictment was quashed. Johnson gave in on June 20, the indictment disappeared, and Grant sent him Lee's application. Perversely, no pardon ever came because when Lee sent in the required oath of allegiance on October 2, someone in the executive branch kept the document as a souvenir.[26]

When no pardon arrived soon after Grant's letter, Lee began to wonder if he would ever have his civil rights fully restored, but he did not broach the matter again to Grant. Meanwhile, he stayed at home and did not travel, unclear even as to restrictions on his movements.[27]

While still at Derwent, Lee sent a verbal message to imprisoned Jefferson Davis that "I have not words warm enough & strong enough to express the deep sympathy & constant solicitude I feel for him." Making it worse, Lee told the messenger, was the distressing feeling that he could do nothing. "I trust it may not always be so."[28] Indeed it might not, if he so chose.

Virtually all former Confederates felt that helplessness the summer after the war, but none more than Lee, who sensed keenly the precariousness of his situation. His position called for great care in what he said and did, not only for himself personally, but for all Southerners to whom he was now a symbol of their failed cause, and their current political condition. Hence Lee took heart at any sign of a conciliatory attitude from Congress and the White House. "I wish that spirit could become more general," he wrote Letcher after the former Virginia governor received a friendly welcome in Washington. "It would go far to promote confidence & to calm feelings which have too long existed." Lee freely acknowledged that having lost their bid for independence, it was now incumbent on the Southern states to yield manfully and openly to the result. The interests of Virginia were once more identical to those of the general government, and their future prosperity inextricably intertwined. "All should unite in honest efforts to obliterate the grievous effects of war," he added, "& to restore the blessings of peace." Virginians should promote good will, and elect to state and federal offices "wise & patriotic men, who devote their abilities to the interests of the Country & the healing of all dissensions." They should also remain in Virginia.[29] Some Confederates had expatriated themselves to Mexico, and other colonization schemes even then attracted more to Brazil, Venezuela, and elsewhere. The way for former Confederates to serve their states was to stay home and rebuild.

Whether he liked it or not, Lee was to be an example to other ex-Confederates who took their cue from his behavior. He had half expected that, and apparently from the day of the surrender never gave a thought to leaving Virginia, but once more to "share the fortunes of my people," for as he told one cousin, his native state "requires the presence of all her sons, more now, than at any period of her history." Beyond that advice, which he would give again and again, he refrained from offering counsel. As for Virginians who had left the country during the war and wanted to return, he suggested that they secure a pardon "So Called" before entering the country just to be safe.[30] By the fall, however, he allowed an occasional letter to this effect to be handed to the press, or else was not consulted in the matter. A September letter to a man in Petersburg laid out his policy as well as any. "It should be the object of all to avoid controversy, to allay passion, give free scope to reason and every kindly feeling," he wrote. He believed that if people devoted themselves to life's daily duties "with a determination not to be turned aside by thoughts of the past or fears of the future, our country will not only be restored in material prosperity, but will be advanced in science, in virtue and in religion."[31]

Following his unsuccessful meeting with Lee after the surrender at Appomattox, Grant went to Washington to see Lincoln and Stanton, where fortunately he declined an invitation to the theater and instead left for Philadelphia to join Julia. He arrived to the news that Lincoln had been shot and was dying. Grant immediately returned to Washington, stunned by the news, and uneasy that the vindictive Johnson of Tennessee would now be president. Not knowing the extent of the murderous conspiracy, Grant spent his days in an office at his headquarters with a guard, and only appeared outside twice a day to go to his hotel for meals.[32] Forty-eight hours after Lincoln's death Sherman sent word that he and Johnston were going to meet, with surrender a likely result, so Grant decided to shift the crest of the wave west and ordered Pope to send a proposal for surrender to General Kirby Smith in command of Confederates west of the Mississippi.[33] The flurry of activity brought on by the Confederate collapse was so great that Grant could scarcely escape for a meal. On April 21 when the result of Sherman's meeting with Johnston came in, he saw that his subordinate went far beyond just the surrender of the Army of Tennessee, and had negotiated a surrender of all remaining Confederate forces. Grant knew at once that it went too far and would not be approved, and so it was not when the president and cabinet saw the document. Grant had to inform Sherman to resume hostilities and confine any further negotiations to the surrender of Johnston's army only.[34]

The magnitude of what the Union had achieved was beginning to dawn on him more than ever. "What a spectacle it will be to see a country able to put down a rebellion able to put half a Million of soldiers in the field," he wrote Julia that evening. "That Nation, united, will have a strength which will enable it to dictate to all others [to] *conform to justice and right.*" However, its power should go no further than that. "The moment conscience leaves, physical strength will avail nothing."[35] Coincidentally, he wrote that same evening in answer to a cousin's inquiry about his own future that "I can truly say that I am without ambition," though he confessed that he liked public approval, "for it is in their interest I am serving."[36]

Grant went immediately to North Carolina to meet with Sherman and stayed several days until Johnston finally surrendered on April 26. He sent renewed instructions to army commanders elsewhere to initiate surrender talks on the basis of the terms given Lee and Johnston, and then turned to an aspect of being general-in-chief that he never anticipated. The rejection of Sherman's first agreement commenced a feud between Stanton and Sherman that became embarrassingly public, with Grant trying to arbitrate in the middle. It was only a hint of the job ahead, for now that the Confederacy was virtually conquered, the whole subject of the military's role in the subsequent reconstruction remained to be seen. Would the army be reassigned as an occupying force, or would it be disbanded? What was to happen to the men like Sherman, Sheridan, Thomas, Meade, and many more who were the architects of victory? For that matter, what was to happen to Grant himself?

At the end of May, Johnson issued a proclamation outlining the procedure to be followed by those former Confederates who wanted to seek pardon and amnesty. When Grant heard Lee might apply, he was pleased, though he expected it would be opposed by a vengeful faction in the North and among the Radical Republicans. "I think it would have the best possible effect towards restoring good feeling and peace in the South," he told Halleck. "All the people except a few political leaders South will accept what ever he does as right and will be guided to a great extent by his example."[37] It was what he had believed all along. When Underwood's grand jury handed down Lee's indictment, Grant took Lee's application to the president and stood his ground when Johnson argued that the Appomattox terms and parole only had effect while Lee was a soldier. Now that he was a civilian he enjoyed no protection from civil prosecution. Grant met him argument for argument, telling Johnson he could do what he pleased about civil rights and other questions, but the surrender terms had to be honored. To do otherwise brought dishonor on the government for breaching its own terms, and undid all that Grant had tried to accomplish by way of easing Confederates from resistance toward citizenship. Moreover, Lincoln had in part inspired the Appomattox terms, and tacitly approved them after the fact. Johnson was probably already tired of hearing what Lincoln had done or would do, and demanded to know when the general-in-chief believed any former Confederate leaders could be brought to trial. Grant responded, "Never." At an impasse, Grant closed the conversation with a threat to resign his office if the president dishonored the Appomattox accord. Johnson, already in a weak position, and faced with having to explain to the administration and people how he lost the most popular man in America, finally relented. The indictment against Lee would be dropped and he would be free from any further prosecution for his Confederate service.

By late June all organized Confederate forces had surrendered, and Grant felt it was time to prepare a final report on the actions of the armies since he assumed overall command. He opened with a statement of his conviction early in the war that continuous operations on all fronts were the way to bring down the rebellion, not eastern and western armies acting independent of each other, and sitting out winters in the East and hot summers in the West. They must defeat the military capability of the foe, and then the rebellion would be extinguished. He closed complimenting Lee that "great consideration is due him for his manly course and bearing shown in his surrender." Grant wrote then crossed out a passage condemning Lee's indictment and possible prosecution, saying that had Lee known that was ahead, he would have fought his way out and the war in Virginia would still be going on. "Gen. Lee's great influence throughout the whole South caused his example to be followed," and the armies under him were at home desiring peace. He also wrote then crossed out a passage reflecting on reconstruction. Opposing views among the loyal on handling the defated South had led to factionalism, while those who fought largely wanted moderation and forgiveness. "Would it not be well for all to learn to yeald enough of their individual views to the will of the Majority to preserve a long and happy peace?" On reflection, he deleted such passages that overstepped the bounds of his authority, but his desire for a gentle and speedy reconstruction was clear.[38]

Grant made a visit back to Galena in September to find that his old fellow townsmen had collected more than $16,000 to buy his family a large brick home well stocked with wine and cigars, with views from the top floor across the Mississippi to Iowa, and even an indoor bathroom. Grant liked it there when he was able to get away from Washington. He took morning walks into town to talk with old friends in his brother's store just as he had before the war, only now he did not have to put up with cutting remarks from Orville. A custodian lived in the house when the Grants were in Washington, and though originally he thought he wanted to settle there for good, after a time Grant realized he could not stay. The visits to the store paled and he went less and less often. Friends saw "a far-away look" in his eyes, and he told one that "I like Galena, but there is nothing for me to do here. I must have something to do."[39] He thought for a time of indulging his love of travel by making a trip to Europe, but returned to Washington to embark instead on an inspection trip through some of the South late that fall.[40]

He stopped first at Richmond then went on to Wilmington, Charleston, Savannah, Atlanta, and East Tennessee. What he saw encouraged him that former Confederates were anxious for peace and reconciliation. He produced a report, released to the press, in which he stated all this, arguing strongly that sentiment for reconciliation was strong in the South; though he included the caveat that whites who had remained loyal to the Union and freed blacks were going to need protection until all Southerners were willing to accept Federal authority. Reports of violence toward blacks were too frequent to ignore and he wanted them to stop. Grant was evolving toward a reconstruction policy of his own somewhat at variance both with that of the president and Johnson's Radical Republican enemies in Congress. In January 1866 he issued orders to all commanders in the occupied South to protect blacks. Sending subordinates on a tour of Mississippi, Louisiana, and Texas, he learned that resistance sentiment and antipathy toward freedmen was even greater there. It convinced him that civil authorities were as yet helpless, and that only the army could afford safety, thus weakening his belief that reconciliation might be quick and relatively painless. All of that put him between the president and Congress, both sides courting him for his prestige. He was discovering that political warfare could be far more subtle, complex, and messy than the battlefield.

By the time Lee wrote the September letter to the man in Petersburg, he knew the direction his "daily duties" were to take. The trustees of Lexington's Washington College had offered him its presidency. The institution traced its roots back more than a century, but was in poor straits like most higher education in the South immediately after the war. "If I believed I could be of advantage to the youth of the Country, I should not hesitate," he wrote former governor John Letcher.[41] He replied to the trustees that "I think it the duty of every citizen, in the present condition of the country, to do all in his power to aid in the restoration of peace and harmony, and in no way to oppose the policy of the State or general governments directed to that object."[42] On September 18 a gray horse carrying a gray man in an old military coat with neither buttons nor insignia rode into Lexington, and quickly word spread that General Lee had come to take over his school.[43]

The trustees wanted him to expand course offerings to make it more attractive to a postwar generation, and at the same time raise the college's endowment. Lee accepted the challenge, and began to spread the word to potential benefactors.[44] By the next spring, at the end of his first term as president, Washington College graduated sixteen young men, and Lee endured his first commencement. Students and guests that day saw on the dais a man about five feet, ten inches tall standing on surprisingly small feet, with a heavy gray mustache and short cropped gray beard, the hair on his head thin and gray, and almost gone from the top and back. "His eye is *fine*, his walk *military*, and active, his general carriage superb," wrote one who saw him shortly afterward. "If you did not note the glance of his eye and the military carriage you would take him for a well-to-do Va farmer." That observer thought Lee possessed of "an active, acute mind, rather than a mind of great power."[45] Certainly his first graduates were impressed with him, and each had a speech prepared. Most of them repeatedly referred to their admiration for Lee. Sitting on the stand through one after another of these, Lee grew impatient, especially as the school band performed after each peroration. During one musical selection he asked Professor William Allan, "Colonel Allen, how many more of them are to speak?" Told that four remained, Lee leaned over and whispered, "Couldn't you arrange it, Colonel, for all four to speak at once?"[46]

Lee actively promoted the school, telling parents that any student with a desire to learn ought to do well, yet he did not tout it at the expense of other state institutions.[47] He went to work on a new catalog and prepared synopses of course offerings, proudly announcing an expanded curriculum for the fall 1866 term and four new professors.[48] Lee echoed his style at West Point. He knew every pupil, corresponded directly with parents when grades were in, and admonished them that "your influence & advice will prevail with them more than that of any one else."[49] To prospective students he stressed that "you should the more earnestly devote yourself to the acquisition of an education, by preparing yourself to fulfill well all the duties of life."[50]

Lee always stressed duty. The college was a member of the Educational Association of Virginia, which in the spring of 1867 invited him to coauthor an address to parents. The finished piece came almost entirely from Lee, and he could have been writing his own personal credo.[51] He stressed obedience, self-control, consistency, and setting a good example for their children. Parents must be truthful, sincere Christians, and demand hard work. "If habits of self-control and self-denial have been acquired during the season of education," he wrote, "the great object has been accomplished."[52] With 410 students in the school, Lee knew each by name, and his standing in his studies. If he decided to discipline a student, he called him to his office where, instead of scolding or a lecture, he shamed the boy with kindness.[53] At the same time, exemplary performance earned Lee's compliments, and a laudatory letter to parents.[54] He did impose summary discipline when necessary, expelling three who verbally abused a Northern-born storekeeper who had threatened a boy with a pistol after being insulted.[55] Unfortunately, that incident was grossly exaggerated in the

Northern press after a meeting in New York saw Horace Greeley, Garrett Smith, Henry Ward Beecher, and others make and call for donations for the college's endowment, while speaking respectfully of Lee as a man.[56] Outraged anonymous writers soon said the storekeeper had been attacked by seventy-five students and driven from town in fear of his life, that the faculty and students were all "thoroughly rebel in sentiment," and the school itself "a hot-bed of proscription and embryo treason."[57]

That and similar incidents soon led to an investigation by the military authorities running the state, which absolved Lee and the school, but not before more letters hit the press charging abuse and intimidation of blacks and teachers of the local freedmen's school.[58] Soon sensationalist accounts appeared of nightly rioting in Lexington's streets, blacks being murdered indiscriminately, and Lee "a perfect nonentity" doing nothing but running a school where classrooms were "a bed of rampant secession" and students were taught "to be ready at any time to turn against the General Government."[59] One of the professors supposedly said that if the Southern states should rise again, "I have General Lee to think for me, and when he acts, I will follow in his steps."[60] For a change, Lee wrote a public denial, but to little effect, and in any case the bad press did no lasting damage.[61] After three years Washington College appeared to be flourishing, and even some in the Northern press acknowledged that it was due to "the admirable qualifications of its President."[62] By 1869 Lee had commenced schools of law, business, and journalism, meanwhile promoting agricultural and mechanical studies. [63]

Everyone wanted to capitalize on his fame, or so it seemed. Life insurance companies offered him figurehead presidencies.[64] Railroads approached him. Wilmer McLean, in whose parlor Lee agreed to surrender, asked to have a portrait of Lee made to sell along with a photo of his house, which Lee declined.[65] Still, the manufacturers of a sewing machine took a private letter from Lee, saying how much his daughters liked their machine, and turned it into a product endorsement appearing all across the country in newspaper advertisements, probably to his embarrassment.[66] Yet Lee did take one approach quite seriously. Informed of a proposed merger of the Virginia Central and Chesapeake & Ohio Railroads that would connect Richmond with the

Ohio River, he predicted great benefits for Virginia in a letter that promoters used to raise capitalization.[67] Rumor soon said that Lee had accepted the line's presidency, which he had not, but three years later the company did offer him its top job and he agreed to accept when the construction was completed, so long as it allowed him to continue his work at the college.[68]

He wanted to do something else as well. Just three months after Appomattox he decided to write a history of his army's campaigns as "the only tribute I can pay to their valour & devotion." Sadly, most of his war papers and reports were gone, and he felt real doubts that his book would be possible.[69] He decided to collect papers and recollections from his senior officers, and sent a circular to many asking for what they could send, saying his object was "to transmit, if possible, the truth to posterity and to do justice to our brave soldiers." Reflecting his continuing anger at the destruction of property, he also wanted statistics on Yankee damage, and accurate numbers so he could "get the world to understand the odds against which we fought," a special fixation for the rest of his life.[70] Besides defending himself and his army, he wanted to defend his cause, shifting his loyalty as a Confederate to the preservation of Confederate memory.

By early 1866 material enough came in to encourage him that he might be able "to do justice to those who fell," especially since he could rely on the documents "better than my own memory."[71] Generals like Breckinridge who were compiling their own narratives happily shared copies, but after a year Lee had yet to write a line, especially on learning that almost all of the official papers of Longstreet's corps had been lost.[72] Soon publishers hovered, sensing a big seller. One was rumored to have offered a $10,000 gift to the college in return for a series of weekly articles, which Lee declined. He first spoke of the book with Charles B. Richardson of New York, who specialized in works by Confederates about the war, and met with him more than once in 1865 and 1866. Richardson wanted to publish in August 1866, but Lee thought that too soon, as the public mind was "not yet ready to receive the truth." When the publisher told him that the work would sell better sooner rather than later, Lee agreed, but sales were "not altogether my object," besides which he still had written nothing.[73] By December 1866 Lee told a friend that "I progress slowly," and kept collecting materials in a desultory fashion but never felt he had enough to begin the work.[74] In March 1869 when a report appeared in the press that he had actually finished his book and it would appear that summer, he sent a correction that there was no present prospect for the book either to be written or published.[75]

Even before that Lee told one of his professors that he was "hardly calculated for a historian," and feared he was "too much interested and might be biassed."[76] He apparently intended a "history" rather than a memoir, with heavy reliance on official reports, and he made it clear that his real motive was defensive, to show that only overwhelming numbers and resources beat him. His abhorrence of controversy virtually guaranteed few candid opinions about subordinates. Hence, the consequent loss to Confederate literature is hard to assess, but it may not have been great. Meanwhile, in discussions with professors at Washington College, he dwelled on the same themes. He spoke of his resignation from the Army in 1861, still sensitive over charges of treason, and of his opposition to secession. Antietam would have been a victory but for the "lost dispatch," and he implied some blame to D. H. Hill. The defeat at Gettysburg was due to the absence of Stuart, and the failure of Ewell, Longstreet, and A. P. Hill to launch coordinated attacks. He was even mildly critical of Stonewall, revealing a shadow of chagrin that Jackson got the credit for movements Lee had planned. All he said of the Confederate government was that Davis's refusal to conciliate his opposition crippled his power, and that he lamented that Breckinridge, "a lofty, pure, strong man," was not made secretary of war sooner.[77]

If he did not write his history, at least he gave encouragement to others. He mildly, and reluctantly, critiqued a new biography of Jackson, concerned that it claimed too much for Stonewall's command, and that men from the other corps of his army might feel slighted and respond in the press. He recoiled at the thought of former Confederates embarrassing themselves in print by fighting over credit.[78] Apparently he was happy to encourage such feuds between Yankee generals. He corresponded with Fitz-John Porter, a Union general court-martialed and dismissed on charges by Pope after Second Manassas. Lee detested Pope, and gave Porter permission to use his letters in a campaign to regain his commission and reputation.[79]

Lee sent small donations to several associations formed to care for orphans of slain soldiers and their fathers' graves.[80] When the Hollywood Memorial Association of Richmond wanted to bring the Confederate dead at Gettysburg home, he approved.[81] "The graves of the Confederate dead will always be green in my memory, and their deeds be hallowed in my recollection."[82] Yet he opposed erecting monuments on the battlefields of the Confederacy. "I think it wiser," he wrote, "not to keep open the sores of war, but to follow the examples of those nations who endeavored to obliterate the marks of civil strife, to commit to oblivion the feelings it engendered."[83] Unfortunately, some of Lee's "sores" would not be allowed to heal, like the seemingly senseless hanging of Orton Williams. A cruel reminder of it came in November 1869 when a bizarre rumor circulated that he did not die in June 1863, but was smuggled from the country, and now lived in Cuba under the name Brigadier General Don Emanuel, commanding a regiment of black cavalry in a revolt against Spain.[84]

Lee's lasting anger toward the Yankees colored his view of the postwar political situation, which he thought precarious, and worsened by partisanship. "I yet believe that the maintenance of the rights and authority reserved to the States, and to the people, [are] not only assential [sic] to the adjustment and balance of the general system, but the safeguard of the continuance of a free government," he wrote in December 1866. The consolidation of power into a central authority was sure to produce domestic despotism and foreign aggression. He accepted one of the myths enthusiastically embraced by secessionists in the 1850s that New England's Hartford Convention of 1814 had endorsed secession as a last resort to fight centralization. Then in 1861 reason had been displaced by war waged for the "avowed" maintenance of the Union, while he suspected the real reason was to concentrate all power in Washington. Republicans now made conditions for the "readmission" of states, but Lee argued that if victory decided that secession was unlawful, then those states never really left the Union. All of the states must be perfectly equal now as before, meaning they still had the right to decide for themselves who should vote, and even the nature of their "domestic institutions." He claimed that an end to slavery by different means had long been a goal, and especially for Virginians, which certainly would have been a surprise to a great many

Southerners, but complained that requiring states to ratify emancipation as a condition of readmission was unconstitutional.

The South was willing in 1861 to accept the Crittenden compromise but Republicans would not. "Who, then, is responsible for the war?" Lee asked. The South would have preferred any compromise to what followed, but now must accept its results and embrace the amendment without resistance.[85] Ironically, in 1860 and 1861 Lee condemned the extremists who brought on the crisis, but the effects of the war shifted him toward their positions on the political and social issues driving them. Simply put, he could hardly repudiate the Southern position in 1860 without in effect saying that hundreds of thousands of Confederates died for nothing. They could have had peace. War came when it did only because the North refused to compromise.

Lee found himself drawn into the public arena in February 1866, when called by a congressional committee to testify on current Southern sentiment and treatment of the freed slaves. He gave evasive answers to sometimes loaded questions. Virginians wanted peace, he said, and the best way to achieve that would be liberal treatment by Washington. Blacks were not ready for the vote. Give it to them now and they might easily be led astray. No one could say when or if they would be better qualified in the future. Lee hardly expected his testimony to reawaken the old whipping story, but in March a deposition by Wesley Norris appeared in the press, probably to counter Lee's public stance as a moderate with no special dislike of blacks.[86] "There is not a word of truth in it," he complained privately, averring that "no servant, soldier, or citizen that was ever employed by me can with truth charge me with bad treatment."[87] A few weeks later the story hit the Baltimore press and spread across the country with the headline GEN. LEE A WOMAN-WHIPPER. Again he denied it privately, though he never said what was untrue.[88] Even if he did order the whippings, they were punishment for insubordination, like the execution of deserters, which could hardly be unfair. Still, making no public response, he could remember *Don Quixote*, when Sancho Panza complained at being criticized and the don told him, "Let it alone Sancho I tell you, the more that you stir it, the more it will stink."[89]

Lee's views came before the public even more in the spring of 1867 when Congress divided the South into military districts to be garrisoned. It further mandated the election of delegates to constitutional conventions to revise state constitutions. Blacks were to have the vote in selecting delegates, but former Confederates who had not applied for pardons or taken the oath of allegiance would not. Once a new constitution was approved, and once a sitting state legislature ratified the Fourteenth Amendment guaranteeing rights of citizenship and equal protection, then that state might apply for readmission. The exclusion of former Confederates virtually guaranteed Republican control of the conventions.

Saying he could "suffer nothing more than Appomattox," he reportedly counseled Virginians to accept the situation and make the best of it. "General Lee can now be placed among the advocates of reconstruction," a Boston paper alleged, and men in Richmond argued that Virginia could hardly degrade herself if he supported a convention.[90] To see if the reports were true, the New York *Herald* sent a correspondent to Lexington, but Lee backed away from a direct answer. "I am a paroled prisoner, and have no right to speak upon political matters," he protested. All he would say for publication was that he wanted his people to "take such measures as will most speedily restore to them their prosperity," and that he was in favor of a convention. When Congress passed a second act requiring commanders of the military districts to supervise elections, Lee said he hoped every citizen eligible to vote would do so, "to secure the speedy restoration and welfare of the country."[91]

The press continued to garble Lee's sentiments, and he felt the need to explain himself more fully.[92] "My opinion would have no influence in correcting the misunderstanding which has existed between the North and South," he wrote in April, "and which I fear is still destined to involve the country in greater calamities."[93] Still, to a few friends he reiterated that there was "no doubt" the conventions must be held. "The people are placed in a position where no choice in the matter is left them," and everyone able to vote had a duty to do so "to elect the best available men." He deplored seeing Southerners dividing into parties on the issue, and urged all to yield on all minor points to unite in what was best for the general welfare. Moreover, when the states' conventions revised their constitutions, the people ought to approve and carry out their decrees "in good faith and kind feeling."[94]

"It is difficult to see what may eventually be the best," he wrote a friend in May 1867. "I think it is the duty of all citizens not disfranchised to qualify themselves to vote, attend the polls, and elect the best men in their power." He feared that conservatives might boycott the elections, leaving the convention to be dominated by wartime Unionists "and the negroes." He did not regard a new constitution with enthusiasm, but he was a pragmatist. "I look upon the southern people as acting under compulsion, not of their free choice," he said, "and that it is their duty to consult the best interests of their States, as far as may be in their power to do." They could not control national politics, "but by united efforts, harmony, prudence and wisdom, we may shape and regulate our domestic policy." In time, he thought their political disabilities ought to be relieved and business and economy in the South rebuilt.[95] Yet he had no illusions about the shift in American public life. "Notwithstanding our boastful assertions to the world, for nearly a century, that our government was based on the consent of the people," he declared, "it rests upon force; as much as any government that ever existed." The bitterness lingered.

Meanwhile, Lee looked on with dismay as military reconstruction commenced, and Virginia became subject to Major General John Schofield, of whose administration he did not approve. Of the five military commanders overseeing districts in the South, Lee thought Major General Winfield Scott Hancock, in charge of Texas and Louisiana, was "the only one of the District Commanders who seems to have taken a right conception of his duties, & to understand the necessities of the country." He watched in grief the impositions on the rights of Southerners, trusting that an end to their duress would come one day, "for time, at last, sets all things even."[96] When subpoenaed to appear before a grand jury attempting to try Jefferson Davis for treason, Lee resolutely refused to lay responsibility for his acts as a general at the former president's feet, taking full responsibility onto himself. In these postwar years Lee never spoke of himself again as an American, but only as a Virginian or a Southerner. His comments on public affairs rarely touched on national events or issues, but only on those affecting the South. He might acquiesce, but he would never assimilate.

Like Lee, Grant had hoped to see civil government restored quickly, for otherwise the army would have to maintain order, which invited confrontation and irritated the already sore feelings of ex-Confederates, especially with black regiments among the occupiers. To forestall race-based clashes, he transferred many black units to the North, and ordered the predominantly black XXV Corps to Texas to guard the border with Mexico. In 1862 the French invaded and occupied Mexico, and by 1863 controlled most of the country. The following year they installed their puppet Maximilian as emperor. Grant felt from the first that the French invasion was almost part of the Southern rebellion, for what he believed to be French aid to the Confederacy was "little less than open war." The defiance of the Monroe Doctrine in taking by the bayonet a "friendly but downtroden Nation" was "an act of hostility to the United States." He would have been happy to send an army to Mexico immediately after the surrenders to help the legitimate government of Benito Juarez expel the invaders. When he learned that after surrendering, but before handing over their arms, Kirby Smith and several thousand of his men and officers expatriated themselves to Mexico to support Maximilian, he recommended sending a force into Mexico to capture and return them.[97]

He spoke publicly, though briefly, of his belief in Mexico's "coming deliverance" from foreign oppression.[98] Until the French were out, he favored boycotting international events hosted by France, leaving one visitor with the clear impression that "should the general ever be President, no European emperor in Mexico will be long without a war on his hands."[99] Lee's view of Maximilian was exactly the opposite, evidence of his rather parochial view of world affairs, and continuing disdain for Mexico's native people. When the *Juaristas* captured and executed Maximilian, Lee deplored the act. Dismissing the blatant French usurpation, he argued that the emperor "went to Mexico at the formal invitation of her people."[100]

Violence erupted in the South, as riots in Memphis and elsewhere gave evidence that white Southerners were not ready to accept the freedmen, and Grant concluded that military occupation was going to be needed awhile longer. He was not at all pleased at the state of affairs a year after Appomattox. Southerners seemed more resistant than immediately after the surrenders, and he complained in May 1866 that "now they regard themselves as masters of the situation." Grant even mused that perhaps the war should have lasted a little longer so that places like Texas, largely untouched, could feel what he called the "blighting effects of war." Worse, Lee frustrated him. "Lee is behaving badly," he groused, "conducting himself very differently from what I had reason, from what he said at the time of the surrender, to suppose he would." No other man in the South could exert a tenth of the influence for good that Lee might wield, but instead Grant saw him "setting an example of forced acquiescence so grudging and pernicious in its effects as to be hardly realized." So long as former Confederate leaders acted as if the cause they lost in war could be won in peace, he feared that the military must remain in the South to prevent open resistance.[101] Despite his disappointment, Grant said in private that personally he liked his old foe and that Lee was "a gentleman."[102]

In July 1866, largely in an effort to win Grant to his side, Johnson secured legislation creating the new rank of "general of the army," giving Grant a fourth star. Meanwhile, as the nation wearied of the impasse between Johnson and the Radical Republicans, and with the next election just two years distant, the dormant talk of Grant and the presidency reemerged. Still inclined to disclaim all ambition in that direction, Grant distanced himself from Johnson, especially after the president used some subtle maneuvers to put abroad the impression that Grant stood with him. Then that fall he was caught in the middle of a feud between Johnson and Stanton, and when Johnson tried to get him out of the way on a mission to Mexico, Grant refused.

Johnson's war with the Republican Congress backfired that fall when Republicans won sweeping victories in midterm elections. When Congress reconvened in January 1867 the Republicans had a virtually veto-proof majority and began passing legislation that Johnson could not stop. He fought back by demanding Stanton's resignation, then suspended him when he refused to leave his office. Grant reluctantly agreed to sit as interim secretary of war, and his sense of duty left him no choice but to obey several commands from the president that he found ill advised. When Congress reconvened there was talk of arresting or forcibly removing Johnson from office, but Grant made it clear that as commanding general he would use force if necessary to prevent any such act. While he did not support impeachment, when the Senate ordered Stanton reinstated in January 1868, Grant handed over the office, which effectively broke all ties with Johnson. Ironically, being Johnson's enemy now made Grant quite palatable to Johnson's other enemies, the Radical Republicans, bedfellows for whom Grant had little more taste than he did the president. A few weeks later Congress impeached Johnson.

 ℮‿◡

"My feelings induce me to prefer private life," Lee told Robert Ould in February 1867, "which I think more suitable to my condition and age, and where I believe I can better subserve the interests of my State."[103] In the fall of 1866 a bizarre rumor circulated that he had shown some interest in the governorship of Virginia before the war.[104] He had not, but that did not stop Ould approaching him to say that leading men in the state wanted him to run. Lee could hardly fail to appreciate that it was an effort to capitalize on his status as easily the most popular man in the state, and at the same time a gesture of defiance. They should nominate men solely for their capability, he replied. "This is no time for the indulgence of personal or political considerations in selecting a person to fill that office," he told Ould, "nor should it be regarded as a means of rewarding individuals for supposed former services." Electing him would be used by the Republicans to incite more hostility to Virginia and the South than already existed and bring distress on his fellow Virginians rather than the full return of their civil liberties and rights. He specifically told Ould that his letter was not to be released to the press. Lee wanted no words of his to leak into the public arena, where their meaning could be twisted to suit others.[105]

With or without his permission, some in the South determined to use his name all the same. The Mobile *Register* created a minor sensation in May 1866 when it placed Lee's name at the head of a column as its choice for nominee of the States Rights Democrats for the presidency in 1868.[106] No groundswell followed, and Lee ignored the defiant gesture, but then in January 1867 a Maryland newspaper suggested a reunification ticket for 1868 headed by Grant for president and Lee for vice president.[107] The Macon, Georgia, *Daily Telegraph* immediately commented that the wrong name was on the top of the ticket but that "all creation would not whip it." A Michigan editor sarcastically commented that a President Grant would likely not live long in office "with an ex-rebel General waiting for his shoes."[108]

It became more serious when James Gordon Bennett's New York *Herald* proposed a Grant and Lee ticket to "unite the North and South in a solid bond of practical union." While the Republicans recoiled in shock, Bennett argued that "the election of these two soldiers would insure to the country union and fraternity at home, respect and influence abroad."[109] In April he went on to suggest that the newly enfranchised black men of the South should begin their voting careers by nominating Grant and Lee in the most effective gesture they could make to demonstrate fitness for citizenship.[110] One Northern journal in Evansville, Indiana, even placed Lee's name on top, believing that he could get the Democratic nomination.[111] Neither Grant nor Lee commented on this strange juxtaposition of their names.

Still, Lee's name was introduced into the 1868 presidential campaign, but in quite a different manner. That summer the Republican Party nominated Grant for the presidency and the Democrats put forward Horatio Seymour of New York. The Democrat Rosecrans, hoping to win support for Seymour and at the same time defeat his old foe Grant, approached Lee to ask for the viewpoint of men of the South on important campaign issues. Were Southerners willing to treat the freed slaves fairly and humanely, as opposed to Republican claims that blacks were being oppressed in the former Confederate states, and were Southerners reconciled to the result of the war and ready to work with the rest of the nation in moving forward? Lee did not presume to speak for the South, but he agreed to present a letter with Rosecrans's questions to other leading Southern men. Lee turned his letter over to two friends who drafted a reply, and Lee took it to show to Generals John Echols and Beauregard and consult with them.

With Echols acting as secretary, Lee dictated changes and cuts.[112] The missive mirrored his oft-expressed sentiments, and in places used almost verbatim his testimony before the congressional committee in February 1866.[113] The result of the war had settled the slavery and secession questions for good. Southerners wanted only to resume their old relations with the United States and to return to peace and harmony, nor were they hostile to blacks. Rather, the letter pointed out that Southern agriculture was just as dependent on black labor as those former slaves were

dependent on white planters for employment. Lee opposed putting political power in the hands of the freedmen, not from enmity, but from
"a deep-seated conviction that at present the negroes have neither the
intelligence nor the qualifications which are necessary to make them
safe depositories of political power." He deprecated all disorder and violence. "The great want of the South is peace" and "relief from oppres-
sive misrule."[114] Though they had no impact on the election of Grant
that November, the sentiments attributed to Lee were not incompatible
with the incoming president's. Moreover, the impression remained that
Lee was willing to speak out as the leading representative of the old
Confederacy, and a possible molder of Southern opinion.

When Virginia's new constitution was ready to be submitted to
Congress, some feared its rejection over several clauses, in particular
the one covering suffrage and office holding for blacks. A committee of
nine Virginians representing all regions of the state was self-appointed
to go to Washington and make known to Congress that, despite the
feeling that blacks were not yet ready to exercise the vote intelligently,
Virginians would accept the clause rather than see their constitution
rejected. The resolutions creating the committee were drafted by the
same man who wrote the response to the Rosecrans letter, and the
similarity of language quickly gave rise to rumors that Lee was himself a prime mover to get the committee in operation.

In fact, he played no active role whatever, though he did have a conversation with one of the organizers of the committee about the voting clause.[115] Lee told him that slaves were freed without any fault or
agency of their own, that they were among whites now and could
not be got rid of, so whites should do the best they could with them.
To make them useful citizens, he thought qualified suffrage ought to
be extended to those who were educated and owned property. That
would be only about one-tenth of them, so hardly enough for them to
do real harm at the polls, he thought. Lee did not envision universal
suffrage, telling General Jubal Early in April, "I never thought that all
the white men were qualified to vote." A Whig patrician to the last,
Lee doubted even Congress would give all blacks the vote. Anxious for
something to be done to remove military rule, he admitted that he was
"no politician," and hoped others might put their heads together and
agree on something to relieve the people.[116]

18

THE LAST MEETING

A LOOMING QUESTION during the first postwar years was whether Grant and Lee would meet again. There was no particular reason for them to do so, yet the two names had been so intertwined since 1864 that the public imagination was naturally primed to take a deep interest in the possibility. At first it seemed it might happen in December 1867, at the first postwar reunion of the old Aztec Club that both had joined in Mexico. The first announcement said the club would meet at the Astor House, and that both generals were expected to attend. When it was learned that McClellan was absent in Europe and could not come, both Grant and Lee suggested postponement until the fall of 1868, but by that time Grant was busy running for the presidency, and the reunion was postponed yet again until September 1870, and neither attended.[1]

By that time they had met a fourth and last time. Shortly after Grant's inauguration, knowing that he must make a business trip to Baltimore in the spring of 1869, and would necessarily pass through Washington, Lee decided to seek "a quiet social interview." Not thinking it proper to write to or call on the president himself, and wary of publicity that would do neither any good, he asked an old friend to approach Grant on his behalf. Grant may not have received the request, for he did not respond, but Lee's friend then called on Julia's brother Frederick Dent, who immediately arranged everything. Lee was in Baltimore the last week of April when a letter conveyed to him "the kind sentiments of Pres: Grant" and a request to come to the White House when he reached Washington. Lee said he would send his calling card to Dent when he arrived, and wait to learn if Grant could see him, enjoining that there be no public notice given of his coming, to "divest my visit of all unnecessary publicity, which will I think be the more agreeable to Pres: Grant as well as myself."[2]

Lee arrived by train from Baltimore on the morning of May 1 and rushed through a gawking crowd at the station to board a carriage to Georgetown. Then he drove to the White House, arriving about eleven o'clock, and was ushered into the Red Room where he found about twenty other callers waiting, including at least one senator. He sent his card in to the president, and waited while around him a sudden buzz arose when he was recognized. Someone audibly said, "There's Gen. Lee—wonder what he wants here?" When an aide brought Lee's card in to him, Grant was meeting with half a dozen congressmen, but he told them, "Gentlemen, you will have to excuse me. I have an engagement with General Lee, who is now waiting outside to keep it, and I wish our interview to be private." They left grumbling, one senator muttering that "the President sees us in a crowd, and thereby exposes our private business; but when a rebel comes along he is given a private audience." Another was heard to grouse, "Yes, and we are driven out as if we had no business here, when we are looking after the interests of the country." And yet another sarcastically observed that "being a rebel is a good card of admission here, it appears."

Lee was ushered into the reception room and the two who last met as generals shook hands as presidents. They spoke privately for perhaps half an hour. After some courteous but reserved pleasantries, it became evident to Grant that Lee was not going to volunteer much in ordinary conversation. Speaking "always to the point" as associates noted, Grant told him he wanted to talk about affairs in the South, and especially Virginia and the forthcoming vote on its new constitution. Typically, Lee replied that he preferred not to be understood as speaking for his state or region, but only for himself.[3] Grant then asked him a series of direct questions on the matters of interest to him. He asked about sentiment in Virginia, and Lee replied that it was much the same as that expressed in the Rosecrans letter the year before. Virginians accepted the obligations of the reconstruction acts in good faith and wanted good relations between the races and with immigrants. In return they wanted full restoration to the Union and assistance in developing their own internal resources. The new constitution required for readmission would probably be approved; Lee believed that the "best men" in the state would vote for it, but he thought the clauses proscribing and disenfranchising certain classes ought to be voted on separately from the constitution as a whole, so they could be defeated and deleted. Grant agreed entirely and had wanted that from the first, and promised Lee there would be a fair election when the time came. What remained ought to pass handily.

Lee also referred to the committee of Virginians who came to Washington the previous winter to repudiate their slate of candidates for state office in favor of a conservative Republican ticket endorsed by the state convention, and said he approved of the candidates. In fact, Lee thought there was slight difference between the Republican and Democratic Parties in his state at the moment. Pleased at that, the president said he hoped Virginia would be ready for full restoration of rights soon, and Lee added that he thought all of the former Confederate states could be readmitted quickly so that elected representatives could be sent to Congress. That done, all other outstanding questions should settle themselves. At some point in the discussion, Lee also said he did not think giving black men the vote would be as harmful as many feared.[4]

Outside, the speculation began immediately, and continued after Lee left. Some said it was simply a courtesy call, and the two spoke of nothing but the weather, crop prospects, and the new Virginia railroad. Others said Grant talked about the troublesome reconstruction business in Virginia, the new Fifteenth Amendment to the Constitution, and voting rights. Some said Lee frankly condemned some Virginia politicians as corrupt and incompetent. At least one speculated that Grant asked Lee to act as a special envoy to Cuba to investigate affairs there.[5] Lee, it was said, spoke "less as a politician than as a leader who possesses the entire confidence of his followers."[6]

That was rather a lot of ground to cover in half an hour. Grant had been disappointed with Lee's posture three years before, but the answers he got in this discussion seemed much in line with his own views. Lee, for his part, may have been dismayed that the meeting was so short.[7] It was a great departure from his customary demeanor for him to seek an audience with Grant, and clearly he would not have done so had he not wanted to speak on some matters of importance. If Grant's questions touched on them, discussion was necessarily brief, and it seems that the main obstacle to any more extended conversation was the evident discomfort felt by both. Already there were grumblings outside Grant's door over the president entertaining a former Confederate, and Lee could well expect much the same reaction in Virginia if he appeared to get too friendly with the man who crushed the Confederacy. In contrast to their last meeting, in which so much was accomplished to put the country on the road to peace, this conversation seems to have accomplished little more than to make the two greatest soldiers of their age painfully aware that they were warriors no more.

Grant may not have volunteered that his own ideas were in perfect accord with Lee's to a point. He, too, favored submitting the new Virginia constitution to voters without the disenfranchisement clause, and then holding a separate referendum on that. He could see that in the Old Dominion the Democrats and moderate Republicans were unhappy with the excesses of the Radicals, and ready to make common cause to exchange resistance to black suffrage for restoration of rights to whites. As summer arrived, and with it nominations for Virginia's governorship, Grant withheld support from the Radicals' candidate and tacitly supported a coalition ticket of moderate Republicans headed by Gilbert C. Walker, a Northern-born moderate widely supported by former Whigs in the commonwealth. That put him much in tune with Lee's antebellum political stance before the war experience made him more conservative. Walker was also aligned with Grant and Lee on the issue of submitting the new constitution and the difficult voting rights clause to separate referenda. Though he could not vote, Lee watched elective politics in Virginia closely, and in June word leaked out that he favored the Walker ticket, as did Grant.[8]

In a close election, Walker won in November to become Virginia's first Republican governor. As a result, once the constitution passed and it and the Thirteenth and Fourteenth Amendments were ratified, military rule ended and Virginia would be readmitted to the Union on January 26, 1870, making it the only state to escape enduring radical reconstruction. Lee may have declined to speak out as Grant wanted, but his views and support for Walker nevertheless became known, and to the extent that Grant was right about Southerners following Lee's example, the Confederate had an impact. At arm's length to be sure, Grant and Lee had helped to shape the peace with a template for other states to follow if they chose.

Meanwhile, the advice Lee most commonly gave was that "work is what we now require, work by everybody." Labor and thrift would get Southerners through this difficult period. "The good old times of former days," he told his cousin Hill Carter, "will return again." They might not see them, but their children would. Despite what he said about the interdependence of white planters and black workers in the letter to Rosecrans, he believed that if they should have to hire workers, they must "get white labour on every account," that they needed work done "especially by white hands."[9] That was so important to him that, despite his earlier prejudices, he favored European immigration as the best source of "a respectable class of laborers from Europe." They needed not only white reliable laborers, "but good citizens, whose interests and feelings would be in unison with our own." For that reason, he rejected bringing in Chinese or Japanese workers, fearing their presence might result in injury to the country and its institutions. He endorsed state-sponsored immigration societies to attract "honest, steady, willing men," care for them on arrival, and make arrangements for their new homes and jobs. Families would be better yet, for that promoted contentment and permanency, something else his experience told him black laborers would not provide. He actually endorsed the Virginia Immigration Society in a public letter in September 1869 saying, "I should rejoice to see a plan in successful operation calculated to develop the wealth and to promote the prosperity of the South."[10]

Meanwhile, he advised friends that the people of the South should pay less attention to national politics, and more to their own fortunes. If they had done that from the founding of the old Union, the Southern view of the Constitution might have carried more weight in Washington. "It was from the want of this weight," he said, "that it failed, when it attempted to maintain its views." The war to maintain those views he now described as "the struggle of the states for their rights & for Constitutional Government."[11]

Over and again he counseled developing the untapped resources of the South as a means to make it a phoenix rising from the ashes of war. Virginia would never recover its former position of leadership in the nation until it capitalized on its resources and rebuilt its population.[12] "There is no subject upon which the material interests of the country now so much depend, in my opinion, as upon agriculture," he told a Georgian, "nor is there one more worthy of the earnest attention of the people."[13] In their small way the Lee family encouraged Southern manufacture, among other things, by using South Carolina gingham for his daughters' dresses, declaring that "no silks or any other dress would be so well suited to his views as this article manufactured in the Southern country."[14] Invited to attend the Memphis Commercial Convention in 1869, he declined, but added that "it would afford me great gratification to aid in every way in my power the efforts that [you] are making to restore the prosperity of the country."[15] He also begged off attending a similar meeting in Louisville that fall, but responded with perhaps his most optimistic estimate:

> If we turn to the past history of the country and compare our material condition with that of our forefathers when they undertook, in the face of the difficulties which surrounded them, its organization and establishment, it would seem to be an easy task for us to revive what may be depressed and to encourage what may be languishing in all the walks of life. We shall find it easy if we will cherish the same principles and practice the same virtues which governed them. Every man, however, must do his part in this great work. He must carry into the administration of his affairs industry, fidelity and economy, and apply the knowledge taught by science to the promotion of agriculture, manufactures and all industrial pursuits. As individuals prosper, communities will become rich, and the avenues and depots required by trade and commerce will be readily constructed.[16]

By the time he had his last meeting with Grant, it was plain for all to see that Lee's health was waning. He no longer felt up to riding Traveller every day, but he soldiered on.[17] By late summer of 1870 he felt wretched much of the time. Then on September 29 he came home late from a church vestry meeting for the evening meal. "We have been waiting for you," Mary scolded him, asking where he had been, but he could not speak to answer. Doctors diagnosed a stroke, bled him, and he slept for a solid two days. He spoke occasionally in his sleep, muttering things that suggested his mind had gone back to the old battlefields. Once he turned his head over his shoulder and said,

"Tell [A. P.] Hill he must come up. Strike my tent." Able to sit up, he ate a little but muttered only a few occasional words. Still, he squeezed Mary's hand when she spoke to him, and physicians thought he might recover, though they doubted he wanted to when he said "tis no use" to medicines. Thus he lingered, and in his last forty-eight hours he seemed largely unaware of those around him. On October 12 he gave a deep sigh and died.[18] A few days later the city of Lexington laid him to rest in a tomb beneath the college chapel, where Mary joined him three years later. A century afterward Traveller's bones were buried just outside the chapel, a few yards away from his master. Long before then, the college changed its name to Washington and Lee University.

Grant was nineteen months into his presidency when Lee died. At forty-six he was the youngest elected president to date, running on the motto "Let us have peace." The first chief executive to serve two full terms since Andrew Jackson, he was the most productive of all save Lincoln. Just as he had as a general, he consulted no one on cabinet appointments and some other issues before simply announcing his decisions, a policy he later admitted caused him some trouble.[19] His choice of cabinet also reflected his conciliatory approach by avoiding leading Republicans who expected portfolios. He pushed successfully for passage of the Fifteenth Amendment, and thereafter strove to ensure safety for freed blacks and their full civil rights, an approach that led to the creation of the Department of Justice in 1870, the Enforcement Acts of 1870–1871, and a concerted effort to put down the Ku Klux Klan and other groups intimidating black voters. The collapse of the KKK in 1872 was largely due to Grant's efforts, and in the elections that year blacks in great numbers voted for the first tine. The Civil Rights Act of 1875 sought to guarantee them further equal treatment.

Grant's relations with the South were strained, though his Amnesty Act restoring political rights to all ex-Confederates was a sincere gesture of conciliation, and Lee would not be the last former enemy Grant welcomed to the White House. Unfortunately, violence against blacks and Republicans, especially a deadly riot in New Orleans, forced him to retain military garrisons in several former Confederate states to keep civil order, as a group called the Redeemers gradually regained white Democratic control over one Southern state after another. In the election of 1876 his support was of course behind Republican candidate Rutherford B. Hayes, but he also acknowledged that the Democrat Samuel J. Tilden might have legitimately won the contest with the disputed electoral votes of three former Confederate states. Since the settlement was handled entirely by Congress, Grant did not influence the final decision by which Democrats agreed to give the presidency to Hayes in return for virtually ending reconstruction, but he did honor the compromise by commencing the removal of Federal occupying troops before he left office.

Meanwhile, Grant sought reform in Indian policy, believing that the continuing friction with the native peoples "were entirely owing to the bad faith kept towards the Indians by the white settlers."[20] He promoted free public schooling for all children, and reinforced separation of church and state. Seeking a platform for the American navy in Caribbean waters, he unsuccessfully negotiated for the annexation of the Dominican Republic, which he also thought might act as a safety valve in race relations by attracting blacks from the South to emigrate. He made a special effort to redress his offense to American Jews during the war, paying tribute to their contribution to the Union war effort, and began appointing Jews to public positions within days of taking office. For all the failures and occasional scandals of Grant's tenure, he was the first two-term chief executive to display a modern approach to domestic involvement and world outlook.

Yet the scandals dogged him for the rest of his life. He made several unwise appointments, starting with making Rawlins secretary of war. Rawlins's feud with Sherman, whom Grant made commanding general of the army, strained relations between the two friends. His appointed heads of the Treasury and Interior Departments, and the New York Customs House, all became linked either to corruption and bribery, or to covering up cases of malfeasance, and Grant loyally clung to them far too long. He had always been too trusting, and especially naïve, especially when it came to friends, and it seriously tarnished his administration.

Grant left Galena in the summer of 1861 as largely unmolded clay politically. The war itself gave him political form. His indifference to slavery and emancipation became a commitment both to freedom for the slaves and civil rights for the freedmen. His realization of the power of the United States in fielding its armies and defeating the rebellion gave him an awareness that his country was now a major actor on the world stage, capable of making itself felt anywhere as a force for justice and fair government, though he recognized how that power could be misused. At home, he assumed the primacy of the central authority, a view shaped by the unwillingness of many in the former Confederacy to acquiesce in Federal actions without Federal force. Throughout, his attitude toward the Constitution and the laws remained what it had been during the war. Like it or not, law was law and he would enforce it to the full.

Grant never lost his passion for travel and new scenes. On leaving office in 1877 he continued expanding his horizons by taking Julia on a two-year trip around the globe, from England and Europe, to Palestine, India, Southeast Asia, and finally China and Japan. While in Japan he voluntarily negotiated a settlement to a territorial dispute that averted war between China and Japan, the first time an American president acted as diplomat without portfolio in using personal prestige to keep peace abroad. He returned with renewed respect and reputation, and almost won nomination for a third term. Having nearly gone broke paying for the world tour, he invested in a brokerage firm in which his son Ulysses Jr. was partner. The firm lost everything in questionable trading practices, though Grant himself had no knowledge of them, and in 1884 at age sixty-two he was nearly as bankrupt as he had been thirty years before. Worse, there was cancer in his throat.

Typically, he sought renewal elsewhere, and found it in writing, first articles for popular magazines, and then a memoir of his life contracted for publication by his friend Samuel L. "Mark Twain" Clemens. He began writing in New York City, then moved to the cooler air of Mount McGregor. There, bundled in a blanket, Grant wrote in a wicker chair on the veranda of a summer home, often interrupted by hundreds of the curious and well-wishers who walked past, or by calls from old friends like Sherman, Sheridan, and Buckner.[21] Racing against his own mortality, he finished the two-volume narrative in mid-July 1885. He knew he had little time left. "There never was one more willing to go than I am," he scrawled on July 16. He had willed himself to live to finish the book, and now it was done. "There is nothing more I should do to it now, and therefore I am not likely to be more ready to go than at this moment." A week later he left.[22] Eminently fair, though not entirely unprejudiced, and occasionally defensive, *Personal Memoirs of U. S. Grant* not only saved his family financially, but also became— and remains—perhaps the greatest of American autobiographies. It is thoroughly reflective of its author, the writing crisp, the humor self-deprecating, and most of all "to the point."

The opportunity to look back on his life given him by writing his memoir was one that he welcomed. Grant hosted many dinners at the White House. At one a guest suggested that each diner recall the period of his life he might most like to relive. Naturally, everyone chose the brightest moments to reprise. Then it was the president's turn. "What part of your life would you like to live over again?" someone asked. Grant dropped his head to his chest in his usual thoughtful pose, then raised it and replied, "All of it. I should like to live all of my life over again. There isn't any part of it I should want to leave out." His answer stunned the others. "He was the only man in the room who was ready to take the bitter with the sweet in his life," a senator recalled. Only Grant "had the courage to live his whole life over again."[23] More than thirty years earlier, when just in his late teens, Grant forthrightly told a cousin that "I am not one to show fals[e] colors [or] the brightest side of the picture."[24] He took dark and light with equanimity. The contrast gave his life texture.

Even in death Grant made a conciliatory gesture. His pallbearers were Sherman, Sheridan, Logan, and Porter, and Confederates Buck-ner and Joseph E. Johnston. The nation averted an even more elo-quent, as well as potentially controversial, gesture when they laid him to rest in New York City, where a dozen years later he would be moved to a massive new mausoleum. Before his death Grant feared that the people would want him to rest in the national cemetery just across the Potomac from Washington, where lay thousands of other veterans of the war, soldiers and generals alike. He wanted to be buried with only Julia beside him. When she died in 1902 he got his wish. Otherwise, he might have suffered the irony of going to his rest in the sod of Lee's Arlington.[25]

Both men lost speech in their last days and hours. Both died at age sixty-three, Lee long since weary of life, and Grant ready to live it again. Their war made them national icons, and their war reputations dictated the balance of their lives, careers, and posterity. Even before Lee's death his former associates were crafting what would become known as the Lost Cause myth, its major tenets being that secession was lawful, the war was not over slavery, Yankees won by sheer force of overwhelming numbers, and Confederate generals were chivalric Christian knights pitted against mechanistic vandals. It enshrined Lee as a second Washington who embodied Southern manhood. "By the Christ-like spirit of self-sacrifice," one of his officers later wrote, "the sign of the Cross was upon his life."[26] Lee's supposed agony over the decision to resign his commission in April 1861 was likened to Christ's temptation on the mountain, myth makers calling it Lee's "crucifix moment." Gettysburg transfigured him, they said, where "the Divinity in his bosom shone translucent through the man, and his spirit rose up into the God-like."[27]

While Lee's place in American memory only rose, Grant's, clouded by the scandals of his presidency, never again matched what it had been in 1865 and the years immediately following, when he was easily the most popular man in the nation. Ironically, having been defeated by him in war, Confederates thoroughly defeated Grant for the verdict of popular history, reducing him to "the Butcher," whose only redeeming feature was leniency at Appomattox when Lee decided to "allow" the conflict to end by "withdrawing" from the war. Grant's place in American memory is further complicated by his seemingly inexplicable meteoric rise from obscurity. Even Sherman, who knew him as well as anyone, remained mystified by his friend. "Grants whole character was a mystery even to himself," Sherman wrote after Grant's death, "a combination of strength and weakness not paralleled by any of whom I have read in Ancient or Modern History."[28]

Grant's and Lee's opinions of each other's generalship are muddied by time and human nature, and rest chiefly in what they said about other generals. Typical of his reticence, Lee's survive only in second-hand after-the-fact comments, and many may not be authentic. The only recorded expression during his lifetime came sometime prior to January 1870, when he reportedly told a cousin that the Federals' finest commander was McClellan. "Oh yes!" Lee reportedly exclaimed, "he was the ablest soldier they had."[29] Eighteen years later a letter he supposedly wrote after the war circulated in Washington. In it he declared that the Yankee with "the greatest ability" was Meade, and that "he feared Meade more than any man that he ever met upon the field of battle."[30] In 1904 Lee's nephew Cazanove Lee recalled a conversation at least thirty-five years earlier in which Lee supposedly said the greatest Union general was "McClellan by all odds."[31] Grant's opinions survive in contemporary and more candid versions, though only after Lee's death. Admitting that Lee was "a patriotic and gallant soldier, concerned alone for the welfare of his army and his State," Grant declared that "I never ranked Lee as high as some others of the army." He found Joseph E. Johnston more intimidating. "Lee was a good man, a fair commander, who had everything in his favor," he went on. "Lee was of a slow, conservative, cautious nature, without imagination or humor, always the same, with grave dignity." Unable to see that Lee's achievements justified his reputation, Grant concluded that "he was a man who needed sunshine."[32]

Both were human. Lee's strength at the outset of their campaign against each other was 65,000–70,000, but he argued that it was never more than 50,000. Grant asserted that it was 80,000 or above, and that Lee's advantages of fighting on the defensive on home ground virtually evened the odds. Thus, each erred by an almost equal amount in his own favor. Lee routinely defeated McClellan, and believed he had to a degree beaten Meade in the drawn battle at Gettysburg. If McClellan was the Union's best, and Lee consistently bested him, then what did that say about Lee? Intending a book to demonstrate that Grant only prevailed by numbers, Lee would hardly accord him surpassing skill. There was no conceit in him, but there was pride, and if he really entertained these opinions, they compensated forgivably for his far heavier burden of defeat. As for Grant, the years of being portrayed as a lucky bumbler too powerful not to win had an effect in the end. Nothing in Johnston's wartime performance offered any justification for Grant claiming him as a feared adversary, but somehow in Grant's mind that deflected the endless comparisons of himself to Lee in which he came out second best.

Experience forged their characters. Those characters defined the war they fought against others and each other. Each in his way helped shape the direction of a postwar nation that would take far longer than either imagined to escape the effects of their war.

The simple fact neither ever admitted is that, in each other, they faced their preeminent adversaries.

NOTES

Works frequently cited have been identified by the following abbreviations or shortened forms.

Adams, Letters	Francis Raymond Adams Jr., ed. *An Annotated Edition of the Personal Letters of Robert E. Lee, April 1855–April 1861*
AG	Adjutant General
CCL	Charles Carter Lee
CSR	Compiled Service Record
DeButts, "Lee in Love"	Robert E. L. DeButts Jr., "Lee in Love: Courtship and Correspondence in Antebellum Virginia"
GWCL	George Washington Custis Lee
JEJ	Joseph E. Johnston
Julia	Julia Dent Grant
LC	Library of Congress, Washington, DC
Lee	Douglas Southall Freeman, *R. E. Lee*
MCL	Mary Custis Lee
NA	National Archives, Washington, DC
OR	*War of the Rebellion: Official Records of the Union and Confederate Armies*
PMJDG	*Personal Memoirs of Julia Dent Grant*
PMUSG	*Personal Memoirs of U. S. Grant*
PUSG	*Papers of Ulysses S. Grant*
REL	Robert Edward Lee
RG	Record Group
SPC	Shirley Plantation Collection, Colonial Williamsburg Foundation Library, Williamsburg
USAMHI	United States Army Military History Institute, Carlisle, PA
USG	Ulysses S. Grant
USGA	Ulysses S. Grant Association
UVA	University of Virginia, Charlottesville
VHS	Virginia Historical Society, Richmond
VSL	Virginia State Library
Wartime Papers	Clifford Dowdey and Louis H. Manarin, eds., *The Wartime Papers of R. E. Lee*
WHFL	William Henry Fitzhugh Lee

INTRODUCTION: ICONS

1   Alexandria, *Gazette*, April 29, 1869; Boston, *Post*, May 6, 1869.
2   This story has had a checkered history. It originated in a brief article by S. D. McCormick, "Robert E. Lee as College President, The Recollections of a Student," in *The Outlook* 56 (July 17, 1897), p. 686. McCormick entered Washington College in 1866 and had the usual student's exposure to Lee, but he certainly was not present at faculty and staff

meetings, nor did he claim to have witnessed this episode. Rather, he described it as "another occurrence, which was currently reported among the students"; in other words a campus rumor, and one not set down by him until some thirty years later. McCormick used the episode as an example of Lee's supposed complete unwillingness to discuss the war, whereas in fact he discussed it often and at length with friends and faculty, and of course wanted to write a book about his army's experience. In 1912 Gamaliel Bradford used the anecdote in *Lee the American* (Boston: Houghton, Mifflin), p. 226, acknowledging that "Lee is said to have once spoken sharply" in defense of Grant, but then cited page 586 of *The Outlook* rather than 686. Most recently Charles Bracelin Flood, *Lee: The Last Years* (Boston: Houghton, Mifflin, 1981), p. 188, took the story from Bradford, but misquoted Lee's exclamation.

3   A typical example of this line of argument can be found at http://www.rulen.com/myths/, which offers a fair diet of other blatant fictions about North, South, slavery, and the war.

CHAPTER 1: SONS AND FATHERS

1   Robert E. Lee to John Eaton, August 21, 1829, Letters Received by the Adjutant General, 1861–1870, 1861, File L60, National Archives, Washington, DC.

2   Henry Lee to Charles Carter Lee, February 9, 1817, Edmund Jennings Lee, *Lee of Virginia, 1642–1892, Biographical and Genealogical Sketches of the Descendants of Col. Richard Lee* (Philadelphia: Franklin Printing Co., 1895), p. 349.

3   Ann Lee to Philip Fendall Jr., September 21, 1811, Lee Family Digital Archive, Washington and Lee University, Lexington, VA; Alexandria, *Herald*, December 27, 1822; Benjamin Hallowell, *Autobiography of Benjamin Hallowell* (Philadelphia: Friends Book Association, 1883), p. 104. Ann's letter is headed "Eastern View" and she mentions expecting to be in Alexandria to look at the house in a few days.

4   Anna Modigliani Lynch and Kelsey Ryan, comps., "Antebellum Reminiscences of Alexandria, Virginia." Extracted from the Memoirs of Mary Louisa Slacum Benham. Unpublished paper, Alexandria, 2009, p. 3.

5   Alexandria, *Daily Advertiser*, February 6, 1807.

6   The story of Lee's impecunious youth has been much overstated, starting with Freeman. Reconstructing Ann Carter Hill Lee's finances for that period is very difficult, and no conclusion can ever be more than approximate, yet it is apparent that she did have an income, and not a bad one either, at least prior to 1819.

7   Will of Charles Carter, May 10, 1803, Shirley Plantation Collection, Colonial Williamsburg Foundation Library, Williamsburg, VA.

8   Will of Mildred W. Carter, May 31, 1807, Legislative Petitions, Virginia State Archives, Richmond, in Loren Sweninger, ed., Race, Slavery, and Free Blacks. Series I: Petitions to Southern Legislatures, 1777–1867, reel 18 Virginia (1816–1826), Accession 11681612. Bethesda, MD: University Microfilms, 2003. frame 0063.

9   Ann's December 1816 petition said that the inheritance was "in part" slaves, not specifying the nature of the other property or money inherited. Ann Lee to Carter Lee, July 17, 1816, Charles Carter Lee Collection, Major Henry Lee Papers 1813–1841, VSL.

10   Based on the sources cited below, Ann's annual income from dividends in 1810 was $1,800. Figures for the Bank of Virginia shares cannot be found for the years 1811–1813, but given that those for the Potomac Bank remained virtually unchanged during those years, it seems reasonable to presume that the same was the case with the Bank of Virginia. Hence, it is estimated that her dividend income in these years was 1811, $1,800; 1812,

$1,800; 1813, $1,800. Complete figures being available for subsequent years, her income can be put at 1814, $1,675; 1815, $1,675; 1816, $1,825; 1817, $2,050.

11 Douglas Southall Freeman, *R. E. Lee, A Biography* (New York: Scribner's, 1934–1935), 4 vols., I, pp. 30–31, relates an extremely suspect brief episode suggesting Lee's need to be disciplined in his preteens, based on an account told him verbally by a woman who got the story from her mother, who remembered a letter she claimed to have read prior to the Civil War. Thus it is second- or thirdhand, removed by at least seventy years from the time any such letter was seen.

12 Emily V. Mason, *Popular Life of General Robert Edward Lee* (Baltimore: John Murphy & Co., 1871), p. 24.

13 Henry Lee to Carter Lee, June 18, 1817, Lee, *Lee of Virginia*, p. 355 makes it clear that he did receive letters from his wife.

14 Henry Lee to Carter Lee, September 30, 1816, ibid., pp. 345–46, p. 348, February 9, 1817, p. 348, April 19, 1817, pp. 350–51, 353.

15 Henry Lee to Carter Lee, June 26, 1818, ibid., pp. 343–44, August 8, 1816, pp. 344–45, September 30, 1816, p. 345.

16 Charles Royster, *A Revolutionary People at War: The Continental Army and American Character, 1775–1783* (New York: W. W. Norton & Company, 1979), p. 76–77.

17 Henry Lee to Carter Lee, September 30, 1816, Lee, *Lee of Virginia*, p. 345, December 1, 1816, pp. 346–47, May 5, 1817, p. 353.

18 Ibid.

19 Henry Lee to Carter Lee, December 1, 1816, pp. 346–47, ibid., April 19, 1817, pp. 352–53.

20 Henry Lee to Carter Lee, December 1, 1816, ibid., pp. 34–48; Robert E. Lee, "Biography of the Author," in Henry Lee, *Memoirs of the War in the Southern Department of the United States* (New York: University Publishing Co., 1869), p. 78.

21 Ann Hill Lee to Charles Carter Lee, May 8, 1816, Charles Carter Lee Collection, Major Henry Lee Papers 1813–1841, Virginia State Library.

22 Richmond, *Virginia Argus*, August 14, 1816; Richmond, *Whig*, September 22, 1826.

23 Ann Hill Lee to Charles Carter Lee, May 8, 1816, Charles Carter Lee Collection, Major Henry Lee Papers 1813–1841, VSL.

24 Ann Hill Lee to Charles Carter Lee, July 17, 1816, ibid.

25 Ann Hill Lee to Charles Carter Lee, May 8, 1816, VSL. It is evident that the Lees moved back to Oronoco Street on an unknown date, from Alexandria, *Herald*, December 27, 1822, which lists that house for auction and describes it as "now occupied by Mrs. Lee." Benjamin Hallowell, *Autobiography of Benjamin Hallowell* (Philadelphia: Friends Book Association, 1883), pp. 96, 100, places the Lees at 607 Oronoco in November 1824.

26 Bernard M. Carter & others Petition, December 12, 1816, Legislative Petitions, Virginia State Archives, Richmond, in Sweninger, Race, Slavery, and Free Blacks. I: reel 18, Virginia, Accession 11681612.

27 *Journal of the House of Delegates of the Commonwealth of Virginia* (Richmond: Thomas Ritchie, 1816), pp. 94, 138, 169, 186, 205, 209.

28 Ann Hill Lee to Charles Carter Lee, July 17, 1816, Charles Carter Lee Collection, Major Henry Lee Papers 1813–1841, VSL; Alexandria, *Gazette*, December 31, 1817.

29 According to her will, at her death she owned stock in the Potomac Bank and the Bank of Virginia totaling *at least* $20,000 by her estimate. This has sometimes carelessly been read to mean that $20,000 is all she had, but her will explicitly stated that a trust for her two younger daughters was to be made up of "all my Potomac bank stock, and so much of my Virginia bank stock, as (estimating both at their par value) will make up the sum of twenty thousand dollars." In other words, not all of her Bank of Virginia stock was to go

into that trust, and the balance was to be liquidated along with other assets to settle her debts, the residue going to her sons (Will of Ann H. Lee, July 24, 1829, Will Book P-1 1827–1830, Fairfax County Court House, Fairfax, VA). Just how many shares of either stock she actually owned is unknown. In 1816 she wrote that prior to about 1812 her annual income had been running approximately $1,440 per year in dividends from the Bank of Virginia stock. Dividend figures gleaned from the contemporary press (see below) indicate that in the years preceding 1816 the annual dividends had been running an average of 9.75 percent, which would mean that her total par value of stock would have been about $14,400 (Ann H. Lee to Charles Carter Lee May 8, 1816, Charles Carter Lee Collection, Major Henry Lee Papers 1813–1841, VSL). Share prices were running about $130 per share. The fact that the Bank of Virginia stock was to fill out the amount to $20,000 could be read to suggest that most of the trust was covered by Potomac Bank stock, but that would only be supposition. Still, a rough *minimum* annual income from dividends can be approached. Except for the anomalous year 1819, the Bank of Virginia shares consistently paid higher dividends than the Potomac Bank stock, once as much as 3.5 percent, though usually more like 1–2 percent.

Since there is no alternative but to make some assumptions, the figures here assume that the $20,000 trust was made up of $10,000 in shares at par value from both banks. The semiannual dividend percentage payments for both have been gleaned from the sources cited below for the years 1807–1829. Statements of dividend percentages for the Bank of Virginia have not been found for 1808, 1809, 1811, 1813, 1820, the last half of 1819, and the first halves of 1820, 1826, and 1827. However, from 1821 onward all other dividend statements are consistent at 3 percent so that assumption has been used for the missing periods. From 1820 to 1825 the Bank of Virginia shares consistently ran one-half of a percent higher than the Potomac Bank shares. Hence, if the Potomac Bank shares really made up more than half of the trust, then the income figures suggested for Ann Lee will be slightly elevated by an undue proportion of Bank of Virginia shares in the mix. Also in 1824 the actual dividend payment made a deduction per share for a "bonus" to the state before payment. On the other hand, all annual totals are understated to some degree by the fact that Ann had more Bank of Virginia shares remaining than needed to fill out the $20,000 trust, how many we cannot know, and more income from them. Allowing for both of these caveats, it seems reasonable to conclude that the figures arrived at for her annual income for these years is close to accurate or slightly understated.

The dividend figures for the Potomac Bank are compiled from Alexandria, *Daily Advertiser*, November 28, 1807, May 16, 1808; Alexandria, *Daily Gazette, Commercial and Political*, November 7, 1808, November 6, 1809, May 18, November 1, 1810, May 28, 1811, May 1, 1812, May 10, October 30, 1813, November 17, 1814, May 11, 1815, May 18, 1816, May 5, 1817; Alexandria, *Gazette*, May 4, 1822; Alexandria, *Gazette & Advertiser*, November 2, 1822, November 1, 1823, May 1, October 30, 1824; Alexandria, *Gazette & Daily Advertiser*, May 4, 1818, November 19, 1818, May 18, 1819, November 5, 1821, May 11, 1822; Alexandria, *Herald*, November 11, 1811, November 4, 1812, May 6, 1814, November 10, 1815, November 15, 1816, November 17, 1817, May 4, 1818, May 8, November 1, 1820, May 7, 1823; Alexandria, *Phenix Gazette*, May 5, November 1, 1825, May 5, October 28, 1826, April 28, November 6, 1827, May 3, November 3, 1828, May 7, 1829. The dividend figures for the Bank of Virginia are compiled from Alexandria, *Gazette*, July 23, 1819, January 8, 1822; Alexandria, *Phenix Gazette*, January 13, 1829; Norfolk, *American Beacon*, July 17, 1817, January 14, 1818, January 16, 1819; Norfolk, *Gazette and Publick Ledger*, July 10, 1812, July 27, 1814, July 27, 1815, January 18, July 6, 1816; Richmond, *Enquirer*, July 11, 1823, January 8, July 13, 1824, January 12, 1825, January 14, 1826, January 12, 1827, January 11, July 11, 1828, January 17, 1829; Richmond, *Vir-*

ginia Argus, July 11, 1807, January 11, 1818; Richmond, *Virginia Patriot*, July 10, 1810, January 11, 1815, January 7, 1817, May 19, 1818.

30   The Montgomery County land was at Spring Camp in what is now Floyd County, part of a 19,000-acre grant from the state to Lee for his Revolutionary War services (Amos D. Wood, *Floyd County, A History of the People and Places* [Blacksburg, VA: Southern Printing Co., 1981], pp. 28–29). At Harpers Ferry Henry Lee sold the mineral rights under his property in 1800, while the surface ownership remained his (Warranty deed, Henry Lee et ux to the United States, May 8, 1800, Harpers Ferry Laminated Material, Public Buildings Service, RG 121, NA).

31   Ann H. Lee to Sydney Smith Lee, April 10, 1827, Jessie Ball duPont Library, Stratford Hall, Stratford, VA.

32   Ann H. Lee to Sydney Smith Lee, May 17, 1822, Gary L. Sisson, Montross, VA.

33   Ann H. Lee to Sydney Smith Lee, April 10, 1827, Jessie Ball duPont Library, Stratford Hall, Stratford, VA.

34   Richmond, *Times-Dispatch*, December 5, 1932; Charleston, *State Gazette of South Carolina*, March 20, 1786.

35   Alfred J. Morrison, *The Beginnings of Public Education in Virginia, 1776–1860* (Richmond: Superintendent of Public Printing, 1917), p. 114n states that Leary took over as principal in 1807, which is manifestly incorrect in that Harrison was principal in 1818–1819.

36   Alexandria, *Herald*, July 28, 1820; Alexandria, *Gazette & Daily Advertiser*, September 5, 1820. A thorough search of the Alexandria papers for December 1820 has found no announcement of examinations, nor the usual publication of resulting awards. This is not conclusive that no term was held, but certainly is suggestive.

37   Ann H. Lee to Sydney Smith Lee, May 17, 1822, states that "Robert continues to go to school to Mr. Leary." This is a letter that brings Sydney up to date on what has happened in the past year, and her use of the word "continues" would imply that Robert was at the Academy when she saw Sydney last, or in the spring of 1821. Gary L. Sisson, Montross, VA.

38   As with fall 1820, no announcements of examinations or results can be found in the city's press for this period. Ann Lee to Sydney Smith Lee, cited above, definitely establishes that the academy was open for spring 1822.

39   This conclusion is admittedly an interpolation from his statement on January 7, 1823, in announcing the move of his school out of the academy premises, that now he would have an opportunity "of devoting his exclusive attention to the duties of his profession." Alexandria, *Gazette & Advertiser*, January 7, 1823, March 2, 1822.

40   Ibid., January 7, 1823. Harold W. Hurst, *Alexandria on the Potomac: The Portrait of an Ante-Bellum Community* (Lanham, MD: University Press of America, 1991), p. 64, says the academy closed in 1821 due to economic depression in Alexandria, but manifestly it held terms in 1822 and then closed.

41   Alexandria, *Gazette & Advertiser*, October 28, 1823, May 1, 1824.

42   If Leary commenced a spring 1824 term he did not finish it. He still lived in Alexandria in February when he wrote his recommendation for Lee to the Military Academy, but by late April his uncollected letters accumulated in the city post office. He soon went on to St. John's College at Annapolis, where he earned a master's degree and became a professor of grammar. In April 1829 the state legislature incorporated the Academy and elected trustees still included Edmund J. Lee. By 1830 the Academy was back in operation, though moved to Prince Street, and still with a revolving door of principals. Alexandria, *Gazette & Advertiser*, May 1, 1824, and subsequent issues through August; *Register of the Graduates and Alumni of St. John's College at Annapolis, Maryland* (Baltimore: Williams & Wilkins, 1908), p. 26; Alexandria, *Phenix Gazette*, April 25, 1829, May 24, 1831.

43   R. E. Lee to [John C. Calhoun], February 28, 1824, San Francisco, *Post*, February 18, 1886.
     This document, the earliest known Lee letter to date, was clearly stolen sometime prior
     to 1886 from the War Department in Washington, where it would have been in Lee's
     application file for the Military Academy.

44   William Maynadier spent four years at the academy, from 1818 to 1822, first under Harri-
     son and then Leary, and describes virtually this same series of studies except that he did
     not progress beyond the fifth book of Euclid. William Maynadier to John C. Calhoun,
     March 15, 1822, William Maynadier File 060-991/2, U.S. Military Academy, Cadet Applica-
     tion Papers, 1805–1866, Records of the Adjutant General's Office, RG 94, NA.

45   The only directly contemporaneous confirmation of Lee's attendance at the academy
     is Ann Lee's statement that "Robert continues to go to school to Mr. Leary" in Ann H.
     Lee to Sydney Smith Lee, May 17, 1822, Gary L. Sisson, Montross, VA. In February 1824
     Leary himself said nothing more than that "Robert Lee was formerly a pupil of mine,"
     but he did not state where or when (William B. Leary to John C. Calhoun, n.d. [February
     1824], Robert E. Lee File, Cadet Applications, etc., RG 94). As for Lee, in December 1866
     he recalled to Leary the days "when I was under your tuition," but nothing more, and in
     1904 Lee's son Robert E. Lee Jr. wrote that "Mr. Leary . . . was my father's teacher when
     a boy in Alexandria," but again said neither where nor when (Robert E. Lee, *Recollections
     and Letters of General Robert E. Lee by His Son* [New York: Doubleday, 1904], p. 417). Writing
     prior to June 1871, Mason, *Popular Life*, pp. 23–24, said "his first teacher was an Irish gentle-
     man, Mr. William B. Leary," but that is all.

46   Since Leary taught both at the academy and on St. Asaph and Cameron Streets, Lee might
     have studied at any or all venues. The common assumption has taken hold that it had
     to be at the Alexandria Academy, and probably it was, but all we have to that effect is a
     secondhand recollection by Lee's cousin Cazenove Lee recounting his father Cassius F.
     Lee's conversation with Robert E. Lee in July 1870. As Cassius related it, the two old men
     recalled their days with Leary, whom Cazanove identified as "their old teacher at the Al-
     exandria Academy" (Lee, *Recollections*, pp. 415, 417). Lee's time with Leary at the academy
     could have been anytime between the spring 1820 term and the spring or fall 1822 terms,
     but he certainly did not study under him there for a full four years. Still, Lee completed
     virtually the same work as his contemporary William Maynadier, just a few weeks Lee's
     junior, who entered the academy in the fall of 1818 under Harrison. Indeed, Lee mastered
     one more book of Euclid than did Maynadier. William Maynadier entered the academy
     at age eleven and finished aged fifteen after four years (Maynadier to Calhoun, March 15,
     1822, Maynadier File 060-991/2, Cadet Application Papers, 1805–1866, RG 94, NA).
         Lee biographers have used the academy as a convenient way to fill the years 1818 to
     1824 for which Lee left no trace. In 1928 Mary Gregory Powell, *The History of Old Alexan-
     dria, Virginia: From July 13, 1749 to May 24, 1861* (Alexandria: William Byrd Press, 1928), p. 154,
     said without authority that Lee entered at age thirteen, or in 1820, and stayed until 1824.
     In December 1932 Douglas Southall Freeman's own newspaper—and possibly Freeman
     himself writing in it—claimed that Lee spent six years at the school from 1818 to 1824
     (Richmond, *Times-Dispatch*, December 5, 1932). Two years later Freeman, taking Powell as
     his source, put Lee there in 1820 and possibly a year before, and had him staying "approx-
     imately three years" until "the end of 1823, and perhaps earlier" (*Lee*, 1, pp. 36–37). Most
     biographers since have borrowed Freeman's estimate, though Elizabeth Brown Pryor,
     Reading the Man: A Portrait of Robert E. Lee Through His Private Letters (New York: Viking,
     2007), pp. 25–26, has Lee entering the academy when "he was about fourteen," which
     would mean the spring term in 1821, and staying "three years," or until early 1824. Like
     Freeman she appears to interpret Lee's February 1824 application to West Point as signal-

ing a terminus to his time at the academy, whereas that definitely could not have gone later than the fall term of 1822, after which Leary left the academy. If Lee had any formal schooling in 1823, it was either under Leary on St. Asaph Street, or at the academy under someone else, and quite possibly neither. What is certain, however, is that Lee was not a student at the academy itself anytime beyond the fall term of 1822, after which Leary moved to St. Asaph Street, and possibly not after spring 1822 if Leary did not hold a fall session.

Thus it is possible that Lee attended the academy in the Harrison years, perhaps commencing in 1818 as did Maynadier. Since the academy admitted students at least as young as ten, an eleven-year-old Lee could have been admitted the same time as Maynadier in 1818. Meanwhile, the average age of the award-winning students at the academy was thirteen, with average birth dates in May 1807. Robert E. Lee, of course, was born in January of 1807, meaning his age fit him very close to that average for all of Leary's terms. (These figures are based on thirteen of the students named for awards and premiums in 1819, 1820, and 1820, whose birth dates can be found, plus Cassius Lee, born in 1808, who is known to have attended at that time. No records of enrollments survive.)

It has often been assumed that the prospect of free tuition at the academy would have been a strong inducement to send Robert there, beginning at least with Powell, *Old Alexandria*, p. 155, which says that the academy became free of charge to all Alexandria boys from January 1821. She gave no source for this claim, whereas the trustees' 1822 complaint of recurring deficits and resorts to loans hardly sounds like the academy was an institution that could afford to ignore tuition as a source of revenue. In fact tuition was being charged at least as early as 1818. More conclusive is the fact that when Leary moved to St. Asaph Street in 1822 he announced he would be charging the same for tuition at his new venue as he had at the academy (Alexandria, *Gazette & Daily Advertiser*, October 20, 1821, January 7, 1823). Hence the assertion that the academy was free is erroneous, and likely a confusion with its original intent in 1786.

It is improbable that Lee enrolled with others during those terms that Leary may not have held classes. Lee sent only Leary's recommendation with his application to West Point. Had he studied under others it is reasonable to expect that he would have sent certificates from them as well. Moreover, Leary published lists of the outstanding students for the 1820 and 1821 spring terms, as his predecessor did for spring 1819, but no such lists were published for the fall terms. Overlooking one might be attributed to chance oversight, but to fail to do so three years in a row, after regularly doing it for each spring term in those same years, suggests that the school held no fall terms. However, on September 2, 1820, an announcement appeared in the local press that the fall term at the academy would commence three days later (Alexandria, *Gazette and Daily Advertiser*, September 5, 1820). There is no further record of the term's actual commencement or conclusion. So we are left with more questions than answers about the possible extent of young Lee's education at the academy.

47 Mason, *Personal Life*, p. 23; Henry Lee to Carter Lee, February 9, 1817, Lee, *Lee of Virginia*, p. 350.
48 REL to MCL, August 7, 1864, *Wartime Papers*, p. 829.
49 Henry Lee to Carter Lee, February 9, 1817, Lee, *Lee of Virginia*, p. 348.
50 REL to MCL, March 14, 1862, *Wartime Papers*, p. 128; Mason, *Popular Life*, p. 24. While there is no record of Lee's baptism, it is inferred from his mother's reference to a godfather (*Lee*, 1, p. 28).
51 Ann Hill Lee to Charles Carter Lee, July 17, 1816, Charles Carter Lee Collection, Major Henry Lee Papers 1813–1841, VSL.

52   Mason, *Popular Life*, p. 23. Mason says she was told this by one of Robert E. Lee's family "who knew him best," probably Cassius Lee.

53   Alexandria, *Gazette*, July 23, 1819; Richmond, *Virginia Patriot*, March 10, 1819; Richmond, *Enquirer*, August 27, 1819, December 14, 1822.

54   Ann Lee's annual income for these years, as reconstructed from the dividend percentages in the sources previously cited, was roughly the following (the figures under "Other" represent the fact that in 1816 she stated that her income from other sources was less than half her dividend income, then running $1,210. The vector signs indicate < for less than and > for more than):

	Bank of Virginia	Potomac Bank	Other	Total
1816	$1,188	----	<$1,210	<2,400
1817	$1,800	----	<$1,210	<3,000
1818	$1,332	$1,725	<$1,210	>4,255
1819	unknown	$600–$700	<$1,210	<1,860
1820	unknown	$1,100	<$1,210	<2,310
1821–26	$864	$983 average	<$1,21	0 >3,050
1827	$720	$900	<$1,210	>2,830
1828	$864	$1,000	<$1,21	0 >3,074
1829	$432 Jan.–June	$500 Jan.–June	<$605	>1,537

55   Alexandria, *Gazette & Advertiser*, December 11, 1823; Ann Hill Lee to Sydney Smith. Lee, April 10, 1827, duPont Library, Stratford.

56   Mason, *Popular Life*, p. 23. Pryor, *Reading the Man*, offers good general observations on Ann Carter Lee's illness and personality.

57   Mason, *Popular Life*, p. 23; Robert E. L. DeButts Jr., "Lee in Love: Courtship and Correspondence in Antebellum Virginia," *Virginia Magazine of History and Biography*, 115, no. 4 (2007), pp. 488–89.

58   REL to Mary Custis Lee, June 15, 1857, Francis Raymond Adams Jr., ed., *An Annotated Edition of the Personal Letters of Robert E. Lee, April 1855–April 1861* (Doctoral thesis: University of Maryland, 1955), p. 365.

59   A. L. Long, *Memoirs of Robert E. Lee, His Military and Personal History* (New York: J. M. Stoddart, 1887), p. 26.

60   REL to Mary Custis, October 30, 1830, DeButts, "Lee in Love," pp. 517–18.

61   REL to Anna Fitzhugh, June 6, 1860, Adams, *Letters*, p. 638.

62   REL to Mary Custis, March 8, 1831, DeButts, "Lee in Love," p. 534.

63   REL to Custis, April 16, 1860, Adams, *Letters*, p. 611.

64   REL to Charles Lee, May 10, 1855, ibid., p. 13; REL to Martha Custis Williams, January 2, 1854, Avery O. Craven, ed., *"To Markie": The Letters of Robert E. Lee to Martha Custis Williams* (Cambridge, MA: Harvard University Press, 1933), p. 39.

65   These are the only terms for which examination results and honors have been found in the Alexandria press.

66   William B. Leary Certificate, February 3, 1822, Maynadier File 060-991/2, Cadet Application Papers, 1805–1866, RG 94, NA.

67   William B. Leary statement, n.d. [February 1824], Robert E. Lee File L60, RG 94, NA.

68   W. B. Leary statement, February 15, 1824, ibid.

69   Lee to [John C. Calhoun], February 28, 1824, San Francisco, *Post*, February 18, 1886.

70   Rose Mortimer Ellzey MacDonald, *Mrs. Robert E. Lee* (Boston: Ginn and Company, 1939), pp. 22–23.

71   Hallowell, *Autobiography*, p. 100.

72   Alexandria, *Gazette & Advertiser*, October 19, 1824.

73   REL to Albert Sydney Johnston, October 25, 1857, Marilyn McAdams Sibley, ed., "Robert E. Lee to Albert Sydney Johnston, 1857," *Journal of Southern History*, 29 (February 1963), p. 104.

74   Lee to Mary Custis, May 13, 1831, DeButts, "Lee in Love," p. 541.

75   Long, *Memoirs*, p. 28. *Lee*, p. 44n, cites a tradition that Jackson got involved in Lee's appointment. The reference to a Jackson letter in Lee's application papers below confirms this.

76   On June 14, 1861, Scott issued an order that Mary Fitzhugh was to have "the safeguard of the army" for her property, calling her "a lady of great excellence, connected with the family of the father of his country." Springfield, MA, *Republican*, May 22, 1872.

77   William Fitzhugh to John C. Calhoun, February 7, 1824, Statement of William B. Leary, [February 1824], R. S. Garnett to Calhoun, February 16, 1824, C. F. Mercer et al to Calhoun, February 23, 1824, Charles Carter Lee to Calhoun, February 28, 1824, Henry Lee to Calhoun, March 6, 1824, Robert E. Lee File, U.S. Military Academy, Cadet Application Papers, 1805–1866, Records of the Adjutant General's Office, RG 94, NA. The Jackson letter is not in this file, and Freeman was unaware of it in the 1920s and 1930s, which means he only looked at the Cadet Application File for Lee. Long, *Memoirs*, p. 28, states that Lee was taken to Washington by Nellie Custis Lewis and introduced to Jackson, "who was so much pleased with him that he got him the appointment." In Record for Robt E. Lee, U.S. Military Academy, Cadet Records and Applications, 1805–1898, Register of Cadet Applications, 1819–1867, 1, 1819–1927, #101, RG 94, NA, the annotation lists the letters that Freeman found in the application file and also one from "Genl Jackson," which confirms that Jackson took some interest in Lee's application. The letters and statements supporting Lee's application are numbered enclosures one through eight, but number three is missing. That may be the Jackson letter, which was probably subsequently lost or stolen from the file, as was Lee's February 28, 1824 letter.

78   Lee to [Calhoun], February 28, 1824, San Francisco, *Post*, February 18, 1886. This letter, and other sources here cited, have raised discussion on the possibility that Lee was really born in 1806 (see Pryor, *Reading*, p. 498n). For instance, the Lee family Bible in the Lee Family Papers at VHS originally had 1806 beside his birth, but it was later amended to 1807. Fitzhugh's endorsement letter said Lee was eighteen "I believe," and Garnett's letter of the same month said he was "about 18." Pryor speculates that "it seems that the family at least thought for a time that this (1806) was the correct date, and changed it for unknown reasons." Lee's own February 28, 1824, letter would seem to support that. The annual registers of officers and cadets at the Academy for the years 1826, 1827, 1828, and 1829, further confuse the issue by consistently giving his age at admission as nineteen years and four months, placing his birth in March 1806. Even more confusing is Record for Robt E. Lee, Cadet Records and Applications, 1805–1898, Register of Cadet Applications, 1819–1867, 1, 1819–1927, #101, RG 94, NA, in which Lee's age at application in 1824 is noted as fourteen.

Countering all this, it seems probable that the Bible entry was simply an example of the commonplace error of inadvertently writing the old year some days or even weeks into the new year. In their letters Fitzhugh and Garnett both freely admit uncertainty as to Lee's age, and Lee himself in his 1824 letter had just given his day of birth wrong, so he could have been equally careless with his age. On September 25, 1828, when he signed his oath of allegiance after admission, Lee stated his age as "18 years and nine months," which placed his birth squarely in January 1807 (*Lee*, 1, p. 51n). The family's—and Lee's— later consistency in using the 1807 date should be conclusive, as should be Ann H. Lee's letter to Calhoun dated March 1824 (Robert E. Lee File L60, RG 94, NA) in which she gives her permission for her son to accept the appointment. If born in 1807, Lee would have been seventeen when she wrote that note. If born in 1806 he would have been eighteen, making her permission unnecessary.

79 Record for Robt E. Lee, Register of Cadet Applications, 1819–1867, I, 1819–1927, #101, RG 94. The final remark after noting the date of the appointment are the words "sent to Genl Jackson." As this notation does not appear attached to any other statements of appointment in this register, it seems to be best understood as additional confirmation that Jackson had interested himself personally in Lee's case and Calhoun obliged him. Lee's acceptance is in Lee to Calhoun, April 1, 1824, File 160, RG 94, NA.

80 *Obituary Record of Graduates of Yale College Deceased from June, 1870, to June, 1880. Presented at the Annual Meetings of the Alumni, 1870–1880* (New Haven, CT: Tuttle, Morehouse & Taylor, 1880), pp. 335–36; "James Watson Robbins," *Boston Medical and Surgical Journal,* 100 (January 30, 1879), p. 169; Rushton Dachwood Burr, ed., *Address Delivered at the Unitarian Church, in Uxbridge, Mass., in 1864, . . . by Harry Chapin* (Worcester, MA: Press of Charles Hamilton, 1881), p. 116. Mason's reference to "Lee of Fauquier" might suggest that he associated Lee with Fauquier because of Robbins's recommendation. Robbins collected specimens extensively in Fauquier, and around the Potomac and Pamunky Rivers in 1824–25 (James Watson Robbins Field Notes, 1824–1826, Field Book Project, 1855–2008, Acc. 12–339, Smithsonian Institution Archives, Capital Gallery, Washington, DC).

81 Alexandria, *Gazette & Advertiser,* October 5, 1824.

82 Hallowell, *Autobiography,* p. 100. Hallowell actually says that Lafayette called on the Lees on October 14, a forgivable lapse of memory after almost sixty years.

83 Alexandria, *Gazette & Advertiser,* December 4, 1824.

84 Hallowell, *Autobiography,* pp. 101, 103.

85 Ibid., pp. 96–97.

86 Washington, *Daily National Intelligencer,* November 4, 1829.

87 Alexandria, *Phenix Gazette,* February 24, 1826.

88 Alexandria, *Gazette,* November 24, 1851; Hallowell, *Autobiography,* p. 109.

89 Ibid., April 30, 1827.

90 REL to Mackay, June 26, 1834, Gilder Lehrman Collection, New-York Historical Society. Hallowell's letters are so written and, presumably, his speech was the same. Hallowell to Robert W. Miller, November 14, 1873, Lee Family Papers, Washington and Lee University, Lexington, VA.

91 Long, *Memoirs,* p. 26; Mason, *Popular Life,* pp. 22–23. Long's source is identified only as a cousin of Robert E. Lee writing to his widow sometime between 1870 and 1886. It is Sally Lee writing to Mary Custis Lee, October 27, 1870, DeButts-Ely Papers, LC. Mason's account here cited sounds very much like it may have based on the same letter.

92 REL to MCL, March 24, 1848, DeButts-Ely Papers, LC.

93 Mason, *Popular Life,* pp. 25–26.

94 Hallowell, *Autobiography,* p. 214.

95 REL to John B. Floyd, February 1, 1860, Adams, *Letters,* p. 561.

96 Mason, *Popular Life,* p. 23.

97 Mary Custis Lee to Louise H. Carter, November 9, 1870, Shirley Plantation Collection.

98 This is the version Jesse Grant gave to P. C. Headley in an undated letter, probably written in 1864 or early 1865, quoted in P. C. Headley, *The Life and Campaigns of Lieut.-Gen. U. S. Grant* (New York: Derby and Miller, 1866), p. 19. Headley actually stated essentially the same thing before his book appeared, in a letter to the New York, *Times,* quoted in Lowell, MA, *Daily Citizen and News,* November 21, 1865. Jesse told substantially the same story in a letter dated January 21, 1868, addressed to Robert Bonner, proprietor of the New York *Ledger,* though it is probable that a reporter actually wrote this and other letters attributed to

Jesse at the time, basing them on oral interviews ("Grant as Remembered by His Father," *Ulysses S. Grant Association Newsletter*, 8 [October 1970], pp. 4–5). Eight months later Jesse had embellished the story, turning the choice of names into a lottery whereby several names were put in a hat and the name Ulysses was drawn out, while Hiram was added at the request of not Hannah's father but Jesse's, though at that point he had been dead for seventeen years (Providence, RI, *Evening Press*, September 25, 1868)! See also Hamlin Garland, "The Early Life of Ulysses Grant," *McClure's Magazine*, 8 (December 1896), p. 130.

99 *PMUSG*, 1, p. 20. Some biographers mention Jesse's early association with John Brown and others do not. Jesse Grant made no mention of it in his January 17, 1868, sketch of himself in Jesse R. Grant, *"Grant as Remembered by His Father," Ulysses S. Grant Association Newsletter* 8 (October, 1970), 6. Still, by the end of the nineteenth century the story had gained some currency, probably because of USG's own account of the stories told him by his father in *PMUSG*, which is ultimately the earliest and most likely reliable source.

100 United States Census, Georgetown, Brown County, Ohio, 1830.

101 Daniel Ammen in Philadelphia, *Inquirer*, April 23, 1893; James A. Sanderson in New York, *Times*, July 30, 1885.

102 Daniel Ammen in Philadelphia, *Inquirer*, April 23, 1893.

103 James Sanderson in Cincinnati, *Commercial Tribune*, August 1, 1885. Sanderson differs from other and better sources in maintaining that Grant loved guns, especially pistols, and was rarely without one, being a crack shot. It sounds fanciful.

104 James A. Sanderson in New York, *Times*, July 30, 1885; Daniel Ammen in Philadelphia, *Inquirer*, April 23, 1893. Sanderson says that Grant loved guns and was a skilled marksman, but that fails to ring true, and is probably a false recollection fifty years after the fact.

105 Jesse Grant to Bonner, January 17, 1868, "Grant as Remembered by His Father," p. 7.

106 *PMUSG*, 1, p. 212.

107 Garland, "Early life," p. 127.

108 Ibid., p. 129.

109 Ibid., p. 127.

110 Daniel Ammen in Philadelphia, *Inquirer*, April 23, 1893.

111 "Grant as Remembered by His Father," p. 9; Garland, "Early Life," p. 138; USG note, 1864–1866, *PUSG*, 32, p. 187.

112 Garland, "Early Life," p. 134.

113 In USG to McKinstry Griffith, September 22, 1839, *PUSG*, 1, pp. 6–7, Grant indicates some special fondness for his grandmother as he asks that all of his letters written from West Point be shown to her.

114 *PMUSG*, 1, pp. 30–31.

115 Ibid., pp. 30–31; Washington, *Evening Star*, April 4, 1885.

116 USG to Julia, December 19, 1852, *PUSG*, 1, p. 277.

117 Daniel Ammen in Philadelphia, *Inquirer*, April 23, 1893.

118 James A. Sanderson in New York, *Times*, July 30, 1885.

119 Daniel Ammen in Philadelphia, *Inquirer*, April 23, 1893.

120 James A. Sanderson in New York, *Times*, July 30, 1885. Sanderson's claim that Grant did not like to read books is at odds with Grant's own statements about his reading habits in his memoirs.

121 Garland, "Early Life," p. 137.

122 James A. Sanderson in New York, *Times*, July 30, 1885.

123 Garland, "Early Life," p. 137.

124 James A. Sanderson in New York, *Times*, July 30, 1885.

125 Ibid.

126 Daniel Ammen in Philadelphia, *Inquirer*, April 23, 1893.

127 James A. Sanderson in New York, *Times*, July 30, 1885.

128 The actual date of this circus episode is conjectural. No performances of any circus can be found in southern Ohio during the 1830s except for two in 1837, both of them featuring equestrian acts that seem compatible with the pony and monkey attraction. Either could have stopped in Georgetown. Canton, Ohio, *Repository*, June 8, 1837; Cincinnati, *Daily Gazette*, March 30, 1837.

129 This story first appeared in the *Chicago Home Visitor* of unknown date in 1865. It hit the newspaper press as early as May 31, 1865, in the Sandusky, Ohio, *Register*, and soon spread across the country. The writer of the story is unidentified, but said that he spent part of his boyhood in Georgetown with Grant. Jesse Grant, or the reporter who wrote most of the January 18, 1868, letter attributed to Jesse that appeared in the March 7, 1868, issue of the New York, *Ledger*, included this episode, only enlarged on it to have the monkey jumping on the horse behind young Grant and eventually jumping onto his shoulders and grabbing Grant's hair with its paws. *Ulysses S. Grant Association Newsletter*, VIII, 1 (October, 1970), pp. 8–9.

130 Portland, ME, *Daily Eastern Argus*, August 20, 1868. Somehow this story was omitted from those in the New York, *Ledger* letters.

131 Cleveland, *Leader*, October 3, 1865.

132 Garland, "Early Life," pp. 133–34.

133 Jesse Grant to Robert Bonner, January 20, 1868, "Grant as Remembered by His Father," pp. 8–10, 11–13.

134 Garland, "Early Life," p. 127.

135 Albany, NY, *Evening Journal*, December 22, 1863. In the original newspaper article the teller of the story is identified only as a member of Congress who went to school with Grant in Georgetown. In 1863 White was the sitting member from Georgetown's district. In 1885 in *PMUSG*, 1, pp. 29–30, Grant credited White with telling the story. In 1863 White said this incident took place when Grant was "about twelve," or circa 1834, while Grant twenty years later wrote that "this story is nearly true," but added that he "could not have been over eight" at the time, putting it at 1830. There were several Ralston families living together in Pleasant Township at the time, making it impossible to identify which one sold Grant the horse. 1830 United States Census, Pleasant Township, Brown County, Ohio.

136 *PMUSG*, 1, p. 30.

137 Ibid., pp. 26–27

138 Columbus, OH, *Crisis*, November 21, 1861; Cincinnati, *Commercial Tribune*, July 28, 1885.

139 Daniel Ammen in Philadelphia, *Inquirer*, April 23, 1893.

140 Thomas E. Pickett, "W. W. Richeson, The Kentuckian That 'Taught' Grant," *Register of the Kentucky State Historical Society*, 9 (September 1911), p. 20.

141 New York, *Herald*, December 20, 1879.

142 Pickett, "W. W. Richeson," pp. 16 and passim.

143 Ibid., pp. 14, 15, 17.

144 A. H. Markland and W. W. Richeson in Washington, *Evening Star*, April 4, 1885.

145 Garland, "Early Life," p. 138.

146 W. W. Richeson in New York, *Herald*, December 13, 1879.

147 *PMUSG*, 1, pp. 30–31.

148 Ibid., 1, pp. 34–35.

149 Frankfort, KY, *Argus*, October 31, 1832.

150 New York, *Times*, April 28, 1897. Peyton placed Grant's visit in 1840, not 1837, and said Grant brought Payne's niece not his brother.

151 *PMUSG*, 1, pp. 27–29

152 Columbus, *Ohio State Journal*, November 17, 1832; Columbus, *Ohio Monitor*, January 28, 1833.

153 Michael Speer, ed., "Autobiography of Adam Lowry Rankin," *Ohio History*, 79 (Winter 1970), pp. 27–28.

154 In his memoir Grant tersely dismissed his term there with a reference to it as a "school at Ripley" and "a private school." *PMUSG*, 1, pp. 25, 32.

155 New York, *Emancipator*, October 3, 1839; Andrew Ritchie, *The Soldier, the Battle, and the Victory: Being a Brief Account of the Work of Rev. John Rankin in the Anti-Slavery Cause* (Cincinnati: Western Tract and Book Society, 1870), pp. 105–107; Ann Hagedorn, *Beyond the River: The Untold Story of the Heroes of the Underground Railroad* (New York: Simon & Schuster, 2002), pp. 135–139. The Rankin story of the escaping slave woman seems not to have hit the newspaper press until the 1890s, by which time it was already well established in Ohio lore. See, for instance, Aberdeen, SD, *Daily News,* March 30, 1890.

156 He does not mention Rankin or the story in his memoirs.

157 *PMUSG*, 1, p. 25.

158 None of the essays and speeches he had composed later survived to attest to his literacy, but later this year he wrote his earliest surviving letter, and its display of vocabulary and ease and facility of expression are surety that it was not his first, and that he felt comfortable and confidant with a pen in his hand. *PUSG*, 1, p.

159 Columbus, *Ohio State Journal*, November 17, 1832. Grant may have boarded in the home of Marion Johnson or Johnston, who boarded several young males at the time. United States Census, Brown County, Ohio, 1840.

160 Cincinnati, *Daily Gazette*, January 19, 1837.

161 Jesse R. Grant to Thomas L. Hamer, February 19, 1839, Cincinnati, *Commercial Tribune*, September 7, 1885.

162 Thomas Hamer in Chicago, *Daily Inter Ocean*, April 30, 1887.

163 U.S. Military and Naval Academies, Cadet Records and Applications, 1805–1898, Register of Cadet Applicants, 1819–1867, volume 10, 1838–1839, Records of the Adjutant General's Office, RG 94, NA.

164 Jesse Grant to Robert Bonner, January 21, 1868, "Grant as Remembered by His Father," p. 13; Garland, "Early Life," p. 138.

165 *PMUSG*, 1, p. 32.

166 James Sanderson in Cincinnati, *Commercial Tribune*, August 1, 1885.

167 *PMUSG*, 1, pp. 32–33.

CHAPTER 2: SCHOOL OF THE SOLDIER

1 REL to Mary Custis, June 21, 1831, DeButts, "Lee in Love," p. 549.

2 *Register of the Officers and Cadets of the U.S. Military Academy, June 1826* (New York: N.p., 1826), pp. 3, 12.

3 As of the spring term in 1827 Lee told his mother, in her words, that he had "never . . . received a mark of demerit." Receiving no demerits, and having none on his record, were two different things of course, and read literally—assuming he was being truthful—her comment seems weighted toward the former. Ann Hill Lee to Sydney Smith Lee, April 10, 1827, duPont Library, Stratford.

Of the forty-four months Lee spent at the Academy, September 1825–June 1829 (he was home on leave July and August 1827), the reports for sixteen are missing from the files, presumably lost or destroyed as many are in fragile condition. Of the twenty-eight that are extant, Lee appears on every one with no demerits. Taking at face value his statement to his mother as of March–April 1827 that he had no demerits to date (fourteen extant reports for his nineteen months to date at the Academy confirm this), that leaves eleven of his remaining twenty-five months unaccounted for. Given the absolute consistency of his performance on the extant reports it is not unreasonable to conclude that his performance would have been the same in those months for which reports are missing, though it is always possible that he in fact did garner a demerit or two and remove them from his record.

Nothing on these monthly reports indicates whether the demerits shown are total actually received or "net" after any being remitted. However, the January 1829 monthly report shows one demerit each for Jesse H. Leavenworth and Thomas Stockton, whereas *Register of the Officers and Cadets of the U.S. Military Academy, June, 1829* (New York: United States Military Academy, 1884; reprint), p, 19, shows both Leavenworth and Stockton with no demerits for the academic year. Thus the single demerit against each on the January 1829 report has disappeared, meaning they must have been expunged. Hence, demerit figures on the monthly reports are actual, not net. (Monthly Class Reports and Conduct Rolls, United States Military Academy, 1820–1830, RG 94, Entry 231, NA).

4   *Lee*, 1, pp. 61–62.
5   Ibid., 1, p. 64n. Freeman erroneously gives the author of the last book as someone surnamed Light.
6   Sylvanus Thayer to Alexander McComb, December 13, 1827, AG 1822–1860, NA.
7   Ann Hill Lee to Sydney Smith Lee, April 10, 1827, duPont Library, Stratford.
8   *Register of the Officers and Cadets of the U.S. Military Academy, June 1827* (New York: New York: N.p., 1827), pp. 10, 19; *Lee*, 1, pp. 67–68.
9   Just when Ann Lee moved to Georgetown is uncertain, but she was there at least as early as June 1826 when her daughter was married in the house (Philadelphia, *National Gazette*, July 4, 1826). Ethel Armes, *Stratford Hall: the Great House of the Lees* (Richmond: Garrett and Massie, 1936), p. 388, says she moved there in 1825 without citing a source, but that would make sense. With Smith gone and Robert leaving in the summer of 1825, she needed less space. On January 22, 1824, the Oronoco Street house was to be auctioned, but she could have stayed on as a tenant (Alexandria, *Herald*, December 27, 1822). She remained in the Georgetown house until her death, after which it was briefly a seminary for young women (Washington, *Daily National Intelligencer*, September 7, 1829). Today Second Street is O Street.
10   Ann Hill Lee to Sydney Smith Lee, April 10, 1827, duPont Library, Stratford.
11   REL to Mary Custis, September 11, 1830, DeButts, "Lee in Love," p. 514.
12   Marietta Fauntleroy Turner Powell reminiscence, July 17, 1886, Marietta Minnegerode Andrews, comp., *Scraps of Paper* (New York: E. P. Dutton, 1929), p. 199. *Lee*, 1, p. 68 and n, states that at the Academy by this time Lee was so handsome and soldierly that he was being called the "Marble Model." He gave his source as "General L. L. Lomax, quoted in Walter Watson's *Notes on Southside Virginia*." As Freeman often did, he took the printed word at face value and either ignored or dismissed fuller context that compromised the content. In fact Walter A. Watson, "Notes on Southside Virginia," *Bulletin of the Virginia State Library*, 15 (No's. 2–4, September 1925), pp. 244–45, repeats from notes taken in January 1914 the substance of recent interviews with John S. Mosby, who had just turned eighty. In them it is Mosby who states that Lunsford L. Lomax years before had told him that "he [Lomax] was at West Point with him [Lee]," and that "he [Lee] was then known as 'The Marble Model.'" Lomax was not born until November 1835, more than six years after Lee left West Point, and thus obviously had no direct personal observation or knowl-

edge of what anyone was calling Lee in 1827. Lomax was a cadet at West Point 1852–1856 during the period that Lee was superintendent, and in the Elizabeth Lindsay Lomax diary, December 20, 1854, Lindsay Lomax Wood, ed., *Leaves from an Old Washington Diary, 1854–1863* (New York: E. P. Dutton, 1943), p. 29, the diarist writes that "Lindsay wrote me from West Point that Colonel Lee was the handsomest man he had ever known, just like a 'marble model.'"

13 At Christmas 1824 they did something over cake in a store room at Arlington, but neither illuminated the event. REL to Mary Custis, December 28, 1830, DeButts, "Lee in Love," p. 526.

14 REL to Mary Custis, May 13, 1831, ibid., p. 541.

15 Mary Custis to Edward G. W, Butler, n.d. (August 10, 1827?), Edward G. W. Butler Papers, Williams Research Center, Historic New Orleans Collection, New Orleans, LA.

16 *Lee*, I, pp. 72–73. Freeman got a list of Lee's books taken from the West Point library from the then assistant librarian M. L. Samson. Either the librarian in 1828 was careless, or Samson was careless, or Freeman, for the author names and titles of some of the books listed are corrupted. Warnery, for instance, appears as Wamery.

17 *Register of the Officers and Cadets of the U.S. Military Academy, West Point, N.Y. June 1828* (New York: N.p., 1828), pp. 8, 19.

18 Register 600, Entry 544, Field Records of Hospitals. West Point Cadets' Hospital, January 1, 1827–May 22, 1833, RG 94, NA.

19 *Lee*, I, pp. 72–73, 80.

20 Ibid., pp. 81–82; *Register of the Officers and Cadets of the U.S. Military Academy, West Point, N.Y. June 1829* (New York: N.p., 1829), pp. 6, 19. For that year twenty-six cadets from all classes combined showed no demerits.

21 Twenty-two of the forty-four monthly reports are extant in RG 94, and his name is on the "distinguished" list in each. Moreover, in the Academy register for conduct infractions, the page with Lee's name on it has had his name crossed out so it could be used for another cadet who did receive demerits.

22 Unknown woman to "My dear Sally," July 2, 1829, Raynors Historical Collectible Auctions catalog for November 17, 2005 sale, item #97, Burlington, NC.

23 Ann Hill Lee to Sydney Smith Lee, April 10, 1827, duPont Library, Stratford.

24 Some sources at the time and later claimed that Ann died in Georgetown, but her Alexandria obituary made it clear that her death came at Ravensworth. Alexandria, *Phenix Gazette*, July 28, 1829.

25 Long, *Memoirs*, p. 26; Lee, *Recollections*, p. 363; Edmund Jennings Lee, "The Character of General Lee," Robert A. Brock, ed., *Gen. Robert Edward Lee: Soldier, Citizen and Christian Patriot* (Richmond: Johnson Publishing Co., 1897), p. 383.

26 Mary Custis Lee to James Callaway, April 20, 1918, Montgomery, *Advertiser*, May 7, 1918.

27 Copy in files of U. S. Grant Association, Mississippi State University, Starkeville, MS. Mary King's sister Hattie King owned the album in which he wrote the poem, but said he wrote it when he was on vacation, meaning his leave in the summer of 1841.

28 USG to cousin McKinstry Griffith September 22, 1839, *PUSG*, I, p. 6; *PMUSG*, I, pp. 35–38.

29 USG to Julia Dent, August 31, 1844, *PUSG*, I, p. 36. USG shows as Ulysses S. Grant on U.S. Military Academy, Cadet Records and Applications, 1805–1898, Register of Cadet Applications, 1819–1867, 11, 1839–1840, RG 94, NA.

30 USG to McKinstry Griffith, September 22, 1839, *PUSG*, I, pp. 5, 7.

31 Ibid.

32 U. S. Grant Class and Conduct Report, September 1839, copy at USGA.

33 *PMUSG*, I, pp. 41–42. Here Grant says Scott and Van Buren came in succeeding years, but

his 1839 letter makes it clear that they both came during the early months of his fourth class year.

34 USG to McKinstry Griffith, September 22, 1839, *PUSG*, 1, pp. 6–7.

35 Register 604, Entry 544, Field Records of Hospitals, West Point Cadets' Hospital, January 1, 1838–July 31, 1840, RG 94, NA.

36 USG to R. McKinstry Griffith, July 18, 1840, *PUSG*, 32, pp. 3, 5. USG's monthly conduct reports show him a total of 51 and 5/6 demerits, but the published Official Register shows him with 59, an unexplained anomaly. Monthly Class Report and Conduct Roll, September 1839–June 1840, Entry 232, RG 94, NA; *Official Register of the Officers and Cadets of the U.S. Military Academy, West Point, New York. June 1840* (New York: J. P. Wright, 1840), pp. 13, 18, 23.

37 *Official Register of the Officers and Cadets of the U.S. Military Academy, West Point, New York. June 1840*, pp. 23–24, USG to Charles F. Smith, July 13, 1840, *PUSG*, 1, pp. 9–10.

38 USG to Julia, August 31, 1844 1, *PUSG*, pp. 34–36.

39 *PMUSG*, 1, p. 39.

40 Monthly Class Report and Conduct Roll, January 1841, Entry 232, RG 94, Entry 232, NA.

41 *Official Register of the Officers and Cadets of the U.S. Military Academy, West Point, New York. June 1841* (New York: J. P. Wright, 1841), pp. 13, 20. The Official Register shows USG with 67 demerits, while the monthly reports July 1840–June 1841 show him with a total of 62½. Monthly Class Reports and Conduct Rolls, July 1840–June 1841, Entry 232, RG 94, NA.

42 Melancthon T. Burke memoir, 1896, Hamlin Garland Papers, University of Southern California, Los Angeles.

43 *PMUSG*, 1, p. 40.

44 Years later several women emerged as claimants to romance with the young Grant, among them Hannah Richey. Fifty-five years after the fact Samuel Walker of Cincinnati claimed that Grant had courted her (the surname appears in several variants) from 1841 to 1843, but Walker won her favors instead. The two certainly did marry, and appear on the 1860 census as Samuel and Hannah Walker, with her brother Robert Ritchie living with them in Cincinnati. The story as told by Walker says that Grant was a classmate of Hannah's brother John Alexander Richey and that Grant met her in 1841 when the two returned to Ohio on their furlough and Grant visited Richey's home. However, John A. Richey did not actually enter West Point until the fall of 1841, so though they certainly would have been acquainted after that, and may even have become friends, he and Grant were not classmates, and the story of Grant meeting Hannah while visiting Richey is probably just the seventy-four-year-old Walker's conflation with the genuine story of how Grant met Julia Dent when visiting his classmate Frederick Dent. Lieutenant John A. Richey was killed in Mexico in January 1847, but Grant makes no mention of it in his correspondence, which may suggest that the two were not close, though Walker in 1896 spun quite a story of intimate friendship, supposedly referring to Grant's letters to Richey's family after his death. The letters have not come to light if they ever existed (Omaha, *World Herald*, April 24, 27, 1896). Most of the claimants are certainly fictional, such as Eleanor Brandon Spaulding in 1882 (San Francisco, *Bulletin*, March 25, 1882), and most bizarrely the woman calling herself Queen Katherine who claimed to have been his lover in Washington during the Civil War (New York, *Morning Telegraph*, September 5, 1875). For others see Jackson, MI, *Citizen*, June 4, 1897, Omaha, *World Herald*, April 27, 1896. The San Diego, *Evening Tribune*, September 6, 1901, says Lucinda Powers of Georgetown, Ohio, was a sweetheart of Grant's, and that as president he made her postmistress at Georgetown. Then there is Mary King of Georgetown. In addition to the poem in her album, Grant sent her from Mexico a drawing of Tehuantepec. Grant supposedly liked her but lost interest when he finished at

West Point due to some misunderstanding. As president he did appoint her postmistress of Thibodeaux when she was Mrs. John Fulford. Grant also supposedly got attached to Sarah Clarke, sister of Congressman R. W. Clarke. She married Charles Hunt and died in 1850. He also liked Carrie Tice, later Richards, and a widow Hubbell of Mt. Carmel in Clermont County (Washington, *Critic-Record*, January 4, 1886). A longer-standing claim has been accorded to Katherine "Kate" Lowe, who lived with her father John W. Lowe at Batavia. Grant supposedly sent her one of his watercolors when he was at West Point. The Melanchthon T. Burke Memoir (Garland Papers), claims that Grant actually went to Batavia to visit "Miss Kate Lowe," whom he had known as a cadet because she sometimes came to New York. Hamlin Garland, *Ulysses S. Grant, His Life and Character* (New York: Doubleday, 1898), p. 49, used this and other half-century-old recollections of Bethel residents to state that Grant visited the home of John W. Lowe "in whose home Miss Kate Lowe was staying," without mentioning the precise relationship between these two Lowes. Carl Becker, "Was Grant Drinking in Mexico?" *Bulletin of the Cincinnati Historical Society*, 24, no. 1 (January 1966), p. 69, transmutes this into saying Grant was attracted to the Lowe home by "the presence of young Kate Lowe, one of Lowe's relatives visiting from the East." Those memories and local traditions more than half a century after the fact were seriously confused, for Kate Lowe was John W. Lowe's daughter, born in 1850, nine years after Grant's furlough home.

45 *PMUSG*, 1, p. 41.

46 *Official Register of the Officers and Cadets of the U.S. Military Academy, West Point, New-York. June 1842* (New York: J. P. Wright, 1842), p. 23.

47 Ibid., pp. 7–14.

48 Several of Grant's drawings and watercolors appear in *PUSG*, 1, pp. 13–19.

49 Monthly Class Report and Conduct Roll, February, May, 1842, Entry 232, RG 94, NA.

50 *Official Register of the Officers and Cadets of the U.S. Military Academy, West Point, New-York, June 1842*, pp. 19, 21, shows USG with 98 demerits. However, the tally from the actual monthly reports for September 1841 to June 1842 is 127⅓ . Monthly Class Reports and Conduct Rolls, United States Military Academy, 1831–1866, RG 94, Entry 232 NA.

51 *PUSG*, 1, p. 41.

52 *Official Register of the Officers and Cadets of the U.S. Military Academy, West Point, New York. June 1843* (New York: Burroughs & Co., 1843), p. 20.

53 Certificate, June 20, 1843, *PUSG*, 1, p. 21, USG to Carey and Hart, March 31, April 8, 1843, p. 11, USG to Julia, May 6, 1845, pp. 43–44.

54 Monthly Class Report and Conduct Roll, March 1843, Entry 232, RG 94, NA.

55 The 78 total comes from the monthly reports for July 1842–June 1843, and the September report shows 12 demerits removed, which agrees with the 68 shown in *Official Register of the Officers and Cadets of the U.S. Military Academy, West Point, New York. June 1843*, p. 18.

56 *PMUSG*, 1, pp. 42–43; *Official Register of the Officers and Cadets of the U.S. Military Academy, West Point, New York. June 1843*, p. 2, 3, 7, 17.

57 USG to Julia, July 13, 1851, *PUSG*, 1, p. 219.

58 Daniel Ammen in Philadelphia, *Inquirer*, April 23, 1893; W. W. Richeson in New York, *Herald*, December 13, 1879; *PMUSG*, 1, p. 42.

59 USG, Oath of Office July 28, 1843, *PUSG*, 1, pp. 21–22, USG to Adjutant General's Office, July 31, 1843, p. 22.

60 Lee biographers, following the lead of Freeman, assume that he assisted in settling his mother's estate, but there is no evidence for such an assumption. Her named executor William Carter likely handled all of that, perhaps assisted by lawyer Charles Carter Lee (*Lee*, 1, p. 92). REL to CCL, October 12, 1830, Lee Papers, UVA, makes it clear that he left

the details to brothers Smith and Carter, even when he was himself at hand in Arlington. Other correspondence with CCL also suggests that Lee's involvement was mainly if not exclusively division of slaves and other property among them after the estate was settled.

61 REL to Mary Custis, December 1, 1830, DeButts, "Lee in Love," p. 523.

62 CCL to Henry Lee, August 6, 1829, quoted in Armes, *Stratford*, p. 394, states that Lee had left Georgetown that day.

63 DeButts, "Lee in Love," p. 490.

64 File L60, AG.

65 REL to CCL, May 8, 1830, Lee Papers, UVA.

66 REL to CCL, September 22, 30, 1830, Lee Papers, UVA.

67 REL to Mary Custis, October 30, 1830, DeButts, "Lee in Love," pp. 517–18.

68 REL to Mary Custis, November 19, 1830, ibid., p. 522. See also REL to John Mackay, June 26, 1834, Gilder Lehrman Collection, for his familiarity with Cervantes and Goethe.

69 Mary Custis to REL, September 20, 1830, DeButts, "Lee in Love," p. 515.

70 REL to Mary Custis, November 11, 1830, ibid., p. 520.

71 REL to Mary Custis, November 19, 1830, ibid., p. 522.

72 REL to Mary Custis, November 19, 1830, ibid., p. 521.

73 REL to Mary Custis, December 1, 1830, ibid., p. 524.

74 REL to Mary Custis, November 19, 1830, ibid., p. 522, December 28, 1830, p. 526.

75 REL to Mary Lee Fitzhugh Custis, January 10, 1831, ibid., p. 531.

76 REL to Mary Custis, January 10, 1831, ibid., p. 529.

77 REL to Mary Custis, March 8, 1831, ibid., pp. 532, 534.

78 REL to Mary Custis, March 8, 1831, ibid., p. 533.

79 REL to Mary Custis, December 1, 1830, ibid., p. 523, April 3, 1831, p. 538, June 5, 1831, p. 543, June 12, 1831, p. 547, Mary Custis to REL, June 11, 1831, p. 545, REL to Mary Custis, June 21, 1831, p. 549.

80 REL to Mary Custis, December 28, 1830, ibid., p. 528.

81 Worcester, MA, *National Aegis*, January 26, 1831; Portland, ME, *Advertiser*, December 7, 1830; Bangor, ME, *Weekly Register*, April 6, 1830.

82 REL to Mary Custis, April 3, 1831, DeButts, "Lee in Love," p. 535.

83 REL to Mary Custis, May 13, 1831, ibid., pp. 505, 540.

84 REL to Mary Custis, June 5, 1831, ibid., p. 542.

85 REL to Mary Lee Fitzhugh Custis, June 15, 1831, Profiles in History, Calabasas, CA, Auction July 11, 2014, "The Property of a Distinguished American Private Collector," Auction Part IV-54D, page 110, item #61.

86 REL to Mary Custis, June 21, 1831, DeButts, "Lee in Love," pp. 549–50.

87 CCL to Henry Lee, July 21, 1831, Lee-Jackson Collection, Washington and Lee.

88 Pryor, *Reading the Man*, p. 86.

89 REL to MCL, November 27, 1833, Norma B. Cuthbert, ed., "Five Early Letters from Robert E. Lee to his Wife, 1832–1835," *Huntington Library Quarterly*, 15 (No 3, May 1951), p. 267.

90 REL to MCL (June 6, 1832), Cuthbert, "Letters," p. 264, REL to MCL, November 27, 1833, p. 268.

91 MCL and REL to Mary Fitzhugh Custis, Sunday, Lee Family Papers, VHS. Internal evidence establishes that MCL's portion of this letter was written August 28, 1831.

92 REL to MCL, November 27, 1833, Cuthbert, "Letters," p. 269.

93 Document signed, n.d. [1833], Alexander Autographs catalog for sale June 24, 1997, p. 10, item #99.

94 REL to CCL, April 6, 1833, Lee Papers, UVA.

95 MacDonald, *Mrs. Robert E. Lee*, p. 42.

96 REL to MCL, August 21, 1835, Cuthbert, "Letters," pp. 271–73.

97 MCL to Mary Custis, August 1832, MacDonald, *Mrs. Robert E. Lee*, p. 44.

98 *PMUSG*, 1, pp. 43–44. John Fishback, a young man in Bethel at the time, later related this story to the New York, *Herald*, November 22, 1878, but said it occurred during Grant's 1841 visit home.

99 Burke Memoir, Garland Papers.

100 USG to Roger Jones, November 17, 1843, *PUSG*, 1, p. 23.

101 John Y. Simon, ed., *The Personal Memoirs of Julia Dent Grant* (New York: G. P. Putnam's, 1975), p. 48.

102 Ibid., p. 50; *PMUSG*, 1, pp. 48–51.

103 USG to Mrs. G. B. Bailey, June 6, 1844, New Orleans, *Daily Picayune*, August 9, 1885.

104 USG to Julia, September 7, 1844, *PUSG*, 1, p. 37.

105 USG to Julia, January 12, 1845, ibid., pp. 40–41, July 6, 1845, p. 48.

106 USG to Julia Dent, June 4, 1844, ibid., 1, p. 23–24, July 28 , 1844, pp. 30–31, 32–33.

107 USG to Mrs. G. B. Bailey, June 6, 1844, New Orleans, *Daily Picayune*, August 9, 1885

108 USG to Julia, July 28, 1844, *PUSG*, 1, p. 30.

109 USG to Julia, August 31, 1844, ibid., pp. 34–36.

110 *PMJDG*, p. 49.

111 USG to Julia, May 6, 1845, *PUSG*, 1, p. 43.

112 *PMJDG*, p. 51.

113 USG to Julia, July 6, 1845 *PUSG*, 1, p. 48.

114 USG to Julia, July 11, 1845, ibid., p. 50, July 28, 1844, p. 30.

115 USG to Julia October 10, 1845, ibid., p. 56–57.

116 USG to Julia, October 1845, ibid., pp. 58–59; Columbus, *Ohio State Journal*, August 16, 1843.

117 USG to Julia, November 11, 1845, *PUSG*, 1, p. 63, January 12, 1846, p. 69.

118 USG to Julia, November–December 1845, ibid., p. 65, January 2, 1846, p. 68.

119 USG to Julia, October 1845, ibid., p. 60.

120 Charles Gratiot to Lewis Cass, March 7, 1832, Letters Received by the Office of the Adjutant General 1822–1860, RG 94, NA.

121 REL to CCL, February 24, 1835, Lee Papers, University of Virginia.

122 *Lee*, 1, pp. 135–36.

123 REL to John Mackay, June 27, 1837, Gilder Lehrman Collection.

124 MacDonald, *Mrs. Robert E. Lee*, p. 66.

125 REL to Mackay, June 27, 1838, November 7, 1839, Gilder Lehrman Collection.

126 Ibid.

127 Ibid.

128 Ibid.

129 REL to MCL, June 5, 1839, J. William Jones, *Life and Letters of General Robert Edward Lee: Soldier and Man* (New York: Neale, 1906), p. 369, October 16, 1837, pp. 368–69.

130 REL to Mackay, November 7, 1839, Gilder Lehrman Collection.

131 Ibid.

132 REL to Mary Custis, November 7, 1839, Lee Papers, Virginia Historical Society.

133 Ibid.; *Lee*, 1, p. 177.

134 *Lee*, 1, p. 177.

135 Ibid.

136 REL to Mackay, January 23, 1833, Fort Pulaski National Monument, Savannah, GA.

137 REL to Talcott, December 7, 1832, Talcott Family Papers, VHS; REL to Mackay, January 23, 1833, Fort Pulaski.

138 REL to CCL, February 1, 1833, Lee Papers, UVA; Cincinnati, *Commercial*, August 9, 1879.

The *Commercial's* account comes from an interview Lee gave to George Pepper, a Union chaplain, shortly after Appomattox. Since it was not committed to paper until fourteen years later, it is probable that Pepper's memory embellished in places. Still, Lee's correspondence does confirm that he did attend some of the debates involving Clay, Webster, and Calhoun; hence he was in a position in 1865 to speak from memory, though perhaps with his own embellishments more than thirty years after the fact.

139 REL to Mackay, June 26, 1834, Gilder Lehrman Collection.

140 REL to Hill Carter, January 25, 1840, Shirley Plantation Collection.

141 REL to Jack Mackay, June 27, 1838, March 18, 1841, February 6, 1843, Gilder Lehrman Collection.

142 REL to Louis Marshall, February 25, 1844, RWA Auction Catalog #39, June 1, 1996, p. 34, item 156.

143 REL to Henry Kayser, December 23, 1843, May 19, 1844, Robert E. Lee Collection, Missouri Historical Society, St. Louis, MO.

144 REL to CCL, September 1, 1844, Lee Papers, UVA.

145 MacDonald, *Mrs. Robert E. Lee*, p. 52; REL to Hill Carter February 1, 21, 1842, REL to A. S. White, February 21, 1845, Lee Family Papers, VHS.

146 MCL and REL to Mary Fitzhugh Custis, Sunday, Lee Family Papers, VHS [Internal evidence establishes that REL's portion of this letter was written August 29, 1831].

147 REL to Mary Custis, November 11, 1830, DeButts, "Lee in Love," p. 519, April 3, 1831, p. 536.

148 REL to Mary Custis, January 10, 1831, ibid., p. 531, June 21, 1831, p. 548.

149 REL to Mary Custis, December 1, 1830, ibid., p. 525.

150 REL to Mary Custis, November 19, 1830, ibid., p. 522, May 24, 1831, p. 562 n.83.

151 Historians have never agreed on how many slaves Lee owned personally, or who they were. The most common mistake is to conflate his slaves with the Custis slaves at Arlington, White House, and Romancoke plantations, which never belonged to him or his wife. Lee's letters often mention names such as Jane and Philip Meriday and others as servants with his family, but they were Arlington slaves. A subsequent chapter will deal with the Burke family, usually—and erroneously—accepted as having belonged to Lee.

152 Ann Carter Lee Will, July 24, 1829, Will Book P-1 1827–1830, Fairfax County Courthouse, Fairfax, VA. Pp. 277–28.

153 REL to MCL, March 28, 1832, DeButts-Ely Papers, LC. Emory M. Thomas, *Robert E. Lee. A Biography* (New York: Norton, 1995), p. 108, says that Ann Lee left thirty slaves to her three sons, citing REL to CCL, February 24, 1835, Lee Family Papers, UVA. That letter, however, makes no mention of this, and there seems to be no source suggesting thirty slaves, whereas Charles Carter's will, cited previously, makes it clear that he left no slaves to his daughter Ann Hill Lee, but did bequeath thirty slaves to be divided between daughters Mildred and Lucy. Mildred's fifteen—and any others she may have had—passed at her death to Ann in 1817. Since R. E. Lee received apparently four adult females and one adult male from his mother's estate, that would suggest that his brothers Carter and Smith each received five as well, adding up to the fifteen that Mildred left Ann (not counting minor children born to any of Mildred's fifteen, as with Nancy Ruffin's three offspring). As Robert had no farm to work, his brother Carter probably kept most of the males. In 1833 Carter Lee traded Gardner for R. E. Lee's Sam (REL to CCL, October 12, 1830, April 6, 1833, February 14, 1843, Lee Papers, UVA). Hill Carter managed Gardner's hire since at least 1824 on behalf of Ann Hill Lee. In 1830 and 1831 Hill Carter paid the proceeds to executor William Carter, then there is a gap in the records until 1836 when he paid the Gardner hire to Lee to cover the years 1833–1835, and thereafter paid it annually until 1845. Gardner is not mentioned in R. E. Lee's will in 1846, as were Nancy Ruffin and her three children,

suggesting that Lee no longer owned him. A slave male named Gardner appears in the first entry of Hill Carter's Memorandum Book for Hirelings, dated September 15, 1850, and almost every entry thereafter through the final entry on August 20, 1853, suggesting that between 1845 and 1850 Lee gave or sold Gardner to Hill. CCL to Hill Carter, March 10, 1824, receipt to CCL, March 20, 1827, receipts from William Carter, January 1, 1830, REL to Hill Carter, February 10, 1836, April 24, 1837, January 31, 1838, February 1, 1840, May 8, 1841, January 22, 1842, January 21, 1843, February 19, 1844, February 1, 1845, Hill Carter Memorandum Book for Hirelings, 1850–1853, Shirley Plantation Collection, John D. Rockefeller Library Jr., Colonial Williamsburg Foundation, Williamsburg, VA.

154 REL to Mary Custis, April 17, 1831, Cuthbert, "Letters," p. 262. This letter's reference to Catty (which could be a misreading of the old style "double "f" that Lee occasionally used, hence Cassy), Jane, and Letitia is usually read to suggest that these women were also Lee's property, and they probably were since he gave Mary permission to deal with them, but there was also a Cassy and a Jane Meriday among the Custis slaves at Arlington. By the 1840s Cassy was married to a man named Louis and both were free and living in New York. MacDonald, *Mrs. Robert E. Lee*, pp. 38, 52, 54, 56, 91–93. In 1850 the Custises at Arlington had an infant slave Cassy Branham, suggesting the name may have been common among their slaves. 1850 census, Alexandria County. Cassy was the daughter of "Old Nurse," who had helped raise Mary Custis Lee. Both names were common among slaves.

155 REL to CCL, February 24, 1835, Lee Papers, UVA. For "plagues" see, for instance, this same letter and also REL to MCL, May 24, 1831, DeButts, "Lee in Love," p. 562 n.83.

156 Receipt, February 10, 1836, Shirley Plantation Collection, covers Gardner's hire for the years 1833, 1834, and 1835. Lee's notes on receipt of rent payments are in REL to Hill Carter, January 22, 1842, January 21, 1843, February 1, 1845, Lee Family Papers, VHS. Hill Carter paid Gardner's hire to Ann Lee from 1822 until 1829, then to her executors for 1830, then directly to Carter Lee for 1831 and 1832. Thereafter his hire went to REL. Hill Carter Hireling Book, 1822–1848, Shirley Plantation Collection. In 1834, writing from Arlington, Lee made reference to sending something by "my man Dick." This is clearly not Gardner, who was then hired out in Charles City County, yet there is no other known reference by Lee to owning any other male slave. This Dick is probably one of the Arlington slaves loaned to Lee for his use by father-in-law Custis. REL to Eben Eveleth, November 13, 1834, Signature House Sale catalog Sale January 7, 2000, p. 46, item #233.

157 Nancy and her three children were still owned by Lee and still at White House as of August 1, 1846, when he wrote his will (Last Will and Testament of Robert E. Lee, Rockingham County Courthouse, Lexington, VA). The 1847 Alexandria County Property Tax Book shows "Col. Lee" owning four slaves over the age of sixteen, which are presumably Nancy and her three children, though that could just be the slaves that he owned in that county, while Nancy and children might still be at White House in New Kent County. (Joseph C. Robert, "Lee the Farmer." *Journal of Southern History*, 4 [November 1937], p. 429.)

158 REL to Hill Carter, January 25, 1840, Shirley Plantation Collection.

159 REL to Mary Custis, December 28, 1830, DeButts, "Lee in Love," p. 527; REL to CCL, January 4, 1831, Lee Papers, UVA.

160 REL to Mary Custis, April 3, 1831, DeButts, "Lee in Love," p. 537–38, December 28, 1830, p. 527.

161 Mason, *Popular Life*, p. 23.

162 REL to Hill Carter, February 25, 1840, Shirley Plantation Collection.

163 REL to Hill Carter, January 25, 1840, ibid.

164 REL to Mackay, March 18, 1841, Gilder Lehrman Collection.

165 REL to CCL, February 14, 1843, Lee Papers, UVA.

166 REL to MCL, March 24, 1843, Ferdinand Dreer Collection, Historical Society of Pennsylvania, Philadelphia.
167 REL to CCL, June 7, 1839, Lee Papers, UVA.

CHAPTER 3: FIGHTING ON THE SAME SIDE

1 USG to Julia, February 5, 1846, *PUSG*, 1, p. 71, April 20, 1846, p. 80–81, March 3, 1846, p. 75.
2 USG to Julia, May 3, 1846, ibid., p. 83.
3 USG to Julia, May 11, 1846, ibid., p. 85.
4 USG to Julia, May 11, 1846, ibid., pp. 85–86.
5 USG to Julia, May 24, 1846, ibid., p. 88.
6 USG to John W. Lowe, June 26, 1846, ibid., p. 97.
7 USG to Julia, August 14, 1846, ibid., p. 105.
8 USG to Julia, September 6, 1846, ibid., p. 108–109, October 3, 1846, p. 113.
9 USG to John W. Lowe, May 3, 1847, ibid., p. 137.
10 Alexandria, *Gazette*, May 27, 1846, is one of dozens of papers that spread the Walker account across the United States.
11 USG to Julia, September 1847, *PUSG*, 1, pp. 147–48.
12 New York, *Commercial Advertiser*, August 31, 1846.
13 This letter has apparently not survived.
14 New York, *Herald*, November 22, 1878.
15 USG to Julia, November 7, 1846, *PUSG*, 1, 117.
16 USG protest, n.d. [August 1846], John W. Emerson, "Grant's Life in the West and His Mississippi Valley Campaigns," *Midland Monthly*, 6 (No. 1, January 1897), p. 36. This and other letters that appear in the Emerson article are to be found nowhere else, and present something of a problem; namely, how did Emerson come by them? Emerson said in a preface that he had lived most of his life near St. Louis, close to Grant and Grant's friends, "in touch with Grant himself and with Grant's associates and intimate friends." (5 [No. 11, November 1896], p. 395n.) Frederick D. Grant addressed him as "My Dear Emerson" and applauded his 1889 article(s) on USG. So Emerson was acquainted with the family. In the segment in 6 (No. 6, June 1897), pp. 498, he reproduced a sketch by Lieutenant Calvin Benjamin of a cabin where he and Grant stayed between Austin and Corpus Christi, so Emerson apparently had access to Benjamin's papers. In places, Emerson indicates that some of what he said came from conversations with Grant. Grant mentioned Benjamin only in passing in *PMUSG* and not as a bosom friend as Emerson has it. During the Civil War John Wesley Emerson was briefly a field officer of the 47th Missouri Volunteer Infantry from his hometown Ironton, Missouri. In August 1861, Grant chose Emerson's home as his headquarters, and Emerson later claimed that Grant conceived his strategy for conquest of the Mississippi while there, which seems unlikely, though possible. Some of the letters like the one here cited ought to have been in official archives with others of their kind, while personal letters and some fragmentary lines attributed to Grant could have come from anywhere, possibly Grant himself. Emerson gives no clues in his lengthy work to indicate sources. Given that the editors of the USG Papers have accepted the letters Emerson published as genuine, this author will do likewise, though with a reservation or two where noted. See *PUSG*, 1, p. 107n.
17 USG to Julia, June 5, 1846, *PUSG*, 1, p. 90.
18 USG to Julia, June 10, 1846, ibid., pp. 92–93.
19 USG to Julia, September 6, 1846, ibid., pp. 108–109.
20 *PMUSG*, 1, pp. 110–11, 115–16.

21 USG to Julia, September 23, 1846, *PUSG*, 1, p. 111.

22 USG to Julia, October 3, 1846, ibid., p. 112.

23 USG to ?, [December 1846], Emerson, "Grant's Life in the West," *Midland* Monthly, VII, 2 (February 1897), pp. 139–40. Emerson says only that Grant wrote this "as Christmas approached."

24 USG to Julia, October 20, 1846, *PUSG*, 1, p. 114.

25 USG to James Hazlitt, November 23, 1846, *PUSG*, 32, pp. 6–7.

26 Thomas L. Hamer to ?, August 1846, Emerson, "Grant's Life in the West," p. 34. Emerson states that Hamer's letter to a friend quoted here was written from Camargo, which dates it to August 1846. Hamer's mention that he and Grant had been struggling to control several wagons and teamsters suggests that it would date from after August 14 or 16 when Grant became acting regimental quartermaster. While Emerson's account of Grant in essence tutoring Hamer is not illogical given their acquaintance years before, Emerson's claim that a father-son intimate relationship grew up between the two should not be taken at face value. In his own *PMUSG* almost forty years later, Grant wrote of Hamer joining the army but said nothing of any personal relations between them other than a comment Hamer made on his gaining his commission. Later in his memoir Grant wrote of Franklin Pierce that "I knew him more intimately than I did any other of the volunteer generals," which certainly diminishes the degree of intimacy with Hamer claimed by Emerson. *PMUSG*, 1, pp. 103, 147.

27 Houston, *Texas Telegraph*, January 4, 1847.

28 USG to [Mrs. Thomas L. Hamer], n.d. [December 1846], Emerson, "Grant's Life in the West," p. 35. Again, while Emerson's text for Grant's presumed letter to Hamer's widow is probably genuine, the background he spins of Grant ministering to the dying man is largely nonsense. In part it reads:

> Every moment Grant was free from imperative duties he was with his friend in his struggle with that enemy whose eventual triumph is always certain. No kindness was omitted. His own hands ministered to his dying comrade. Grant returned from a charge through shot and shell, black and besmeared with smoke and dust and blood, and hastened to the tent and cot of the dying Hamer. The earth was trembling, and the air reverberating with the thunder of artillery, and the shriek and explosion of shells; and the moans of the wounded were sounding on every ear as men limped, or crawled, or were carried to the rear. With this music, the dirge of woe and death about them, Grant stood bent over the cot of his dying friend, holding his hand, looking into his eyes as their light slowly faded away and the pallor of death touched the parted but speechless lips. Tears came into the eyes of the young soldier; the rays of the receding sun struggled at the tent door with the smoke of battle that covered the scene, and in the dull gloom of eventide, thus surrounded, Hamer died.

> In fact, on the day Hamer died, and for two months leading up to it, the garrison at Monterey had seen no action at all and Mexican forces were many miles away. There was no artillery fire to shake the ground, no fighting for Grant to slip away from to tend his friend, no blood or powder grime to smear Grant's face. When he wrote the widow that Hamer died "within the sound of battle" he was simply inventing to console her. He could not lie and tell her Hamer died in action, but he could paint the scene of the conventionally accepted manner of the ideal death of the soldier.

> Emerson based his account on a letter from a Lieutenant Benjamin "to a friend at home," dated "the next day after the surrender of Monterey," which would make it September 25, 1846. In that letter Benjamin describes *my dear friend, Lieutenant Grant* tending to a dying Lieutenant Haskins, having "come up all the way from the death-bed of his friend, Major Hamer." Again, on September 25 Hamer was in wonderful health, and temporarily commanding a divi-

sion in the operations at Monterey. Benjamin was Lieutenant Calvin Benjamin, adjutant of an artillery battalion, and Haskins was Lieutenant Charles Hoskins, adjutant of the 4th Infantry, whom Grant replaced on his death (*PMUSG*, 1, pp. 111–12). This portion of the Benjamin letter is obviously a fabrication, either by Emerson or someone who furnished him documents, and inevitably it must raise questions about all documents that Emerson quotes, including those purportedly by Grant. The orthography in the alleged Grant items is somewhat better than in his holograph letters, though that could simply be editorial cleanup by Emerson. Otherwise there is nothing anachronistic in their texts.

29 *PMUSG*, 1, pp. 212–13.

30 Ibid., p. 147.

31 USG to John W. Lowe, June 26, 1846, *PUSG*, 1, p. 97–98.

32 USG to Julia, August 14, 1846, ibid., p. 105.

33 USG to Julia, February 1, 1847, ibid., p. 124.

34 USG to ?, [December 1846], Emerson, "Grant's Life in the West," *Midland* Monthly, VII, 2 (February 1897), pp. 139–40. Emerson says only that Grant wrote this "as Christmas approached."

35 *PMUSG*, 1, p. 119.

36 USG to Julia, April 3, 1847, *PUSG*, 1, p. 129, USG to John W. Lowe June 26, 1846, p. 97.

37 USG to Julia September 6, 1846, ibid., pp. 108–109, November 7, 1846, p. 118.

38 USG to Julia, February 5, 1847, ibid., p. 128. Interestingly, the play with words here is exactly the same as a Grant comment customarily regarded as apocryphal, in which he said he only knew two songs, one being "Yankee Doodle" and the other one not.

39 USG to Julia, July 6, 1845, ibid., p. 49, September 14, 1845, p. 54.

40 USG to Julia, April 3, 1847, ibid., p. 130.

41 *PMUSG*, 1, p. 118.

42 USG to Julia, May 24, 1846, *PUSG*, 1, p. 88.

43 USG to Julia, May 17, 1847, ibid., p. 138.

44 USG to Julia, January 9, 1848, ibid., p. 149.

45 USG to Julia, July 25, 1846, ibid., p. 102.

46 USG to Julia, February 25, 1847, ibid., p. 127.

47 USG to Julia, June 5, 1846, ibid., p. 91, February 1, 1847, p. 124, April 3, 1847, p. 129, May 17, 1847, pp. 138–39.

48 REL to MCL, May 12, 1846. February 13, 1848, DeButts-Ely Collection, LC. Freeman offers only a single paragraph about Lee's feelings as the war started, and all of that is unsubstantiated invention about Lee fearing he would be left out of the war. *Lee*, 1, p. 202.

49 REL to CCL, March 4, 1848, Lee Family Papers Digital Library, Washington and Lee.

50 Joseph Totten to Lee, August 17, 1846, File L60, AG.

51 REL to A. S. White, February 21, 1845, Lee Family Papers, VHS.

52 Lee's most recent payment for Gardner's hire covered 1844. On February 1, 1845, he told his cousin Hill Carter to continue to hire the man, but Carter noted in Hill Carter Hireling Book, 1822–1848, that "Gardner could not be made to pay any hire this year [1845]." He further noted Gardner was not hired in 1846 or 1847. This is probably on account of age or infirmity. Assuming Gardner to have been one of the slaves Ann Lee inherited from her sister Mildred, the terms of Charles Carter's 1806 will specified that the slaves given to Mildred had to be born between 1772 and 1795. Meanwhile, Gardner's hire, as detailed in Hill Carter's 1822–1848 book, ran $70 per annum 1821–1828, then $60 per annum 1829–1841, then $50 per annum 1842–1843, then $30 for 1844, and nothing thereafter. That suggests the declining value of his labor for which age would be the most logical explanation. In 1844 Gardner would have been aged forty-nine to seventy-two. Lee's August 1846 will does not

list Gardner among his assets, though it lists Nancy Ruffin and her three children, yet Hill Carter still carries Gardner in his hireling book, even though there is no mention of Lee and Gardner was not hired after 1844. However, the daily entries in Hill Carter Memorandum Book for Hirelings, 1850–1853, show sums paid by Carter to Gardner for various odd jobs, along with notes indicating that Gardner left work when he chose, and finally on August 20, 1853, Carter noted that he paid Gardner $9 "when he left off working here." So Gardner was working for Carter and being paid directly, rather than his wages going to another owner. Thus by 1850 at least, Gardner must have been a free man. Lee may have freed him between February 1845, when he told Carter to hire him again, and August 1846, when Gardner was not an asset mentioned in Lee's will. Lee could have freed him since he was no longer an income-producing asset, or he may have given him to Hill Carter, which would account for Carter still carrying Gardner on his hireling account for 1846 and 1847. Or Gardner may have earned enough to purchase his freedom from either Lee or Carter. Gardner was allowed to earn money for himself even while a slave, as witness Carter's notation for December 30, 1837, that Gardner paid $25 for the hire of a slave named Jack George, with the notation that Jack George drowned January 25, 1838, and Gardner paid for his coffin "so as to square his hire." REL to Hill Carter, February 1, 1845, Hill Carter Hireling Book 1822–1848, Hill Carter Memorandum Book for Hirelings, 1850–1853, Shirley Plantation Collection. Gardner does not appear in the List of Free Negroes and Mulattoes in the County of Charles City Over Twelve Years of Age for the Year 1859, or in the Charles City County Register of Free Negroes, 1835–1864 (Library of Virginia), which would suggest that he was deceased or moved prior to 1859, and that if he was freed, by whatever means, his freedom was not registered with the county. If he was sold, the transaction does not appear in Charles City County Deed Book 10, 1846–1856, Library of Virginia.

53 Last will and Testament of R. E. Lee, August 2, 1846, Rockingham County Courthouse, Lexington, VA. Nancy Ruffin here disappears from the documentary record. If she remained at the White House plantation after 1846, unfortunately registers of free blacks for that county are missing.

54 REL to GWCL and WHFL, February 27, 1847, Lee, *Lee of Virginia*, p. 432.

55 Winchester, VA, *Times*, June 3, 1896. McClellan told this story of their first meeting in 1878.

56 W. A. Croffut, ed., *Fifty Years in Camp and Field: Diary of Major-General Ethan Allen Hitchcock, U.S.A.* (New York: G. P. Putnam's, 1909), p. 243.

57 REL to Winfield Scott, August 11, 1857, Adams, *Letters*, p. 395.

58 USG to Julia, April 3, 1847, *PUSG*, I, p. 129.

59 USG resignation, n.d. [April 1847], with endorsement, Emerson, "Grant's Life in the West," *Midland Monthly*, VII, no. 3 (March 1897), p. 219.

60 Thomas L. Hamer to ?, August 1846, Emerson, "Grant's Life in the West," p. 34.

61 *PUSG*, I, p. 130n.

62 USG to Julia, February 1, 1847, ibid., p. 124.

63 USG to Julia, February 5, 1847, ibid., p. 128.

64 REL to John Mackay, October 2, 1847, General Stephen Elliott Papers, United States Army Military History Institute, Carlisle Barracks, PA.

65 *Lee*, I, pp. 247–48.

66 REL to Mackay, October 2, 1847, Elliott Papers, USAMHI.

67 REL to MCL, April 25, 1847, Lee, *General Lee*, pp. 40–41.

68 USG to Julia, April 3, 1847, *PUSG*, I, p. 129, April 24, 1847, p. 131.

69 Emerson, "Grant's Life in the West," February, 1897, p. 221, has USG and REL doing reconnaissance together during the siege of Vera Cruz with P. G. T. Beauregard, George B.

McClellan, and G. W. Smith. *PMUSG*, 1, 131–32 mentions these men doing reconnaissances but gives no indication that USG was with them. All were engineers; USG was not.

70 *PMUSG*, 1, p. 137.

71 Grant to ?, n.d. [August 22, 1847], Emerson, "Grant's Life in the West," *Midland Monthly*, VII, 4 (April 1897), p. 324. Emerson describes this statement as coming from "a letter written by him during this armistice."

72 Emerson, "Grant's Life in the West," January 1897, p. 33, says Grant's map was so good and so well known throughout the army that Lee often consulted with him over it. The next page invents Grant tending Hamer during battle at Monterey, and on p. 40 Emerson quotes a letter in which Lieutenant Benjamin calls Hamer "Major," whereas all would know he was a brigadier general by then, a big difference.

73 USG to ?, n.d. [September 12, 1847], Emerson, "Grant's Life in the West," *Midland Monthly*, VII, 5 (May 1897), p. 433. Emerson gives no more information on this statement of Grant's than to note that it was in "a private letter" in which Grant described the advance of the army on Mexico City. Interestingly, though, Emerson quotes none of that campaign narrative, or if he does he gives no indication of it coming from Grant. In *PMUSG*, Grant makes no allusion whatever to this map or to his own presumed *contemporary* assessment of Scott's strategy. However, he did muse that "in later years" that he felt some of the battles Scott fought were unnecessary, and that the northern approach to Mexico City would have been better (*PMUSG*, 1, pp. 154–55, 165–66).

74 *PMUSG*, 1, pp. 138–39.

75 REL to Mary, November 8, 1856, Adams, *Letters*, p. 202.

76 Francis Lee to Roger Jones, January 16, 1849, *PUSG*, 1, p. 381.

77 *PMUSG*, 1, pp. 152–59.

78 USG to Julia, January 8, 1848, *PUSG*, 1, pp. 149–50, February 4, 1848, p. 151, March 22, 1848, pp. 153–54, May 7, 1848, pp. 155–56, June 4, 1848, p. 160.

79 Lowe arrived in Mexico City sometime between April 28 and May 5, 1848, and left by about May 10. On May 12 Lowe wrote: "I saw Lieut. Grant. He has altered very much: he is a short thick man with a beard reaching half way down his waist and I fear he drinks too much but don't you say a word on that subject" (John Lowe to Manorah Lowe, May 12, 1848, Becker, "Was Grant Drinking in Mexico," pp. 70–71). Lowe said "I fear he drinks too much," which sounds as much like an apprehension as a statement of fact. What did Lowe regard as drinking "too much"? Did he actually *see* Grant drinking or drunk, or was he repeating hearsay? Was Grant just happily inebriated, or sloppy drunk? Lowe was not there long enough to tell if any such behavior was chronic or just an isolated incident. It seems unlikely that Lowe felt any animus against Grant, else why would Lowe bother to see him? If the stories were true of Grant having a pre-war involvement with a member of Lowe's family—though certainly not his as yet unborn daughter Kate—Lowe might have been miffed on learning that Grant was engaged to Julia (see chapter 2, note 39). Yet Grant was certainly under the impression that he was still on good, even close, terms with Lowe in June 1846 when he said he would like to see Lowe in Mexico commanding a company of volunteers. Becker also notes (p. 68) that Hamlin Garland in 1898 said Grant "learned the use of liquor in Mexico," but added that there was "little reliable evidence of excess in its use." Garland's statement nevertheless *implies* that there was still *some* evidence of heavy drinking that he thought reliable, but he failed to back that up with any specific attribution (Garland, *Grant*, p. 124). Since most of the recollections on which Garland based his book were taken down fifty years after the fact, all statements that Grant drank in Mexico, or had drinking problems later, were subject to heavy influence by the extensive and very public literature regarding Grant and liquor that emerged during and after the Civil War.

Meanwhile, and significantly, in his letters to Julia written May 7 and May 22 immediately following Lowe's visit, Grant made no mention of Lowe whatever. It is reasonable to suppose that he would have commented on seeing an old friend from Ohio, since it was hardly a common occurrence. After all, Grant mentioned seeing Julia's brother Fred in every letter. (USG to Julia, May 7, 1848, *PUSG*, 1, pp. 155–57, May 22, 1848, pp. 158–59).

80 USG to ?, [August 22, 1847], Emerson, "Grant's Life in the West," April 1897, p. 324.

81 Francis Lee to Roger Jones, January 16, 1849, *PUSG*, 1, p. 382.

82 Emerson, "Grant's Early life in the West," VII, 5 (May 1897), p. 430.

83 REL to Matilda Mason, November 1, 1847, Profiles in History Catalog, Calabasas Hills, CA, December 2007, p. 20, item #24.

84 REL to Mackay, October 2, 1847, Elliott Papers, USAMHI.

85 Ibid.

86 Ibid.

87 REL to CCL, February 13, 1848, Lee Papers, UVA.

88 REL to CCL, March 4, 1848, Lee Family Papers Digital Library, Washington and Lee.

89 REL to Matilda Mason, November 1, 1847, Profiles in History Catalog, Calabasas Hills, CA, December 2007, p. 20, item #24.

90 REL to CCL, March 18, May 15, 1848, Lee Papers, VHS.

91 REL to Sidney Smith Lee, May 21, 1848, Gilder Lehrman Collection.

92 Raphael Semmes, *Service Afloat and Ashore During the Mexican War* (Cincinnati: William H. Moore, 1851), p. 379.

93 Both officers became members of the Aztec Club, founded by Scott in October 1847. Lee appears to have been an original member, whereas Grant was elected to membership two years later (*PUSG*, 1, pp. 388–89).

CHAPTER 4: TIMES OF TRIAL

1 John Livingston to USG, July 5, 1854, *PUSG*, 1, p. 425; REL to John Livingston, October 20, 1854, Charles R. Bowery and Brian D. Hankinson, eds., *The Daily Correspondence of Brevet Colonel Robert E. Lee Superintendent, United States Military Academy September 1, 1852 to March 24, 1855* (West Point, NY: United States Military Academy Library Occasional Papers #5, 2003), p. 231.

2 REL to CCL, March 4, 1848, Lee Family Papers Digital Library, Washington and Lee.

3 Engineer Order 19, July 21, 1848, Order 32, Sept. 13, 1848, File L60, AG.

4 REL to GWCL, August 3, 1851, Gilder Lehrman Collection.

5 REL to Totten, November 23, 1852, Bowery and Hankinson, *Correspondence*, pp. 24–25; REL to Totten, September 1, 1853, REL to Totten, July 31, 1854, REL to Totten, September 12, 1854, File L60, RG 94, NA.

6 See for instance, REL to Solon Borland, October 19, 1854, Bowery and Hankinson, *Correspondence*, p. 230, REL to William Terrell, September 3, 1852, p. 2, REL to Mrs. Hetzel, January 31, 1855, p. 274.

7 REL to Totten, October 9, 11, 1852, *Correspondence*, pp. 13–14, 16.

8 REL to Totten, November 30, 1852, ibid., pp. 25–26, December 9, 1852, ibid., pp. 27–29.

9 REL to C. M. Conrad, February 10, 1853, ibid., p. 52.

10 REL to Totten, January 7, 1853, ibid., p. 40.

11 REL to Louis Marshall, February 25, 1844, RWA Auction Catalog #39, June 1, 1996, p. 34, item 156.

12 Walter A. Watson, "Notes on Southside Virginia," *Bulletin of the Virginia State Library*, 15 (Nos. 2–4, September 1925), pp. 244–45.

13 Thomas H. Ruger to Thomas J. Ruger, December 11, 1853, HCA Auction Sale, July 22, 2010.

14 Agnes Lee Journal, November 8, 1853, Mary Custis Lee deButts, *Growing Up in the 1850s: The Journal of Agnes Lee* (Chapel Hill: University of North Carolina Press, 1984), p. 27.

15 Peter W. Houck, ed., *Duty, Honor, Country: The Diary and Biography of General William P. Craighill, Cadet at West Point 1849–1853*. Lynchburg, VA: Warwick House, 1993), p. 522.

16 REL to George Dutton, October 19, 1854, eBay listing April 10, 2012; REL to Totten, February 14, 1853, Bowery and Hankinson, *Daily Correspondence*, pp. 52–54.

17 See Bowery and Hankinson, *Daily Correspondence*, pp. 6, 8, 30.

18 REL to Totten, June 21, 1853, ibid., p. 99.

19 REL to J. R. Torbert, October 6, 1852, ibid., p. 12, REL to B. O'Connor, December 17, 1852, pp. 31–32.

20 REL to Alpheus Frank, June 29, 1853, ibid., p. 103.

21 REL to Samuel Cooper, March 15, 1855, File L60, AG.

22 REL to George W. Cullum, March 13, 1855, Swann Auction Galleries, Sale 2333, New York, November 16, 2013, item 14.

23 REL to Charlotte Wickham, October 10, 1857, Adams, *Letters*, p. 432, REL to Martha Custis Williams, March 14, 1855, p. 2.

24 REL to Totten, September 6, 1855, AG 1822–1860; REL to William Wickham, January 2, 1856, Adams, *Letters*, pp. 81–82.

25 REL to MCL, April 12, 1856, Adams, *Letters*, p. 114, July 28, 1856, p. 134, August 25, 1856, p. 162, January 24, 1857, p. 276, REL to Mary Ann Mackay Stiles, May 24, 1856, pp. 122–23.

26 REL to MCL, August 26, 1855, ibid., p. 56.

27 REL to MCL, July 19, 1855, ibid., pp. 29–30.

28 REL to MCL, August 26, 1855, ibid., p. 57, June 9, 1857, p. 362.

29 REL to Mary Anna Randolph Custis, February 14, 1831, Mary Custis Lee Papers, VHS.

30 REL to Mackay, October 2, 1847, Elliott Papers, USAMHI; Dr. May to Cassius F. Lee, April 22, 1861, Lee, *Lee of Virginia*, p. 418.

31 REL to Sidney Smith Lee, June 20, 1848, Gilder Lehrman Collection.

32 REL to MCL, July 8, 1849, Lee Family Papers, VHS.

33 Pryor, *Reading the Man*, pp. 231–32.

34 MacDonald, *Mrs. Robert E. Lee*, p. 111.

35 REL to MCL, July 1, 1855, Adams, *Letters*, p. 23, REL to MCL, April 19, 1857, p. 330.

36 REL to MCL, August 26, 1855, ibid., p. 56.

37 REL to MCL, April 12, 1856, ibid,, p. 113, REL to MCL, September 3, 1855, pp. 62–63.

38 See, for instance, REL to MCL, August 11, 1856, ibid., p. 144, to Mary Ann Mackay Stiles, August 14, 1856, p. 149.

39 REL to MCL, September 20, 1857, ibid., p. 429. See Harry S. Stout, *Upon the Altar of the Nation* (New York: Viking, 2006), p. 93 and passim.

40 REL to MCL, July 5, 1857, Adams, *Letters*, p. 379, November 15, 1856, pp. 206–207.

41 REL to MCL, December 5, 1856, ibid., p. 221.

42 REL to MCL, June 18, 1860, ibid., p. 654.

43 REL to MCL, November 15, 1856, ibid., p. 206.

44 REL to MCL, December 13, 1856, ibid., p. 233, December 27, 1856, p. 247.

45 REL to MCL, June 18, 1860, ibid., p. 654.

46 REL to MCL, November 19, 1856, ibid., p. 214.

47 REL to MCL, December 13, 1856, ibid., p. 233, REL to MCL, February 7, 1857, p. 287.

48 Sibley, ed., "Robert E. Lee to Albert Sidney Johnston, 1857," October 25, 1857, p. 104.

49 Sandusky, *Register*, January 19, 1858; REL to Custis Lee, January 17, 1858, Adams, *Letters*, p. 457.

50 Karl Decker and Angus McSween, *Historic Arlington: A History of the National Cemetery from Its Establishment to the Present Time* (Washington: Decker and McSween, 1892), pp. 80–81.

51 REL to Anna Fitzhugh, November 22, 1857, Adams, *Letters*, p. 442.

52 REL to GWCL, January 17, 1858, ibid., p. 456.

53 REL to GWCL, February 15, 1858, ibid., p. 469.

54 REL to GWCL, January 17, 1858, ibid., p. 456; Boston, *American Traveller*, December 17, 1864.

55 REL to GWCL May 30, 1859, Adams, *Letters*, p. 529. A good study of Lee's efforts at Arlington will be found in Joseph C. Robert, "Lee the Farmer," *Journal of Southern History*, 3, no. 4 (November 1937), pp. 422–40.

56 July 16, 1854, deButts, *Growing Up in the 1850s*, p. 40. According to his son Robert Jr., at one time Lee owned several slave families that he inherited from his mother, but he freed them before the Civil War without registering manumission papers. That, claimed Robert Jr., was because Virginia statute required freed slaves to leave the state within a year or be returned to slavery. Pryor, *Reading the Man*, pp. 148–49, discusses slaves of Lee's but confuses those he owned with the Custis slaves at Arlington, like Perry Parks, whom he managed both before and after Custis's death.

57 REL to WHFL, July 9, 1860, George Bolling Lee Papers, VHS.

58 REL, Expense Account, December 31, 1858, Gary Hendershott catalog, December 1995, p. 55 item #129; REL to MCL September 25, 1849, Lee Family Papers, VHS.

59 Ibid. There has been much confusion over the years about this Burke family, and Lee is often mistakenly credited as having been their owner and emancipator; see *The African Repository and Colonial Journal*, 30, no. 1 (January 1854), p. 21. There is no question that they belonged to Custis and not Lee. More members of the family were still at Arlington when Custis died (Inventory of Custis slaves, September 11, 1858, Alexandria County Court, Alexandria, VA), and in 1867, writing from Liberia, William Burke referred to "my dear old mother" still at Arlington (William C. Burke to Ralph R. Gurley, February 9, 1867, VHS). The Burke family appear as free mulattoes in the 1850 census for Baltimore where the Lees were then living, and Burke himself was apparently enumerated twice, since he also appears living as a free mulatto with the Lees. Yet in the *African Repository* the Burke family appear as slaves, emancipated by Lee. Lee handled the arrangements for the Burkes' departure from Baltimore on November 9, 1853, presumably at Custis's request, as he sometimes handled other slave matters for his father-in-law. Applicants for Emigration to Liberia, 1826–1855, American Colonization Society Papers, Series VI, vol. 18, LC, shows "Col. R. E. Lee" of Arlington and West Point as the applicant for "Self wife 4 chil'n." Of course, Lee was not applying for his family to emigrate. Most of the other applicants listed were the actual emigrants themselves or the masters who freed them. In deriving its published listings from this register, the *African Repository* quite logically concluded from this listing that Lee was the emancipator. The listing further shows that Lee actually called at the society's office in Baltimore to make the arrangements.

In 1885 John Leyburn claimed that during a conversation in Baltimore in 1869, Lee told him that "he had emancipated most of his slaves years before the war, and had sent to Liberia those who were willing to go; that the latter were writing back most affectionate letters to him, some of which he received through the lines during the war." The conversation almost certainly took place, but Leyburn misunderstood, or misremembered, Lee's obvious remarks about the Burkes as meaning he had emancipated them himself. John Leyburn, "An Interview with General Robert E. Lee," *Century Magazine*, 30, no. 1 (May, 1885), p. 167.

60 REL to James Everett, August 1, 1852, Lee Family Papers, VHS.

61 REL to C. C. Baldwin, October 18, 1854, Bowery and Hankinson, *Daily Correspondence*, p. 229; Joseph Glover Baldwin, *Party Leaders: Sketches of Thomas Jefferson, Alex'r Hamilton, Andrew Jackson, Henry Clay, John Randolph of Roanoke, including Notices of Many Other Distinguished American Statesmen* (New York: D. Appleton, 1854), pp. 238–39, 355. See John Grammer, "The Republican Historical Vision: Joseph Glover Baldwin's *Party Leaders*," *Southern Literary Journal*, 25, no. 2 (Spring, 1993), pp. 3ff.

62 REL to C. C. Baldwin, October 18, 1854, Bowery and Hankinson, *Daily Correspondence*, p. 229.

63 REL to MCL, August 20, 1855, Adams, *Letters*, p. 51.

64 William Moran, *The Belles of New England: The Women of the Textile Mills and the Families Whose Wealth They Wove* (New York: St. Martin's, 2002), p. 68.

65 REL to MCL, December 27, 1856, Adams, *Letters*, pp. 245–46.

66 Boston, *American Traveller*, December 28, 1857.

67 REL to the Editor, January 4, 1858, Arlington, *Gazette*, January 5, 1858.

68 Decker and McSween, *Historical Arlington*, pp. 80–81.

69 Pryor misreads the will when she states that it "called for land to be sold to pay the debts and legacies, and never states that these obligations should take precedence over freeing the slaves" (*Reading the Man*, p. 265). The Custis will is clear that lands are to be sold "to *assist* in paying my granddaughters' legacies," "to *aid* in paying my granddaughters' legacies," and "are charged with the payment of the legacies of my granddaughters" (italics author's). Nowhere does he state or imply that the legacies are *solely* to be funded from land sales. And the will could not be more clear that the estates must be cleared of debt and the bequests funded *before* the slaves were to be emancipated. Indeed, the land could only be sold after cleared of debt, and after it had time to produce income to fund the legacies.

70 MCL to William G. Webster, February 17, 1858, quoted in Michael Fellman, *The Making of Robert E. Lee* (New York: Random House, 2000), p. 71.

71 REL to Edward Turner, February 12, 1858, Adams, *Letters*, pp. 459; 1860 Census, Fairfax County, Virginia. McQuinn's family is enumerated immediately next to the Lees, indicating that he was living on the property.

72 REL to GWCL, January 17, 1858, Adams, *Letters*, pp. 456–57.

73 REL to MCL, January 7, 1857, Adams, *Letters*, pp. 257–58, REL to A. E. S. Keese, April 28, 1858, p. 473, REL to William O. Winston, July 8, 1858, July 10, 1858, Lee Family Papers, VHS; REL to Winston, July 12, 1858, Gilder Lehrman Collection.

74 REL to A. E. S. Keese, April 28, 1858, Adams, *Letters*, pp. 472–73; Baltimore, *Sun*, April 21, 1858.

75 REL to MCL, March 3, 1860, Adams, *Letters*, p. 579, REL to GWCL, December 5, 1860, pp. 702–703.

76 REL to GWCL, January 17, 1858, Adams, *Letters*, p. 456.

77 REL to Irvin McDowell, October 22, 1858, ibid., p. 504.

78 Wesley's reference to his sister and fellow runaway Mary is somewhat confusing. Census records do not show a Mary Norris connected to the family until the 1900 census for Fairfax County, when a Mary Norris is shown living with her sister Selena Norris Gray, but her birth is given as December 1865 and her age as thirty-four. So she cannot be the Mary who escaped with Wesley in 1859. There is no question he had a sister known by that name at least between 1858 and 1862, for she appears as such on An Inventory of the Slaves at Arlington belonging to the Estate of G. W. P. Custis taken January 1, 1858 (reproduced in *Arlington House* [Washington: National Park Service, n.d.], p. 7), which lists Leonard and Sallie Norris and their children Wesley, Mary, and Sally, a "child." Their other daughter

Selina appears as Selina Grey on the list with her husband Thornton Grey. On December 29, 1862, in the document of final emancipation of the Custis slaves, the Norrises again appear as Leonard, Sallie, Wesley, Mary, and Sally (Robert E. Lee Papers, Museum of the Confederacy, Richmond, VA). In 1866 Wesley refers to her as Mary. Yet in the 1870 census for Fairfax County, Virginia, the Norrises enumerated are Leonard, Sallie, Wesley, and Sarah, now Sarah Hoffman, whom the 1900 Fairfax County census shows being born in February 1838. She is almost certainly the "Sally" referred to in the 1858 inventory and 1862 emancipation, though at age nineteen in 1858 her listing as a "child" seems odd. Wesley stated in 1866 that Mary was then living and working in Washington, and while several black and mulatto Mary Norrises can be found there in 1870 and beyond, none seem to fit her admittedly skimpy description.

79 Westminster, MD, *Carroll County Democrat*, June 2, 1859.

80 It is not possible to date the actual punishment, but extant sources combined would suggest sometime during the week of June 10–17, 1859.

81 Anonymous to the editor, June 19, 1859, New York, *Tribune*, June 24, 1859.

82 Ibid. The writer signed himself only as "A," but he may have given away his identity when he ended his letter with a rant. "Next to Mount Vernon, we associate 'the Custis place' with the 'Father of the free country'," he wrote. "Shall 'Washington's body guard' be thus tampered with, and never a voice raised for such helplessness?" Eighteen months earlier the Washington letter writer "Alpha" raised the same questions about the timing of freedom for the Custis slaves, and the supposed sequestering of the will, closing his letter with a similar allusion to Washington: "It would be awful if the last remaining member of the household of Washington should not be allowed, should be prevented by fraud, from carrying out those precepts which he had learned, standing by the knee, and hearing from the lips, of that immortal Sage." (Boston, *American Traveller*, December 28, 1857.)

83 REL to Custis Lee, July 2, 1859. RR Auction Autograph Blog, August 3, 2011

84 Alexandria, *Gazette*, June 30, 1859.

85 Washington, *Post* in Rockford, IL, *Republican*, July 25, 1861; Hartford, CT, *Daily Courant*, May 14, 1863.

86 Sibley, "Robert E. Lee to Albert Sidney Johnston, 1857," p. 102n.

87 REL to Lorenzo Thomas, June 16, 1859, Adams, *Letters*, pp. 534–35.

88 Milwaukee, *Semi-Weekly Madison*, March 31, 1866. This is the earliest appearance of the Norris statement found to date, though it could have appeared earlier.

89 No record of Lee ordering other whippings has come to light. Fellman, *Lee*, p. 65, says that "enlightened masters" often sent their unruly slaves to local jails to be whipped by constables, but provides no source.

90 Wesley Norris returned to Arlington within days of arriving at Union lines. On September 22 Union authorities gave Wesley a pass to enter Washington for ten days, and then again ten more days from October 6, to check on the safety of family members, perhaps looking for Mary. She found her way home, too, and got a pass into Washington on October 21, and again November 16, to visit the Syphax family, former Arlington slaves themselves. By the end of 1864 she was living with or near her parents at Arlington once more (Boston, *Liberator*, December 9, 1864). Over the next two years Mary got employment with the French legation in Washington, and then fell out of sight, while Wesley returned to Arlington and his family. There he lived with first his parents, and then his sister Sarah Hoffman and her family, until 1900, when he disappeared from the record (United States Census, 1870, 1880, 1900, Fairfax County, VA.

91 USG to Julia, August 7, 1848, *PUSG*, 1, p. 163.

92 USG to Roger Jones, December 17, 1848, ibid., p. 168.

93 USG to Oscar Winship, March 9, 1849, ibid., p. 181.

94 USG to John B. Grayson, November 12, 1851, ibid., pp. 231–32.

95 USG to Julia, April 27, 1849, ibid., p. 184, May 20, 1849, p. 187, May 26, 1849, pp. 188–89, USG to Ellen Dent, May 26, 1849, pp. 189–90.

96 USG to Oscar F. Winship, June 14, 1850, ibid., p. 194 and n. On August 10, 1850 a census taker found the Grants living with Julia's parents in the 2d Ward, St. Louis, St. Louis County, Missouri. However, they appeared again on the census for the 4th Ward on September 9, 1850, as passengers enumerated aboard the *Excelsior*. 1850 Census, St. Louis County, Missouri.

97 Deposition, January 10, 1851, *PUSG*, 1, p. 195 and n. This is a curious document. As cited it comes from the original at the Detroit Historical Museum, which says the property owner was Antoine Beaubien, who had been a prominent early settler and city father. But Beaubien died in 1850, so would not have been the occupant in January 1851.

The document first appeared in print in the Cincinnati, *Daily Enquirer*, March 10, 1868, but in this case shows the property owner as "Zachary" Chandler. The story first broke into print in that same issue of the *Daily Enquirer*, an anti-Grant paper whose story maintained that Grant was "drunk all the time" while in Detroit, and that after the court ruling in his favor he lashed Chandler with a rawhide whip on Jefferson Street. A pro-Grant rejoinder soon appeared, written by James Brisbin, who was working at the time on a biography of Grant, and claimed that he had the story from "an officer who was serving in Grant's regiment at the time of the occurrence." It appeared in the Cincinnati, *Daily Gazette*, April 14, 1868, and told a different story. Both versions agree that Grant himself suffered an injured leg and that Chandler defended himself before a jury by charging that the soldiers would not fall on his walk "if you soldiers would keep sober." This was not necessarily a specific allegation of drunkenness aimed at Grant, but it is certainly implied. Supposedly Grant talked for several days about whipping Chandler, but then calmed and the affair ended. Brisbin's April 1868 account is the earliest pro-Grant version, and was clearly the major source for Albert D. Richardson's account appearing in *A Personal History or Ulysses S. Grant* (Hartford: American Publishing, 1868), pp. 134–35, in September 1868. Richardson amended the story by maintaining that fifteen years later in 1866, when Grant visited Chandler in Detroit, the two men laughed over the incident. Grant did, in fact, visit Detroit on September 4, 1866 (Salem, MA, *Register*, September 6, 1866), but at that time Chandler was in Philadelphia attending a convention (Boston, *Daily Advertiser*, September 5, 1866). Grant did not mention the subject in his memoirs, though he did describe Chandler running for mayor at the time he was stationed at Detroit. Consequently, it is uncertain just how much to make of either version of the document. It may be worth remembering that Richardson was probably the first pro-Grant biographer to assert that Grant did battle the bottle a few years later.

98 USG to Julia, May 28, 1851, *PUSG*, 1, p. 203, June 4, 1851, p. 205, June 7, 1851, p. 207.

99 USG to Julia, June 16, 1851, ibid., p. 210.

100 USG to Julia, June 22, 1851, ibid., p. 211, June 29, 1851, p. 214, July 3, 1851, pp. 216–17, July 13, 1851, pp. 219–20.

101 USG to Jesup, May 26, 1852, ibid., p. 232.

102 USG to Julia, June 24, 1852, ibid., p. 238, June 28, 1852, pp. 240–41, July 1, 1852, p. 243.

103 USG to Julia, July 5, 1852, ibid., p. 247.

104 USG to Julia, July 15, 1852, ibid., p. 248.

105 For an excellent, and generally reliable, extended account of this journey, see Charles G. Ellington, *The Trial of U. S. Grant: The Pacific Coast Years, 1852–1854* (Glendale, CA: Arthur H. Clark, 1986), pp. 39–70 *passim*. See also Henry D. Wallen to "My Dear Colonel," August 2,

1852, Plattsburgh, NY, *Republican*, September 11, 1852, and "An Officer of the Army to "My Dear Sir," August 16, 1852, Washington, *Daily National Intelligencer*, September 16, 1852.

106 USG to Julia, August 9, 1852, *PUSG*, 1, pp. 251–52, October 26, 1852, p. 269–70; "An Officer of the Army to "My Dear Sir," August 16, 1852, Washington, *Daily National Intelligencer*, September 16, 1852; St. Louis, *Daily Missouri Republican*, December 5, 1852.

107 New London, CT, *Democrat*, October 9, 1852.

108 USG to Julia, August 16, 1852, *PUSG*, 1, p. 255.

109 USG to Julia, July 15, 1852, ibid., p. 248.

110 USG to Julia, August 20, 1852, ibid., pp. 257–58.

111 USG to Julia, December 3, 1852, ibid., pp. 274–75.

112 USG to July, July 13, 1853, ibid., p. 307.

113 USG to Julia, August 16, 1852, ibid., p. 255.

114 USG to Julia, September 14, 1852, ibid., p. 263.

115 USG to Julia, August 20, 1852, ibid., p. 257, September 9, 1852, p. 266.

116 USG to Jesup, September 8, 1853, ibid., p. 312n.

117 USG to Julia, September 19, 1852, ibid., p. 266.

118 USG to Julia, October 7, 1852, ibid., pp. 267–68.

119 USG to Julia, October 26, 1852, ibid., p. 269.

120 USG to Julia, December 3, 1852, ibid., p. 275.

121 USG to Julia, December 19, 1852, ibid., p. 278.

122 USG to Julia, January 29, 1853, ibid., p. 285, March 19, 1853, p. 294.

123 USG to Julia, February 15, 1853, ibid., p. 289.

124 USG to Julia, March 4, 1853, ibid., p. 291.

125 USG to Julia, March 19, 1853, ibid., p. 295.

126 USG to Julia, March 31, 1853, ibid., p. 297.

127 USG to Julia, May 20, 1853, ibid., p. 299.

128 USG to Julia, March 19, 1853, ibid., p. 296.

129 USG to Osborn Cross, July 25, 1853, ibid., pp. 308–10.

130 USG to Julia, June 15, 1853, ibid., p. 301, June 28, 1853, pp. 304–305.

131 USG to Julia, June 15, 1853, ibid., p. 301, June 28, 1853, pp. 304–305. During his California visit he made arrangements to "do a conciderable business, in a commission way, if I could but stay."

132 USG to Thomas H. Stevens, July 13, 1853, *PUSG*, 32, p. 12, Court Docket, August 1853, 1, p. 416.

133 USG to Julia, June 28, 1853, *PUSG*, 1, p. 304, July 13, 1853, p. 306.

134 Letter of George Phelan to *Sporting Life*, 1900, Portland, *Oregonian*, July 15, 1900.

135 George Alfred Townsend, writing as "Gath" in the Philadelphia, *Press*, seemed to have considerable knowledge of this enterprise. Augusta, GA, *Chronicle*, December 28, 1879.

136 Lease, October 5, 1853, San Francisco, *Bulletin*, November 5, 1879. This lease has been a bit confused from careless readings. It is referenced in "Scraps," *Historical Magazine*, 2d Series, 2 (September 1867), p. 179, mistakenly saying that Hall was Grant and Wallen's partner, while the lessor was Stevens. The *Historical Magazine* is calendared in *PUSG*, 32, p. 144, where it is further confused by saying Grant had three officer partners, and that the lease stipulates that it is to be used "only as a private billiard room." The original says nothing about the billiard room being "private," only specifying that no business other than billiards was to be pursued on the premises. The day after signing the lease, Isaac M. Hall advertised the opening of the Union Hotel Billiard Saloon, suggesting that he operated it on behalf of the officer partners, since their postings required them to be elsewhere. San Francisco, *Evening Journal*, October 11, 1853.

137 Grant's authorization is attached to Lease, October 5, 1853, San Francisco, *Bulletin*, November 5, 1879. It is printed with the date 1855, but this is clearly a typographical error. First Grant states that he is "of the 4th U.S. Infantry," which was not the case in 1855, and he signs and dates the document "San Francisco," whereas on that date in 1855 he was in St Louis. Augusta, GA, *Chronicle*, December 28, 1879.

138 USG to Vogelsandt & Gulliper, June 28, 1855, *PUSG*, 32, p. 144.

139 USG to Julia, May 20, 1853, *PUSG*, 1, p. 300, Z. Holt to USG, October 17, 1865, 32, p. 421. The Holt letter mentions a note Grant owed Hiram Thorn, or Thorns, dated January 4, 1854. Grant told Julia in his January 18, 1854, letter (p. 315) that it took him two days to reach Fort Humboldt by ship, and other records date his arrival at January 5. Hence, if the dates are all correct, Grant signed the note due to Thorns the same day his ship left San Francisco.

140 USG to Julia, February 2, 1854, *PUSG*, 1, p. 317, March 6, 1854, p. 323.

141 It may be significant that no letters from Grant to Julia have survived for the six months prior to his arrival at Fort Humboldt. This could be read as a sign of withdrawal and depression, though more likely it is simply a case of failure to survive the years. Grant's January 18, 1854, letter clearly implies that Julia already knew where he was going, which in turn is evidence of earlier correspondence now lost.

142 USG to Julia, February 2, 1854, ibid., pp. 316–18.

143 USG to Julia, February 6, 1854, ibid., pp. 320–22.

144 USG to Julia, March 6, 1854, ibid., pp. 323–24, March 25, 1854, p. 326.

145 USG to Julia, February 6, 1854, ibid., pp. 320, March 25, 1854, p. 326.

146 "The Brett Street Idea," *Architectural Legacy*, 2, no. 3 (Spring/Summer 2011), p. 2. The barkeeper's given name is sometimes stated as William, but in the 1850 census for Eureka he gave his name as Richard Brett and in the 1860 census for Eureka as Richard W. Brett. See Ellington, *Trial*, p. 176.

147 There is an extensive body of legend that Grant at this stage in his life was either an alcoholic or at least drank so excessively at Fort Humboldt and elsewhere on the Pacific Coast that he was virtually forced to resign in disgrace to avoid dismissal. This is all based on a considerable array of mythology, and virtually no contemporary evidence. Some appears in Clara McGeorge Shields, "General Grant At Fort Humboldt In The Early Days," Eureka, CA, *Humboldt Times*, November 10, 1912, in *Ulysses S. Grant Association Newsletter*, 8, no. 3 (April 1971), pp. 23ff, a highly unreliable retailing of recollections that were, for the most part, almost sixty years old when the author collected them. More will be found in the recollections collected by Hamlin Garland for his Grant biography; they are almost as old, being for the most part written in the 1890s. Moreover it should be remembered that, in fact, up until 1862, there is only one directly contemporaneous source claiming that Grant drank too much, the John W. Lowe letter May 12, 1848 (see chapter 2), and context makes its veracity muddy at least. Only one extant document from Grant's Pacific Coast period directly links him with alcohol, and that is his purchase, as quartermaster and commissary, of a dozen bottles of brandy for one of the railroad survey expeditions he fitted out (Invoice, July 23, 1853, *PUSG*, 32, p. 144). Not one of the other sources associating Grant with alcohol in California or Oregon 1852–1854 are contemporaneous. For instance, the earliest known claim that Grant drank to excess in California dates from 1863, and is a ten-year-old thirdhand account of Grant's supposedly spending a winter at Knight's Ferry where "he did nothing but drink whiskey and get tight" (Ellington, *Trial*, p. 88). Grant spent only two winters on the Pacific Coast, the first (1852–1853) entirely in Oregon more than seven hundred miles from Knight's Ferry, and the second (1853–1854) uninterruptedly at Fort Humboldt almost three hundred miles distant. In fact, Grant's only visits to Knight's Ferry were in August 1852 for no more than a few days, something

less than a week in late May 1853, and possibly a week or more in May 1854 on his way home (USG to Julia, August 20, 1852, *PUSG*, 1, p. 256, August 30, 1852, p. 258, May 20, 1853, p. 299, May 2, 1854, p. 332). After this one deeply flawed source (which could have been influenced by the 1862 press reports on Grant's drinking), almost a quarter century passed before anyone else came forward claiming to have knowledge of Grant's drinking habits in California. A good compilation of these various sources is in Ellington, *Trial*, pp. 165–89, though the author fails to adequately assess the context of some of the examples he includes. Several indicate that Grant was not a drunkard or habitual drinker, though he might go on "a spree" two or three times a year, while others attest that he suffered alcoholism, knew it, and drank spirits only sparingly as a result. One former officer of the 4th Infantry did claim that Grant was a habitual drinker of whisky, gulping down large glasses of it several times a day. However, that same officer was dismissed from the service for disloyalty in 1863. After the Civil War Grant lent him no assistance as he fought for reinstatement, hence his account of Grant's drinking, written in 1897, can hardly be accepted as disinterested.

Moreover, virtually all of the recollections of Grant's drinking in California were set down years after the growth of popular mythology about Grant and the bottle, and can hardly have been unaffected. Even those by men of kindly sentiments toward him had a motive in confronting the allegations head on, accepting them in order to follow up by praising him for overcoming his weakness. Hence, they almost make presumed alcoholism a virtue by the fact that it gave Grant a vehicle by which to demonstrate his superior willpower and character.

Corollary to Grant's reputed excess is the story that he fell afoul of Lieutenant Colonel Buchanan, who supposedly entertained some prejudice against Grant from the first. As commander of the 4th Infantry, Buchanan allegedly had Grant arrested more than once for his drinking, and demanded from him an undated letter of resignation that Buchanan could use to force Grant out of the army if his behavior became intolerable. The origin of this story lies in comments Buchanan supposedly made to Thomas Anderson in 1862 and afterward, but not written down until 1896, so it is secondhand and forty-four years after the fact (Ellington, *Trial*, pp. 171–72). It is worth noting that in 1862 Buchanan was a brigadier general of volunteers, whereas Grant had risen to major general, and when the war ended Buchanan was a lowly colonel of the 1st Infantry, whereas Grant was commander of all Union armies. An aged veteran's resentment of a one-time subaltern who had far surpassed him to the top of the ladder could certainly account for some overzealous invention in a recollection.

The story about the signed and undated resignation is clearly and completely gainsaid by Grant's actual resignation letter dated April 11, 1854, since if it had been written earlier, there would be no way at the time of its writing for Grant or Buchanan to know when or even if it might be used, making the internal requested effective date of July 31 a serious anachronism (*PUSG*, 1, p. 329). Moreover, nothing in Grant's personal correspondence or Buchanan's official correspondence gives any evidence of ill feeling between the two, though Grant's friend and fellow officer Lewis Cass Hunt did not care for Buchanan. In fact, they shared a house together at Fort Humboldt, while Hunt lived alone. Logically, if Grant shared Hunt's distaste for Buchanan, he would have roomed with Hunt instead. (USG to Julia, June 15, 1853, *PUSG*, 1, p. 302, February 6, 1854, p. 322).

Finally, Buchanan would have been the officer to approve Grant trading positions with Captain Henry M. Judah at Fort Jones, yet Judah was notorious for his drinking habits. It hardly seems probable that Buchanan would want to force Grant out of the army over drink, while bringing Judah to Fort Humboldt.

Local lore in Humboldt County, especially from 1900 onward, often retold the stories of Grant's drinking, now considerably exaggerated, even though local historians exploded them as erroneous, one declaring that "most of the stories are absolute fiction" (Ellington, *Trial*, p. 174). Indeed they are.

148 USG to Julia, February 6, 1854, *PUSG*, 1, p. 322.

149 USG to Julia, February 15, 1853, ibid., p. 289.

150 USG to Julia, March 25, 1854, ibid., p. 327.

151 USG to E. D. Townsend, October 12, 1853, ibid., p. 313.

152 Edward Coffman, *The Old Army: A Portrait of the American Army in Peacetime 1784–1898* (New York: Oxford University Press, 1988), p. 49.

153 USG to Samuel Cooper, April 11, 1854, and resignation of same date, *PUSG*, 1, pp. 328–29.

154 USG to Julia, March 6, 1854, ibid., p. 323.

155 *PMJDG*, p. 75.

156 *PMUSG*, 1, p. 210.

157 *PUSG*, 1, p. 328 n2.

158 USG to Julia, March 31, 1853, ibid., 1, p. 297.

159 USG to Charles Thomas, September 4, 1851, ibid., p. 229, USG to Jesup, April 14, 1851, p. 198, April 17, 1858, p. 199.

160 USG to Julia, March 4, 1853, ibid., p. 291.

161 USG to Julia, June 15, 1853, ibid., p. 302, June 28, 1853, p. 303.

162 Jesup to USG, December 2, 1853, ibid., pp. 311–12n.

163 USG to Osborn Cross, July 25, 1853, ibid., pp. 308–309.

164 USG to Jesup, November 26, 1853, ibid., p. 314, February 3, 1854, pp. 318–19, November 13, 1853, *PUSG*, 32, p. 12. See also *PUSG*, 32, pp. 14–15n.

165 USG to Board of Survey, September 2, 1852, *PUSG*, 1, pp. 261–62.

166 Panama, *Herald*, August 17, 1852, in Schenectady, NY, *Cabinet*, September 7, 1852; St. Louis, *Daily Missouri Republican*, December 5, 1852.

167 USG to Julia, October 26, 1852, *PUSG*, 1, pp. 270–71.

168 USG to Julia, June 15, 1853, ibid., p. 301,

169 USG to Cooper, April 11, 1854, ibid., p. 329.

170 USG to Julia, May 2, 1854, ibid., p. 332.

171 Jesse Grant to Jefferson Davis, June 21, 1854, ibid., pp. 330–31, to Jonathan D. Morris, February 21, 1848, p. 375.

172 USG to Jesse R. Grant, December 28, 1856, ibid., p. 334.

173 USG to Jesse R. Grant, February 7, 1857, ibid., p. 336–37.

174 Pawn Ticket, December 23, 1857, ibid., p. 339.

175 Grant must have redeemed it, or Freligh's son Louis H. Freligh, who had taken over as pawn broker by 1860 census, would not have had the ticket in 1910.

176 USG to Mary Grant, March 21, 1858, ibid., pp. 340–41.

177 USG to Mary Grant, September 7, 1858, ibid., p. 343. *PMJDG*, p. 80, says that Grant's illness was malarial.

178 USG to Jesse R. Grant, October 1, 1858, *PUSG*, 1, p. 344.

179 Hartford, CT, *Connecticut Courant*, November 26, 1864.

180 Augusta, GA, *Chronicle*, December 28, 1879.

181 USG to Jesse R. Grant, March 12, 1859, *PUSG*, 1, pp. 345–46.

182 George A. Townsend, in 1879, alleged that at this time Grant had "about three slaves," probably confusing the two hired from Dent as being Grant's. Augusta, *Chronicle*, December 28, 1879.

183 In her memoirs Julia Grant refers more than once to "servants my father had given me."

See for instance *PMJDG*, pp. 81–83. However, she never explicitly defined what was meant by "given."

184 *PMJDG*, p. 80; USG to Mary Grant, March 21, 1858, *PUSG*, 1, p. 341.

185 USG to Jesse R. Grant, March 12, 1859, *PUSG*, 1, pp. 345–46.

186 Manumission of slave, March 29, 1859, ibid., p. 347. It is faintly possible, though hardly likely, that Jones purchased his freedom from Grant, but in that case the appropriate document would have been a bill of sale from Grant to Jones, and not Grant's manumission. Allowing slaves to earn their own money was illegal in Missouri, though often done nevertheless, but considering what an adult slave might be able to learn in any spare time left after doing the owner's work, it would have taken Jones more years to earn something like $1,000 than Grant had been in Missouri. On the other hand, Grant left nothing behind explicitly explaining the emancipation of Jones. He might have decided to divest himself of Jones the previous fall when he briefly intended to go to Covington, knowing that his father surely would not allow a slave to be brought into his business, and just delayed getting around to it. Jones's manumission may have been a condition of Dent's transfer of title to the slave, though that seems unlikely given Dent's apparently whole-hearted belief in slavery.

187 USG to Jesse R. Grant, March 12, 1859, ibid., p. 345.

188 USG to Mary Grant, September 7, 1858, ibid., p. 343; St. Louis, *Daily Missouri Republican*, July 8, 1858. Grant merely says he went to St. Louis "to hear a political speech." The internal evidence in his letter indicates that the occasion was at least three weeks prior to the letter cited, and probably longer. The election in St. Louis was August 3, so the speech must have been prior to that. While the July 7 speeches at Carondelet seem perhaps too early, they are the only ones that seem to fit, and in any case would be virtually the same in substance as any other stump meetings of the candidates.

189 *PMUSG*, 1, pp. 235, 573.

190 Ibid., p. 212.

191 USG to Julia, July 4, 1852, *PUSG*, 1, pp. 245–46.

192 *PMUSG*, 1, pp. 212–13.

193 In 1850 the percentage of foreign born citizens in St. Louis was 49.3 with only Chicago having a higher proportion. By 1860 foreigners in St. Louis totaled 50.4 percent, and in Chicago it had receded to exactly 50 percent. United States Census Bureau, Nativity of the Population for the 25 Largest Urban Places and for Selected Counties: 1850, Table 21 (Internet release March 9, 1999); United States Census Bureau, Nativity of the Population for the 25 Largest Urban Places and for Selected Counties: 1860, Table 20 (Internet release March 9, 1999).

194 USG to Jesse R. Grant, August 20, 1859, *PUSG*, 1, p. 350, September 23, 1859, p. 351. There is still a hint of this feeling in *PMUSG*, 1, p. 213.

195 *PMJDG*, pp. 34–35, says this anyhow, writing many years later. Julia Grant's comments on the family slaves are all glowing.

196 Julia was emphatic in *PMJDG* (pp. 82–83) that Grant never attempted to sell "her" slaves, erroneously maintaining that they remained hers until freed by the Emancipation Proclamation, whereas in fact they were not legally free until Missouri abolished slavery in January 1865.

197 Hartford, CT, *Connecticut Courant*, November 26, 1864.

198 REL to Samuel Cooper, December 24, 1859, Adams, *Letters*, pp. 556–57.

199 REL to MCL, December 1, 1859, ibid., pp. 550–51.

200 James M. Mason to John B. Floyd, December 13, 1859, File L60, AG.

201 REL to T. P. August, December 20, 1859, Adams, *Letters*, pp. 554–55.

202 REL to MCL, August 26, 1855, ibid., p. 57, REL to Custis Lee, March 13, 1860, p. 585.

203 REL to MCL, November 8, 1856, ibid., p. 202, December 20, 1856, p. 239.

204 REL to MCL, September 3, 1855, ibid., p. 63.

205 REL to MCL, March 28, 1856, ibid., p. 104.

206 REL to Martha Williams, December 5, 1857, ibid., p. 451, December 27, 1857, p. 453.

207 REL to Anna Fitzhugh, September 13, 1858, ibid., pp. 498–99, REL to MCL, August 12, 1857, p. 398.

208 REL to Charlotte Wickham, October 10, 1857, ibid., p. 432, REL to MCL, March 20, 1857, p. 307.

209 REL to GWCL, May 30, 1859, ibid., p. 531, REL to MCL, April 25, 1860, p. 621.

210 REL to MCL, May 2, 1860, ibid., p. 626.

211 REL to MCL, November 8, 1856, ibid., p. 207.

212 REL to MCL, November 19, 1856, ibid., p. 212.

213 REL to MCL, December 12, 1856, ibid., pp. 232–33.

214 REL to MCL, July 27, 1857, ibid., p. 384, August 12, 1857, pp. 397–98, REL to Annie Lee, August 8, 1857, p. 393.

215 REL to MCL, April 25, 1860, ibid., pp. 621–22.

216 REL to MCL, June 18, 1860, ibid., p. 653.

217 REL to Annie Lee, August 27, 1860, ibid., pp. 686–87.

218 REL to GWCL, May 30, 1859, ibid., p. 529.

219 REL to Anna Fitzhugh, February 9, 1860, ibid., p. 565.

220 REL to MCL, July 15, 1860, ibid., p. 677.

221 REL to Annie Lee, August 27, 1860, ibid., pp. 686–87.

222 REL to Mildred Lee, October 22, 1860, ibid., pp. 691–92.

223 REL to MCL, June 22, 1857, ibid., p. 370.

224 REL to MCL, November 19, 1856, ibid., pp. 212–13.

225 REL to MCL, March 13, 1857, ibid., p. 302.

226 REL to MCL, August 11, 1856, ibid., p. 145, September 13, 1856, p. 171, October 3, 1856, p. 173, July 5, 1857, p. 377, REL to GWCL, January 30, 1861, pp. 737–38.

227 REL to MCL, March 17, 1856, ibid., p. 91, March 3, 1860, p. 579.

228 deButts, ed., *Growing Up in the 1850s*, p. 118.

229 March 11, 1855, ibid., p. 47.

230 REL to MCL, November 5, 1855, Adams, *Letters*, p. 73.

231 Ibid.

232 REL to MCL, January 7, 1857, ibid., pp. 257–58.

233 REL to MCL, June 3, 1860, ibid., p. 630.

234 Lee wrote almost weekly in 1855, weekly in 1856, and weekly in 1860, until the period July 15 1860 to January 21 1861, for which most of his letters must have been lost.

235 REL to MCL, March 3, 1860, Adams, *Letters*, p. 578.

236 REL to GWCL, May 30, 1859, ibid., p. 530.

237 REL to MCL, January 31, 1857, ibid., p. 283.

238 REL to MCL, January 31, 1857, ibid., p. 284.

239 REL to GWCL, May 30, 1858, ibid., p. 487.

240 REL to GWCL, August 3, 1851, Gilder Lehrman Collection.

241 REL to GWCL, February 1, 1852, Washington, *Evening Union*, April 1, 1864. The letter was found at Arlington in 1864 by occupying Union soldiers.

242 REL to MCL, May 18, 1857, Adams, *Letters*, p. 343.

243 REL to WHFL, June 2, 1853, Gilder Lehrman Collection.

244 REL to MCL, August 4, 1856, Adams, *Letters*, p. 140, August 11, 1856, p. 146.

245 REL to MCL, January 9, 1857, ibid., p. 268.

246 REL to Nathan G. Evans, August 3, 1857, ibid., pp. 387–88, September 15, 1857, p. 388. Lee asked Mary to send him a small cask of wine and one of brandy not long after they were married. REL to MCL, June 6, 1832, deButts, "Lee in Love," p. 265.

247 REL to WHFL, January 1, 1859, Lee, *Lee of Virginia*, p. 437.

248 REL to WHFL, May 30, 1858, Adams, *Letters*, p. 488.

249 REL to MCL, August 18, 1856, ibid., pp. 156–57.

250 REL to MCL, September 9, 1857, ibid., p. 418.

251 REL to R. Jacqueline Ambler, February 4, 1860, ibid., p. 563.

252 REL to MCL, July 27, 1857, ibid., pp. 383–84.

253 REL to MCL, June 18, 1860, ibid., pp. 653–54, REL to Mildred Lee, October 22, 1860, pp. 689–90.

254 REL to Mildred Lee, January 9, 1857, ibid., p. 265.

255 REL to Mildred Lee, October 22, 1860, ibid., pp. 689–90.

256 REL to MCL, June 15, 1857, ibid., pp. 365–66, August 18, 1856, pp. 156–57.

257 REL to Mildred Childe Lee, January 9, 1857, ibid., pp. 263–64.

258 Agnes Lee to REL, April 9, 1857, deButts, *Growing Up in the 1850s*, p. 138.

259 REL to MCL, August 12, 1857, Adams, *Letters*, p. 397.

260 REL to GWCL, May 30, 1858, ibid., pp. 487–88.

261 REL to Anne Lee, February 22, 1860, ibid., p. 571.

262 Ibid., p. 572.

263 REL to MCL, April 25, 1860, ibid., p. 621.

264 REL to MCL, March 7, 1857, ibid., p. 295.

265 REL to Anna Fitzhugh, June 6, 1860, ibid., p. 638.

266 REL to MCL, August 12, 1857, ibid., p. 397.

267 REL to MCL, December 13, 1856, ibid., pp. 233–34, REL to Mrs. Stiles, August 14, 1856, p. 152.

268 REL to MCL, October 24, 1856, ibid., p. 186.

269 REL to MCL, August 4, 1856, ibid., pp. 140–41.

270 REL to GWCL, December 5, 1860, ibid., p. 702.

271 REL to GWCL or WHFL, August 22, 1860, ibid., p. 682.

272 USG to Board of County Commissioners, August 15, 1859, *PUSG*, 1, p. 348.

273 USG to Jesse R. Grant, August 20, 1859, ibid., pp. 350–51.

274 USG to Jesse R. Grant, September 23, 1859, ibid., p. 351.

275 USG to Jesse R. Grant, September 23, 1859, ibid., p. 351–52, USG to Simpson Grant, October 24, 1859, pp. 353–45.

276 Augusta, GA, *Chronicle*, December 28, 1879; William W. Averell speech, ca. 1887, Alexander Autographs Catalog, October 14, 2006, sale, #item 57; USG to J. H. Lightner, February 13, 1860, *PUSG*, 1, pp. 354–55. Grant did not mention applying for work moving cattle or supplies for the army in *PMUSG*. Averell in his speech dated it to the winter of 1857, when he recalled seeing Grant at the time in St. Louis. The correspondent George A. Townsend, quoted in the Augusta *Chronicle* dated the episode in the winter of 1859, which seems the better fit in Grant's chronology.

277 USG to Jesse R. Grant, August 20, 1859, *PUSG*, 1, pp. 350–51.

CHAPTER 5: A CRISIS MADE FOR THEM

1 *PMJDG*, p. 82.

2 USG to Julia, March 14, 1860, *PUSG*, 1, pp. 355–56.

3   *PMJDG*, pp. 81, 82–83. The June 13, 1860 Census for Galena, Jo Davies County, IL, shows the Grant family living there. Julia's memoir accounts of these slaves are somewhat confused, written many years after the fact. She lists her four servants' names as Eliza, Don, Julia, and John, and their ages in 1859 as ranging from twelve to eighteen, meaning they would have been born between 1841 and 1847 (p. 83). She usually refers to having four, but in her account of the Civil War years it is usually just one, Julia, who is intermittently with her.

4   Providence, RI, *Evening Press*, August 23, 1865.

5   Newark, NJ, *Centinel of Freedom*, December 15, 1874; Providence, RI, *Evening Press*, August 23, 1865. Almost no letters from Grant survive from his Galena period, thus this narrative of his time there relies heavily on early newspaper accounts from the 1860s and 1870s by men who knew him there, due allowance being made for hindsight on their part, and supplemented by *PMUSG*, which in general is accurate though occasionally confused as to chronology.

6   Providence, RI, *Evening Press*, August 23, 1865; United States Census, 1860, Jo Daviess County, IL. George A. Townsend in Philadelphia *Press*, as given in Augusta, GA, *Chronicle*, December 28, 1879, says Grant paid $125 a year, or a little more than $10 per month.

7   George A. Townsend in Philadelphia *Press*, as given in Augusta, GA, *Chronicle*, December 28, 1879.

8   A Galena correspondent in San Francisco, *Bulletin*, November 12, 1879.

9   Chicago, *Herald*, August 16, 1891; Burke memoir, 1896, Garland Papers; *PMUSG*, I, p. 212.

10 Newark, NJ, *Centinel of Freedom*, December 15, 1874. Another source, George A. Townsend writing in the Philadelphia *Press*, as quoted in the Augusta, GA, *Chronicle*, December 28, 1879, said Grant was paid $50 monthly.

11 New York, *Tribune*, in Providence, RI, *Evening Press*, August 23, 1865.

12 Newark, NJ, *Centinel of Freedom*, December 15, 1874; New York, *Tribune*, in Providence, RI, *Evening Press*, August 23, 1865; George A. Townsend in Philadelphia *Press*, as given in Augusta, GA, *Chronicle*, December 28, 1879.

13 USG to Julia, December 31, 1860, *PUSG*, I, p. 358; *PMUSG*, I, p. 222.

14 *PMUSG*, I, p. 233.

15 George A. Townsend in Philadelphia *Press*, as given in Augusta, GA, *Chronicle*, December 28, 1879; John E. Smith in Philadelphia, *Inquirer*, July 3, 1865.

16 New Orleans, *Times*, September 24, 1865.

17 Providence, RI, *Evening Press*, August 23, 1865.

18 New York, *Herald*, November 22, 1878.

19 New Orleans, *Times*, September 24, 1865.

20 Philadelphia, *Inquirer*, July 3, 1865; George A. Townsend in Philadelphia *Press*, as given in Augusta, GA, *Chronicle*, December 28, 1879.

21 Newark, NJ, *Centinel of Freedom*, December 15, 1874.

22 John A. Rawlins in San Francisco, *Bulletin*, September 26, 1868.

23 Letter from Galena in Newark, NJ, *Centinel of Freedom*, December 15, 1874; Philadelphia, *Inquirer*, July 3, 1865.

24 New York, *Tribune*, in Providence, RI, *Evening Press*, August 23, 1865; Cleveland, *Plain Dealer*, February 6, 1868; Macon, GA, *Weekly Telegraph*, August 30, 1867.

25 Cleveland, *Plain Dealer*, February 6, 1868; Providence, RI, *Evening Press*, August 23, 1865; Macon, GA, *Weekly Telegraph*, August 30, 1867.

26 New Orleans, *Times*, September 24, 1865; Letter from Galena in Newark, NJ, *Centinel of Freedom*, December 15, 1874.

27 Macon, GA, *Weekly Telegraph*, August 30, 1867.

28 New Orleans, *Times*, September 24, 1865.

29 Cincinnati, *Daily Enquirer*, January 23, 1874; Letter from Galena in Newark, NJ, *Centinel of Freedom*, December 15, 1874; Providence, RI, *Evening Press*, August 23, 1865; George A. Townsend in Philadelphia *Press*, as given in Augusta, GA, *Chronicle*, December 28, 1879.

30 Chicago, *Herald*, August 16, 1891; Burke Memoir, Garland Papers. It is interesting that there are absolutely no religious references in any of his letters to Julia, and he only mentions attending church once while on the Pacific Coast.

31 Providence, RI, *Evening Press*, August 23, 1865.

32 San Francisco, *Bulletin*, September 26, 1868.

33 George A. Townsend in Philadelphia *Press*, as given in Augusta, GA, *Chronicle*, December 28, 1879; Providence, RI, *Evening Press*, August 23, 1865.

34 USG to John H. Vincent, May 25, 1862, *PUSG*, 5, p. 132.

35 Chicago, *Herald*, August 16, 1891; Burke Memoir, Garland Papers; Augustus L. Chetlain, *Recollections of Seventy Years* (Galena, IL: Galena *Gazette*, 1899), p. 66.

36 Providence, RI, *Evening Press*, August 23, 1865; Letter from Galena in Newark, NJ, *Centinel of Freedom*, December 15, 1874.

37 Providence, RI, *Evening Press*, August 23, 1865.

38 USG to Mr. Davis, August 7, 1860, *PUSG*, 1, p. 357.

39 USG to Charles Ford, December 10, 1860, *PUSG*, 32, p. 16.

40 *PMUSG*, 1, p. 216.

41 USG to Mr. Davis, August 7, 1860, *PUSG*, 1, p. 357.

42 Providence, RI, *Evening Press*, August 23, 1865.

43 San Francisco, *Bulletin*, September 26, 1868. Rawlins says in this interview that Grant slowly began to lean toward the Republicans after hearing Douglas speak in Galena in 1860, but Douglas did not make a speech there, and Rawlins, speaking in 1868, was probably retroactively trying to make the earlier Grant more of a Republican than he had been, if at all. Grant was more honest in his memoirs.

44 Cleveland, *Plain Dealer*, February 6, 1868.

45 San Francisco, *Bulletin*, September 26, 1868; Providence, RI, *Evening Press*, August 23, 1865.

46 *PMUSG*, 1, p. 217.

47 Cleveland, *Plain Dealer*, February 6, 1868.

48 George A. Townsend in Philadelphia, *Press*, as given in Augusta, GA, *Chronicle*, December 28, 1879.

49 For a full explanation of the twisted and confusing business of Johnston's brevet ranks, see Robert K. Krick, " 'Snarl and Sneer and Quarrel': General Joseph E. Johnston and an Obsession with Rank," Gary W. Gallagher and Joseph T. Glatthaar, eds., *Leaders of the Lost Cause: New Perspectives on the Confederate High Command* (Mechanicsburg, PA: Stackpole, 2004), pp. 172–73 and notes.

50 REL to GWCL, April 16, 1860, Adams, *Letters*, pp. 612–13.

51 REL to Earl Van Dorn, June 27, 1860, ibid., pp. 661–63.

52 REL to Custis Lee, October 2, 1860, ibid., p. 704.

53 REL to Van Dorn, July 1860, ibid., p. 671.

54 Thoughts on Politicians, n.d., Robert E. Lee Headquarters Papers, 1850–1876, VHS. While this is undated, it most aptly fits Lee's thoughts during the 1860–1861 crisis. It does not appear to have been part of a letter or other document, but three separate yet related musings.

55 REL to Mildred Lee, October 2, 1860, Adams, *Letters*, p. 697.

56 REL to GWCL, November 24, 1860, ibid., p. 693.

57 REL to GWCL, December 5, 1860, ibid., p. 703.

58 REL to GWCL, October 2, 1860, ibid., p. 704.

59 REL to GWCL, December 5, 1860, ibid., p. 702, December 14, 1860, pp. 710–11; Charles Anderson, *Texas, Before and on the Eve of the Rebellion* (Cincinnati: Peter G. Thompson, 1884), pp. 27–31.

60 REL to GWCL, December 14, 1860, ibid., pp. 710–11.

61 REL to WHFL, December 3, 1860, Lee Family Papers, VHS.

62 REL to Nellie Whitely, January 1, 1861, Adams, *Letters*, p. 714.

63 REL to Annette Carter, January 16, 1861, San Francisco, *Bulletin*, May 3, 1875.

64 REL to Martha Williams, January 22, 1861, Adams, *Letters*, pp. 717–19.

65 REL to WHFL, January 29, 1861, Lee Family Papers, VHS.

66 REL to GWCL, February 23, 1861 [misdated January 23], Adams, *Letters*, pp. 721–22.

67 Ibid.

68 Ibid., pp. 723–25.

69 REL to Agnes Lee, January 29, 1861, ibid., p. 728–29, REL to MCL, February 23, 1861 [misdated January 23, 1861], pp. 723–25, REL to GWCL, January 30, 1861, pp. 737–38.

70 REL to Agnes Lee, January 29, 1861, ibid., p. 728–29, REL to MCL, February 23, 1861 [misdated January 23], pp. 723–25.

71 REL to GWCL, February 1, 1861 Ibid., pp. 741–42.

72 REL to MCL, February 23, 1861 [misdated January 23], ibid., pp. 723–24.

73 *Lee*, 1, p. 432, speculates on a range of discussion when the two met, but all based on much later testimony, none of it from Lee or Scott. Lee did not have to come to Washington just to receive his promotion, of course, but he was also being transferred to a different regiment in a different department. That was sufficient cause for Lee to be called to see Scott, though of course it may not have been Scott's only reason.

74 REL to Lorenzo Thomas, March 30, 1861, File L60, 1861, Letters Received by the Office of the Adjutant General, 1861–1870, M619, Records of the Adjutant General's Office, RG 94, NA.

75 REL to Mildred Lee, April 1, 1861, Adams, *Letters*, pp. 746–47.

76 Leroy P. Walker to REL, March 15, 1861, United States War Department, *War of the Rebellion: Official Records of the Union and Confederate Armies* (Washington: Government Printing Office, 1880–1901), Series IV, 1, pp. 165–66. A quarter century later John H. Harmon, one-time Democratic mayor of Detroit and editor of its influential paper the *Free Press*, recalled this season in Washington. He spent that congressional session in the city mainly as a hanger-on with Southern politicians, and much of it imbibing more than was good for him. He claimed that in December, as was their wont, a group of Southern senators gathered at Arlington after the close of the Friday session to dine and socialize as the Lees' guests. Harmon and Jesse D. Bright of Indiana were the only Northerners in the group, which included Senators James Mason of Virginia, John Slidell of Louisiana, Jefferson Davis of Mississippi, Clement C. Clay of Alabama, Robert Toombs of Georgia, Congressman William Smith of Virginia, Governor John Letcher of Virginia, and former governor Henry A. Wise, Secretary of the Interior Jacob Thompson of Mississippi, Secretary of the Treasury Howell Cobb of Georgia, Secretary of War John B. Floyd of Virginia, Vice President John C. Breckinridge of Kentucky, and others. Over dinner Slidell said that in the wake of Lincoln's election, all Southern members of Congress ought to resign. Harmon recalled Lee's shock at the suggestion, and he responded temperately, admitting that things looked gloomy, but that he believed when Lincoln took office he would not unlawfully interfere with slavery where it existed. Some of the more radical men at the table disagreed, and began peppering Lee with questions on what Virginia would do, finally forcing him to admit that as a Virginian and a believer in the state-rights doctrine, he would go with his state if she left the Union. Breckinridge tearfully spoke against

secession, but admitted that he would follow Kentucky. Davis did not urge secession, but spoke of a more general revolution. Some spoke of a new confederation, while Toombs said that if they did not resign, they would all be expelled anyhow as their states seceded. No one spoke of war as a serious possibility, while some averred that there might be one battle and that would decide the issue. Slidell and Mason joked that all Southerners would need to whip the Yankees with a good supply of broomsticks.

Of course, no such dinner took place. Lee was in Texas that December, and had been for months, and did not return to Arlington until February 1861, by which time many of the men named had already resigned and gone home. Yet in Lee's response to Slidell's proposition there may be a germ of genuine recollection, for surely this was Lee's posture that winter. New Orleans, *Times-Picayune*, August 25, 1884. This is a portion of Harmon's memoirs being published in the summer of 1884 in the Detroit, *Free Press* (Cleveland, *Plain Dealer*, December 31, 1884).

77 Alexandria, *Gazette*, October 18, 1872.
78 Washington, *Evening Star*, April 18, 1861; Alexandria, *Gazette*, April 18, 1861.
79 William W. Averell speech, ca. 1887, Alexander Autographs Catalog, October 14, 2006 sale, #item 57.
80 Benson Lossing, notes on conversation with Winfield Scott, August 5, 1864, Alexander Autographs Catalog for May 13, 2009, sale item #206.
81 REL to Sydney Smith Lee, April 20, 1861, Adams, *Letters*, pp. 752–53.
82 Anna Maria Mason Lee to Daniel Murray Lee, May 27, 1861, Lee and Ficklin Family Archives, Robert K. Krick, Fredericksburg, VA.
83 John S. Mosby, *Memoirs of Colonel John S. Mosby* (Boston: Little, Brown, 1917), 379.
84 REL to Sydney Smith Lee, April 20, 1861, Adams, *Letters*, pp. 752–53.
85 REL to Simon Cameron, April 20, 1861, File L60, RG94, NA.
86 REL to Winfield Scott, April 20, 1861, *Wartime Papers*, p. 9.
87 REL to Sydney Smith Lee, April 20, 1861, Adams, *Letters*, pp. 752–53.
88 Mary Custis Lee to Charles Marshall, January-February 1871, Mary Custis Lee Papers, VHS.
89 REL to Anne Marshall, April 20, 1861, *Wartime Papers*, p. 10.
90 REL to Roger Jones, April 20, 1861, Adams, *Letters*, p. 756.
91 REL to Anne Marshall, April 20, 1861, *Wartime Papers*, p. 10.
92 Ludwell Lee Montague, ed., "Memoir of Mrs. Harriotte Lee Taliaferro Concerning Events in Virginia, April 11–21, 1861," *Virginia Magazine of History and Biography*, 57 (October 1949), pp. 416–20.
93 Statement by Ward Burke for the Southern Claims Commission, Portland, *Oregonian*, November 15, 1872.
94 Benjamin Hallowell letter, n.d., in Mason, *Popular Life*, p. 26.
95 REL to P. G. T. Beauregard, October 3, 1865, DeButts-Ely Collection, LC.
96 REL to MCL, November 8, 1856, Adams, *Letters*, p. 202.
97 Alexandria, *Gazette*, October 18, 1872.
98 Thoughts on Politicians, n.d., Robert E. Lee Headquarters Papers, 1850–1876, VHS.
99 *PMJDG*, pp. 86–87; George A. Townsend in Philadelphia *Press*, as given in Augusta, GA, *Chronicle*, December 28, 1879; San Francisco, *Bulletin*, September 26, 1868.
100 USG to Charles Ford, December 10, 1860, *PUSG*, 32, pp. 16–17.
101 George A. Townsend in Philadelphia *Press*, as given in Augusta, GA, *Chronicle*, December 28, 1879; San Francisco, *Bulletin*, September 26, 1868.
102 San Francisco, *Bulletin*, September 26, 1868; Providence, RI, *Evening Press*, August 23, 1865.
103 *PUSG*, 2, p. 7n; Newark, NJ, *Centinel of Freedom*, December 15, 1874. Both Rawlins in his

1868 interview and Grant in *PMUSG* conflate events of this meeting with the one that followed on April 18.

104 *PMUSG*, 1, pp. 230–31.

105 Ibid., p. 231.

106 San Francisco, *Bulletin*, September 26, 1868. Rawlins said that getting command of a regiment was all Grant talked about at this time.

107 Ibid.; Chetlain, *Recollections*, p. 71.

108 USG to Frederick Dent, Sr., April 19, 1861, *PUSG*, 2, pp. 3–4, USG to Jesse Grant, April 21, 1861, pp. 6–7.

109 Philadelphia, *Inquirer*, July 3, 1865.

110 USG to Jesse Grant, April 21, 1861, *PUSG*, 2, pp. 6–7.

111 Chetlain, *Recollections*, p. 72.

112 Ibid., p. 72; *PMUSG*, 1, pp. 231–32.

113 Chetlain, *Recollections*, pp. 72–73.

114 San Francisco, *Bulletin*, September 26, 1868.

CHAPTER 6: "WHAT HAS BECOME OF GEN. LEE?"—
"WHO IS GENERAL GRANT?"

1   USG to Julia, April 27, 1861, *PUSG*, 2, p. 9.

2   Chetlain, *Recollections*, p. 73.

3   USG to Julia, April 27, 1861, *PUSG*, 2, p. 9, USG to Richard Yates, April 29, 1861, p. 12.

4   USG to Julia, May 1, 1861, ibid., p. 16; Chetlain, *Recollections*, p. 73.

5   *PMUSG*, 1, p. 233; USG to Julia, May 3, 1861, *PUSG*, 2, p. 19; Chetlain, *Recollections*, p. 75; Providence, RI, *Evening Press*, August 23, 1865.

6   USG to Julia, May 3, 1861, *PUSG*, 2, p. 19.

7   USG to Jesse Grant, May 2, 1861, ibid., p. 18, May 6, 1861, p. 21.

8   USG to Julia, April 27, 1861, ibid., p. 9.

9   USG to Jesse Grant, May 6, 1861, ibid., p. 21–22, USG to Julia, May 6, 1861, p. 24.

10   USG to Jesse Grant, May 6, 1861, ibid., pp. 21–22, USG to Julia, May 6, 1861, p. 24.

11   USG to Julia, May 10, 1861, p. 26, May 15, 1864, ibid., pp. 31–32.

12   USG to Julia, May 10, 1861, ibid., pp. 26, 28.

13   *PMUSG*, 1, pp. 234–38.

14   USG to Thomas, May 24, 1861, *PUSG*, 2, pp. 35–36.

15   USG to Jesse Grant, May 30, 1861, ibid., p. 37, August 3, 1861, p. 81, USG to Julia, June 6, 1861, pp. 38–39.

16   Cleveland, *Leader*, June 10, 1861.

17   Quincy, IL, *Whig*, August 19, 1868, as republished in St. Paul, *Daily Press*, August 30, 1868. The other man is identified only as "Colonel W." Of the Ohio regiments then in service, only the 2d Ohio had a colonel or lieutenant colonel whose surname fits, Lewis Wilson, and in May his regiment was in Pennsylvania. Mace told this story in Lafayette in the winter of 1865–66, and it was related to the *Whig* by an unidentified officer who heard Mace tell it on that occasion.

18   This Reynolds family tradition originally appeared in Robert R. Hitt, "A Historic Yuletide," Springfield, *Daily Illinois State Journal*, December 24, 1905, and was later included in Richard Patten DeHart, *Past and Present of Tippecanoe County, Indiana* (Indianapolis: B. F. Bowen, 1909). 1, pp. 227–28. In *PMUSG*, 1, pp. 240–41, Grant recalled some uncertainty of his fitness to lead a regiment.

19   USG to Julia, June 17, 1861, *PUSG*, 2, p. 42.

20 Philadelphia, *Inquirer*, July 3, 1865.
21 *PUSG*, 2, pp. 44–45n; Cleveland, *Plain Dealer*, February 6, 1868.
22 Springfield, *Daily Illinois State Journal*, June 19, 1861.
23 *PUSG*, 2, pp. 46–47.
24 Orders No. 14, June 26, 1861, ibid., p. 48.
25 Orders, July 6, 1861, ibid., pp. 58–59, USG to Julia, July 7, 1861, pp. 59–60.
26 Springfield, *Daily Illinois State Journal*, June 29, 1861.
27 *PUSG*, 2, p. 59n.
28 Springfield, *Daily Illinois State Journal*, June 19, 1861.
29 USG to Jesse Grant, July 13, 1861, *PUSG*, 2, pp. 66–67.
30 USG to Stephen A. Hurlbut, July 16, 1861, ibid., p. 71.
31 USG to Julia, July 19, 1861, ibid., p. 73; *PMUSG*, 1, pp. 249–50.
32 USG to Julia, August 3, 1861, *PUSG*, 2, p. 83.
33 USG to Mary Grant, August 12, 1861, ibid., p. 105.
34 USG to Mary Grant, August 12, 1861, ibid., p. 105, USG to John C. Kelton, August 12, 1861, p. 102, USG to Warren E. McMackin, August 12, 1861, p. 104, USG to Peter E. Bland, August 16, 1861.
35 USG to Kelton, August 14, 1861, ibid., pp. 111–12.
36 USG to Jesse Grant, August 3, 1861, ibid., pp. 80–81.
37 In a somewhat confused secondhand account, Logan said in 1864 that Grant was one of several Illinois men put forward by the caucus, and that everyone in the delegation voted in his favor. Philadelphia, *Inquirer*, July 3, 1864.
38 San Francisco, *Bulletin*, September 26, 1868.
39 USG to Julia, August 10, 1861, *PUSG*, 2, p. 96, USG to McMackin, August 12, 1861, p. 104.
40 USG to Julia, August 15, 1861, ibid., p. 115.
41 The orders detailing these movements are in Ibid., pp. 106–121. See also, *PMUSG*, 1, p. 257.
42 USG to Jesse Grant, August 31, 1861, *PUSG*, 2, p. 158.
43 USG to Prentiss, September 2, 1861, ibid., p. 169, USG to Frémont, September 2, 1861, pp. 173–75.
44 USG to Kelton, September 2, 1861, ibid., p. 175, USG to Prentiss, September 3, 1861, p. 177.
45 USG to Frémont, September 4, 1861, ibid., p. 186, September 5, 1861, pp. 190–92.
46 USG to Frémont, September 5, 1861, ibid., p. 190.
47 Proclamation, September 6, 1861, ibid., p. 194, USG to Frémont, September 6, 1861, pp. 196–97.
48 USG to Julia, September 25, 1861, ibid., p. 311.
49 USG to McKeever, October 9, 1861, *PUSG*, 3, p. 30.
50 USG to Julia, September 8, 1861, *PUSG*, 2, p. 214, September 22, 1861, p. 300.
51 USG to McKeever, October 9, 1861, *PUSG*, 3, p. 30.
52 Richmond, *Daily Dispatch*, April 23, 1861.
53 Davis to Letcher, April 22, 1861, Executive Papers, Virginia.
54 Speech to Virginia Convention, April 23, 1861, *Wartime Papers*, p. 11.
55 Alexandria *Gazette*, April 20, 1861.
56 Cassius F. Lee to REL, April 23, 1861, Lee, *Lee of Virginia*, p. 417.
57 James May to Cassius F. Lee, April 22, 1861, Lee, *Lee of Virginia*, pp. 417–19.
58 REL to Cassius F. Lee, April 25, 1861, Lee, *Lee of Virginia*, pp. 419–20.
59 REL to MCL, April 26, 1861, Adams, *Letters*, p. 758.
60 REL to MCL, April 30, 1861, ibid., pp. 760–62.
61 REL to "My Dear Little H," May 5, 1861, Washington, *Daily National Intelligencer*, August 5, 1861. This letter seems to be genuine as it was published in the Confederacy after first

appearing in the New York *Express*. Context suggests that the addressee was the daughter of an old friend. *Lee*, 1, p. 475 n9, says that this use of "my section of country" shows how quickly Lee's loyalty to Virginia "became blended with allegiance to the South." This seems like wishful thinking. Virginia was part of the Confederacy on May 5 when Lee wrote. Therefore any Virginia soldier took on an automatic allegiance to the larger nation. A more interesting question would be to ask if Lee's allegiance to Virginia still trumped that to the Confederacy, as it had to the old Union, a question that never arose directly, but which events in 1865 came close to testing, as will be seen.

62 REL to MCL, May 2, 1861, *Wartime Papers*, pp. 18–19.

63 REL to MCL, May 2, 1861, ibid., p. 18; REL to MCL, July 12, 1861, Lee, *Recollections*, p. 36.

64 William C. Rives to Judith Page Rives, June 3, 1861, William C. Rives Papers, LC.

65 Milwaukee, *Journal of Commerce*, November 1, 1871. This is an account by Virginian brigadier general John D. Imboden, whose writings are rarely to be trusted entirely, even from this early date, hence his extended account of Lee's conversation has been summarized rather than quoted.

66 REL to Jane Peter, May 11, 1861, George Washington and Jane Peter Papers. In the early 1960s these papers were apparently on loan to the Maryland Historical Society in Baltimore, and were excerpted in an undated essay by Lee Wallace. Their whereabouts today are unknown. Robert K. Krick collection.

67 REL to Cassius F. Lee, April 25, 1861, Lee, *Lee of Virginia*, pp. 419–20.

68 REL to MCL, April 30, 1861, *Wartime Papers*, p. 15

69 REL to MCL, May 2, 1861, ibid., p. 18.

70 REL to Francis Boykin, April 30, 1861, ibid., p. 16.

71 REL to William B. Taliaferro, May 8, 1861, ibid., p. 21.

72 REL to Jackson, April 27, 1861, ibid., p. 13.

73 REL to Jackson, May 6, ibid., p. 20.

74 REL to Jackson, May 9, 1861, ibid., p. 22, May 10, 1861, p. 24.

75 REL to Jackson May 12, 1861, ibid., p. 27.

76 REL to James M. Mason, May 21, 1861, ibid., p. 32.

77 REL to Cocke, May 15, 1861, ibid., p. 30.

78 REL to Cocke, May 6, 1861, ibid., p. 19–20, May 10, p. 23.

79 REL to George H. Terrett, May 10, 1861, ibid., p. 24, May 15, 1861, p. 29.

80 REL to Davis, May 7, 1861, ibid., p. 21.

81 REL to Bonham, May 22, 1861, ibid., p. 33.

82 Samuel Melton to wife, May 29, 1861, Samuel Melton Papers, South Caroliniana Library, University of South Carolina, Columbia.

83 REL to Joseph E. Johnston, May 30, 1861, *Wartime Papers*, p. 40.

84 REL to Johnston, June 1, 1861, ibid., p. 41.

85 REL to Letcher, June 15, 1861, ibid., pp. 51–52.

86 REL to MCL, June 9, 1861, ibid., p. 46.

87 REL to MCL, May 25, 1861, ibid., p. 36.

88 REL to MCL, June 11, 1861, ibid., p. 47.

89 REL to MCL, April 30, 1861, p. 15.

90 Rives to Judith Page Rives, June 3, 1861, Rives Papers, LC.

91 Ibid.

92 Charles Bracelen Flood, *Lee: The Last Years* (Boston: Houghton, Mifflin, 1981), p. 220.

93 REL to JEJ, June 7, 1861, *Wartime Papers*, p. 43.

94 REL to Magruder, June 13, 1861, ibid., p. 49.

95 REL to MCL, June 24, 1861, ibid., p. 54.

96 Charles S. Morton to his mother, July 4, 1861, www.vmb-collection.com/AandDPages/AandDP47.html.

97 REL to MCL, July 27, 1861, Lee, *Recollections*, p. 37.

98 Ibid.

99 REL to Jane Peter, July 27, 1861, Peter Papers, Krick collection.

100 REL to MCL, July 27, 1861, Lee, *Recollections*, p. 37; REL to Jane Peter, July 27, 1861, Peter Papers, Krick collection.

101 REL to MCL, August 4, 1861, *Wartime Papers*, p. 61.

102 His mandate was so understood in Richmond. Richmond *Examiner*, July 31, 1861.

103 REL to MCL, August 4, 1861, *Wartime Papers*, p. 62.

104 REL to William W. Loring, July 20, 1861, *OR*, I, 2, p. 986.

105 Loring to George Deas, July 28, 1861, ibid., p. 1006; REL to MCL, July 27, 1861, Lee *Recollections*, p. 37.

106 John Kennedy Howard to wife, August 4, 1861, Patricia Chatham, "Letters Home," *Newsletter of the North Suburban Genealogical Society* 17 (September-October 1992), p. 35; William Preston Johnston, "Reminiscences of General Robert E. Lee," *Belford's Magazine* 25 (June 1890), p. 86.

107 Wise to REL, August 7, 1861, *OR*, I, 5, p. 773.

108 No correspondence with Floyd survives from this period, though that is hardly conclusive. Still, copybooks of Lee's correspondence should contain his communications to Floyd, but do not.

109 REL to Wise, August 8, 1861, *Wartime Papers*, p. 62; Floyd to Wise, August 8, 1861, *OR*, I, 5, pp. 774, August 9 1861, p. 776, Wise to Floyd, August 8, 1861, pp. 774–76, August 9, 1861, p. 776, August 11, 1861, p. 779, Floyd to Davis, August 11, 1861, pp. 780–81. More of this sort of correspondence continues on pp. 781–93.

110 D. H. Hill to John W. Ellis, June 16, 1861, Lee Family Papers Washington and Lee.

111 REL to WHFL, September 3, 1861, *Wartime Papers*, September 3, 1861, p. 69.

112 REL to MCL, September 1, 1861, ibid., pp. 68–69.

113 REL to WHFL, September 3, 1861, ibid., p. 69.

114 Salem, NC, *Peoples Press*, November 15, 1861.

115 There is precious little in the way of relevant contemporary documentation to limn the Lee-Loring relationship at this time. Freeman and Jack Zinn, *R. E. Lee's Cheat Mountain Campaign* (Parsons, WV: McLain, 1974), both rely almost exclusively on an account by A. L. Long years after the fact, and Long is not always the most reliable source. Long, *Memoirs*, pp. 120ff.

116 REL to MCL, August 9, 1861, *Wartime Papers*, pp. 63–64.

117 *Lee*, 1, pp. 559–60, implies that Lee got word of the promotion on August 31, but in fact cites no source making such a claim. He also states that Lee had been signing letters as "general" for some time, again implying that Lee knew he was to assume that rank. Again this is misleading. Lee signed himself as both "general" and "major general" and with no rank at all in correspondence in late May, and usually as "general commanding" after that, a reference to his immediate position rather than an actually designated rank, especially since Davis did not even put his name forward for full general until August 31.

118 Samuel Cooper to Lee, September 4, 1861, *OR*, I, 5, pp. 828–29.

119 Zinn, *Cheat Mountain*, pp. 112–14, is the best estimate, though adequate sources are almost nonexistent.

120 *OR*, I, 51, part 2, pp. 282–83.

121 Easton, MD, *Gazette*, July 13, 1861. This last appears to be the main substance of Mary's August 30, 1861, letter to Lee, not to date found, but referenced in his to her of September

9, 1861, *Wartime Papers*, p. 71. Neither Freeman nor Pryor dealt with this matter, though both were aware of Lee's letter. To date, efforts to find any such allegations in the press of the time have failed, which is not to say they were not published.

122 REL to MCL, September 9, 1861, *Wartime Papers*, p. 71.

123 Special Order, September 9, 1861, ibid., p. 73.

124 REL to MCL, September 17, 1861, ibid., p. 74.

125 Special Order, September 14, 1861, *OR*, I, 5, pp. 192–93.

126 Peter W. Hairston to Fanny Hairston, September 28, 1861, Robert J. Trout, *With Pen & Saber* (Harrisburg, PA: Stackpole Books, 1995), p. 40.

127 REL to Letcher, September 17, 1861, *Wartime Papers*, pp. 75–76.

128 Alexandre DeClouet to Paul DeClouet, September 23, 1861, Raab Autographs, Ardmore, PA, catalog January 2003, p. 12, item #11.

129 REL to Wise, September 21, 1861, *OR*, I, 5, p. 76.

130 Wise to REL, September 21, 1861, ibid., pp. 868–69.

131 REL to Wise, September 25, 1861, *Wartime Papers*, p. 77.

132 REL to MCL, October 7, 1861, ibid., p. 80.

133 REL to Floyd, October 20, 1861, *OR*, I, 5, pp. 908–909, Judah P. Benjamin to Loring, November 24, 1861, p. 969.

134 REL to Jane Peter, July 27, 1861, Peter Papers, Krick collection.

135 REL to Edward C. Turner, September 14, 1861, Lee Family Papers, UVA.

136 John Kennedy Howard to wife, August 4, 1861, Chatham, "Letters Home," p. 36.

137 Hairston to Fanny Hairston, September 28, 1861, Trout, *With Pen & Saber*, p. 40.

138 USG to Frémont, September 5, 1861, *OR*, I, 3, p. 169, September 10, *PUSG*, 2, p. 225.

139 For an excellent account of the subsequent campaign see Nathaniel Cheairs Hughes, *The Battle of Belmont: Grant Strikes South* (Chapel Hill: University of North Carolina Press, 1991).

140 USG to Mary Grant, September 11, 1861, *PUSG*, 2, p. 238.

141 USG to Julia, October 20, 1861, *PUSG*, 3, pp. 64–65, USG to Mary Grant, October 25, 1861, pp. 75–76.

142 USG to McKeever, October 16, 1861, ibid., pp. 42–43.

143 Ibid., p. 79n, USG to McKeever, October 27, 1861, p. 78.

144 USG to Julia, October 6, 1861, ibid., p. 23.

145 USG to Mary Grant, October 25, 1861, ibid., p. 76.

146 USG to Julia, September 25, 1861, *PUSG*, 2, p. 311.

147 San Francisco, *Bulletin*, September 26, 1868.

148 USG to Julia, August 31, 1861, *PUSG*, 2, p. 161, September 12, 1861, p. 247, September 20, 1861, p. 290.

149 USG to Mary Grant, October 25, 1861, *PUSG*, 3, p. 76.

150 McKeever to USG, November 2, 1861, ibid., p. 268.

151 USG to Oglesby, November 3, 1861, ibid., p. 109.

152 USG to Joseph B. Plummer, October 18, 1861, ibid., p. 57.

153 *PMUSG*, I, p. 269.

154 Frémont to USG, September 5, 1861, *OR*, I, 3, p. 150.

155 See, for instance, Springfield, *Daily Illinois State Journal*, October 21, 1861.

156 USG to McClernand, November 5, 1861, *PUSG*, 3, p. 113.

157 USG to Smith, November 6, 1861, ibid., p. 120.

158 USG to Oglesby, November 6, 1861, ibid., p. 123, USG to W. H. L. Wallace, November 6, 1861, p. 124.

159 USG to Oglesby, November 8, 1861, ibid., p. 135 and n; Grant's Report of Belmont, November 17, 1861, *OR*, I, 3, p. 269. This report was actually written in 1864.

160 Smith to Grant, November 8, 1861, *PUSG*, 3, pp. 134–35n. This is of course only conjecture as to Grant's intent after Belmont, but such a plan is exactly what he employed in the spring and summer of 1863 against Vicksburg. Further support is that Grant sent orders to Fort Holt outside Paducah to send about 1,000 men on a day's march toward Columbus on November 7. By that time he would know the outcome of his Belmont move, after which they were to return unless Grant sent them further instructions. At the same time another column was to move out of Cape Girardeau toward Charleston and then return (USG to John Cook, November 6, 1861, *PUSG*, 3, p. 121, USG to Marsh, November 6, 1861, p. 123).

161 Grant Report, November 17, 1861, *OR*, I, 3, p. 269.

162 For a fine discussion of this supposed note, see *PUSG*, 3, pp. 149–52n, and Hughes, *Belmont*, pp. 51–55. The consensus suggests that the message never existed, and was perhaps invented by Rawlins and others in April 1864 as a justification for the attack when they compiled Grant's revised report. The fact that by that time Grant's success made him virtually untouchable begs the question of why they would bother, especially when the report was not submitted until the war was over. Moreover, Grant's September 8, 1861, message to McKeever, written just two days after the battle, spoke of learning that Polk had "a large force" ready to cross the river to join Confederates confronting Frémont in southwestern Missouri (*PUSG*, 3, p. 133). That is not the same as a threat to one of Grant's columns in south*eastern* Missouri. Yet the basic matter of Confederates crossing, or preparing to cross, to endanger Federals in Missouri is a common thread. This suggests that some such threat was perceived by Grant as real at the time, and since garbled or confused in his memory and his staff's. See also William B. Feis, "Grant and the Belmont Campaign: A Study in Intelligence and Command," in Steven E. Woodworth, ed., *The Art of Command in the Civil War* (Lincoln: University of Nebraska Press, 1998), pp. 17–49. Brooks D. Simpson in *Ulysses S. Grant: Triumph over Adversity* (Boston: Houghton, Mifflin, 2000), p. 477 n.7, says the message was perhaps oral or maybe written, though there is no evidence either way.

163 Much of the foregoing narrative has been drawn from Hughes, *Belmont*.

164 USG to McKeever, November 7, 1861, *PUSG*, 3, p. 128.

165 USG to McKeever, November 8, 1861, ibid., p. 133.

166 Hughes, *Belmont*, pp. 184–85 provides casualties unit by unit taken from contemporary newspapers, which seem more accurate than the official figures for both sides given in *PUSG*, 3, p. 129n, USG to Smith, November 8, 1861, p. 134.

167 Report to Seth Williams, November 10, 1861, ibid., pp. 141–43.

168 Orders, November 8, 1861, ibid., p. 130.

169 USG to Jesse Grant, November 8, 1861, ibid., pp. 137–38.

170 November 11, 1861.

CHAPTER 7: LEE FRUSTRATED AND GRANT VICTORIOUS

1 REL to Annie Lee, November 15, 1861, *Wartime Papers*, p. 86.

2 Special Orders 206, November 5, 1861, *OR*, I, 6, p. 213, Benjamin to Pickens, November 9, 1861, p. 313.

3 William K. Scarborough, ed., *The Diary of Edmund Ruffin, Volume II: The Years of Hope April, 1861–June, 1863* (Baton Rouge: Louisiana State University Press, 1976), November 28, 1861, p. 177.

4 Thomas Henry Carter to wife, December 11, 1861, Thomas Henry Carter Letters, VHS.

5 REL to Mildred Lee, November 15, 1861, *Wartime Papers*, p. 86.

6 REL to Annie Lee, December 8, 1861, ibid., p. 91.

7   REL to Benjamin, November 9, 1861, ibid., pp. 85–86.
8   Lawton to REL, November 10, 1861, *OR*, I, 6, pp. 313–14.
9   Trapier to Benjamin, November 10, 1861, ibid., p. 313.
10   Brown to Benjamin, November 11, 1861, Pickens to Benjamin, November 11, 1861, ibid., p. 315.
11   Benjamin to REL, November 11, 1861, ibid., p. 314.
12   Special Orders 1, November 16, 1861, ibid., p. 322, Special Orders 2, November 17, 1861, p. 323.
13   REL to Annie and Agnes Lee, November 22, 1861, *Wartime Papers*, p. 9.
14   William C. Davis, *"A Government of Our Own": The Making of the Confederacy* (New York: Free Press, 1994), p. 373.
15   Pickens to Milledge L. Bonham, July 71, 1861, Milledge L. Bonham Papers, South Caroliniana Library, University of South Carolina, Columbia.
16   REL to William Elliott, Edmund Rhett, and Leroy Youmans, December 3, 1861, *Wartime Papers*, p. 90.
17   REL to Andrew G. Magrath, December 24, 1861, ibid., pp. 93–94.
18   Ibid., p. 95.
19   REL to Benjamin December 20, 1861, ibid., pp. 92–93
20   REL to Annie Lee, December 8, 1861, ibid., p. 91.
21   REL to Cooper, January 8, 1861, ibid., p. 102.
22   Special Orders 17, December 10, 1861, *OR*, I, 6, pp. 344–45.
23   States Rights Gist to REL, December 12, 1861, ibid., p. 345.
24   REL to MCL, December 25, 1861, *Wartime Papers*, p. 96.
25   Ibid., p. 95
26   REL to GWCL, January 19, 1862, ibid., p. 106.
27   REL to GWCL, December 29, 1861, ibid., p. 98.
28   REL to Annie and Agnes Lee, November 22, 1861, ibid., p. 88, REL to MCL, December 25, 1861, p. 96, REL to Annie Lee, March 2, 1862, p. 122.
29   REL to MCL, December 25, 1861, ibid., p. 96.
30   REL to GWCL December 29, 1861, ibid., p. 99.
31   REL to Annie Lee, December 8, 1861, ibid., pp. 90–91.
32   REL to MCL, January 28, 1862, ibid., p. 107, January 18, 1862, pp. 103–104, REL to GWCL, January 19, 1862, p. 106.
33   REL to MCL, December 25, 1861, ibid., p. 96, REL to GWCL, December 29, 1861, p. 98.
34   REL to MCL, January 18, 1862, ibid., pp. 103–104, January 28, 1862, p. 107.
35   REL to Annie Lee, December 8, 1861, ibid., p. 91.
36   REL to Benjamin, December 3, 1861, *OR*, I, 6, p. 335.
37   REL to GWCL, January 4, 1862, *Wartime Papers*, p. 101.
38   REL to GWCL, January 19, 1862, ibid., p. 106.
39   REL to MCL, January 28, 1862, ibid., p. 107.
40   REL to Joseph R. Anderson, January 28, 1862, ibid., pp. 108–109.
41   REL to Benjamin, February 6, 1862, ibid., p. 110.
42   REL to MCL, February 8, 1862, ibid., p. 111.
43   Ibid., REL to Benjamin, February 10, 1862, p. 112.
44   REL to Brown, February 10, 1862, ibid., p. 113.
45   REL to MCL, May 11, 1861, ibid., p. 26.
46   REL to Cooper, February 18, 1862, ibid., p. 115; Portland, ME, *Weekly Advertiser*, March 15, 1862; REL to Brown, February 18, 1862, *OR*, I, 6, p. 391, Brown to Lee, February 21, 1862, p. 396.

47 REL to Ripley, February 19, 1862, *Wartime Papers*, p. 116, REL to Trapier, February 19, 1862, p. 117.

48 REL to John Milton, February 24, 1862, ibid., pp. 119–20.

49 REL to MCL, February 8, 1862, ibid., p. 111.

50 REL to GWCL, February 23, 1862, Museum of the Confederacy.

51 Benjamin to REL, February 18, 1862, *OR*, I, 6, p. 390.

52 Benjamin to REL, February 24, 1862, ibid., p. 398, REL to Benjamin, March 1, 1862, p. 400.

53 REL to MCL, February 8, 1862, *Wartime Papers*, pp. 111–12.

54 REL to Ripley, February 15, 1862, *OR*, I, 6, p. 386, REL to John C. Pemberton, February 20, 1862, p. 395, REL to Lt. Col. Gill, February 15, 1862, pp. 384–85; REL to Brown, February 22, 1862, *Wartime Papers*, pp. 117–18.

55 REL to Annie Lee, March 2, 1862, *Wartime Papers*, pp. 121–22.

56 For illuminating reflections on this posture, hardly unique to Lee, see James M. McPherson, *For Cause and Comrades*, 62–67, and Gerald F. Linderman, *Embattled Courage: The Experience of Combat in the American Civil War* (New York: The Free Press, 1987), 102–10.

57 REL to MCL, February 23, 1862, *Wartime Papers*, p. 118.

58 Carter to wife, March 1, 1862, Carter Letters, VHS

59 Davis to REL, March 2, 1862, *OR*, I, 6, p. 400; REL to Davis, March 2, 1862 telegram, *Wartime Papers*, p. 123.

60 REL to Annie Lee, March 2, 1862, *Wartime Papers*, pp. 121–22.

61 New York, *Evening Post*, November 11, 1861.

62 Columbus, OH, *Crisis*, November 21, 1861.

63 USG to Williams, November 20, 1861, *PUSG*, 3, p. 192, USG to Washburne, November 20, 1861, pp. 204–205.

64 USG to Polk, November 8, 1861, ibid., p. 131.

65 *OR*, I, 3, p. 310.

66 Boston *Evening Transcript*, December 6, 1861.

67 Nashville, *Union and American*, November 19, 1861; Charleston, *Courier*, November 25, 1861.

68 Leonidas Polk to Fanny Polk, November 15, 1861, Leonidas Polk Papers, University of the South, Sewanee, Tennessee.

69 USG to Joseph P. Taylor, November 10, 1861, *PUSG*, 3, p. 157, USG to McClellan, November 13, 1861, p. 161.

70 Testimony, October 31, 1861, ibid., p. 95, USG to Hatch, January 4, 1862, pp. 371–72.

71 USG to Kelton, December 22, 1861, ibid., pp. 324–28, USG to Montgomery Meigs, December 29, 1861, pp. 351–52.

72 USG to P. Casey, December 31, 1861, *PUSG*, 32, p. 27, USG to Meigs, January 2, 1862, *PUSG*, 3, pp. 361–62.

73 USG to Thomas J. Haines, December 17, 1861, *PUSG*, 3, p. 299, USG to William Leland, January 1, 1862, pp. 359–61.

74 USG to Jesse Grant, November 27, 1861, ibid., p. 227.

75 USG to Kelton, January 2, 1862, ibid., pp. 363–64, USG to Robert Allen, January 3, 1862, p. 370–71.

76 USG to Washburne, November 20, 1861, ibid., pp. 204–207. There is no explicit statement by Grant or the others as to this suggestion, but it is the most logical scenario to fit the details in Grant's November 20 letter, and it makes sense of his comment that he knew that "the plan proposed by Gen. McClernand and myself" would come to nothing when he saw in the press "the new assignment of Military Departments."

77 New York, *Tribune*, November 13, 1861.

78 USG to Henry W. Halleck, November 20, 1861, *PUSG*, 3, p. 202.

79 November 27, 1861, ibid., pp. 227–28.

80 General Orders 22, December 23, 1861, ibid., pp. 330–31.

81 USG to Kelton, November 22, 1861, ibid., p. 212.

82 Portsmouth, OH, *Times*, November 23, 1861.

83 USG to Jesse Grant, November 29, 1861, *PUSG*, 3, pp. 238–39.

84 USG to Samuel P. Curtis, November 16, 1861, ibid., p. 177

85 USG to John Cook, December 23, 1861, ibid., pp. 334–35, General Orders 26, December 28, 1861, p. 349, USG to Polk, December 5, 1861, p. 259, Rawlins to Ross, January 5, 1862, pp. 372–73.

86 USG to John Cook, December 25, 1861, ibid., pp. 342–43.

87 USG to Jesse Grant, November 27, 1861, ibid., pp. 226–27.

88 USG to Mary Grant December 18, 1861, ibid., p. 307–308.

89 USG to Jesse Grant, November 27, 1861, ibid., p. 227.

90 USG to Halleck, December 20, 1861, ibid., pp. 316–18.

91 Cleveland, *Leader*, June 28, 1875. In 1864 Kountz was nominated for a seat in Congress from Pennsylvania. Cincinnati, *Daily Enquirer*, October 3, 1864.

92 USG to William J. Kountz, December 21, 1861, *PUSG*, 3, pp. 320–22.

93 USG to Kelton, November 29, 1861, ibid., p. 234.

94 USG to Kelton, December 29, 1861, ibid., pp. 353–54.

95 USG to Kelton, January 6, 1862, ibid., p. 375.

96 USG to Kelton, January 3, 1862, ibid., p. 368.

97 USG to Kelton, January 6, 1862, ibid., pp. 375–76.

98 Halleck to Grant, January 6, 1862, *OR*, I, 7, pp. 533–34.

99 Halleck to Buell, January 10, 1862, ibid., p. 543.

100 Grant to Halleck, January 8, 1862, ibid., pp. 537–38.

101 USG to McClernand, January 14, 1862, *PUSG*, 4, p. 56.

102 USG to Kelton, January 14, 1862, ibid., pp. 53–54. See also pp. 110–11n.

103 Springfield, *Daily Illinois Journal*, March 8, 1862.

104 USG to Hatch, January 12, 1862, *PUSG*, 4, p. 44.

105 USG to Lincoln, February 8, 1863, *PUSG*, 7, pp. 297–98.

106 Halleck to Grant, January 10, 1862, *OR*, I, 7, p. 543, January 11, 1862, p. 544.

107 USG to McClernand, January 18, 1862, ibid., p. 560.

108 USG to Mary Grant, January 23, 1862, *PUSG*, 4, p. 96.

109 USG to Washburne, March 22, 1862, ibid., p. 409.

110 USG to Halleck, January 28, 1862, ibid., p. 99 and n.

111 USG to Halleck, January 29, 1862, ibid., pp. 103–104.

112 McClellan to Halleck, January 29, 1862, *OR*, I, 7, p. 571, Halleck to McClellan, January 30, 1862, pp. 571–72.

113 Halleck to Grant, January 30, 1862, *PUSG*, 4, pp. 121–22.

114 Ibid.

115 Ibid., pp. 110–14n.

116 USG to Julia, February 4, 1862, ibid., p. 149.

117 Field Orders 1, February 5, 1862, ibid., pp. 150–51.

118 USG to Julia, February 5, 1862, ibid., p. 153.

119 USG to Kelton, February 6, 1862, ibid., p. 157.

120 USG to Julia, February 6, 1862, ibid., p. 163.

121 USG to George W. Cullum, February 8, 1862, ibid., pp. 171–72.

122 USG to Mary Grant, February 9, 1862, ibid., pp. 179–80.
123 Halleck to McClellan, February 6, 1862, *OR*, I, 7, pp. 586, 587, Halleck to Buell, February 6, 1862, p. 588.
124 McClellan to Halleck, January 29, 1862, ibid., 930.
125 McClellan to Halleck, February 6, 1862, ibid., p. 587. Halleck's exact proposal to McClellan has not been found, but in this telegram McClellan responds that "I will push Hitchcock's case."
126 Halleck to Secretary of War, February 8, 1862, ibid., p. 594.
127 Halleck to McClellan, February 8, 1862, ibid., p. 595.
128 USG to Foote, February 10, 1862, *PUSG*, 4, p. 182.
129 Hillyer to McClernand, February 10, 1862, ibid., pp. 183–85.
130 General Field Orders 11, February 11, 1862, *OR*, I, 7, p. 605.
131 USG to Julia, February 10, 1862, *PUSG*, 4, p. 188.
132 Grant is virtually silent on his personal movements in *PMUSG*.
133 *PMUSG*, 1, p. 300.
134 USG to Walke, February 13, 1862, *PUSG*, 4, pp. 202–203.
135 USG to Julia, February 13, 1862, ibid., p. 203.
136 USG to Halleck, February 14, 1862, ibid., pp. 206–207.
137 USG to Cullum, February 14, 1862, ibid., p. 209.
138 USG to Foote, February 14, 1862, *PUSG*, 32, p. 29.
139 *PMUSG*, 1, pp. 302–304.
140 USG to Julia, February 14, 1862, *PUSG*, 4, p. 211.
141 USG to Foote, February 15, 1862, ibid., p. 214.
142 USG to Buckner, February 16, 1862, ibid., p. 218.

CHAPTER 8: SHILOH AND SEVENS

1 REL to CCL, March 14, 1862, R. E. Lee Collection, Leyburn Library, Washington and Lee. Contrary to *Lee*, 2, p. 254, which says Lee did not see Mary until June 10, Lee's letter to his brother establishes that he saw Mary on Sunday March 9.
2 REL to CCL, March 14, 1862, Lee Collection, Washington and Lee. The Richmond, *Examiner* of March 7, 1862 stated that Lee was expected to arrive the day before. MacDonald, *Mrs. Robert E. Lee*, p. 164, says Lee found Mary in worse health than he expected, so crippled by her arthritis that she could barely walk. Lee's letter to his brother refutes this. Freeman relies on the MacDonald account without citing it (*Lee*, 2, p. 254).
3 General Orders No. 14, March 13, 1862, *Wartime Papers*, p. 127.
4 Richmond, *Whig*, March 14, 21, 1862.
5 Charleston, *Mercury*, March 10, 1862; Augusta, GA, *Chronicle*, March 2, 1862.
6 Richmond, *Examiner*, March 13, 1862.
7 REL to MCL, March 14, 1862, *Wartime Papers*, pp. 127–28.
8 REL to John Milton, April 25, 1862, Profiles in History Catalog, December 2007, p. 22, item #25; REL to Joseph Brown, May 13, 1862, Alexander Autographs Catalog sale November 6, 2008, p. 55, item #209.
9 REL to Nathan G. Evans, early 1862, Jason Silverman, Samuel N. Thomas Jr., and Beverly D. Evans, IV, *Shanks: The Life and Wars of General Nathan George Evans, C.S.A.* (New York: Da Capo Press, 2002), pp. 100–101.
10 REL to Theophilus H. Holmes, March 16, 1862, *Wartime Papers*, pp. 130–31.
11 REL to Johnston, March 17, 1862, ibid., pp. 131–32.
12 REL to MCL, March 15, 1862, ibid., p. 129.

13   REL to Johnston, March 25, 1862, Gilder Lehrman Collection; REL to Johnston, March 28, 1862, *Wartime Papers*, pp. 138–39.

14   REL to Huger, March 25, 1862, *Wartime Papers*, pp. 135–36, REL to Magruder, March 26, 1862, pp. 136–37.

15   REL to MCL, March 15, 1862, ibid., p. 129.

16   REL to MCL, April 4, 1862, ibid., p. 142.

17   REL to Magruder, March 26, 1862, ibid., pp. 136–37, April 9, 1862, p. 144.

18   Richmond, *Whig*, March 3, 1874.

19   REL to Johnston, April 21, 1862, *Wartime Papers*, p. 152, April 23, 1862, p. 155, May 17, 1862, p. 175.

20   REL to Johnston, May 8, 1862, ibid., p. 166, May 10, 1862, p. 169, May 12, 1862, p. 171.

21   REL to Johnston, May 17, 1862, ibid., p. 175.

22   *OR*, IV, 1, p. 1095 ff; Albert Burton Moore, *Conscription and Conflict in the Confederacy* (New York: Macmillan, 1924), pp. 12–14; *Lee*, 2, p. 28.

23   REL to Albert Sidney Johnston, March 26, 1862, The Rhode Scholar Catalog, Upper Marlboro, MD, September 1998, p. 25, item #84.

24   USG to Polk, October 14, 1861, *PUSG*, 3, p. 39.

25   Boston *Evening Transcript*, December 6, 1861.

26   USG to Julia, February 16, 1862, *PUSG*, 4, p. 229.

27   Ibid., pp. 113–16n, 222n.

28   Halleck to Buell, February 13, 1862, *OR*, I, 7, p. 609.

29   *PUSG*, 4, pp. 272–73n.

30   USG to Julia, February 22, 1862, ibid., p. 271.

31   Halleck to McClellan, February 16, 1862, *OR*, I, 7, pp. 624–25; USG to Halleck, February 13, 1862, *PUSG*, 4, pp. 200–201, February 14, 1862, pp. 206–208, February 16, 1862, p. 226n, USG to Cullum, February 14, 1862, p. 209, February 15, 1862, pp. 212–13.

32   Halleck to Lincoln, February 17, 1862, *OR*, I, 7, p. 628.

33   Halleck to Buell, February 18, 1862, ibid., p. 632, Halleck to McClellan, February 19, 1862, p. 637.

34   USG to Cullum, February 19, 1862, ibid., p. 636.

35   Halleck to Thomas A. Scott, February 20, 1862, ibid., p. 643.

36   Halleck to McClellan, February 19, 1862, ibid., p. 636.

37   USG to Julia, February 16, 1862, *PUSG*, 4, pp. 229–31.

38   USG to Hempstead Washburne, December 11, 1864, *PUSG*, 32, p. 70. Grant carried the pistol with him until the end of 1864 when he gave it to Washburne.

39   USG to Washburne, February 21, 1862, ibid., p. 264.

40   USG to Sherman, February 25, 1862, *OR*, I, 7, p. 667, USG to Cullum, February 25, 1862, p. 666.

41   USG to Julia, February 24, 1862, *PUSG*, 4, p. 284.

42   USG to Buell, February 27, 1862, *OR*, I, 7, p. 671.

43   USG to Julia, February 28, 1862, *PUSG*, 4, p. 292.

44   USG to Julia, March 1, 1862, ibid., p. 306.

45   Halleck to USG, March 1, 1862, *OR*, I, 7, p. 674.

46   McClellan to Halleck, March 3, 1862, ibid., p. 680.

47   C. F. Smith to ?, March 17, 1862, Philadelphia, *Inquirer*, August 12, 1885.

48   USG to Halleck, March 5, 1862, *PUSG*, 4, p. 318.

49   Ibid., p. 320n.

50   Springfield, *Daily Illinois State Journal*, March 8, 1862.

51   USG to Julia, March 5, 1862, *PUSG*, 4, pp. 326–27.

52 USG to Foote, March 3, 1862, ibid., p. 313.

53 USG to Halleck, March 7, 1862, ibid., p. 331.

54 See, for instance, Boston, *Evening Transcript*, February 18, 1862.

55 Springfield, *Daily Illinois State Register*, March 3, 1862.

56 New York, *Frank Leslie's Illustrated Newspaper*, March 8, 15, 1862; New York, *Tribune*, March 15, 1862.

57 Boston, *Evening Transcript*, March 17, 1862.

58 Halleck to USG, March 10, 1862, *PUSG*, 4, p. 342n.

59 USG to Smith, March 11, 1862, ibid., p. 343.

60 On that same March 11 Grant wrote that "I will not probably be here" in speaking of the return of a cavalry unit he that day ordered out to protect loyal citizens in the area. USG to William W. Lowe, March 11, 1862, ibid., p. 346.

61 USG to Julia, March 11, 1862, ibid., p. 348.

62 Ibid., p. 349.

63 USG to Halleck, March 13, 1862, ibid., pp. 353 54.

64 Halleck to USG, March 13, 1862, ibid., pp. 354–55n.

65 USG to Julia, March 15, 1862, ibid., p. 375.

66 Halleck to USG, March 16, 1862, *OR*, I, 10, pt. 2, p. 41.

67 USG to Halleck, March 14, 1862, ibid., p. 35.

68 USG to Halleck, March 18, 1862, *PUSG*, 4, pp. 386–87, USG to Nathaniel H. McLean, March 19, 1862, p. 393.

69 USG to Julia, March 18, 1862, ibid., p. 389.

70 General Orders No. 24, March 19, 1862, ibid., pp. 390–91.

71 USG to McLean, March 20, 1862, ibid., pp. 396–97.

72 USG to Halleck, March 21, 1862, ibid., p. 400, USG to Washburne, March 22, 1862, p. 408, USG to Smith, March 23, 1862, p. 411.

73 USG to Julia, March 23, 1862, ibid., p. 413.

74 USG to Halleck, March 25, 1862, ibid., p. 421.

75 USG to Ellen Ewing Sherman, July 7, 1862, *PUSG*, 5, p. 201.

76 See *PUSG*, 4, pp. 190–91.

77 USG to Julia, March 29, 1862, ibid., p. 443–44.

78 Buell to Halleck, April 1, 1862, *OR*, I, 10, pt. 2, p. 85.

79 USG to Alexander M. McCook, March 31, 1862, *PUSG* 4, p. 455; *OR*, I, 10, pt. 2, p. 84.

80 USG to Sherman, April 4, 1862, *OR*, I, 10, pt. 2, p. 91.

81 USG to Buell, April 3, 1862, ibid., p. 89.

82 USG to Sherman, April 4, 1862, ibid., p. 91.

83 Buell to Grant, April 4, 1862, ibid., p. 91.

84 General Orders No. 33, April 2, 1862, ibid., pp. 87–88, Special Orders No. 43, April 2, 1862, p. 88.

85 USG to McLean, April 3, 1862, *PUSG*, 5, p. 3.

86 USG to Julia, April 3, 1862, ibid., p. 7.

87 Ibid.

88 USG to Buell, April 5, 1862, *OR*, I, 10, pt. 2, p. 93, Sherman to Grant, April 5, 1862, pp. 93–94; Sherman to Rawlins, April 5, 1862, *PUSG*, 5, p. 16n, Grant to Halleck, April 5, 1862, pp. 13–14.

89 Jacob Ammen Diary, April 5, 1862, *OR*, I, 10, pt. 1, pp. 330–31.

90 USG to Nelson, April 6, 1862, USG to Thomas J. Wood, April 6, 1862, *OR*, I, 10, pt. 2, p. 95; USG to Buell, April 6, 1862, *PUSG*, 5, p. 17. While Grant later said he was not quite certain where the threatened point was, the fact that he ordered Nelson to Pittsburg Landing and

not Crump's Landing would seem to conclusively establish that by the time his boat left Savannah Grant had little doubt.

91   In his memoirs Grant said he reached the battlefield at eight o'clock, which was impossible.

92   USG to Comd'g Officer, April 6, 1862, *PUSG*, 5, p. 18.

93   USG to Nelson, April 6, 1862, *OR*, I, 10, pt. 2, pp. 95–96.

94   Report of Lieut. Col. William Hall, April 9, 1862, *OR*, I, 10, pt. 1, pp. 130–31.

95   Report of Brig. Gen. B. M. Prentiss, November 17, 1862, ibid., pp. 278–79.

96   Report of Brig. Gen. William Nelson, April 10, 1862, ibid., p. 323.

97   Ammen diary, April 6, 1862, ibid., p. 333.

98   *PMUSG*, 1, p. 348.

99   Ibid., p. 349.

100 See USG to Buell, April 7, 1862, *PUSG*, 5, pp. 20–21, April 8, 1862, p. 24, April 10, 1862, pp. 38–39, for instance. *PMUSG*, 1, p. 355.

101 *PMUSG*, 1, pp. 350–51.

102 USG to Halleck, April 9, 1862, *PUSG*, 5, p. 31.

103 USG to Julia, April 8, 1862, ibid., p. 27.

104 USG to Julia, April 15, 1862, ibid., p. 47.

105 REL to Pemberton, April 10, 1862, *OR*, I, 6, p. 432, Pemberton to REL, April 10, 1862, p. 432.

106 REL to Pickens, May 29, 1862, Gilder Lehrman Collection.

107 *OR*, I, 11, pt. 3, pp. 530–31.

108 Jefferson Davis, *Rise and Fall of the Confederate Government* (New York: D. Appleton, 1881), 2, p. 120.

109 REL to Johnston, May 30, 1862, *OR*, I, 11, pt. 3, p. 560.

110 William Preston Johnston, "Reminiscences of General Robert E. Lee," *Belford's Magazine*, 25 (June 1890), pp. 86, 89.

111 Davis, *Rise and Fall*, 2, pp. 122–24, says Lee met with Smith. Gustavus W. Smith, *The Battle of Seven Pines* (New York: C. C. Crawford, 1891), p. 104, says tersely that "Lee gave him [Smith] no instructions."

112 REL to Smith, June 1, 1862, Smith, *Seven Pines*, p. 130. *Lee*, 2, p. 74 gives a fanciful—and entirely invented—account of Davis telling Lee on the ride back to Richmond on May 31 that he would have to take command of the army, and to prepare to take over as soon as he reached his quarters. Yet hours later, at five in the morning June 1, Lee's letter cited above clearly addresses Smith as "Commd Army of N. VA," saying "you are right in calling upon me for what you want," and expressing the hope that "you can gain a complete victory." Lee at that moment clearly regarded Smith as being in command of the army, and his own role as one of support and succor. Moreover, if given command of the army the night before, Lee would certainly have been back with the army in person before daylight to be present for the renewed fighting, rather than waiting until the following afternoon. Davis in *Rise and Fall*, 2, p. 130, says he told Lee he would take the command during the ride to Richmond on May 31, but Smith, *Seven Pines*, p. 137, said in 1891 that Davis told him he had notified Lee "early in the morning" of June 1 that he was to take command. That sounds more likely, and perfectly fits with Lee still regarding Smith as commander at five that morning. Both sources are too many years after the fact to be regarded as conclusive.

113 Davis to REL, June 1, 1862, *OR*, I, 11, pt. 3, pp. 568–69.

114 Smith, *Seven Pines*, pp. 129, 137.

115 REL to Charlotte Lee, June 2, 1862, Lee Papers, VHS.

116 Special Orders No. 22, June 1, 1862, *Wartime Papers*, pp. 181–82.

117 Davis, *Rise and Fall*, 2, p. 131.

118 Melton to wife, June 6, 1862, Melton Papers, University of South Carolina.

119 Beth Gilbert Crabtree and James W. Patton, eds., *"Journal of a Secesh Lady": The Diary of Catherine Ann Devereaux Edmondston, 1860–1866* (Raleigh: North Carolina Division of Archives and History, 1979), p. 189.

120 REL to Randolph, June 5, 1862, *Wartime Papers*, p. 185.

121 Stephen W. Sears, *To the Gates of Richmond: The Peninsula Campaign* (Boston: Ticknor & Fields, 1992), pp. 153–54.

122 Alexandria, *Gazette*, June 3, 1862.

123 *Lee*, 2, p. 254 and n.

124 Smith to Johnston, July 18, 1862, *OR*, I, 51, pt. 2, pp. 593–94.

125 REL to Jackson, June 16, 1862, *Wartime Papers*, p. 194, REL to Theophilus H. Holmes, June 18, 1862, p. 195.

126 There are no contemporaneous accounts of this council of war, and what we have comes from postwar writings of Longstreet, who is not always reliable.

127 REL to MCL, June 25, 1862, Heritage Auction, Dallas, November 20–21, 2008, item #57137.

128 REL to Davis, June 27, 1862, *Wartime Papers*, p. 202.

129 REL to Davis, June 29, 1862, ibid., pp. 205–206.

130 REL to Magruder, June 29, 1862, ibid., p. 205.

131 Robert William Sidwell, "Maintaining Order in the Midst of Chaos: Robert E. Lee's Usage of His Personal Staff" (Master's Thesis: Kent State University, 2009), pp. 19–20, 25, 29, 31, 33, 36.

132 Ibid., pp. 35, 36, 39, 46.

133 John Goode, *Recollections of A Lifetime* (New York: Neale, 1906), p. 58.

134 REL to MCL, July 9, 1862, *Wartime Papers*, p. 230.

CHAPTER 9: LEE VICTORIOUS AND GRANT FRUSTRATED

1 General Orders No. 34, April 8, 1862, *PUSG*, 5, pp. 21–22.

2 USG to Halleck, April 8, 1862, ibid., p. 23.

3 See, for instance, Boston, *American Traveller*, April 12, 1862, and Philadelphia, *Public Ledger*, April 14, 1862.

4 USG to Julia, April 15, 1862, *PUSG*, 5, p. 47, March 23, 1862, *PUSG*, 4, p. 413.

5 USG to George P. Ihrie, April 25, 1862, *PUSG*, 5, pp. 74–74, USG to Julia, May 4, 1862, p. 111.

6 USG to Jesse Grant, April 26, 1862, ibid., p. 78.

7 Ibid., pp. 48–50n.

8 Ibid., pp. 50–51n.

9 USG to Julia, April 25, 1862, ibid., p. 72.

10 USG to Julia, May 4, 1862, ibid., p. 110.

11 USG to Julia, April 30, 1862, ibid., p. 102.

12 USG to Halleck, May 11, 1862, ibid., p. 114.

13 USG to Julia, May 11, 1862, ibid., p. 116, May 13, 1862, p. 118.

14 USG to Washburne, May 14, 1862, ibid., pp. 119–20 and n.

15 USG to Julia, May 24, 1862, ibid., p. 130.

16 USG to Julia, May 31, 1862, ibid., p. 134.

17 USG to Julia, June 9, 1862, ibid., pp. 140–41 and n.

18 See, for instance, USG to Halleck, June 19, 1862, ibid., p. 169.

19 USG to Hillyer, July 1, 1862, ibid., p. 181.

20 USG to Julia, May 16, 1862, ibid., p. 124.

21 *PMJDG*, pp. 101, 105. For a thoughtful and persuasive discussion of Julia and slaves, see

"Did Julia Grant Own Slaves," *Yesterday and Today*, April 2, 2011, http://www.yandtblog .com/?p=298.

22 USG to Julia, March 24, 1862, *PUSG*, 4, p. 418. See, for instance, Cleveland, *Leader*, February 26, 1862.

23 USG to Washburne, March 22, 1862, ibid., p. 408.

24 USG to Jesse Grant, August 3, 1862, *PUSG*, 5, p. 263.

25 USG to Mary Grant, August 19, 1862, ibid., p. 311.

26 USG to Lincoln, February 9, 1863, *PUSG*, 7, pp. 301–303n.

27 *Register of the Officers and Cadets of the U.S. Military Academy, June 1828*, p. 22.

28 USG to McLean, August 10, 1862, *PUSG*, 5, pp. 281–82n.

29 USG to Stanton, March 14, 1862, *PUSG*, 4, p. 357.

30 USG to McLean, April 21, 1862, *PUSG*, 5, p. 63.

31 USG to McClernand, August 17, 1862, ibid., pp. 299–301n.

32 USG to Jesse Grant, August 3, 1862, ibid., p. 263.

33 USG to Jesse Grant, September 17, 1862, *PUSG*, 6, pp. 61–62.

34 USG to Kelton, June 30, 1862, *PUSG*, 5, p. 178.

35 USG to Halleck July 8, 1862, ibid., p. 199.

36 USG to Washburne, July 22, 1862, ibid., p. 225.

37 Ibid., p. 207n.

38 USG to Washburne, July 22, 1862, ibid., p. 226.

39 USG to Halleck, August 9, 1862, ibid., p. 278.

40 USG to Halleck, August 1, 1862, ibid., p. 257.

41 USG to Hillyer, August 14, 1862, *PUSG*, 32, p. 35.

42 USG to Julia, August 18, 1862, *PUSG*, 5, p. 308.

43 USG to Mary Grant, August 19, 1862, ibid., p. 311.

44 USG to Julia, August 18, 1862, ibid., p. 308.

45 USG to Halleck, June 30, 1862, ibid., p. 175.

46 USG to Halleck, September 7, 1862, *PUSG*, 6, p. 34.

47 USG to Julia, September 14, 1862, ibid., p. 43.

48 USG to Halleck, June 19, 1862, *PUSG*, 5, p. 169.

49 REL to William C. Rives, July 4, 1862, William C. Rives Papers, LC.

50 REL to Davis, July 9, 1862, *Wartime Papers*, p. 229, REL to MCL, July 9, 1862, pp. 229–30.

51 REL to Davis, July 18, 1862, ibid., p. 232.

52 REL to Jackson, July 23, 1862, ibid., p. 235.

53 REL to Jackson, July 27, 1862, ibid., pp. 239–40.

54 REL to McClellan, July 21, 1862, Philadelphia, *Inquirer*, August 14, 1862.

55 REL to Mildred Lee, July 28, 1862, *Wartime Papers*, p. 240.

56 REL to Jackson, August 4, 1861, ibid., p. 245.

57 REL to Jackson, August 7, 1862, ibid., p. 248.

58 REL to Jackson, August 12, 1862, ibid., p. 251.

59 REL to Davis, August 14, 1862, ibid., p. 254.

60 John H. Chamberlayne to Lucy Parke Chamberlayne, August 15, 1862, Churchill Gibson Chamberlayne, ed., *Ham Chamberlayne—Virginian: Letters and Papers of an Artillery Officer in the War for Southern Independence 1861–1865* (Richmond: Dietz Press, 1932), p. 93.

61 REL to Longstreet, August 14, 1862, *Wartime Papers*, p. 253.

62 John Hennessy, *Return to Bull Run: The Campaign and Battle of Second Manassas* (New York: Simon and Schuster, 1992), p. 226.

63 REL to Davis, August 29, 1862, *Wartime Papers*, p. 266.

64 San Francisco, *Bulletin*, March 20, 1863; Thomas Claybrook Elder letter to unidentified addressee, September 4, 1862, Thomas Claybrook Elder Papers, VHS.

65 REL to Davis, August 30, 1862, *Wartime Papers*, pp. 266–67.

66 REL to Davis, August 30, 1862, ibid., p. 268.

67 USG to Julia, September 14, 1862, *PUSG*, 6, p. 43.

68 USG to Halleck, September 15, 1862, ibid., p. 46.

69 USG to Rosecrans, September 18, 1862, ibid., p. 64.

70 Ibid., p. 66n.

71 REL to Davis, September 3, 1862, *Wartime Papers*, pp. 292–93.

72 REL to Davis, August 14, 1862, ibid., p. 254.

73 REL to Davis, September 12, 1862, ibid., pp. 304–305.

74 REL to Davis, September 4, 1862, ibid., p. 294. It is sometimes stated that one of Lee's goals was to influence the British cabinet to consider, even grant, diplomatic recognition to the Confederacy, by invading the North to demonstrate the South's capability of defending its independence. In fact, eight months earlier Lee told his son Custis that he had no expectation of foreign intervention, and nothing suggests that he had changed his mind at this time. Nothing from him survives even mentioning the diplomatic impact of this campaign, and the only hint that he considered political impact at all is the above cited very general mention to Davis in this letter. Three years after the close of the war Lee stated his campaign aims in Maryland as threatening Washington to draw away the combined forces of Pope and McClellan, and subsisting his own army off Maryland for a while to relieve Virginia. He said nothing at all about influencing either the fall elections in the North, or diplomatic affairs in England. REL to William M. McDonald, April 15, 1868, New Orleans, *Times-Picayune*, August 30, 1903.

75 REL to Davis, June 5, 1862, *Wartime Papers*, pp. 183–84. Despite its sometimes hyperbolic conclusions, James A. Kegel's *North with Lee and Jackson: The Lost Story of Gettysburg* (Mechanicsburg, PA: Stackpole Books, 1996) is an insightful investigation of the origins and evolution of the dream of invading Pennsylvania.

76 REL to Davis, September 5, 1862, *Wartime Papers*, p. 295.

77 REL to Davis, September 6, 1862, ibid., p. 296.

78 REL to Davis, September 7, 1862, ibid., p. 298.

79 Broadside, September 8, 1862, Gilder Lehrman Collection.

80 REL to Davis, September 8, 1862, *Wartime Papers*, p. 301.

81 Davis to REL, Bragg, et al, September 12, 1862, Lynda Lasswell Crust, ed., *The Papers of Jefferson Davis* (Baton Rouge: Louisiana State University Press, 1995), 8, p. 386.

82 Special Orders No. 191, September 9, 1862, *Wartime Papers*, pp. 301–303.

83 James Longstreet, *From Manassas to Appomattox* (Philadelphia: J. B. Lippincott, 1895), p. 285, claimed that it was intended all along that Davis should accompany the invasion. This is clearly gainsaid by Lee's September 3 letter to Davis proposing the invasion, and the fact that none of Lee's correspondence with Davis makes any mention of an expectation of his presence.

84 REL to Davis, September 9, 1862, *Wartime Papers*, p. 303.

85 R. H. Chilton to Lafayette McLaws, September 14, 1862, ibid., p. 307.

86 Thomas Henry Carter to Susan Carter, October 4, 1862, Thomas Henry Carter Letters, VHS.

87 Ibid. There are several good accounts of the campaign and battle, all of which detail Lee's movements during the day. See Stephen W. Sears, *Landscape Turned Red: The Battle of Antietam* (New York: Houghton, Mifflin, 1983) and Joseph T. Harsh, *Taken at the Flood:*

Robert E. Lee & Confederate Strategy in the Maryland Campaign of 1862 (Kent, OH: Kent State University Press, 1999).

88 The vaunted fact that the outcome failed to influence Great Britain to intervene on behalf of the Confederacy seems colossally irrelevant since that was never one of Lee's goals, there being no reason to think he was aware of such discussions, and Britain's presumed willingness to intervene in the fall of 1862 is open to serious question. On this point see "The Turning Point That Wasn't: The Confederates and the Election of 1864," in William C. Davis, *The Cause Lost: Myths and Realities of the Confederacy* (Lawrence, KS: University Press of Kansas, 1996), pp. 137–39.

89 Sidwell, "Maintaining Order," pp. 52, 53, 73, 79.

90 This theme is developed in Gary W. Gallagher's essay "The Net Result of the Campaign Was in Our Favor: Confederate Reaction to the Maryland Campaign," in Gallagher, ed., *The Antietam Campaign* (Chapel Hill: University of North Carolina Press, 1999), pp. 6–7.

91 USG to Kelton, October 22, 1862, *PUSG*, 6, pp. 172–73.

92 Ibid., p. 73n.

93 USG to Halleck, September 20, 1862, ibid., p. 72.

94 USG to Rosecrans, September 22, 1862, *PUSG*, 32, p. 39.

95 USG to Halleck, October 1, 1862, *PUSG*, 7, pp. 96–97.

96 USG to Rosecrans, October 2, 1862, ibid., p. 99.

97 USG too Hurlbut, October 3, 1862, ibid., p. 103.

98 USG to Hurlbut, October 3, 1862, ibid., pp. 104–106.

99 I. N. Haynie to USG, October 3, 1862, *OR*, I, 17, pt. 2, pp. 257–58.

100 Haynie to USG, October 3, 4, 1862, ibid., p. 258.

101 USG to Hurlbut, October 4, 1862, *PUSG*, 6, pp. 112–13, 114.

102 Ibid., p. 108n.

103 USG to Rosecrans, October 4, 1862, ibid., p. 114.

104 Ibid., p. 115n.

105 USG to Rosecrans, October 5, 1862, ibid., p. 123.

106 Ibid., 123n.

107 USG to Rosecrans, October 7, 1862, ibid., p. 131. For modern works on Iuka and Corinth see Peter Cozzens, *The Darkest Days of the War: The Battles of Iuka & Corinth* (Chapel Hill: University of North Carolina Press, 1997) and Timothy B. Smith, *Corinth, 1862: Siege, Battle, Occupation* (Lawrence: University Press of Kansas, 2012). Though they do not always agree, both are fine studies.

108 USG to Rosecrans, October 6, 1862, *PUSG*, 6, p. 129.

109 USG to Halleck, October 8, 1862, ibid., p. 134.

110 USG to Julia, September 15, 1862, ibid., p. 51.

111 USG to Mary Grant, October 16, 1862, ibid., p. 154.

112 USG to Halleck, October 8, 1862, ibid., pp. 133–34. Frank P. Varney, *General Grant and the Rewriting of History: How the Destruction of General William S. Rosecrans Influenced Our Understanding of the Civil War* (El Dorado Hills, CA: Savas Beatie, 2013) has some good background on the development of the breakup of the Grant-Rosecrans friendship and working relationship thanks to Iuka and Corinth, but is often unconvincing due to its unrelenting defensiveness over criticism of Rosecrans. Grant was not objective toward Rosecrans in *PMUSG* after more than two decades of hearing and reading "Rosey's" attacks on himself, but to thereby condemn Grant's entire memoir oversteps reasonable bounds.

113 USG to Mary Grant, October 16, 1862, *PUSG*, 6, pp. 154–55.

114 USG to Halleck, October 26, 1862, ibid., p. 200.

CHAPTER 10: "WHAT HAVE WE TO LIVE FOR IF NOT VICTORIES?"

1   Springfield, *Daily Illinois State Journal*, December 8, 1862.

2   General Orders No. 88, October 7, 1862, *OR*, I, 17, pt. 1, p. 159, Rosecrans to USG, October 11, 1862, p. 165.

3   *PUSG*, 6, p. 167n.

4   J. Cutler Andrews, *The North Reports the Civil War* (Pittsburgh: University of Pittsburgh Press, 1955), pp. 438–39.

5   Keene, *New Hampshire Sentinel*, October 16, 1862.

6   Milwaukee, *Sentinel*, November 8, 1862.

7   See *PUSG*, 6, p. 87. The letter purports to be by Franklin A. Dick, dated September 28, and telling a story secondhand from Congressman Henry T. Blow of seeing Grant "as tight as a brick" on September 26. In fact, on that date Grant was in Corinth, having left St. Louis the day before. In October 1863 Blow denied having made any such statement, in November Dick denied any recollection of writing the letter, and Bates stated he had never received such a letter. Sacramento, *Daily Union*, December 7, 1863. Blow and Grant were friends both before and after the war, and Dick did not mention the incident in his surviving journals, but was highly complimentary of Grant as a commander. Gari Carter, *Troubled State: Civil War Journals of Franklin Archibald Dick* (Kirksville, MO: Truman State University Press, 2008), p. 77.

8   *PUSG*, 6, p. 167n.

9   USG to Rosecrans, October 21, 1862, ibid., pp. 163–64.

10 USG to Rosecrans, October 21, 1862, ibid., p. 166n.

11 USG to Halleck, September 20, 1862, ibid., p. 72.

12 USG to Kelton, October 22, 1862, ibid., pp. 168–76.

13 Rosecrans to Halleck, October 22, 1862, OR, I, 17, pt. 2, pp. 286–87; Halleck to USG, October 23, 1862, *PUSG*, 6, p. 182, USG to Rosecrans, October 23, 1862, p. 182.

14 USG to Ord, October 24, 1862, *PUSG*, 6, p. 184.

15 USG to Washburne, November 7, 1862, ibid., p. 275.

16 USG to Halleck November 10, 1862, ibid., pp. 288–89n.

17 USG to Sherman, November 14, 1862, ibid., pp. 310–11.

18 General Orders No. 1, October 25, 1862, ibid., p. 186.

19 USG to Halleck, October 17, 1862, ibid., p. 155.

20 USG to Rosecrans, September 22, 1822, *PUSG*, 32, p. 39; USG to Halleck, October 26, 1862, *PUSG*, 6, p. 200–201n.

21 USG to McPherson, November 1, 1862, *PUSG*, 6, p. 235, November 2, 1862, pp. 244–45, USG to Halleck, November 2, 1862, p. 243.

22 USG to Halleck, November 4, 1862, ibid., p. 256, USG to Sherman, November 6, 1862, pp. 262–63.

23 USG to Halleck, November 7, 1862, ibid., p. 268.

24 Springfield, MA, *Republican*, November 29, 1862.

25 USG to Sherman, November 10, 1862, *PUSG*, 6, pp. 291–92.

26 Special Field Orders No. 1, November 7, 1862, ibid., pp. 266–67.

27 Special Field Orders No. 6, November 16, 1862, ibid., pp. 321–22.

28 USG to Webster, November 13, 1862, ibid., p. 304, USG to Isaac F. Quinby, November 18, 1862, p. 331.

29 John Eaton, *Grant, Lincoln and the Freedmen: Reminiscences of the Civil War* (New York: Longmans, Green, 1907), pp. 10–15. Writing forty-five years after the fact, Eaton's recollec-

tion may well be influenced by subsequent events, attributing greater forecast to Grant than he actually had in 1862, but the outline presented here fits with Grant's thinking processes and what little he wrote at the time.

30 USG to Halleck, November 15, 1862, *PUSG*, 6, p. 315.

31 USG to Halleck, November 9, 1862, ibid., p. 279, General Orders No. 6, November 11, 1862, pp. 294–95.

32 USG to Kelton, December 3, 1862, ibid., pp. 377–85, 391–92.

33 Porter claims this, at least, though his memoir is heavily fictionalized in places, and he could be quite loose with facts. David D. Porter, *Incidents and Anecdotes of the Civil War* (New York: D. Appleton, 1885), p. 125.

34 The date of this meeting is confirmed in Springfield, *Daily Illinois State Journal*, November 22, 1862.

35 USG to David D. Porter, November 22, 1862, *PUSG*, 6, p. 340, USG to McPherson, November 21, 1862, p. 338.

36 USG to Jesse Grant, November 23, 1862, ibid., p. 345.

37 USG to Halleck, November 24, 1862, ibid., p. 346,

38 USG to Hamilton, November 26, 1862, ibid., pp. 350–51.

39 USG to Sherman, November 29, 1862, ibid., pp. 360–61, November 30, 1862, pp. 364–65.

40 Springfield, MA, *Republican*, November 29, 1862.

41 USG to Halleck, December 3, 1862, *PUSG*, 6, p. 371–72.

42 Ibid., p. 372n.

43 USG to Halleck, December 5, 1862, ibid., p. 390.

44 USG to Halleck, December 7, 1862, ibid., p. 401.

45 Halleck to USG, December 9, 1862, *OR*, I, 17, pt. 1, p. 474.

46 USG to Halleck, December 8, 1862, *PUSG*, 6, p. 403.

47 USG to Sherman, December 8, 1862, ibid., p. 404.

48 Ibid., pp. 406–407.

49 USG to Commanding Officer, December 8, 1862, *PUSG*, 6, p. 411, USG to Frederick Steele, December 8, 1862, pp. 408–409.

50 USG to Halleck, December 9, 1862, *PUSG*, 7, p. 6.

51 USG to Halleck, December 14, 1862, ibid., p. 29.

52 USG to McClernand, December 18, 1862, ibid., pp. 61–63.

53 USG to McPherson, December 19, 1862, ibid., p. 69.

54 Richmond, *Times-Dispatch*, June 2, 1918.

55 REL to MCL, October 26, 1862, Lee, *Recollections*, pp. 79–80.

56 REL to Mary Lee, November 1862, ibid., p. 80.

57 REL to CCL, October 26, 1862, transcript, Keith Kehlbeck, Marshall, MI.

58 REL to Jackson, November 9, 1862, *Wartime Papers*, p. 331.

59 REL to George W. Randolph, November 10, 1862, ibid., p. 332.

60 REL to Custis Lee, November 10, 1862, ibid., p. 333.

61 *Lee*, 2, p. 428, says Lee learned on November 10 and cites *OR*, I, 21, p. 83 as his source. That citation in fact is to Burnside's report of the Fredericksburg campaign and has nothing at all to do with when Lee learned of the change.

62 REL to Jackson, November 12, 1862, *Wartime Papers*, p. 334.

63 REL to Jackson, November 19, 1862, ibid., p. 340, REL to Davis, November 20, 1862, p. 341.

64 REL to MCL, November 22, 1862, ibid., p. 343.

65 REL to William M. McDonald, April 15, 1868, New Orleans, *Times-Picayune*, August 30, 1903.

66 REL to Cooper, November 22, 1862, *Wartime Papers*, pp. 341–42.

67 REL to MCL, November 22, 1862, ibid., p. 343.

68 REL to Davis, November 25, 1862, ibid., p. 345.
69 REL to Jackson, November 23, 1862, ibid., p. 344.
70 REL to Davis, November 25, 1862, *OR*, I, 21, pp. 1029–30, REL to Secretary of War, November 25, 1862, p. 1030.
71 D. H. Hill to R. L. Dabney, July 21, 1864, Charles S. Venable to Dabney, December 21, 1864, R. L. Dabney Collection, Union Theological Seminary, Richmond, VA.
72 Longstreet to Joseph E. Johnston, October 5, 1862, Marshall Coyne Collection, Fredericksburg, VA.
73 REL to Jackson, November 28, 1862, *OR*, I, 21, p. 1037.
74 REL to Jackson, November 27, 1862, *Wartime Papers*, p. 347.
75 Abstract from field return, December 10, 1862, *OR*, I, 21, p. 1057.
76 REL to MCL, December 7, 1862, *Wartime Papers*, p. 354.
77 REL to Mrs. W. H. F. Lee, December 10, 1862, ibid., p. 357.
78 REL to MCL, December 11, 1862, ibid., pp. 357–58.
79 REL to Gustavus W. Smith, December 12, 1862, *OR*, I, 21, p. 1060.
80 This is the point in the battle when Lee supposedly said to Longstreet words to the effect that it was a good thing war was so horrible, or else men would come to love it too much. This comes from John Esten Cooke's 1871 biography of Lee, though Cooke was on Jeb Stuart's staff and almost certainly could not have been present to hear anything said by Lee, since Stuart and his division were posted at the extreme right flank of the Confederate line almost five miles from Telegraph Hill. If Cooke did not invent the expression, it was at best hearsay sometime after the fact. Longstreet never wrote about Lee making such a statement. E. P. Alexander did, but forty-five years after the fact, and obviously taking it from Cooke's book, by which time the expression was firmly fixed in the Lee mythology. Freeman further muddied the issue by altering the quotation. See Gary W. Gallagher's introduction in Gary W. Gallagher, ed., *The Fredericksburg Campaign: Decision on the Rappahannock* (Chapel Hill: University of North Carolina Press, 1995), p. xii note, for a brief though incisive discussion of this famous quotation.
81 REL to William M. McDonald, April 15, 1868, New Orleans, *Times-Picayune*, August 30, 1903.
82 REL to MCL, December 16, 1862, *Wartime Papers*, p. 365.
83 REL to MCL, December 25, 1862, ibid., p. 380. In June 1877 Major General Henry Heth wrote a letter recalling a conversation of Lee's supposedly shortly after Gettysburg when Lee said "I was much depressed" after Fredericksburg and that "we had really accomplished nothing; we had not gained a foot of ground, and I knew the enemy could easily replace the men he had lost." Heth may overstate his recollection, assuming the conversation took place. "Letter from Major-General Henry Heth, of A. P. Hill's Corps, A. N. V.," *Southern Historical Society Papers*, 4 (October 1877), p. 153.
84 REL to James A. Seddon, December 14, 1862, *Wartime Papers*, pp. 363–64.
85 REL to MCL, December 16, 1862, ibid., p. 364.
86 REL to GWCL, January 4, 1862, ibid., p. 100.
87 REL to WHFL, July 9, 1860, George Bolling Lee Papers, VHS.
88 REL to GWCL, January 19, 1862, *Wartime Papers*, pp. 105–106, REL to MCL, January 28, 1862, p. 108.
89 MCL to Eliza A. Stiles, July 6, 1862, Hugh S. Golson Collection of Stiles Family Papers, Georgia Historical Society, Savannah.
90 REL to MCL, December 16, 1862, *Wartime Papers*, p. 365, December 21, 1862, p. 379.
91 The Seligmans sold primarily ladies' fashion items, so Julia may have been the reason Grant and Jesse met. Watertown, *New York Reporter*, April 3, 1851.

92   *In Memoriam: Jesse Seligman* (New York: Philip Cowen, 1894), p. 20.

93   Pawn Ticket, December 23, 1857, *PUSG*, 1, p. 339.

94   USG to Thomas J. Haines, December 17, 1861, *PUSG*, 3, p. 299, USG to William Leland, January 1, 1862, pp. 359–61.

95   Grant to Isaac F. Quinby, July 26, 1862, *PUSG*, 5, pp. 238–41n.

96   *PUSG*, 5, p. 240n.

97   Charles A. Dana to Stanton, January 21, 1863, Charles A. Dana, *Recollections of the Civil War* (New York: D. Appleton, 1913), p. 18.

98   USG to Washburne, November 7, 1862, *PUSG*, 6, p. 273.

99   USG to Hurlbut, November 9, 1862, ibid., p. 283 and n.

100 USG to Sherman, December 5, 1862, ibid., p. 393.

101 USG to John V. D. Du Bois, December 9, 1862, *PUSG*, 7, pp. 8–9n.

102 Ibid., p. 9n.

103 Ibid., p. 52n.

104 Ibid., p. 51n.

105 Boston, *Herald*, January 29, 1863.

106 Richmond, *Examiner*, December 25, 1862.

107 Springfield, *Daily Illinois State Journal*, December 18, 1862.

108 Macon, *Telegraph*, December 20, 1862.

109 USG to Mary Grant, December 15, 1862, *PUSG*, 7, pp. 43, 44.

110 Ibid., pp. 44–45n.

111 Jesse R. Grant to Washburne, January 20, 1863, Elihu B. Washburne Papers, LC; Jesse R. Grant Statement, December 31, 1863, Cincinnati, *Daily Enquirer*, September 16, 1872; New York, *Tribune*, January 31, 1872.

112 *PUSG*, 7, p. 24n, says Julia arrived December 19, but the sources are an undated memoir written some years later that may not be accurate, and Julia's statement says that she arrived the day before the Holly Springs raid, which was December 20 (*PMJDG*, pp. 107–108). She could not have arrived any earlier than December 16 if the rail line was completed by then, as Grant believed it would be when he wrote to his sister Mary the day before (USG to Mary Grant, December 15, 1862, *PUSG*, 7, p. 43). Julia Grant makes no mention of Jesse Grant being with her on the visit. She does by her chronology suggest that Grant had issued Orders No. 11 before he notified her that the road to Oxford was completed.

113 USG to Mary Grant, December 15, 1862, *PUSG*, 7, p. 44.

114 USG to McPherson, December 16, 1862, ibid., p. 47.

115 USG to Jesse Grant, November 23, 1862, *PUSG*, 6, p. 344–45.

116 William S. Hillyer to New York *World*, January 29, 1868, *PUSG*, 19, pp. 20–21n. Hillyer says this telegraphic exchange took place December 17 and Grant wrote the order immediately afterward, but his memory is surely in error. USG's letter to Mary Grant on December 15 states he had received a telegram from Jesse at Holly Springs. It seems more likely that if Jesse was going to ask for permission to come on to Oxford he would have done it then rather than wait two days. Moreover, as of December 15 Grant only expected to be at Oxford until the next day or December 17 at the latest, which Julia surely knew, so Jesse should have too, more reason that he would not wait until December 17 to wire for permission, when for all he knew his son would not be in Oxford when he got there.

It appears questionable that Jesse Grant ever got the permit from his son. He later maintained that he did, and in 1864 filed a suit against the Marks for $10,000 as his share of the cotton they purchased thanks to his good offices. The Marks, however, testified that Jesse never met his obligations under the contract, did not get them a permit, but only furnished a letter of introduction to USG. They did buy cotton at Lagrange from

January to March 1863, but that was after revocation of Grant's expulsion order, and Jesse had nothing to do with it since it was not purchased under a permit from his son. Their defense was that Jesse rendered no "lawful service" to them. On October 23, 1866, Jesse's suit was dismissed by mutual assent with each side paying its own court costs, though some accounts allege that the Macks paid him a small settlement. Jesse Grant Statement December 31, 1863 Cincinnati Superior Court, Jesse R. Mack vs. Harmon Mack and others, Cincinnati, *Daily Enquirer*, September 16, 1872; New York, *Tribune*, January 31, 1872; Matthew Carey, Jr., comp., *The Democratic Speaker's Hand-book: Containing Every Thing Necessary for the Defense of the National Democracy in the Upcoming Presidential Campaign, and for the Assault of the Radical Enemies of the Country and Its Constitution* (Cincinnati: Miami Print and Publishing, 1868), pp. 42–43. This reprints an account that first appeared in the Cincinnati, *Commercial*, May 17, 1864.

117 An anonymous writer ironically styling himself "Gentile" wrote to the Cincinnati, *Commercial*, in mid-January, 1863, attesting that he had been at Grant's headquarters in Oxford on the evening of December 17 when an aide brought in a telegram from Washington that Grant read aloud. "We are reliably advised that Jews are buying up the gold in the various cities of the Union, for the purpose of investing in cotton in the South," the writer remembered it saying. "This should be prevented. You will, therefore, issue an order expelling from your lines *all* Jews who can not give satisfactory evidence of their honesty of intentions" (Columbus, OH, *Crisis*, January 21, 1863). Thereupon, it said, Grant immediately issued General Orders No. 11.

"Gentile's" story may have been a hoax, or a truth stretched to falsehood. Certainly Grant had received forged telegrams in the past. The Cincinnati, *Commercial*, was no apologist for Grant, having itself published some scathing criticism of his actions at Shiloh, as well as Bickham's insinuations, while puffing for Rosecrans. Just days before the order appeared it predicted that "too much must not be expected of Gen. Grant" (quoted in Augusta, GA, *Daily Constitutionalist*, December 25, 1862). That would make it seem unlikely that the paper would publish something amounting to a defense of Grant after General Orders No. 11 caused a firestorm of protest. Yet it was also the *Commercial* that published his letter to his father defending himself against charges of being surprised at Shiloh, and Jesse Grant had placed other items in its pages in his often bumbling efforts to advance his son. Jesse did not get to Oxford on this trip, apparently, at least not on December 17. "That Jew order so much harped on in congress," he told Washburne six weeks later, "was issued on express instructions from Washington" (Jesse Grant to Washburne, January 20, 1863, Washburne Papers). He could only know that—or purport to know it—if his son told him, or if he read the "Gentile" statement in the *Commercial*. One other possibility offers an explanation: Jesse Grant himself was "Gentile." The heavy-handed irony of the nom de plume was typical of his ham-fisted efforts at wit, as would be such a retroactive attempt to relieve his son of responsibility for the controversial order. Speculation on that can go no further.

The alleged December 17 telegram or packet of letters is a controversial issue and cannot be fully resolved. If such a telegram was actually sent and received, no copy or record of it survived, which would be unusual in Grant's headquarters, and even more so in the War Department at Washington. That argues more for a letter if anything, and the testimony is strong that something came to headquarters that day that influenced Grant's action. Certainly the alleged telegram just reiterated reports common in the department for some time. Others later testified to the general authenticity of the "Gentile" statement, if not the telegram quoted, and all agreed that Grant received some kind of communication on December 17 that led directly to issuance of the order. Jesse Grant's

January 30, 1863, letter to Washburne is the earliest, and though it does not mention the supposed telegram received December 17, it substantively corroborates its import. The New York, *World,* on August 18, 1863, ran a letter from a correspondent with Grant's army observing that his policy at that time seemed to be "what he was instructed by the department at Washington to attempt six months ago, namely, the expulsion of the 'Jews,'" a pretty clear reference to the supposed order received by Grant on December 17, 1863. On January 29, 1868, William S. Hillyer wrote an account that unequivocally stated that Grant wrote General Orders No. 11 after receiving a telegram that his father was at Holly Springs with a Jewish trader, Goldsmith, who wanted to come see him (William S. Hillyer to New York *World,* January 29, 1868, *PUSG,* 19, pp. 20–21n). On May 6, 1868, writing on behalf of Grant, Rawlins addressed an open letter to Lewis Dembitz, in which he gave a lengthy justification of the order, noting that on the evening of December 17 Grant received a number of complaints referred to him by Halleck, all citing Jews for violating orders prohibiting alleged acts. On reading them, Grant, said Rawlins, felt that "some immediate action was demanded of him," hence the order (Rawlins to Dembitz, May 6, 1868, New York, *Tribune,* June 23, 1868).

On July 6, 1868, David Eckstein of Cincinnati, who had three days earlier published a denial that Jews were opposed to Grant's presidential candidacy, made an unannounced call on Grant while the general was in Covington for a few hours visiting his parents (San Francisco, *Bulletin,* August 15, 1868). Grant discussed the order with him for some two hours and gave him permission to publish "the substance of our conversation" if he wished (New York, *Herald,* October 23, 1868). Eckstein certainly drafted an account of Grant's explanation for General Orders No. 11 and sent it to Grant a few weeks later, for in an August 14 letter to his father Grant mentioned "the Israelite who called on me," and added that he got a letter from him in late July or early August and that Eckstein had "written out our conversation substantially correct," mentioning that the account contained "an allusion to a letter received by me before the publication of my Jew orders, correctly given, as I recollect it." Thus Grant confirmed the receipt of an unspecified communication just before he issued General Orders No. 11, though he did not state that it was an order for him to do so, or even that it was the proximate cause for him doing so, though the context clearly implies that was the case. Grant further stated that he sent Eckstein's account to Rawlins for verification (USG to Jesse Grant, August 14, 1868, *PUSG,* 19, p. 17).

Interestingly, Eckstein's papers in private hands contain an unsigned and undated account written in the first person as a witness present on December 17, 1862, that almost quotes the "Gentile" item verbatim. Bertram Korn, *American Jewry and the Civil War* (New York: Athenaeum, 1970), p. 141, sees the similarity in wording between the Eckstein document and the "Gentile" original as corroboration of its content, but it argues just as strongly that whoever wrote this account had "Gentile's" item before them and rephrased it in the form of a personal recollection. The unnamed writer also says that he sent his "recollection" to someone in Washington who had been present at Grant's headquarters on December 17, 1862, asking for his opinion, and that he replied that the account was "substantially correct." The man in Washington is obviously Rawlins (*PUSG,* 19, pp. 26–27n). The fact that Grant in his letter to his father and the unnamed writer of the Eckstein account both state that an account was sent to Rawlins suggests that they are both talking about the same statement, a conclusion circumstantially reinforced by the fact that both Grant and the authority in Washington use exactly the same phrase "substantially correct" in evaluating what Eckstein showed Grant, and what the unnamed writer sent to Rawlins. Moreover, if Jesse Grant was in fact the author of the "Gentile" statement, the fact that Eckstein met Grant in his father's Covington home would mean that Jesse very likely had a copy of the newspaper item readily at hand to display, accounting for the similarity in wording. The fact that the unsigned account is written in the first person is challenging. Korn, *American Jewry*, p. 141, states that other papers of Eckstein's establish that he was in the Oxford, Mississippi, area in December 1862, but makes no specific citations.

Finally, on September 18, 1868, USG wrote to Isaac N. Morris in explanation of the order, saying, "I do not pretend to sustain the order. At the time of its publication I was incensed by a reprimand received from Washington for permitting acts which the Jews, within my lines, were engaged in." The supposed telegram quoted by "Gentile" was hardly a reprimand, but Grant's letter corroborates the statement that he issued the order in response to a communication from Washington (USG to Morris, September 14, 1868, *PUSG*, 19, p. 37).

The most outlandish explanation came five years later when Grant was running for the presidency and a newspaper stated that Jesse told his son that the Macks were refusing to pay him his share of their cotton profits, and Grant threatened to expel Jews from his department in retaliation, and finally did (Camden, NJ, *Democrat*, August 15, 1868).

118 USG to Christopher P. Wolcott, December 17, 1862, *PUSG*, 7, pp. 56–57. Grant's failure to mention General Orders No. 11 in his letter argues strongly that it was written prior to his drafting the order that day, though clearly he had an order of expulsion on his mind.

119 It is often asserted that Grant's "last straw" was his father arriving with one or more of the Macks to apply for a permit to buy cotton. See, for instance, *PUSG*, 7, p. 53n, and John Y. Simon, "Ulysses S. Grant and the Jews: An Unsolved Mystery," *The Record* (Washington: Jewish Historical Society of Greater Washington, 1995), 21, pp. 24–33; Simpson, *Ulysses S. Grant: Triumph Over Adversity*, p. 164. However, this seems highly improbable, at least as traditionally presented. Simon Mack, in testimony cited below, stated that Jesse Grant only gave him a letter of introduction to USG and did not secure a permit. Solomon Goldsmith said he went to Holly Springs with Jesse, made no mention of going on to Oxford to meet Grant in person, and then said he returned North with Jesse. If the railroad line from Holly Springs to Oxford was not open for Julia to make the trip to her husband until December 19, then Jesse could have made it no sooner unless somehow he made the trip overland. Solomon Goldsmith said he bought $6,000 worth of cotton at Holly Springs that was destroyed in the Confederate raid on December 20, and presumably was not allowed to buy any after December 18, when Grant's expulsion order was known. Indeed, that order would have required Goldsmith to leave Holly Springs within twenty-four hours of the post commander there being notified of General Orders No. 11, which he would have been the first to receive as it went out on the telegraph from Oxford. Thus Goldsmith would have been required to leave by December 18, or the 19th at the latest. The fact that Julia's memoir does not mention Jesse Grant being with her is not conclusive of anything, since it was written years later and is often fallible, but it is suggestive of the possibility that Jesse never came on to Oxford but left when Goldsmith left, and thus never had an opportunity to apply personally to his son for a permit. That would agree with the Macks' later statement that no such permit was issued and that all Jesse did for them was give Simon Mack a letter of introduction, which he very well might have, since the Macks were certainly buying cotton from January to March 1863 in that department after General Order No., 11 was revoked.

120 General Orders No. 11, December 17, 1862, *PUSG*, 7, p. 50.

121 Jonathan D. Sarna, *When General Grant Expelled the Jews* (New York: Schocken Books, 2012) is the fullest modern treatment of the whole subject, though its emphasis is on the aftermath of the order. Korn, *American Jewry* is also very useful.

122 USG to Isaac N. Morris, September 14, 1868, *PUSG*, 19, p. 37.

123 REL to M. J. Michelbacher, August 22, 1861, Herbert T. Ezekiel and Gaston Lichtenstein, *The History of the Jews of Richmond from 1769 to 1917* (Richmond: Herbert T. Ezekiel, 1917), pp. 161–62.

124 REL to MCL, December 7, 1862, *Wartime* Papers, p. 354; Emancipation document, December 29, 1862, Eleanor Brockenbrough Library, Museum of the Confederacy, Richmond.

125 Interview with Thomas M. Cook, April 23, 1865, New York, *Herald*, April 29, 1865.

126 REL to E. D. Eacho, January 3, 1863, Macon, *Telegraph*, February 19, 1886.

127 REL to MCL, January 8, 1863, Lee Family Papers, VHS.

128 REL to GWCL, January 11, 1863, Massachusetts Historical Society, Boston.

129 REL to Captain Peters, September 25, 1861, William N. Palmer Collection, Western Reserve Historical Society, Cleveland, OH.

130 REL to MCL, December 7, 1862, *Wartime Papers*, p. 354, February 8, 1863, p. 402. While Perry's identity is clear, there were two Georges at Arlington: George Clarke and George Parks. Lee's cook could have been either, but since Lee had had George Parks whipped along with the Norrises, it seems more likely he would opt for the other.

131 Thomas M. Cook, reporting on April 24, 1865, an interview with Lee held the day before, stated that Lee said of the Custis manumission that "they were all thus liberated, together with a number who were either the General's or Mrs. Lee's private property." It has been assumed by some, without evidence, that this included Nancy Ruffin and her grown children. Perhaps it did, perhaps not. They are not named on the December 29, 1862, deed of manumission, but that was only intended to cover the Custis slaves. Lee may have freed others by separate deeds not extant, or without filing documentation so that they would not be forced to leave Virginia when the Lee's could not employ them (New York, *Herald*, April 29, 1865). Joe Ryan, "The Lee Family Slaves," at http://americancivilwar.com/authors/Joseph_Ryan/Articles/General-Lee-Slaves/General-Lee-Family-Slaves.html, claims that Lee included Nancy and her children "as part of his action as executor as the Custis estate." There is no evidence for this, and he offers none. As stated, their names do not appear on the emancipation document.

132 Springfield, *Daily Illinois State Journal*, January 1, 1863.

133 See, for instance, the Washington, *Evening Star*, January 6, 1863.

134 USG to Halleck, December 21, 1862, *PUSG*, 7, p. 83, USG to McPherson, December 21, 1862, p. 84.

135 REL to MCL, December 21, 1862, *Wartime Papers*, p. 379.

136 REL to MCL, December 25, 1861, ibid., p. 96.

137 REL to Mildred Lee, December 25, 1862, ibid., p. 381.

138 REL to MCL, December 25, 1862, ibid., p. 380.

139 REL to Mildred Lee, December 25, 1862, ibid., p. 381.

140 REL to GWCL, January 11, 1863, Massachusetts Historical Society; REL to GWCL, January 19, 1863, *Wartime Papers*, pp. 105–106.

141 REL to GWCL, November 28, 1862, *Wartime Papers*, p. 351.

142 REL to Pickens, May 29, 1862, Gilder Lehrman Collection.

143 REL to Cooper, December 13, 1862, *OR*, I, 21, p. 1061.

144 REL to Seddon, January 10, 1863, *Wartime Papers*, pp. 389–90. Lee's comments have often been interpreted to be a reaction to recent actions by General Robert Milroy making local citizens pay for damage done by Confederate raiders in western Virginia. However, those acts utterly fail to merit Lee's references to "saving families from pollution" or a "social system from destruction." The Emancipation Proclamation, issued just ten days before, is the only such event to draw forth accusations like this from Confederates during the war.

145 Cleveland, *Plain Dealer*, November 24, 1862; Boston, *Evening Transcript*, November 25, 1862; New Haven, CT, *Columbian Register*, November 29, 1862.

146 REL to MCL, January 8, 1863, Lee Family Papers, VHS.

147 REL to GWCL, February 1863, *Wartime Papers*, p. 411.

148 REL to John D. Imboden, February 6, 1863, *OR*, I, 51, pt. 2, p. 677.

149 REL to GWCL, February 12, 1863, Jones, *Life and Letters*, p. 226.

150 REL to Andrew G. Magrath, December 24, 1861, *Wartime Papers*, pp. 93–94.

151 Gary Gallagher develops this theme perceptively, and persuasively, in "Conduct Must Conform to the New Order of Things: R. E. Lee and the Question of Loyalty," *Becoming Confederates: Paths to a New National Loyalty* (Athens: University of Georgia Press, 2013), pp. 8–34.

CHAPTER 11: TWO RIVERS TO CROSS

1 General Orders No. 138, December 31, 1862, *OR*, I, 21, pp. 549–50.

2 Lynchburg, VA, *Republican*, quoted in Cleveland, *Plain Dealer*, February 19, 1863.

3 Macon, *Telegraph*, January 7, 1863.

4 Atlanta, *Southern Confederacy*, December 5, 1862.

5 Chattanooga, *Daily Rebel*, January 31, 1863; New York, *Frank Leslie's Illustrated Newspaper*, February 28, 1863.

6 Fayetteville, NC, *Carolina Observer*, February 16, 1863.

7 E. W. Hubard to the editor, Lynchburg *Republican*, December 10, 1862; Richmond, *Whig*, January 6, 1863.

8 George C. Rable, *God's Almost Chosen People: A Religious History of the American Civil War* (Chapel Hill: University of North Carolina Press, 2010), pp. 136–37. Rable notes Lee's fatalism, and that Lee rarely if ever went beyond that in finding theological justification for his actions.

9 Lynchburg, *Virginian* quoted in Augusta, GA, *Daily Constitutionalist*, August 11, 1861; Fayetteville, NC, *Carolina Observer*, November 25, 1861; Richmond, *Whig*, July 1, 1862; Hillsborough, NC, *Recorder*, December 17, 1862.

10 Quoted in Augusta, GA, *Chronicle*, January 21, 1863.

11 Thomas R. R. Cobb to Marian Cobb, July 11, 1862, Thomas R. R. Cobb Papers, University of Georgia, Athens.

12 William McCash, *Thomas R. R. Cobb: The Making of a Southern Nationalist* (Macon, GA: Mercer University Press, 1983), p. 312.

13 REL to Howell Cobb, December 18, 1862, Augusta, GA, *Daily Constitutionalist*, February 10, 1863.

14 REL to Pickens, December 18, 1862, Charleston, *Mercury*, January 8, 1863.

15 Macon, *Weekly Telegraph*, March 28, 1862.

16 REL to MCL, April 19, 1863, *Wartime Papers*, p. 438; REL to A. E. Dickinson, n.d., 1862, Macon, *Telegraph*, December 11, 1862.

17 REL to Joseph S. Key, November 17, 1862, Mobile, *Register*, March 8, 1863.

18 Chattanooga, *Daily Rebel*, January 23, 1863; Macon, *Telegraph*, January 7, 1863.

19 REL to Mildred Lee, December 25, 1862, *Wartime Papers*, p. 381.

20 REL to Agnes Lee, December 26, 1862, ibid., p. 382.

21 REL to MCL, March 27, 1863, ibid., p. 419.

22 REL to MCL, April 5, 1863, ibid., p. 429.

23 REL to MCL, April 24, 1863, ibid., p. 440.

24 Samuel Merrifield Bemiss to My dear Children, April 10, 1863, Bemiss Family Papers, VHS.

25 [Garnet Wolseley], "A Month's Visit to the Confederate Headquarters," *Blackwood's Edinburgh Magazine*, 93 (January 1863), p. 21.

26 Atlanta, *Southern Confederacy*, December 5, 1862.

27 San Francisco, *Bulletin*, March 20, 1863. The writer visited Lee on November 21, 1862.

28 [Wolseley], "A Month's Visit to the Confederate Headquarters," p. 21.

29 Richmond, *Enquirer*, January 5, 1863.

30 Baltimore, *Sun*, January 13, 1863.

31 Richmond, *Whig*, January 27, 1863.

32 REL to MCL, March 9, 1863, *Wartime Papers*, p. 413.

33 Augusta, GA, *Chronicle*, January 23, 1863.

34 Francis Lawley to London, *Times*, November 14, 1862; Charleston, *Mercury*, February 5, 1863.

35 Chattanooga, *Daily Rebel*, February 20, 1863.

36 REL to GWCL Lee, January 5, 1863, *Wartime Papers*, p. 385.

37 REL to Cooper, January 9, 1863, ibid., p. 388.

38 REL to Seddon, January 10, 1863, ibid., pp. 388–90.

39 REL to Davis, January 13, 1863, ibid., pp. 390–91.

40 REL to Gustavus W. Smith, January 4, 1863, ibid., p. 384.

41 REL to Davis, January 13, 1863, ibid., pp. 390–91.

42 REL to Seddon, January 5, 1863, ibid., pp. 385–86, REL to Davis, January 6, 1863, p. 388.

43 William Allan, "Memoranda of Conversations with General Robert E. Lee," Gary W. Gallagher, ed., *Lee the Soldier* (Lincoln: University of Nebraska Press, 1996), pp. 11–12.

44 REL to Davis, January 19, 1863, *Wartime Papers*, pp. 391–92.

45 REL to Wade Hampton, January 20, 1863, ibid., p. 393.

46 REL to Davis, January 23, 1863, ibid., p. 394.

47 REL to MCL, January 29, 1863, ibid., pp. 395–96.

48 REL to Agnes Lee, February 6, 1863, ibid., p. 400.

49 REL to Davis, February 16, 1863, ibid., p. 376.

50 REL to Davis, February 18, 1863, ibid., p. 405.

51 REL to Seddon, February 4, 1863, ibid., p. 398, REL to Davis, February 5, 1863, p. 399, February 16, 1863, p. 376, February 18, 1863, p. 405, REL to Longstreet, February 18, 1863, p. 406.

52 REL to MCL, February 23, 1863, ibid., p. 407.

53 REL to Davis, February 26, 1863, ibid., p. 409.

54 REL to GWCL Lee, February 28, 1863, ibid., p. 411.

55 REL to MCL, March 9, 1863, ibid., p. 413.

56 REL to CCL, March 24, 1863, Special Collections, UVA.

57 REL to MCL, December 21, 1862, *Wartime Papers*, p. 378, REL to Mildred Lee, December 25, 1862, p. 381.

58 REL to MCL, January 29, 1863, ibid., p. 396.

59 REL to Mary, February 8, 1863, ibid., p. 401.

60 REL to MCL, March 9, 1863, ibid., p. 413.

61 New London, CT, *New London Daily Chronicle*, February 20, 1863.

62 REL to MCL, March 27, 1863, *Wartime Papers*, p. 419.

63 REL to MCL, April 5, 1863, ibid., pp. 427–28.

64 REL to Seddon, March 27, 1863, ibid., p. 419.

65 REL to Longstreet, March 27, 1863, ibid., p. 417.

66 REL to CCL, March 24, 1863, Special Collections, UVA.

67 REL to MCL, February 8, 1863, *Wartime Papers*, p. 401.

68 REL to MCL, February 23, 1863, ibid., p. 408, REL to GWCL, February 28, 1863, pp. 411–12.

69 REL to Davis, January 6, 1863, ibid., p. 387.

70 REL to MCL, April 3, 1863, ibid., p. 427.

71 REL to Michelbacher, April 2, 1863, Ezekiel and Lichtenstein, *Jews of Richmond*, p. 162.

72 REL to Seddon, April 9, 1863, *Wartime Papers*, p. 430.

73 REL to Davis, April 16, 1863, ibid., p. 435.

74 REL to Cooper, April 16, 1863, ibid., p. 434.

75 REL to MCL, April 19, 1863, ibid., pp. 437–38.

76 REL to Jackson, April 25, 1863, photocopy provided by Robert K. Krick, from Clifford Dowdey, *Lee* (Boston: Little, Brown, 1965), p. 741, which misdates the document to 1862.

77 Richmond, *Examiner*, May 1, 1863; REL to MCL, March 21, 1863, *Wartime Papers*, p. 416, April 24, 1863, p. 440. The *Examiner* notice says Minnis went to the army with his camera. Lee's April 24 letter refers to "Mr. Carole" coming to photograph him, an obvious error in transcription of "Cowell." The inference that Mary might have had something to do with the photographer(s) coming to the army is drawn from that same letter.

78 REL to MCL, April 24, 1863, *Wartime Papers*, pp. 439–40, REL to Longstreet, April 27, 1863, p. 441.

79 See communications in Ibid., pp. 441–45.

80 USG to Kelton, December 25, 1862, *PUSG*, 7, p. 105, USG to Halleck, January 4, 1863, p. 170.

81 USG to John K. Mizner, December 21, 1862, ibid., p. 88, USG to McPherson, December 25, 1862, p. 110.

82 USG to Hurlbut, January 3, 1863, ibid., p. 167, USG to James C. Veatch, January 22, 1863, p. 245.

83 USG to McPherson, December 31, 1862, ibid., p. 150.

84 USG to McPherson, January 1, 1863, ibid., p. 155.

85 USG to McPherson, December 31, 1862, ibid., p. 148, January 4, 1863, pp. 174–75, USG to Hamilton, January 1, 1863, p. 156, USG to Halleck, January 2, 1863, pp. 158–59, USG to Halleck, January 4, 1863, p. 171, USG to Washburne, January 7, 1863, p. 196, USG to Halleck, January 9, 1863, p. 204.

86 USG to Porter, January 10, 1863, ibid., p. 206.

87 For a detailed examination of Grant's several attempts to approach Vicksburg, and of the campaign itself, see Edwin Cole Bearss, *The Campaign for Vicksburg* (Dayton, OH: Morningside House, 1985–1986), 3 vols. A very good general account in briefer compass is William L. Shea and Terrence J. Winschel, *Vicksburg Is the Key: The Struggle for the Mississippi River* (Lincoln: University of Nebraska Press, 2003).

88 USG to Halleck January 11, 1863, *PUSG*, 7, p. 209.

89 USG to McClernand, January 11, 1863, ibid., p. 210, January 13, 1863, p. 218.

90 USG to Halleck, January 18, 1863, ibid., p. 231.

91 USG to Halleck, January 20, 1863, ibid., pp. 233–35.

92 USG to McClernand, January 18, 1863, ibid., p. 231.

93 USG to Julia, January 28, 1863, ibid., p. 253, USG to Julia, January 31, 1863, p. 270.

94 USG to McClernand, January 31, 1863, ibid., p. 264 and ff.

95 USG to Kelton, February 1, 1863, ibid., pp. 274–75n. In fact, Grant was out on a rigorous personal reconnaissance with Porter on that day, nowhere close enough for Kountz to have seen him personally, though the two were briefly at Milliken's Bend at the same time on March 16, when Grant got back and before Kountz left that same day. Thus Kountz could have heard something from someone who had been on the reconnaissance, but the claim of officers of high rank as substantiation, in that brief interval, strains credulity.

96 USG to Kelton, February 4, 1863, ibid., p. 281.

97 USG to Porter, January 30, 1863, ibid., p. 257, USG to McClernand, January 30, 1863, pp. 257–58.

98   USG to McPherson, February 5, 1863, ibid., pp. 284–85.

99   USG to Halleck, March 7, 1`863, ibid., pp. 399–400, USG to McPherson, March 11, 1863, p. 411.

100 USG to McPherson, March 16, 1863, ibid., p. 422, USG to Halleck, March 17, 1862, p. 427, USG to David G. Farragut, March 23, 1863, pp. 458–59.

101 USG to McClernand, January 22, 1863, ibid., p. 239.

102 USG to Halleck, January 29, 1863, ibid., pp. 253–54, USG to Kelton, February 4, 1863, p. 281, USG to Kelton, February 6, 1863, p. 286, USG to Commanding Officer, February 7, 1863, pp. 296–97.

103 USG to Porter, February 14, 1863, ibid., p. 323.

104 USG to Halleck, February 16, 1863, ibid., pp. 333–34, USG to McPherson, February 27, 1863, p. 366, March 5, 1863, pp. 388–89.

105 USG to Halleck, March 7, 1863, ibid., p. 400, USG to Washburne, March 10, 1865, p. 409.

106 USG to Halleck, March 17, 1863, ibid., pp. 427–28, USG to Prentiss, March 17, 1863, pp. 429–30, USG to McClernand, March 18, 1863, p. 441, Grant to Nathaniel Banks, March 23, 1863, p. 446.

107 USG to McPherson, March 14, 1863, ibid., USG to Sherman, March 16, 1863, pp. 424–25, USG to Halleck, March 17, 1863, p. 428.

108 USG to Prentiss, March 17, 1863, ibid., p. 430, USG to Banks, March 23, 1861, p. 446.

109 USG to Quinby, March 23, 1861, ibid., p. 463, USG to Halleck, March 27, 1863, p. 478.

110 USG to Julia, February 9, 1863, ibid., p. 309.

111 USG to Julia, February 11, 1863, ibid., p. 311, February 14, 1863, p. 325, March 6, 1863, p. 396.

112 USG to Julia, February 15, 1863, ibid., pp. 330–31.

113 New York, *Tribune*, May 25, 1866.

114 USG to Hillyer, February 5, 1862, *PUSG*, 32, p. 43.

115 USG to Julia, February 11, 1863, *PUSG*, 7, p, 311.

116 USG to William F. Raynolds, February 23, 1863, *PUSG*, 32, p. 45.

117 USG to Halleck, February 2, 1863, *PUSG*, 7, p. 280.

118 USG to Halleck, March 27, 1863, ibid., p. 478.

119 USG to Sherman, February 27, 1863, ibid., p. 367.

120 USG to Porter, March 23, 1863, ibid., pp. 456–57.

121 USG to Porter, March 26, 1863, ibid., p. 475.

122 USG to Charles A. Reynolds, March 25, 1863, ibid., p. 471, USG to Robert Allen, March 26, 1863, p. 476.

123 USG to Sherman, March 22, 1863, ibid., pp. 455–56.

124 USG to Julia, March 27, 1863, ibid., pp. 479–80.

125 USG to Porter, April 2, 1863, *PUSG*, 8, pp. 3–4.

126 USG to Porter, March 29, 1863, *PUSG*, 7, p. 486.

127 USG to Julia, March 30, 1863, ibid., pp. 490–91.

128 USG to Julia, April 3, 1863, *PUSG*, 8, p. 9.

129 USG to Halleck, April 4, 1863, ibid., p. 12.

130 USG to Halleck, April 19, 1863, ibid., p. 91.

131 USG to Halleck, April 12, 1863, ibid., p. 53, USG to McClernand, April 11, 1863, p. 47, April 12, 1863, p. 56, April 18, 1863, p. 88.

132 USG to Jesse Grant, April 21, 1863, ibid., pp. 109–10.

133 USG to Sherman, April 24, 1863, ibid., p. 117.

134 USG to McClernand, April 25, 1863, ibid., 119.

135 USG to Halleck, April 27, 1863, ibid., p. 122, USG to McClernand, April 27, 1863, pp. 126–27.

136 USG to Sherman, April 27, 1863, ibid., p. 130.

137 USG to Julia, April 28, 1863, ibid., p. 132.

138 USG to Halleck, April 29, 1863, ibid., p. 133, USG to Sherman, April 29, 1863, p. 135.

139 *PMUSG*, 1, pp. 482–84, 487.

140 Bearss, *Campaign for Vicksburg*, 2, p. 385.

141 USG to Porter, May 1, 1863, *PUSG*, 8, p. 139, USG to Halleck, May 3, 1863, pp. 144–48.

142 USG to Porter, May 1, 1863, ibid., p. 139.

143 The unnamed member of Jackson's staff is quoted in D. H. Hill to R. L. Dabney, July 21, 1864, R. L. Dabney Collection, Union Theological Seminary, Richmond, VA. Hill was not present, of course, and said that Jackson pressed the flank movement while Lee preferred a frontal assault. Three years later Lee said that he had wanted to attack Hooker's exposed flank as soon as possible. REL to Anna Jackson, January 25, 1866, Dabney Collection, Union Theological Seminary.

144 New Orleans, *Picayune*, June 5, 1863.

145 Richmond, *Examiner*, May 19, 1863.

146 Two notes REL to Stuart, May 5, 1863, James E. B. Stuart Papers, Huntington Library, San Marino, CA.

147 REL to GWCL, May 11, 1863, *Wartime Papers*, p. 484.

CHAPTER 12: JULY 1863

1 Lafayette Guild to Samuel P. Moore, May 22, 1863, Jeffrey L. Raw, comp., Outgoing Correspondence of Lafayette Guild, Medical Director, Army of Northern Virginia, Chapter 6, vols. 641–42, RG 109, NA.

2 REL to MCL, February 23, 1862, *Wartime Papers*, p. 118.

3 Krick, "'The Great Tycoon' Forges a Staff System," p. 84n.

4 REL to MCL, May 23, 1863, *Wartime Papers*, p. 491, REL to GWCL, December 29, 1861, p. 98, March 29, 1864, p. 686, April 9, 1864, p. 695.

5 Mobile, *Advertiser & Register*, March 16, 1864.

6 REL to GWCL, January 5, 1863, *Wartime Papers*, p. 385, REL to MCL, June 11, 1863, p. 512.

7 The author is indebted to Robert E. L. Krick for sharing his opinions and insight on this admittedly subjective area.

8 REL to Edward Sparrow, March 20, 1863, *OR*, IV, 2, pp. 446–47.

9 Jeffry D. Wert, "The Tycoon: Lee and His Staff," *Civil War Times Illustrated*, 11 (July 1972), pp. 12–13.

10 Ibid., p. 13.

11 Mobile, *Advertiser & Register*, March 16, 1864.

12 Charles S. Venable to Margaret Venable, June 21, 1863, Venable Papers, UVA.

13 REL to Chilton, n.d. [April 22, 1863], REL to Seddon, December 19, 1863, Robert H. Chilton Combined Service Record, RG 109, NA.

14 Report of a Board of Officers for the examination of the system of military signals devised by Assistant Surgeon A. J. Meyer, March 12, 1859, Letters Received by the Office of the Adjutant General, 1822–1860, RG 94, NA.

15 Jeffry D. Wert, "The Tycoon: Lee and His Staff," p. 11.

16 Sidwell, "Maintaining Order," pp. 19–20, 25, 26, 29, 33–35, 36, 39, 46.

17 Ibid., 53, 73, 79.

18 Ibid., p. 12. Sidwell disagrees with most of Freeman's overall analysis, finding Lee's staff usually highly capable and emphasizing that it improved in the performance of its duties as the war progressed.

19 J. Boone Bartholomees Jr., *Buff Facings and Gilt Buttons: Staff and Headquarters Operations*

in the Army of Northern Virginia, 1861–1865 (Columbia, SC: University of South Carolina Press, 1998), pp. 7–12.

20 REL to Edward Sparrow, March 20, 1863, *OR*, IV, 2, pp. 446–47.

21 REL to Davis, March 21, 1863, ibid., pp. 447–48.

22 REL to A. P. Hill, May 8, 1863, *OR*, I, 25, pt. 2, pp. 786–87.

23 Unless otherwise cited, much of this discussion is drawn from the excellent Krick, "'The Great Tycoon,'" pp. 82–106 passim. Some useful information may be found in R. Steven Jones, *The Right Hand of Command: Use and Disuse of Personal Staffs in the American Civil War* (Mechanicsburg, PA: Stackpole Books, 2000), but it is in the main an operational history of the generals dealt with, with relatively little discrete comment on staff operations.

24 New Orleans, *Picayune*, June 5, 1863.

25 D. Lyon Jr. to My dear Annie, May 14, 1863, copy in Krick collection.

26 Fayetteville, NC, *Observer*, in Augusta, GA, *Chronicle*, June 27, 1863.

27 Springfield, MA, *Republican*, May 30, 1863.

28 REL to Longstreet, May 7, 1863, *Wartime Papers*, p. 458.

29 REL to Seddon, May 10, 1863, ibid., p. 482.

30 REL to Davis, May 11, 1863, ibid., pp. 483–84.

31 REL to CCL, May 24, 1863, transcript, Keith Kehlbeck, Marshall, MI.

32 This planning is ably discussed in Stephen W. Sears, *Gettysburg* (Boston: Houghton, Mifflin, 2003), pp. 5–9.

33 A good essay on this subject is Peter S. Carmichael, "Lee's Search for the Battle of Annihilation," in Carmichael, ed., *Audacity Personified: The Generalship of Robert E. Lee* (Baton Rouge: Louisiana State University Press, 2004), pp. 1–26.

34 REL to CCL, May 24, 1863, transcript, Keith Kehlbeck, Marshall, MI.

35 David Watson to Susan Watson, April 15, 1863, David Watson Letters, copies at Louisa County Historical Society, Louisa, VA.

36 REL to William C. Rives, May 21, 1863, Lee Papers, UVA. Lee expressed almost identical thoughts that same day in REL to John B. Hood, May 21, 1863, *Wartime Papers*, p. 490.

37 REL to Davis, May 20, 1863, ibid., pp. 488–89.

38 REL to Hood, May 21, 1863, ibid., p. 490.

39 Sidwell, "Maintaining Order," p. 15.

40 REL to Seddon, May 20, 1863, *Wartime Papers*, p. 489, REL to Davis, May 20, 1863, p. 489.

41 REL to D. H. Hill, May 25, 1863, ibid., p. 493, REL to Seddon, May 30, 1863, p. 498.

42 REL to MCL, May 23, 1863, ibid., p. 491.

43 REL to Davis, May 29, 1863, ibid., p. 495.

44 REL to D. H. Hill, May 30, 1863, ibid., 497, REL to Davis, May 30, 1863, p. 496.

45 REL to Davis, May 30, 1863, ibid., p. 496.

46 REL to Agnes Lee, May 25, 1863, ibid., p. 492.

47 REL to MCL, May 31, 1863, ibid., p. 499.

48 REL to MCL, June 3, 1863, ibid., p. 500.

49 REL to Cooper, June 4, 1863, ibid., p. 501, REL to A. P. Hill, June 5, 1863, p. 502, REL to Davis, June 7, 1863, p. 502.

50 REL to Seddon, June 8, 1863, ibid., p. 504.

51 REL to MCL, June 9, 1863, ibid., p. 507.

52 REL to Davis, June 10, 1863, ibid., pp. 507–509.

53 REL to MCL, June 11, 1863, ibid., p. 511.

54 REL to A. P. Hill, June 16, 1863, ibid., p. 517, C. S. Venable to Stuart, June 9, 1863, p. 505, REL to Seddon, June 13, 1863, p. 513, REL to GWCL, June 13, 1863, p. 514.

55 Richmond, *Examiner*, June 12, 1863.

56 C. S. Venable to Stuart, June 9, 1863, *Wartime Papers*, p. 505, REL to Cooper, June 15, 1863., pp. 515–16, REL to Mrs. WHFL, June 11, 1863, p. 512.

57 REL to Seddon, June 13, 1863, ibid., p. 513; Richmond, *Whig*, June 12, 1863.

58 Charleston, *Mercury*, June 24, 1863.

59 Fayetteville, NC, *Observer*, in Augusta, GA, *Chronicle*, June 27, 1863.

60 REL to Ewell, June 17, 1863, *Wartime Papers*, p. 518.

61 REL to Longstreet, June 17, 1863, ibid., p. 518.

62 REL to Ewell, June 22, 1863, ibid., p. 524.

63 REL to Davis, June 23, 1863, ibid., p. 527.

64 REL to Stuart, June 22, 1863, ibid., p. 523, June 23, 1863, p. 526.

65 REL to Davis, June 23, 1863, ibid., p. 529.

66 REL to Davis, June 23, 1863, ibid., p. 527, REL to Davis, June 25, 1863, pp. 530–31, REL to Davis, June 25, 1863, p. 532.

67 REL to Davis, June 25, 1863, ibid., pp. 530–31, REL to MCL, May 31, 1863, p. 499, June 3, 1863, p. 500.

68 REL to Ewell, June 28, 1863, ibid., p. 534.

69 REL to MCL, June 30, 1863, ibid., pp. 535–36.

70 Sidwell, "Maintaining Order," pp. 105, 108; Robert K. Krick, *The Smoothbore Volley That Doomed the Confederacy: The Death of Stonewall Jackson and Other Chapters on the Army of Northern Virginia* (Baton Rouge: Louisiana State University Press, 2002), pp. 69–70.

71 Wert, "The Tycoon," p. 16.

72 Justus Scheibert, *Seven Months in the Rebel States During the North American War, 1863* (Tuscaloosa, AL: Confederate Publishing Company, 1958), p. 75n.

73 Sidwell, "Maintaining Order," pp. 109, 112.

74 Ibid., 117.

75 Ibid., pp. 85–86, 115, 119, 120.

76 Ibid., pp. 127–28, maintains that Lee's reluctance to let staff officers give orders in his name was due to the Southern culture of resistance to authority, as he did not want to risk having mere captains delivering orders, which might be offensive to prickly generals. The argument is unconvincing.

77 REL to William M. McDonald, April 15, 1868, New Orleans, *Times-Picayune*, August 30, 1903.

78 Allan, "Memoranda," February 19, 1870, Gallagher, *Lee the Soldier*, p. 18.

79 USG to Sherman, May 3, 1863, *PUSG*, 8, p. 152.

80 USG to Halleck, May 3, 1863, ibid., p. 148.

81 USG to Sherman, May 9, 1863, ibid., p. 183.

82 USG to Sherman, May 3, 1863, ibid., pp. 151–52, USG to Sullivan, May 3, 1863, p. 153, USG to Hillyer, May 5, 1863, p. 163.

83 USG to Hillyer, May 5, 1863, ibid., pp. 162, 163.

84 USG to Halleck, May 6, 1863, ibid., p. 169.

85 USG to Sherman, May 9, 1863, ibid., p. 183–84.

86 USG to McClernand, May 10, 1863, ibid., p. 193.

87 USG to Sherman, May 9, 1863, ibid., p. 183–84.

88 USG to Julia, May 9, 1863, ibid., p. 19.

89 General Orders No. 32, May 7, 1863, ibid., p. 171.

90 USG to Halleck, May 11, 1863, ibid., p. 196.

91 USG to McPherson, May 11, 1863, ibid., p. 200.

92 USG to McClernand, May 12, 1863, ibid., p. 205.

93 USG to Sherman, May 13, 1863, ibid., p. 212.

94   USG to Halleck, May 15, 1863, ibid., p. 220.
95   USG to McClernand, May 13, 1863, ibid., p. 208.
96   USG to Blair, May 16, 1863, ibid., pp. 222–23, USG to McClernand, May 16, 1863, p. 224.
97   USG to Sherman, May 16, 1863, 5:30 a.m., ibid., pp. 227–28.
98   USG to Sherman, May 16, 1863, ibid., pp. 228, 229.
99   USG to Sherman, May 17, 1863, ibid., p. 232.
100 Special Field Orders No. 134, May 19, 1863, ibid., p. 237, USG to Porter, May 19, 1863, p. 239.
101 USG to McClernand, May 19, 1863, ibid., p. 240–41.
102 General Field Orders, May 21 1863, ibid., pp. 245–46, USG to Porter, May 21, 1863, pp. 246–47.
103 USG to Porter, May 23, 1863, ibid., p. 257.
104 USG to Halleck, May 22, 1863, ibid., p. 249.
105 USG to Hurlbut, May 31, 1863, ibid., p. 297.
106 USG to Banks, May 31, 1863, ibid., p. 294.
107 USG to Halleck, May 25, 1863, ibid., p. 267, May 29, 1863, p. 283.
108 USG to Sherman, May 22, 1863, ibid., p. 255.
109 USG to Halleck, June 3, 1863, ibid., p. 304.
110 Rawlins to Grant, June 6, 1863, ibid., pp. 322–23n. Rawlins refers to "the condition of your health" as a reason Grant should have been in bed. In 1898 Dana (*Recollections*, p. 83) said that Grant was ill at this time and went to bed early on June 6, and was unable to make a decision when told it was too dangerous to go on to Haynes' Bluff. Yet Grant wrote to Julia, June 9, 1863, ibid., p. 332, that "I have enjoyed most excellent health during the campaign." In 1887, recounting the same trip, Dana said Grant was "stupidly drunk." Wilson's diary entry would seem to be conclusive, and is the only directly contemporary source.
111 *PUSG*, 8, p. 325n. Wilson's diary entry is dated June 7, yet both of Dana's accounts indicate that whatever Grant did it happened on the evening of June 6, and Grant arose on June 7 in perfect control and feeling fine.
112 USG to Julia, June 9, 1863, ibid., p. 332.
113 USG to Julia, June 15, 1863, ibid., pp. 376–77.
114 USG to Jesse Grant, June 15, 1863, ibid., p. 376.
115 USG to Halleck, May 24, 1863, ibid., p. 261.
116 Ibid., pp. 81n, 254–55n.
117 USG to Thomas, June 26, 1863, ibid., p. 428.
118 Dana to Stanton, June 19, 1863, OR, I, 26, pt. 1, p. 103.
119 General Orders No. 72, May 30, 1863, OR, I, 24, pt. 1, pp. 159–61.
120 McClernand to Grant, June 4, 1863, ibid., pp, 165–66.
121 McClernand to Grant, June 9, 1863, OR, I, 24, pt. 2, p. 48. The earliest identified appearance of the questioned report is in Springfield, *Daily Republican*, May 25, 1863.
122 Sherman to Rawlins, June 17, 1863, OR, I, 24, pt. 1, pp. 162–63, McPherson to Grant, June 18, 1863, pp. 163–64.
123 USG to McClernand, June 17, 1863, PUSG, 8, pp. 384–85.
124 McClernand to USG, June 17, 1863, OR, I, 24, pt. 1, p. 162.
125 Report of Maj. Gen. John A. McClernand, June 17, 1863, ibid., pp. 137–57.
126 USG Endorsement, July 19, 1863, ibid., p. 157.
127 Special Orders No. 164, June 18, 1863, ibid., pp. 164–65, USG to Halleck, June 19, 1863, p. 43, Charles A. Dana to Stanton, June 19, 1863, pp. 102–103.
128 USG to Julia, May 3, 1863, PUSG, 8, p. 155.
129 USG to Kelton, August 9, 1861, PUSG, 2, p. 91, August 11, 1861, p. 98, USG to Julia, August 10, 1861, p. 96, August 26, 1861, p. 141.

130 USG to Thomas, August 31, 1861, ibid., p. 156, General Orders No. 4, September 8, 1861, p. 206.
131 Jones, *Right Hand of Command*, p. 61, argues unconvincingly that Grant made these first staff selections because of a need for "familial comradeship," yet excepting Rawlins, Grant had not been really close with any.
132 USG to Mary Grant, September 11, 1861, *PUSG*, 2, p. 238.
133 USG to Julia, May 24, 1862, *PUSG*, 5, p. 130.
134 General Orders No. 22, December 23, 1861, *PUSG*, 3, p. 331, USG to Simon Cameron, September 16, 1861, p. 268.
135 General Orders No. 21, March 15, 1862, *OR*, I, 10, pt. 2, p. 41.
136 USG to McLean, April 9, 1862, *PUSG*, 5, pp. 34–35.
137 USG to George G. Pride, April 23, 1863, *PUSG*, 8, p. 113.
138 USG to Thomas, April 14, 1863, ibid., p. 69.
139 Jones, *Right Hand*, pp. 86ff.
140 General Orders No. 9, November 11, 1863, *PUSG*, 6, pp. 294–95.
141 Jones, *Right Hand*, p. 97.
142 USG to Kelton, January 23, 1863, *PUSG*, 7, p. 246.
143 USG to Julia, February 9, 1863, ibid., p. 309.
144 USG to Halleck, December 14, 1862, ibid., pp. 28–29.
145 Endorsement May 23, 1863, *PUSG*, 8, p. 548.
146 Ibid., 219n.
147 USG to Julia, June 15, 1863, ibid., p. 377.
148 Jones, *Right Hand*, pp. 117–18.
149 USG to Silas Hudson, November 16, 1862, *PUSG*, 6, p. 320.
150 USG to Washburne, March 10, 1863, *PUSG*, 7, p. 409.
151 USG to Sherman, April 24, 1863, *PUSG*, 8, p. 118, April 27, 1863, p. 130.
152 USG to Joseph B. Plummer, October 18, 1861, *PUSG*, 3, p. 57.
153 USG to Julia, April 20, 1863, *PUSG*, 8, p. 101.
154 "Our New President," *Atlantic Monthly*, 23 (March 1869), p. 380.
155 USG to Prentiss, February 21, 1863, *PUSG*, 7, p. 347, USG to Hillyer, February 27, 1863, p. 368.
156 General Field Orders, June 19, 1863, *PUSG*, 8, p. 394.
157 USG to Sherman, June 25, 1863, ibid., p. 423, USG to Halleck, June 27, 1863, p. 434.
158 USG to Julia, June 29, 1863, ibid., p. 444–45.
159 USG to Pemberton, July 3, 1863, ibid., p. 455.
160 USG to Pemberton, July 3, 1863, ibid., p. 457.
161 USG to Pemberton, July 4, 1863, ibid., p. 467.
162 Special Orders No. 180, July 4, 1863, ibid., pp. 464–65.
163 USG to Porter, June 22, 1863, ibid., p. 402.
164 USG to Pride, June 15, 1863, ibid., p. 379.
165 USG to Sherman, July 3, 1863, ibid., p. 460, July 4, 1863, p. 476.
166 USG to Sherman, July 4, 1863, ibid., p. 477.
167 USG to Halleck, July 4, 1863, ibid., p. 469.

CHAPTER 13: HINTS OF THE INEVITABLE

1 REL to MCL, July 12, 1863, *Wartime Papers*, p. 547.
2 REL to Davis, July 4, 1863, ibid., pp. 538–39.
3 REL to Davis, July 8, 1863, ibid., p. 543.
4 REL to MCL, July 12, 1863, ibid., pp. 547–48.

5   REL to MCL, July 15, 1863, ibid., p. 551.

6   REL to Davis, July 16, 1863, ibid., pp. 552–53.

7   REL to MCL, July 26, 1863, ibid., p. 560.

8   REL to GWCL, August 18, 1863, ibid., p. 592.

9   Order No. 44, Office of the U.S. District Attorney for the Eastern District of Virginia, Confiscation and Seizure Book, box 207, Alexandria Public Library.

10 Salem, MA, *Register*, January 18, 1864.

11 REL to MCL, February 8, 1863, *Wartime Papers*, p. 401.

12 The Putnam letter, dated Fort Albany, VA, April 16, 1863, first appeared in an extract in the May 13, 1863 Springfield, MA, *Republican*, and then in full on May 14, 1863 in the Hartford, CT, *Daily Courant*.

13 Lee to William G. Webster, September 23, 1852, Bowery and Hankinson, *Correspondence*, p. 288.

14 Alexandria, *Gazette*, May 27, 1863. Webster had little reason to love his former friend Lee after the war commenced. His son Calvert Stuart Webster served in the 15th New York Engineers and died August 9, 1862, of disease. His other son William E. Webster supposedly idolized Lee so much that he enlisted in the Confederate army, and was killed at the battle of Cold Harbor, June 27, 1862. Thus the Websters lost two sons in a span of six weeks. This is what Webster refers to in his letter of May 10–12, 1863, when he says "bitterly and immediately as I have suffered from Gen. Lee's defection from his former loyalty, in the loss of everything that made life dear to me." Boston, *Liberator*, May 29, 1863.

15 Boston, *Liberator*, May 29, 1863.

16 Putnam to Editor of the Boston, *Journal*, May 17, 1863, Boston, *Liberator*, May 29, 1863.

17 Washington, PA, *Reporter*, July 1, 1863.

18 Greenfield, MA, *Gazette & Courier*, June 15, 1863. This comes from a blog post at http:// southernhistorian.wordpress.com/2011/06/11/12/. The writer somewhat confuses things himself by referring to the newspaper with the story as the Greenfield, MA, *Courier & Gazette*, whereas its actual name was the *Gazette & Courier*.

19 REL to MCL, June 14, 1863, DeButts-Ely Papers, LC.

20 Richmond, *Examiner*, June 13, 1863.

21 Anne Butler Moore Carter Wickham Memoranda, Henry T. Wickham, comp., and Lois Wingfield Wickham, ed., *Memoirs of the Wickham Family of Hickory Hill, Hanover County, Virginia, 1791–1988* (N. p.: privately published, 2008), p. 39.

22 REL to Floyd, February 1, 1860, Adams, *Letters*, p. 560–61.

23 Williams to Thomas, March 26, 1861, E. D Townsend to Williams, April 15, 1861, Williams to Thomas, June 6, 1861, Letters Received by the Office of the Adjutant General, RG 94, NA; Post Return, Fort Columbus, New York, May 1861, Returns from U.S. Military Posts, 1806–1916, RG 94, NA; REL to Mildred Lee, April 1, 1861, Adams, *Letters*, p. 746; Allan, "Memoranda," p. 10; W. H. Carter, *From Yorktown to Santiago with the 6th U.S. Cavalry* (Baltimore: Lord Baltimore Press, 1900) p. 36.

24 MCL to Anne Carter Wickham, August 7, 1863, Wickham and Wickham, *Memoirs of the Wickham Family*, p. 42; Patrick J. Griffin III, "Tragedy of Two Cousins—Adventurers or Spies?" *The Montgomery County Story*, 34 (November 1991), p. 181. Unless otherwise cited, material in this sketch is drawn from Lawrence Williams Orton CSR, NA.

25 Carter, *Yorktown to Santiago*, pp. 36–38.

26 Bragg to Cooper, December 6, 1862, Special Orders No. 55, December 6, 1862, William Orton Williams to Cooper, December [15], 1862, Lawrence Williams Orton CSR, NA.

27 Anne Butler Moore Carter Wickham Memoranda, Wickham and Wickham, *Memoirs of*

the Wickham Family, p. 39; Henry T. Wickham recollections, Winchester, *Evening Star*, February 23, 1940.

28 REL to William Orton Williams, April 7, 1863, Mary Custis Lee Papers, VHS; Special Orders No. 86, April 2, 1863, *OR*, 52, pt. 2, p. 451.

29 Terry L. Jones, ed., *Campbell Brown's Civil War: With Ewell and the Army of Northern Virginia* (Baton Rouge: LSU Press, 2001), pp. 184–85; William B. Richmond to Alexander Polk, April 1, 1863, Swann Auction Galleries Catalog 2163, lot 86, November 18, 2008. The woman was almost certainly Mrs. Francis H. Lamb, who had been resident in Charleston at least the previous winter (Charleston, *Mercury*, February 27, 1863), and with whom Williams's companion left his valise before his death to be returned to his family (Fannie H. Lamb to Walter Henderson, October 10, 1863, Armistead Peter Papers, Tudor Hall, Washington, DC).

30 Griffin, "Tragedy of Two Cousins," p. 182. Even the Confederate press said Williams was "brave to rashness," but his "courage was not tempered with prudence." The Richmond, *Whig* dismissed him as "a hair-brained, reckless soldier of fortune." While granting his daring, it said "he was all 'dash'" with "little solidity about him, or ballast," concluding, "poor fellow! What was he about?" The whole business was "strange, strange, very strange." Not surprisingly, the Northern press was even less sympathetic, one Washington paper saying that "he died the death of a fool." (Augusta, *Daily Constitutionalist*, June 21, 1863; Richmond, *Whig*, June 30, 1863; Washington, *Evening Star*, June 10, 1863). The novelist Alfred R. Calhoun published a serialized novella based on the story titled "A Mad Exploit," in the Canton, OH, *Repository*, April 7, 14, 21, 1895, and probably syndicated in other papers at the time.

31 Jones, *Campbell Brown's Civil War*, pp. 184–85; Carter, *Yorktown to Santiago*, p. 41.

32 Chattanooga, *Daily Rebel*, June 17, 1863, in Baltimore, *Sun*, June 23, 1863.

33 Letter of Surgeon W. H., June 9, 1863, Richmond, *Whig*, June 19, 1863.

34 REL to MCL, June 14, 1863, DeButts-Ely Papers, LC.

35 REL to MCL, August 17, 1863, ibid.

36 REL to Martha Custis Williams, December 1, 1866, Avery Craven, ed., *"To Markie": The Letters of Robert E. Lee to Martha Custis Williams* (Cambridge: Harvard University Press, 1933), pp. 71–72.

37 REL to MCL, July 7, 1863, *Wartime Papers*, p. 542.

38 It has been claimed erroneously that the Federals beat Williams Carter to death. Not so. He did not die until August 1864.

39 REL to MCL, July 12, 1863, *Wartime Papers*, p. 547.

40 Ibid.

41 Boston, *Daily Advertiser*, August 12, 1863.

42 REL to MCL, August 2, 1863, *Wartime Papers*, p. 566.

43 REL to Davis, June 25, 1863, ibid., pp. 530–31.

44 David G. Smith, "Race and Retaliation: The Capture of African-Americans during the Gettysburg Campaign," Peter Wallenstein and Bertram Wyatt-Brown, *Virginia's Civil War* (Charlottesville: University of Virginia Press, 2005), pp. 137–51 passim.

45 REL to MCL, October 28, 1863, *Wartime Papers*, p. 615.

46 REL to MCL, December 27, 1863, ibid., p. 645, July 26, 1863, p. 559.

47 REL to Margaret Stuart, July 26, 1863, ibid., p. 561, REL to Davis, July 31, 1863, p. 565.

48 REL to Davis, August 8, 1863, ibid., pp. 589–90.

49 Thomas Henry Carter to Susan Carter, September 18, 1863, Carter Letters, VHS.

50 REL to Davis, August 22, 1863, *Wartime Papers*, p. 593.

51 REL to Longstreet, August 31, 1863, ibid., p. 594.

52   REL to MCL, September 4, 1863, ibid., p. 595.

53   REL to Davis, September 11, 1863, ibid., p. 599.

54   REL to Davis, September 14, 1863, ibid., p. 600.

55   REL to Michelbacher, September 20, 1864, Ezekiel and Lichtenstein, *Jews of Richmond*, pp. 162–63.

56   REL to Davis, September 23, 1863, *Wartime Papers*, pp. 602–603.

57   REL to Longstreet, September 25, 1863, ibid., p. 605.

58   William H. Perry, Jr. to William H. Perry, Sr., November 3, 1863, William Hartwell Perry Letters, 1860–1865, UVA. Long, *Memoirs*, p. 311, gives nearly the same quotation.

59   David Gregg McIntosh to Mary G. Lee, November 5, 1863, David Gregg McIntosh Papers, VHS.

60   Thomas H. Carter to Susan Carter, November 10, 1863, Carter Letters, VHS.

61   REL to MCL, October 28, 1863, *Wartime Papers*, p. 616.

62   REL to MCL, October 19, 1863, ibid., p. 611.

63   REL to Polk, October 26, 1863, ibid., pp. 614–15.

64   REL to MCL, November 11, 1863, ibid., p. 622.

65   REL to MCL, November 21, 1863, ibid., p. 625.

66   Benjamin Wesley Justice to Ann Justice, November 22, 1863, Benjamin Wesley Justice Papers, Emory University, Atlanta.

67   Allen, "Memoranda," p. 11.

68   Donald C. Pfanz, *Richard S. Ewell, A Soldier's Life* (Chapel Hill: University of North Carolina Press, 1998), p. 346.

69   Pfanz, *Ewell*, p. 347.

70   REL to MCL, December 4, 1863, *Wartime Papers*, p. 631.

71   San Francisco, *Bulletin*, July 12, 1865; Portland, ME, *Daily Advertiser*, July 4, 1863.

72   Portland, *Oregonian*, April 15, 1864.

73   Providence, *Evening Press*, December 31, 1863.

74   USG to Halleck, July 4, 1863, *PUSG*, 8, p. 469, July 6, 1863, p. 484–85, USG to Banks, July 4, 1863, p. 472.

75   USG to Halleck, July 18, 1863, *PUSG*, 9, p. 70.

76   USG to Julia, June 29, 1863, *PUSG*, 8, pp. 444–45.

77   USG to Julia, February 14, 1863, *PUSG*, 7, p. 325.

78   USG to Hurlbut, February 13, 1863, ibid., p. 316.

79   USG to Jesse Grant, April 21, 1863, *PUSG*, 8, p. 110.

80   USG to Thomas Knox, April 6, 1863, ibid., pp. 30–31, USG to Napoleon Buford, April 8, 1863, pp. 37–38, USG to Hurlbut, April 9, 1863, pp. 38–39.

81   USG to Halleck, January 6, 1863, *PUSG*, 7, pp. 186–87.

82   USG to Lincoln, June 11, 1863, *PUSG*, 8, pp. 342–43.

83   USG to Lincoln, August 23, 1863, *PUSG*, 9, pp. 196–97.

84   USG to Halleck, July 24, 1863, ibid., p. 110.

85   USG to Halleck, April 19, 1863, *PUSG*, 8, pp. 91–92, USG to Richard Taylor, June 22, 1863, pp. 400–401, July 4, pp. 468–69, USG to McPherson, July 5, 1863, pp. 483–84.

86   USG to Washburne, August 30, 1863, *PUSG*, 9, pp. 218.

87   USG to Lincoln, June 19, 1863, *PUSG*, 8, p. 395.

88   USG to Lincoln, August 23, 1863, *PUSG* 9, pp. 195–96, USG to Halleck, July 18, 1863, p. 70, July 24, 1863, p. 109, August 1, 1863, pp. 137–38, USG to Dana, August 5, 1863, p. 146.

89   USG to Lincoln, August 23, 1863, ibid., pp. 195–95.

90   Boston, *Saturday Evening Gazette*, July 18, 1863.

91   USG to Dana, August 5, 1863, *PUSG*, 9, pp. 146–47.

92 USG to Dana, August 5, 1863, ibid., p. 146, USG to Washburne, August 30, 1863, pp. 217–18.

93 Dana to Stanton, July 5, 1863, Dana, *Recollections*, p. 102.

94 USG to Halleck, August 31, 1863, *PUSG*, 9, p. 219.

95 Portland, ME, *Daily Eastern Argus*, September 18, 1863. Since Grant was injured and bed-ridden from September 4 on, he could only have risen from bed September 2 or 3. While this source does not make clear which day it was, September 2 seems the more likely, as he would be tired from the trip, and admirers would most likely gather on his first night in the city.

96 New York, *World*, September 12, 1863. Many sources erroneously have the levee on the same day as the review where Grant was injured. See, for instance, Springfield, MA, *Republican*, September 14, 1863; Washington, *Evening Union*, September 12, 1863.

97 The day after the accident Banks implied that Grant was drunk when his horse fell and that this was the cause of the accident. More likely Banks, knowing the rumors about Grant, just assumed that drink was behind the mishap, a common assumption every time Grant fell or stumbled during the war. Yet all other witnesses and reports agree that Grant's horse was spooked either by being clipped by a cart or carriage, or by a railroad whistle, both events for which Grant, drunk or sober, was hardly responsible. What Grant did do was keep his seat on a powerful animal as it reacted wildly, not the act of an inebriated man. General Cadwallader Washburn, whose corps Grant and Banks reviewed, wrote the next day to his brother Elihu Washburne (the brothers used different spellings) and said nothing about Grant being drunk either at the review or in the accident. Bruce Catton, *Grant Takes Command* (Boston: Little, Brown, 1968), pp. 26–27, has a good discussion on the matter. In Benjamin P. Thomas, ed., *Three Years with Grant as Recalled by War Correspondent Sylvanus Cadwallader* (New York: Alfred A. Knopf, 1955), p. 117, Cadwallader refers to the accident and states that he was told it was caused by Grant's being drunk, but makes it clear that he was not himself in New Orleans at the time, and only repeated hearsay. The only reliable source for Grant drinking at all while in New Orleans is Rawlins's reference to "his New Orleans experience" in a November 17, 1863, letter discussing Grant's recent alleged drinking. *PUSG*, 9, p. 475n.

98 USG to Halleck, September 19, 1863, *PUSG*, 9, p. 221.

99 *PMJDG*, p. 121; USG to Kelton, September 25, 1863, *PUSG*, 9, p. 238.

100 USG to Kelton, September 25, 1863, *PUSG*, 9, p. 237, USG to Halleck, September 30, 1863, pp. 251–53,

101 USG to Halleck, October 15, 1863, ibid., p. 284n, Halleck to USG, October 16, 1863, p. 296n.

102 *PMJDG*, p. 123; Halleck to USG, October 16, 1863, *PUSG*, 9, p. 297n.

103 The coolness between Grant and Thomas has never been adequately explained, and virtually no contemporary evidence from either of them or their immediate intimates sheds much light. Catton, *Grant Takes Command*, p. 40, and Peter Cozzens, *The Shipwreck of their Hopes: The Battles for Chattanooga* (Urbana: University of Illinois Press, 1994), pp. 45–46, offer brief but inconclusive discussions of the matter.

104 Quoted in Simpson, *Grant*, p. 231.

105 USG to Halleck, October 28, 1863, *PUSG*, 9, p. 335.

106 USG to Julia, November 2, 1863, ibid., pp. 352–53 and n.

107 USG to Halleck, November 6, 1863, ibid., p. 364.

108 USG to Halleck, November 7, 1863, ibid., p. 368, USG to Burnside, November 7, 1863, pp. 368–69, USG to Thomas, November 7, 1863, p. 371.

109 USG to Burnside, November 8, 1863, ibid., pp. 374–75.

110 USG to Sherman, November 11, 1863, ibid., p. 380.

111 USG to Julia, November 14, 1863, ibid., p. 396–97.

112 USG to Burnside, November 14, 1863, ibid., p. 391, USG to Halleck, November 15, 1863, p. 400.

113 USG to Burnside, November 15, 1863, ibid., p. 401.

114 USG to John Riggin Jr., November 18, 1863, ibid., p. 413.

115 USG endorsement, November 20, 1863, *PUSG*, 32, pp. 178–79; USG to Bragg, November 20, 1863, p. 60.

116 USG to Halleck, November 21, 1863, *PUSG*, 9, p. 428.

117 USG to Orlando B. Willcox, November 23, 1863, ibid., p. 436.

118 USG to Thomas, November 24, 1863, ibid., p. 443.

119 USG to Halleck, November 23, 1863, ibid., p. 434.

120 The facts of the matter on the assault up Missionary Ridge are still not entirely understood, and most of the testimony comes from memoirs written years after the fact, seasoned with considerable hindsight. It is often stated that Grant was angry when he saw it, demanding to know if Thomas had ordered it, and threatening that someone would pay for it if the assault failed. Montgomery Meigs was with Grant at the time, however, and in his diary that night he wrote only that Grant was surprised, said he had not ordered it, but immediately adapted his plans to the moment and ordered a general attack. *PUSG*, 9, p. 448n. See also Simpson, *Grant*, pp. 495–96.

121 USG to Halleck, November 25, 1863, *PUSG*, 9, p. 446.

122 USG to Julia, November 30, 1863, ibid., p. 478.

123 USG to McPherson, December 1, 1863, ibid., pp. 480–81.

CHAPTER 14: "IF DEFEATED NOTHING WILL BE LEFT US TO LIVE FOR."

1   USG to J. Russell Jones, December 5, 1863, *PUSG*, 9, p. 496.

2   USG to Halleck, December 7, 1863, ibid., pp. 500–502n.

3   USG to Washburne, December 12, 1863, ibid., p. 522–23.

4   USG to Barnabas Burns, December 17, 1863, ibid., p. 541.

5   Easton, MD, *Gazette*, November 21, 1863.

6   New York, *Herald*, December 11, 15, 23, 1863.

7   Washburne to Grant, January 24, 1864, *PUSG*, 9, p. 523n.

8   *PUSG*, 9, p. 543n.

9   USG to Jesse Grant, December 13, 1863, ibid., p. 524.

10   USG to Halleck, December 17, 1863, ibid., p. 534.

11   Portland, *Oregonian*, April 15, 1864.

12   USG to Thomas, December 22, 1863, *PUSG*, 9, p. 549.

13   Portland, *Oregonian*, April 15, 1864.

14   USG to Halleck, December 23, 1863, *PUSG*, 9, pp. 551–52.

15   USG to Julia, December 28, 1863, ibid., p. 576.

16   USG to Henry Wilson, February 3, 1864, *PUSG*, 10, p. 77.

17   USG to Halleck, January 15, 1864, ibid., pp. 14–16.

18   USG to Halleck, January 19, 1864, ibid., pp. 39–41n.

19   USG to ?, [August 22, 1847], Emerson, "Grant's Life in the West," 7 (April 1897), p. 324.

20   USG to Julia, February 10, 1864, *PUSG*, 10, p. 100.

21   USG to Isaac Morris, January 20, 1864, ibid., p. 53, USG to Daniel Ammen, February 16, 1864, pp. 132–33.

22   New York, *Herald*, February 3, 1864.

23   USG to Jesse Grant, January 31, 1864 *PUSG*, 10, p. 75n.

24   USG to Julia, February 3, 1864, ibid., p. 76.

25 USG to Daniel Ammen, February 16, 1864, ibid., pp. 132–33.
26 *PUSG*, 9, pp. 475–76n. William F. Smith wrote at the time that Grant broke up Lagow's spree but made no mention of Grant drinking as well. Wilson agreed, and David Hunter shared a room with Grant at the time and wrote that Grant was sober throughout and "seldom drinks," having no more than two drinks in three weeks.
27 Ibid., p. 476n.
28 USG to Alvin P. Hovey, February 9, 1864, *PUSG*, 10, pp. 96–97, USG to Halleck, February 11, 1864, p. 101.
29 USG to Julia, February 17, 1864, ibid., p. 138.
30 USG to Sherman, March 4, 1864, ibid., pp. 186–87.
31 USG to Francis Preston Blair, Jr., February 28, 1864, ibid., pp. 166–67.
32 USG to Julia, February 17, 1864, ibid., p. 138.
33 USG to Sherman, March 4, 1864, ibid., pp. 187–88n.
34 *PMUSG*, 2, pp. 122–23; Interview, May 9, 1878, *PUSG*, 28, p. 382.
35 New York, *Herald*, July 24, 1878.
36 REL to Davis, December 3, 1863, *Wartime Papers*, pp. 641–42.
37 Davis to Lee, December 5 [6], 1863, *OR*, I, 31, pt. 3, p. 785.
38 REL to Davis, December 7, 1863, *Wartime Papers*, p. 642.
39 Davis to REL, December 8, 1863, Lynda Lasswell Crist, ed., *The Papers of Jefferson Davis: Volume 10, October 1863–August 1864* (Baton Rouge: Louisiana State University Press, 1999), p. 104.
40 REL to Stuart, December 9, 1863, *Wartime Papers*, p. 642.
41 These several reports will be found calendared in Crist, *Davis Papers*, 10, pp. 105–109.
42 Polk to Davis, December 8, 1863, *OR*, I, 31, pt. 3, pp. 796–97.
43 Taylor to Bettie Saunders, December 20, 1863, R. Lockwood Tower, ed., *Lee's Adjutant: The Wartime Letters of Colonel Walter Herron Taylor, 1862–1865* (Columbia: University of South Carolina Press, 1995), p. 101.
44 REL to Davis, January 2, 1863, *Wartime Papers*, p. 647.
45 REL to Lucius B. Northrop, January 5, 1864, ibid., pp. 647–48.
46 General Orders No. 7, January 22, 1864, ibid., p. 659.
47 REL to Seddon, January 22, 1863, ibid., pp. 659–60.
48 REL to MCL, January 24, 1864, ibid., p. 661.
49 REL to James L. Kemper, January 29, 1864, ibid., pp. 663–64.
50 REL to MCL, January 24, 1864, ibid., p. 661.
51 Boston, *Daily Advertiser*, May 13, 1864, taken from the Mobile *Register*.
52 Milwaukee, *Journal of Commerce*, November 1, 1871.
53 Taylor to Saunders, December 20, 1863, Tower, *Lee's Adjutant*, p. 101.
54 Taylor to Saunders, February 21, 1864, Tower, *Lee's Adjutant*, p. 123; REL to MCL, February 21, 1864, *Wartime Papers*, p. 671.
55 REL to WHFL, April 24, 1864, Gilder Lehrman Collection.
56 Taylor to Saunders, December 20, 1863, Tower, *Lee's Adjutant*, p. 101.
57 REL to Davis, February 3, 1864, *Wartime Papers*, p. 667.
58 REL to Davis, February 18, 1864, ibid., p. 675.
59 REL to Seddon, April 30, 1864, in the Michael Masters collection as of 2002.
60 REL to Davis, March 25, 1864, *Wartime Papers*, pp. 682–84.
61 REL to Longstreet, March 28, 1864, ibid., pp. 684–85.
62 REL to GWCL, March 29, 1864, ibid., p. 686.
63 Taylor to Bettie Saunders, April 3, 1864, Tower, *Lee's Adjutant*, p. 148.
64 REL to Bragg, April 13, 1864, *Wartime Papers*, p. 698.

65   REL to Seddon, April 12, 1864, ibid., pp. 696–97.

66   REL to Davis, April 15, 1864, ibid., pp. 699–700.

67   REL to Davis, April 30, 1864, ibid., p. 709.

68   Thomas J. Goree to Sarah Goree, April 26, 1864, Thomas W. Cutrer, ed., *Longstreet's Aide: The Civil War Letters of Major Thomas J. Goree* (Charlottesville: University Press of Virginia, 1995), p. 123.

69   REL to Davis, April 25, 1864, *Wartime Papers*, p. 706.

70   Taylor to Saunders, December 27, 1863, Tower, *Lee's Adjutant*, p. 104.

71   Taylor to Saunders, December 5, 1863, ibid., p. 94.

72   General Orders No. 15, February 7, 1864, *Wartime Papers*, pp. 668–69.

73   Edward Richardson Crockett Diary, April 29, 1864, Center for American History, University of Texas, Austin.

74   Gary W. Gallagher, ed., *Fighting for the Confederacy: The Personal Recollections of General Edward Porter Alexander* (Chapel Hill: University of North Carolina Press, 1989), pp. 345–46; *Lee*, 3, p. 267.

75   REL to MCL, April 23, 1864, *Wartime Papers*, p. 705.

76   REL to MCL, April 9, 1864, ibid., p. 695, REL to Davis, April 19, 1864, p. 704.

77   REL to Blair Robertson, April 30, 1864, Richmond, *Times-Dispatch*, July 14, 1907.

78   USG to Banks, March 15, 1864, *PUSG*, 10, pp. 200–201.

79   USG to T. Lyle Dickey, March 15, 1864, ibid., p. 208.

80   USG to Halleck, March 28, 1864, ibid., p. 232.

81   USG to Halleck, March 25, 1864, ibid., p. 222.

82   USG to Sherman, April 4, 1864, ibid., pp. 252–53.

83   USG to Benjamin F. Butler, April 2, 1864, ibid., pp. 246–47.

84   USG to Julia, March 25, 1864, ibid., p. 225.

85   USG to Julia, April 17, 1864, ibid., p. 315.

86   New York, *Herald*, July 24, 1878.

87   USG to Meade, April 9, 1864, *PUSG*, 10, p. 274.

88   USG to Meade, April 17, 1864, ibid., p. 309, USG to Butler, April 19, 1864, p. 328.

89   USG to Julia, April 24, 1864, ibid., p. 350.

90   USG to Butler, April 19, 1864, ibid., p. 328.

91   USG to Halleck, April 22, 1864, ibid., p. 340.

92   USG to Halleck, April 29, 1864, ibid., p. 371.

93   USG to Julia, April 30, 1864, ibid., p. 377.

94   USG to Lincoln, May 1, 1864, ibid., p. 380.

95   USG to Julia, May 2, 1864, ibid., p. 394.

96   USG to Halleck, May 4, 1864, ibid., p. 397.

97   Robert K. Krick, *Civil War Weather in Virginia* (Tuscaloosa: University of Alabama Press, 2007), p. 129.

98   USG to Halleck, May 4, 1864, *PUSG*, 10, p. 397.

99   USG to Burnside, May 2, 1864, ibid., p. 388.

100 REL to Davis, May 4, 1864, *Wartime Papers*, p. 719.

101 USG to Meade, May 5, 1864, *PUSG*, 10, p. 399.

102 C. Marshall to Ewell, May 6, 1864, *Wartime Papers*, p. 721.

103 Robert K. Krick, "Lee to the Rear," the Texans Cried," Gary W. Gallagher, ed., *The Wilderness Campaign* (Chapel Hill: University of North Carolina Press, 1997), pp. 161, 178–86.

104 USG to Halleck, May 6, 1864, *PUSG*, 10, p. 400.

105 USG to Halleck, May 7, 1864, ibid., p. 405.

106 New York *Herald*, July 24, 1878.

107 Gordon C. Rhea, *The Battle of the Wilderness, May 5–6, 1864* (Baton Rouge: Louisiana State University Press, 1994), pp. 435, 440. Rhea's study is the most detailed narrative to date of this action.

108 USG to Halleck, May 8, 1864, *PUSG*, 10, p. 411.

109 W. H. Taylor to Stuart, May 7, 1864, *Wartime Papers*, p. 723.

110 Taylor to Ewell, May 7, 1864, ibid., p. 724.

111 REL statement April 27, 1864, Museum of the Confederacy.

112 USG to Burnside, May 8, 1864, *PUSG*, 10, p. 413.

113 USG to Halleck, May 9, 1864, ibid., p. 418.

114 REL to MCL, May 16, 1864, *Wartime Papers*, p. 731.

115 USG to Stanton, May 11, 1864, *PUSG*, 10, p. 422.

116 USG to Halleck, May 12, 1864, ibid., p. 428.

117 Gordon C. Rhea, *The Battles for Spotsylvania Court House and the Road to Yellow Tavern, May 7–12, 1864* (Baton Rouge: Louisiana State University Press, 1997), pp. 249–50. For extensive accounts of the Spotsylvania fighting, see this, and also William D. Matter, *If It Takes All Summer: The Battle for Spotsylvania* (Chapel Hill: University of North Carolina Press, 1988).

118 USG to Stanton, May 13, 1864, *PUSG*, 10, p. 434.

119 Ibid., p. 460n.

120 REL, Message to the Army of Northern Virginia, ca. May 14, 1864, Gilder Lehrman Collection.

121 USG to Julia, May 13, 1864, *PUSG*, 10, p. 444.

CHAPTER 15: "A MERE QUESTION OF TIME."

1   USG to Julia, May 19, 1864, *PUSG*, 32, p. 63.

2   REL to Davis, May 22, 1864, *Wartime Papers*, p. 746.

3   REL to Davis, May 23, 1864, ibid., p. 747.

4   REL to MCL, May 23, 1864, ibid., p. 748.

5   REL to T. V. Moore, May 30, 1864, Gilder Lehrman Collection.

6   Gordon C. Rhea, *To the North Anna River: Grant and Lee, May 13–25, 1864* (Baton Rouge: Louisiana State University Press, 2000), pp. 325–26. This is a fine and densely detailed account of the North Anna operations.

7   New York, *Tribune*, May 25, 1866.

8   USG to Halleck, May 26, 1864, *PUSG*, 10, p. 491.

9   Pfanz, *Ewell*, pp. 397–401.

10 USG to Julia, June 1, 1864, *PUSG*, 11, p. 5.

11 USG to Halleck, June 3, 1864, ibid., p. 9.

12 Krick, *Weather*, pp. 129, 132.

13 USG to Halleck, June 5, 1864, *PUSG*, 11, pp. 19–20.

14 USG to Washburne, June 9, 1864, ibid., p. 32.

15 J. William Jones, *Personal Reminiscences, Anecdotes and Letters of Gen. Robert E. Lee* (New York: D. Appleton, 1875), p. 40, quoting Jubal Early's January 19, 1872, address at Washington and Lee University.

16 Abner Embry McGarity to wife, June 12, 1864, Edmund C. Burnett, ed., "Letters of a Confederate Surgeon: Dr. Abner Embry McGarity, 1862–1865," *Georgia Historical Quarterly* 29 (December 1945), p. 243.

17 REL to Davis, June 14, 1864, *Wartime Papers*, pp. 777–78.

18 REL to Davis, June 14, 1864, ibid., p. 779.

19 USG to Meade, June 18, 1864, *PUSG*, 11, p. 78.

20　Frank Buchser Diary, October 1869, quoted in Charles Bracelen Flood, *Lee, Last Years* (New York: Houghton, Mifflin, 1981), p. 220.

21　REL to Davis, July 26, 1862, *Wartime Papers*, p. 238, August 14, 1862, p. 254.

22　REL to Davis, June 5, 1862, ibid., p. 184.

23　REL to Davis, August 14, 1862, ibid., p. 254.

24　Davis to REL, August 11, 1863, Crist, *Papers of Jefferson Davis*, 9, p. 338.

25　Stephen R. Mallory Diary, n.d., Stephen R. Mallory Papers, Southern Historical Collection, University of North Carolina, Chapel Hill.

26　REL to MCL, August 5, 1855, Adams, *Letters*, p. 41.

27　Joseph T. Glatthaar, *General Lee's Army: From Victory to Collapse* (New York: Free Press, 2008), p. 409.

28　William Harmon to J. H. Pierce, August 16, 1863, William H. Crawford CSR.

29　This figure is very approximate, of course, given the destruction of many records at the end of the war. It is compiled from the surviving general orders and other sources as presented in Thomas P. Lowry and Lewis Laska, *Confederate Death Sentences: A Reference Guide* (Charleston, SC: Booksurge, 2009), pp. 9–24, 55ff, with the addition of 27 additional cases from Lee's Special Orders No. 96 of April 7, 1864 (Orders and Circulars Issued by the Army of the Potomac and the Army and Department of Northern Virginia, C.S.A., 1861–1865, M921, National Archives, Roll 4). The figures in Lowry and Laska for those actually executed have been adjusted by examination of the combined service records in the National Archives of the men involved, and the elimination of cases shown to have been pardoned or suspended.

30　Thomas P. Lowry, *A Thousand Stories You Didn't Know About the Civil War* (N.p.: Published by author, 2014), pp. 46–50, states that 133 were executed, a figure apparently based on the assumption that if general orders did not announce a reprieve or suspension, then the sentence was carried out. However, examination of the compiled service records of all the 218 men condemned reveal that besides the 53 known to have been shot, almost all of the others were suspended indefinitely with no further action, or the men were returned to their units; the ultimate disposition of a dozen or so cannot be determined. Also, the 27 condemned men given pardon by Lee in Special Orders No. 96, April 7, 1864, cited above have been factored out.

31　Special Orders No. 96, April 7, 1864, M921, Roll 4, NA.

32　General Orders No. 2, February 11, 1865, *OR*, I, 46, pt. 2, pp. 1229–30.

33　Lowry, *A Thousand Stories*, p. 48.

34　Circular, January 11, 1864, Olde Soldier Books, Inc. Catalog #192, December 2003, item #118.

35　USG to John J. Abercrombie, May 31, 1864, *PUSG*, 10, pp. 500–501.

36　*PUSG*, 6, p. 91n.

37　USG to Lorenzo Thomas, October 28, 1862, *PUSG*, 10, p. 204 and n.

38　Case files nn1694, mm997, mm995, Court Court-martial Case Files, Records of the Judge Advocate General's Office (Army), Entry 15, RG 153, NA; USG to Stanton, June 30–July 2, 1864, *PUSG*, 11, p. 442.

39　Case files mm2377, mm28, mm984, mm980, mm1019, mm98, RG 153, NA.

40　USG to Yates, February 26, 1863, *PUSG*, 7, pp. 534–35.

41　Endorsement, October 7, 1863, *PUSG*, 32, pp. 57–58.

42　Case file nn3058, mm992, RG 153, NA.

43　*PUSG*, 13, p. 521.

44　USG to Thomas Hendrickson, June 26, 1863, *PUSG*, 8, pp. 432–33.

45　Halleck to USG May 12, 1864, *PUSG*, 10, p. 428n.

46 Case file nn2163, RG 153, NA.

47 Case file mm189, ibid.; USG Endorsement, March 26, 1863, *PUSG*, 7, pp. 547–48.

48 Case file 00114, 00111, RG 153, NA.

49 Case file mm971, mm984, ibid.

50 Case files 00307, 00483, nn348, ibid.; *PUSG*, 13, p. 535.

51 Case file mm1035, RG 153, NA.

52 Edward C. Johnson, Gail R. Johnson, and Melissa Johnson Williams, *All Were Not Heroes: A Study of "the List of U.S. Soldiers Executed by U.S.: Military Authorities During the Late War"* (Chicago: privately published, 1997), pp. 430–39. In this admittedly incomplete "official" list, only one execution is listed for Grant's commands from fall 1861 to spring 1864.

53 *PUSG*, 12, p. 467n.

54 Case file nn1750, RG 153, NA.

55 Case file 11875, ibid.

56 Case files mm358, mm556, ibid.

57 Case files nn355, mm158, ibid.

58 *PUSG*, 14, p. 148n.

59 *PUSG* 13, p. 374–75, USG to Stanton February 6, 1865, pp. 378–79.

60 Thomas P. Lowry, *Don't Shoot That Boy! Abraham Lincoln and Military Justice* (Mason City, IA: Savas Publishing, 1999), pp. 261–62. While according to RG 153 the number of capital court-martial sentences Grant definitely reviewed totaled just thirty-seven, it seems probable that a few are missing or incomplete. The author is indebted to Thomas and Beverly Lowry for access to the results of their path-breaking work in these files.

61 San Francisco, *Bulletin*, October 9, 1862.

62 Lowell, MA, *Daily Citizen and News*, August 6, 1864; Richmond, *Whig* June 10, 1864.

63 Troy, NY, *Times*, October 8, 1864.

64 New York, *Tribune*, May 25, 1866.

65 USG to J. Russell Jones, July 5, 1864, *PUSG*, 32, p. 176.

66 REL to MCL, June 19, 1864, *Wartime Papers*, p. 793, November 16, 1864, p. 869, November 30, 1864, p. 873.

67 REL to MCL, September 18, 1864, ibid., p. 855.

68 REL to A. R. Lawton, July 21, 1864, Augusta, GA, *Chronicle*, November 11, 1903.

69 REL to Lawton, July 27, 1864, in Michael Masters collection as of 2002.

70 Mobile, *Advertiser & Register*, September 25, 1864.

71 REL to Mildred Lee, July 5, 1864, *Wartime Papers*, p. 814.

72 REL to MCL, June 30, 1864, Lee Family Papers, VHS.

73 REL to MCL, December 30, 1864, *Wartime Papers*, p. 880.

74 Proclamation, November 7, 1864, Gilder Lehrman Collection.

75 REL to MCL, July 10, 1864, *Wartime Papers*, p. 818.

76 REL to GWCL, July 24, 1864, ibid., p. 825.

77 REL to Seddon, August 23, 1864, ibid., pp. 843–44.

78 REL to Davis, June 26, 1864, ibid., pp. 807–808.

79 REL to Davis, September 2, 1864, ibid., pp. 847–49.

80 Venable to Taylor, March 29, 1878, Walter Herron Taylor Papers, duPont Library, Stratford.

81 William K. Boyd and William H. Wannamaker, eds., "Reminiscences of General Robert E. Lee, 1865–1868, by George Taylor Lee," *The South Atlantic Quarterly*, 26 (July, 1927), pp. 236–37.

82 REL to Louis T, Wigfall, February 8, 1865, Gilder Lehrman Collection.

83 REL to Haywood Brahan, January 30, 1865, Houston, *Telegraph*, May 17, 1865.

84 REL to Henry A. Wise, February 4, 1865, Richmond, *Daily Dispatch*, February 17, 1865.

85 REL to Davis, September 2, 1864, *Wartime Papers*, pp. 847–49.

86 REL to Andrew Hunter, January 11, 1865, *OR*, IV, 3, pp. 1012–13.

87 REL to Davis, March 10, 1865, *Wartime Papers*, p. 914.

CHAPTER 16: MEETING AGAIN

1   USG to Jesse Grant, July 5, 1864, *PUSG*, 32, p. 65.

2   USG to Julia, July 12, 1864, *PUSG*, 11, p. 226.

3   USG to Julia, August 1, 1864, ibid., p. 371.

4   USG to Julia, September 7, 1864, *PUSG*, 12, p. 136, USG to J. Russell Jones, October 4, 1864, p. 278, USG to Julia, August 25, 1864, p. 90, USG to Julia, October 2, 1864, p. 262.

5   USG to Julia, October 24, 1864, ibid., p. 345.

6   USG to William W. Smith, January 1, 1865, *PUSG*, 13, p. 204.

7   USG to Julia, November 25, 1864, ibid., p. 26.

8   Providence, *Evening Press*, June 3, 1864.

9   USG to Isaac N., Morris, August 10, 1864, *PUSG*, 11, pp. 396–97.

10 Lowell, MA, *Daily Citizen and News*, March 18, 1865.

11 USG to Washburne, September 21, 1864, *PUSG*, 12, p. 185.

12 USG to Stanton, September 27, 1864, ibid., pp. 212–13.

13 USG to J. Russell Jones, November 13, 1864, ibid., p. 416.

14 USG to Julia, September 30, 1864, ibid., p. 250.

15 Lincoln to USG, August 17, 1864, *PUSG*, 32, p. 184.

16 Dunbar Rowland, comp., *Jefferson Davis, Constitutionalist* (Jackson, MS: Mississippi Department of Archives and History, 1923), 7, p. 284.

17 USG to Halleck, July 24, 1863, *PUSG*, 9, p. 110, USG to Sherman, March 4, 1864, *PUSG*, 10, p. 190. *PUSG*, 9, pp. 583–84.

18 USG to Sherman, April 4, 1864, *PUSG*, 10, p. 255.

19 USG to Stanton, February 26, 1865, *PUSG*, 14, p. 55.

20 USG to Stanton, July 15, 1864, *PUSG*, 11, p. 250, USG to Halleck, July 24, 1863, *PUSG*, 9, p. 110, USG to Julia, July 1, 1863, *PUSG*, 8, p. 454, USG to Lorenzo Thomas, July 11, 1863, *PUSG*, 9, p. 23, USG to Halleck, August 19, 1864, *PUSG*, 12, pp. 38–39, USG to Ord, August 26, 1864, p. 95.

21 USG to Elias S. Dennis, June 15, 1863, *PUSG*, 8, p. 375.

22 USG to Taylor, July 4, 1863, ibid., p. 468.

23 USG to Lorenzo Thomas, July 11, 1863, *PUSG*, 9, p. 24.

24 USG to Richard Taylor, June 22, 1863, *PUSG*, 8, pp. 400–401.

25 USG to REL, October 2, 1864, *PUSG*, 12, p. 258, REL to USG, October 3, 1864, p. 263.

26 USG to REL, October 20, 1864, ibid., pp. 323–26n.

27 USG to Thomas, December 22, 1864, *PUSG*, 13, p. 151, USG to J. Russell Jones, December 26, 1864, *PUSG*, 32, p. 73.

28 USG to Canby, February 27, 1865, *PUSG*, 14, p. 62.

29 USG to Banks, July 11, 1863, *PUSG*, 9, p. 31.

30 USG to Lincoln, July 25, 1864, *PUSG*, 11, p. 309, USG to Sherman, August 7, 1864, *PUSG*, 11, p. 381.

31 USG to Julia, July 18, 1864, ibid., p. 278.

32 USG to Rawlins, October 29, 1864, *PUSG*, 12, pp. 363–65n.

33 USG to Stanton [January 1–3, 1865], *PUSG*, 13, pp. 199–200. A report of a conversation with Grant in the Cleveland, *Plain Dealer*, March 3, 1865, had him saying Rosecrans took thirty

days to obey the order, which was not true, but it does reflect the special impatience Grant showed toward him.

34 USG to Washburne, July 23 1864, *PUSG*, 11, p. 300.

35 USG to Sherman, December 6, 1864, *PUSG*, 13, p. 73.

36 USG to Thomas, December 6, 1864, ibid., p. 77, USG to Stanton, December 7, 1864, pp. 78–79.

37 USG to Thomas, December 8, 1864, ibid., p. 88, December 9, 1864, p. 96, December 11, 1864, p. 107.

38 USG to Thomas, December 15, 1864, ibid., p. 124, USG to Logan, December 17, 1864, p. 127.

39 USG to Halleck, August 29, 1864, *PUSG*, 12, p. 102.

40 USG to Edward R. S. Canby, February 9, 1865, *PUSG*, 13, p. 397.

41 USG to Sherman, December 18, 1864, ibid., p. 129–30.

42 USG to Sherman, March 16, 1865, *PUSG*, 14, pp. 173–75.

43 USG to Lydia Slocum, August 10, 1864, *PUSG*, 11, p. 397.

44 USG to Julia, January 1, 1865, *PUSG*, 13, p. 203.

45 USG to Sherman, September 10, 1864, *PUSG*, 12, p. 144, September 12, 1864, p. 155, USG to Stanton, October 13, 1864, pp. 302–303.

46 USG to Halleck, November 30, 1864, *PUSG*, 13, pp. 35–36.

47 USG to Sherman, September 12, 1864, *PUSG*, 12, p. 155

48 USG to Irvin McDowell, January 8, 1865, *PUSG*, 13, pp. 250–51.

49 USG to Washburne, February 23, 1865, *PUSG*, 14, p. 31.

50 USG to James L. Crane, January 2, 1865, *PUSG*, 32, p. 73.

51 Meade to Margaretta Meade, December 20, 1863, George Meade, ed., *Life and Letters of George Gordon Meade* (New York: Scribner's, 1913), 2, p. 162.

52 Meade to Margaretta Meade, March 10, 1864, ibid., 2, p. 177, March 14, 1864, p. 178, March 16, 1864, p. 181, March 22, 1864, p. 182, March 24, 1864, p. 183.

53 Meade to Margaretta Meade, March 26, 1864, ibid., p. 183 March 27, 1864, p. 184, April 23, 1864, p. 190.

54 Meade to Margaretta Meade, April 18, 1864, ibid., p. 190.

55 Meade to Margaretta Meade, April 24, 1864, ibid., p. 191.

56 Meade to Margaretta Meade, May 19, 1864, ibid., p. 197.

57 Meade to Margaretta Meade, May 23, 1864, ibid., p. 198, June 5, 1864, p. 201, June 9, 1864, p. 202.

58 Meade to Margaretta Meade, September 15, 1864, ibid., p. 228, November 24, 1864, p. 246.

59 USG to Julia, December 22, 1864, *PUSG*, 13, pp. 152–53.

60 USG to Julia, December 24, 1864, ibid., p. 163.

61 USG to Jesse Grant, September 5, 1864, *PUSG*, 12, p., 130, USG to Julia, October 28, 1864, p. 362.

62 USG to Sherman, December 18, 1864, *PUSG*, 13, p. 129–30.

63 USG to Isaac N. Morris, February 15, 1865, ibid., p. 429.

64 REL to MCL, July 31, 1864, *Wartime Papers*, p. 828, August 7, 1864, p. 829.

65 REL to MCL, August 14, 1864, ibid., p. 837.

66 REL to MCL, October 25, 1864, ibid., p. 865.

67 REL to MCL, August 7, 1864, ibid., p. 829.

68 J[ohn]. W[illiam]. J[ones]., "General Lee's Letter to His Son," *University Monthly*, 2 (March 1872), pp. 68–69.

69 Speech of Benjamin Hill, February 18, 1874, Augusta, GA, *Daily Chronicle & Sentinel*, March 11, 1874.

70 Davis to REL, February 25, 1865, *OR*, I, 46, pt. 2, p. 1, 256.

71 Venable to Taylor, March 29, 1878, Taylor Papers, duPont Library, Stratford.

72 Venable to Taylor, March 29, 1878, Taylor Papers, duPont Library, Stratford; Tower, *Lee's Adjutant*, p. 228.

73 REL to MCL, September 5, 1864, *Wartime Papers*, p. 851.

74 Alfred P. Aldrich to Lewis M. Ayer, January 9, 1865, Lewis M. Ayer Papers, South Caroliniana Library, University of South Carolina, Columbia.

75 Raleigh, NC, *Progress*, n.d., in Hartford, CT, *Daily Courant*, January 14, 1864; Worcester, MA, *National Aegis*, January 30, 1864; New York, *Herald*, December 30, 1864.

76 William C. Davis, ed., *A Fire-Eater Remembers: The Confederate Memoir of Robert Barnwell Rhett* (Columbia: University of South Carolina Press, 2000), pp. 80–81. Rhett does not date the sending of the Stephens letter, though the context would suggest that it was in the summer of 1863. However, Rhett's chronology in his fragmentary memoir is often off, and late 1864 or early 1865 seem more probable.

77 Charles Minnegerode to Mary Carter Minnegerode, November 17, 1864, Charles Minnegerode Letters, copies on file at Richmond National Battlefield Park.

78 Charleston, *Mercury*, February 7, 1865.

79 United States Congress, *Journal of the Congress of the Confederate States of America, 1861–1865* (Washington: Government Printing Office, 1904–1905), 4, pp. 456–58, 510–11.

80 New York, *Herald*, February 5, 1865.

81 REL to Davis, January 19, 1865, *Wartime Papers*, pp. 884–85.

82 REL to Seddon, February 4, 1865, ibid., pp. 888–89, General Orders No. 1, February 9, 1865, p. 891.

83 REL to Beauregard, March 9, 1865, William Reese Company Americana, New Haven, CT, website item 46845.

84 Richmond, *Sentinel*, January 16, 1865; Baltimore, *Sun*, January 21, 1865.

85 Boston, *American Traveller*, July 8, 1865; Norwich, CT, *Aurora*, February 11, 1865. Some of Singleton's claims are more than suspect, especially the involvement of Grant, who scarcely knew Singleton and regarded him as just another speculator trying to profit from the war. In a few weeks, in fact, Grant would revoke Singleton's pass to go through the lines. Still, it was common rumor in the army and in the North that the Illinoisan was on some kind of peace mission (USG to Stanton, March 8, 1865, *PUSG*, 14, pp. 113–15n, 13, p. 283n.). Even in Richmond his mission was no secret, as one paper commented on his arrival that the city was experiencing "a Perfect Diarrhoea of Peace Commissioners" (Richmond, *Whig*, January 16, 1865). Yet elements of his story are corroborated. He and Breckinridge did arrive in Richmond on the same day. Stephens, Campbell, Ould, and Hunter were among the men then seeking a means to peace, even at the price of reunion, and so were Longstreet and Ewell, and perhaps even Lee.

86 Boston, *American Traveller*, July 8, 1865.

87 REL to Henry A. Wise, February 4, 1865, Richmond, *Daily Dispatch*, February 17, 1865.

88 James Longstreet, *From Manassas to Appomattox* (Philadelphia: Lippincott, 1896), p. 584.

89 REL to Davis, March 2, 1865, *Wartime Papers*, p. 911, REL to Grant, March 2, 1865, pp. 911–12.

90 USG to REL, March 4, 1865, *PUSG*, 14, pp. 98–99n, USG to Stanton, March 4, 1865, p. 100.

91 R. M. T. Hunter to William Jones, n.d. [November 1877], Rowland, *Jefferson Davis, Constitutionalist*, 7, pp. 576–77.

92 REL to Breckinridge, March 9, 1865, *Wartime Papers*, pp. 912–13.

93 Edward Younger, ed., *Inside the Confederate Government: The Diary of Robert Garlick Hill Kean* (New York: Oxford University Press, 1957), p. 203; Burton Harrison to Davis, May 24, 1877, Rowland, *Jefferson Davis, Constitutionalist*, 7, p. 551; John A. Campbell to Joshua

Speed, August 31, 1865, "Papers of John A. Campbell," *Southern Historical Society Papers*, 42 (September 1917), p. 69.

94 George G. Vest in the Sedalia, MO, *Democrat*, in Macon, *Weekly Telegraph*, June 15, 1875.

95 John B. Jones, *A Rebel War Clerk's Diary at the Confederate States Capital* (Philadelphia: Lippincott, 1866), 2, p. 454; Nelson D. Lankford, ed., *An Irishman in Dixie: Thomas Conolly's Diary of the Fall of the Confederacy* (Columbia: University of South Carolina Press, 1988), pp. 60–61.

96 REL endorsement, March 23, 1865, on John Bell Hood, "Notes on the Spring Campaign of 1865" addressed to Davis, n.d., Civil War Collection, Huntington Library.

97 USG to Dana, February 23, 1865, *PUSG*, 14, p. 26.

98 USG to Julia, March 30, 1865, ibid., p. 273.

99 USG to Julia, April 1, 1865, ibid., p. 311.

100 Venable to Taylor, March 29, 1878, Taylor Papers, duPont Library, Stratford.

101 REL to Edward G. W. Butler, March 2, 1868, Swann Auction Galleries, Sale 2333, New York, November 16, 2013, item 15.

102 David Gregg McIntosh Diary, April 2–3, 1865, Gregg Papers, VHS.

103 USG to Julia, April 2, 1865, *PUSG*, 14, p. 330.

104 The correspondence between Grant and Lee will be found in Ibid., pp. 361–73, and *Wartime Papers*, pp. 931–34.

105 This theme is developed in Elizabeth R. Varon, *Appomattox: Victory, Defeat, and Freedom at the End of the Civil War* (New York: Oxford University Press, 2014), pp. 35–37 and passim.

106 Colonel T. P. Shaffner in Louisville, *Courier-Journal*, in Philadelphia, *Inquirer*, December 16, 1879.

107 *PMUSG*, 2, p. 489.

108 Horace Porter, "The Surrender at Appomattox Court House," Robert Underwood Johnson and Clarence Clough Buel, eds., *Battles and Leaders of the Civil War* (New York: The Century Company, 1888), 4, p. 743.

109 Ibid., p. 496.

CHAPTER 17: GRANT AND LEE IN 1868

1 USG to Washburn, April 10, 1865, *PUSG*, 32, p. 78.

2 New York, *Tribune*, May 25, 1866.

3 *PMUSG*, 2, p. 497. Sadly, this is the only firsthand account of the private meeting between the two. Lee never wrote of it, and the staff member and bugler with Grant presumably waited out of earshot. That night Grant told members of his staff about the conversation, and Horace Porter later wrote his recollection of what Grant told them, which agrees substantially with Grant's account, adding only that Lee said emancipation would not be an obstacle to reunion. Porter, "The Surrender at Appomattox Court House," in Johnson and Buel, *Battles and Leaders*, 4, pp. 745–46.

4 Theodore Lyman to Elizabeth Lyman, April 23, 1865, George R. Agassiz, ed., *Meade's Headquarters 1863–1865: Letters of Colonel Theodore Lyman from the Wilderness to Appomattox* (Boston: Massachusetts Historical Society, 1922), pp. 360–61; Meade to Margaretta, April 10, 1865, Meade, *Life and Letters*, 2, p. 270.

5 REL to Davis, April 12, 1865, *Wartime Papers*, pp. 935–38.

6 General Orders No. 9, ibid., pp. 914–15.

7 Giles B. Cooke Diary, April 10–13, 1865, excerpted on February 20, 1923, Profiles in History Auction, Calabasas, CA, July 11, 2014, "The Property of a Distinguished American Private Collector, Part IV-54D, p. 49, item #22.2; MCL to Louisa Snowden, April 16, 1865,

T. Michael Miller, "My Dear Louisa: Letters from Mrs. Mary Custis Lee to the Snowden Family of Alexandria, Virginia," *The Fireside Sentinel*, 5 (June 1991), p. 72. Cooke's dairy—as excerpted, anyhow—says they left April 11, but virtually all other sources unite in saying April 12.

8   Milwaukee, *Sentinel*, May 1, 1865.

9   MCL to Mary Meade, April 23, 1865, MacDonald, *Mrs. Robert E. Lee*, p. 197.

10   REL to Davis, April 20, 1865, *Wartime Papers*, pp. 938–39.

11   Lyman to Elizabeth Lyman, April 23, 1865, Agassiz, *Meade's Headquarters*, p. 362.

12   MCL to Mary Meade, April 23, 1865, MacDonald, *Mrs. Robert E. Lee*, p. 198.

13   Keowee, SC, *Courier*, June 2, 1866.

14   J. Stoddard Johnston interview, December 1879, Trenton, *State Gazette*, December 18, 1879.

15   Cincinnati, *Commercial*, August 9, 1879.

16   Boston, *Daily Advertiser*, May 5, 1865; Philadelphia, *Inquirer*, May 3, 1865.

17   New York, *Tribune*, May 9, 1865.

18   Washington, *Evening Union*, June 3, 1865.

19   This episode, which is almost certainly apocryphal, has enjoyed enormous popularity in Lee biographies and other works, and been misquoted and carelessly embellished to become an example of his magnanimity, charity, and good feeling toward the newly freed slaves. As usually given, it presents Lee attending communion service at St. Paul's Episcopal Church early in June, when the congregation is stunned that a black man went first to the communion table at the call for communicants. No one else would go forward until Lee did, knelt beside the man, and they took communion together, Lee accepting the black man's equality before God.

The episode stems from the article "Negro Communed at St. Paul's Church" in the *Confederate Veteran*, 13 (August 1905), p. 360. It is based on a conversation with T. L. Broun, who was in St. Paul's that day and according to the unidentified transcriber said that when the invitation to take communion was announced, a tall, well-dressed, and very black man went to the communion table, apparently before anyone else. White would-be communicants were so shocked that they remained immobile in their pews, "deeply chagrined at this attempt to inaugurate the 'new regime' to offend and humiliate them during their most devoted Church services." Lee, however, "ignoring the action and presence of the negro," walked up the aisle to the chancel rail and stopped not far from the black man, then knelt to receive the host. Lee's act, "under such provoking and irritating circumstances had a magic effect," and Broun and the rest rose and joined him. "By this action of Gen. Lee the services were conducted as if the negro had not been present. It was a grand exhibition of superiority shown by a true Christian and great soldier under the most trying and offensive circumstances."

Immediately evident, of course, is that Lee's is an act of defiance, not charity or welcome to the black man as it is usually depicted. Other questions arise as well. For instance, given that blacks, slave or free, customarily sat in the western gallery at St. Paul's, how did this man get downstairs and past the entire white congregation to be first at the rail? Had he taken a seat beforehand in one of the front rows, that in itself would have been as much an outrage as what Broun described, and he would have been evicted before the service commenced.

The *Confederate Veteran* actually appeared four months after the first publication of Broun's story, and made some subtle alterations. The Richmond, *Times-Dispatch*, April 16, 1905, recounted a conversation with Broun the previous day in which he told the story. So Broun orally recounted the tale to a reporter who presumably tried to transcribe it carefully, and then four months later an unidentified person somewhat carelessly transcribed it again to send to the *Confederate Veteran*. Hence the *Confederate Veteran* version is thirdhand and forty years after the fact, which alone would make it highly suspect. Broun originally said that the black man was "among those who first arose," not the very first as implied in the later version. Broun also originally said that the man "walked with an air of military authority," and that when the rest of the congregation remained seated, their shock was at "this attempt of the Federal authorities to offensively humiliate them." The suggestion is strong, though not explicit, that this was a black Union soldier, which someone four months later chose to leave out. However, by June 4 the Army of the Potomac had gone to Washington to be disbanded, and Grant had ordered all black units out of Richmond to other duty, so there should have been no black soldiers in the city.

Finally, any incident such as this, whether involving a black soldier or civilian, occurring as described, would have left an indelible memory that would not have had to wait four decades to see print. It is likely that white males in the congregation would have forcibly ejected the offender, causing enough of a scene to attract notice in contemporary diaries and in the Richmond press, yet the newspapers are silent, as are the diarists. Broun did know Lee somewhat, for his brother sold the horse Traveller to the general in early 1862. By 1905, when he told his story to the *Times-Dispatch* reporter, Broun was eighty-one years old, adding the probability of faulty memory, or even possible dementia, to the usual problems of recollections that far from the event.

In the end, the whole incident is probably fantasy, though Broun had no reason to lie, so it is *possible* that some sort of minor incident took place at that communion that was exaggerated and grossly reshaped by forty years of failing memory. For more on this questionable incident, see Philip Schwarz, "General Lee and Visibility," at http://www.stratalum.org/leecommunion.htm.

20   REL to A. L. Long, May 24, 1865, Robert E. Lee Papers, Washington and Lee.
21   MacDonald, *Mrs. Robert E. Lee*, p. 199.
22   REL to Robert E. Lee Jr., July 10, 1865, Lee-Jackson Collection, Washington and Lee.
23   Trenton, NJ, *State Gazette*, August 19, 1865
24   Undated endorsement by GWCL attached to REL to Andrew Johnson, June 13, 1865, Sotheby's Presidential and Other American Manuscripts Sale Catalog, April 3, 2008, item #13.
25   REL to Beauregard, October 1865, Gary W. Gallagher "A Question of Loyalty," *Civil War Times*, 52 (October 2013), p. 30.
26   Alexandria, *Gazette*, September 14, 1876; USG to Halleck, May 6, 1865, *PUSG*, 15, p. 11, June 16, 1865, p. 150, USG to REL, June 20, 1865, pp. 210–11. Lee's amnesty oath of allegiance is in General Records of the Department of State, RG 59, NA.
27   REL to Robert E. Lee Jr., July 10, 1865, Lee-Jackson Collection, Washington and Lee.
28   REL to Charles Minnegerode, July 29, 1865, ibid.
29   REL to John Letcher, August 28, 1865, Gilder Lehrman Collection.
30   REL to Louise H. Carter, November 16, 1865, SPC.
31   REL to "A gentlemen in Petersburg," n.d. [September 1865], Washington, *Evening Union*, September 30, 1865.
32   USG to Julia, April 16, 1865, *PUSG*, 14, p. 396.
33   USG to Pope, April 17, 1865, ibid., p. 403.
34   USG to Sherman, April 21, 1865, ibid., pp. 424–25.
35   USG to Julia, April 21, 1865, ibid., p. 429.
36   USG to Silas Hudson, April 21, 1865, ibid., pp. 429–30.
37   USG to Halleck, May 6, 1865, *PUSG*, 15, p. 11.
38   USG, Report, June 20, 1865, ibid., pp. 204–206.
39   New Orleans, *Times*, September 24, 1865; Macon, GA, *Weekly Telegraph*, August 30, 1867; Providence, RI, *Evening Press*, August 23, 1865; Burke memoir, 1896, Garland Papers.
40   New Orleans, *Times*, September 24, 1865.

41 REL to Letcher, August 28, 1865, Gilder Lehrman Collection.

42 REL to Trustees of Washington College, August 24, 1865, Washington and Lee Archives.

43 MacDonald, *Mrs. Robert E. Lee*, p. 206–207.

44 REL to M. G. Harmon, November 22, 1865, Philadelphia, *Illustrated New Age*, December 4, 1865.

45 Rufus L. Patterson to Mrs. Lisetta Maria Fries, July 31, 1866, Thomas Felix Hickerson, *Echoes of Happy Valley: Letters and Diaries, Family Life in the South, Civil War History* (Chapel Hill, NC: privately published, 1962), p. 111. Patterson had seen Lee at Alum Springs in Rockbridge County the day before, July 30, 1866.

46 Cleveland, *Plain Dealer*, June 29, 1872.

47 REL to ? at Fort Riley, KS, May 23, 1866, Richmond, *Times Dispatch*, January 23, 1922.

48 REL to M. O. McLaughlin, April 27, 1866, Dallas, *Morning News*, December 19, 1928; REL to W. G. Morgan, March 16, 1867, Lexington, KY, *Morning Herald*, May 19, 1901.

49 REL to Catherine Carson, July 9, 1866, Breckinridge Family Papers, LC.

50 REL to W. G. Morgan, March 16, 1867, Lexington, KY, *Morning Herald*, May 19, 1901.

51 REL to J. B. Minor, January 17, 1867, Lee Papers, UVA.

52 "An Address to the Parents and Public of Virginia, by General R. E. Lee and Professors Minor and Dabney," Macon, *Weekly Telegraph*, March 29, 1867.

53 Columbus, GA, *Daily Enquirer*, July 7, 1868.

54 REL to R. W. Jemison, June 18, 1870, Macon, *Weekly Telegraph*, July 12, 1870.

55 Letter April 10, 1868, New York, *Tribune*, April 20, 1868.

56 Richmond, *Whig*, March 6, 1868.

57 Anonymous letter, March 17, 1868, Cleveland, *Leader*, April 17, 1868; Cincinnati, *Daily Gazette*, April 6, 1868.

58 Jamestown, NY, *Journal*, April 24, 1868.

59 New York, *Commercial Advertiser*, October 22, 1868.

60 MacDonald, *Mrs. Robert E. Lee*, p. 222.

61 Augusta, GA, *Daily Constitutionalist*, June 11, 1868.

62 Albany, NY, *Daily Argus*, July 24, 1868.

63 REL to ?, n.d. [September–October 1869], Baltimore, *Sun*, October 18, 1869.

64 Macon, GA, *Weekly Telegraph*, November 17, 1868.

65 Wilmer McLean to REL, April 2, 1866, Lee Collection, Washington and Lee.

66 REL to Wilcox & Gibbs Sewing Machine Company, January 12, 1867, Augusta, GA, *Daily Constitutionalist*, August 20, 1868; REL to William J. Rivers, March 25, 1869, item 76, Civil War Auction Catalog No. 155, Antebellum Covers, Ron and Anne Meininger, Gaithersburg, MD.

67 REL to John B. Baldwin, May 20, 1867, John B. Baldwin to Robert H. Maury, June 5, 1867, Richmond, *Whig*, June 11, 1867.

68 Richmond, *Dispatch*, August 20, 1867; REL to M. G. Harman, H. W. Sheffey, John B. Baldwin et al., July 28, 1870, Alexandria, *Gazette*, August 1, 1870.

69 REL to Charles Minnegerode, July 29, 1865, Lee-Jackson Collection, Washington and Lee.

70 REL Circular Letter, July 31, 1865, Lee Collection, Missouri Historical Society, St. Louis; REL to Early, November 22, 1865, March 15, 1866, New Orleans, *Times-Picayune*, March 16, 1886; REL to John B. Gordon, July 31, 1865, John B. Gordon Papers, University of Georgia, Athens.

71 R. M. Smith to REL, November 24, 1865, item 13, Gary Hendershott Catalog, August 1999, Little Rock, AK; Alexandria, *Gazette*, February 11, 1874; REL to Charles Venable, March 1866, Minor-Venable File, University of Virginia.

72 REL to J. Stoddard Johnston, January 2, 1866, Lee-Jackson Collection, Washington and Lee; Macon, *Telegraph*, June 17, 1866; REL to Osman Latrobe, June 8, 1866, sold at auction in 1980, present location unknown.

73 Dallas, *Weekly Herald*, August 4, 1866; REL to Charles Marshall, December 4, 1865, item 77, Alexander Autographs "War Between the States" catalog, 2008; New Orleans, *Daily Picayune*, January 5, 1866; Augusta, GA, *Chronicle*, March 23, 1866.

74 REL to John Dalberg Acton, December 15, 1866, Richmond, *Times-Dispatch*, January 20, 1924.

75 Richmond, *Southern Opinion*, March 27, 1869.

76 William Preston Johnston, "Memoranda of Conversations with General R. E. Lee," Gallagher, *Lee the Soldier*, p. 32.

77 Allan et al., "Memoranda," Gallagher, *Lee the Soldier*, pp. 7–34 passim.

78 REL to Anna Jackson, January 25, 1866, Dabney Collection, Union Theological Seminary.

79 Fitz-John Porter to Charles Marshall, January 22, 1870, January 24, 1882, Swann Galleries Catalog Sale March 24, 1988, item #142.

80 REL to Mrs. A. M. Keiley, n.d. [March, 1867], Richmond, *Whig*, April 5, 1867; REL to Mrs. E. A. F. Mears, March 27, 1867, Washington, *Evening Star*, April 5, 1867; REL to Mrs. J. C. Thompson, January 28, 1867, Baltimore, *American*, May 28, 1905; REL to Julia Gratiot Chouteau, March 21, 1866, Augusta, GA, *Chronicle*, May 3, 2000.

81 Richmond, *Whig*, October 12, 1869.

82 REL to J. G. Arrington, January 25, 1867, Macon, *Weekly Telegraph*, March 22, 1867.

83 REL to [D. McConaghy], August 5, 1869, Norwich, CT, *Aurora*, September 1, 1869.

84 Washington, *Critic-Record*, November 8, 1869.

85 REL to John Dalberg Acton, December 15, 1866, Richmond, *Times-Dispatch*, January 20, 1924. John Leyburn, "An Interview with General Robert E. Lee," *Century Magazine*, 30 (No. 1, May, 1885) p. 167, says that in 1869 Lee told Leyburn "he had emancipated most of his slaves years before the war, and had sent to Liberia those who were willing to go; that the latter were writing back most affectionate letters to him, some of which he received through the lines during the war." He went on to quote Lee as saying, "So far from engaging in a war to perpetuate slavery, I am rejoiced that slavery is abolished. I believe it will be greatly for the interests of the South. So fully am I satisfied of this, as regards Virginia especially, *that I would cheerfully have lost all I have lost by the war, and have suffered all I have suffered, to have this object attained.*" Lee, 4, pp. 400–401, accepts Leyburn's account without question, but it is highly suspect. Like so many, Leyburn confused the Custis slaves Lee emancipated as being Lee's own, and did the same with the family sent to Liberia, neither of which was a mistake Lee would make if he was being honest. As for Lee's supposed comments on slavery and abolition, they hardly square with everything else he wrote about doubting that the time was right for emancipation, or what place blacks should have in the postwar South. If Lee said anything to Leyburn on slavery, Leyburn badly garbled the recollection of it in the ensuing sixteen years.

86 Milwaukee, *Semi-Weekly Madison*, March 31, 1866. Lee's name and the whipping episode had appeared in the press in May and again in November 1865 when he was dubbed a "whipper of slaves," but he ignored those at the time. Columbus, *Daily Ohio Statesman*, November 2, 1865.

87 REL to E. S. Quick, March 1, 1866, Lee Papers, VHS. It is hard to say just what Lee was responding to, though it could be the accounts appearing in May 1865 starting with the New York, *Tribune*, May 9, 1865, article rehashing the whipping episode. The Wesley Norris account seems not to have started circulating until early April, a month after Lee's letter.

88 REL to [George K. Fox], April 13, 1866, in Lee, *Recollections*, pp. 224–25. The Baltimore, *American* was not available to locate the date of the article's appearance, but Lee's letter is in response to one dated April 5, and extracts of the Wesley Norris statement began appearing at least as early as April 5 in the New York, *Independent* and perhaps elsewhere.

89 REL to Mackay, June 27, 1838, Gilder Lehrman Collection. In fact, it is Sancho who says this, his words being "the more you stir this business the more it will stink." By 1888 the remaining slaves at Arlington remembered Lee as "a kind master" who sometimes worked in the fields with them, and held Sunday services for them if they did not go to church. "The negroes at Arlington remember the Lees, and speak of them with uniform kindness," wrote a reporter. "Colonel Lee must have been a kind master." His informant was Mariah Syphax, who also said that old Custis was her father. Rockford, IL, *Morning Star*, September 4, 1888.

90 Boston, *Journal*, March 23, 1867.

91 Richmond, *Whig*, April 9, 1867.

92 Atlanta, *Era*, April 2, 1867, quoted in New Orleans, *Times*, April 5, 1867; Augusta, GA, *Daily Constitutionalist*, April 9, 1867.

93 REL to Frank Fuller, April 20, 1867, The Raab Collection Catalog, January 2012, pp. 5–6.

94 REL to "My Dear Major," April 3, 1867, Augusta, GA, *Chronicle*, November 28, 1880. Content in the letter indicates that the addressee had been a commissary officer on Lee's staff. The best match is Robert G. Cole. Though he finished the war as a lieutenant colonel, he lived after the war in Georgia, and this letter surfaced and was used in a political speech in Georgia in 1880.

95 REL to D. H. Maury, May 23, 1867, New Orleans, *Times-Picayune*, February 28, 1871.

96 REL to Edward G. W. Butler, October 11, 1867, Gilder Lehrman Collection; REL to Edward G. W. Butler, March 2, 1868, Swann Auction Galleries, Sale 2333, New York, November 16, 2013, item 15.

97 New York, *Tribune*, May 25, 1866; USG Report, June 20, 1865, *PUSG*, 15, pp. 205–206.

98 New York, *Herald*, November 17, 1865.

99 Marquis De Lorne, *A Trip Through the Tropics and Home Through America* (London: Hurst and Blackett, 1867), pp. 249–50.

100 REL to Edward G. W. Butler, October 11, 1867, Gilder Lehrman Collection.

101 New York, *Tribune*, May 25, 1866.

102 De Lorne, *A Trip Through the Tropics*, p. 250

103 REL to Robert Ould, February 4, 1867, Richmond, *Dispatch*, May 29, 1890.

104 Dallas, *Weekly Herald*, August 4, 1866.

105 REL to Robert Ould, February 4, 1867, Richmond, *Dispatch*, May 29, 1890.

106 Macon, *Daily Telegraph*, May 4, 1866.

107 Trenton, NJ, *State Gazette*, January 23, 1867.

108 Jackson, MI, *Daily Citizen*, January 28, 1867.

109 Philadelphia, *Evening Telegraph*, March 13, 1867.

110 Augusta, GA, *Daily Constitutionalist*, April 9, 1867, quoted the New York, *Herald*, April 1, 1867.

111 Galveston, *Flake's Bulletin*, November 16, 1867; New York, *Herald*, June 10, 1867.

112 John Echols to Beauregard, March 11, 1874, item 145, Signature House Catalog, n.d., Bridgeport, WV, p. 39.

113 A. H. H. Stuart to Nathaniel B. Meade, January 29, 1874, Richmond, *Whig*, March 3, 1874.

114 Rosecrans to REL, August 26, 1868, REL et al. to Rosecrans, August 26, 1868, Richmond, *Whig*, September 8, 1868.

115 A. H. H. Stuart to Nathaniel B. Meade, January 29, 1874, Richmond, *Whig*, March 3, 1874; Alexandria, *Gazette*, February 5, 1869.

116 Richmond, *Whig*, January 27, 1874.

CHAPTER 18: THE LAST MEETING

1 New York, *Herald*, November 25, 1867, December 8, 1867; Boston, *American Traveller*, November 30, 1867; New York, *Herald*, December 8, 1867; Memphis, *Daily Avalanche*, October 17, 1868.

2 James May to USG, June 2, 1869, REL to May, April 28, 30, 1869, *PUSG*, 19, pp. 488–89.

3 New York, *Herald*, July 24, 1878; Richmond, *Dispatch*, May 8, 1869. This is a secondhand account given to a New York, *Herald* reporter in Alexandria the next day, by someone repeating what Lee had told him. As such it is suspect, especially since Grant is stated as wanting a long interview while Lee cuts it short and leaves, while May to Grant, June 2, 1869, *PUSG*, 19, p. 489, says that Lee "was deeply mortified that the interview was *so short & formal.*"

4 Quincy, IL, *Daily Whig*, May 7, 1869; Cincinnati, *Commercial Tribune*, May 3, 1869.

5 Boston, *Journal*, May 4, 1869; Cleveland, *Plain Dealer*, May 4, 1869.

6 New York, *Commercial Advertiser*, May 3, 1869; Richmond, *Whig*, May 4, 1869.

7 May to Grant, June 2, 1869, *PUSG*, 19, p. 489, says that Lee "was deeply mortified that the interview was *so short & formal.*"

8 New York, *Herald*, June 15, 20, 1869.

9 REL to Hill Carter, April 25, 1868, May 28, SPC.

10 REL to Thomas H. Ellis, September 30, 1869, Cincinnati, *Commercial Tribune*, February 1, 1870.

11 REL to William G. Bullock, March 26, 1869, Alexander Autographs Catalog Sale, November 6, 2008, item #119.

12 REL to Edward G. W. Butler, February 10, 1870, item 211, Swann Auction Catalog, April 17, 2012.

13 REL to H. D. Capers, July 8, 1868, Philadelphia, *Inquirer*, August 25, 1868.

14 REL letter n.d. [1869] paraphrased in Charleston, *Daily News*, April 30, 1869.

15 REL to "My Dear Sir," May 17, 1869, Richmond, *Whig*, May 21, 1869.

16 REL to Blanton Duncan, September 13, 1869, Charleston, *Courier*, September 25, 1869.

17 Columbus, GA, *Daily Enquirer*, July 7, 1868.

18 MacDonald, *Mrs. Robert E. Lee*, pp. 278–79; MCL to Louise H. Carter, November 9, 1870, SPC; Macon, *Weekly Telegraph*, November 1, 1870. It is noteworthy that in Mary's November 9 letter, Lee's famous "strike the tent" is not given as his last words, and context places them perhaps a day or two before his death. Also, Mary wrote to Mary Meade the evening of his death and made no mention of such final words (MacDonald, *Mrs. Robert E. Lee*, p. 283).

19 New York, *Herald*, July 24, 1878.

20 De Lorne, *Trip to the Tropics*, p. 250.

21 *PMJDG*, pp. 330–31.

22 USG to John H. Douglas, July 16, 1885 *PUSG*, 31, p. 437.

23 San Diego, *Union*, April 26, 1885.

24 USG to McKinstry Griffith, September 22, 1839, *PUSG*, 1, p. 5.

25 Omaha, *Omaha World Herald*, April 8, 1895.

26 Randolph H. McKim, *The Soul of Lee* (New York: Longmans, Green, 1918), pp. 200, 202,

210; J. William Jones, *Army of Northern Virginia Memorial Volume* (Richmond: Randolph and English, 1880), p. 120. Perhaps the height of this deification of Lee came in 1964: a United Kingdom branch of a tiny Nashville group calling itself the Confederate High Command wrote a letter to the home group averring that no human since Jesus had demonstrated his qualities to the extent Lee had; it concluded by declaring that "the patron saint of the Confederate High Command is that great general, Robert E. Lee, our Commander in Chief, the Lord in Heaven." Marcus Hinton, "Christmas Greetings," *Rebel* No. 9 (United Kingdom Division, Confederate High Command, 1964), n.p.

27 Jones, *Army of Northern Virginia*, p. 120.

28 Sherman to John E. Tourtellotte, February 4, 1887, *PUSG*, 8, pp. 323–24n.

29 J. F. Lee to Fitz-John Porter, January 24, 1870, "Knapsack," *North & South*, 5 (July 2002), p. 11.

30 New York, *Tribune*, May 31, 1886.

31 Lee, *Recollections*, p. 416.

32 Interview, July 6, 1878, *PUSG*, 28, pp. 414–15, 419.

BIBLIOGRAPHY

MANUSCRIPTS

Alexandria County Court, Alexandria, VA. Inventory of Custis slaves, September 11, 1858

Alexandria Public Library, Alexandria, VA. Order No. 44, Office of the U. S. District Attorney for the Eastern District of Virginia, Confiscation and Seizure Book, box 207

Colonial Williamsburg Foundation, Williamsburg, VA, John D. Rockefeller Jr. Library. Shirley Plantation Collection: Hill Carter Hireling Book, 1822–1848; Hill Carter Memorandum Book for Hirelings, 1850–1853

Marshall Coyne Collection, Fredericksburg, VA

Emory University, Atlanta, GA. Benjamin Wesley Justice Papers, Emory University, Atlanta

Fairfax County Court House, Fairfax, VA. Anne Carter Lee Will, July 24, 1829, Will Book P-1 1827–1830, pp. 277–28

Fort Pulaski National Monument, Savannah, GA. Robert E. Lee to John Mackay, January 23, 1833

Georgia Historical Society, Savannah, GA. Hugh S. Golson Collection of Stiles Family Papers

Historic New Orleans Collection, New Orleans, LA, Williams Research Center. Edward G. W. Butler Papers

Huntington Library, San Marino, CA. Civil War Collection; James E. B. Stuart Papers

Indiana State Library, Indianapolis. Calvin Benjamin Papers

Keith Kehlbeck, Marshall, MI. Robert E. Lee Letters, 1862–1863, transcripts

Robert K. Krick, Fredericksburg, VA. Lee and Ficklin Family Archives: D. Lyon Jr. to My dear Annie, May 14, 1863, copy in George Washington and Jane Peter Papers. In the early 1960s these papers were at the Maryland Historical Society in Baltimore, and were excerpted in an undated essay by Lee Wallace, copy in this collection. Their whereabouts today are unknown.

Library of Congress, Washington, DC. American Colonization Society Papers: Applicants for Emigration to Liberia, 1826–1855, Series VI, vol. 18; Calvin Benjamin Letters; Breckinridge Family Papers; DeButts-Ely Papers; William C. Rives Papers; Elihu B. Washburne Papers

Louisa County Historical Society, Louisa, VA. David Watson Letters, copies

Massachusetts Historical Society, Boston. Robert E. Lee to George Washington Custis Lee, January 11, 1863

Michael Masters Collection, NC

Mississippi State University, Starkeville. Papers of the U. S. Grant Association

Missouri Historical Society, St. Louis. Robert E. Lee Collection

Museum of the Confederacy, Richmond, VA. Robert E. Lee Emancipation document, December 29, 1862; Robert E. Lee Papers

National Archives, Washington, DC. General Records of the Department of State, RG 59; R. E. Lee Amnesty Oath, October 2, 1865. Records of the Adjutant General's Office, RG 94; Field Records of Hospitals, West Point Cadets' Hospital, January 1, 1827–May 22, 1833, Register 600, Entry 544; Field Records of Hospitals, West Point Cadets' Hospital, January 1, 1838–July 31, 1840, Register 604, Entry 544; Letters Received by the Office of the Adjutant General, 1861–1870, File L60, 1861, M619; Records of the U.S. Military Academy, Entry 231 Monthly Class Reports and Conduct Rolls, 1819–1830; Records of the U.S. Military Academy, Entry 232 Monthly Class Reports and Conduct Rolls, 1831–1866; Records of the U.S. Military Academy, Entry 232 Monthly Class Reports and Conduct Rolls, March 1843; Records of the U.S. Military Academy, Entry 232 Monthly Class Reports and Conduct Rolls, September 1839–June 1840, Entry 232; Records of the U.S. Military Academy. Monthly Class Reports and Conduct Rolls, January 1841, Entry 232; Records of the U.S. Military Academy. Monthly Class Reports and Conduct Rolls, July 1840–June 1841, Entry 232; Records of the U.S. Military Academy, Monthly Class Reports and Conduct Rolls, February, May, 1842, Entry 232; Records of the U.S. Military Academy, Monthly Class Reports and Conduct Rolls, 1831–1866, Entry 232; Returns from U.S. Military Posts, 1806–1916; U.S. Military Academy, Cadet Application Papers, 1805–1866, Robert E. Lee File; U.S. Military Academy, Cadet Records and Applications, 1805–1898, Register of Cadet Applications, 1819–1867, 1, 1819–1927, Record for Robt E. Lee, #101; William Maynadier File, #060-991/2; U.S. Military Academy, Cadet Records and Applications, 1805–1898, Register of Cadet Applications, 1819–1867, volume 11, 1839–1840; U.S. Military and Naval Academies, Cadet Records and Applications, 1805–1898, Register of Cadet Applicants, 1819–1867, volume 10, 1838–1839; U.S. Military and Naval Academies, Cadet Records and Applications, 1805–1898, Register of Cadet Applicants, 1819–1867, volume 10, 1838–1839, Records of the Adjutant General's Office, Records of the Judge Advocate's Office, RG 153; Court Martial Case Files (Army), Entry 15. War Department Collection of Confederate Records RG 109; Compiled Service Records, RG 109 J. C. Brown (Broun), Robert H. Chilton, William H. Crawford, Robert E. Lee, Lawrence Williams Orton [William Orton Williams]; Orders and Circulars Issued by the Army of the Potomac and the Army and Department of Northern Virginia, CSA, 1861–1865, M921, Roll 4; Jeffrey L. Raw, comp., Outgoing Correspondence of Lafayette Guild, Medical Director, Army of Northern Virginia, Chapter 6, vols. 641–42

United States Census, Alexandria County, VA, 1850

United States Census, Brown County, Ohio, IL, 1830

United States Census, Jo Davies County, IL, 1860

United States Census, Fairfax County, VA, 1860, 1870, 1880, 1900

United States Census, St. Louis County, MO, 1850

New-York Historical Society, New York. Gilder Lehrman Collection

Historical Society of Pennsylvania, Philadelphia. Ferdinand J. Dreer Collection

Richmond National Battlefield Park, Richmond, VA. Charles Minnegerode Letters

Rockingham County Courthouse, Lexington, VA. Last Will and Testament of Robert E. Lee

Gary L. Sisson, Montross, VA. Ann H. Lee to Sydney Smith Lee, May 17, 1822

Smithsonian Institution Archives, Capital Gallery, Washington, DC. James Watson Robbins Field Notes, 1824–1826, Field Book Project, 1855–2008, Acc. 12–339

Stratford Hall, Stratford, VA, Jessie Ball duPont Library. Ann Hill Carter Lee Letters; Walter Herron Taylor Papers

Tudor Hall, Washington, DC. Armistead Peter Papers

Union Theological Seminary, Richmond, VA. R. L. Dabney Collection

United States Army Military History Institute, Carlisle Barracks, PA. General Stephen Elliott Papers

University of Georgia, Athens. Thomas R. R. Cobb Papers; John B. Gordon Papers

University Microfilms, Bethesda, MD. Loren Sweninger, ed., Race, Slavery, and Free Blacks. Series I: Petitions to Southern Legislatures, 1777–1867, reel 18, Virginia (1816–1826), Accession 11681612, 2003

University of North Carolina, Chapel Hill, Southern Historical Collection. Stephen R. Mallory Papers

University of the South, Sewanee, TN. Leonidas Polk Papers

University of South Carolina, Columbia, South Caroliniana Library. Lewis M. Ayer Papers; Milledge L. Bonham Papers; Samuel Melton Papers

University of Southern California, Los Angeles. Hamlin Garland Papers

Center for American History, University of Texas, Austin. Edward Richardson Crockett Diary

University of Virginia, Charlottesville. Lee Papers; Robert E. Lee to Charles Carter Lee, March 24, 1863; William Hartwell Perry Letters, 1860–1865; Minor-Venable File; Charles S. Venable Papers

Virginia Historical Society, Richmond. Samuel Merrifield Bemiss Family Papers; William C. Burke to Ralph R. Gurley, February 9, 1867; Thomas Henry Carter Letters; Thomas Claybrook Elder Papers; Lee Family Papers; George Bolling Lee Papers; Mary Custis Lee Collection; Mary Custis Lee Papers; Robert E. Lee Headquarters Papers, 1850–1876; David Gregg McIntosh Papers; Talcott Family Papers

Library of Virginia, Richmond. Charles City County Deed Book 10, 1846–1856; Charles City County, List of Free Negroes and Mulattoes over Twelve Years of Age for the Year 1859; Charles City County Register of Free Negroes, 1835–1864; Charles Carter Lee Collection, Major Henry Lee Papers 1813–1841; Virginia State Executive Papers

Washington and Lee University, Lexington, VA, Leyburn Library. Robert E. Lee Collection; Robert E. Lee Papers; Lee Family Papers; Lee Family Papers Digital Library; Lee-Jackson Collection; Washington and Lee Archives

Western Reserve Historical Society, Cleveland, OH. William N. Palmer Collection

AUTOBIOGRAPHIES, DIARIES, LETTERS, AND MEMOIRS

Adams, Francis Raymond, Jr., ed. *An Annotated Edition of the Personal Letters of Robert E. Lee, April 1855–April 1861.* Doctoral thesis: University of Maryland, 1955.

Agassiz, George R., ed. *Meade's Headquarters 1863–1865: Letters of Colonel Theodore Lyman from the Wilderness to Appomattox.* Boston: Massachusetts Historical Society, 1922.

Anderson, Charles. *Texas, Before and on the Eve of the Rebellion.* Cincinnati: Peter G. Thompson, 1884.

Andrews, Marietta Minnegerode, comp. *Scraps of Paper.* New York: E. P. Dutton, 1929.

Baldwin, Joseph Glover. *Party Leaders: Sketches of Thomas Jefferson, Alex'r Hamilton, Andrew Jackson, Henry Clay, John Randolph of Roanoke, including Notices of Many Other Distinguished American Statesmen.* New York: D. Appleton, 1854.

Bowery, Charles R., and Brian D. Hankinson, eds. The Daily Correspondence of Brevet Colonel Robert E. Lee Superintendent, United States Military Academy September 1, 1852 to March 24, 1855. West Point, NY: United States Military Academy Library Occasional Papers #5, 2003.

Burr, Rushton Dachwood, ed. *Address Delivered at the Unitarian Church, in Uxbridge, Mass., in 1864, . . . by Harry Chapin.* Worcester, MA: Press of Charles Hamilton, 1881.

Carter, Gari. *Troubled State: Civil War Journals of Franklin Archibald Dick.* Kirksville, MO: Truman State University Press, 2008.

Carter, W. H. *From Yorktown to Santiago with the 6th U.S. Cavalry.* Baltimore: Lord Baltimore Press, 1900.

Cary, Matthew, Jr., comp. *The Democratic Speaker's Hand-book: Containing Every Thing Necessary for the Defense of the National Democracy in the Upcoming Presidential Campaign, and for the Assault of the Radical Enemies of the Country and Its Constitution.* Cincinnati: Miami Print and Publishing, 1868.

Chamberlayne, Churchill Gibson, ed. *Ham Chamberlayne—Virginian: Letters and Papers of an Artillery Officer in the War for Southern Independence 1861–1865.* Richmond: Dietz Press, 1932.

Chetlain, Augustus L. *Recollections of Seventy Years.* Galena, IL: Galena Gazette, 1899.

Colton, J. H. *A Guide Book to West Point and Vicinity*. New York: J. H. Colton, 1844.

Crabtree, Beth Gilbert, and James W. Patton, eds. *"Journal of a Secesh Lady": The Diary of Catherine Ann Devereaux Edmondston, 1860–1866*. Raleigh: North Carolina Division of Archives and History, 1979.

Craven, Avery O., ed. *"To Markie": The Letters of Robert E. Lee to Martha Custis Williams*. Cambridge, MA: Harvard University Press, 1933.

Crist, Lynda Lasswell Crist, ed. *The Papers of Jefferson Davis: Volume 8*. Baton Rouge: Louisiana State University Press, 1995.

———. *The Papers of Jefferson Davis: Volume 10, October 1863–August 1864*. Baton Rouge: Louisiana State University Press, 1999.

Croffutt, W. A., ed. *Fifty Years in Camp and Field: Diary of Major-General Ethan Allen Hitchcock, U.SA*. New York: G. P. Putnam's, 1909.

Custis, George Washington Parke. *Recollections and Private Memoirs of Washington, by His Adopted Son George Washington Parke Custis, with A Memoir of the Author, by His Daughter*. New York: Derby and Jackson, 1860.

Cutrer, Thomas W., ed. *Longstreet's Aide: The Civil War Letters of Major Thomas J. Goree*. Charlottesville: University Press of Virginia, 1995.

Dana, Charles A. *Recollections of the Civil War*. New York: D. Appleton, 1913.

Davis, Jefferson. *Rise and Fall of the Confederate Government*. New York: D. Appleton, 1881. 2 vols.

deButts, Mary Custis Lee. *Growing Up in the 1850s: The Journal of Agnes Lee*. Chapel Hill: University of North Carolina Press, 1984.

Dowdey, Clifford, and Louis H. Manarin, eds. *The Wartime Papers of R. E. Lee*. Boston: Little, Brown, 1961.

Eaton, John. *Grant, Lincoln and the Freedmen: Reminiscences of the Civil War*. New York: Longmans, Green, 1907.

Gallagher, Gary W., ed. *Fighting for the Confederacy: The Personal Recollections of General Edward Porter Alexander*. Chapel Hill: University of North Carolina Press, 1989.

Goode, John. *Recollections of a Lifetime*. New York: Neale, 1906.

Hagedorn, Ann. *Beyond the River: The Untold Story of the Heroes of the Underground Railroad*. New York: Simon & Schuster, 2002.

Hallowell, Benjamin. *Autobiography of Benjamin Hallowell*. Philadelphia: Friends Book Association, 1883.

Hickerson, Thomas Felix. *Echoes of Happy Valley: Letters and Diaries, Family Life in the South, Civil War History*. Chapel Hill, NC: privately published, 1962.

Houck, Peter W., ed. *Duty, Honor, Country: The Diary and Biography of General William P. Craighill, Cadet at West Point 1849–1853*. Lynchburg, VA: Warwick House, 1993.

In Memoriam: Jesse Seligman. New York: Philip Cowen, 1894.

Jones, J. William. *Army of Northern Virginia Memorial Volume*. Richmond: Randolph and English, 1880.

———. *Life and Letters of General Robert Edward Lee: Soldier and Man*. New York: Neale, 1906.

———. *Personal Reminiscences, Anecdotes and Letters of Gen. Robert E. Lee*. New York: D. Appleton, 1875.

Jones, John B. *A Rebel War Clerk's Diary at the Confederate States Capital*. Philadelphia: Lippincott, 1866. 2 vols.

Jones, Terry L., ed. *Campbell Brown's Civil War: With Ewell and the Army of Northern Virginia*. Baton Rouge: Louisiana State University Press, 2001.

Lankford, Nelson D., ed. *An Irishman in Dixie: Thomas Conolly's Diary of the Fall of the Confederacy*. Columbia: University of South Carolina Press, 1988.

Lee, Fitzhugh. *General Lee*. New York: Appleton, 1901.

Lee, Robert E. "Biography of the Author," in Henry Lee, *Memoirs of the War in the Southern Department of the United States*. New York: University Publishing Co., 1869.

Lee, Robert E., Jr. *Recollections and Letters of General Robert E. Lee by His Son*. New York: Doubleday, 1904.

Long, A. L. *Memoirs of Robert E. Lee, His Military and Personal History*. New York: J. M. Stoddart, 1887.

Longstreet, James. *From Manassas to Appomattox*. Philadelphia: Lippincott, 1896.

De Lorne, Marquis. *A Trip Through the Tropics and Home Through America*. London: Hurst and Blackett, 1867.

Lynch, Anna Modigliani, and Kelsey Ryan, comps. "Antebellum Reminiscences of Alexandria, Virginia, Extracted from the Memoirs of Mary Louisa Slacum Benham." Unpublished paper, Alexandria, 2009.

MacDonald, Rose Mortimer Ellzey. *Mrs. Robert E. Lee*. Boston: Ginn and Company, 1939.

Mason, Emily V. *Popular Life of General Robert Edward Lee*. Baltimore: John Murphy & Co., 1871.

Meade, George, ed., *Life and Letters of George Gordon Meade*. New York: Scribner's, 1913. 2 vols.

Mosby, John S. *Memoirs of Colonel John S. Mosby*. Boston: Little, Brown, 1917.

Porter, David D. *Incidents and Anecdotes of the Civil War*. New York: D. Appleton, 1885.

Ripley, Roswell. *The War with Mexico*. New York: Harper & Brothers, 1849. 2 vols.

Ritchie, Andrew. *The Soldier, the Battle, and the Victory: Being a Brief Account of the Work of Rev. John Rankin in the Anti-Slavery Cause*. Cincinnati: Western Tract and Book Society, 1870.

Rowland, Dunbar, comp. *Jefferson Davis, Constitutionalist*. Jackson, MS: Mississippi Department of Archives and History, 1923. 10 vols.

Scarborough, William K., ed. *The Diary of Edmund Ruffin, Volume II: The Years of Hope April, 1861–June, 1863*. Baton Rouge: Louisiana State University Press, 1976.

Scheibert, Justus. *Seven Months in the Rebel States During the North American War, 1863*. Tuscaloosa, AL: Confederate Publishing Company, 1958.

Semmes, Raphael. *Service Afloat and Ashore During the Mexican War*. Cincinnati: William H. Moore, 1851.

Sidwell, Robert William. "Maintaining Order in the Midst of Chaos: Robert E. Lee's Usage of His Personal Staff." Master's Thesis: Kent State University, 2009.

Simon, John Y., ed. *The Papers of Ulysses S. Grant*. Carbondale, IL: Southern Illinois University Press, 1967–2012. 32 vols.

———., ed. *Personal Memoirs of Julia Dent Grant*. New York: G. P. Putnam's, 1975.

Smith, Gustavus W. *The Battle of Seven Pines*. New York: C. C. Crawford, 1891.

Thomas, Benjamin P., ed. *Three Years with Grant as Recalled by War Correspondent Sylvanus Cadwallader*. New York: Alfred A. Knopf, 1955.

Tower, R. Lockwood, ed. *Lee's Adjutant: The Wartime Letters of Colonel Walter Herron Taylor, 1862–1865*. Columbia: University of South Carolina Press, 1995.

Wood, Lindsay Lomax, ed. *Leaves from an Old Washington Diary, 1854–1863*. New York: E. P. Dutton, 1943.

Younger, Edward, ed. *Inside the Confederate Government: The Diary of Robert Garlick Hill Kean*. New York: Oxford University Press, 1957.

OFFICIAL PUBLICATIONS

Journal of the House of Delegates of the Commonwealth of Virginia. Richmond: Thomas Ritchie, 1816.

Obituary Record of Graduates of Yale College Deceased from June, 1870, to June, 1880. Presented at the Annual Meetings of the Alumni, 1870–1880. New Haven, CT: Tuttle, Morehouse & Taylor, 1880.

Register of the Graduates and Alumni of St. John's College at Annapolis, Maryland. Baltimore: Williams & Wilkins, 1908.

Register of the Officers and Cadets of the U.S. Military Academy, June 1826. New York: N.p., 1826.

Register of the Officers and Cadets of the U.S. Military Academy, June 1827. New York: N.p., 1827.

Register of the Officers and Cadets of the U.S. Military Academy, West Point, N.Y., June 1828. New York: N.p., 1828.

Register of the Officers and Cadets of the U S. Military Academy, West Point, June 1829. New York: United States Military Academy, 1829.

Official Register of the Officers and Cadets of the U S. Military Academy, West Point, New York, June 1840. New York: J. P. Wright, 1840.

Official Register of the Officers and Cadets of the U.S. Military Academy, West Point, New York, June 1841. New York: J. P. Wright, 1841.

Official Register of the Officers and Cadets of the U.S. Military Academy, West Point, New York, June 1842. New York: J. P. Wright, 1842.

Official Register of the Officers and Cadets of the U.S. Military Academy, West Point, New York, June 1843. New York: Burroughs & Co., 1843.

United States Congress, Journal of the Congress of the Confederate States of America, 1861–1865. Washington: Government Printing Office, 1904–1905. 7 vols.

ARTICLES

Allan, William. "Memoranda of Conversations with General Robert E. Lee," Gary W. Gallagher, ed., *Lee the Soldier.* Lincoln: University of Nebraska Press, 1996: 7–24.

Becker, Carl. "Was Grant Drinking in Mexico?" *Bulletin of the Cincinnati Historical Society* 24 (January 1966): 68–71

Boyd, William K., and William H. Wannamaker, eds. "Reminiscences of General Robert E. Lee, 1865–1868, by George Taylor Lee." *The South Atlantic Quarterly* 26 (July 1927): 236–51.

Burnett, Edmund C., ed. "Letters of a Confederate Surgeon: Dr. Abner Embry McGarity, 1862–1865." *Georgia Historical Quarterly* 29 (December 1945): 222–53.

Chatham, Patricia. "Letters Home." *Newsletter of the North Suburban Genealogical Society* 17 (September–October 1992): 35–36.

Childe, Blanche Lee. "Le Général Robert E. Lee." *Revue des Deux Mondes* 43 (June 1873): 497–537.

Cuthbert, Norma B., ed. "Five Early Letters from Robert E. Lee to His Wife, 1832–1835." *Huntington Library Quarterly* 15 (May 1951): 257–76.

DeButts, Robert E. L., Jr. "Lee in Love: Courtship and Correspondence in Antebellum Virginia." *Virginia Magazine of History and Biography* 115 (October 2007): 486–575.

Emerson, John W. "Grant's Life in the West and His Mississippi Valley Campaigns." *The Midland Monthly* 6 (October 1896): 291–303; (November 1896): 387–99; (December 1896): 488–99; 7 (January 1897): 30–41; (February 1896): 138–47; (March 1897): 218–26; (April 1897): 316–29; (May 1897): 430–38; (June 18, 1897): 497–501; 8 (July 1897): 3–9; (August 1897): 138–43; (September 1897): 206–20.

Garland, Hamlin. "The Early Life of Ulysses Grant." *McClure's Magazine* 8 (December 1896): 125–39.

Grant, Jesse R. "Grant as Remembered by His Father." *Ulysses S. Grant Association Newsletter* 8 (October, 1970): 1–10.

"James Watson Robbins." *Boston Medical and Surgical Journal* 100 (January 30, 1879): 169.

Johnston, William Preston. "Memoranda of Conversations with General R. E. Lee." Gallagher, *Lee the Soldier*: 29–34.

———. "Reminiscences of General Robert E. Lee." *Belford's Magazine* 25 (June 1890): 8—91.

Jones, J[ohn]. W[illiam]. "General Lee's Letter to His Son." *University Monthly* 2 (March 1872): 68–69.

"Knapsack." *North & South* 5 (July 2002), 8–11.

Lee, Edmund Jennings. "The Character of General Lee." Robert A. Brock, ed. *Gen. Robert Edward Lee: Soldier, Citizen and Christian Patriot*. Richmond: Johnson Publishing Co., 1897: 379–413.

"Letter from Major-General Henry Heth, of A. P. Hill's Corps, A. N. V." *Southern Historical Society Papers* 4 (October 1877): 151–60.

Leyburn, John. "An Interview with General Robert E. Lee." *Century Magazine* 30 (May, 1885): 166–67.

"List of Emigrants." *The African Repository and Colonial Journal* 30 (January 1854): 19–24.

McCormick, S. D. "Robert E. Lee as College President. The Recollections of a Student." *The Outlook* 56 (July 17, 1897), 684—87.

Miller, T. Michael, ed. "My Dear Louisa: Letters from Mrs. Mary Custis Lee to the Snowden Family of Alexandria, Virginia." *The Fireside Sentinel*, 5 (June 1991): 69–77.

Montague, Ludwell Lee, ed., "Memoir of Mrs. Harriotte Lee Taliaferro Concerning Events in Virginia, April 11–21, 1861." *Virginia Magazine of History and Biography* 57 (October 1949): 416–20.

"Negro Communed at St. Paul's Church." *Confederate Veteran* 13 (August 1905): 360.

"Our New President." *Atlantic Monthly*, 23 (March 1869): 378–83.

"Papers of Hon. John A. Campbell, 1861–1865." *Southern Historical Society Papers* 42 (September 1917): 3–81.

Porter, Horace. "The Surrender at Appomattox Court House." Robert Underwood Johnson and Clarence Clough Buel, eds. *Battles and Leaders of the Civil War*. New York: The Century Company, 1888. 4: 729–46.

"Scraps," *Historical Magazine* 2d Series, 2 (September 1867): 176–80.

Shields, Clara McGeorge. "General Grant at Fort Humboldt in the Early Days." Eureka, CA, *Humboldt Times*, November 10, 1912, in *Ulysses S. Grant Association Newsletter* 8 (April 1971): 23–28.

Sibley, Marilyn McAdams, ed. "Robert E. Lee to Albert Sydney Johnston, 1857." *Journal of Southern History* 29 (February 1963): 102–107.

Speer, Michael, ed., "Autobiography of Adam Lowry Rankin." *Ohio History* 79 (Winter 1970): 18–55.

Watson, Walter A. "Notes on Southside Virginia: Extracts from Diaries, 1914." *Bulletin of the Virginia State Library*, 15 (September 1925): pp. 244–58.

[Wolseley, Garnet]. "A Month's Visit to the Confederate Headquarters." *Blackwood's Edinburgh Magazine* 93 (January 1863): 1–29.

NEWSPAPERS

Aberdeen, SD, *Daily News*, 1890.

Albany, NY, *Daily Argus*, 1868.

Albany, NY, *Evening Journal*, 1863.

Alexandria, *Daily Advertiser*, 1807, 1808.

Alexandria, *Daily Gazette, Commercial and Political*, 1808–1817.

Alexandria, *Gazette*, 1817, 1819, 1822, 1851, 1859, 1861–1864, 1869, 1870, 1872, 1876.

Alexandria, *Gazette & Advertiser*, 1822–1824.

Alexandria, *Gazette & Daily Advertiser*, 1818–1823.

Alexandria, *Herald*, 1811–1812, 1814–1818, 1820, 1822–1823.

Alexandria, *Phenix Gazette*, 1825–1829, 1831.

Arlington, *Gazette*, 1858.

Atlanta, *Era*, 1867.

Atlanta, *Southern Confederacy*, 1862.

Augusta, GA, *Chronicle*, 1862–1863, 1866, 1879–1880, 1903, 2000.

Augusta, GA, *Daily Chronicle & Sentinel*, 1874.

Augusta, GA, *Daily Constitutionalist*, 1861–1863, 1868, 1867.

Baltimore, *Sun*, 1858, 1863, 1865, 1869.

Bangor, ME, *Weekly Register*, 1830.

Boston, *American Traveller*, 1857, 1862, 1864–1865, 1867.

Boston, *Daily Advertiser*, 18631866.

Boston, *Evening Transcript*, 1861–1862.

Boston, *Herald*, 1863.

Boston, *Journal*, 1867, 1869.

Boston, *Liberator*, 1863–1864.

Boston, *Post*, 1869.

Boston, *Saturday Evening Gazette*, 1863.

Camden, NJ, *Democrat*, 1868.

Canton, Ohio, *Repository*, 1837, 1895.

Charleston, *Courier*, 1861, 1869.

Charleston, *Daily News*, 1869.

Charleston, *Mercury*, 1862, 1863, 1865.

Charleston, *State Gazette of South Carolina*, 1786.

Chattanooga, *Daily Rebel*, 1863.

Chicago, *Daily Inter Ocean*, 1887.

Chicago, *Herald*, 1891.

Cincinnati, *Commercial*, 1863–1864, 1879.

Cincinnati, *Commercial Tribune*, 1869–1870, 1885.

Cincinnati, *Daily Enquirer*, 1864, 1868, 1872, 1874.

Cincinnati, *Daily Gazette*, 1837, 1868.

Cleveland, *Leader*, 1861–1862, 1865, 1868, 1875.

Cleveland, *Plain Dealer*, 1862–1863, 1865, 1868–1869, 1872, 1884.

Columbus, GA, *Daily Enquirer*, 1868.

Columbus, OH, *Crisis*, 1861, 1863.

Columbus, *Daily Ohio Statesman*, 1865.

Columbus, *Ohio State Journal*, 1832, 1843.

Columbus, *Ohio Monitor*, 1833.

Dallas, *Morning News*, 1928.

Dallas, *Weekly Herald*, 1866.

Easton, MD, *Gazette*, 1861, 1863.

Fayetteville, NC, *Carolina Observer*, 1861, 1863.

Frankfort, KY, *Argus*, 1832.

Galveston, *Flake's Bulletin*, 1867.

Greenfield, MA, *Gazette & Courier*, 1863.

Hartford, CT, *Connecticut Courant*, 1864.

Hartford, CT, *Daily Courant*, 1863–1864.

Hillsborough, NC, *Recorder*, 1862.

Houston, *Telegraph*, 1865.
Houston, *Texas Telegraph*, 1847.
Jackson, MI, *Citizen*, 1897.
Jackson, MI, *Daily Citizen*, 1867.
Jamestown, NY, *Journal*, 1868.
Keene, *New Hampshire Sentinel*, 1862.
Keowee, SC, *Courier*, 1866.
Lexington, KY, *Morning Herald*, 1901.
Lowell, MA, *Daily Citizen and News*, 1864–1865.
Macon, GA, *Daily Telegraph*, 1866.
Macon, GA, *Telegraph*, 1862–1863, 1866, 1886.
Macon, GA, *Weekly Telegraph*, 1862, 1867–1868, 1870, 1875.
Memphis, *Daily Avalanche*, 1868.
Milwaukee, *Journal of Commerce*, 1871.
Milwaukee, *Semi Weekly Madison*, 1866.
Milwaukee, *Sentinel*, 1862, 1865.
Mobile, *Advertiser & Register*, 1864.
Mobile, *Register*, 1863.
Montgomery, *Advertiser*, 1918.
Nashville, *Union and American*, 1861.
Newark, NJ, *Centinel of Freedom*, 1874.
New Haven, CT, *Columbian Register*, 1862.
New London, CT, *Democrat*, 1852.
New London, CT, *New London Daily Chronicle*, 1863.
New Orleans, *Daily Picayune*, 1866, 1885.
New Orleans, *Picayune*, 1863.
New Orleans, *Times*, 1865, 1867.
New Orleans, *Times-Picayune*, 1871, 1884, 1886, 1903.
New York, *Commercial Advertiser*, 1846, 1868–1869.
New York, *Emancipator*, 1839.
New York, *Evening Post*, 1861.
New York, *Frank Leslie's Illustrated Newspaper*, 1862–1863.
New York, *Herald*, 1863–1865, 1868–1869, 1878–1879.
New York, *Independent*, 1866.
New York, *Ledger*, 1868.
New York, *Morning Telegraph*, 1875.
New York, *Times*, 1885, 1897.
New York, *Tribune*, 1859, 1861–1863, 1865–1866, 1868, 1872, 1886.
New York, *World*, 1863.
Norfolk, *American Beacon*, 1817–1819.
Norfolk, *Gazette and Publick Ledger*, 1812, 1814–1816.
Norwich, CT, *Aurora*, 1865, 1869.
Omaha, *World Herald*, 1895–1896.
Philadelphia, *Evening Telegraph*, 1867.
Philadelphia, *Illustrated New Age*, 1865.
Philadelphia, *Inquirer*, 1862, 1864–1865, 1868, 1879, 1885, 1893.
Philadelphia, *National Gazette*, 1826.
Philadelphia, *Public Ledger*, 1862.
Plattsburgh, NY, *Republican*, 1852.

Portland, ME, *Advertiser*, 1830.

Portland, ME, *Daily Advertiser*, 1863.

Portland, ME, *Daily Eastern Argus*, 1863, 1868.

Portland, ME, *Weekly Advertiser*, 1862.

Portland, *Oregonian*, 1864, 1872, 1900.

Portsmouth, OH, *Times*, 1861.

Providence, RI, *Evening Press*, 1863–1865, 1868.

Quincy, IL, *Daily Whig*, 1869.

Quincy, IL, *Whig*, 1868.

Richmond, *Daily Dispatch*, 1861, 1865.

Richmond, *Dispatch*, 1867, 1869, 1890.

Richmond, *Enquirer*, 1819, 1823–1829, 1863.

Richmond, *Examiner*, 1861–1863.

Richmond, *Sentinel*, 1865.

Richmond, *Southern Opinion*, 1869

Richmond, *Times-Dispatch*, 1905, 1907, 1918, 1922, 1924, 1932.

Richmond, *Virginia Argus*, 1807, 1816, 1818.

Richmond, *Virginia Patriot*, 1810, 1815, 1817–1818.

Richmond, *Whig*, 1826, 1862–1864, 1867–1869, 1874.

Rockford, IL, *Morning Star*, 1888.

Rockford, IL, *Republican*, 1861.

Sacramento, *Daily Union*, 1863.

Salem, MA, *Register*, 1864, 1866.

Salem, NC, *People's Press*, 1861.

San Diego, *Evening Tribune*, 1901.

San Diego, *Union*, 1885.

San Francisco, *Bulletin*, 1862–1863, 1865, 1868, 1875, 1879, 1882.

San Francisco, *Evening Journal*, 1853.

San Francisco, *Post*, 1886.

Sandusky, *Register*, 1858.

Schenectady, NY, *Cabinet*, 1852.

Springfield, *Daily Illinois Journal*, 1862.

Springfield, *Daily Illinois State Journal*, 1861–1863, 1905.

Springfield, *Daily Republican*, 1863.

Springfield, MA, *Republican*, 1862–1863, 1872.

St. Louis, *Daily Missouri Republican*, 1852, 1858.

St. Paul, *Daily Press*, 1868.

Trenton, *State Gazette*, 1865, 1867, 1879.

Troy, NY, *Times*, 1864.

Washington, *Critic-Record*, 1869, 1886.

Washington, *Daily National Intelligencer*, 1821, 1829, 1852, 1861.

Washington, *Evening Star*, 1861, 1863, 1867, 1885.

Washington, *Evening Union*, 1863–1865.

Washington, PA, *Reporter*, 1863.

Watertown, *New York Reporter*, 1851.

Westminster, MD, *Carroll County Democrat*, 1859.

Winchester, VA, *Evening Star*, 1940.

Winchester, VA, *Times*, June 3, 1896.

Worcester, MA, *National Aegis*, 1831, 1864.

AUTOGRAPH DEALER CATALOGS

Alexander Autographs Catalog, June 24, 1997, p. 10, item #99.

Alexander Autographs Catalog, October 14, 2006, sale, item #57.

Alexander Autographs Catalog, November 6, 2008, sale, p. 55, item #119 and #209.

Alexander Autographs Catalog, May 13, 2009 sale, item #206.

Alexander Autographs "War Between the States" catalog, 2008.

Civil War Auction Catalog No. 155, Antebellum Covers, Ron and Anne Meininger, Gaithers-burg, MD.

Gary Hendershott Catalog, December 1995, p. 55, item #129.

Gary Hendershott Catalog, August 1999, Little Rock, AK.

HCA Auction Sale, July 22, 2010.

Heritage Auction, Dallas, November 20–21, 2008, item #57137.

Lee, Robert E., letter to Osman Latrobe, June 8, 1866, sold at auction in 1980, present location unknown.

Olde Soldier Books, Inc., Catalog #192, December 2003, item #118.

Profiles in History Catalog, Calabasas Hills, CA, December 2007, p. 20, item #24 and #25.

Raab Autographs, Ardmore, PA, Catalog, January 2003, p. 12, item #11.

Raab Collection Catalog, January 2012.

Raynors' Historical Collectible Auctions Catalog, Burlington, NC, November 17, 2005, sale, item #97.

Rhode Scholar Catalog, Upper Marlboro, MD, September 1998, p. 25, item #84.

RR Auction Autograph Blog, August 3, 2011.

RWA Auction Catalog #39, June 1, 1996, p. 34, item #156.

RWA Auction Catalog #41, March 15, 1997, p. 59, item #341.

Signature House Sale Catalog Sale January 7, 2000, p. 46, item #233.

Signature House Catalog, n.d., Bridgeport, WV.

Sotheby's Presidential and Other American Manuscripts Sale Catalog, April 3, 2008, item #13.

Swann Auction Catalog, April 17, 2012.

Swann Auction Galleries Catalog 2163, November 18, 2008.

Swann Auction Galleries, Sale 2333, New York, November 16, 2013.

Swann Galleries Catalog Sale, March 24, 1988, item #142.

William Reese Company Americana, New Haven, CT, website item 46845.

SECONDARY WORKS

Andrews, J. Cutler. *The North Reports the Civil War*. Pittsburgh: University of Pittsburgh Press, 1955.

Arlington House. Washington: National Park Service, n.d.

Armes, Ethel. *Stratford Hall: The Great House of the Lees*. Richmond: Garrett and Massie, 1936.

Bartholomees, J. Boone Jr. *Buff Facings and Gilt Buttons: Staff and Headquarters Operations in the Army of Northern Virginia, 1861–1865*. Columbia, South Carolina: University of South Carolina Press, 1998.

Bearss, Edwin Cole. *The Campaign for Vicksburg*. Dayton, OH: Morningside House, 1985–86. 3 vols.

Bradford, Gamaliel. *Lee the American*. Boston: Houghton, Mifflin, 1912.

Catton, Bruce. *Grant Takes Command*. Boston: Little, Brown, 1968.

Coffman, Edward. *The Old Army: A Portrait of the American Army in Peacetime 1784–1898*. New York: Oxford University Press, 1988.

Cozzens, Peter. *The Darkest Days of the War: The Battles of Iuka & Corinth*. Chapel Hill: University of North Carolina Press, 1997.

————. *The Shipwreck of Their Hopes: The Battles for Chattanooga*. Urbana: University of Illinois Press, 1994.

Davis, William C., ed. *A Fire-Eater Remembers: The Confederate Memoir of Robert Barnwell Rhett*. Columbia: University of South Carolina Press, 2000.

————. *"A Government of Our Own": The Making of the Confederacy*. New York: Free Press, 1994.

Decker, Karl, and Angus McSween. *Historic Arlington: A History of the National Cemetery from Its Establishment to the Present Time*. Washington: Decker and McSween, 1892.

DeHart, Richard Patten. *Past and Present of Tippecanoe County, Indiana*. Indianapolis: B. F. Bowen, 1909. 2 vols.

Dowdey, Clifford. *Lee*. Boston: Little, Brown, 1965.

Ellington, Charles G. *The Trial of U. S. Grant: The Pacific Coast Years, 1852–1854*. Glendale, CA: Arthur H. Clark, 1986.

Ezekiel, Herbert T., and Gaston Lichtenstein. *The History of the Jews of Richmond from 1769 to 1917*. Richmond: Herbert T. Ezekiel, 1917.

Fellman, Michael. *The Making of Robert E. Lee*. New York: Random House, 2000.

Flood, Charles Bracelen. *Lee: The Last Years*. Boston: Houghton, Mifflin, 1981.

Freeman, Douglas Southall. *R. E. Lee, A Biography*. New York: Scribner's, 1934–1935. 4 vols.

Gallagher, Gary W. *Becoming Confederates: Paths to a New National Identity*. Athens: University of Georgia Press, 203.

————. *The Fredericksburg Campaign: Decision on the Rappahannock*. Chapel Hill: University of North Carolina Press, 1995.

————. *Lee and His Generals in War and Memory*. Baton Rouge: Louisiana State University Press, 1998.

Garland, Hamlin. *Ulysses S. Grant, His Life and Character*. New York: Doubleday, 1898.

Glatthaar, Joseph T. *General Lee's Army: From Victory to Collapse*. New York: Free Press, 2008.

Harsh, Joseph T. *Taken at the Flood: Robert E. Lee & Confederate Strategy in the Maryland Campaign of 1862*. Kent, OH: Kent State University Press, 1999.

Headley, P. C. *The Life and Campaigns of Lieut.-Gen. U. S. Grant*. New York: Derby and Miller, 1866.

Hennessy, John. *Return to Bull Run: The Campaign and Battle of Second Manassas*. New York: Simon and Schuster, 1992.

Hughes, Nathaniel Cheairs. *The Battle of Belmont: Grant Strikes South*. Chapel Hill: University of North Carolina Press, 1991.

Hurst, Harold W. *Alexandria on the Potomac: The Portrait of an Ante-Bellum Community*. Lanham, MD: University Press of America, 1991.

Johnson, Edward C., Gail R. Johnson, and Melissa Johnson Williams. *All Were Not Heroes: A Study of "the List of U. S. Soldiers Executed by U.S. Military Authorities During the Late War."* Chicago: privately published, 1997.

Jones, R. Steven. *The Right Hand of Command: Use and Disuse of Personal Staffs in the American Civil War*. Mechanicsburg, PA: Stackpole Books, 2000.

Kegel, James A. *North with Lee and Jackson: The Lost Story of Gettysburg*. Mechanicsburg, PA: Stackpole Books, 1996.

Kelsey, Marie Ellen, comp. *Ulysses S. Grant, A Bibliography*. Westport, CT: Praeger, 2005.

Korn, Bertram. *American Jewry and the Civil War*. New York: Athenaeum, 1970.

Krick, Robert E. L. *Staff Officers in Gray: A Biographical Register of the Staff Officers in the Army of Northern Virginia*. Chapel Hill: University of North Carolina Press, 2003.

Krick, Robert K. *Civil War Weather in Virginia*. Tuscaloosa: University of Alabama Press, 2007.

————. *The Smoothbore Volley That Doomed the Confederacy: The Death of Stonewall Jackson and Other Chapters on the Army of Northern Virginia*. Baton Rouge: Louisiana State University Press, 2002.

Lee, Edmund Jennings. *Lee of Virginia, 1642–1892, Biographical and Genealogical Sketches of the Descendants of Col. Richard Lee*. Philadelphia: Franklin Printing Co., 1895.

Linderman, Gerald F. *Embattled Courage: The Experience of Combat in the American Civil War*. New York: The Free Press, 1987.

Lowry, Thomas P. *A Thousand Stories You Didn't Know About the Civil War*. N.p.: Published by author, 2014.

————. *Don't Shoot That Boy! Abraham Lincoln and Military Justice*. Mason City, IA: Savas Publishing, 1999.

Lowry, Thomas P., and Lewis Laska. *Confederate Death Sentences: A Reference Guide*. Charleston, SC: Booksurge, 2008.

Matter, William D. *If It Takes All Summer: The Battle for Spotsylvania*. Chapel Hill: University of North Carolina Press, 1988.

McCash, William. *Thomas R. R. Cobb: The Making of a Southern Nationalist*. Macon, GA: Mercer University Press, 1983.

McKim, Randolph H. *The Soul of Lee*. New York: Longmans, Green, 1918.

McPherson, James M. *For Cause and Comrades: Why Men Fought in the Civil War*. New York: Oxford University Press, 1997.

Moore, Albert Burton. *Conscription and Conflict in the Confederacy*. New York: Macmillan, 1924.

Moran, William. *The Belles of New England: The Women of the Textile Mills and the Families Whose Wealth They Wove*. New York: St. Martin's Press, 2002.

Morrison, Alfred J. *The Beginnings of Public Education in Virginia, 1776–1860*. Richmond: Superintendent of Public Printing, 1917.

Pfanz, Donald C. *Richard S. Ewell, A Soldier's Life*. Chapel Hill: University of North Carolina Press, 1998.

Powell, Mary Gregory. *The History of Old Alexandria, Virginia: From July 13, 1749 to May 24, 1861*. Alexandria: William Byrd Press, 1928.

Pryor, Elizabeth Brown. *Reading the Man: A Portrait of Robert E. Lee Through His Private Letters*. New York: Viking, 2007.

Rable, George C. *God's Almost Chosen People: A Religious History of the American Civil War*. Chapel Hill: University of North Carolina Press, 2010.

Rhea, Gordon C. *The Battle of the Wilderness, May 5–6, 1864*. Baton Rouge: Louisiana State University Press, 1994.

————. *The Battles for Spotsylvania Court House and the Road to Yellow Tavern, May 7–12, 1864*. Baton Rouge: Louisiana State University Press, 1997.

————. *To the North Anna River: Grant and Lee, May 13–25, 1864*. Baton Rouge: Louisiana State University Press, 2000.

Richardson, Albert D. *A Personal History of Ulysses S. Grant*. Hartford: American Publishing, 1868.

Royster, Charles. *A Revolutionary People at War: The Continental Army and American Character, 1775–1783*. New York: W. W. Norton & Company, 1979.

Sarna, Jonathan D. *When General Grant Expelled the Jews*. New York: Schocken Books, 2012.

Sears, Stephen W. *Gettysburg*. Boston: Houghton, Mifflin, 2003.

————. *Landscape Turned Red: The Battle of Antietam*. New York: Houghton, Mifflin, 1983.

————. *To the Gates of Richmond: The Peninsula Campaign*. Boston: Ticknor & Fields, 1992.

Shea, William L., and Terrence J. Winschel. *Vicksburg Is the Key: The Struggle for the Mississippi River*. Lincoln: University of Nebraska Press, 2003.

Silverman, Jason, Samuel N. Thomas Jr., and Beverly D. Evans IV. *Shanks: The Life and Wars of General Nathan George Evans, CSA*. New York: Da Capo Press, 2002.

Simpson, Brooks D. *Let Us Have Peace: Ulysses S. Grant and the Politics of War and Reconstruction, 1861–1868*. Chapel Hill: University of North Carolina, 1991.

———. *Ulysses S. Grant: Triumph Over Adversity, 1822–1865*. Boston: Houghton, Mifflin, 2000.

Smith, Timothy B. *Corinth, 1862: Siege, Battle, Occupation*. Lawrence: University Press of Kansas, 2012.

Stout, Harry S. *Upon the Altar of the Nation*. New York: Viking, 2006.

Thomas, Emory M. *Robert E. Lee. A Biography*. New York: Norton, 1995.

Trout, Robert J. *With Pen & Saber*. Harrisburg, PA: Stackpole Books, 1995.

Varney, Frank P. *General Grant and the Rewriting of History: How the Destruction of General William S. Rosecrans Influenced Our Understanding of the Civil War*. El Dorado Hills, CA: Savas Beatie, 2013.

Varon, Elizabeth R. *Appomattox: Victory, Defeat, and Freedom at the End of the Civil War*. New York: Oxford University Press, 2014.

Waugh, Joan. *U. S. Grant: American Hero, American Myth*. Chapel Hill: University of North Carolina Press, 2013.

Wickham, Henry T., comp., and Lois Wingfield Wickham, ed. *Memoirs of the Wickham Family of Hickory Hill, Hanover County, Virginia, 1791–1988*. Privately published: 2008.

Wilson, David L., and John Y. Simon, eds. *Ulysses S. Grant: Essays and Documents*. Carbondale: Southern Illinis University Press, 1981.

Wood, Amos D. *Floyd County, A History of the People and Places*. Blacksburg, VA: Southern Printing Co., 1981.

Zinn, Jack. *R. E. Lee's Cheat Mountain Campaign*. Parsons, WV: McLain, 1974.

ARTICLES

"The Brett Street Idea," *Architectural Legacy* 2 (Spring/Summer 2011): 2.

Carmichael, Peter S. "Lee's Search for the Battle of Annihilation." Peter S. Carmichael, ed., *Audacity Personified: The Generalship of Robert E. Lee*. Baton Rouge: Louisiana State University Press, 2004. 1–26.

Davis, William C. "The Turning Point That Wasn't: The Confederates and the Election of 1864," in William C. Davis, *The Cause Lost: Myths and Realities of the Confederacy*. Lawrence, KS: University Press of Kansas, 1996. 127–47.

Feis, William B. "Grant and the Belmont Campaign: A Study in Intelligence and Command." Steven E. Woodworth, ed., *The Art of Command in the Civil War*. Lincoln: University of Nebraska Press, 1998. 17–49.

Gallagher, Gary W. "Conduct Must Conform to the New Order of Things: R. E. Lee and the Question of Loyalty." Gary W. Gallagher, *Becoming Confederates: Paths to a New National Loyalty*. Athens: University of Georgia Press, 2013. 8–34.

———. "The Net Result of the Campaign Was in Our Favor: Confederate Reaction to the Maryland Campaign," in Gary W. Gallagher, ed., *The Antietam Campaign*. Chapel Hill: University of North Carolina Press, 1999. 3–43.

———. "A Question of Loyalty," *Civil War Times* 52 (October 2013): 30–37.

Grammer, John. "The Republican Historical Vision: Joseph Glover Baldwin's Party Leaders." *Southern Literary Journal* 25 (Spring 1993): 3–13.

Griffin, Patrick J., III. "Tragedy of Two Cousins—Adventurers or Spies?" *The Montgomery County Story* 34 (November 1991): 177–88.

Hinton, Marcus. "Christmas Greetings," Rebel United Kingdom Division, Confederate High Command, (December 1964): n.p.

Krick, Robert E. L. "The 'Great Tycoon' Forges a Staff System." Peter S. Carmichael, ed., *Audacity Personified: The Generalship of Robert E. Lee*. Baton Rouge: Louisiana State University Press, 2004. 82–106.

Krick, Robert K. "'Lee to the Rear,' the Texans Cried." Gary W. Gallagher, ed., *The Wilderness Campaign*. Chapel Hill: University of North Carolina Press, 1997. 160–200.

———. "'Snarl and Sneer and Quarrel': General Joseph E. Johnston and an Obsession with Rank." Gary W. Gallagher and Joseph T. Glatthaar, eds, *Leaders of the Lost Cause: New Perspectives on the Confederate High Command*. Mechanicsburg, PA: Stackpole, 2004. 165–204.

Pickett, Thomas E. "W. W. Richeson, The Kentuckian That 'Taught' Grant." *Register of the Kentucky State Historical Society* 9 (September 1911): 13–25.

Robert, Joseph C. "Lee the Farmer." *Journal of Southern History* 4 (November 1937): 422–40.

Simon, John Y. "Ulysses S. Grant and the Jews: An Unsolved Mystery." *The Record* 21 (1995): 24–33.

Smith, David G. "Race and Retaliation: The Capture of African-Americans during the Gettysburg Campaign." Peter Wallenstein and Bertram Wyatt-Brown, eds., *Virginia's Civil War*. Charlottesville: University of Virginia Press, 2005.137–51.

Wert, Jeffry D. "The Tycoon: Lee and His Staff." *Civil War Times Illustrated* 11 (July 1972): 11–19.

WEBSITES

"Confederate History—Disspelling the Myths." http://www.rulen.com/myths/.

"Did Julia Grant Own Slaves?" Yesterday and Today, April 2, 2011. http://www.yandtblog.com/?p=298.

Lee Family Digital Archive, Washington and Lee University, Lexington, VA. http://leearchive.wlu.edu/.

Morton, Charles S., to his mother, July 4, 1861. www.vmb-collection.com/AandDPages/AandDP47.html.

Ryan, Joe. "The Lee Family Slaves." http://americancivilwar.com/authors/Joseph_Ryan/Articles/General-Lee-Slaves/General-Lee-Family-Slaves.html.

Schwartz, Philip J., "General Lee and Visibility." http://www.stratalum.org/leecommunion.htm.

United States Census Bureau. Nativity of the Population for the 25 Largest Urban Places and for Selected Counties: 1850, Table 21. https://www.census.gov/population/www/documentation/twps0029/tab21.html.

United States Census Bureau, Nativity of the Population for the 25 Largest Urban Places and for Selected Counties: 1860, Table 20. http://www.census.gov/population/www/documentation/twps0029/tab20.html.

Woodward, Colin. "Slaves at the Lee Family Home." http://southernhistorian.wordpress.com/2011/06/11/12/.

ACKNOWLEDGMENTS

My first debt is to the many friends who have given of their time and expertise. At the front of the line must stand Robert K. Krick of Fredericksburg, Virginia, a friend for forty years. He opened to me his incomparable archive of reference notes on Lee from around the country, and an archive of manuscript and autograph catalog listings of Lee materials going back many years, containing partial or often full transcripts of letters in collectors' hands that could never be found otherwise. On top of that, he carefully read the Lee portions of this book and corrected many a gaffe, while offering suggestions and insights from which I have benefited greatly. Gary W. Gallagher of the University of Virginia, another close friend of more than a quarter century, also read this work and made comments from his vantage as one of our most distinguished commentators on Lee and the Confederate experience. Frank Williams, a longtime friend and president of the Ulysses S. Grant Association, himself a distinguished Lincoln scholar, gave the book a thoughtful reading and raised valuable questions on focus and interpretation from which it has benefited greatly. Another friend for the past quarter century, Joseph T. Glatthaar of the University of North Carolina, one of the nation's outstanding students of military history and theory, kindly commented on major portions of the work.

Numerous other friends and colleagues helped with documents or made suggestions, or otherwise gave of their expertise. National Park Service staff, as always, never failed to be generous, among them Matthew Penrod at Arlington House, the Robert E. Lee Memorial, Dennis Frye at Harpers Ferry National Memorial Park, and Robert E. L. Krick at Richmond National Battlefield Park. Old friends John E. Marsalek, James I. Robertson Jr., David G. Smith, and Richard J. Sommers all lent good counsel. The Reverend Reginald Tuck of Blacksburg United Methodist Church, a keen student of history both lay and ecclesiastical, offered excellent insights into Lee's developing faith.

Archivists are simply indispensable to a historian. Without them the raw materials vital to a work such as this would stay locked away, unknown; and without their knowledge of their institutions' holdings, uncataloged treasures would remain unused, as good as lost. Douglas Mayo, associate librarian at Colonial Williamsburg Foundation's John D. Rockefeller Jr. Library in Williamsburg, lent valuable assistance with the Hill Carter Papers. Deanne Blanton at the National Archives in Washington, DC, bids fair to be a national treasure herself. Her assistance to myriad scholars working in nineteenth-century military documents cannot be overpraised; she certainly unlocked many unknown doors in the research for this volume. The Museum of the Confederacy's John Coski has been a friend and colleague for many years; no one knows its fine collections as well as he. Those collections will soon be housed at the Virginia Historical Society. Paul Reber, executive director of Stratford Hall, Stratford, Virginia, and Judy Hynson, librarian at Stratford's Jesse Ball duPont Memorial Library, were very helpful with materials illuminating Lee's youth, including putting me in touch with Gary L. Sisson of Montross, Virginia, owner of the letter containing Lee's only directly contemporaneous comments on his time at West Point. Suzanne Cristoff, associate director of the United States Military Academy Library at West Point, and archives curator Alicia Mauldin-Ware, were very helpful with records of Grant's and Lee's tenures there as cadets. Graham Dozier of the Virginia Historical Society in Richmond has been especially generous in assistance with the extensive Lee family holdings in that exemplary institution. And special thanks are due to Vonnie Zullo of Fairfax, Virginia, an outstanding freelance researcher who made many a trip to archives in Washington to catch something I overlooked.

My agent Jim Donovan of Jim Donovan Literary in Dallas, Texas, has definitely made me a convert when it comes to the value of working with an agent. He proved invaluable both in finding and working with my publisher, and as an extra set of eyes on the manuscript. Robert Pigeon, executive editor at Da Capo Press, has been unfailingly supportive and patient from the outset, and a keen judge of balance and content in the writing of this book

My thanks are due to all, and most especially to yet another reader, Sandra C. Davis, whose patience with the writing of books seems boundless, and whose love and support are greater still.

INDEX

21st Illinois Infantry, 130–131

2d United States Cavalry, 77, 111, 412

4th United States Infantry, 42, 53, 54, 85ff

A

Adams, John Quincy, 9

Alexander, E. Porter, 388

Alexandria Academy, 6

Alexandria Boarding School, 11

Allan, William, 468

Allen, George, 54

American Colonization Society, 80

Ammen, Daniel, 14, 15, 19, 33, 206, 379

Ammen, Jacob, 14, 206

Anderson, Richard H., 322, 400, 401

Antietam, MD, Campaign, 239–246

Appomattox Campaign, 449–454

Arlington House plantation, 26, 38, 39, 43, 44, 60, 80ff, 151, 166, 347, 349, 490

B

Babcock, Orville, 389, 390

Bailey, George P., 14, 176

Baldwin, Briscoe G., 316

Baldwin, Joseph Glover, 81

Banks, Nathaniel P., 296, 299, 305, 345, 362, 364, 365, 386, 389, 390, 392, 437

Barret, John R., 94, 110

Battles. *See individual battles by name*

Beauregard, Pierre G. T., 141, 143, 189, 207, 209, 314, 325, 380, 381, 386, 403, 405, 412, 414, 444, 461, 479

Beecher, Henry Ward, 469

Bell, John, 109

Belmont, MO, Battle of, 134, 154–157, 158, 173, 174

Benjamin, Judah P., 161, 162, 169, 170, 171, 189, 413

Bickham, William D., 252–253

Big Bethel, VA, Battle of, 142

Blair, Francis Preston, Jr., 94, 110, 129

Blair, Francis Preston, Sr., 118–119, 444

Boggs, Harry, 93, 95, 102

Bonham, Milledge L., 140, 141

Booth, Jack, 108

Bowers, Theodore, 341, 389

Bragg, Braxton, 239, 241, 242, 246, 266, 292, 354–356, 366, 368–370, 372, 380

Brand, Robert, 124

Brandy Station, VA, Battle of, 324

Breckinridge, John C., 41, 109, 110, 112, 403, 405, 408, 420, 444, 445–447, 449, 450, 451, 452, 457, 470, 471

Brett, Richard W., 89

Bristoe Station, VA, Battle of, 355–356

Brown, John, 14, 95–96

Brown, Joseph E., 161, 162, 168, 170, 172

Brown, Owen, 14

Buchanan, James, 79, 95, 110, 113

Buckner, Simon Bolivar, 32, 186, 188, 193, 489, 490

Buell, Don Carlos, 178, 179, 193, 195, 196, 198–199, 228, 229, 251

   at Shiloh 202–207, 222

Buford, Napoleon B., 225

Bull Run, VA, First Battle of, 132, 141, 143

Bull Run, VA, Second Battle of, 232–237

Burke, Melancthon, 31

Burke, William, 80

Burnside, Ambrose E., 263, 264, 268–269, 280, 287–288, 366, 368, 369, 370, 375, 391, 398, 429, 406

Butler, Benjamin F., 390, 392, 400, 403, 405, 408, 409

C

Calderwood, John C., 108

Calhoun, John C., 10, 11, 45

Camp, Elijah, 87, 88

Campaigns. *See individual campaigns*

Campbell, John A., 444, 446, 447, 450–452, 457

Camp Salubrity, LA, 41

Canby, E. R. S., 434, 437

Carter, Ann Hill. *See* Lee, Ann Hill Carter

Carter, Charles (REL grandfather), 1

Carter, Hill (REL cousin), 48, 61, 485

Carter, Williams (REL uncle), 48, 351, 440

Cass, Lewis, 94

Catlin, George, 32

Catty or Cassy (REL slave), 48

Cerro Gordo, Battle of, 64

Cervantes, Miguel, 35

Chancellorsville, VA, Battle of, 293–294, 308–313

Chandler, Zachariah, 85, 526 n97

Chattanooga, GA, Campaign, 366–372

Cheat Mountain, VA, Campaign, 146–149

Chickamauga, GA, Battle of, 355, 365

Chilton, Robert H., 316, 319

Christ Episcopal Church, Alexandria, VA, 2, 7, 121

Churchill, Winston, 409

Churubusco, Battle of, 67

Clarke, George (slave), 278

Clay, Henry, 15, 20, 45, 46, 94

Clemens, Samuel (Mark Twain), 489, 490

Cobb, Thomas R. R., 284

Cocke, Elizabeth Randolph, 460

Cocke, Philip St. George, 136, 140

Cold Harbor, VA, Battle of, 406–408, 438

College of Ripley, OH, 21–22

Collins, E. A., 105

Columbus, KY, 134, 152, 154, 156

Comstock, Cyrus, 377, 379, 389

Cook, John, 153

Cooke, Giles B., 457

Cooper, James Fenimore, 31

Cooper, Samuel, 146

Corinth, MS, Battle of, 247–251

Corinth Campaign, Grant's, 229, 238

Corrick's Ford, VA, Battle of, 144

Cowell, D. T., 293

Crittenden Compromise, 473

Crittenden, John J., 116

Curtis, Samuel, 254, 255, 258, 260

Custis, George Washington Parke (REL father-in-law), 8, 9, 35, 37, 48, 60–61, 270, 271, 278

   death, 79

   estate, 79–82, 113

   will, 524 n69

Custis, Mary Anna Randolph. *See* Lee, Mary Custis

CSA (Confederate States of America). *See* Grant, as general *and various Lee entries*

D

Dana, Charles, 363, 449

Davis, Jefferson, xx, 101, 136, 172, 189, 210, 211, 218, 225, 233, 236, 239, 264, 288, 291, 320–323, 346, 347, 353, 354, 380, 384, 397, 445–447, 449, 452, 456, 458, 462
   makes REL advisor, 142, 150
   relations with REL, 380–381, 387, 411–415, 431, 441

Dent, Emma (USG sister-in-law), 85, 95

Dent, Frederick, Jr. (USG brother-in-law), 32, 70, 85, 389, 390, 481

Dent, Frederick, Sr. (USG father-in-law), 40, 41, 95, 104, 111, 129, 224

Dent, Julia. *See* Grant, Julia Dent

Dent, Lewis (USG brother-in-law), 92

Dominguez, 67, 122

Douglas, Stephen A., 109, 110, 112

Drayton, Thomas, 265

E

Early, Jubal A., 40, 357, 407, 420, 480

Eastern View plantation, 26, 46

Echols, John, 459, 479

Everett, Edward, 116

Ewell, Richard S., 230, 322–330, 354, 357, 381, 398, 401, 406, 407, 444, 471

F

Fishback, John, 107

Fitzhugh, Anna (REL aunt), 121

Fitzhugh, Mary (REL aunt), 10, 49

Fitzhugh, William Henry (REL uncle), 1, 7, 8, 10, 35

Floyd, John B., 111, 144–150, 186, 188, 195

Foote, Andrew H., 135, 178, 179, 180, 181–187

Forrest, Nathan Bedford, 279, 294

Fort Carroll, MD, 75

Fort Donelson, TN, 171–188

Fort Hamilton, NY, 49

Fort Henry, TN, 171–188

Fort Henry–Fort Donelson Campaign, 179–188, 193–194

Fort Monroe, VA, 37, 39, 43, 47

Fort Pickens, FL, 118

Fort Pulaski, GA, 34

Fort Sumter, SC, 118, 124

Foster, John G., 375, 376, 379

Franklin, William B., 32

Frayser's Farm, VA, Battle of, 218–219

Fredericksburg, VA, Battle of, 267–269, 280

Freeman, Douglas Southall, xi

Freligh, J. S., 92, 95, 277

Frémont, John C., 95, 132–135, 152, 153, 158, 175, 389

Frost, Daniel M., 123, 129

G

Gaines's Mill, VA, Battle of, 216

Gardner (REL slave), 48, 61

Garland, John, 54, 56, 63, 66

Garnett, Robert S., 144

Gettysburg, PA, Battle of, 347, 349, 353

Gettysburg, PA, Campaign, 320–330, 346

Goethe, Johann Wolfgang von, 35

Goldsmith, Solomon, 275

Gorman, Willis, 343

Grant, Ellen (USG daughter), 92

Grant, Frederick (USG son), 92, 378

Grant, Hannah Simpson (USG
    mother), 13–16
  as mother, 15, 24
Grant, Jesse (USG son), 92
Grant, Jesse Root (USG father), 158,
    174, 430
  boastfulness, 17–18, 40, 53
  business, 14
  employs USG, 104, 110, 224
  as father, 14–15, 23
  naming USG, 14, 17
  pushes USG, 42, 58, 91
  and slavery, 15
  USG on, 195
  as Whig 15
Grant, Julia Dent (USG wife), 40,
    51–54, 57, 70, 84–88, 123, 223, 224,
    298, 305, 335, 364, 369, 376, 464,
    489, 490
Grant, Mary (USG Sister), 132, 182
Grant, Orville (USG brother), 104–107,
    110, 343, 378
Grant, Simpson (USG brother), 104,
    105, 153
Grant, Ulysses S. (USG), Civil War
    career
  21st Illinois Infantry, training,
    130–131
  army, organization of, 257
  Appomattox Campaign, 449–54
  Battle of Cold Harbor, VA,
    406–408, 438
  Battle of Corinth, MS, 247–51
  Battle of Iuka, MS, 238, 246ff
  Battle of Shiloh, TN, 202–208
  Belmont, strategy post-attack, 158
  Chattanooga Campaign, 366–372
  command in Missouri, 131–134
  Corinth Campaign, 229, 238

Holly Springs, reaction to attack,
    279, 294
Illinois volunteers, organizing,
    125–129
James, crossing of, 409
Lee, April 10 meeting with,
    455–456, 585 n3
Lee surrender, 452–454
Mobile Campaign plan, 362–63, 364,
    365, 373, 437
North Anna, VA, operations,
    405–406
Paducah, occupation of, 134
promotion to brigadier general, 133
promotion to colonel of 21st IL,
    130
promotion to general, 477
promotion to lieutenant general,
    379–380
promotion to major general, 195
and Sherman–Johnston agreement,
    463–464
Shiloh Campaign, 200ff
Siege of Petersburg, 420–449
    passim
Spotsylvania Campaign, 400
Vicksburg Campaign, 255, 258–260,
    295–308, 330–338, 343–345
Wilderness Campaign, 392–393,
    397–400
See also individual attacks, battles,
    campaigns, and sieges
Grant, Ulysses S. (USG), as general,
  1865 peace feelers, 445–446
  army, reforms in, 174
  black soldiers, 360–361, 420, 432–434
  celebrity, 430–431
  characteristics, 130, 134, 157, 158, 174,
    177–179, 193, 194, 200, 203, 208,

225, 226, 229, 250, 255, 257, 294, 338, 343, 390, 398, 402, 403, 405, 407, 408, 421, 439

Constitution, respect for, 359, 363

contrabands, 176, 224–225, 256–257, 360

corruption, combat of, 272–273

CSA (Confederate States of America) citizens, treatment of, 132, 135, 176, 256, 294–295

delegation, 153, 178, 184–185

description of, 173, 358, 379, 396

deserters, 416–419

discipline of soldiers, 130–131, 256, 416–419

economy, 361–362

emancipation, 360

enemy, respect for, 344

enlistments, 361–362

general-in-chief, 434–437

"Jew Order" (Order No. 11), 272–277, 279, 488, 558 n116, 559 n117, 561 n118, n119

judgment of character, 343

Lee, compared with, 393–395

management style, 153–154, 157–158, 178, 184–185, 225–226, 250, 338, 389, 363–364

morale, 416–419

Navy, cooperation with, 158

political generals, 128, 201–202

presidency in 1864, 374

and press, 134, 135, 222, 224, 226, 252–253, 359, 360

prisoner exchange, 433

prisoners, 194

retaliation, 360

slavery, xviii–xix, 92, 360–361, 431–432

slaves, 20, 93–94, 105, 530 n182, n183, 531 n186, n196

staff, 39, 132–133, 175, 338–343, 379

strategic planning, 129, 134–135, 158, 174, 296, 313, 362, 376–377, 389, 391, 448

Union, 124, 361

Unionism, 127

voting, soldiers in field, 431

See also individual attacks, battles, campaigns, and sieges

Grant, Ulysses S. (USG), personal

anti-Semitism, 272–277

anti-slavery influences, 21

appearance, 107–108, 109, 358

birth, 13

character and personality, xvii, 15, 18, 19, 23–24, 86–87, 91, 109, 133, 134–135, 154, 182, 187, 196, 199, 205, 305, 306, 308, 331, 335, 369, 373, 379, 411, 437, 449

courtship, 40

drawing ability, 16–17

drinking, 69–70, 89–90, 94, 108, 131, 180, 194, 197, 252, 299, 335, 364–365, 379, 520 n79, 526 n97, 528 n147, 555 n7, 565 n95, 570 n110, n111, 575 n97, 577 n26

education, primary, 15–16

education, secondary, 19ff

entrepreneurism, 109

as farmer, 92–93

as father, 85–86

finances, 153, 302, 378, 430

health, 197–198, 302, 379, 429, 439

horses, 17, 20

marriage, 84–86, 89, 229, 429

politics, 15, 94, 535 n43

profanity, 108, 131

Grant, Ulysses S. (USG), personal
    (*continued*)
  public speaking, 16, 20
  reading, 16
  religion, 15, 108, 535 n30
  romances, purported, 510 n44
  slave ownership, 92
  smoking, 358
  temperance, 94
  thought process, 302–303
  travel, 20, 22, 28–29, 69, 85–86, 106,
    489
  work habits, 17–18, 153, 175, 429
  writing style, 16, 21, 358, 507 n158
  youth, 14–24
  See also Grant, pre–Civil War life;
    Grant, views on
Grant, Ulysses S. (USG), post–Civil
    War
  administration scandals, 488
  bankruptcy, 489
  Civil Rights Act, 487
  and Fifteenth Amendment, 487
  the French in Mexico, 437, 476
  Galena, return to, 466
  historiography on, xi–xii, xxi
  and Indian policy reform, 488
  and Ku Klux Klan, 487
  Lee in 1869, meeting with, 481–
    484
  Lee pardon, 464–465
  memoirs, 489–490
  military occupation of South,
    476–477
  mythology, xviii–xxi
  presidency, 477–478, 479, 487–489,
    490
  secretary of war, interim, 477
  trip around world, 489

Grant, Ulysses S. (USG), pre–Civil
    War life
  abolitionists, and, 15
  billiard parlor ownership, 88–89,
    527 n136, 528 n137
  in brokerage house, 93
  Chandler in Detroit, and, 85, 526
    n97
  election of 1860, 109–111
  farmer, 91–93
  in Galena, 104ff
  Lee, meeting, xvii
  name, 504 n98
  slave, frees, xviii–xix, 93, 95
  votes in 1856, 94
Grant, Ulysses S. (USG), pre–Civil
    War military experience
  ambition, 22
  army, frustration in, 56–58, 60,
    90–91
  army, resignation from, 90
  Battle of Molina del Rey, 68
  in California, 88
  at Fort Humboldt, 89–90
  at Fort Vancouver, 87
  Mexican War, 50–60, 63–64, 66–70,
    73–74, 84ff
  in Oregon, 87–89
  promotion to captain, 90
Grant, Ulysses S. (USG), relationships
    with
  Buell, Don Carlos, 207
  father (Jesse), 14–15, 18, 23, 24, 177,
    195, 197, 226
  Halleck, Henry W., 177, 183–184,
    194–199, 222–223, 226
  Kountz, William J., 177–180, 181,
    183–184, 194–197, 226
  Lincoln, Abraham, 360, 374, 431–432

McClernand, John A., 226, 242, 243, 254, 258, 260, 297, 299, 330, 336–338
Meade, William, 391, 403, 438–439
Porter, David D., 342
Rawlins, John A., 108
Rosecrans, William S., 228, 252–254, 365
Sherman, William T., 342, 436
Thomas, George H., 365, 366–369, 379, 435–436, 437
Grant, Ulysses S. (USG), views on
black protection and civil rights, 466–467, 487–489
Buchanan, James, 123
Confederate soldiers, 404
Confederate will, 377–378
Democratic Party, 109
Dred Scott decision, 94
education, 488
fighting, 54, 56, 64, 431
freedom, 18–19
government, 59
Grant, Jesse, and speculators, 275–276
Hamer, Thomas L., 517 n26, n28
Indians, 87–88
Lecompton Constitution, 94
Lee, 465, 477, 492
Mexican War, 53, 58, 66, 520 n73
Mexicans, 58–59, 70
Northern dissent, 359
patriotism, 125
Pierce, Franklin, 517 n26
press, 53, 359
reconstruction, 465, 476
Republicans, 95
rivers, control of, 129, 134–135
secession, 123
slavery, 58–59, 125, 129, 176, 224–225
Union army, 437
US future, 464
Virginia, 482–483, 484
war, 152, 465
Grant, Ulysses S., Jr. (USG son), 86, 485
Greene, Nathaniel, 167
Gregg, Maxcy, 284
Grierson, Benjamin, 306, 308, 402

H
Halleck, Henry W., 175, 178, 179, 180, 181, 183–184, 193, 221–222, 226, 248, 250, 253–255, 258, 259, 297, 303, 307, 331, 334, 341, 345, 360, 361, 363, 367, 370, 372, 373, 390, 392, 400, 402, 403, 407, 408, 409, 416, 429, 432, 464
jealousy of USG, 195–199, 201–207 passim
relations with USG, 177
Hallowell, Benjamin, 11–13
on REL, 122
Hamer, Thomas, L., 15, 19, 22, 57, 64
Hamilton, Charles, 258
Hancock, Winfield Scott, 475
Hardee, William J., 133
Hardscrabble (USG farm), 92, 103
Harney, William S., 118
Harpers Ferry, 1859 attack, 95–96
seized 1861, 120
Harris, Thomas, 131
Hatch, Reuben, 174, 179, 225, 343
Hayes, Rutherford B., 488
Hazlitt, Charles, 57
Hickory Hill plantation, 351

Hill, Ambrose P., 213, 214–220, 230, 238, 239, 243, 310, 314, 322–330, 354–357, 398, 401, 405, 471, 487
Hill, Benjamin, 441
Hill, Daniel H., 32, 145, 209, 214–220, 288–289, 322–323, 471
Hillyer, William S., 132, 175, 187, 250, 302, 330, 331, 338–341
Hitchcock, Ethan A., 183
Holly Springs, MS, attack, 279
Holmes, Theophilus H., 213
Hood, John Bell, 322, 434, 435, 447
Hooker, Joseph, 289, 290, 292–294, 308, 310–311, 313, 319, 320, 323, 325, 366–367, 369, 370–371
Hoskins, Charles, 56
Houghton, H. H., 108
Hudson, Peter, 342
Huger, Benjamin, 191, 213, 216
Hunter, David, 379, 389–390
Hunter, R. M. T., 444, 446
Hurlbut, Stephen, 131, 200, 201, 206, 248–250, 260, 334, 359

I

Imboden, John D., 384
Ingalls, Rufus, 32
Irving, Washington, 16, 30, 31
Iuka, MS, Battle of, 238, 246–247

J

Jackson, Andrew, 9–10, 11, 15, 45, 487, 503 n77, 504 n79
Jackson, Thomas J "Stonewall," 139–140, 190, 193, 212, 213, 214, 230, 240, 242–246, 261–268, 286, 293, 308, 310, 313, 317–321, 323–337, 354, 471
Jane (REL slave), 48

Jo Daviess Guard, 124, 125, 126
Johnson, Andrew, 458, 463, 477
Johnston, Albert Sidney, 77, 83, 111, 146, 160, 171, 178, 179, 182, 190, 193, 199, 202, 204, 207
Johnston, J. Stoddard, 459
Johnston, Joseph E., 25, 62, 111, 140, 141, 189, 209, 213, 233, 266, 333, 334, 344, 345, 347, 379, 380–382, 385–386, 395, 412–414, 443–444, 448, 449, 457, 458, 490, 492
    on Peninsula 190–193
Johnston, Samuel, 328
Johnston, William Preston, 211
Jomini, Antoine-Henri, 27
Jones, John Paul, 27
Jones, William (USG slave), 92–94
Juarez, Benito, 476

K

King, Mary, 28
Kirby Smith, Edmund, 266, 463, 476
Knowlton, Miner, 33
Knoxville, TN, Campaign, 356
Kountz, William J., 177–179, 180, 181, 183, 194, 197, 299

L

Lafayette, Marquis de, 9
Lagow, Clark B., 132, 175, 338–341, 364, 379
Lamb, Francis, 350
Lawley, Francis, 286
Lawrence, Abbott, 81
Lawton, A. R., 161
Leary, William B., 6, 7, 9, 10, 131, 499 n35, n37, n39, 499 n40, n42, 500 n45, n46
    on REL, 9

Lee, Ann Carter (REL daughter), 44,
  144, 68, 97, 100, 173, 291
  death 261–262, 270
Lee, Ann (REL sister), 26
Lee, Ann Hill Carter (REL mother)
  death, 28, 48
  on education, 5–6
  finances, 2–5, 7–8, 10, 496 n6, n10,
    497 n29, 502 n54
  health, 8, 26
  moves to Georgetown, 508 n9
  on REL, 13
  slaves and slavery, 2, 4, 5, 48
Lee, Cassius (REL cousin), 7, 11, 121,
  136
Lee, Cazanove (REL nephew), 492
Lee, Charles Carter (REL brother), 3,
  4, 8, 10, 26, 34, 35, 38, 46, 48, 72,
  189, 262, 290, 291, 321
Lee, Charlotte (REL daughter-in-law),
  352
Lee, Edmund Jennings (REL uncle), 6
Lee, Eleanor Agnes (REL daughter),
  49, 100–101, 285, 289, 323, 349,
  350
Lee, Fitzhugh (REL nephew), 284
Lee, Francis, 68, 70
Lee, George Washington Custis (REL
  son), 39, 75, 80, 83, 99–100, 101,
  102, 112, 113, 115, 116, 117, 118, 166,
  167, 171, 271, 280, 290, 291, 314, 347,
  424, 461
Lee, Henry (REL half-brother), 3, 9,
  10, 37
Lee, Henry "Light Horse Harry,"
  (REL father)
  death, 5
  and REL, 1–3, 23
  religion, 7

Lee, Mary Custis (REL daughter), 43
Lee, Mary Custis (REL wife), 26, 43,
  165, 285, 289, 314, 316, 322–324, 347,
  384, 440, 457, 486–487
  courtship, 26, 34–38
  erratic behavior, 98–99
  health, 97, 189, 191, 261, 267, 424
  on REL 26
  religion, 35–36
  and slaves, 349, 351
Lee, Mildred (REL aunt), 2, 4
Lee, Mildred (REL sister), 26, 34, 49
Lee, Mildred Childe (REL daughter),
  50, 98, 112, 166, 285
Lee, Robert Edward (REL), Civil War
  career
  Antietam, MD, Campaign, 239–246
  Appomattox, retreat to, 449–452
  Battle of Bristoe Station, VA,
    355–356
  Battle of Bull Run, VA, First, 141,
    143
  Battle of Bull Run, VA, Second,
    232–237
  Battle of Chancellorsville, VA,
    293–294
  Battle of Cold Harbor, VA, 406–408
  Battle of Petersburg, VA, 410–411
  Cheat Mountain, VA, Campaign,
    146–149
  as chief of military operations, 189
  command, asks to be relieved of,
    353–354
  command in South Carolina,
    160–172
  command in Virginia, 136–141,
    143–152
  command in western Virginia,
    143–152

Lee, Robert Edward (REL), Civil War
    career (*continued*)
  command of Army of Northern
      Virginia, 211, 550 n112
  Davis, Jefferson, advisor to, 142
  Fredericksburg Campaign, 267–269,
      280
  general-in-chief, 443, 444
  Gettysburg Campaign, 320–330, 347,
      351, 353
  Grant, April 10 meeting with,
      455–456, 585 n3
  Mine Run Campaign, 357
  "Mud March," 289
  North Anna, VA, operations, 402,
      405–406
  Petersburg, evacuation of, 449
  Petersburg, Siege of 409, 420–449
  promotion to full general, 146,
      541 n117
  Seven Days' Campaign, 214–220
  Shenandoah Valley Campaign 1862,
      192–193
  Spotsylvania Campaign, 400–402
  surrender, 452–454
  Virginia 1861, defense of, 136–141
  Wilderness, VA, Campaign, 387–388
  *See also individual attacks, battles,
      campaigns, and sieges*
Lee, Robert Edward (REL), as general
  army, reorganization of, 288,
      321–322
  believes cause lost, 425–427, 442–443
  blacks in PA, seizure of, 352
  characteristics, 138, 145, 268–270,
      287–290, 292, 346, 348, 356, 398,
      400, 404, 405, 406, 415–416
  command of Tennessee, declines,
      354, 380–381, 414

criticism of, 149, 151, 163, 172,
      189–190, 212, 283, 284, 319, 356
  and CSA (Confederate States of
      America), 151, 163, 282, 319, 441,
      455–456
  delegation, 139, 232, 317
  descriptions of, 142–143, 149, 243,
      283, 285–286, 319, 324, 354, 356,
      388, 397, 409, 467
  deserters, 382, 415–416, 419
  and dictatorship, 442–443
  discipline of soldiers, 415–416, 419
  dislike of North and Northerners,
      136, 137, 139, 151, 164, 165–166, 314,
      348, 349–350, 352, 439–440, 472
  and Emancipation Proclamation,
      352
  Grant, compared with, 393–395
  headquarters, life at, 290, 291,
      314–315, 383–384, 423–424
  and Jews, 277, 292
  management style, 75–76, 139, 140,
      145–146, 150, 190, 217–218, 219,
      231–232, 235–236, 243–244, 265,
      315–316, 327–329, 357, 383–384, 423
  peace efforts, 444–448, 450, 458
  and press, 281, 287, 349, 385, 413
  prisoner exchange, 433
  reconnaissance, 329–330
  "reconstructionist" in 1861, 137–
      138
  recruiting, 163, 321, 424–425
  risks, physical, 312, 400, 403
  staff, 139, 218, 314–319, 322, 324, 325,
      328–329, 456
  strategic thinking, 141, 143, 147, 149,
      192–193, 214, 233–234, 237, 239,
      240–241, 296, 308–309, 310, 313,
      320–321, 347, 380–381, 384–386

Trent affair, 107

See also individual attacks, battles,
campaigns, and sieges

Lee, Robert Edward (REL), personal
appearance, 138, 142–143, 144–145,
160, 508 n12
birth, 503 n78
character and personality, xvii, 6,
8, 10, 13, 23–24, 41, 44, 76, 98, 127,
137, 146, 210–211, 262, 289–290,
316, 322, 323, 353, 355–356, 388, 406,
421, 440
conflict, avoidance of, 83–84, 118,
145, 209, 265, 284, 288–289, 316,
322–323, 355–357, 407
courtship, 26, 34–38
death, anticipation of, 96, 101, 347,
352, 424, 440–441
depression, 280, 290–291, 293, 347,
453, 557 n83
diet, 267
disappointment, 101
duty, 13, 26, 77, 115, 146, 317, 412
education, demerits during, 507 n3,
509 n21
education, Alexandria Academy,
500 n45, n46
education, Military Academy, 9–11,
25–28
education, primary, 3–5
education, secondary, 6–12
failure, sense of, 347, 353
as father, 39, 44, 99–102, 167
grief, 261–262, 270
health, 97, 290–291, 323, 328, 353–356,
406, 420–421, 423, 440, 486
inheritance, 5, 499 n30, 511 n60
isolation, 97
marriage, 38–40, 44, 98–99, 165, 424

Military academy, appointment to,
9–11
patriotism, 102, 412
political awareness, 44–46, 79, 240,
244, 321, 323, 553 n74, 554 n88
religion, 7, 35–36, 65, 76, 77–79, 101,
137, 149, 151, 172, 280, 284–285, 347,
349, 352, 353, 356, 357, 384, 387, 424,
440, 445
travel, 20
youth, 1–13, 23–24, 497 n11
See also Lee, pre–Civil War life;
Lee, views on
Lee, Robert Edward (REL), post–Civil
War
and CSA (Confederate States of
America) memorial societies, 472
death of, 487, 591 n18
deification of, 591 n26
emigration, opposition to, 459, 462
Grant, in 1869, meeting with,
481–484
historiography, xi–xii, xxi
mythology, xviii–xx
oath of allegiance, 461
pardon application, 461
and presidential campaign, 478
and railroad development, 469–470
retirement to private life, 458
Richmond, return to, 457
symbolic post–war leader, 462–463
treason indictment, 461
and Virginia governorship, 478
war record, defense of, 471
at Washington College, xviii,
467–469
to write history of Army of
Northern Virginia, 470–471
See also Lee, views on

Lee, Robert Edward (REL), pre–Civil War life
 election of 1860, 112
 Grant, meeting, xvii
 inheritance, 5, 499 n30, 511 n60
 Norris (slave) whippings, 348–349, 460, 473
 as slave-owner, 48, 61, 514 n151, n153, 515 n156, 518 n52, 523 n56, n59, 589 n77, 590 n89
 slaves, emancipation of Custis, xviii–xix, 113, 270–272, 277–279, 563 n131
 slaves, management of, 80–84
 Virginia, allegiance to, 113, 114, 115, 117, 122
 as Whig, 44, 45
Lee, Robert Edward (REL), pre-Civil War military experience
 with 2d US Cavalry, 77
 ambition, 9–10
 army, dissatisfaction with, 43, 111–112
 army, resignation from, 112, 114, 115, 120–121, 122–123, 138
 Battle of Cerro Gordo, 64–65
 Battle of Churubusco, 65
 command of US forces, declines, 119
 at Harpers Ferry, 95–96
 in Mexican War, 60–63, 64–65, 67–68, 70–74
 at Military Academy, as superintendent, 75–77
 promotion to colonel, 117
 promotions, 65, 67
Lee, Robert Edward (REL), relationships with
 Davis, Jefferson, 142, 160, 190, 210, 232–233, 239, 291–292, 354–355, 385, 412, 411–415, 431, 441, 475

 Johnston, Joseph E., 190, 191, 209
 Loring, William W., 146
 mother (Ann), 8, 12, 13, 23, 28
 Williams, Orton, 349–351
 Wise, Henry A., 149–150
Lee, Robert Edward (REL), views on
 abolitionists, 84
 Antietam, 471
 Appomattox, 457
 Army of Northern Virginia, 313, 321
 Atlanta, fall of, 442
 black labor, 485
 blacks, freed, 460, 473, 475, 480, 586 n19
 black soldiers, 425–427
 black suffrage, 483
 Catholicism, 70–71, 79
 critics, 148
 CSA (Confederate States of America), 107, 167–168, 171, 292, 356, 388, 427–428, 553 n74, 554 n88
 Davis, Jefferson, 142, 459
 democracy, 116
 education, 25, 99
 education, postwar, 467, 468
 Emancipation Proclamation, 281–282, 352, 562 n144
 emancipation, 61, 472–473
 extremists, 113
 father (Henry Lee), 3, 23–24
 fiction, 100
 foreigners, 137, 191, 485
 the French in Mexico, 476
 Gettysburg, 347, 351, 353, 471
 government, postwar, 472, 475
 Grant, xviii, 386, 409, 424, 459, 491–492
 guerilla warfare, 457
 Hill, A. P., 471

Hill, D. H., 471
honor, 114, 118, 138
Indians, 77
Jackson, Stonewall, 71, 321
Longstreet, James, 471
Manifest Destiny, 71, 72
McClellan, George B., 492
Meade, William, 492
Mexican War, 60, 518 n48
Mexico, 70–71
morale, 382
Nullification, 44, 45
patriotism, 122, 461
political officers, 71–72, 75
politicians, 112, 413, 441, 536 n76
popular will, 281–282
private life, 478
public office, 283
reconciliation, 462–463
Reconstruction, 472, 474–475,
    482–483, 485–486
recruiting, 169, 193
responsibility for war, 473
retaliation, 351–352
Richmond, loss of, 441–442
Scott, Winfield, 65
secession, 113–114, 115, 116, 119,
    120
slavery, 46–47, 81ff, 348–349, 352
slaves, 48, 49, 61, 81
Union, 113–114, 116
Virginia constitutional convention,
    474, 482–483
war, 121, 137–138, 280, 472–473,
    557 n80
war, duration of, 163–164
Washington, George, 116
Lee, Robert E., Jr. (REL son), 50, 100,
    191, 351, 460

Lee, Sidney Smith (REL brother), 4, 7,
    8, 9, 26, 48, 63, 72, 77, 119, 120
Lee, William Henry Fitzhugh
    "Rooney" (REL son), 43, 100, 113,
    115, 146, 191, 267, 324, 351, 352, 384,
    402, 458
LeSage, Alain René, 31
Letcher, John, 120, 121, 139, 141, 143,
    462, 467
Letitia (REL slave), 48
Lever, Charles, 31, 33
Lewis, Nellie, 10
Lincoln, Abraham, xx–xxi, 104, 109,
    110, 112, 117, 123, 125, 152, 195, 260,
    298, 299, 338, 362, 364, 373, 379,
    390, 392, 416, 422, 444, 449, 450,
    452, 457, 459, 463, 465, 487
    relations with Grant, 431–432
Livingston, John, 75
Logan, John, 132, 226, 366, 379, 389, 435,
    490
Long, Armistead L., 315, 318, 324
Longstreet, James, 32, 209, 213, 214–
    220, 232–239, 243, 261–268, 291,
    294, 317, 322–330, 354–357, 368, 369,
    371, 375–377, 379, 381–386, 398–400,
    413, 444, 470, 471
Loring, William W., 144–150
Lowe, Enoch L., 240, 242
Lowe, John W., 31, 69
Lyon, Nathaniel, 129

M

Mace, Daniel, 130
Mack, Simon, 275
Mackay, John "Jaçk," 25, 43, 44, 45, 46,
    71
Macomb, Alexander, 9
Magruder, John B., 191, 192, 209,
    213–220, 314

Mahan, Dennis Hart, 32

Malvern Hill, VA, Battle of, 219

Manassas, First Battle of. *See* Bull Run, VA, First Battle of

Manassas, Second Battle of. *See* Bull Run, VA, Second Battle of

Markland, Absalom, 19

Marryat, Frederick, 31

Marshall, Ann (REL sister), 121

Marshall, Charles, 315, 453, 456

Marshall, Louis, 230–231

Mason, Charles, 26, 27

Matthews, Joseph McDowell, 42

Maximilian, Emperor of Mexico, 437, 476

May, James, 137

Maynadier, William, 9, 39, 500 n44

Maysville Academy, 19, 33, 204

McClellan, George B., 63, 91, 130, 133, 144, 177, 179, 180, 183, 191–193, 195–198, 210, 212, 213, 214–220, 227, 229, 232, 238, 239–246, 261–263, 269, 410, 414, 481, 492

McClernand, John A., 132, 135, 153, 154, 156–158, 173, 174, 175, 177, 181–188, 200, 201, 205, 206, 279, 296–300, 305–307, 330, 331, 334, 336, 341, 363, 389

    relations with USG, 226, 254–261, 336–338

    USG relieves, 338

McDowell, Irvin, 143

McLean, Wilmer, 469

McPherson, James B., 194, 226, 248–250, 255, 258, 260, 300–302, 331, 334, 340–342, 372, 379, 380, 389, 436

McQuinn, John, 82

Meade, George G., 326, 329, 330, 346, 353–356, 363, 366, 373, 377, 381, 382, 384–387, 390, 398–400, 401, 403, 405, 407, 408, 418, 420, 429, 436, 456, 458, 464, 492

    relations with USG, 438–439

Meade, William, 7, 284

Mechanicsville, VA, Battle of, 215

Medary, Samuel, 19

Melton, Samuel, 151

Meriday, Judy (Custis slave), 47, 60

Meriday, Michael (Custis slave), 278

Meriday, Philip (Custis slave), 47, 80

Mexico, French occupation, 362

Mine Run Campaign, 357

Minnegerode, Charles, 443

Mobile, AL, Campaign, 362–363, 364, 365, 373, 437

Molina del Rey, Battle of, 68

Monterey, Mexico, 54–56, 73

Morehouse, D. B., 108

Morris, David, 19

N

Nat (Mildred Lee slave), 8, 46, 49

Nelson, Thomas, 19

Nelson, William, 19, 204–207

Norris, Leonard (Custis slave), 348

Norris, Mary (Custis slave), 83, 84, 278, 348

Norris, Wesley (Custis slave), 83, 84, 278, 348, 473, 524 n78, 525 n88, n90

North Anna, VA, operations, 405–406

Northrop, Lucius B., 382

O

Oak Grove, VA, Battle of, 215–216

Oakland Female Seminary, 42

Oglesby, Richard, 153

Ord, Edward O. C., 238, 248, 250, 345, 363, 390, 445

Orton, Lawrence W. *See* Williams, William Orton
Ould, Robert H., 444, 478

P

Palo Alto, Battle of, 51, 53, 73
Parker, Ely S., 389
Parks, Perry (Custis slave), 278, 383
Payne, Hugh, 20, 21
Pemberton, John C., 69, 172, 208–209, 259, 266, 333, 343–345, 358, 362
Pendleton, William N., 316
Pepper, George W., 459
Perkins, C. R., 124
Petersburg, VA, Battle of, 410–411
Petersburg, VA, Siege of, 420–429 passim
Phelan, Michael, 88
Pickens, Francis W., 161, 162, 165, 208–209
on REL, 163
Pierce, Franklin, 57, 81, 94, 142, 411
Pillow, Gideon J., 57, 71, 72, 186, 188
Polk, James K., 50, 57, 72, 94
Polk, Leonidas, 134, 154, 156, 350
on USG, 173
Pope, John, 32, 198, 226–229, 230, 232, 233, 236, 237, 239, 388, 437, 463, 471
Port Hudson, LA, 296, 299, 305, 306, 345, 358, 359
siege of, 336
Porter, David D., 257–258, 295, 297, 301–308, 334, 345, 390, 490
Porter, Fitz-John, 471
Porter, Horace, 389, 437
Prentiss, Benjamin, 133–134, 201, 205
Price, Sterling, 228, 229, 238, 241, 246–247, 248, 434
Pride, George, 340, 341, 344

Pryor, Elizabeth, xi
Putnam, Samuel, 348–349

R

Rand, Jacob W., 19
Randolph, George W., 213
Rankin, John, 21
Ravensworth plantation, 28, 38, 46, 118, 121–122
Rawlins, John A., 108, 110, 124, 125, 126, 153, 252–254, 315, 335, 338, 339–341, 389, 434, 437, 488
on USG's staff, 132–133
Reid, Whitelaw, 226
Resaca de la Palma, Battle of, 51, 53, 73
Reynolds, Joseph, 130, 392
Reynolds, William, 130
Rhett, Robert Barnwell, 163, 442–443
Rich Mountain, VA, Battle of, 144
Richardson, Charles B., 470
Richeson, William West, 19, 33
Ripley, Roswell S., 162, 170, 171, 209
Robbins, James Watson, 11
Rosecrans, William S., 32, 144, 150, 228, 292, 295, 340, 343, 365, 366, 378, 434–435, 437, 479, 480, 482, 485
at Iuka, 238, 246–247
at Corinth, 248–251, 252–255
Ross, Leonard, 294
Rowley, W. R., 108
Ruffin, Edmund, 161
Ruffin, Nancy (REL slave), 48, 60, 278, 515 n157, 519 n53

S

Sam (REL slave), 48
Sanderson, James, 16, 17
on USG, 505 n103, n104
Santa Anna, Antonio Lopez de, 65, 66

Savage Station, VA, Battle of, 216
Sayler's Creek, VA, Battle of, 450
Schofield, John M., 379, 475
Scott, Dred, 109
Scott, Walter, 31
Scott, Winfield, 10, 30, 33, 58, 60, 62, 63, 65, 66, 71, 72, 96, 111, 117, 118, 119, 136, 329, 349, 350, 374, 394, 411
Seddon, James A., 320, 321, 323, 424
Seligman, Jesse, 272
Semmes, Raphael, 73
Seven Days' Battles, 214–220
Seymour, Horatio, 479
Shenandoah Valley Campaign 1862, 192–193
Sheridan, Philip H., 379, 402, 406, 420, 436, 449, 452, 489
Sherman, William T., 129, , 152, 178, 183, 196, 200, 223226, 248, 254, 255, 258–260, 272, 277, 279, 295, 301, 302, 306, 330, 333, 334, 341, 342, 345, 360, 365, 366, 369, 370–371, 373, 375–376, 379–380, 389, 390, 403, 432, 434, 436, 437, 448, 457, 458, 463, 464, 488, 489–491
    at Shiloh, 201–207, 221
Shiloh, TN, Battle of, 202–208
Shiloh Campaign, 200ff
Sigel, Franz, 390, 403
Simmons, James, 338
Simpson, Brooks D., xi
Singleton, James W., 444–445
Smith, Charles F., 32, 111, 152, 153, 154, 181–188, 197, 198–199, 200–203
Smith, Garrett, 469
Smith, Gustavus W., 32, 209–211, 213, 265
Smith, John, 125
Smith, John E., 107, 108, 110–111
Smith, William F., 367, 373, 377, 379, 390, 407, 411–412
Spotsylvania, VA, Campaign, 400–402
Stansfield, F. W. H., 430
Stanton, Edwin M., 298, 299, 338, 363, 365, 373, 403, 429, 431, 463, 464, 477, 478
Steele, Frederick, 258–260
Steele's Bayou Expedition, 301–302
Stephens, Alexander H., 137, 442–443, 444
Stevens, Thomas H., 88
Stowe, Harriet Beecher, 21
Stratford Hall, 280
Stuart, James Ewell Brown "Jeb," 96, 209, 213, 214, 230, 234, 261, 312, 314, 324–326, 330, 346, 381, 382, 397, 400, 402, 471
Sue, Eugene, 33, 42
Sumner, Edwin V., 117, 119
Swett, Leonard, 273

T

Talcott, Thomas M. R., 315, 318
Taylor, Walter H., 315, 316, 319, 361, 384, 386, 387, 448, 453, 456, 457
Taylor, Zachary, 51, 52, 54, 58, 60, 67, 94, 411, 438
Ten Eyck, John C., 286–287
Thomas, George H., 365–371, 375, 376, 379, 433, 435–436, 437, 464
    relations with USG, 366–367, 369, 379
Tilden, Samuel J., 488
Trapier, James H., 161, 162, 170
Traveller (REL horse), 486
Turner, Nat, rebellion, 47
Twiggs, David E., 113, 119
Tyler, John, 46

U

Uncle Tom's Cabin, 21
Underwood, John, 462, 464
United States Military Academy, Lee superintendent at, 75–77

V

Van Buren, Martin, 30, 45
Van Dorn, Earl, 32, 247–251, 279, 294
Venable, Charles S., 41, 315–319, 388
Vera Cruz, Siege of, 63
Vicksburg, MS, Campaign, 255, 258–260, 294–308, 330–338, 343–345, 358
Vincent, John H., 108

W

Walker, Gilbert C., 484
Wallace, Lew, 186, 188, 200–202, 206, 208, 226, 340
Wallace, W. H. L., 153, 201, 202
Wallen, Henry, 87, 88
Warnery, Charles de, 27
Washburne, Elihu B., 104, 108, 132, 152, 173, 174, 175, 301, 342, 361, 373, 374, 379, 380, 437, 455
Washington, John A., 151, 314
Washington, Martha, 82
Waugh, John, xi
Webster, Daniel, 45
Webster, Joseph D., 175, 339, 340

Webster, Noah, 21, 348
Webster, William G., 348
White Haven plantation, 90, 92, 105
White House plantation, 48
White, Albert S., 60
White, Chilton A., 14, 16
White, John D., 15–16, 18
Whiting, William H. T., 213
Wilderness, VA, Campaign, 387–388, 395–396, 398
Williams, Carter (REL uncle), 7
Williams, Thomas, 298, 299
Williams, William Orton, 115, 349–351, 472, 573 n30
Wilson, Henry, 460
Wilson, James H., 335, 341
Wise, Henry A., 144–150
Wish-ton-wish plantation, 92
Wolseley, Garnet, 286
Wool, John E., 60–62, 118
Worth, William, 62, 68, 69, 70
Wright, Crafts J., 225, 226

Y

Yates, Richard, 128–130, 338
Yazoo Pass Expedition, 301
Yellow Tavern, VA, Battle of, 402

Z

Zantzinger, Franklin, 31